Child & Adult Care Professionals

Karen Stephens, M.S.
Early Childhood Instructor
Director, ISU Child Care Center
Illinois State University
Normal, Illinois

Maxine Hammonds-Smith, Ph.D., CFLE
Professor of Family & Consumer Sciences
Director, Center on Aging & Intergenerational Wellness
Texas Southern University
Houston, Texas

New York, New York   Columbus, Ohio   Chicago, Illinois   Peoria, Illinois   Woodland Hills, California

Safety Notice

The reader is expressly advised to consider and use all safety precautions described in this textbook or that might also be indicated by undertaking the activities described herein. In addition, common sense should be exercised to help avoid all potential hazards and, in particular, to take relevant safety precautions concerning any known or likely hazards involved in caring for children or older adults, or in use of the procedures described in Child & Adult Care Professionals, such as the risk of back injuries when lifting children or assisting older adults.

Publisher and Authors assume no responsibility for the activities of the reader or for the subject matter experts who prepared this book. Publisher and Authors make no representation or warranties of any kind, including but not limited to the warranties of fitness for particular purpose or merchantability, nor for any implied warranties related thereto, or otherwise. Publisher and Authors will not be liable for damages of any type, including any consequential, special or exemplary damages resulting, in whole or in part, from reader's use or reliance upon the information, instructions, warnings, or other matter contained in this textbook.

Brand Disclaimer

Publisher does not necessarily recommend or endorse any particular company or brand name product that may be discussed or pictured in this textbook. Brand name products are used because they are readily available, likely to be known to the reader, and their use may aid in the understanding of the text. Publisher recognizes that other brand name or generic products may be substituted and work as well as or better than those featured in the textbook.

A special thank you to *The Council for Professional Recognition* for granting permission to reproduce the CDA Competency Goals and Functional Areas. *All CDA information is available on the official Council for Professional Recognition website on the Internet.*

The McGraw·Hill Companies

Send all inquiries to:
Glencoe/McGraw-Hill
3008 W. Willow Knolls Drive
Peoria, IL 61614-1083

ISBN 0-07-829013-9
Printed in the United States of America
4 5 6 7 8 9 10   027   07

Contents in Brief

Contributors

Kathleen H. Wilber, Ph.D.
Professor of Gerontology
University of Southern California
Los Angeles, California

Linda R. Glosson, Ph.D.
Family & Consumer Sciences Teacher
Wylie High School
Wylie, Texas

Susan G. Elsasser
Freelance Writer
Sparland, Illinois

Brenda Barrington Mendiola
Curriculum Director
Irion County Independent School District
Mertzon, Texas

Technical Reviewers

Kathleen H. Wilber, Ph.D.
Professor of Gerontology
University of Southern
California
Los Angeles, California

Elaina F. Osterbur, M.A.
Gerontology Lecturer
Illinois State University
Normal, Illinois

Sheri Y. Steinig, M.S.W.
Program Director
Generations United
Washington, DC

Marlene S. Lobberecht, M.S., CFCS
Early Childhood Professions
Instructor & Laboratory Director
Cypress Creek High School
Houston, Texas

Eleanor L. Keppler, M.S., CFCS
Family & Consumer Sciences Department Head
Director, Lawrence Central Child Care Center
Lawrence Central High School
Indianapolis, Indiana

Teacher Reviewers

Margaret-Ann Doak
Early Childhood Education
Instructor
Plant City High School
Plant City, Florida

M. Grace Emmell Leister
Department Chair, Human
Services & Consumer Science
North Penn School District
Lansdale, Pennsylvania

Cynthia D. Elliott
Early Childhood Education
Teacher
New Smyrna Beach High
School
New Smyrna Beach, Florida

Jenefer Rowley
Child & Family Development Specialist
Hunter High School
Salt Lake City, Utah

Barbara A. Scott
Department Chair
Family & Consumer Sciences Teacher
Lindbergh High School
St. Louis, Missouri

Judy Watkinson
Director of Early Childhood Programs
Arizona Western College
Yuma, Arizona

Julene K. Swenson, CFCS
Service Occupations Coordinator
Woodbury High School
Woodbury, Minnesota

Contents

Unit 1—Life Span Development

Unit 2—Career Opportunities

Unit 3—Human Services Basics

Unit 4—Program Operations & Management

Unit 5—Providing Care

Unit 6—Developmentally Appropriate Activities

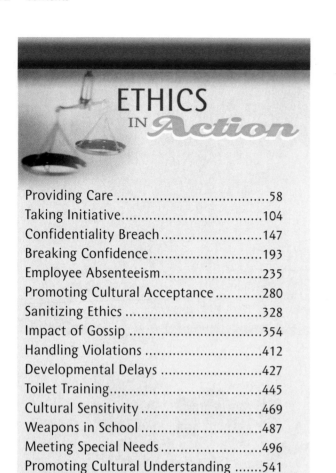

ETHICS IN Action

Boosting Brain Power

Safety First

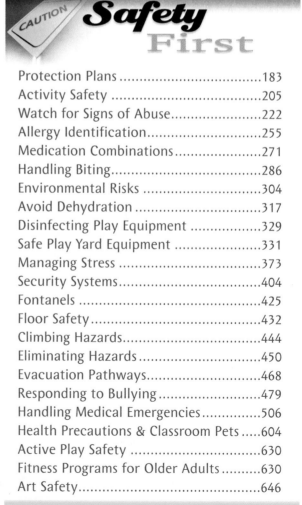

Independence Skills

Intergenerational *Interactions*

How To...

Becoming a
Child Development Associate (CDA)

CDA Eligibility Requirements

Personal
* At least eighteen years of age with a high school diploma.
* Ability to speak, read, and write well enough to fulfill all requirements.
* Must sign a statement of ethical conduct.

Setting
* Must be in a state-approved center.
* Candidate must work as a lead caregiver for a group of at least eight children ages three to five.
* At least ten children must be enrolled in the program with at least two caregivers present.
* No more than twenty percent of those enrolled can be children with special needs.

Experience
* At least 480 hours work experience with three- to five-year-olds in a group setting five years prior to CDA application.

Education
* 120 clock hours with at least ten in each of the eight prescribed areas ranging from planning an environment that is healthy and safe, to principles of child growth and development.

As a student in an occupational early childhood program, you might be wondering, "Why should I work toward acquiring Child Development Associate (CDA) credential?" The internal and external rewards are numerous and include:

* Growing as a professional in knowledge and skill.
* Improving yourself in ways that benefit children.
* Developing a support network of professionals experienced with early childhood development and care.
* Evaluating your knowledge and skills against national standards.
* Acquiring a credential that is nationally recognized by early childhood care providers and educators alike.

The information above offers you an overview of the CDA requirements and assessment process. The training and education required, along with the credential itself, can be a real asset in obtaining gainful employment.

CDA Competency Goals

The Council for Professional Recognition in Washington, D.C. is the sponsoring agency for the CDA credential. As a way to assure families about quality care, the Council created the CDA credentialing program.

The CDA Competency Goals identify the necessary skills for qualified early childhood professionals. They assess the skills necessary in a variety of early childhood settings that include:

A special thank you to *The Council for Professional Recognition* for granting permission to reproduce the CDA Competency Goals and Functional Areas. *All CDA information is available on the official Council for Professional Recognition website on the Internet.*

center-based programs for infants, toddlers, and preschoolers; family day care; and home visitor programs. The six CDA Competency Goals are:

- **Goal I:** To establish and maintain a safe, healthy learning environment.
- **Goal II:** To advance physical and intellectual competence.
- **Goal III:** To support social and emotional development and provide positive guidance.
- **Goal IV:** To establish positive and productive relationships with families.
- **Goal V:** To ensure a well-run, purposeful program responsive to participant needs.
- **Goal VI:** To maintain commitment to professionalism.

All individuals desiring to receive the CDA credential must demonstrate their competence in these six areas. Candidates may also receive endorsement in areas of specialization, such as bilingual education.

The Assessment Process

The process for becoming a CDA involves six steps. It is designed to thoroughly assess each candidate in terms of his or her professional skill. The six steps are described below.

Step 1—Inquiry. Once eligibility requirements as outlined in the chart on page 14 are met, candidates can order an application packet from *The Council for Professional Recognition.*

Step 2—Documentation. Next, the candidate must put together the required documentation showing his or her skills. This documentation includes:

- *Professional Resource File.* This file includes an autobiographical statement, written examples showing the candidate's skills in the CDA Competency Standards, and a collection of resource materials (curriculum and activity ideas) that will be of use to the candidate on the worksite.
- *Parent Opinion Questionnaires.* The parent of each child in the candidate's care completes a questionnaire giving his or her perceptions about the candidate's skill and knowledge.
- *Formal Observation.* A formal observation is completed by an advisor of the candidate's choice—often a program director or college instructor. The observation follows the criteria established by *The Council for Professional Recognition.*
- *Early Childhood Studies Review.* This exam is given during the final assessment visit.
- *Oral Interview.* As a final step in the assessment process, the council representative presents the candidate with ten structured child care situations. The interview is designed to show how the candidate uses knowledge acquired through experience and training.

Step 3—Application. After the candidate and his or her advisor collect the necessary documentation, the application for final assessment is sent (along with the fee) to the Council. You can locate their address and telephone number on the official CDA website on the Internet.

Step 4—On-Site Visit. A council representative will visit the candidate and the candidate's work site to look at documentation, give the written exam, and conduct the oral interview.

Step 5—Credential Award or Denial. A committee from *The Council for Professional Recognition* reviews all of the candidate's documentation. If all of the documentation is favorable, the council awards the CDA credential to the candidate. If for some reason the candidate needs further education and training, he or she will be notified concerning the specifics of that education and training.

Step 6—Renewing the CDA Credential. Once an individual receives the CDA credential, the initial credential is valid for three years. After the first renewal, the credential can be renewed every five years.

The Child Development Associate (CDA) Credential

Note: A CDA correlation to the Child & Adult Care Professionals student edition can be found in the Instructor Resource Guide.

Competency Goal I
To establish and maintain a safe, healthy learning environment.
1. Functional Area: Safe—Candidate provides a safe environment to prevent and reduce injuries. Examples include the following:
Keeps the inside of the center and the outdoor play area free of debris, structural hazards, unguarded space heaters, tools, and dangerous substances, such as medicine, cleaning products, matches, paint, toxic plants, small objects that could be swallowed, balloons, or plastic bags.
Ensures that safety equipment, such as fire extinguisher and smoke detectors, is in place and operable and knows how to use it.
Maintains an easily accessible and current list of phone numbers for contacting parents and emergency services, including poison control, fire company, and medical help.
Uses diagrams, pictures, and words understood by children and adults to post instructions and practice procedures for fires and other emergencies, including safety procedures for children with disabling conditions.
Plans and practices monthly fire drills for moving all children in care to safety as quickly as possible.
Ensures outdoor play equipment is safe for small children and in good repair.
Responds immediately and sympathetically to a child's injury or fear of injury and encourages the same response by the children.
Takes safety precautions in a reassuring manner without overprotecting or making children fearful.
Anticipates and makes plans to prevent potentially dangerous situations, such as children being left alone or separated while on a field trip.
Maintains first aid supplies (including gauze, tape, syrup of ipecac, tweezers, scissors, and soap); knows basic first aid procedures appropriate for young children, such as handling choking, treating cuts, etc.
Uses safe auto/bus travel procedures, including the use of appropriate car seats for children under 4 years and seat belts for self and other children.
Discusses safety information with parents and tells them about resources, such as poison control centers, that provide services to families in their own language.
Supervises all children's activities indoors and outdoors.
Keeps informed about safety standards for toys and equipment and shares this information with parents.
Helps preschoolers stop dangerous actions toward themselves and others.
Explains cause and effect in dangerous situations in simple language, demonstrating as much as possible. Teaches safe use of playground equipment.
Teaches children simple safety rules and enforces rules consistently.
Talks and role plays with preschoolers about safety precautions.
Adapts the indoor and outdoor environment so that children with disabling conditions can maximize their independence (e.g., safely uses mechanical audio equipment).
Requires parents to authorize in writing all persons allowed to pick up children from the program.

Working toward bilingual specialization
Explains and practices safety procedures, such as fire drills, using the language best understood by the children.
Utilizes cultural values and practices in providing safety education.
2. Functional Area: Healthy—Candidate promotes good health and nutrition and provides an environment that contributes to the prevention of illness. Examples include the following:
Learns about good nutrition for children from 3 to 5 years old and provides age-appropriate, nutritious meals and snacks. While respecting family customs and habits, the caregiver shares nutrition information with parents and encourages them to provide healthful foods when they contribute food to the center.
Conducts activities in a positive, relaxed, and pleasant atmosphere to reduce tension and stress.
Washes hands after toileting a child, helping child blow nose, and before food preparation and eating.
Attends to each child's physical needs, such as toileting, eating, exercising, and napping.
Provides affection for all children.
Provides adequate ventilation and lighting, comfortable room temperatures, and good sanitation.
Makes sure play areas and materials are cleaned daily.
Establishes procedures for care of sick children; for example, isolating a child with a contagious illness from well children, contacting parents and medical providers, and administering medicine.
Helps children develop basic health habits.
Keeps handy current emergency telephone numbers for each child's parent(s), nearest relative, and medical providers.
Communicates frequently with parents about children's health, nutrition, communicable diseases and medications, and cooperates with parents and health specialists.
Follows center procedures for maintaining health records and administering medication and first aid and cooperates with health and nutrition staff.
Establishes a relaxed mealtime routine for making eating pleasant for each child.
Limits sugar, salt, processed foods, unnecessary chemical additives, and artificial coloring and flavoring in meals and snacks and encourages parents to do the same.
Informs parents about health resources, such as physicians or community clinics that provide services to families in their primary language.
Recognizes symptoms of possible abuse and neglect and is alert to play or behavior that indicates physical or sexual abuse. If physical or sexual abuse is suspected, the competent Candidate seeks out resources for information and support and follows state laws in response. The Candidate responds sensitively to child and family's needs, and cooperates in carrying out treatment plans.
Uses role playing, modeling, visual material, and real objects to teach healthy physical, mental, dental, and nutritional practices.
Plans health care and educational activities that integrate health and nutrition information from the children's cultures with medically accepted heath and nutrition practices.
Supports children in developing self-help skills in eating, toileting, washing hands, tooth brushing, etc.
Includes children in food preparation and provides other nutrition education activities for children.
Provides opportunities for children to learn about health care by talking about visits to the doctor and dentist, reading books, and encouraging pretend play about health care.
Recognizes unusual behavior and physical symptoms in children and encourages parents to obtain appropriate treatment.
Works cooperatively with health professionals and parents to meet the needs of children with disabling conditions.
Recognizes the signs of a health crisis that children with special needs may have and responds appropriately (e.g., seizures).

Working toward bilingual specialization
Provides written health information for parents (e.g., notices about immunizations) in both languages.
Utilizes cultural values and practices in providing health and nutrition education.
3. Functional Area: Learning Environment—Candidate uses space, relationships, materials, and routines as resources for constructing an interesting, secure, and enjoyable environment that encourages play, exploration, and learning. Examples include the following:
Uses materials, books, and equipment that are stimulating to each child and suitable to individual learning styles, including those of disabled children.
Uses materials that demonstrate acceptance of each child's sex, family, race, language, and culture.
Provides easily accessible learning materials (e.g., puzzles, crayons, markers, and books) that children can explore themselves and puts some materials away for special times or for use at later stages of development.
Organizes space into identifiable areas that encourage appropriate and independent use of materials.
Balances active and quiet, free and structured, individual and group, indoor and outdoor activities.
Provides many opportunities for children to develop their senses and ability to concentrate.
Varies routines spontaneously to take advantage of unusual opportunities; e.g., goes outside in the snow, invites a visiting grandmother to share stories or songs with children, lets the children watch workers and machinery on the street, or plays with one child for an extra period of time when additional adults are available to care for group.
Adapts the schedule to accommodate children with special needs rather than requiring them to fit the schedule.
Working toward bilingual specialization
Uses objects, music activities, and celebrations that are meaningful to young children and encourage development of both languages and cultures.
Helps parents identify resources in their homes, families, and community that will support the development of both languages.
Establishes and maintains a routine for use of the second language in daily activities.

Competency Goal II

To advance physical and intellectual competence.

4. Functional Area: Physical—Candidate provides a variety of equipment, activities, and opportunities to promote the physical development of children. Examples include the following:
Arranges and encourages physical activities, knowing how children's physical development affects their cognitive, social, and emotional development.
Observes and evaluates children's developmental levels in order to provide activities for physical skills and development of the senses at the appropriate level for each child.
Plans and participates daily in appropriate large-muscle activities (e.g., playing ball, running, jumping, climbing with children, both indoors and outdoors).
Provides a variety of activities from children's culture(s), such as dances, music, finger plays, and games.
Provides opportunities for children to develop their senses by noticing colors, smelling odors, distinguishing sounds, feeling and touching a variety of objects, and tasting different foods.
Communicates to children and their parents the importance of outdoor play and physical activity for healthy growth and development.
Plans for and supports children's changing needs for active play, quiet activity, and rest.
Supports and encourages, but never forces, children who are fearful of physical activity because of illness, accidents, abuse, limited opportunity, or overprotective caregivers and parents.

Observes and evaluates children's physical development, recognizes signs of possible physical disabilities and developmental delays, refers parents to appropriate services, and follows up on referrals or individual development plans.

Adapts the program to meet the special needs of children with disabilities, taking into account the importance of physical development to self-concept and social development.

5. Functional Area: Cognitive—Candidate provides activities and opportunities that encourage curiosity, exploration, and problem solving appropriate to the developmental levels and learning styles of children. Examples include the following:

Observes children's play frequently to assess their cognitive development and readiness for new learning opportunities.

Uses techniques and activities that stimulate children's curiosity, inventiveness, and problem-solving and communication skills.

Provides opportunities for children to try out and begin to understand the relationships between cause and effect and means and ends.

Understands the importance of play and often joins children's play as a partner and facilitator.

Uses the center environment, everyday activities, and homemade materials to encourage children's intellectual development.

Helps children discover ways to solve problems in daily activities.

Supports children's repetitions of the familiar and introduces new experiences, activities, and materials as children are interested and ready.

Recognizes differences in individual learning styles and finds ways to work effectively with each child.

Encourages active learning, rather than emphasizing adult talking and children's passive listening.

Provides equipment and materials that children can explore and master by themselves.

Is alert to the task a child is attempting and provides appropriate support.

Encourages children to ask questions and seek help and responds to them in ways that extend their thinking; for example, "That's a good question; let's see if we can find out."

Asks questions that have more than one answer, encouraging children to wonder, guess, and talk about their ideas; for example, "What do you think might happen…?" or "How do you feel when…?"

Encourages children to talk about their experiences and observations.

Provides opportunities to organize, group, and compare and contrast thoughts, words, objects, and sensations.

Involves children in such projects as cooking and gardening as possible.

Reduces distractions and interruptions so that children have opportunities to extend their attention span and work on one activity, such as block building or water play, for a long period of time.

Helps children understand concepts such as space, time, shape, and quantity through many different activities.

Uses field trips as opportunities to expand children's knowledge and understanding of their world, as possible.

Obtains (or makes) and uses special learning materials and equipment for children whose disabilities affect their ability to learn.

Recognizes learning problems and collects good observational examples to support concerns.

Uses written observational examples of children to make and support referrals according to center policy.

Working toward bilingual specialization

Provides learning experiences that lead to the understanding of basic concepts in the language most familiar to each child.

Encourages learning of both languages through everyday experiences and activities.

6. Functional Area: Communication—Candidate actively communicates with children and provides opportunities and support for children to understand, acquire, and use verbal and nonverbal means of communicating thoughts. Examples include the following:

Has realistic expectations for each child's understanding and use of speech based on knowledge of language development and each child.

Talks often with individual children and stimulates conversation among children and with adults in the room.

Provides activities that encourage children to develop listening and comprehension skills.

Helps children connect word meaning(s) to experiences and real objects.

Respects the language of non-English-speaking families, encourages them to communicate freely with their children in the language parents prefer, and helps them find opportunities to learn English.

Listens attentively to children, tries to understand what they want to communicate, and helps them to express themselves.

Shares children's communication/language achievements with parents.

Uses a variety of songs, stories, books, and games—including those from the children's cultures—for language development.

Talks with children about special experiences and relationships in their families and home lives.

Uses conversations with children to enrich and expand their vocabulary.

Provides opportunities for children to represent their ideas nonverbally through activities such as painting, music, and creative movement.

Helps children learn, understand, and use words to express thoughts, ideas, questions, feelings, and needs.

Writes children's stories and labels their drawings showing the relationship between spoken and printed words.

Introduces longer storybooks gradually as children become interested.

Encourages children to take turns talking and listening instead of interrupting each other or adults; ensures that each child has a chance to talk.

Recognizes possible impairments or delays that affect hearing and speech, helps families find resources, cooperates with treatment plans, and finds ways to communicate positively with children.

Working toward bilingual specialization

Demonstrates ability to understand, speak, read, and write both languages.

Understands the principles and characteristics of bilingual language development in children and explains these to parents.

Assesses each child's language abilities and uses activities that are appropriate to the child's level of development in each language.

Allows children opportunities to express themselves in the language of their choice.

Uses lullabies, songs, games, stories, books, and finger plays, from both languages, asking parents for examples from their childhood.

7. Functional Area: Creative—Candidate provides opportunities that stimulate children to play with sound, rhythm, language, materials, space, and ideas in individual ways and to express their creative abilities. Examples include the following:

Recognizes that the process of creating is important—and sometimes more important—than the product.

Understands that each child's creative expression is unique and does not encourage uniformity.

Allows time for spontaneous and extended play within the daily routine.

Includes a variety of music, art, literature, dance, role playing, celebrations, and other creative activities from the children's culture(s) in program activities.

Participates in make-believe games with children.

Models and encourages children's creativity in language; for example, through rhymes, imaginative stories, and nonsense words.

Provides unstructured materials (such as blocks, paint, clay, or musical instruments).

Models creativity by using homemade materials and found objects.

Helps parents understand the importance of creative expression in children's development and the need to provide children with opportunities for creative activities.

Provides for messy activities with children, such as water and sand play, finger painting, and drawing with markers.

Encourages children to try new and different activities.

Provides and rotates a variety of male and female dress-up clothes and other "props," including those from the children's culture(s).

Keeps informed about cultural resources in the community and uses them with children when possible.

Provides crayons, paper, paste, and scissors in a place where children can use them independently.

Working toward bilingual specialization

Helps children develop creative abilities through activities and discussion in both languages.

Helps children identify and imitate creative forms found in the art, music, and dance of their cultures.

Competency Goal III

To support social and emotional development and provide positive guidance.

8. Functional Area: Self—Candidate provides physical and emotional security for each child and helps each child to know, accept, and take pride in himself or herself and to develop a sense of independence. Examples include the following:

Treats each child as an individual with his or her own strengths and needs and unique characteristics.

Is sensitive to differing cultural values and expectations concerning independence and expression of feelings.

Addresses each child by name, talks with every child every day, and encourages each child to call other children and adults by name.

Helps children through stress, separations, transition, and other crises.

When possible, offers children choices in activities, materials, and foods and respects their choices.

Encourages and helps children practice skills when eating, getting dressed, using toys and equipment, cleaning up, and helping others.

Gives one-to-one attention to each child as much as possible.

Enjoys children and directly expresses the enjoyment to them.

Delights in each child's success, expresses kindness and support when a child is having trouble, and helps him/her learn from mistakes.

Helps children recognize and accept their feelings, such as joy, affection, anger, jealousy, sadness, and fear, and express feelings in culturally appropriate ways.

Supports child's developing awareness of him- or herself as a member of a family and of an ethnic or social group by talking about families (using photographs, mirrors, and other appropriate objects) and by celebrating cultural events with children.

Uses books, pictures, stories, and discussion to help children identify positively with the experiences in their lives; for example, single-parent families, extended families, divorce, moving, or birth of siblings.

Comments directly, sincerely, and positively to children about their performance and ideas.

Helps children recognize and appreciate racial, ethnic, and ability differences and similarities.

Emphasizes cooperation in games and activities so that each child experiences success.

Provides many opportunities for all children, including those with disabling conditions, to feel effective, experience success, and gain the positive recognition of others.
Understands the effect of abuse and neglect on children's self-concept and works sensitively with them.
Working toward bilingual specialization
Supports the child's attempts to use the second language.
9. Functional Area: Social—Candidate helps each child feel accepted in the group, helps children learn to communicate and get along with others, and encourages feelings of empathy and mutual respect among children and adults. Examples include the following:
Learns about children's stages of social development and helps children and parents deal with such typical issues as separation anxiety, negative behavior, shyness, sexual identity, and making friends.
Has realistic expectation for young children's social behavior based on their level of development.
Serves as a social model by building a positive relationship with each child and parent and by maintaining positive relationships with other adults in the center.
Responds quickly and calmly to prevent children from hurting each other.
Helps children learn to respect the rights and possessions of others, in light of local expectations about sharing.
Encourages children to ask for, accept, and give help to one another.
Encourages children to make friends.
Helps the children become aware of their feelings and those of others by talking about feelings with each child.
Encourages play and relationship among all children across racial, language, ethnic, age, and gender groupings, including children with special needs.
Encourages children to express their feelings and assert rights in socially acceptable ways.
Encourages children to comfort and help each other.
Encourages children's attempts to use words to resolve conflicts.
Encourages cooperation rather than competition.
Helps children recognize their own and others' feelings, similarities, and differences and helps them empathize with others.
Encourages children to share stories and activities from their families and cultures.
Uses stories, pictures, and other materials to help children deal with issues such as sharing, separation, negative behavior, and disabilities.
Working toward bilingual specialization
Understands that the social roles and expectations for bilingual children in their family setting may be different from those of the child care program and helps the children to behave appropriately in each.
10. Functional Area: Guidance—Candidate provides a supportive environment in which children can begin to learn and practice appropriate and acceptable behaviors as individuals and as a group. Examples include the following:
Knows a variety of positive guidance methods—such as listening, reinforcement, and redirection—and uses each appropriately.
Relates guidance practices to knowledge of each child's personality and level of development.
Avoids negative methods, such as spanking, threatening, shouting, isolating, or shaming children.
Establishes guidelines for children's behavior that encourages self-control and that are simple, reasonable, and consistent.
Alerts children to changes in activities or routines well in advance and handles transitions from one activity to another with clear directions and patience.
Is able to modify play when it becomes over stimulating for any of the children, including children with disabling conditions.

Builds a trusting relationship with children as a foundation for positive guidance and self-discipline.
Anticipates confrontations between children and defuses provocative behavior.
Addresses the problem behavior or situation rather than labeling the child involved.
Helps parents develop realistic expectations for children's behavior in ways that help avoid disciplinary problems (e.g., discussing how long children can sit still).
Knows parents' disciplinary methods and expectations and selects those appropriate for use in the center.
Has realistic expectations about the children's attention spans, interests, social abilities, and physical needs, including disabled children.
Gives children real choices and accepts the choices made: for example, "Do you want to read a book with me or play on the climber?" or "Shall we have the apples or bananas for snack today?"
Lets children solve their own problems whenever possible.
Explains the reasons for limits in simple words, demonstrating whenever possible.
Uses firm and friendly techniques, such as reminding and persuading, when rules are forgotten or disobeyed.
Uses positive language with children: for example, "walk" rather than "don't run."
Involves children in establishing guidelines and limits.
Recognizes that sometimes serious behavior problems are related to developmental or emotional problems and works cooperatively with parents towards solutions.
Is aware of each child's limitations and abilities, uses guidance techniques accordingly, and explains rules at the child's level of understanding.
Working toward bilingual specialization
Uses the language in which each child understands expectations, limits, and guidance.

Competency Goal IV

To establish positive and productive relationships with families.

11. Functional Area: Families—Candidate maintains an open, friendly, and cooperative relationship with each child's family, encourages their involvement in the program, and supports the child's relationship with his or her family. Examples include the following:
Recognizes that children's primary caregivers may be single mothers or fathers, both parents, stepparents, grandparents, uncles, aunts, sisters, brothers, foster parents, or guardians.
Helps parents understand the development of their child and understand the child's point of view.
Provides opportunities for parents and other family members to share their skills and talents in the program.
Recognizes that caregivers can support parents in their role.
Offers parents information about health and social services and other resources in the community.
Respects each family's cultural background, religious belief, and childrearing practices.
Observes strict confidentiality regarding children and families and makes parents aware of this policy.
Encourages parents to talk about important family events and their children's special interests and behavior at home. Shares information frequently with parents about the child's experiences in the center.
Is able to discuss problem behavior with parents in a constructive, supportive manner.
Encourages parents to visit the center, participate in activities, and make suggestions for the daily program.
Respects and tries to understand the parents' views when they differ from the program's goals or policies and attempts to resolve the differences.
Tells parents about children's achievements and shares their pleasure in new abilities.
Helps parents with separations from child, recognizing parents' possible concerns about leaving their child.
Supports children and families under stress, working cooperatively with other professionals, as appropriate.

Sends home projects made by the children.
Shares information with parents about the learning opportunities for children in everyday household tasks and routines.
Helps parents identify resources to diagnose and treat children with disabilities.
Working toward bilingual specialization
Helps parents understand the program goals for bilingual development.
Supports families' desire to communicate their language and cultural heritage to their children through cultural practices.

Competency Goal V

To ensure a well-run, purposeful program responsive to participant needs.

12. Functional Area: Program Management—Candidate is a manager who uses all available resources to ensure an effective program operation. The Candidate is a competent organizer, planner, recordkeeper, communicator, and a cooperative coworker. Examples include the following:
Works with parents to identify the strengths and needs of each child.
Develops skills in observing and recording information about children and their families in a nonjudgmental manner for use in planning and carrying out daily program.
Maintains up-to-date records concerning the growth, health, behavior, and progress of each child and the group and shares the information with parents and appropriate center personnel.
Considers goals and objectives for each child and for the group as a whole. Develops realistic plans responsive to the needs of all, including children with disabling conditions.
Implements plans for each child by identifying developmentally and culturally appropriate activities and materials for each day.
Has a clear understanding of her/his responsibilities within the program.
Discusses issues that affect the program with appropriate staff and follows up on their resolution.
Works as a team member in the classroom and the program, and with substitutes, parents and volunteers. ....
Supports other staff by offering assistance and supervision when needed.
Makes or obtains materials and equipment appropriate to the developmental needs of the children.
Coordinates program plans (including guidance and discipline techniques) with parents, specialists, and program personnel, when appropriate.
Works with appropriate staff to choose substitutes carefully, requiring experience with children of the same ages whenever possible.
Implements procedures that help children make a smooth transition from one group to another.
Knows the social service, health, and education resources of the community and uses them when appropriate.
Recognizes possible learning problems and works with parents and specialists to develop plans specific to the needs of each child. Implements recommended treatment by following up on referrals, and working with the family to meet goals for the child.
Establishes liaison with community services that respond to family violence (e.g., Parents Anonymous, Child Protective Services, and shelter programs).
Working toward bilingual specialization
Recognizes and helps others recognize the needs of children and families who speak a different language and operate in a different cultural context.

Competency Goal VI

To maintain a commitment to professionalism.

13. Functional Area: Professionalism—Candidate makes decisions based on knowledge of early childhood theories and practices; promotes quality in child care services; and takes advantage of opportunities to improve competence, both for personal and professional growth and for the benefit of children and families. Examples include the following:

Enjoys working with young children in a group setting and demonstrates a positive attitude in her/his role.
Understands the philosophy of the program and can describe its goals and objectives to others.
Continues to gain knowledge of physical, cognitive, language, emotional, and social development as a basis for planning program goals.
Keeps all personal information about children and families confidential.
Participates in peer evaluation and is able to accept comments and criticism from colleagues, supervisors, and parents in a constructive way.
Takes advantage of opportunities for professional and personal development by joining appropriate professional organizations and attending meetings, training courses, and conferences.
Keeps informed about child care practices, research, legislation, and other developments in early childhood education.
Keeps current on regulatory, legislative and workforce issues and knows how they affect the welfare of young children and families.
Seeks information relevant to the needs of the children she/he is serving—for example, information on school readiness, bilingual development, and special needs—from professional magazines, community colleges, community services, other caregivers, and community members.
Recognizes that caregiver fatigue, low morale, and lack of work satisfaction decrease effectiveness and finds ways to meet her/his own needs and maintain energy and enthusiasm.
Works cooperatively with other staff members, accepts supervision, and helps promote a positive atmosphere in the center.
Learns about new laws and regulations affecting center care, children, and families.
Advocates quality services and rights for children and families.
Develops the ability to request additional resources for individual children or some aspect of the program.
Is aware that some of the normal developmental characteristics of children (e.g., crying, messiness, dependency, willfulness, negative behavior, curiosity about genital differences, etc.) often make adults uncomfortable. The caregiver can acknowledge these feelings in her- or himself, coworkers, and parents while minimizing negative reactions toward children.
Seeks information about sexual abuse and child abuse and neglect, keeps current on laws and policies concerning reporting and treatment of abuse, and learns effective ways of working with affected children and families.
Working toward bilingual specialization
Demonstrates the ability to understand, speak, read, and write in both languages and uses these skills in all aspects of the program.
Increases knowledge about bilingual education by reading, attending workshops, and consulting professionals.
Maintains and works to increase fluency in her/his second language.
Consistently provides opportunities for all children to acquire a second language.
Promotes the effective functioning of the bilingual program by attempting to clarify issues relating to bilingualism and multiculturalism.

Chapter 1

Child Development Principles

Section 1-1
Understanding Child Development

Section 1-2
Influences on Development

Section 1-1

Understanding Child Development

OBJECTIVES

- Describe the areas of child development.
- Explain three of the theories about child development.
- Identify the general principles of child development.
- Explain how children progress through developmental stages.

KEY TERMS

cognitive
sensorimotor
sensory
temperament
environment
heredity
neurons
synapses

Child development is the pattern of changes that scientists study in how children grow from birth to teen years. As you study this section, you will learn how, when, why, and in what order these changes happen. After you understand how a child might act or what a child might learn at different ages, you will better know what to expect from a child in your care.

Understanding Child Development

As an early childhood professional, you must pay attention to children's development so you can help them grow and learn. By watching and reacting to signs of progress, you can encourage all children to learn. Early childhood professionals can give extra help to children with developmental delays and tell their parents about special services.

Researchers who study development look at four areas: physical, intellectual, emotional, and social development. In this section, you'll learn about how children change at different ages in each of these areas.

Physical Development

Physical development includes the ways a child's body grows and what all the body can do. Growing taller and learning to walk are parts of physical development. The most dramatic changes in growth happen during infancy and the teen years.

Large Motor. As children grow, they gain muscle strength. They learn to move and control their muscles. When they can move and control their larger muscles, they have developed large motor skills. For example, when infants develop large muscles in their upper bodies, they hold up their heads. Later, when they develop large muscles in their lower bodies, they learn to creep and crawl. See Fig. 1-1A.

FIG. 1-1A. **Crawling is a large motor skill.** At what age do most infants start crawling?

FIG. 1-1C. **Running requires skill and good balance.**

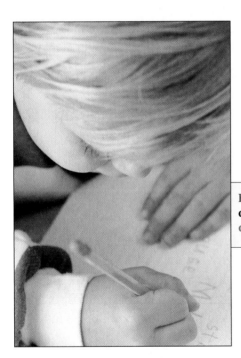

FIG. 1-1B. **Small motor skills allow children to do more detailed tasks.** What small motor skills should a child develop before learning how to cut with a scissors?

Small Motor. Children also develop small muscles, such as moving and controlling their fingers and wrists. For example, an infant who holds a rattle with the thumb and forefinger has developed small motor skills. As they grow, children further develop these skills. In time, they draw on paper and write their ABCs. See Fig. 1-1B.

Balance and Motor Coordination. Muscle growth alone doesn't allow children to develop

new skills. Their eyesight and balance affect how well their large and small motor skills help them perform tasks. Children must concentrate as they control their muscles. They must repeat the movement over and over. For example, children who walk, run, and jump have learned balance. Children who hop, skip, or throw have also learned to coordinate, or use many muscles at the same time. As children move on to even more complex motions, such as bike riding or playing the piano, they must further refine and strengthen their large and small motor skills. See Fig. 1-1C.

Intellectual Development

Intellectual development—often called **cognitive** development—includes how children think, communicate, make decisions, and solve problems. Researchers in cognitive science study how people think and learn. They found that infants develop these skills as they make sense of their experiences. Children learn best as they move within their surroundings. They explore it through their senses of sight, touch, taste, hearing, or smell. This is called **sensorimotor** (sen-suh-ree-MOH-tuhr) learning.

Sensory Skill Development. Children use their senses to learn about the objects around them. These are called **sensory** experiences because they involve the senses. For example, children notice if an item is soft or hard, bitter or sweet, loud or quiet. As children gather such information through their senses, their brains explain the information and store it.

Concept Development. As children gather information, they gradually develop concepts. Sight allows them to learn that objects vary. A young child's brain thrives on noticing the differences. While playing with colored building blocks, for example, children learn the concepts of size, color, and shape. With further intellectual development, children learn to make more difficult comparisons, such as realizing that some objects are heavier than others. See Fig. 1-2.

Language Development. Language allows children to organize and express their thoughts and ideas. It helps them ask questions to better understand experiences. Children use language to explore what interests them.

Development of Thinking Skills. A child's early years bring rapid changes in thinking abilities. Over time, intellectual development becomes more complex, slows down, and continues to develop gradually throughout childhood. This process includes learning to analyze, evaluate, and solve problems. As children grow intellectually, they also learn to understand cause and effect. As a result, they understand the consequences of their actions.

FIG. 1-2. Learning to sort by color and shape is a process children go through in their early years. What other factors indicate children are developing intellectually?

Emotional Development

Emotional development takes place as children form feelings about themselves and others. They experience such feelings as happiness, excitement, fear, frustration, and anger. In learning effective ways to react to children's emotions, early childhood professionals are more helpful to children in understanding their feelings and accepting them in positive ways.

Trust and Attachment. Healthy emotional development begins during the first days and years of life. When children form emotional bonds, or a special attachment, to a small circle of people, they learn trust. If you are consistent and responsive in providing care to infants and toddlers, you will generate and reinforce their trust in you.

Temperament. Research shows that each child is born with an individual **temperament**, or a typical way he or she responds to people and situations. From birth, some children are easygoing and accept change well. Others are anxious and cannot sit still or finish a task. Some children are friendly and look for more ways to play and be with others. Some children are slow to warm up to people and like to play alone. When caring for children, you must identify and respect their individual temperaments and react with sensitivity.

Identity and Self-Esteem. Over time, children create an individual identity, separate from their parents. It becomes a mental picture they form of who they are and whether or not they are attractive, capable, and likable. Self-esteem is the overall feeling children have about themselves. They may have positive or negative pictures of themselves. How other people treat a child in his or her early years greatly influences the child's identity and self-esteem. Children learn to think favorably of themselves when care providers show them love, respect, and support. See Fig. 1-3.

FIG. 1-3. Care providers who respond effectively to children's emotions help children grow in trust and self-esteem.

Self-Control. As children mature, they better understand their emotions and learn to control them. Toddlers have a reputation for temper tantrums. Yet with guidance, they learn to use words to express their needs and wants. When you show children that you know how to control your own feelings, you help children learn how to manage their emotions. Children gain better self-control as they accept that everyone has feelings they must respect.

Social Development

Social development builds as children learn how to get along with others and make friends. Children learn to play together, share, and trade. They find ways to settle disagreements through the use of words, rather than hitting, kicking, pushing, or biting.

Children also learn that society has rules to follow. Getting along with others means knowing and obeying these rules. For example, children learn to reply when someone speaks to them. They learn to give a person a chance to finish talking before they say something. They learn to whisper in certain places.

As children master social skills, peers and adults are more likely to accept them. This acceptance gives children positive feelings about themselves. Without social skills and the acceptance that comes with them, children feel alone and unworthy.

Family Relationships. Families influence social development when they talk to their children about their beliefs and values. The practices parents develop over time for their families reveal their values. Special traditions, for example, introduce children to their heritage. Traditions also show the love within the family and how important the family is to each person. Family love and values shape the children's values.

FIG. 1-4. **Group play gives children an opportunity to develop and practice social skills.**

Peer Relationships. As children interact with others, they learn that everyone has different ideas and ways of doing things. Children in early childhood programs gradually develop skills that allow them to adjust to ways other than their own. Such skills may include listening and taking turns. As a result, they make friends and become accepted members of a group. See Fig. 1-4.

Child Development Research

Hundreds of years ago, many people thought children were just miniature adults. Few realized that children have specific needs and characteristics. As adults grew more concerned about children's ways, they asked more questions of doctors and other scientists. In order to learn more, researchers developed and tested theories using the scientific method. They watched children, collected data, and drew conclusions. Researchers today continue to study child development.

Researchers Describe Development

The findings of many researchers have created a body of knowledge about how children develop. Some findings have had greater impact than others. Keep in mind that some scientists do not always accept another's conclusion as true. Over time, however, new research may reveal that older research was true or not. It may also offer new information and ideas.

Child Development Researchers

The findings of certain researchers have gained wider acceptance among scientists and child development experts. They are described as follows:

- **Jean Piaget** (psychologist; 1896-1980). According to Piaget, children develop cognitive skills based on how they mature, interact with others, and react and adapt to their physical surroundings. After observing his own children, Piaget defined stages that children pass through in developing thinking and intellectual skills. See Fig. 1-5.

FIG. 1-5.

- **Lawrence Kohlberg** (cognitive development researcher; 1927-1987). Kohlberg's research also listed developmental stages, but in how children learn right from wrong. Young children choose by what seems in their best interests. By the teen years, children are influenced by what their parents and friends would think best. Kohlberg said adults who are mature go with what is best and just for society as a whole.

- **Eric Erikson** (psychoanalytical researcher; 1902-1994). Erikson saw a person's identity and self-esteem as results of how a person handles life's challenges, such as learning to toilet and becoming a parent. His social development stages ranged from a baby's developing trust to an older adult's thinking back positively about major life decisions.

- **Alfred Binet** (psychologist; 1857-1911). Binet believed intelligence increases with age. He said that children show their intelligence by how they make judgments, understand word meanings, and solve problems. Based on these skills, he created the IQ test, or the intelligence quotient (KWOH-shuhnt) test, called the Stanford-Binet Intelligence Scale.

- **Urie Bronfrenbrenner** (developmental psychologist; 1917-present). Bronfrenbrenner emphasized that a child develops within a context of many environments, each one influencing the others. A child's **environment** includes the people, culture, and physical and social surroundings in which the child lives. Bronfrenbrenner believes children develop socially the way they do because they are born in a particular culture, during a certain period of history, in a particular community, and within a distinct family.

- **Benjamin Bloom** (psychologist; 1913-present). Bloom ranked thinking skills from least to most difficult. He said that memorizing facts, for example, is easier than solving problems. His ranking is called Bloom's Taxonomy of Educational Objectives.

- **Lev Vygotsky** (psychologist; 1896-1934). Vygotsky studied cognitive development, as did Piaget. He emphasized that the social interactions children have with the people around them greatly influence children's intellectual ability to gain knowledge, think, and learn a language.

- **Abraham Maslow** (personality theorist; 1908-1970). Maslow proposed a motivation theory based on a hierarchy of needs. The lowest and most basic needs are physical, such as food and shelter. Higher levels include safety, love and belongingness, esteem, and self-actualization. Maslow believed people must first meet their basic needs before they can focus on achieving higher needs. See Fig. 1-6.

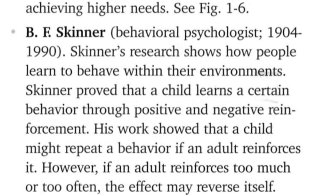

FIG. 1-6.

- **B. F. Skinner** (behavioral psychologist; 1904-1990). Skinner's research shows how people learn to behave within their environments. Skinner proved that a child learns a certain behavior through positive and negative reinforcement. His work showed that a child might repeat a behavior if an adult reinforces it. However, if an adult reinforces too much or too often, the effect may reverse itself.

- **Sigmund Freud** (neurologist, psychoanalyst; 1856-1939). Freud believed a child's personality develops through a predictable pattern of psychosexual stages, which he linked to natural biological needs. Freud believed any emotional or psychological problems people have as adults are connected to how their parents and care providers met their basic needs as children.

- **Bruce Perry** (medical researcher; 1956-present). Perry has helped determine how the brain grows before and after birth. His findings explain how the brain processes, stores, and retrieves information. He believes brain growth and functioning, which affect all areas of human development, come from a continuous interaction between heredity and life experiences.

FIG. 1-7.

Heredity is the passing of parents' qualities and traits through genes at their child's conception. See Fig. 1-7.

- **Howard Gardner** (education professor; 1943-present). Gardner disagrees with Binet's belief that a single test can prove a person's intelligence. Gardner proposes that many kinds of intelligence exist, and that the IQ test focuses on only a few. Gardner's multiple intelligences theory allows that a person has a fuller range of skills and abilities that may lead to a successful life. It recognizes, for example, Michael Jordan's exceptional athletic ability as kinesthetic, or bodily movement, intelligence. It recognizes Oprah's interpersonal intelligence, or her noted ability to understand and motivate people.

- **Stella Chess & Alexander Thomas** (psychologists; unknown-present, 1914-present). Chess and Thomas studied birth temperaments. Their findings encouraged care providers to identify and respond sensitively to children's temperaments. In doing so, they properly nurture children, according to each child's needs.

Principles of Child Development

Children in every part of the world develop in similarly predictable patterns and stages. Many factors influence their growth, but the foundation of their development is the brain. The four general principles of child development include:

- The brain coordinates development.
- The development rate is individual.
- Development is sequential.
- Development is interrelated.

The Brain Coordinates Development

The brain records and interprets a child's mental and sensory experiences. Before the child's body understands information and puts it to good use, it must pass through the child's brain.

Although an infant's brain is not fully formed at birth, it has about 100 billion nerve cells, called **neurons**. At birth, the infant's brain is about 25 percent of its adult weight. By age six, a child's brain reaches its full adult weight. The brain continues to grow throughout childhood but not in weight or neurons. What develops is the number of **synapses**, or electrical connections between the neurons. Some experts say that, by adulthood, the brain has more than 100 trillion such connections. As they increase, neuron pathways develop. This brain wiring permits all parts of the body to receive information, which then tells the body how to function. Having more and more neuron pathways leads to a greater capacity for thinking and learning. They are actually learning pathways. Scientists say a child's synapse activity is two and one-half times faster than an adult's. As a result, children learn much faster than adults.

Sensory Experiences Encourage Brain Development. A child's early experiences and heredity affect brain development. If children experience a secure, engaging environment from infancy, brain function develops as it should. A child's synapses increase with proper nurturing and plenty of sensory and movement

FIG. 1-8. Using one or more senses while playing helps encourage brain growth in children. Identify at least five activities in which children would use two or more senses.

FIG. 1-9. **Learning experiences that are repeated help children accurately learn concepts. What repeated experiences might help children learn to read?**

experiences. Sensory experiences, such as squeezing a ball or singing a song, naturally engage children's interests. Because they enjoy such activities, children continue to explore and learn. See Fig. 1-8.

Repeated and Related Experiences Build Brain Connections. Children enjoy learning by copying their parents' behaviors. They also love to repeat favorite activities, such as listening to nursery rhymes and bedtime stories. This repetition exercises the brain in retaining information. Babies grasp the concept of cause and effect by playing peek-a-boo or stacking and knocking down blocks. If you plan related experiences for preschoolers, it will help them gain and retain knowledge better. For example, if children watch birds, draw birds, pretend to fly like birds, and later listen to stories about birds, their concept of bird features is more accurate and detailed. See Fig. 1-9.

Brain Development Occurs During Critical Periods. Scientists have discovered that different parts of the brain develop at different times. Certain types of learning occur during a single period of a child's early years. Each development area has its own "window of opportunity." The part of the brain that controls language develops during the first two years of life. It's critical that parents and care providers respond to children's babbling and attempts to communicate during this time to help them develop language skills. The part of the brain that controls social development begins developing from birth. Practices and routines that encourage a child's attachment to others are very important. The critical period for learning to play an instrument or learning a second language ends by age ten. Children can learn these skills later, but their brains offer the learning pathways in early childhood.

FIG. 1-10.

SEQUENCE PRINCIPLES OF CHILD DEVELOPMENT

From Top to Bottom	Children progressively master body movement and coordination from the head downward. First, children can lift their head and then the trunk of their body. Eventually, they coordinate their whole body to walk.	
From Center to Outside	 Children develop from the center of their bodies outward. Development progresses from the spine to the arms and legs, and then to the fingers and toes. Children can use their shoulders and swing their arms in large circles before they can coordinate and maneuver their wrists and fingers.	
From Large to Small	Children develop control over large muscles before small muscles. For example, children can run and jump before they can throw or catch a ball.	
From General to Specific	 Development progresses gradually from general to specific. Children's attempts to develop new abilities start out simple and become increasingly complex. For instance, children jump up and down with both feet before they can hop on one foot. Running comes first, skipping later. Babies make sounds before saying words.	

Development Rate Is Individual

The interesting thing about development—and the challenging part for you as a care provider—is that it doesn't occur at exactly the same time or rate for every child. All children experience growth and develop new abilities at a unique pace.

Researchers have found that developmental stages are predictable, especially during early childhood. The rate at which each child progresses through a stage may vary, but the child must pass through all stages to grow and mature. When you notice that a child's progress through a stage is significantly delayed or advanced, plan to give extra attention or help to the child.

Sometimes a child may experience different rates of development in each area. A child with strong intellectual abilities may not have developed age-appropriate social skills. Researchers have found that boys tend to develop more slowly than girls, as much as two to six months behind girls of the same age. Detecting and understanding the difference helps caregivers react and respond more relevantly to both boys and girls.

Development Is Sequential

The skills children learn develop gradually, building one upon another. Development follows an orderly sequence, or in a step-by-step pattern. For example, children learn the letters of the alphabet before learning to spell words. Motor learning also progresses from simple to complex. For example, when learning to play with a ball, children first hold the balls—touching them to sense their shapes and textures. Then they experiment by rolling, dropping, and bouncing the balls. After much play, a child's brain eventually learns to coordinate eye and hand movements, which, in time, gives the child the ability to throw and catch a ball. The following chart describes the four sequence principles of child development. See Fig. 1-10.

Development Is Interrelated

Increasing connections between developmental areas is very important. Growth in one area can affect growth in another. For example, it is easier for children to work out a fight with another child (emotional development) once they speak a language (intellectual development). Before children can master drawing or writing skills, they must experience many different play activities that aid in large and small motor development. Early childhood professionals must consider the total child when planning activities that will promote growth, development, and learning.

Section *1-1* Knowledge Check

1. Name the four areas of child development.
2. Contrast Binet's ideas on intelligence with Gardner's ideas.
3. What specific types of experiences assist children's brain development?

Mini-Lab

In teams, choose a child researcher or theorist and prepare a report about his or her research. Use print and Internet resources to prepare your report. Share your findings with the class.

Section **1-2**

Influences on Development

| OBJECTIVES | KEY TERMS |

OBJECTIVES

- Differentiate between heredity and environment in child development.
- Identify other important factors that affect proper child development.
- Describe potential characteristics of children at risk.
- Explain how prevention and intervention services help at-risk children and their families.

KEY TERMS

**at risk
prenatal
cesarean birth
intervention
    services
referral**

The basic principles of child development apply to all children, but the rate and success of each developmental stage vary with each child. As you study this chapter, you will learn about the factors that affect the proper growth and development of children. After you understand the impact each factor might have, you will better know how to identify characteristics in children who may be at risk of developmental delays. You will also learn about resources and services that help parents avoid such risks or assist their children with special needs.

Factors That Affect Proper Development

Proper growth and development depends on heredity and environment. Heredity may pass on to children serious diseases or physical or mental disabilities. Children who live in **at-risk** environments—those that interfere with proper development and well-being—may not receive enough nurturing and stimulation from their parents or care providers. This can cause them to developmentally fall behind other children their age.

Heredity & Environment

Heredity and environment are the two general factors that affect how well children grow and develop. Researchers have debated for many decades which of the two has the greater impact. Many scientists today believe that heredity and environment each plays a very important part.

A child's heredity is set before birth and is unchangeable. Parents form a unique biological set of genes for their child at conception. These genes decide which of the parents' traits the child will have. Heredity influences how the

Prenatal Development

As you learned in Section 1-1, the rate of development varies with each child and for many reasons. For example, a child may experience problems before birth or during delivery. Injury or illness during the earliest years of life may also slow down the typical rate of development.

Maternal Health Before Delivery. An unborn infant relies completely on the mother for nutrients during her pregnancy. The infant is more likely to be born healthy if the mother is healthy. The mother needs ample nutrition not only for her own energy and health, but also for her rapidly developing child. To ensure a healthy child, a pregnant woman must receive competent **prenatal**, or before birth, health care, especially during the first three months of pregnancy.

Prenatal Drug Use. By using drugs, such as alcohol, caffeine, nicotine, or illegal drugs, a pregnant woman may hurt her infant's development. Depending on the drug, the infant may have physical deformities or mental disabilities. For example, infants born with Fetal Alcohol Syndrome may have deformed hearts or faces or slow physical growth. They may also show poor motor coordination and other learning disabilities. Mothers who use such addictive drugs as cocaine or heroin often deliver their infants early. Usually born addicted to the drug, these babies also have very fragile nervous systems. They go through a painful withdrawal from the drug. Many have severe learning disabilities.

The Birth Process. Most births are routine and predictable, but some are risky. For example, an infant's oxygen flow may be cut off during delivery, causing brain damage. Some infants do not enter the birth canal with their heads down. Their delivery may require the use of forceps or a surgical delivery, called a **cesarean birth.** Each may cause further delays and higher risks.

FIG. 1-11. Although heredity strongly influences development (as shown with these twins), it is important to remember that heredity and environment work together to influence how children use their inherited abilities. Other than physical characteristics, what are some other ways that heredity can influence development?

child will look, such as hair and eye color, adult height, and body shape. It also influences a child's physical, intellectual, emotional, and social strengths and weaknesses, such as overall health and learning ease. See Fig. 1-11.

A child's environment after birth is ever-changing. Parents and care providers help in giving an infant a stable environment. Researchers have found that such environmental experiences as good nutrition and health care, responsive care and nurturing, and an engaging play environment lead to proper growth and development.

Health & Nutrition

Growth and development moves along properly if children are well fed and healthy. Basic health care and nutrition help development. Parents and care providers who ensure that children have well-child preventive and routine health care services help the children avoid severe illness. Illness or injury slows down growth and learning.

Children are well fed if they eat food that gives them at least the minimum daily requirements of nutrients, such as protein, vitamins, and minerals. Only when children receive a variety of nutritious foods—such as whole grains, proteins, and fresh fruits and vegetables—can they receive the fuel they must have for growth and energy. See Fig. 1-12.

Boosting Brain Power

Nutrition Impacts Brain Development. Proper nutrition plays an important role in everyone's life. Poor nutrition during pregnancy and during the first few years of a child's life can result in neurological and behavioral disorders and possibly mental retardation. In order to avoid the serious affects of poor nutrition, developing a lifelong habit of proper nutrition is essential. Care providers play an important role in providing proper meals and snacks to children and teaching children and their parents about proper nutrition.

FIG. 1-12. **Children need nutritious foods at regular intervals in order to grow and develop. List at least three foods that would make good snack choices for young children.**

FIG. 1-13. Every child brings unique family and cultural experiences to the early childhood classroom. How can you affirm each child's diversity?

Responsive Care & Nurturing

Children need nurturing from their parents and other special people around them. An attentive care provider responds quickly to children's basic needs for comfort, love, and assistance. Nurturing is effective if a care provider genuinely enjoys interacting with children. Such caregivers show enthusiasm and encourage children with each new task. A care provider's calm dialogue and warm facial expressions during feeding times, for example, communicate love and worth to the child.

Developing routines—such as bathing, feeding, diapering, and dressing—help nurture a child's overall development. For example, when a care provider tickles a baby's tummy during diapering, a foundation for the child's social development begins building. When a care

provider sings lullabies and rocks the baby to sleep, the child begins to build trust and a bond with the provider.

Parents nurture their children within the setting of their family's values and goals. Their ethnicity, homeland, religion, and unique experiences affect the family's beliefs, traditions, and other practices. Make it a priority to become familiar with the cultural beliefs of the families and children you serve. See Fig. 1-13.

Economic Resources

While parents at all income levels can love and nurture their children, families with very limited economic resources often may not afford the preventive health care services their children need.

Children in families with few economic resources are more likely to be poorly nourished than children in more financially stable families. Poor nutrition affects the child's brain development. It also lowers her energy level for play and taxes her stamina for learning.

Poor living conditions also influence children's development. Crowded, unsanitary, or unsafe conditions may jeopardize children's sense of safety and security. These conditions have a negative impact on children's social development, too. Children may not often play outside if safety is an issue.

Children at Risk

Many people are alarmed when they hear an adult call a child "at risk." They believe it's a label that lowers a child's self-esteem. Children at risk are those who experience any condition that interferes with proper development and well-being. Children at risk have a greater chance of developmental delays. You must use

care to use this term only with other early childhood professionals and parents, but not with children.

Risk Characteristics

Characteristics of children at risk vary widely. Some children are at risk of learning failure because their language development is slow or their behavior in groups is unacceptable. Other children are at risk of child abuse or malnutrition. As a care provider, you must be alert to the at-risk indicators for the children under your care. See Figures 1-14A and 1-14B.

Risk Intervention & Prevention

Early childhood professionals help children at risk when they spot signs of problems and take action. They must be hardworking in observing each child under their care for signs of slow development. If ignored, developmental problems can become more serious and interfere with a child's life.

FIG. 1-14A.

CHARACTERISTICS OF CHILDREN AT RISK

Physical Development
- Drug exposure prior to birth or during breast-feeding.
- Premature birth, low birth weight, or birth delivery problems.
- Physical disability or other special needs.
- Malnutrition, poor overall health, or low energy level.

Intellectual Development
- Inability to listen, concentrate, or participate according to expected age and abilities.
- Significantly delayed language for child's age and experiences.
- Mental disability or other special needs.

Emotional Development
- Behavior problems, especially aggression toward self or others.
- Signs of childhood depression, such as sleep or toileting problems.

Social Development
- Early isolation from others.
- Family moves often.

Environmental Factors
- Poverty.
- Signs of neglect or abuse.
- Untreated mental illness of family member.
- Exposure to domestic or community violence.

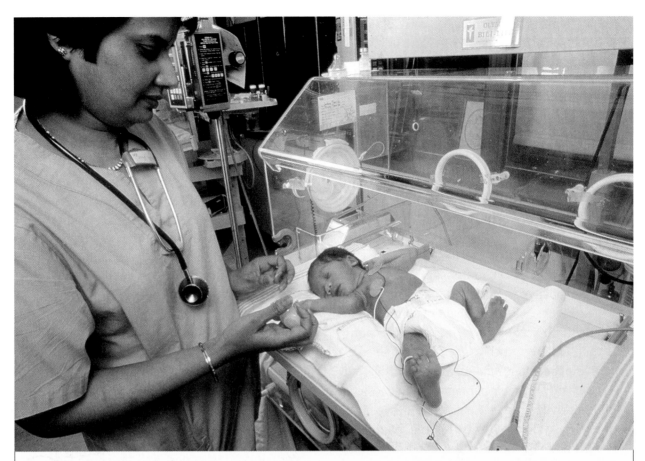

FIG. 1-14B. **Premature birth can cause developmental problems during early childhood.** Investigate ways that early childhood professionals can provide specialized help for children with developmental delays.

After you identify a developmental problem, it is your responsibility as a professional to help the child's parents understand the problem and seek further help. Resources and specialized help are called **intervention services**. When you help the family pursue such services, you reduce or eliminate the risks for the child.

Parent Education. Helping parents understand the prenatal influences on child development means that parent education must begin before pregnancy. Parents also need help in learning how to give safe and proper care to their child. Parents can meet childrearing challenges if they know about developmental needs and how they should respond to them.

- Parent education during pregnancy helps parents learn how to balance all the new responsibilities that come with raising a family. Typical parent education programs include such topics as time management, basic first aid, and childhood nutrition. Helping parents learn positive ways of guiding children's behavior lessens child abuse and neglect.

- Parent education can take many forms. Some parents like formal classes. Other parents like support group meetings at which they casually discuss topics with other parents. Many parenting books and videos offer necessary information and wise advice. Good early childhood programs have parent lending libraries, stocked with such resources. See Fig. 1-15 on page 45.

Intergenerational *Interactions*

Support for Grandparents Raising Grandchildren

Today, more and more grandparents face the unique challenge of raising their grandchildren in their homes. The child's parents often face a life crisis that renders them incapable of caring for their children, such as the death of a spouse or child or substance abuse. Single teen parents may also rely on their parents to become the child's primary care provider while the teen completes school or works full-time. Many groups and networks exist to provide valuable information, education, and even legal assistance for grandparents raising grandchildren:

- **Support Groups.** Grandparents can contact community service agencies that work with older adults and children, local health departments, religious organizations, or school counselors to locate grandparenting support groups. Many states offer special assistance: for example, The Illinois Senior Helpline sponsored by the Illinois Administration on Aging has a Web site that directs grandparents to support groups.

   Organizations such as AARP, Inc., can help grandparents contact local support groups through their Grandparent Information Center. You can locate AARP on the Internet or call your local office. The YWCA and Cooperative Extension Services conduct grandparenting workshops and publish newsletters to inform and educate grandparents raising grandchildren.
- **Monetary and Legal Issues.** Grandparents can contact local family service or public

health agencies or their local Social Security Administration Office for information on monetary and legal issues that arise when raising grandchildren. Many states offer specific assistance to caregiving grandparents. In Illinois, for example, the Land of Lincoln Legal Assistance Foundation, Inc., offers statewide legal aid.
- **Housing Opportunities.** Grandparents can contact their state's Department on Aging for information and referrals about special housing needs when raising grandchildren. In Massachusetts, for example, new residential facilities have been designed specifically for intergenerational living. In Florida, the Kinship Care Warmline provides grandparents with referral information on housing needs as well as medical care, child care, educational services, and emotional support. You can find more information about the Kinship Care Warmline on the Internet.

By reaching out to a variety of governmental or consumer groups, organizations, and networks, grandparents can discover vital resources to help them successfully raise their grandchildren.

Follow-Up

Research local community groups, state agencies, and national organizations that offer support to grandparents and their grandchildren. Interview a grandparent who utilizes these community services. Write a summary of the benefits these services offer grandparents.

FIG. 1-15. **Parent education may be part of an early childhood program.** How can parent education benefit young children?

Support Services. Parents usually receive information on child rearing first from family members, especially from their parents and grandparents. If their own parents live far away or if their children's needs are unusual, families may need other resources. You should give them a **referral**, or send the parent to another resource. Effective early childhood programs keep a list of local family-centered agencies and parenting Web sites. You will know of hospitals, health departments, schools, and social service agencies that offer low-cost programs for parents and children with special needs. They help children with language delays, poor large motor skills, or mental disabilities, for example.

Section 1-2 Knowledge Check

1. Identify five factors that affect a child's proper development.

2. What are three characteristics of children who may be at risk of developmental delays?

3. What kinds of referrals might you offer a parent of a child at risk?

Mini-Lab

Review three prime-time television programs. Record each type of violence and the number of each violent act for each show—one column for each type of violence. Then list the ways you think violence affects the values and attitudes of young children. Identify three ways you or society can prevent the impact of violence on children. Discuss your findings with the class.

Chapter 1 Review & Activities

Section Summaries

1-1 The four areas of child development are physical, intellectual, emotional, and social.

1-1 Researchers observe children, develop theories, and conduct experiments to draw conclusions about child development.

1-1 Basic developmental principles apply to all children.

1-1 There are four general principles of child development.

1-2 Many factors affect the rate of a child's development.

1-2 Certain characteristics identify children at risk of developmental delays.

1-2 Prevention and intervention services help parents meet the needs of their children at risk.

1-2 Parent education offers parents further help in responding to their children's developmental needs.

Check Your Knowledge

1. Explain the four areas of child development.
2. List four researchers and describe how each influenced the study of child development.
3. What are the four principles of child development? Give an example of each.
4. What makes up the learning pathways of the brain?
5. Why do repeated and interrelated activities promote brain development?
6. Explain the concept of windows of opportunity in brain development.
7. Identify three factors that may affect whether a child is at risk.
8. How might a family's economic resources affect a child's development?
9. Describe two preventive steps a parent might take to avoid certain developmental risks in his or her child.
10. Describe three resources for parent education.

Thinking Critically

1. Read at least three research articles on brain development. Summarize the contents of each article on your own paper. Contrast the information in the articles. Is the information consistent within all of the research articles? Why or why not?

2. If a mother told you she couldn't afford to take her ill child to the doctor, what steps could you take to help her find assistance? Draw conclusions about each option available to her.

3. Contrast the ways heredity and environment influence child development.

4. Analyze how an early childhood professional's own self-esteem level may affect the children in his or her care.

Practical Applications

1. **Video Review.** Watch a parent education video on child development. If you were a child care provider, would you recommend this video to your parents? Why or why not? Rate its quality and effectiveness. Use the following rating scale: **4**=Excellent; **3**=Good; **2**=Fair; **1**=Poor.

2. **Observation.** Locate an early childhood program in your area that serves children with special needs. Observe the teachers and classroom environment. Take notes on how the teachers meet the children's needs. Answer this follow-up question after your observation: How do environmental factors influence the growth, development, and success of the special needs child?

3. **Social Worker Interview.** Interview a social worker or public health care provider who works with children at risk. What are the greatest challenges in this kind of work? What advice does he or she have for someone entering the early childhood profession?

Observing for Development

Request permission from the program director to observe a child in a local early childhood program for one hour. Schedule your observation during a time when active play takes place. Take a pad of paper and a pen to record your observations. Then complete the following steps:

Step 1: Record the date and time of your observation.

Step 2: Select a child to observe, but do not record the child's name. Watch the child closely with patience. What are some of the child's abilities in all four areas of development? What can the child do? Not do?

Step 3: In what ways do the teachers recognize and encourage the child's skills and abilities? How many sensory activities does the child seek out?

Step 4: Describe the child's social interactions with peers. Does the child appear to be learning to view the world from a peer's point of view? Does the child appear able to practice social skills, such as trading, sharing, negotiating, or problem solving?

Step 5: At the end of your observation, write down questions that occur to you about child development. Seek insight or answers to your questions from your instructor or this text.

Step 6: Keyboard your observation notes with a written summary for presentation in your career portfolio.

Chapter 2
Adult Development Principles

Section 2-1
Aging & Adult Development

Section 2-2
Basic Needs of Older Adults

Section 2-1

Aging & Adult Development

OBJECTIVES

- Identify myths and stereotypes about aging.
- Describe three principles of aging.
- Compare the researchers' stages of adult development.
- Discuss two aging issues linked to the increasing older adult population.

KEY TERMS

gerontology
sociology
geriatrics
longevity
generativity
elder
baby boomers

Aging is a natural process that begins at the moment of birth and continues throughout life. As you learned in Chapter 1, changes occur at each stage of child development. Change is also a key element in adult development. Aging issues affect people throughout their lives. Because of improvements in health care and widespread knowledge about healthy lifestyles, you will likely live a healthier and longer life than your great-grandparents. Studying about aging will help you know if you're interested in a career caring for older adults.

Aging

Researchers in many fields study aging, especially with greater numbers of Americans reaching retirement age. For example, **gerontology** (jer-uhn-TAH-luh-jee) is the study of the aging process. It involves information from biology, economics, family and consumer sciences, law, medicine, mental health, political science, and sociology. **Sociology** (soh-see-AH-luh-jee) is the study of society, its institutions, and social relationships. **Geriatrics** (jer-ee-A-trihks) is a field of medicine that focuses on preventing or managing common diseases for older adults. Researchers in these fields look for ways to improve the quality of life for older adults.

As larger numbers of the population enter older adulthood, the demand for more caregivers will also grow. For example, geriatric care managers help older people and their families meet their long-term care needs. Your responsibilities as a geriatric case manager would include helping with money management, family or individual therapy, and decisions on who will supervise their overall care. You would learn about the services available to older people in your community, as well as costs and quality.

Myths & Stereotypes About Aging

Children often get their first insights into aging from myths and stereotypes they hear in jokes and stories. For example, parents use

FIG. 2-1.

MYTHS & STEREOTYPES ABOUT AGING

Myth/Stereotype	Fact
Older adults become intellectually impaired.	As people age, their brains must be challenged for them to continue to learn. Some older adults experience intellectual decline, although not severe enough to interfere with daily living.
All older adults are senile.	As people age, many tend to experience some memory loss for various reasons.
Older adults are depressed and have every right to be.	Older adults tend to have happier moods than do younger adults.
Older adults have nothing to contribute to society.	Older adults contribute greatly to society by volunteering in their communities and helping family members.
Men and women age the same way.	Men and women age differently.
Most older adults live in nursing homes or other facilities for older adults.	The vast majority of older adults live in their own homes.
Most older adults spend much of their time in bed because of poor health.	Approximately three-fourths of older people ages 65 to 75 and two-thirds of people over 75 are in good health.
All older adults drive too slowly.	Older adults drive with caution. As they age, they tend to slow down when they drive because their reaction time is longer.
Older adults do not respect young people, but yet they want younger people to respect them.	Older adults appreciate others showing respect. If they receive respectful treatment, they will return it.

nursery rhymes that tell about the "forgetful old man" or "the little old lady who lived in the shoe; she had so many children that she didn't know what to do." As children grow older, they continue to hear adults use such phrases as "over-the-hill" or "past your prime." Some children may not easily witness the aging process if they don't live near their grandparents or other relatives. Consequently, myths and stereotypes become the basis of these children's ideas about aging. Here are some myths and stereotypes about aging you may have heard about, along with what researchers know as fact. See Fig. 2-1.

Studying aging when you are young enables you to witness the aging process in people of all ages without any preconceived ideas. You will know that some are sick, mentally slow, or physically weak. You will also expect to see many others leading full and active lives. For example, many older adults, even after retirement, serve as mentors to young people in the workplace. See Fig. 2-2.

Studying aging teaches you the facts about growing older. You will better understand how a person's lifestyle choices influence the quality of life and length of lifespan. You will understand the environmental and medical care factors affecting how long people live. For example, immunizations at specific ages and periodic health screenings are critical factors for greater **longevity** (lahn-JEH-vuh-tee), or the length of a life span. Researchers say 50 percent of longevity is linked to a person's lifestyle choices, 20 percent is heredity, and 30 percent is linked to environmental factors.

Principles of Aging

Understanding all aspects of the aging process enables you to improve your insights about those who are older. The following six principles of aging will help you better understand the process. See Fig. 2-3.

The Aging Process

Aging is a gradual process that varies greatly from person to person. Through people's life stages, they make decisions and take actions that affect the ways in which they'll age. Researchers study four kinds of aging.

Chronological Aging. Chronological aging is the number of years from a person's birth. It does not take into account physical health or intellectual ability.

Biological Aging. Biological aging concerns a person's body changes that slow the working ability of its systems, such as the respiratory and circulatory systems. When body strength declines, for example, people may become more susceptible to disease because the immune system is not functioning as well.

FIG. 2-2. **Because of changes in health care and lifestyle, most older adults are leading active and fulfilling lives.**

FIG. 2-3.

PRINCIPLES OF AGING

Aging happens to everyone in every culture.	Every person in the world ages.
Aging is a normal process.	Aging is a lifelong process that starts from birth. People view aging differently at various times in their lives. For example, children look forward to the process of growing up. After they turn 50, people view the aging process as growing old.
Aging varies.	Each person's journey through the aging process is individual. Many factors determine the ways an individual will age throughout life.
Older adults do continue to learn.	Learning is a lifelong process. People may learn differently at each of life's stages.
Older adults can and do adjust to change.	As people age, they must adjust to fit their varying needs through life's stages. For example, spouses may die and financial needs may change. Older adults accept change as they involve themselves in new activities and make new friends.
Older adults want to continue to make decisions about their lives.	As people age, they want to keep control over their lives. To prevent older adults from becoming indecisive, help them through a major life change by giving them any options that exist. This will help maintain their self-esteem. Even if older adults cannot maintain complete control, it is best to keep them involved in making decisions.

Psychological Aging. Psychological aging affects intelligence, learning, personality, and memory due to changes in older adults' sensory and perceptual processes. Aging does not affect everyone's psychological functions in the same way. For example, if a person's thinking capacity has gone down, his or her social functioning may still be as it has always been.

Sociological Aging. Sociological aging deals with how society influences older people's views on aging and their lifestyle choices. Health, income, work, and leisure as they relate to family, friends, and community are all part of sociological aging. See Fig. 2-4.

Adult Development

Few researchers studied how adults develop until the mid-1900s. They became interested when people began to live longer and society became rapidly changing. The following information describes three key researchers and the stages in their theories. Much of the research starts with Erik Erickson's theories of human development.

Erikson's Life Stages

As you read in Chapter 1, Erikson said that self-esteem and identity are results of how well

FIG. 2-4. Once older adults retire from the workforce, they look forward to social opportunities and interacting with friends and family. In what social activities do older adults you know participate?

people deal with life's challenges during certain stages of development. Erikson defined eight stages in life. The first five deal with development from birth to 21 years. The last three deal with adult development. Erikson describes his stages as a person's battle between two forces. If the person has a positive end to the conflict, he or she makes an easier transition to the next stage of development. See Fig. 2-5A.

Young Adulthood—Intimacy vs. Isolation (ages 19 to 40 years). Erikson said that during this stage of life people must develop close relationships with other people. If this does not happen, individuals will be alone and isolated. They may not learn or experience love. The positive end of this stage is love.

Adulthood—Generativity vs. Stagnation (ages 40 to 65 years). Erikson said that people of this age want to find vocations where they can help others or in some other way contribute to society. **Generativity** (JEHN-ruh-TIHV-ih-tee) means the power to generate or produce something of value. If this does not happen, people may become self-absorbed or stagnant, which means to not move ahead. The positive end of this stage is caring.

FIG. 2-5A. Erik Erikson.

Old Age—Ego-Integrity vs. Despair (age 65 years to death). Erikson said that people in the latter part of their lives review their pasts to gain a sense of uniqueness, accomplishment, and fulfillment. If this does not happen, people may become depressed or preoccupied with death. The positive end of this stage is wisdom.

Levinson's Transitions

Erikson's work influenced other researchers to study adult development. Daniel J. Levinson studied the adult population to late adulthood. His theory describes a life structure that adults build and change throughout their adulthood. He speaks of stable times when the structure is solid. At other times, a person sees that his or her life structure has flaws and wants change.

FIG. 2-5B. **Daniel J. Levinson.**

This starts a transition period. Levinson said the transition may last five years, and it may develop into a time of crisis. See Fig. 2-5B.

- **Early Adulthood Transition (ages 17 to 22).** This stage, which begins in adolescence, is a time when a person begins exploring adult-like commitments.

- **Early Adulthood (ages 22 to 40).** People enter the adult world during this time, which for most is a stable phase that lasts about six years. They begin creating and building a life structure. At about age 28, people begin to look ahead to age 30 and what changes they may want to make in their lives. By age 33, people are settling down, thinking about a family, promotions at work, or becoming involved in community service.

- **Midlife Transition (ages 40 to 45).** During this stage, people may question what they have done so far with their lives. They assess life satisfaction and may make new choices. For some, this period becomes a life crisis.

- **Middle Adulthood (ages 45 to 60).** Middle life is usually more satisfying and productive than any other time in life. Some people assess their lives once again at 50 and seek change, but generally this stage is stable.

- **Late Adult Transition (ages 60 to 65).** Most people consider retirement during this stage. Many look forward to it; others think they will be bored and feel unproductive.

- **Late Adulthood (ages 65 and beyond).** Levinson's research did not study people in this age group.

Gould's Life of Change

Another researcher in adult development is Roger Gould, a psychiatrist. He looks upon adulthood as a time of constant change and not a time of stable emotions and motivation. He says that each of life's challenges gives people more chances to grow and move through to mature adulthood. Gould says that people must solve their personal problems on a daily basis and try new approaches to stay mentally healthy. That

FIG. 2-5C. **Roger Gould.**

includes facing childhood fears, prejudices, and bad habits that stand in the way of normal development. See Fig. 2-5C. Gould's stages include:

- **Late Adolescence (ages 16 to 22).** During this stage of uncertainty, people must form an identity separate from their parents' world.

- **Young Adulthood (ages 22 to 28).** People feel empowered to set personal goals.

- **Adulthood (ages 28 to 34).** People rethink their goals, reevaluate their life commitments, and work to make their finances more stable.
- **Midlife Transition (ages 35 to 43).** People may question what they value in this unstable period, which may be full of turmoil and personal discomfort.
- **Middle Adulthood (ages 43 to 50).** During this time of stability, people have marital satisfaction, friends become important, and money seems less important.

Aging Issues

The amount of knowledge about aging has increased since the 1800s and 1900s. In colonial times, Americans treated older people with great respect because living to an old age then was very rare. Today, living to an old age is common. Aging is a common topic of discussion today because the United States is experiencing two major population shifts. Living within a multicultural society, Americans come from many ethnic groups and nations. The second shift is in the large percentage of Americans who will soon enter late adulthood. These people will need services, and social policies must meet the demands of this diverse and aging population.

Cultural Values Affect Aging

Aging experiences differ across cultures because each culture has its own attitudes and values about older people. Learning about various ethnic and minority groups' values and practices will help you take better care of older adults in those groups. For example, an Alaskan family shows respect for its oldest person, who is called the **elder**. Family members honor the elder because the Alaskan Native culture believes that older people have more wisdom. Family members go to the elder when they must make important decisions.

Asian cultures also honor their elders. For example, family members of several generations often live together in many Chinese homes. Research shows that Erikson's life stage of intimacy vs. isolation does not fit Chinese society. Chinese families are very close and they often live in tight quarters. These factors demand intimacy, but make isolation nearly impossible. See Fig. 2-6.

FIG. 2-6. In many ethnic cultures, older adults hold the status of elder due to their ages and acquired wisdom. Research the status of older adults in several cultures.

Increasing Population of Older Adults

People are living longer because of advances in medicine, technology, and healthy living practices. The U.S. Census Bureau suggests that the fastest-growing group is the population range of those 85 years and older. As times change and more advances are discovered, so will older people's needs. The needs of an 80-year-old today will be different from those of an 80-year-old 25 years from now.

In the next 10 to 25 years, **baby boomers**—people born between 1946 and 1964 following World War II—will be within the 65-year-old and older population. The Census Bureau predicts that, by 2050, the average life expectancy will climb from the current 75 years old to 82 years old. It also predicts that, by 2030, the number of people 65 and older will double from 35 million to 70 million. The number of people over 85 will increase by 2030 from 3 million to 9 million. The Census Bureau expects that, by 2030, the number of children under 18 will remain the same, about 24 percent of the population. See Fig. 2-7.

This population shift will greatly expand career options in gerontology and geriatrics. People in this field must have ongoing training on aging and full understanding of the needs of an aging society. Chapter 3 will provide you with more information about serving the aging population.

FIG. 2-7. The proportion of adults age 65 and over has steadily increased since 1960, and will continue to grow.

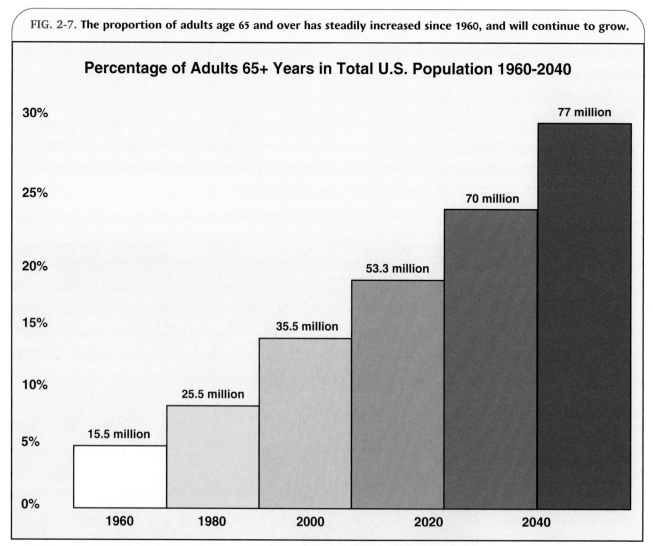

Percentage of Adults 65+ Years in Total U.S. Population 1960-2040

- 15.5 million — 1960
- 25.5 million — 1980
- 35.5 million — 2000
- 53.3 million — 2020
- 70 million — 2020
- 77 million — 2040

Source: US Census, Middle Series Projections

Social Policies for Older Adults

The growth in the older adult population will make greater demands of a society's social, political, and economic institutions. Social policies must change to meet the demands. Baby boomers entering older adulthood will likely move age-related issues to the top of social policy lists. They will have a significant impact on every area of the health-care industry.

Updating Policies. Policy makers must keep informed of the changing needs of older adults. Unlike the older adults of the World War II generation, baby boomers will likely be healthier because of continued improvements in nutrition, fitness programs, and health care. Yet, they will continue to want early detection health-care screenings. They will want preventive programs to maintain good health practices. Many baby boomers are often better educated because their parents had the financial means to send them for further education. Many have higher incomes because of their professional career choices, too. This generation is so different from the previous one that its demands will require new and updated social policies. See Fig. 2-8A.

Policy makers must also consider that some baby boomers will not retire at the government's recommended age, as some experts predict. They must encourage discussions among government, industry, businesses, and families on how each will respond to the needs and lifestyles of these older adults. Other aging issues they must consider are to:

- Address health issues related to various ethnic and minority populations.
- Educate the public about agencies that focus on older adults and their children.
- Expand programs that encourage interactions between children and older adults.
- Develop policies that promote the well-being of children and older adults.
- Facilitate independence and support caregivers.
- Use technology to promote continued education for older adults.
- Address services for the workforce that has held jobs without retirement benefits.

FIG. 2-8A & B. **Meeting the health care needs of the aging baby boomer population will be a great concern for policy makers.** How does meeting health care needs have to change?

Social Security, Medicare, and Medicaid.
Baby boomers will ask their government leaders how Social Security and Medicare benefits fill their needs. Many of them will have the resources to pay for their health care. Individuals who have paid into Social Security will rely on their Medicare insurance. The funds they paid to Social Security and their Federal Insurance Contributions Act (FICA) taxes went into a trust fund. When they reach retirement age, they receive a monthly living wage from their Social Security account. Older adults access the FICA funds to pay for their health-care expenses through a program called Medicare. See Fig. 2-8B.

Individuals who have not paid into Social Security or have no other insurance are eligible for Medicaid. It is a federal- and state-level program that the states and local governments manage. It gives assistance to low-income people of every age. The person's medical bills are paid with federal, state, and local taxes reserved for the needy. In some areas, people with Medicaid coverage must make a small payment, called a copayment, at the time of their health-care appointment.

ETHICS IN Action

Providing Care. An older adult couple have lived in their home for more than 50 years. They both have health problems that require health-care attention every week. The wife is losing her eyesight and the husband is frail, but still holding down a job to ensure their medical benefits. They need a care provider who is sensitive to their specific needs. Their adult children feel responsible for the care of their parents, but the distance they live from their parents keeps them from regular contact. *What would you recommend that the children do to help care for their parents?*

Section 2-1   Knowledge Check

1. Which age group is the fastest growing population?
2. In what ways are Levinson's and Gould's theories about adult development similar?
3. How must social and health-care policies change with an increase in the older adult population?

Mini-Lab

Create a learning activity that will assist older adults in developing and updating their computer skills. This activity should help the older adults access the Internet to get information about preventive health-care services. For example, the older adults might look up information about flu shots and where to get them in the community.

Section *2-2*

Basic Needs of Older Adults

OBJECTIVES

- List the kinds of basic needs of older adults.
- Compare the types of independent living arrangements available to older adults.
- Identify the stages of death and dying.

KEY TERMS

discretionary income
family care manager
self-perception
hospice

As you read in Section 1, adults journey through many life stages. Each stage presents changes and varying needs. Older adults have different needs from those they had when they were younger. In general, older adults' basic needs include social interaction and support, financial security, living arrangements, transportation, health care, and emotional security. As a care provider, you will assess what needs have the highest priority for each person you serve. You will help older adults and their families in ensuring a healthy and happy environment that offers them the physical and emotional security they need.

Social Interaction & Support

After retirement, older people welcome new roles. Some older adults give freely of their time to help others, while others choose to remain at home. Others seek part-time employment. Involvement in these outside activities can help older adults save money, improve their health by staying active, or make a worthwhile contribution to their communities. Many organizations and agencies recruit retirees to assist as tutors and mentors in schools and with after-school programs. Some older adults volunteer in child care centers to read to children and to serve as foster-grandparents.

As the baby boomer generation retires, they will demand various types of social support. Technology will be a must. Many in this "new" generation of older adults will want to continue improving the technological skills they developed in the workplace. They will want access to the Internet and other means of communication so they can stay connected to family and friends who live far away. See Fig. 2-9.

As people age and retire, they often give up roles they have had for most of their adult lives. In younger years, a woman may have been the family manager. She may have balanced the family budget, planned family activities, and supervised household activities. In later years,

FIG. 2-9. **Older adults who have used technology in the workplace will want to continue to maintain their skills.** How can older adults benefit from using computer technology?

Financial Security

As workers approach age 65, the number of them in the workforce drops dramatically. Some older adults will continue to work for various reasons. Some may have poor Social Security benefits and must work to continue earning a living wage. Many who are in good health prefer to continue working. However, research shows that only two percent of people 65 and older remain employed.

Many people who retire sometimes make major lifestyle adjustments. Retirement offers a person a new position in society with its own unique roles, expectations, and responsibilities. After retirement, some may live on less income. During this time, older adults often lower their standards of living because they are now on fixed incomes and have less **discretionary** (dis-KREH-shuh-ner-ee) **income**, or the money left after paying for basic needs. For example, older people may need to look at different housing, ways of transportation, and health-care arrangements because of their financial situations.

she may no longer be able to carry out all these roles. As people age, they may pass on major responsibilities, such as paying bills or handling investments, to other family members or seek social support from social service agencies. Baby boomers and other older adults may also need social support in other areas, ranging from housecleaning to personal shopping, bathing, and home health care. See Fig. 2-10.

FIG. 2-10. **Many older adults rely on family members to help meet their relational needs and other daily living challenges.**

Intergenerational Interactions

Ways Older Adults Can Help Children

There are a number of ways in which older adults can use a wealth of skills to contribute valuable assistance to children and teens, and as a result gain personal enrichment and mutually rewarding relationships. Many groups and networks throughout the country offer a wide variety of programs in which older adults can mentor young people, provide valuable vocational training, or volunteer their services to aid youth with special needs.

- **Foster Grandparents Programs.** Many groups and services exist to connect foster grandparents with young children. For example, LifeSpan Services Network in San Luis Obispo, California, features a Foster Grandparents Program in which low-income seniors spend 20 hours a week working with at-risk children in need of companionship, emotional caring, and guidance. In return, older adults receive ongoing training, a small stipend to cover the cost of volunteering, an annual physical examination, and insurance.

- **Mentoring Programs.** Older adults can establish rewarding relationships with youth in many ways as mentors. They can play with children, help students with homework, or teach at-risk youth skills, such as cooking or carpentry. Big Brothers and Big Sisters of America offer Elder Programs that match the needs of older adults with children based on compatibility of personality, mutual interests,

and the special needs of children. One branch in Prescott, Arizona, for example, matches male adults over 50 with at-risk male youth in need of mentoring.

- **Volunteering Programs.** Older adults can serve as volunteers to children and teens by acting as positive role models and friends, helping children gain greater self-esteem. In some programs, volunteers commit to spending several hours a week with a young person, while professional caseworkers provide supervision and work with the senior volunteer, the child, and his or her family to help establish goals during the volunteering process. One recent study shows that volunteering with at-risk youth leads to a significant drop in the number of such youth who engage in substance abuse or skip school.

Follow-Up

Research community groups and national organizations that offer foster grandparenting, mentoring, or volunteering programs. Write a report on the benefits to older adults from teaching skills to young people.

Living Arrangements

As individuals move through the various stages of life, their living arrangements become an important concern. A housing survey, completed by the AARP Inc., showed that most older Americans prefer to maintain and stay in their own homes. Many older adults want to maintain their own households as long as possible. A majority of people 65 and older are homeowners. For most older people, their homes are their only major asset.

Many programs—including financial, home maintenance, and safety—are available to assist older people in their homes. Older people don't have to stop living independently. These programs offer support to help in meeting the needs for care and socialization without surrendering independence and control. They are designed to prevent uprooting older adults from their homes. The U.S. Department of Health and Human Services funds the Area Agency on

Aging (AAA). The AAA serves as a clearinghouse for all services for older adults who seek to remain in their homes. These services are often operated through a local health department. An AAA geriatrics care manager or case manager evaluates the needs of older people and makes the appropriate referrals based on these needs. See Fig. 2-11.

Older people prefer to live separately from their adult children. Many grown children want to honor their parents' wishes. Unfortunately, many don't know about the services that can help their parents live independently.

Homes may be assets, but they are also older adults' number one financial liability. As older people with their family members decide that they can no longer maintain and manage their homes, they must consider other housing alternatives. The eight basic types of independent living arrangements are described as follows.

Apartments for Older Adults. The advantages of targeted apartments include special features or services, such as ramps, elevators, bath rails, etc. They may be very similar to apartments in public housing or other subsidized housing, or they may be private. Some key disadvantages include fewer chances for interaction with younger people, less privacy, and limited space. See Fig. 2-12.

Congregate Housing. This type of housing provides supportive services, such as meals, recreational and social activities, housekeeping, laundry, and transportation. Services are tailored to the needs of each resident. Government agencies may subsidize the cost of congregate housing. Its disadvantages echo those of apartments for older adults.

Public Housing. Local authorities operate these dwellings, and the federal government supports them, both clear advantages. Individuals or families pay 30 percent of their income toward the cost of the home. The housing units, however, may not be wholly designed as apartments for older adults. Housing choices are generally limited in any area.

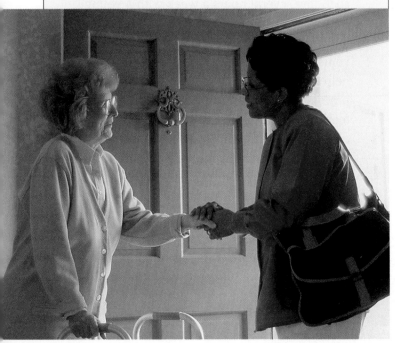

FIG. 2-11. Many services are available which enable older adults to remain in their own homes and maintain a level of independence. Why is independence important for older adults?

FIG. 2-12. Apartments for older adults often include special features that are needed by people as they age. How might apartments for older adults be different than others?

Subsidized Housing. In this low-income housing, residents pay 30 percent of their adjusted income for rent. The rent, fortunately, is lower than that for comparable private housing. This housing includes any style of government-subsidized home. The key disadvantages include limited choices and no specific features for older adults.

Section 8 Vouchers. The U.S. Department of Housing and Urban Development (HUD) designed this rental-assistance program. It allows people with low incomes to rent a dwelling of their choice if the dwelling meets HUD standards. HUD will then pay a portion of the rent based on the tenant's income. Vouchers are available to adults of all ages. The key disadvantages include limited choices and long waiting lists for vouchers in many communities.

Adult Communities. These communities are often designed to attract retirees, although they are not limited to older adults. Many provide social activities and recreational facilities that interest retired people. Some consist of stand-alone, single-family dwellings, while others may consist of duplexes (two-family rentals), parks of manufactured homes (trailers), condominiums, or apartment-type homes. Many of these communities are expensive and may prohibit some older adults from choosing this option. See Fig. 2-13.

Naturally Occurring Retirement Communities. These communities attract older adults for various reasons, including location, services and amenities of interest, nearness to health care, shopping, affordability, and ease of upkeep. Some also consist of stand-alone, single-family dwellings, while others may consist of duplexes (two-family rentals), parks of manufactured homes (trailers), condominiums, or apartment-type homes. However, these facilities are not specifically planned and designed for older adults and can be expensive.

FIG. 2-13. **Whether a dwelling is in an adult retirement community or an individual shared housing arrangement, the dwelling should meet the needs of the older adults who live in it.** What are the benefits of each option?

Shared Housing. With shared group residences, none of the residents owns the dwelling, but each pays rent for a private room and bath and shared common areas. Nonprofit organizations often manage or sponsor shared housing. These residences may offer support services, such as transportation and meals, through agreements with human services providers. In contrast to shared group housing, home sharing differs in that one of the residents may own the home. The key disadvantages of either may be cost and lack of privacy.

Multiunit Assisted Housing with Services. These housing units enable residents with special needs to live in an independent, multiunit setting. Minimum services may include one meal a day, housekeeping services, and personal care services. Licensed home care providers may give hands-on personal care and nursing care, as outlined in a written care plan. Housing management generally arranges the plan with the resident and his or her family. The key disadvantage is that this housing does not welcome residents who need 24-hour supervision.

Transportation

The automobile serves as the primary means of transportation in the United States. Although older adults prefer the independence of driving themselves, at some age many must give up their driving licenses and cars and rely on other means. These older adults have become unsafe drivers either because of a decline in health or other physical or emotional limitations. They are no longer fully capable of the complexities of driving.

Older adults may rely on family members for transportation, but they are often not available during the daytime. Their own family commitments may prevent them from helping, especially with trips to the supermarket and medical appointments.

Older adults may turn to public transportation. Urban areas are known for developing safe and reliable systems of public transportation, but this is not the case in other cities and rural areas, where the car remains the preferred means of transportation. Older adults may become overwhelmed when looking at a bus or subway route map. As a care provider, you can assist older adults by familiarizing them with the map key colors and locations they know. You may also help them obtain other means of transportation available in your area, such as:

- Services for residents of housing facilities.

- Public means, such as taxis and buses. See Fig. 2-14.

- Special van fleets for older adults and people with disabilities.

Health Care

The health care that older adults need will vary according to lifestyle, heredity, and other factors. Common health problems include heart disease, Type II diabetes, and osteoporosis. People who were basically healthy when they were younger may have fewer problems as they age. Their health-care needs may be more routine. However, health care for some older adults makes up the majority of their daily activities.

When older people develop health problems, they may depend on family members to assist them. Younger family members may take on the role of **family care manager**, a person who assesses and directs the care of older adults. They may seek help from such social agencies as community centers and the local health department to assist them in obtaining services for their older family member.

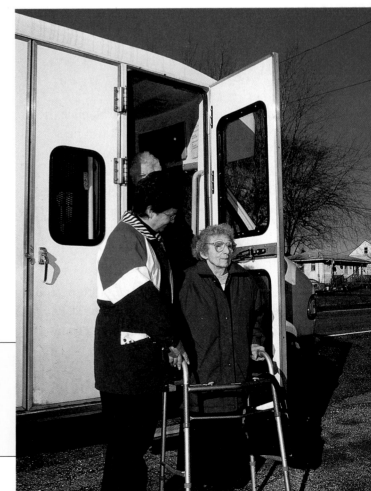

FIG. 2-14. **As people grow older, their transportation needs change. What are** some ways that communities can meet the transportation needs of older adults?

FIG. 2-15. **The need for retaining respectful peer relationships is strong in older adults.** What other relational needs might older adults have?

Emotional Security

Because a person's emotions influence the quality of life, as a caregiver you will need to consider the emotional needs of older adults as well as their basic functional needs. Emotional security comes from feeling good about oneself and being with people who share those feelings.

Relationships

Older people continue to need interpersonal connections with family and friends. They want to maintain loving relationships with friends and family. They thrive on their family's displays of appreciation and respect. Older adults want to feel they still contribute to family decision making. They also like to maintain relationships with health care professionals whom they have come to know. See Fig. 2-15.

Self-Perception

Unlike babies and children, who depend on their parents for their emotional needs, older adults rely primarily on themselves and their loved ones. Their **self-perception**, or how they picture themselves, is very important to their emotional well-being. This self-portrait might evolve from personal insights, what other people have told them, and from how they think others view them. Self-respect and respect from peers greatly affect an older adult's self-perception. For some older adults, their standing in their community may contribute to their self-perception. For example, older adults serving as neighborhood watch volunteers may think of themselves as part of community law enforcement.

The changes an older person experiences also affect self-perception. For example, if a person retires, loses a spouse, or develops a disability, he or she may have to depend more on others. This may change self-perception. Older people who have faced extreme loss may experience severe drops in self-esteem and a reduced sense of self-worth.

Death & Grief

Older adults must deal with very strong emotions when they face death themselves or the death of loved ones. Older adults know that death is part of life and that they are more likely to experience the loss of a loved one as they age. When a spouse dies, the survivor may face new challenges. Tasks done by the person who died can be overwhelming. The support of family and care providers can help smooth the transition into these new roles.

Dr. Elisabeth Kübler-Ross was a pioneer in the study of death and dying. While working with her terminally ill patients, she observed how they acted as they approached death. She identified five stages of death and dying. See Fig. 2-16.

Dying

Researchers observed that people who are dying have five basic needs: food, clothing, shelter, rest, and warmth. They often seek relief from pain. These people want reassurance that their close friends and family will not abandon them to die alone. They desire the comfort of family and friends as they face the end of life.

FIG. 2-16.

STAGES OF DEATH & DYING

Denial	A person may be in shock about the likelihood of dying. Denial acts like a barrier between an individual and the reality of death. During this stage, a person may avoid talking about terminal illness, may claim test results are wrong or mishandled, and may avoid saying much to family and friends. People don't want to believe they are dying. Sometimes denial and isolation are the best devices a dying person uses, however, to cope with the idea of death. **Care provider recommendations:** As a care provider, lend support. Listen when the dying person wants to talk and avoid judging behavior.
Anger	At this stage, a dying person may feel furious that others will go on living while he or she is dying. "Why me?" is a question often asked. Accusing family and friends of being uncaring and questioning religious beliefs are common reactions during this stage. **Care provider recommendations:** When providing care, remember that a person's anger is not directed at you, even though it may feel like it is. Think about what your feelings would be if you were in the person's situation. Recognize that anger is a sign of change in the process and a step toward acceptance.
Bargaining	At this stage, the dying person may try to make a deal with a higher power—such as agreeing to make changes in his or her life if allowed to live. The dying person may appeal to doctors to postpone death by any medical means. **Care provider recommendations:** Listen, and give the person a chance to talk out his or her feelings. Do not try to argue with logic about any unrealistic views.
Depression	With depression, a dying person realizes death is approaching. **Care provider recommendations:** Point out the signs of depression to family members. Encourage them to tell the dying person how important he or she has been in their lives. Encourage them to listen and just be with the person.
Acceptance	During this stage, which is a time of resolution, the dying person may desire less communication. Acceptance of dying eases the person into death. **Care provider recommendations:** Encourage family members to hold the person's hand and talk or sing to him or her. Recite familiar prayers or poems. Limit the number of visitors to the immediate family. If there is no family, the care provider should act as family.

Some special programs and facilities exist to assist and comfort dying people and their families. A **hospice** is a facility or program with staff members who are specially trained to provide a caring environment that will meet the physical and emotional needs of the terminally ill. Hospice care focuses on helping to maintain satisfactory qualities of life by easing suffering through relief of pain. With painful symptoms under control, the terminally ill can focus on personal relationships.

Maintaining a sense of self-worth and dignity is important to people at the end of life. Many welcome the opportunity to talk about their lives with loved ones. They want to complete unfinished business, such as putting personal affairs in order and making funeral and burial plans. They may desire to make amends with siblings or friends they have not spoken to for years. An opportunity to rebuild relationships helps bring closure.

Grief

Grief is a complex set of experiences common to all who experience the death of someone they love. Mourning is the expression of grief. Emotional reactions during periods of grief and mourning may include anger, guilt, depression, relief, anxiety, and preoccupation with death or thoughts about the person who died. Other normal physical and emotional reactions are also possible, such as frustration and the lack of ability to sleep.

Grieving is also a process. Those who grieve often follow common stages that may include:

- **Shock and denial.** Following the death of a loved one, family members and friends often feel an overwhelming sense of loss and confusion. Periods of extreme sadness and frequent crying are common.

- **Preoccupation with thoughts of a loved one.** During this middle stage, those who survive the loss of a loved one are often consumed with memories of that person. As they struggle to accept the death, family members may attach themselves to personal possessions of their loved one or go to places that were meaningful to the relationship. During this time survivors may also experience feelings of depression or despair.

- **Acceptance and recovery.** As survivors begin accepting the death, many struggle with what is often called "a year of firsts" after the death of a loved one—the first holiday, birthday, or an important anniversary. Feelings of loneliness and separation are painful. It is important to remember that with time, these painful experiences diminish in varying degrees. In most cases, time does bring healing. During this stage of acceptance and recovery, grieving people develop renewed interests in activities and continue on with the normal routines of life.

FIG. 2-17. **The desire to comfort someone in need transcends generations.**

FIG. 2-18. **Older adults will experience grief over the loss of a loved one in many ways. How can you as a care provider assist them in coping with their grief?**

The grief process will vary in how long individuals grieve, the order of the stages, and how strong emotions will be during the time. The grieving process is often compared to being on an emotional roller coaster. See Fig. 2-17.

Keep this process and its individual variations in mind as you assist older adults as they grieve. While the stages and emotions are normal, staying in those highly emotional states is not normal. The objective of the grieving process is that the person will mourn and move through the grief process into a healthy acceptance of the changes that the loved one's death has created. As a care provider, here are some things you can do to assist the older adults in your care who experience grief:

- Encourage the older adult to talk about his or her loss.
- Be a good listener. Allow grieving older adults to express their feelings. They may want to tell you repeated stories about their relationships with the deceased.
- Offer practical assistance. Choose something that you know you can do that would be helpful.
- Encourage grieving older adults to attend to their personal needs.

Remember that grieving takes time. No two people experience grief in the same way. As a care provider, offer continuous support, but also be sensitive to the fact that an older adult may need additional help in coping with grief. You or your supervisor may need to refer an older adult to a counselor for additional assistance. See Fig. 2-18.

Section **2-2** Knowledge Check

1. What are the seven kinds of basic needs of older adults?
2. What are the basic types of independent living arrangements for older adults?
3. What are Kübler-Ross's five stages of death and dying?

Mini-Lab

With a partner, create a scenario in which you help a friend who is grieving the loss of an older relative. Act out your scenario for the class.

Chapter **2**
Review & Activities

Section Summaries

2-1 Gerontology is the study of aging.

2-1 People are living longer because of modern medicine, technology, and the practice of healthier lifestyles.

2-1 The process of aging includes chronological, biological, psychological, and sociological aspects of aging.

2-1 Adult development theories by Eric Erikson, Daniel J. Levinson, and Roger Gould outline adulthood periods of stability and change, with transitional periods in between.

2-1 The fastest-growing population in the 2000s is those 85 years and older.

2-1 Because of increases in the older adult population, social policies must change to meet new demands.

2-2 Older adults' basic needs include social interaction and support, financial security, living arrangements, transportation, health care, and emotional security.

2-2 Choices in living arrangements for older adults vary depending on level of privacy, costs, and whether they need health care services.

2-2 Family members must often attend to the transportation needs and health care arrangements of older adults.

2-2 Self-respect and respect from peers greatly affect an older adult's self-perception and emotional security.

2-2 Researcher Kübler-Ross identified five common stages of death and dying.

2-2 Older adults must face their own death and the death of loved ones.

Check Your Knowledge

1. What is the difference between gerontology and geriatrics?
2. How do young people benefit from studying aging?
3. What are four of the general principles of aging?
4. How can understanding the theories of adult development help you handle your own adulthood?
5. In what areas will the increase in older people increase the cost to society?
6. Differentiate between Social Security, FICA, Medicare, and Medicaid.
7. Identify the basic needs of older adults.
8. Why might financial security be difficult for many older adults?
9. What are the needs of a dying person?

Thinking Critically

1. How might you as the care provider of a shy and isolated older adult help her to satisfy her need for greater social interaction and support?
2. Contrast Kübler-Ross's stages of dying with the stages of grief. Refer to Fig. 2-16, then describe what grieving people might be experiencing in each stage as they mourn the loss of their loved one.

Practical Applications

1. **Create a Word Picture.** Write a word picture to describe how an older person's self-perception might be at 65 years of age, 75 years, and 85 years.

2. **Writing.** Develop a story that illustrates how a teen student might view the aging process. Select one of the following situations: (1) a teen who was raised by his grandmother; (2) a grandmother who is ill moves into a teen's family household; and (3) a teen must share with other family members in providing daily care for her dying grandfather.

3. **Internet Research.** Search the Internet to identify state-sponsored services for older adults and their families in your state. Summarize your findings, and share them with the class.

4. **Making a Recommendation.** What living arrangements options would you recommend to a family whose mother can no longer maintain her home and is under a doctor's care for diabetes and heart disease? Explain your reason for each option.

Building Your PORTFOLIO

Understanding Perspectives on Aging

Your future employer will expect you to have a clear understanding of the aging process and of the basic needs of older adults.

Step 1: Develop a questionnaire to identify perceptions people of different ages have about aging. Include questions about aging and what older adults are like. Have your instructor review your questions for clarity and appropriateness. Ask people of different ages to respond to the questionnaire. Include responses from teens, young adults, middle-aged adults, and older adults. Compare their answers. How were the beliefs of those surveyed similar? How did their beliefs differ? Write a one- to two-page paper describing your findings. Include a copy of your questionnaire and your findings in your portfolio.

Step 2: Use your local telephone directory or social services directory to determine what services are available in your community to meet the basic needs of older adults for social interaction and support, financial security, living arrangements, transportation, health care, and emotional security. Summarize your findings and rate your community's ability to meet these needs. What additional services may be needed in your community? In your portfolio, include your analysis of services available to older adults in your community.

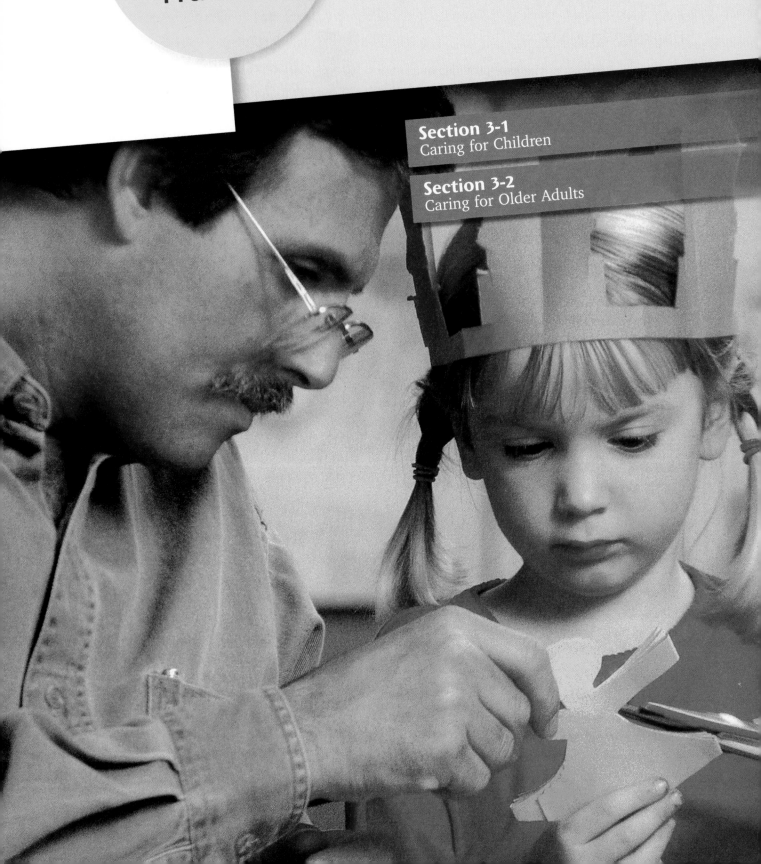

Chapter 3
Human Services Careers

Section 3-1
Caring for Children

Section 3-2
Caring for Older Adults

Section 3-1

Caring for Children

OBJECTIVES

- Identify three factors that contribute to an increasing demand for early childhood providers.
- Describe ten characteristics of a successful early childhood professional.
- Identify places to work and positions in early childhood care and education.
- Summarize three major legal responsibilities of early childhood professionals.

KEY TERMS

trend
entrepreneur
Child Development
  Associate (CDA)
mandated

Today more children than ever are cared for by trained professionals outside of the family home. As you have read in Chapter 1, a child experiences critical development during the early years. Early childhood providers must understand the stages of child development and develop keen skills in caring for, and educating, young children. If you are willing to gain this knowledge and know-how, many employment opportunities await you. As you read this section, think about the ways your current traits, attitudes, skills, and abilities might direct you toward a successful career as an early childhood professional.

Demand for Early Childhood Professionals

Well-trained early childhood professionals are in great demand in nearly all parts of the United States. Yet, shortages are very common often due to low pay and minimal benefits. Within the past 20 years, more Americans rely on early childhood professionals to care for their infants and toddlers outside of their homes. This development is called a **trend**, or the overall direction in which a society moves within a given time frame. Several factors con-

tribute to this trend. The United States is a mobile society with many families moving from community to community to find satisfying employment. Grandparents, who, in earlier times, might have assisted parents with child care, often live far away. Fewer and fewer grandparents can provide daily daytime care for their grandchildren.

Recent studies show more than half of infants under age one and more than 12 million children under age five spend at least sometime in someone's care other than the parents. During the mid-1980s, researchers studied the benefits to young children of daytime child care programs. Their findings showed that the early education experience had a positive impact on some children's social and psychological development. It helped some children's intellectual development, too. Because of this research, parents during the 1990s became more willing to enroll their children in child care programs or centers, especially if they had a reputation of quality care.

Likely the most influential factor for this trend is the increasing numbers of dual-career families and single parents. In almost 75 percent of families with young children, both parents must work outside of the home to support the family's needs. Recent shifts in economic and job security, plus the expenses children require, have made two incomes a necessity. This is more often seen in regions where the U.S. economy's downturn led to business failures and job cuts. Whether a parent is unmarried due to teen pregnancy, divorce, or adopting a child while single, the number of single parents has increased dramatically. According to the *2001 Kids Count Data Book*, the number of children living in single-parent families rose from 5.8 million in 1960 to 19.8 million in 1999. Without outside help with child care, single parents cannot work full-time and care for their children.

Child Care Services

No two children or two families are exactly alike; therefore, no one type of care is right for all families. Parents scout for early childhood care options and providers that suit their needs. Early childhood providers often work in center-based child care, family child care homes, or part-day nursery or preschools.

In the past, providers offered simple custodial care. They offered parents a safe place for their children. They served children meals and watched over them as the children played and napped. The provider did not plan or conduct any educational activities.

Today, good programs go far beyond custodial care. Early childhood programs focus on meeting children's overall developmental needs, such as secure attachments and positive self-esteem, while nurturing their emerging skills and abilities. See Fig. 3-1.

Inclusive & Diverse Environments

Early childhood programs and centers must comply with Title III of the *Americans with Disabilities Act (ADA)*. These programs and centers cannot discriminate against people with disabilities including children and their parents or guardians. They must provide equal participation opportunities for all people. Exceptions to Title III include:

- An *individualized assessment* shows the presence of children with disabilities would pose a *direct threat* to the health or safety of others or require a *fundamental alteration* of the program or facility.
- Centers operated by religious organizations.

If a center can meet a child's needs, it is required by law to include the child. See the ADA Web site for more information.

Early childhood professionals ensure that the children's classroom environment and routines—such as discipline, meal service, and toilet training—respect individual family traditions and beliefs. They encourage children of varying abilities and diverse backgrounds to enroll in their programs. Professional staff members become acquainted with the varying needs of these children and their families and accommodate them. Today's professionals show their respect of children and families of all racial, ethnic, and cultural backgrounds. This includes providing information to children and their parents in their native languages. In addition, early childhood providers often provide opportunities for all children to acquire a second language. They strive to communicate effectively with everyone and work in a professional manner.

FIG. 3-1. Many program options are available for children and early childhood professionals ranging from early childhood centers to family day care homes. What options might fit your needs and skills?

Family-Friendly Environments. Early childhood professionals create a family-friendly environment in their center. They know that children develop within a family unit, so good providers encourage parents to participate. They may ask parents, whenever possible, to serve as a field trip chaperone or a monitor for outdoor play periods.

Early childhood staff members also help parents better manage their child-rearing responsibilities by offering parent education classes. Referring families to services they need, such as family counseling, is another important role for early childhood professionals.

Your Potential as a Professional

Your success as an early childhood professional depends not only on doing the best job you can, but also on being the best person you can be. Education and experience can help prepare you for a career with children. In addition, you must have or develop certain positive traits and attitudes to be successful as a child care provider. Not everyone is suited for the responsibilities of an early childhood professional or to the child care center environment.

Traits & Attitudes

In early childhood programs, providers work with people of all ages. It is a complex task to maintain good working relations with parents, children, and coworkers. A caregiver with most of the following traits and attitudes will have a greater chance of performing well under the demands of the profession. As you review the list, ask yourself which of these traits and attitudes describe you, as you are today.

- High energy.
- Good physical health.
- Positive, "can-do" attitude.
- Sense of humor, especially in uncomfortable situations.
- Dedication to serving children and families.
- Respect for diverse family backgrounds.
- Appreciation of children's ages and stages of development.
- Patience with children's inappropriate behavior.
- Understanding the world from a child's point of view, as well as a parent's point of view.

Skills & Abilities

Settings with children are very busy places because they typically involve games, activities, meals, naps, and other daily routines. These routines and other demands require that providers respond immediately and consistently. See Fig. 3-2. The ability to "think on your feet" in a child care setting is a necessity. In addition, you must apply the following skills consistently when working with children.

FIG. 3-2. **Communicating with children on their level both physically and verbally increases the effectiveness of communication.** What are the benefits of being on the same physical level with children when you are talking with them?

- Communicate directly and clearly, both in oral and written forms.
- Arrive to the workplace on time. Many employers cite employee absences to be an ongoing problem.
- Display a consistent temperament, with no great mood swings.
- Show consistency in ways of responding to children.
- Adapt easily to changes in schedule and plans, as needed.
- Show creativity and resourcefulness in solving problems.
- Make decisions as a team player.
- Manage time with flexibility.
- Display self-starting initiative.
- Show willingness to work hard to complete a project.

Managing the Stress Factors

Early childhood professionals work in a stressful environment. Working with children and families is not always easy. Anticipating and meeting so many needs can seem overwhelming. The work, for example, can be physically and mentally tiring. Some duties are not at all glamorous, such as wiping noses, changing diapers, and cleaning up spills. Here are some causes of potential stress in a care provider's daily routine:

- Exposure to minor illnesses, such as colds, flu, and chicken pox.
- Back strain from frequent or improper lifting of children. See Fig. 3-3.
- Low wages (often minimum wage) with few fringe benefits.
- Long hours with 15-minute breaks, rather than hour-long lunches.
- Unpaid planning and preparation time, requiring evening or weekend work.
- Excessive workload because of minimal staff in each classroom.

FIG. 3-3. Back injuries from improper lifting can add stress to the early childhood professional's work load.

- Continual adjustment to new coworkers due to frequent staff changes.
- Infrequent recognition for excellent job performance.
- Mentally reviewing concerns for children in troubling situations after the workday.

When a care provider's stress level is overwhelming, job performance declines. A care provider's family life can suffer, too. Choosing to ignore the stress often results in providers leaving their early childhood careers.

The care provider, instead, must find ways to manage the stress. A care provider must balance work responsibilities along with responsibilities at home. When you manage work stress well, your job remains fulfilling and enjoyable. Here are some ways to help you manage stress at work and home:

- Eat nutritious meals and snacks.
- Eat three meals a day.
- Exercise regularly.
- Set realistic expectations for yourself.
- Practice good time management.
- Learn to say "no" to avoid taking on too many commitments.
- Set goals, and prioritize them.
- Break each goal into tasks, and begin to work on one task.
- Share home and work responsibilities with others, whenever possible.
- Maintain friendships by spending time regularly with friends.
- Take up a hobby, and do it regularly. See Fig. 3-4.
- Seek help from a trusted counselor if you continue to feel powerless.

See Section 2 of this chapter for more ways to balance work and home responsibilities.

Working with Children

Working in an early childhood program helps you stay young because you continually see and hear about the world from a child's perspective. Children's natural curiosity and high activity levels create an interesting environment. Teaching and guiding children allow you practice in developing many talents and skills. Each early childhood professional chooses the field for his or her own reasons. Most agree that a love of children is at the top of the list.

Early Childhood Careers

Children usually view anyone who spends time with them in a classroom setting as a teacher. However, the people who make up a child care center staff have different titles, such as director, teacher, care giver or provider, child care worker, teacher's assistant, or teacher's aide. The title generally refers to the level of training the position requires. Note that job titles and training requirements may vary from program to program and state to state.

The following chart includes an array of programs or settings that involve working with young children and their parents. Which ones appeal to you for your professional career? See Fig. 3-5 on page 79.

Choosing a Career Path

If you pursue a career in early childhood care, you must prepare for the responsibilities you will have. The education, training, and experience you need, however, will depend upon the specific job you seek and where you live.

FIG. 3-4. **Taking time for personal hobbies and interests is part of maintaining balance between work and personal life.** What hobbies or outside interests do you have that help bring balance to your life?

FIG. 3-5.

PLACES YOU CAN WORK WITH CHILDREN

- Boys and Girls Clubs
- Boy Scouts district office
- Child care centers
- Child care resource and referral agencies
- Children's hospital or hospice
- Children's section of a library
- Children's zoo
- Cruise ships, shopping malls, fitness centers, or supermarkets
- Crisis nurseries
- Day care homes
- Domestic violence shelters
- Early childhood professional organizations
- Elementary school after-school child care programs
- Employer-sponsored child care programs
- Faith-based early childhood centers
- Family education agencies
- Girl Scouts district office
- Head Start programs
- High school lab schools
- Homeless shelters
- Hospital pediatric units
- Human services departments in government agencies
- Ill-child child care services

- Intergenerational care centers
- Kindergartens
- Law firm that specializes in family law
- Mental health agencies
- Migrant worker programs
- Montessori preschool programs
- Museums
- Nursery schools or preschools
- Parks and recreation programs
- Prisons with in-house child visitation
- Public school pre-kindergarten programs

- Salvation Army child care centers
- School health center or office
- State education boards
- Summer camps and sports clinics
- Tribal child care centers on Native American reservations
- United Way agencies, e.g., Big Brothers & Big Sisters
- University lab schools
- U.S. military bases
- Visiting nurses associations
- YWCA or YMCA child care centers

The United States has no uniform national licensing or registration standards for education, training, and experience in the early childhood care profession. Each state sets its own standards. Different job titles have different standards and requirements. Contact your local agency that licenses or regulates early childhood centers to find out about your state's requirements. See Chapter 14 for more information on licensing and registration.

Programs in public schools usually have higher requirements than those of privately owned early childhood centers. You may obtain a school district's standards directly from the school board office or from the state board of education. See Fig. 3-6 for more information regarding career options with children.

As you may have observed, people in interesting, challenging, and higher-paying jobs generally have achieved higher levels of education.

Some jobs in early childhood care and education require at least a high school diploma. But many more positions require education beyond high school. After reading about child development in Chapter 1, you can imagine how effectively you could work with children if you have the knowledge that post-high school education provides.

Setting educational goals is the first step in planning your career. Gaining the education that qualifies you for early childhood positions leads to the achievement of your career goals and the rewards it brings.

You can also look for practical intern or volunteer experiences in early childhood careers before you graduate. During high school, you can gain firsthand experience in working with young children. By serving as a volunteer, your training and the rewards it brings can begin today. Exposure to and comparing various early childhood careers will also help you confirm whether you have the traits, attitudes, skills, and abilities

FIG. 3-6.

WHAT COULD I BE?

Not everyone who works with children is a teacher or a care provider. Have you ever thought about training for one of these positions? How could you benefit from comparing the rewards of various levels of early childhood careers? Choose four careers from the list below and compare the rewards they offer.

- Adoption counselor
- Amusement park guide
- Architect who designs child care settings
- Art, music, or dance instructor
- Athletic coach or assistant
- Child care center owner or director
- Child care law secretary or attorney
- Child care licensing specialist
- Child care resource & referral specialist
- Child custody mediator
- Child development specialist for toy or children's food corporations
- Children's book author
- Children's book illustrator
- Children's clothing designer
- Children's clothing or toy store owner
- Children's librarian
- Children's museum guide
- Children's photographer
- Children's television programmer
- Children's zoo guide
- District manager of a child care center chain
- Family and consumer sciences community college instructor or university professor
- Family therapist
- Funeral home bereavement counselor

- Home visitor
- Montessori program director or teacher
- Nanny
- Nature educator
- Newspaper or magazine reporter/columnist specializing in children
- Parent educator
- Play therapist
- School nurse or nurse practitioner
- School psychologist
- Social worker
- Summer camp or sports clinic instructor, counselor, or director

FIG. 3-7.

HOW MUCH EDUCATION DO I NEED?

High School diploma	Associate's degree (2-year college)	Bachelor's degree (4-year college)	Master's degree (bachelor's plus graduate school)
• Amusement park guide • Athletic assistant • Care provider • Children's library assistant • Children's museum guide • Children's zoo guide • Summer camp counselor • Teacher's aide or assistant	• Child care center owner or director • Child care center teacher • Child care law secretary • Child care licensing specialist • Child care resource & referral specialist • Children's book illustrator • Children's clothing designer • Children's clothing or toy store owner • Children's photographer • District manager of child care center chain • Funeral home bereavement counselor • Home visitor • Montessori program teacher • Nanny	• Adoption counselor • Art, music, or dance instructor • Child custody mediator • Children's book author • Children's television programmer • Director of child care resource & referral agency • Family and consumer sciences high school or community college instructor • Nature educator • Newspaper or magazine reporter/columnist specializing in children • Parent educator • Play therapist in children's hospital • School nurse • Summer camp or sports clinic instructor, counselor, or director	• Architect who designs child care settings • Child care attorney • Child development specialist for toy or children's food corporations • Children's librarian • Director of play therapy department in hospital • Family and consumer sciences university professor • Family therapist • School nurse practitioner • School psychologist • Social worker • Textbook author

you said you did earlier in this section. It is an excellent way to watch how professionals teach and care for young children. See Fig. 3-7.

Entrepreneurship Opportunities

As you examine your interests and abilities, you may discover things about yourself that guide you toward other career directions. Perhaps you could be a successful **entrepreneur** (AHN-truh-pruh-NUR), or a person who owns and operates a business. Here are some questions to ask yourself if owning a child-centered business appeals to you:

- Do I have the necessary experience and knowledge of child development and child care or education? If not, what education and experience must I have before I open my business?

- From what sources will I obtain the financial backing I need to start my business?

- Have I saved enough money to pay for at least six months of personal living expenses?
- Am I willing to research the laws in my city and state related to operating a business, such as taxes, safety regulations, and zoning?
- Am I willing to research the licensing requirements for my type of business?
- Am I willing to research the need for my business in the area and the prices that customers will pay?
- Do I have the time and energy to start a business and maintain it daily?
- Am I mature enough to accept ultimate responsibility for a business?
- Do I have the patience and commitment to see a business through problems and slow periods?
- How might my business affect my family and personal life?

Provider Certification and Credentials

In order to identify individuals who can successfully perform the duties of an early childhood professional, federal, state, and county or city government agencies have created certification and credentialing programs.

To earn a certificate or a credential, you must satisfactorily complete on-the-job training and formal education. Public schools typically use certification for early childhood educators. The board of education in each state determines certification requirements. A nationally recognized credential program for early childhood professionals is the **Child Development Associate (CDA)** credential, although this credential is not mandated by state or national governments. (See Chapter 5 for more information on the CDA credential.) Meeting this credential's standards prepares people for entry-level positions in early childhood programs. More and more states also offer the director credential to prepare administrators for managing children's programs.

Legal Responsibilities

Early childhood professionals must abide by the laws that apply to their job responsibilities. Laws help protect the rights and welfare of children, families, and staff. Three major legal responsibilities in the early childhood profession are criminal background checks, maintaining privacy and confidentiality, and mandated reporting of abuse and neglect.

Criminal Background Checks

Many states now require confidential criminal background checks before a person can be employed in early childhood care and education. If a background check reveals a person has been convicted of a crime against children, state law requires that the center or employer reject the prospective candidate, or dismiss him, if already hired. See Fig. 3-8.

FIG. 3-8. **Fingerprinting for criminal background checks is often customary to work in early childhood centers.** How can this practice benefit the children and the profession?

Privacy & Confidentiality

The Family Educational Rights and Privacy Act (FERPA) is a federal law that protects the privacy of personal and educational records. It says that only parents or legal guardians may have access to their children's records. To share the information with others, such as a counselor, the parents or guardians must give written permission.

Although it is tempting to discuss children's development issues with fellow staff members, it is your professional responsibility to maintain confidentiality. FERPA specifies that personal, developmental, or educational information about a child should only be shared with staff members who have necessary involvement in a child's care and education.

Mandated Reporting

All states have child abuse and neglect laws, which protect children from harm inside or outside of their homes. Anyone can report a case of child abuse or neglect. Early childhood professionals, however, along with health care workers and teachers, are **mandated**, or required by law, to report each suspected abuse or neglect case. People in these professions are called *mandated reporters.*

Most states have hotlines that make it easier to make mandated-reporter calls to the appropriate office. Licensing laws often require that staff members receive training in identifying symptoms of child abuse and neglect and in reporting these incidents. See Fig. 3-9.

FIG. 3-9. Mandated reporting is just one of the professional requirements for those who work with children.

Section 3-1   Knowledge Check

1. List at least two factors that contribute to the demand for early childhood providers.

2. In what ways can your personal traits and the required level of education influence the careers you select?

3. Describe the three major legal responsibilities of early childhood care providers.

Mini-Lab

Investigate the rewards and challenges of a variety of levels of early childhood careers. What education and training is required for those careers? What personal traits and characteristics would you recommend for a person seeking any early childhood career?

Section **3-2**

Caring for Older Adults

OBJECTIVES

- Differentiate Medicare from Medicaid.
- Describe the characteristics of a successful care professional of older adults.
- Describe the traditional models for adult day care and intergenerational care programs.
- Identify places to work and positions in older adult care.
- Identify issues related to balancing work and home responsibilities.

KEY TERMS

ageism
Medicare
Medicaid
intergenerational
  programs
multidisciplinary
burnout

As you have read in Chapter 2, growing numbers of baby boomers will soon become part of the aging population. These older adults will need services and programs to meet their medical, social, psychological, and even political needs. Demand for older adult care professionals will be high. These professionals must understand the complexities of late adulthood development and acquire keen skills in communicating with, and caring for, older adults. If you are willing to gain this knowledge and know-how, many employment opportunities await you. As you read this section, think about the ways your current traits, attitudes, skills, and abilities might direct you toward a successful career as an older adult care professional.

Demand for Older Adult Care Professionals

As baby boomers (those born between 1946 and 1964) turn 65, well-trained older adult care professionals will be in great demand in all parts of the United States. These career opportunities will differ from those in the past. The new population of older people will likely have improved health, higher incomes, and better education. Most will have taken better care of themselves. They will live longer. Rather than

primarily providing medical care, care professionals may serve, for example, as tour companions, geriatric fitness trainers, and personal secretaries or shoppers. They may own their own businesses in geriatric care and care management. See Fig. 3-10.

Older Adult Care Policies

Just as the kinds of older adult care careers will increase, the programs for older adults will become more diverse than those in the past. These programs will assist older adults in main-

FIG. 3-10. **As baby boomers age, their needs will likely be different from the current generation of older adults.** What career opportunities may exist for these varying needs?

taining healthy practices and will advocate changes in policies for the aging population.

Social and health policies will need to change to address older adults' needs. In 1950, the first national conference on aging led to major amendments to the Social Security Act and its provisions. This major federal law reform led the way for other program and policy reforms for older adults. See Fig. 3-11 for these reforms.

FIG. 3-11.

CONFERENCES LEADING TO LAW REFORM

Year	Conference
1950	**The National Conference on Aging** Significance: Sponsored the Federal Security Agency.
1961	**The First White House Conference on Aging** Significance: The Social Security Administration lowered the retirement age for men from 65 to 62; relaxed the requirements for retirement, increased minimum benefits, and increased benefits to older widows.
1971	**The Second White House Conference on Aging** Significance: Established a means for income assistance for older adults on low incomes, reducing poverty among this population.
1981	**The Third White House Conference on Aging** Significance: Focused on supportive services to help older people remain independent. Addressed **ageism** (discrimination against older people), intergenerational programs, and long-term health care.
1995	**The Fourth White House Conference on Aging** Significance: Celebrated the 30th anniversaries of the Older Americans Act, Medicare, Medicaid, and the Foster Grandparent Program. Increased focus on intergenerational issues.

FIG. 3-12. **Nutrition programs, such as Meals-on-Wheels, help older adults meet their nutritional needs and maintain their independence.** Which programs and services interest you most?

As a result of the Older Americans Act, career opportunities in aging have grown in such agencies as the Area Agency on Aging, AARP, Inc., and many other profit and nonprofit organizations. Several amendments added to the Older Americans Act provide for additional programs and services for older adults. These programs offer an array of careers for individuals to work with older people as well as on their behalf. These include:

- Studies concerning personnel needs in the aging field.
- Grants and model demonstration projects.
- Foster grandparent programs.
- Retired senior volunteer programs.
- **Intergenerational programs**, or those that involve two or more generations, such as older adults and children.
- Transportation services.
- Home care, legal services, and home renovation/repair services.
- Nutrition programs and congregate housing services. See Fig. 3-12.

Older Adult Care Environments

Career and job opportunities will require some people to work directly with older people in a variety of older adult care settings. Traditional care centers serve older adults' need for socialization or health care. Some offer both kinds of services in the same facility. A recently developed concept for care centers addresses the socialization needs of older adults with children.

The Older Americans Act of 1965 established the Administration on Aging as part of the U.S. Department of Health, Education, and Welfare. This legislation also called for each state to establish its own unit on aging. In addition, this law created two key programs as part of the Social Security Act:

- **Medicare and Title XVIII.** Established as part of the Social Security Act, Medicare and Title XVIII offer a health insurance program for older adults.
- **Medicaid and Title XIX.** The Social Security Act also provides a health insurance program for low-income people through Medicaid and Title XIX.

Traditional Adult Day Care. Traditional adult day centers may be based on one of three models: social, medical, and a combination of these two, the social-medical model. Career opportunities in gerontology and geriatrics services exist in each model. See Chapter 15 for more information on these models.

- **Social Model.** A center with a social model provides activities for its participants. For example, healthy adults may volunteer in a center to assist more physically challenged or frail adults with crafts and table games, such as checkers or chess. In addition, the older adult volunteers may help by serving meals.

- **Medical Model.** A center with a medical model primarily manages the health care of participants. A medical staff is part of the day care staff, and may include a licensed practical nurse (LPN), who is supervised by a registered nurse (RN). An on-site or off-site physician may supervise both. If a participant has physician's orders for a daily blood pressure check, a medical staff person would be available for this service. See Fig. 3-13. Also, if a person must go to a clinic for medical services, the center would ensure that he or she was taken there.

- **Social-Medical Model.** A center with a social-medical model combines activities with medical care. The day care center would provide health services for well and frail adults. All participants interact in activities based on their abilities.

Intergenerational Programs. Care providers in intergenerational programs develop activities to encourage interactions between two or more generations. In this environment, the staff members must be skilled or trained to direct programs to meet the needs of each generation. A number of models exist for intergenerational programs. Each program offers a number of career opportunities and requires specialized care providers:

- **Older Adult Day Care and Child Care Offered in the Same Center.** Although housed in the same facility, adult day care programs and child care programs each has its own designated space and staff to meet the unique needs of each group. The older adults and children meet together for activities.

- **Long-Term Care Centers with On-Site Child Care.** Care providers in these centers combine their activities and resources for the older and younger populations. On-site child care is also a benefit for employees of long-term care centers. The activity interactions between the old and young are generally planned, but can also be spontaneous.

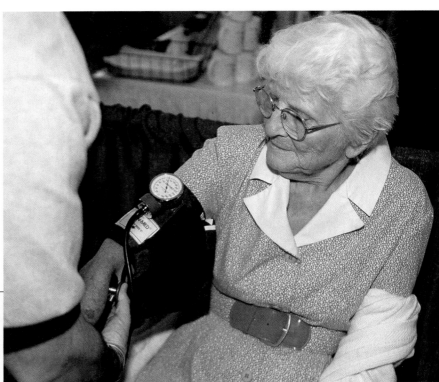

FIG. 3-13. **Providing some basic health services is part of adult day care programs that follow the medical model.**

- **Older Adults as Family Day Care Providers.** Some older adults receive training as family day care providers. Special funding is often available for this training. After becoming certified, older adults can then provide child care in their homes. This provides them with income and a chance to develop new relationships.

- **Interactive Visitation Services.** When children visit older adults at long-term care facilities or adult day care centers, or older adults visit children at child care centers, many chances for intergenerational activities occur. Center staff may plan these activities because the centers are near one another or somehow affiliated. Activities may center on special celebrations of the subjects children are studying in school.

- **Volunteer Service Programs.** Many chances for interaction between children and older adults exist in volunteer service programs. With these programs, youth and older adults volunteer their time and abilities for activities, such as tutoring, playing cards and games, dictating letters, and reading books. They meet regularly with one another and develop friendly relationships. See Fig. 3-14.

Your Potential as a Professional

To be successful as a professional in the field of gerontology or geriatric services, you should have an understanding of later life development. It will help you to know what people experience as they age. Just as children develop and act in a certain way as they get older, so do older people. Understanding that people are different in their cultural and ethnic backgrounds is also necessary.

Traits & Attitudes

Positive traits and attitudes are essential tools you need when working with older adults. You must develop professional skills to be successful in your career and to enjoy your work. A care provider with most of the following traits and attitudes will have a greater chance of performing well under the demands of the profession. As you review the list, ask yourself which of these traits and attitudes describe you, as you are today.

FIG. 3-14. Intergenerational care programs provide many opportunities to work with older adults. How can intergenerational care benefit the younger and older generations?

- **Dependability.** Arriving at work on time and working independently on assigned tasks show your employer that you are dependable.

- **Honesty and Integrity.** Older adults have a long life experience and can often detect when someone is not telling them the truth. They appreciate someone communicating with them directly and honestly.

- **Respect and Courtesy.** Care providers must always communicate truthfully, but avoid confidential issues. Showing older adults kindness, patience, and consideration is critical. Older adults who doubt their self-worth due to failing health or other circumstances especially appreciate respectful and courteous interactions with younger people. Care providers should also address older adults by their preferred name, respect individual privacy, and avoid gossip.

- **Calm Temperament.** Remaining calm in stressful situations and reporting incidents in an unemotional and factual manner are necessary professional qualities. You must work hard to handle any anger and frustration you feel as a professional. Be conscientious and timely in handling matters and complaints. Reporting complaints in appropriate ways and times is critical.

- **Hard Worker.** Working hard and being willing to work show your genuine intention. Others can see if you are actually working hard and not just talking about how hard you work. Some care providers work too hard. They do not balance their work and home responsibilities, and, in time, feel powerless with stress from the job demands. Balance and managing stress are necessary to sustain a career as a care provider. See Section 1 of this chapter for ways to manage stress.

- **Positive Attitude.** A friendly smile and tone of voice, a good sense of humor, and showing interest in others all display a positive attitude. See Fig. 3-15. You must have a supportive outlook in working with adults who want to enjoy their lives even as they age.

FIG. 3-15. **Having a good sense of humor is a positive attribute for those who work with older adults.** Why is having a sense of humor important?

Skills & Abilities

Working with older adults requires effective oral communication skills—speaking and listening. The challenge is to hear, listen, understand, and respect what an older adult says to you. An older adult might speak slowly, have trouble thinking of a word, or follow several trains of thoughts within a single conversation with you. Make certain that you repeat what you heard, which confirms to the older adult that you were listening. Help the older adult stick to the topic by asking a question. You must take into account the speaker's views and preferences. Use "I" statements, such as "I believe," "I think," "I want," and so on, to help the older adult understand what you are saying.

In addition to communication, you must apply the following skills consistently when working in an older adult care environment:

- Arrive to the workplace on time.
- Display a consistent temperament, with no great mood swings.
- Show consistency in ways of responding to older adults.
- Adapt easily to changes in schedule and plans as needed.
- Show creativity and resourcefulness in solving problems.
- Make decisions as a team player.
- Manage time with flexibility.
- Display a self-starting initiative.
- Show willingness to work hard to complete a project.

Working with Older Adults

Gerontology is stimulating and challenging. Because it is very diverse, this field offers several employment opportunities. Throughout their lives, people have various needs and require different services. People's needs, resources, and abilities change as they age. Their gender, race, ethnicity, health, and economic status may contribute to how and when change takes place.

The relative newness of gerontology means many opportunities are available for new and different ideas, programs, and products to serve older adults. Some might work directly with older adults in care settings. Others may work on behalf of older people in such areas as research, advocacy, and teaching about aging. The goal of both is to improve the quality of life for an aging population. See Fig. 3-16 for more information about where you can work with older adults.

FIG. 3-16.

PLACES TO WORK WITH OLDER ADULTS

- Alumni associations
- Community health clinics
- Cruise ships
- Elderhostels
- Faith-based community centers
- Gerontology community college instructor or university professor
- Gerontology research institutions
- Group homes for older adults
- Health care centers
- Homeless shelters
- Hospitals
- Human resources departments in corporations
- Human services departments in government agencies
- Intergenerational care centers
- Mental health hospitals or agencies
- Museums
- Nursing homes
- Parks & recreation programs

- Religious organizations
- Retirement communities
- Retirement residences
- Travel study tours & pilgrimages
- Veterans' hospitals

Starting a business related to gerontology may be another option. For example, you might coordinate home health care services or consult with businesses about how to develop services or design products for older consumers. See Section 1 about whether you may be well suited for being a business owner.

Choosing a Career Path

If you pursue a career in older adult care, you must prepare for the responsibilities you will have. The education, training, and experience you need, however, will depend upon the specific job you seek and where you live. Colleges and universities, community colleges and community-based organizations have dramatically increased their programs in gerontology, geriatrics, and related fields. If you are interested in such a career, you can begin at any educational level and choose more education later, if desired. Fields that offer such opportunities are adult education, counseling, family and consumer sciences, long-term care administration, medicine, nursing, psychology, public policy making, recreation, rehabilitation therapy, and social work.

Careers in Gerontology & Geriatrics

Gerontology is a **multidisciplinary** field, which means it combines two or more fields of study. In gerontology, you would focus on meeting the social, economic, or political needs of older people. You may work side-by-side with people from such areas as housing, law, transportation, family counseling, and teaching. As a gerontology professional, you may serve on a family care team that provides family counseling, day care, or home care. As an educator, you might teach a course on work and retirement to individuals thinking about leaving the work force. Depending upon your career goals, gerontology offers some career choices.

Careers in geriatrics are more numerous and diverse. Geriatrics is a branch of medicine that deals with the problems and diseases of older people. A career in geriatrics can be in any area that helps people stay healthy. Geriatric physicians, nurses, dietitians, and nutrition educators all work to meet the health needs of older adults. See Fig. 3-17.

Education Requirements for Gerontology and Geriatrics Careers. Positions are available in these fields at all levels of education. See Fig. 3-18. If you choose to work in gerontology immediately after high school, for example, you may obtain an entry-level job as a certified nursing assistant (CNA), home health aide, certified home health aide, or physical and occupational therapy assistant. You may be required to take short courses and participate in on-the-job training for hands-on positions. On any job, you will be expected to participate in training to help you keep current. In order to move into middle-level and higher-level positions, you will be required to take more courses or earn a college degree.

Provider Certification & Credentials

In order to identify individuals who are adequately prepared to perform the duties of an adult care professional, federal, state, and county or city government agencies have created certification and credentialing programs. To earn a certificate or a credential, you must satisfactorily complete on-the-job training and formal education. Meeting this credential's standards prepares people for entry-level positions in older adult care programs. The National Association for Adult Day Centers oversees state credentialing agencies. More and more states also offer the director credential to prepare administrators for managing adult care programs.

FIG. 3-17.

WHAT COULD I BE?

Not everyone who works with older adults is a nurse, doctor, or care provider. Have you ever thought about training for one of these positions?

- Architect who designs retirement residences
- Art therapist
- Care center aide
- Care center care provider
- Care center director
- Community outreach aide
- Elderhostel instructor
- Food and nutrition educator
- Food services cook
- Food services coordinator
- Funeral home bereavement counselor
- Funeral home director or owner
- Geriatric counselor or therapist
- Gerontology community college instructor
- Gerontology textbook author
- Gerontology university professor
- Gerontology program coordinator

- Home visitor
- Homebound shopper aide
- Homebound shopper program director
- Hospital orderly
- Long-term care insurance salesperson
- Museum guide
- Music instructor
- Newspaper or magazine reporter/columnist specializing in older adult issues
- Nurse or nurse practitioner
- Ombudsman program coordinator
- Physical fitness aide
- Recreation director
- Retirement and pension adviser
- Social worker
- Social activity leader
- Tour guide

Legal Responsibilities

Professionals in gerontology and geriatrics services must follow the laws that apply to their jobs. Laws help protect the rights and welfare of employees, older adults (especially those who are unable to help themselves), and family members. Social-medical and medical model adult day facilities require criminal background checks, the protection of confidentiality, and the mandate to report suspected abuse and neglect to help ensure a safer environment for older adults.

Criminal Background Checks. Many states make provisions for older adult care programs to conduct criminal background checks for prospective employees. These laws often permit background checks in all states in which the prospective employee has lived during the past seven years. Some state laws mandate adult care programs to perform a state criminal background check or a private agency background check if they are suspicious of a person's background.

Privacy and Confidentiality. In some cases, providing care for older adults involves handling medical records. Medical records are among the most important documents in a person's life and must be handled with confidentiality. The Medical Records Confidentiality Act of 1995 was established to protect personal health information for all people. By law, each state must guarantee strong and consistent privacy safeguards whether the health information is in paper or electronic form.

Mandated Reporting. Unfortunately abuse and neglect of older adults are prevalent in the United States. People that work with the older population are required to report the suspected abuse, neglect, and exploitation of persons who are unable to report it themselves. Adult protective services agencies exist by law in every state

FIG. 3-18.

HOW MUCH EDUCATION DO I NEED?

High School diploma	Associate's degree (2-year college)	Bachelor's degree (4-year college)	Master's degree (bachelor's plus graduate school)
Gerontology			
• Care center care provider • Community outreach aide • Fitness aide • Food services cook • Homebound shopper aide • Home cook • Hospital orderly • Housekeeper • Tour guide • Transportation attendant • Van driver	• Activity or recreation director • Care center assistant director • Food services coordinator • Homebound shopper program director • Human services assistant • Paralegal in gerontological issues • Speakers' bureau coordinator	• Art therapist • Care center director • Elderhostel instructor • Food and nutrition educator • Gerontology community college instructor • Gerontology program coordinator • Legal specialist in gerontology • Music instructor or song leader • Retirement and pension adviser	• Architect who designs retirement residences • Attorney specializing in gerontological issues • Gerontology university professor • Social worker
Geriatrics			
• Hearing center aide • Hospice services clerk • Meal planner assistant • Nurse's aide • Occupational therapist aide • Recreational equipment aide • Respite care aide	• Hearing center assistant • Hospice care assistant • Licensed practical nurse (LPN) • Meal planner • Occupational therapist assistant • Respite care coordinator	• Health services manager • Registered nurse (RN) • Occupational therapist • Respiratory therapist • Speech and language therapist • Therapeutic recreation specialist	• Audiologist • Dietitian • Hospice director • Nurse practitioner

to investigate cases of possible abuse and neglect. States require the reporting of elder abuse. People working with older adults can be held responsible if they fail to report suspected abuse. If an older adult with a possible history of abuse dies, a complete investigation is needed including reporting the death to law enforcement, the coroner, or the medical examiner as required by state law.

Intergenerational *Interactions*

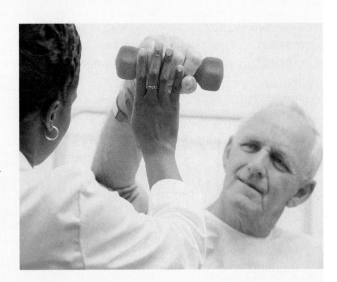

Job Bank for Gerontology & Geriatrics

Opportunities for careers and jobs in gerontology and geriatrics will comprise one of the leading areas for employment growth. As the population ages, job opportunities will be available in all areas of human services, education, research, and health care. Here are some ways that you can research careers in gerontology and geriatrics:

1. **Collect Information.** Use your local newspaper and the Internet "job opportunity" section to identify jobs in areas related to gerontology.

2. **Design a Job Bank Listing.** Develop a chart that has four columns and head each column as follows: Job title; Type agency/organization; Qualification for the job; and Salary range.

3. **List Jobs.** Identify at least 10 job positions from the newspaper.

4. **Conduct a Needs Assessment.** Identify one older person in your family or community. Outline questions to ask an older family member about the types of services that are needed to help maintain a quality of life. Ask the following questions: What services do you need to help you maintain good health? Where would you want the services to be offered? Do you think there is a trained workforce to assist you with the services you want and need? How will you pay for these services?

5. **Discuss Your Findings.** Attach your job listing to create your job bank. Design an attractive caption for your job bank listing.

Follow-Up

Check your local newspaper to find job listings in gerontology or geriatrics. Then explore after-school volunteer opportunities to work in adult day settings. Volunteer to assist an older adult with chores. Investigate current trends, issues, or technologies associated with aging services. How do these factors affect your career choice?

Balancing Work & Home Life

As you develop professional skills in gerontology or geriatrics services, you must also learn to balance your work life with your family life. Because jobs in these fields are rewarding but demanding, you may become so involved in your work that you may neglect your family.

For example, if you work with an older person who doesn't have family nearby, your family may become a surrogate, or substitute, to that older adult. This situation is positive for the older person; however, it may have a negative impact on your family because you spend time with that person during the day and then again at night. See Fig. 3-19.

Balancing work and life is a skill you must learn and practice. You must gain a clear understanding of what is most important to you. You might ask yourself: Must this work be done today? If it must, is it more important to stay longer at work to complete it or to bring it home to finish? How will each choice affect me and my family and our plans? Your family environment, finances, and career goals influence how you will make these decisions.

You must learn what *balance* is for you. You may feel you do not have enough time and energy for yourself and your family. When you are overworked, you can experience **burnout**, or physical and mental exhaustion due to long periods of stress and frustration.

A growing body of research shows that employers and employees benefit when workers are given appropriate flexibility and control in structuring when and where they do their work. When employees are able to manage a work schedule that complements their chosen way of life, employers often see more productivity. When people can balance their work and home lives, they are absent less from work.

FIG. 3-19. **Learning to balance work and personal or family life is beneficial to avoiding burnout on the job.** What are some ways you might balance work and personal or family life?

Section 3-2 Knowledge Check

1. List three traits of a successful care provider.
2. Contrast traditional adult day care with intergenerational care.
3. What are the consequences of failing to balance work and home life?

Mini-Lab

Investigate three careers in either adult day care or intergenerational care. What qualifications, both educational and personal, are necessary for each career? Write a summary of your findings to share with the class.

Chapter **3**

Review & Activities

Section Summaries

3-1 The need for quality child care is greater than the available supply.

3-1 Early child care professionals find success when they have or develop certain traits, attitudes, skills, and abilities.

3-1 A broad range of careers involves working with children.

3-1 Certificates and credentials promote professional success.

3-1 Licensing and registration procedures allow child care programs to operate legally.

3-2 Growing numbers of older adult baby boomers will need services and programs for older adults to meet their needs, increasing demand for older adult care professionals.

3-2 Traditional adult day centers focus on the social and/or medical needs of older adults, but a growing trend is intergenerational care programs.

3-2 Older adult care professionals find success when they have or develop certain traits, attitudes, skills, and abilities.

3-2 A range of careers in gerontology and geriatrics involves working with older adults.

3-2 Social-medical and medical model adult day facilities require criminal background checks, the protection of confidentiality, and the mandate to report suspected abuse and neglect.

3-2 Care professionals, whether caring for children or older adults, must practice ways to manage stress and balance work and family responsibilities.

Check Your Knowledge

1. Cite two factors that led to more parents needing child care services outside the home.
2. What can child care professionals do to create a quality child care environment?
3. Describe five ways a care provider can help herself in managing stress.
4. List ten traits, attitudes, skills, or abilities required of a successful care professional.
5. What is the purpose of the Family Educational Rights & Privacy Act?
6. Describe the responsibilities of a mandated reporter.
7. What determines if an older adult care program is intergenerational?
8. What education is required for mid-level and high-level careers in gerontology or geriatrics?
9. Why is confidentiality a legal requirement for adult care providers?
10. Why are employees more productive when their employers are flexible in letting them set up their work schedules?

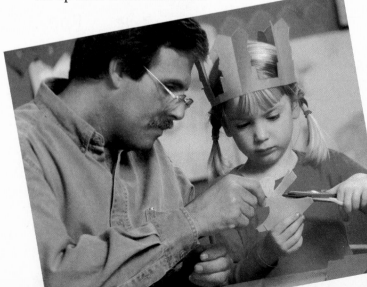

Thinking Critically

1. Draw conclusions about how the child care industry (or the older adult care industry) influences the local, national, and global economies. Use research from print and Internet sources to support your conclusions.

2. Care provider fatigue, low morale, and lack of work satisfaction can decrease care provider effectiveness. Analyze how care providers can find ways to meet their own needs and maintain personal energy and enthusiasm.

Practical Applications

1. **Examine Career Choices.** Choose several careers in early childhood or older adult care, then investigate the traits, attitudes, skills, and abilities associated with each career. Write a summary of your findings.

2. **Observation and Evaluation.** Obtain a copy of your state's licensing laws for child care centers. Read the laws thoroughly. Then visit a NAEYC accredited early childhood program in your area. Record the indicators of high quality that you observe. How do these indicators compare to standards set by the state licensing laws? Write a summary of your observation.

3. **Graphing Job Opportunities.** Use the Internet and library reference resources to research potential job opportunities in the fields of geriatrics and gerontology from 2001 to 2040. Draw a graph showing the predictions of the number of job opportunities over the years. Write a brief summary of your findings.

Building Your PORTFOLIO

Child & Adult Care Entrepreneurs

Some child and adult care providers are family day care home entrepreneurs. Follow the steps below to find out how to become a quality home care provider.

Step 1: Use print and Internet resources to obtain the quality standards for family child care homes from the National Association for Family Child Care (NAFCC). Or, contact your local Area Agency on Aging for quality standards for adult day care homes.

Step 2: Investigate state licensing laws for family child or adult care homes.

Step 3: Write a business plan for your business based on quality standards and licensing laws. Include the following components in your business plan:

- **Vision:** Include your services, start-up and operating costs, the business location, and the cost to your customers for services.

- **Goals:** Your goals must be specific, concrete, and measurable.

- **Strategies:** Include strategies for meeting each of your goals.

- **Action plan:** Your plan will help you reach your business goals by giving a specific course of action. It shows how you will meet licensing laws and quality standards.

Step 4: Compile the information from Steps 1, 2, and 3 to put in your career portfolio.

Chapter *4*

Employability Skills

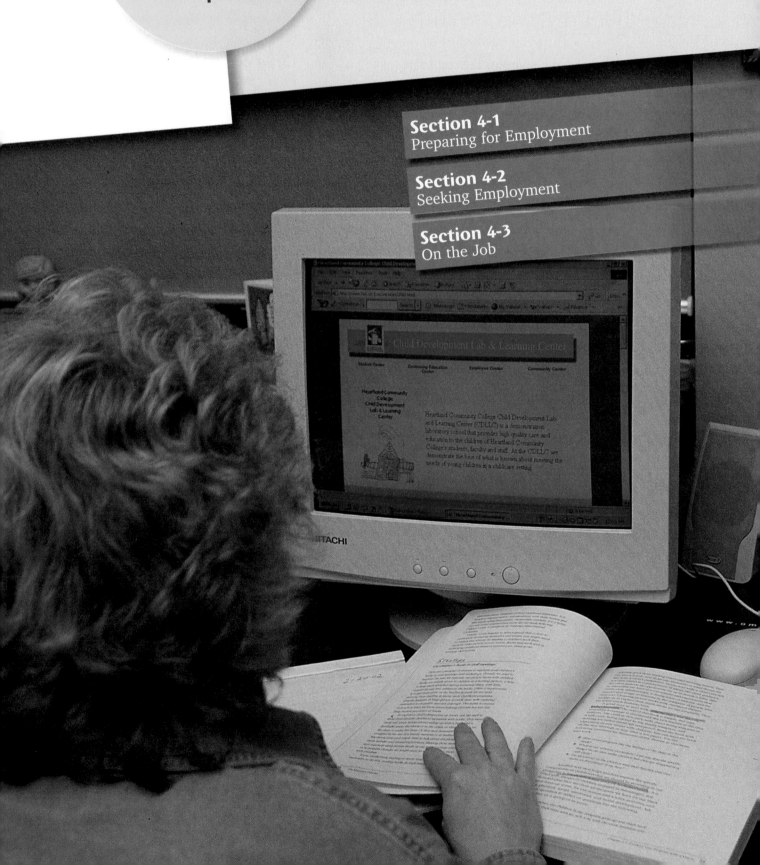

Section 4-1
Preparing for Employment

Section 4-2
Seeking Employment

Section 4-3
On the Job

Section 4-1

Preparing for Employment

OBJECTIVES

- Describe the basic employability skills that applicants for positions in early childhood care and older adult care need.
- Identify effective verbal, nonverbal, written, and electronic communication skills.
- Identify the traits and behaviors of a worker with a positive work ethic.
- Compare the types of resources care professionals use in their careers.

KEY TERMS

active listening
body language
work ethic
flexibility
prioritize

Congratulations! You have decided to consider a career in early childhood care or older adult care services. Whether you see yourself as a facility director, care provider, geriatric nurse practitioner, or activity coordinator, your next step is to develop the knowledge and skills you need to start your professional career. The skills you need to be hired are the same ones you will draw on to find and keep a job in any field. You may already have many of these basic skills. This section will help you identify those you have and those you must develop during your studies. You will also learn how you will apply these employment skills in your position as a care professional.

Sharpening Your Basic Skills

Imagine you are a care center director looking for the right person to hire. What would you look for in a potential employee? Depending on the position, you would look for someone with specific education, training, or work experience. For example, to hire a head teacher, you would look for someone with activity planning experience.

Beyond this specialized knowledge and experience, however, every employer expects you to

have certain basic skills. These are generic skills that are needed and used in almost all employment opportunities. They provide you with a strong foundation for finding a job, staying employed, and advancing on the job. Basic skills can also transfer from job to job. The basics include communication skills, math skills, and thinking skills. These critical skills will help you acquire the knowledge and experience you will need to pursue your career goals. They will also help you pursue further education, if you are interested.

Communication Skills

Effective communication skills are basic to any career. As a care professional, your skills in speaking, writing, reading, and listening will play an important role in how well you give information to children, parents, older adults, and their families. See Fig. 4-1.

Speaking Skills. How well other people understand you depends upon how clearly you speak. Follow these steps to clear speech:

- **Pronounce Words Clearly and Correctly.** If you are unsure how to pronounce a word or a name, ask someone or check a dictionary.

- **Do Not Use Slang.** Slang is not acceptable in the workplace. It can confuse children, older adults, and those who speak a language other than English.

FIG. 4-1. **Using effective communication skills on the job is foundational for any career. How can you benefit from polishing your communication skills?**

- **Try to Speak at a Medium Pace.** If you speak too quickly, your listener may miss words or your message. If you speak too slowly, your listener may become distracted or think you are talking down to him or her.

- **Speak Each Syllable of a Word.** Do not slur your words together or drop the endings of words.

- **Check Your Volume.** How loud is your everyday speaking voice? Ask someone to judge it for you. If you speak too softly, people will not hear you. If you speak too loudly, you will annoy your listeners.

Telephone Use. When using the telephone, speak clearly at a moderate volume. Even though your listener cannot see you, smile while you speak on the telephone. The person can sense when you are smiling. Your voice on the telephone may be a family member's first or only impression of the care you provide his or her child or older adult.

Writing Skills. Your ability to communicate in writing will help you find a job and perform well on the job. The two most common forms of business writing are memos and business letters. In providing care services, you must also document or log the care that you provide within the child's or older adult's records. Whether you are writing a letter to a parent, filling out a request form for supplies, or sending a memo to the staff, your writing will improve every time you write if you pay attention to the following points. See Fig. 4-2.

- **Your Audience.** Before you write anything, picture the person or group who will be reading your writing. Tailor what you write to what the reader needs to understand your message. If you have never met the person, you may want to start with a sentence that briefly introduces you to the person.

- **Your Purpose.** Choose words that suit the purpose of your writing. Read what you have written, and decide if your writing meets its purpose.

FIG. 4-2. **Written communication is important in all businesses, but is especially important for care professionals when documenting or seeking information.**

- Carry out general job responsibilities by reading workplace policies and communications.
- Carry out care instructions from family members.
- Share literature with children and older adults. See Fig. 4-3.
- Communicate with other care team members.
- Keep updated on research findings in journal articles for ongoing professional development.

Here are some basic reading skills you will practice on the job:

- **Previewing.** Read the headlines and sub-heads to get an overview.

- **Your Writing Style.** The style of your written communication comes from your choice of words and the tone—or attitude—that your words convey to the reader. Be direct in stating your purpose in your writing and use a professional tone. Always follow basic grammar and punctuation rules. Be sure to use the spell-checker and grammar-checker features on the computer to check your writing. Also have someone else proofread your business letters before mailing them.

It will also be to your benefit to demonstrate effective electronic communication skills. Many of the above forms of communication are often performed electronically, or with the use of a computer.

Reading Skills. Because you read much of the information you receive on the job, reading is a very important skill. Care professionals use their reading skills to:

FIG. 4-3. **Whether you are reading through care instructions or reading a story to children, effective reading skills are important for care providers.** What other ways do effective reading skills benefit care providers?

- **Skimming.** When reading, you should always look over the reading material for key points.

- **Focusing.** After you have previewed or skimmed material, give what you are reading your full attention. Begin reading, and as you read, think about what you are reading.

- **Visualizing.** If the reading material has no illustrations, imagine a set of photographs or charts that you would find suitable for the material.

- **Checking Comprehension.** Ask yourself how well you understand what you just read. If there are words you do not understand, look for each one in a dictionary. Then reread the paragraph, inserting the meaning of each word.

Listening Skills. You will be listening and speaking almost constantly at work. The kinds of listening and speaking skills you must demonstrate on the job promote understanding—between you and the child and parents or between you and the older adult and family members.

Listening is not just appearing to hear what a person has said to you. It is hearing the message and responding to it. To listen, you must avoid distractions. Whether you are listening to an older adult's health concerns or stopping a fight between two children, you must learn to practice **active listening**. This skill requires paying attention to and interacting with the speaker. See Fig. 4-4.

Body Language. Whether you are aware of it or not, you also speak without saying a word through your **body language**. This form of nonverbal communication does not use words but communicates through what a person sees when he speaks or listens to you. Body language "speaks" through the ways you move your hands or head, sit, stand, look, even smile or frown. It reveals your reactions and feelings to what you say or hear. By paying attention to your body language, you can demonstrate effective nonverbal communication skills.

Math Skills

The ability to work with numbers is a fundamental part of almost every job. You will find yourself adding, subtracting, multiplying, and dividing in countless ways. For example, you will use basic math skills to keep track of your work hours and wages, vacation days, and sick days. Care directors, for example, use math skills to order supplies, schedule deliveries, set up employee work rosters, complete payroll and tax forms, and maintain budgets. See Fig. 4-5.

Sharpening your basic math skills will improve your chances of employment as a care professional.

FIG. 4-4. Active listening involves maintaining eye contact. Why is active listening especially important in working with older adults?

FIG. 4-5. **Math skills can be used in a variety of ways in human services careers.** Investigate ways that human services employees use math skills in their daily work.

Thinking Skills

In addition to needing basic communication and math skills, you also must demonstrate that you can think critically, make decisions, and solve problems.

Think Critically. An employee who can think critically can respond quickly and properly to a variety of situations. For example, if a fire alarm sounds during nap or rest time, you must react immediately to evacuate children and older adults as safely as possible.

Make Decisions. An employee who can consistently make good decisions demonstrates the responsibility needed to succeed in the workplace. For example, when a person other than a child's custodial parent arrives to pick up a child in your care, you reveal your good decision-making abilities by asking for photo identification. You may also want to check the child's file for a completed and required written authorization for the child's release to this parent.

Solve Problems. An employee who finds quick, practical solutions to problems will help the professional team offer quality care. For example, if your care facility's sanitizing automatic dishwasher breaks down, you can suggest using disposable meal service supplies, such as paper plates, cups, and plastic utensils. With this solution, the facility continues to provide sanitary conditions in its meal service, until the dishwasher is repaired. In another instance, you may be called upon to use your interpersonal skills of conflict resolution and negotiation when dealing with children and older adults and conflict. You will learn more about conflict resolution and negotiation in Chapters 5 and 11.

Developing a Strong Work Ethic

In addition to skills, employers also look for certain key qualities in prospective employees. Demonstrating these traits shows a strong **work ethic**—a personal commitment to do your very best. Employers want employees that exhibit productive work habits and attitudes. The qualities that mark a strong work ethic include responsibility, teamwork, reliability, flexibility, commitment, and honesty.

Responsibility. Showing responsibility is one of the most important qualifications for success in any job. Responsibility means showing up for work on time, even when you would rather be late or vacationing. It means correctly carrying out your job duties, even when your boss is gone for the day. When you are responsible, you know right behavior from wrong. You are able to accept the consequences of your actions rather than blaming others. See Fig. 4-6.

Teamwork. As a care provider, you will often find yourself part of a large care team. A team, however, is more than a set of individuals. If you've ever played a team sport or served on a committee, you know how important it is that

FIG. 4-6. There are many ways to show responsibility in the workplace, including being on time for work. What other ways show responsibility?

every member participates and completes his or her assignment. You will practice teamwork on the job by completing your duties, and in doing so, you are supporting the efforts of your coworkers.

Reliability. Reliability means that you perform as your employer expects time after time. Reliable people are more likely to advance on the job to higher-level positions than employees who are inconsistent in their performance. Reliable employees carry out a variety of assigned tasks without constant prompting. They direct themselves to do the next right thing. They take on extra work when unusual circumstances require it.

Flexibility. In today's rapidly changing work environment, **flexibility**—the ability to adapt willingly to changing circumstances—is very important. Flexibility on the job means approaching change without complaining. The more confident that you are in your skills, the easier you will find it to be flexible when certain times demand it.

Commitment. Commitment is the quality that supports all your other abilities and skills. You show that you are committed to quality care and to the mission of your facility or employer by following all procedures and rules, supporting the other employees with whom you work, and performing your duties exceptionally well. Demonstrating your commitment to quality and excellence on the job will set you apart as a valuable employee.

- **Quality.** A commitment to quality means doing pride-worthy work. When you are committed to quality, you strive to meet the highest standards. For example, you may ask permission to attend workshops or conferences where you learn about new techniques and care practices. You may keep certificates renewed, such as your first aid/CPR certification, or work toward the next level of certification. You may meet licensing laws completely.

- **Excellence.** Employees committed to excellence strive to do their very best at all times. They make the most of opportunities to improve their abilities and learn new skills.

ETHICS in *Action*

Taking Initiative. As you are finishing up an activity with a small group of young children, you notice two of your coworkers sitting off to the side of the room talking. Although it is the end of the day and few children remain at the center, there are still numerous tasks to be done to get the center ready for the next day. Your coworkers don't appear to be taking the initiative to do these tasks without prompting from your supervisor who is in her office. *What can you do about your coworkers' lack of initiative?*

People who are committed to excellence are not willing to settle for work that is adequate or "just good enough."

Honesty. Honesty is an important part of a strong work ethic. You practice honesty on the job when you are truthful in what you say and in what you do. For example, if you make a mistake, you are honest, admit your error, and find out ways to prevent making it again. You do not cover up the mistake or blame someone else. Employers insist on honesty, and some consider dishonesty immediate grounds for firing. See Fig. 4-7.

Developing Leadership Skills

In addition to a strong work ethic, employers look for employees with leadership qualities. Leadership is the ability to motivate others to accomplish goals. Although leadership qualities vary from person to person and group to group, effective leaders get the job done and keep the group together.

Qualities of Effective Leaders

Effective leaders have certain qualities that are helpful in cultivating a productive work environment. These qualities include:

- **Integrity.** Good leaders are honest and trustworthy. They are dependable and straightforward in their communication with others. They use good judgment based on solid values and principles in working with others.
- **Vision.** Good leaders are open-minded and future-oriented. They look to the future for opportunities and challenges. They use their vision and creativity to motivate others.
- **Perseverance.** Good leaders are persistent even when faced with difficult challenges. They keep focused and seek to find and use resources to achieve desired goals.
- **Consideration.** Effective leaders are aware and considerate of the feelings of others.

FIG. 4-7. **Honesty is essential for care providers.** In what ways is honesty shown in the workplace?

They take time to listen to others' ideas. They recognize the worth of each team member and encourage a sense of belonging to a group.

- **Team-Oriented.** Good leaders are committed to the team effort. They collaborate, or work well with others, to achieve a common goal. They value the differing backgrounds and viewpoints of others on the team.

In addition to the above qualities, effective leaders maintain a high level of commitment to their goals and the workers who help them achieve these goals. Effective leaders also desire to reach the highest standards of quality in any task. In achieving these high standards, good leaders regularly monitor team members' work. Effective leaders are also committed to self-improvement. One way to improve leadership skills is through participation in educational and professional organizations.

FCCLA Leadership Programs

Many organizations and programs have been designed to help students develop leadership skills. One such group is Family, Career and Community Leaders of America (FCCLA). See Fig. 4-8A below. FCCLA is a national organization of students that are either currently taking or have taken Family and Consumer Sciences courses through grade 12. About 20 to 25 percent of the FCCLA membership is from middle and junior high schools. FCCLA activities provide opportunities for career and leadership development. Some of the FCCLA programs that contribute to student development include:

FIG. 4-8A

- **Leaders at Work.** Student members working in the unit on "Early Childhood, Education and Services" have opportunities to create projects to strengthen their communication, interpersonal, management, or entrepreneurship skills.

- **STAR Events.** Student members also participate in challenging competitions, such as the Students Taking Action with Recognition (STAR) Events. For example, student members may compete in the "Occupational Child Care" event that recognizes participants who submit a prepared portfolio, develop a lesson plan, and present the lesson to demonstrate their ability in this career area. Additional STAR Events include: Entrepreneurship, Focus on Children, and Interpersonal Communications.

- **Career Connection.** Student members participating in Career Connection activities learn different aspects of career development. Students might focus on learning how to find a job or how to be a more productive worker.

- **Dynamic Leadership.** Success in careers requires integrity, persistence, and teamwork. The Dynamic Leadership program provides

information, activities, and project ideas to help young people: learn about leadership, recognize the lifelong benefits of leadership strength, practice leadership through FCCLA involvement, and become strong leaders for families, careers, and communities. Through this program, dynamic leaders model good character, solve problems, foster positive relationships, manage conflict, build teams, and educate peers.

SkillsUSA-VICA

Another organization that helps students develop leadership skills is SkillsUSA-VICA. SkillsUSA-VICA is a national organization of high school and college students enrolled in training programs for technical, skilled, and service occupations. SkillsUSA-VICA programs partner students with industry professionals to provide the SkillsUSA Championships.

Students enrolled in occupational child care and early childhood programs can participate in the "Preschool Teaching Assistant" contest. Students are judged on their abilities to plan and present appropriate activities for preschool children relating to a specific theme and their general knowledge of quality child care. You can learn more about this competition on the SkillsUSA-VICA Web site. See Fig. 4-8B below.

FIG. 4-8B

Developing your leadership skills will help you as you move along your career path. Employers look among their employees for those whom others respect who can also handle more responsibility. They consider these employees first when higher-level positions become open.

Using Resources Effectively

As a care professional, it is to your advantage to use all available resources wisely because they are the raw materials with which you work. Your resources include people, information, technology, time, energy, money, equipment, and supplies.

People. Care professionals have constant interaction with people. You must take care to respect and communicate with children, older adults, and coworkers effectively. See Fig. 4-9. In addition, building positive relationships with parents and family members benefits both children and older adults.

Information. Information comes from countless sources all during your workday. You must learn and practice how to acquire, understand, and use information appropriately. See Fig. 4-10.

- **Acquiring Information.** From TV headlines to Internet listings, information is everywhere. Learn the difference between reliable and useful information and false or mislead-

FIG. 4-10. **Reliable information is important for updating your knowledge and skills. How can you determine if information is reliable?**

ing opinions. Be careful when retrieving information from the Internet because some Web sites contain unreliable information.

- **Sharing Information.** Effective care professionals share the important information they acquire. The whole team benefits from shared knowledge. They also recognize the difference between sharing useful job information and negative information, such as gossip.

Technology. Technology is an employee resource, not a replacement for a skilled employee. You must learn to use technology as effectively as you use any other resource. Depending on your care responsibilities, you may need to learn how to operate a security system or the latest portable oxygen supply technology. All care careers rely on computer technology. Here are some tips to keep in mind:

- **Do Not Expect Computers to Do Your Job.** Computers assist you enormously, but a computer cannot think or solve problems. Be sure

FIG. 4-9. **As a human service professional, part of your job will be to use all resources wisely, including human resources.**

your basic communication skills are strong enough to compensate when the computer system goes down. Learn and maintain the technological processes and software that apply to your job. See Fig. 4-11.

- **Respect Computer Resources on the Job.** If your employer provides you with access to a computer, remember to use it for business purposes only. Personal e-mail, Web surfing, on-line chatting, and computer games are inappropriate uses of employer-owned computers and a waste of your employer's resources.

Time. You can use time effectively by planning and completing tasks quickly and carefully. You must also learn to **prioritize**, or put tasks in the order of importance, not in the order of your preference. You may need to ask your supervisor to help you prioritize your assigned tasks, especially if you have been told to do more in your workday than is humanly possible.

Energy. Use personal energy resources effectively by taking good care of yourself. Working with children and older adults demands good physical and mental health. Be sure to get the right amount of nutrition, exercise, rest, and health care to do your job well. Good physical and mental health can lead to success and achievement in the workplace. What could happen to a care provider who doesn't maintain good physical and mental health?

FIG. 4-11. **Keeping up-to-date with the latest technology in your profession helps you do your job more effectively.** How might technology be used in human services careers?

Money. Whenever you perform a job transaction that involves money, double-check yourself and be honest. If you are responsible for making purchases, look for good values when you spend the facility's budget.

Equipment and Supplies. The materials, equipment, and supplies are key resources for providing care to children or older adults. Use these supplies properly and carefully. Immediately report any problems with or damage to equipment and supplies.

Section Knowledge Check

1. What kinds of basic skills will you need to practice on the job? Give an example of each.
2. What qualities contribute to developing a strong work ethic?
3. What kinds of resources will care professionals need to do their jobs effectively?

Mini-Lab

Imagine you have been asked to lead a team that will open a new intergenerational care center. Write a short "help wanted" ad, listing the qualities you want in team members who will help you carry out that task.

Section 4-2

Seeking Employment

OBJECTIVES

- Describe four resources for job leads.
- Contrast employment agencies and temporary employment agencies.
- Prepare a résumé and cover letter.
- Practice skills needed for job interviewing.

KEY TERMS

networking
referral
trade publications
service learning
résumé
keywords

As you have read in earlier chapters, the employment picture is bright in the early childhood care and education industry and the older adult care industry. Your career as a care professional begins with your first job. Whether you enter child care or older adult care, obtaining a job will involve following very clear steps within a hiring process common among most employers. This section will familiarize you with this process and the actions you must take to find, apply for, and secure a job as a care professional.

Employment Resources

Many first-time job seekers mistakenly believe that the local newspaper's classified ads are the only place to search for job openings. While it is true that some jobs are frequently listed there, especially entry-level positions, job opportunities are listed in many other resources. Your job search will demand that you tap many kinds of resources.

Job Search Journal

Your job search will become at least a part-time job in itself. Because you will learn of many job possibilities and meet many people, you will need to keep records for successful follow-up. Since you are serious about getting your first professional job, you will also want a record of all your hard work. Buy a conveniently sized notebook to use as a daily log or journal of your job search activities. As another option, you may prefer to use a set of index cards or create an electronic file for your journal. See Fig. 4-12.

The journal's organization is a personal matter. You may organize your journal chronologically, by listing the date on the top of each page and recording what you did to find a job that day. Or, you may organize your journal topically, by listing each opening you investigate and the information you find in each instance.

Job Lead

Job: *Activities Director*

Key Details: *35 hours per week, mostly week days but may include some weekends, technical education or associate's degree required*

Employer: *Brookdale Care Center; 5555 Brookdale Court; Anytown, USA*

Contact Person: *Mark Smith, Executive Director*

Source of Lead: *JoAnna Applegate, high school teacher/mentor*

Next Steps: *Complete and return job application by November 10*

FIG. 4-12. **Develop an organized system for keeping track of job leads, such as using index cards, a digital planner, or your computer.**

Networking

Networking is the most direct and successful way of finding a job. **Networking** means making use of all your personal and professional contacts to further your career goals. If you have ever asked a family member or friend about a job possibility, you have practiced networking. In addition to networking with family, you can also network with:

- **Teachers and Mentors.** These adults know your strengths and how you could apply those attributes in a care team setting. These are also individuals whom you may ask for reference letters, if a job application calls for one. See Fig. 4-13.

- **Friends and Classmates.** Others who are interested in careers similar to yours also will be researching jobs. They may be willing to share information with you. You may even want to organize a small group that

meets regularly to share job leads and help and encourage one another through the often-frustrating steps in the hiring process.

- **Employers and Coworkers.** If you already have a job, your workplace may be a source of information about other openings. Most companies post job opportunities for advancement before advertising to the general public. Your coworkers also may know about upcoming job openings within or outside of your workplace.

- **Organizations.** School organizations and community groups can often provide job information. See pages 111 and 112 for more information on organizations.

Building a strong network takes time. You may not view your family, friends, or coworkers as a solid network base for gaining employment, but you must trust the fact that research shows that the more people who know you are looking for a job, the more likely you will hear of job leads. Many of your contacts know other people you know, and they will talk.

FIG. 4-13. **Maintaining connections with teachers and mentors, the people who know your job strengths well, is one form of networking.**

FIG. 4-14. **Maintaining contact with others in order to exchange information about careers is an important aspect of networking.** What are some ways that you can network with others to achieve your career goals?

Be courteous in all networking situations, and show your gratitude with a handshake or a "thank you" and a genuine smile. You will need to demonstrate appropriate business and personal etiquette at all times. When your networking is successful, and you begin to receive good leads on jobs, you will feel more confident during the application process.

Every **referral**, or job lead, you receive through networking is a gift. Treat it with respect. If someone you know gives you a job lead, follow up with the employer responsibly. Return phone calls and be on time for interviews, if your referral leads to one. Always present yourself professionally. Your dress, communication skills, and behavior not only reflect you but the person who recommended you. See Fig. 4-14.

Remember to return the favor—when you become aware of job information that people in your network may need, share it.

The Internet

Thousands of employment resources are available on the Internet. You can:

- Review job postings.
- Network with other people.
- Contact professional organizations.
- Read on-line versions of professional publications.
- Register with on-line employment agencies.

Professional Organizations

Another source of finding job openings is professional organizations, many of which have members involved in various aspects of caring for children and older adults. Many have Web sites that list jobs on their staffs, as well as in member companies or member programs. Here are a few you may wish to investigate:

- National Association for the Education of Young Children (NAEYC)
- National Child Care Resource and Referral Agencies (NCCRRA)
- National Coalition for Campus Children's Centers (NCCCC)
- Association for Childhood Education International (ACEI)
- National Council on Aging (NCOA)
- Council for Professional Recognition (CDA)
- Administration on Aging (AOA)
- Gerontological Society of America (GSA)
- National Association of Social Workers (NASW)
- AARP, Inc.
- American Association of Family and Consumer Sciences (AAFCS)
- National Council on Family Relations (NCFR)

Although you may have to pay a membership fee to join a professional organization, the benefits outweigh the investment. Many organizations have student chapters in high schools,

FIG. 4-15.

Child Care Information Exchange

Young Children

Child Care Action Campaign News

The Gerontologist

Journals of Gerontology

Elderhostel

community colleges, and colleges and universities. The services they offer their members may include job listings, job placement services, scholarships, workshops, and conferences, which provide networking opportunities. Early childhood care and older adult care positions listed with professional organizations usually require more education and skills than those listed in local newspapers and, consequently, offer higher salaries.

Trade Publications

Most early childhood care and older adult care professional organizations publish professional magazines and newsletters for their members. Because they are written for people in an industry by organizations that support the industry, they are called **trade publications**. Membership fees may include a subscription to the organization's publications. These publications contain helpful articles on all aspects of the industry and often list job opportunities. Fig. 4-15 lists some of these publications. Some also can be found on the Internet.

Employment Agencies

At some point it may be best to work with an employment agency to assist in your job search. Employment agencies are businesses that work for employers and seek potential employees for them. They maintain lists of their clients' job openings and interview potential applicants. For a fee—charged to the applicant or employer or shared by both—they will submit the applicant's credentials to the employer for consideration.

Temporary agencies offer fast placement for people looking for an entry-level position. Employers who have an ongoing need for care professionals may rely on temporary agencies to fill their ever-growing demand. This hiring arrangement gives the employer a chance to assess each agency employee as a potential team member without going through the company's hiring process.

Working through a temporary agency gives you a chance to see what the child care field or the older adult care field is like without committing to a certain employer. Most temporary agencies allow their short-term employees to report whether they wish to continue working at their current placement.

Volunteering & Internships

Although volunteers don't usually get paid, they do gain valuable career experience. Never underestimate the value of volunteering to gain information about your chosen career. The information you learn can help you make valuable career decisions in the future. To gain experience in working with children or older adults, consider volunteering at hospitals, child care centers, or adult day centers.

Internships are another way to gain valuable career experience. An internship is a more formal position and requires a longer time commitment than a volunteer position. Internships may be unpaid or paid depending upon the situation. Through hands-on experience at the worksite, interns gain vital job skills. Internships can sometimes lead to fulltime, paid employment.

In addition to volunteering and internships, many schools offer **service learning** opportunities. Through service learning opportunities, community service becomes part of your schoolwork. For example, you might work at your community senior center or early childhood center. Service learning gives you another opportunity to expand your career horizons.

Applying for a Job

When you have identified several job leads, rank the possible jobs in order of your preference. Apply for the job you want most first.

You will need to request, complete, and return a job application. Some job leads may require you to begin the application process with a telephone call. Other job leads will ask you to contact the employer by mail, sending a letter of application and a résumé (REH-zuh-may). A **résumé** is a summary of your career objectives, work experience, job qualifications, education, and training. The second step in responding to a job lead will be one or more interviews. It is important to perform each step of the job application process in a professional manner.

Filling Out an Application

Remember to make a good impression from the beginning. Do not walk into a potential workplace, even to ask for an application, unless your clothing is neat and appropriate and you are clean and well groomed. It is absolutely essential that you demonstrate appropriate grooming and appearance for the workplace including when applying for a job. A job posting will not disappear in the time it takes you to clean up and change clothes.

Even if an application form is not your first step, you will be asked to complete one at some point during the process. You must fill out the form correctly and completely. Job application forms vary, but they all ask for the same kinds of information. See Fig. 4-16. Keep these tips in mind when completing an application:

- Print neatly, using blue or black ink. Use cursive handwriting for your signature only.

- Read the instructions for completing each section before responding. Try not to make errors. If you must correct something, draw a line through it.

- Carry important information with you. This includes your Social Security number; driver's license number; and the names, addresses, and phone numbers of previous employers along with the dates of your employment.

FIG. 4-16. Carry relevant employment application information with you at all times as you search for work.

- Carry your list of references with you. This includes the complete names, addresses, and telephone numbers of your personal references. Be sure to get permission from those people who are on your reference list before using their names.

- Do not leave any part of the application form blank unless you are asked to do so. If a question does not apply, put NA, which means *not applicable*, in the space provided.

- Always tell the truth. Submitting false information is illegal.

Responding by Telephone

Job leads may list phone numbers and ask you to call for more information. When making these calls, follow these guidelines:

1. Tell the person who answers the phone that you are calling in response to a job opening you saw in [name the resource].

2. State your name and which job opening interests you. If someone referred you, mention that person's name.

3. The contact person may ask you to send a letter of application and a résumé. Or, the contact person may send you a job application, or set up an interview appointment.

4. Write down everything you are told to do. Repeat it back to the contact person to make sure you understood the next steps correctly. In addition, write down the name of the person with whom you talked.

5. Ask any questions you may have about the application process. Answer any questions the contact person asks you.

6. Thank the contact person for his or her time.

Responding in Writing

Responding to a job lead in writing means including an effective letter of request or a cover letter to accompany your résumé.

Letter of Request. Write a letter of request when you need to ask for an application form or request an interview. Include a brief summary of your education, experience, and qualifications in the letter.

Cover Letter. A cover letter is used when a job lead asks you to send a written response and résumé. Your cover letter should introduce you to your prospective employer without repeating your résumé. Fig. 4-17.

Before mailing an application letter, be sure to double-check the letter, the contact name, and the address. Sign your letter in black ink and use the correct postage.

Preparing Your Résumé

Your résumé is a very important job-seeking tool. It gives a prospective employer the information he or she needs to help determine if you are suitable for a position. Always be truthful and accurate. List your work experience, skills, and education or training that will convince an employer that you are the best candidate for the job. See page 117 for more details on preparing your résumé.

The Interview Process

Once you have completed the application process, you must prepare for your interview. During this important face-to-face meeting, you will have a chance to convince an employer that you are the right person for the job. The employer will evaluate your appearance, attitude, personality, and answers to his or her questions.

Before the Interview

The interview process begins when an employer schedules an appointment. Write down the date, time, and place of the interview in your job search journal along with the name of the contact person.

Do Your Homework. The more you know about your prospective employer and the job

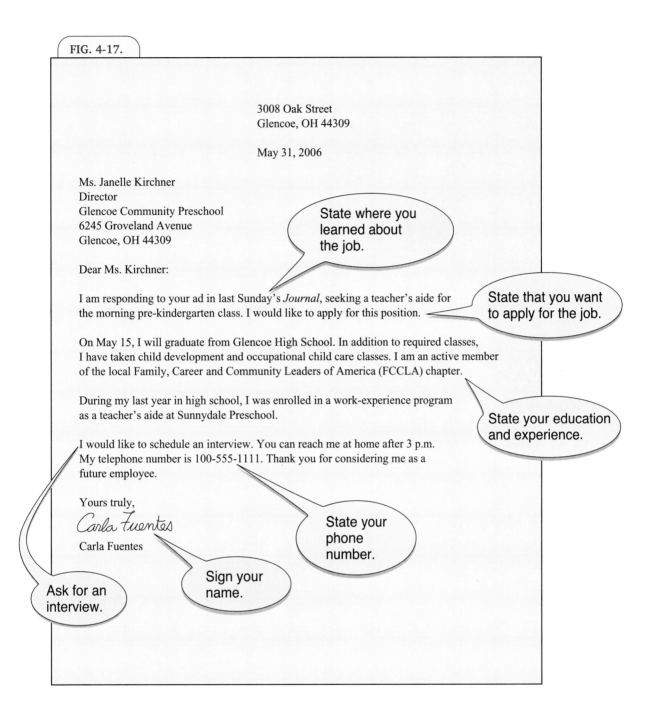

FIG. 4-17.

3008 Oak Street
Glencoe, OH 44309

May 31, 2006

Ms. Janelle Kirchner
Director
Glencoe Community Preschool
6245 Groveland Avenue
Glencoe, OH 44309

Dear Ms. Kirchner:

I am responding to your ad in last Sunday's *Journal*, seeking a teacher's aide for the morning pre-kindergarten class. I would like to apply for this position.

On May 15, I will graduate from Glencoe High School. In addition to required classes, I have taken child development and occupational child care classes. I am an active member of the local Family, Career and Community Leaders of America (FCCLA) chapter.

During my last year in high school, I was enrolled in a work-experience program as a teacher's aide at Sunnydale Preschool.

I would like to schedule an interview. You can reach me at home after 3 p.m. My telephone number is 100-555-1111. Thank you for considering me as a future employee.

Yours truly,

Carla Fuentes

Carla Fuentes

State where you learned about the job.

State that you want to apply for the job.

State your education and experience.

State your phone number.

Sign your name.

Ask for an interview.

you are seeking, the better you will do in the interview. Check such resources as community business publications, local newspapers, Internet directories, and professional organizations. Take notes in your journal.

Choose Appropriate Clothing. Your employer's first impression of you will be based on your appearance. Choose appropriate clothing that fits properly and is clean, pressed, and in good condition. Your grooming habits can make or break a job interview. You should be

clean, your hair well trimmed and conservatively styled, and your fingernails clean and neatly trimmed. See Fig. 4-18.

Be Prompt and Courteous. On the day of the interview, allow plenty of time to locate your destination. Arrive early and practice appropriate business and personal etiquette. As you introduce yourself to a receptionist, guard, or other person before meeting with the interviewer, be polite and respectful. The interviewer may check with these people later.

FIG. 4-18. The first impression you make on an employer will be through your appearance. How should you dress for an interview for a human services career?

Speak Clearly. Use correct grammar and speak clearly. The interviewer will ask you questions designed to determine if you are the person the company needs.

Use Good Manners. Sit up straight, with both feet on the floor. Avoid nervous gestures such as tapping. Never chew gum during an interview.

Answer Thoughtfully and Completely. Do not interrupt the interviewer or become sidetracked. If you do not understand a question or do not know the answer, say so politely. See Fig. 4-20.

Ask Questions. The interview process is meant to help you gain information, too. Do not hesitate to ask the interviewer about:

- The nature of the job.
- Your responsibilities.
- The working environment.

During the Interview

Because the interview is so important in the hiring process, you will do well if you are prepared, positive, and relaxed. Keep the following points in mind.

Shake Hands. The interviewer will introduce him- or herself to you. Introduce yourself in return, and offer your hand for a firm, confident handshake. Remain standing until the interviewer asks you to take a seat. He or she will probably begin with a few simple questions to help you feel more at ease. Smiling never hurts. See Fig. 4-19.

Make Eye Contact. Throughout the interview, maintain eye contact with the interviewer. Eye contact helps show that you are listening and are interested in what the interviewer is saying.

FIG. 4-19. A confident handshake makes a positive impression on a prospective employer.

How To...

Prepare Your Résumé

Your résumé will likely be the first contact an employer has with you. As with all first impressions, you want to leave a good one. Here are some guidelines for preparing an effective résumé:

- Keep it brief, using the front side of each page only.

- Include your accurate contact information.

- Begin with a clear career objective. Your objective should be short and to the point—specifically stating the type of position for which you are looking. If you have found a specific job you are interested in, focus your career objective on that job.

- Stress relevant work experience, key skills, education, and training. Be sure to include any early childhood or older adult care experience. If your work experience has been limited, you may wish to organize your résumé by the kinds of skills you have, such as organizational skills, communication skills, technical skills, listing below each the responsibilities you had that match each category. Use active verbs in describing your skills and experience.

- Use correct spelling and grammar. Have someone else who is good with the English language proofread the cover letter and résumé.

- Avoid using decorative graphics and pictures.

- Prepare an electronic version of your résumé. Many employers will ask you to send them a copy electronically. You want to be prepared to do so.

- Use keywords to describe your work experience. **Keywords** are significant words that make it easier for employers to search for relevant information. If your résumé contains keywords, such as early childhood, older adult care, or aging, employers using the Internet will be more likely to call up your résumé in an electronic search. Employers also look for keywords as they review paper résumés.

APPLY IT!

Write your résumé focusing on a specific career in either early childhood care and education or older adult care.

You should not raise questions about the rate of pay and employee benefits, such as insurance, during the first interview unless the interviewer addresses them. Most employers use the first interview to narrow the applicants to one or two. In the second interview, employers will get more specific about pay and benefits.

Leave Gracefully. Regardless of how the interview ends, thank the interviewer for his or her time. A professional attitude will always be remembered. Shake hands as you leave. The interviewer will signal the end of the interview in one of the following ways:

- The interviewer may tell you that you will be contacted later. If the interviewer does not specify a time period, politely ask, "How soon will the second round of interviews begin?"

FIG. 4-20.

QUESTIONS OFTEN ASKED IN A JOB INTERVIEW

- Why would you like to work for this company?
- What do you want to be doing in five years?
- What are your qualifications for this job?
- What are your strengths and weaknesses?
- Why did you leave your last job?
- Tell me about a challenge you met or a problem you solved in school or on the job.
- Have you ever been part of a team or a club? What did you like best and least about the experience?
- What questions do you have about the job or this company?
- Why should we hire you?

- You may be asked to contact the employer later. Note the telephone number, the preferred time to call, and the contact person's name.

- You may be offered the job and asked to decide right away whether you will take it. If you are unsure, ask the interviewer if you may think about the offer for 24 hours. If he or she agrees, be sure to follow up by responding promptly.

- You may not be offered the job. Do not be discouraged by being turned down for a job. You may not have the necessary qualifications or the employer may have found another applicant more suited to the job. The interviewer is under no obligation to tell you why you are not being offered the job. Accept the decision gracefully. See Fig. 4-21.

After the Interview

The interview process does not end when the interview is over. After each interview, you have the following responsibilities.

Send a Thank-You Letter. The day after the interview, send the interviewer a handwritten "thank-you" letter for the interview. Do this even if you have been turned down for the job. Be sure the employer's correct address and the right amount of postage are on the envelope.

Follow-Up. If you have been asked to contact the employer, do so at the specified time. Send or deliver any materials or information requested, such as reference letters or names and phone numbers of references. If the employer has promised to contact you, wait the specified amount of time. If this time passes, telephone the employer and politely request information about the status of your application. You may be asked to go through a second interview. Keep a record of these events and comments in your job search journal so you will remember to follow-up at the proper time. If the employer is vague about when to follow up, call every week and ask, "Could you please tell me what step is next in hiring someone for the position?"

FIG. 4-21. **Presenting yourself properly at an interview is essential in making a good impression.** How should you present yourself for an interview at a care center?

Review the Session. As soon as possible after the interview, go over the session in your mind. Think about the impression you made. Make notes on what questions you were asked and anything you could do to improve during the next interview. Note any key information, such as employer expectations and job responsibilities. List any unanswered questions you have about the job. See Fig. 4-22.

Responding to a Job Offer

When you receive an offer of employment, you have three options.

1. **Accept the Offer.** The employer will give you information on when you can begin work. You may be asked to participate in employee orientation or a training session before formally beginning your job. The employer will usually set up another interview during which you will be given specific details on pay, benefits, schedules, and job expectations.

2. **Ask for Time to Consider the Offer.** This is the time to bring up any unanswered questions that might affect your decision. With the employer, come to an agreement on when you will notify him or her of your decision. Do not put off responding to the employer.

3. **Turn Down the Job Offer.** Perhaps you will decide that the job is not right for you. Or,

FIG. 4-22. **Taking time to review an interview and make plans for future improvements will help you achieve your career goals.**

maybe you have been offered a better job in the meantime. Whatever the case, if you do not intend to take the position, say so. You do not need to supply reasons for turning down a job offer. Simply say, "Thank you for considering me, but I am not interested in taking the position."

S e c t i o n **4-2** Knowledge Check

1. What resources for job leads do you plan to use, and why?

2. What are the key elements of a résumé?

3. What are the actions you should take before, during, and after an interview?

Mini-Lab

Write a cover letter in response to a job ad from a newspaper or the Internet.

Section **4-3**

On the Job

Whether you work for a large or small business, what really matters to your professional success is the relationship between you and your employer. In this relationship, both parties have rights and responsibilities. When you begin your job, your employer will explain to you specific expectations and regulations. In accepting the job, you agree to these responsibilities. In this section, you will learn about your rights as an employee and your responsibilities to your employer. You will become familiar with wages, taxes, and benefits. You will practice skills for getting along with others on the job. This section will also identify some of the qualities you must develop to advance in your career as a care professional.

Employee Responsibilities

As an employee, your main responsibility is to do the very best job possible for your employer and for the people in your care. In most cases, your responsibilities to your employer are the employer's rights in the relationship. Successful employees do more than just show up for the job. They are proactive and involved in their work. In addition, they have the exact skills needed to do their jobs well. Here are some general ways to carry out your responsibilities:

- **Earn Your Pay.** Complete each task you are assigned, respecting the employer's priority. Keep your work area neat and well organized. Use employer resources responsibly. Sometimes going the "extra mile" with your work leads to greater success.

- **Use Time Responsibly.** Be on time for work. Return promptly from designated breaks and meal periods. Caring for children and older adults requires your full attention. Do not waste time chatting with coworkers and ignoring those in your care. Never use work time or resources to do personal business.

- **Respect the Rules.** Learn and follow your employer's rules, regulations, and policies, typically spelled out in an employee handbook. If you are in doubt about a company policy, ask your employer, and if necessary, ask if it is available in writing.

- **Work Safely.** Familiarize yourself with your job's safety requirements. Learn how to operate and maintain equipment safely. Ask your supervisor to observe you to ensure that you have learned properly. Report any unsafe conditions or practices to your supervisor immediately. See Fig. 4-23.

- **Maintain Confidentiality.** As you work with older adults and children, much of the information you gain about individuals may be private and personal. It is up to you to respect the rights of the people you care for and maintain confidentiality about any information concerning your clients.

In addition to the above responsibilities, success as an employee depends upon willingness to work as a team, show a positive attitude and respect, and resolve conflicts effectively.

Positive Attitude

An upbeat, positive outlook contributes to team spirit. Complaining can bring the whole team down and affect your job performance. A positive attitude, along with carefully thought out responses, leads to effectiveness in the workplace and your personal life. Look beyond your personal views and understand the reality of a situation before you respond.

Respect

When you respect and appreciate the differences in people, you will be more likely to have good work relationships. You demonstrate self-respect when you accept responsibility for your actions and learn from your mistakes. Disrespectful actions can result in unemployment. Learn to practice **empathy** (EHM-pah-thee), the skill of putting yourself in another's place. Empathy will help you understand your coworkers and the people for whom you care.

Teamwork

Besides the employer-employee relationship, you also form a relationship with your coworkers. Every worker is an individual, with his or her own personality traits, strengths, and weaknesses. In order to bring individuals together into an effective team, each employee must practice good teamwork. As you build and maintain relationships at work, you are investing in your career and the people with whom you work, as well as those in your care. You must get along to work well together.

FIG. 4-23. **Reporting unsafe conditions or equipment in need of repair to your supervisor is an important part of your job responsibility.**

Intergenerational Interactions

Discovering the Benefits of Intergenerational Programs

As a result of differing lifestyles among older-adult and younger generations, age-related differences thrive throughout America. Older adults sometimes think children and teens are disorderly and lazy. Similarly, younger people often think older adults are senile and feeble. When intergenerational programs bring these age groups together, ways of thinking change and everyone benefits. The following are just some of the benefits that may be gathered from an intergenerational program.

- **Encourage Learning.** In 1999, the Current Population Survey conducted by the U.S. Census Bureau showed that high school graduates made an average of 32 percent more than those workers who did not complete high school. Programs that enable older adults to help children and teens with schoolwork increase child literacy levels and encourage young people to stay in school. As the statistics show, children who complete high school increase their chances of finding good paying jobs in adulthood.

- **Promote Communication.** Today's job market often pushes adults to relocate their families as they transfer to better paying jobs. These moves, which often take children away from grandparents and other influential older adults, lessen opportunities for intergenerational communication. After-school programs that use older adult volun-

teers enable children to "adopt" grandparents who will listen to their joys and concerns. At the same time, older adults can share tales of their youth with youngsters who enjoy hearing about the past.

- **Boost Self-Esteem.** When children and teens have a chance to speak with an older adult who is willing to listen without judgment, those young people are sure to feel better about themselves. Likewise, older adults sharing stories and historical views on subjects that are important to today's youth will experience a boost in self-esteem through the curiosity of their captive younger audiences.

- **Maintain Health and Wellness.** Older adults who live alone are at greater risk of depression as well as personal injury. Intergenerational programs that include in-home visits have great effects on the mental health of older adults. Those programs that include low-impact exercise like walking also contribute to the physical well-being of older adults.

Follow-Up

Team up with a partner to discuss the benefits of intergenerational communication. Then, using the bullet items as a starting point, make a list of additional practices an intergenerational program can use to benefit older adults as well as children and teens.

Resolving Conflicts

No matter how well you and your coworkers get along, you will not always agree. Disputes and conflicts are an inevitable part of team interaction. Use your negotiation and compromise skills to lead the way to effective problem solving. While conflict can be unpleasant, you can learn something from the process of resolving conflicts respectfully. See Fig. 4-24.

You may encounter conflicts that cannot be resolved, no matter how much you want to settle a disagreement. Remember to focus on the problem, not the personalities involved.

Employer Responsibilities

The employer-employee relationship works both ways. Your employer has responsibilities to you, too. Your employer's chief responsibilities include supplying you with what you need to do your job, providing safe working conditions, and making sure you are treated fairly. In most cases, your employer's responsibilities to you are your rights in the relationship.

Employee Support

Your employer will outline your responsibilities and expectations clearly. Your employer is responsible for supplying you with all the equipment or training you need to do your job well. You and your employer may not agree on what are necessities. If you observe that you lack what you need, ask your supervisor to tell or show you how to go about an assigned task with the available resources.

Safe Working Conditions

Federal, state, and local regulations require your employer to provide you with safe working conditions. This responsibility includes:

- Providing equipment and materials necessary to do the job safely.
- Eliminating any recognized health and safety hazards.
- Informing employees when conditions or materials pose dangers to health and safety.
- Maintaining records of job-related illnesses and injuries.
- Complying with environmental protection policies for safely disposing of waste materials.

Workers' Compensation. If you are injured on the job and cannot work, state laws require your employer to provide financial help—called **workers' compensation**—to cover medical expenses and lost wages. However, employers with fewer than four employees do not have to carry this type of insurance. If your employer does not, you might consider buying your own personal disability insurance.

FIG. 4-24. Treating your coworkers with respect can help you resolve conflicts effectively. What characteristics show respect?

Injury Prevention. Another important part of your employer's safety responsibility is to provide conditions or equipment known to prevent injury. For example, workers who must perform the same motions repeatedly, such as lifting clients, can develop stress injuries that may disable them. Research on such injuries has led to some employers investigating other equipment and procedures, different ways to run equipment, and rotating workers' schedules on the equipment or performing certain repetitive procedures.

Fair Labor Practices

Your employer has a legal responsibility to protect you from unfair treatment on the job. U.S. labor laws are meant to protect the following rights of employees:

- To have an equal opportunity to obtain and keep employment.
- To be paid a fair wage.
- To be considered fairly for promotion.

Among other legally mandated responsibilities, employers must pay their employees at least the federal **minimum wage**, the lowest hourly amount a worker can earn. See Fig. 4-25. Some locations pay entry-level employees a wage higher than the federal government requires. Employers must compensate hourly employees who work overtime (more than 40 hours per week) with extra pay or time off, called **compensatory time**.

U.S. workers are guaranteed the right to join a **labor union**, an organization of workers in a similar field. Leaders of labor unions act as the voice of their members in **collective bargaining**, the process of workers and employers agreeing to working conditions, contracts, and other job benefits. Labor unions represent about 15 percent of U.S. workers. Some labor unions include child care teachers and aides and some older adult care employees.

Employers must also protect their employees from **discrimination**—unfair treatment based on

FIG. 4-25. Employers are required to post government information that impacts employees.

age, gender, race, ethnicity, religion, physical appearance, disability, or other factors. For example, **sexual harassment** is an act of discrimination. It is any unwelcome verbal or physical behavior of a sexual nature. It is illegal behavior in the workplace. If you think someone has sexually harassed you, report the incident to your supervisor immediately so the employer can investigate the matter and take action.

Performance Evaluations

Your employer also is responsible for giving you feedback on your job performance. Some employers consider an employee's first few months on a new job as probationary. **Probation** is a period in which an employer observes the employee's work and behavior in order to assess whether the employee is fit to remain with the company. Your employee handbook should include details about how often the employer conducts performance evaluations. It may state a more frequent schedule during the employee's first year. Your employee handbook will also identify what your employer looks for during a performance evaluation and the procedure an employee should follow in responding to the evaluation. During a performance evaluation, an employer may examine such things as the employee's:

- Job knowledge and how the employee applies that knowledge.
- Willingness to work cooperatively as a team member.
- Ability to communicate effectively on the job.
- Positive attitude and workplace ethic.

Wages

When you agree to take a job, you trade your skills and efforts for money. Your employer sets your pay, influenced by your level of skills and experience, the difficulty of the work, and the number of people competing for the same job. Many companies will advertise the salary range or the hourly wage they plan to pay. If they do not, you would be wise to search on the Internet to obtain examples of pay for the same job in cities in your region. This will give you a fair market value of the position so you know whether the pay rate you are offered is fair.

FIG. 4-26.

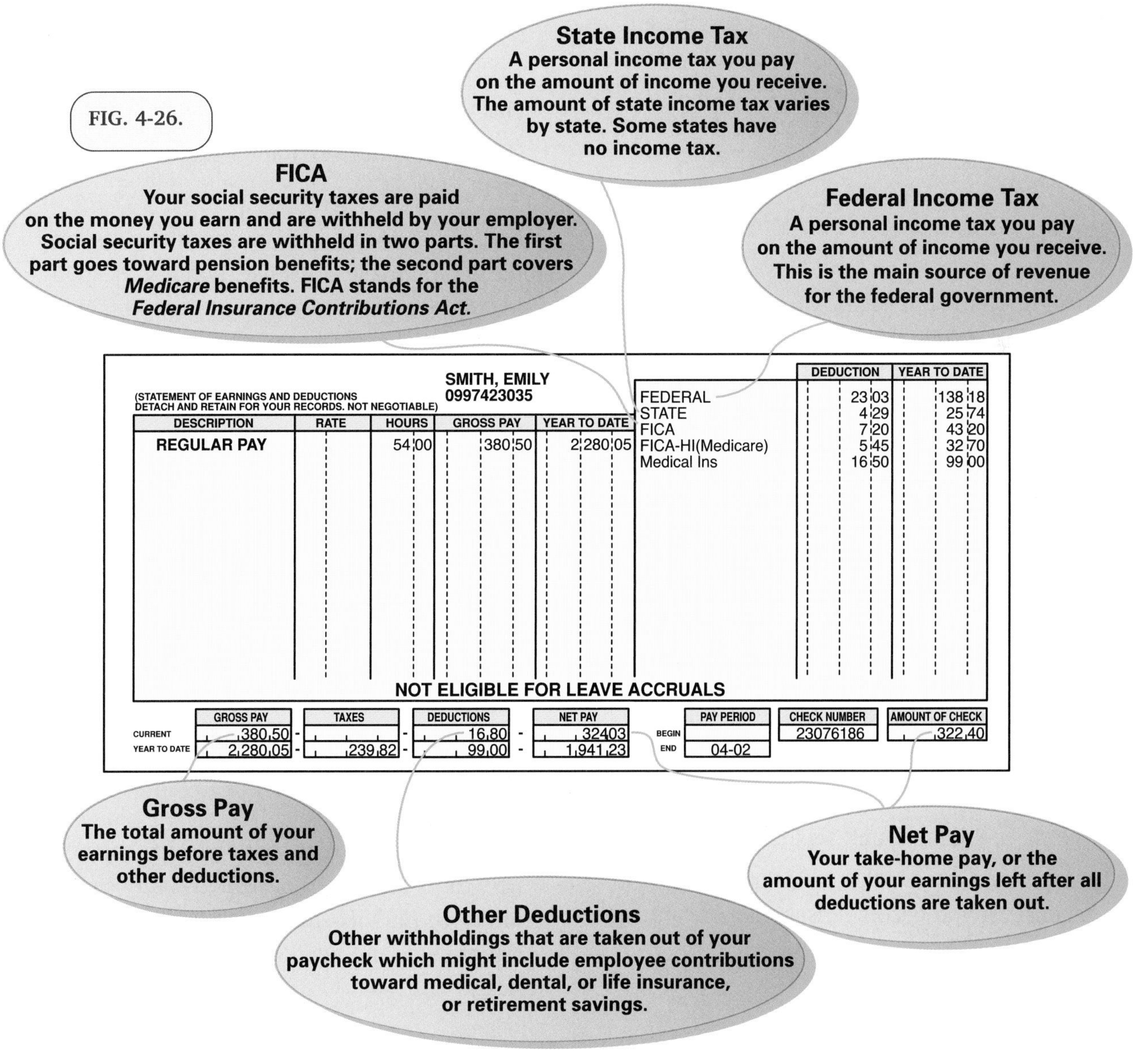
State Income Tax
A personal income tax you pay on the amount of income you receive. The amount of state income tax varies by state. Some states have no income tax.
FICA
Your social security taxes are paid on the money you earn and are withheld by your employer. Social security taxes are withheld in two parts. The first part goes toward pension benefits; the second part covers *Medicare* benefits. FICA stands for the *Federal Insurance Contributions Act.*
Federal Income Tax
A personal income tax you pay on the amount of income you receive. This is the main source of revenue for the federal government.
SMITH, EMILY
0997423035
(STATEMENT OF EARNINGS AND DEDUCTIONS DETACH AND RETAIN FOR YOUR RECORDS. NOT NEGOTIABLE)
DESCRIPTION | RATE | HOURS | GROSS PAY | YEAR TO DATE
REGULAR PAY | | 54.00 | 380.50 | 2,280.05
DEDUCTION | YEAR TO DATE
FEDERAL 23.03 138.18
STATE 4.29 25.74
FICA 7.20 43.20
FICA-HI(Medicare) 5.45 32.70
Medical Ins 16.50 99.00
NOT ELIGIBLE FOR LEAVE ACCRUALS
GROSS PAY | TAXES | DEDUCTIONS | NET PAY
CURRENT 380.50 - - 16.80 - 32403
YEAR TO DATE 2,280.05 - 239.82 - 99.00 - 1,941.23
PAY PERIOD BEGIN END 04-02
CHECK NUMBER 23076186
AMOUNT OF CHECK 322.40
Gross Pay
The total amount of your earnings before taxes and other deductions.
Net Pay
Your take-home pay, or the amount of your earnings left after all deductions are taken out.
Other Deductions
Other withholdings that are taken out of your paycheck which might include employee contributions toward medical, dental, or life insurance, or retirement savings.

Pay Periods. Pay periods differ. Some employers pay weekly, every two weeks, or once a month. Your employer will pay you in one of two ways. If you are paid an hourly wage, your employer will pay you a certain amount for each hour you work. With an hourly wage, your pay will vary depending on how many hours you work each pay period. If you receive a salary, your employer will pay you a set amount of money, regardless of the hours worked.

Deductions. The total amount of money you earn is your gross pay. If you are paid an hourly wage, calculate your gross pay by multiplying the number of hours you work by your hourly wage. The amount of money you actually receive after deductions are taken out is called your net pay, or take-home pay. Deductions are amounts of money withheld from your gross pay for taxes, insurance, and other fees. Ask your employer to explain the types and amounts of deductions that will be taken out of your pay. Fig. 4-26 on page 125 lists some common deductions.

Benefits

In addition to your salary, your employer may offer benefits. While most workers do not think of benefits the same way they think about their take-home pay, the employer pays out money for both wages and benefits. In the employer's mind, they are both money earned for your work. Be sure to figure your benefits as cash when you calculate your total job compensation. Add wages and benefits together, as best as you can, and then calculate what you make per pay period. A generous benefits package can compensate for a lower wage. Likewise, a higher wage may make up for few benefits. Among the benefits your employer may offer are:

- Paid vacation and sick days.
- Health, life, dental, and accident insurance.
- Disability insurance that helps pay your expenses if you become disabled and cannot work.
- Savings and investment plans, such as a 401K plan, to help you earn money for retirement.
- Tuition reimbursement for tuition and fees you pay for education courses that are directly related to your career.

Ethics

Your **ethics** (EH-thicks) are your internal guidelines for distinguishing right from wrong. Ethical behavior consists of doing what is right. Some choices, however, are more difficult. When two choices appear equally right or equally wrong, ask yourself the following questions:

- Does the choice comply with the law?
- Is the choice fair to those involved?
- Does the choice harm anyone?
- Has the choice been communicated honestly?
- Can I live with the choice without embarrassment or guilt?

Behaving ethically also means taking responsibility. If you make a mistake, admit it. Responsible employees learn from their mistakes and adapt their behavior to make better choices.

Advancing on the Job

Advancement opportunities in early childhood education and older adult care services vary. Advancement may involve a promotion. It also can be at the same job level but with more responsibilities at a higher rate of pay. Advancement may also involve leaving for a better job elsewhere, or beginning your own business. Here are some qualities that will help you advance in your career:

- **Show Initiative.** The willingness to take on new tasks and levels of responsibility shows initiative (ih-NIH-shuh-tihv). Workers with initiative do not wait to be told what to do next.

- **Show Desire to Learn.** Continuing your education or training through formal classes, workshops, or independent study shows a desire to learn. See Fig. 4-27.

Terminating Employment

The main focus in this chapter has been on selecting and landing a job. There may come a time in the future in which you want to change careers or jobs. When considering a job change, keep the following points in mind:

- Keep your job search to yourself until you have a new job. You do not want to make your work situation difficult with your current employer while you search for a new job.

- Research and list the jobs or careers in which you are interested. Analyze each in regard to your skills and experience.

- Set up interviews so that you do not miss work. If necessary, use vacation time.

- After finding a new job, be sure to give notice to your employer that you are terminating your employment. Check your employee handbook to find out how much notice you must give your employer.

- Until you leave your place of employment, work just as hard as you always have. You want to leave a good impression. How you perform during your last few weeks of work is what people will remember about you.

FIG. 4-27. Showing a desire to learn and grow will help you advance on the job. How can you show your willingness to learn and grow?

Section **4-3** Knowledge Check

1. What are the main responsibilities of an employee?
2. What are the main responsibilities of an employer?
3. Contrast a salary and an hourly wage.

Mini-Lab

Assume you have been hired as a teacher aide at a local preschool. You will be working 40 hours per week for $8.50 per hour. You have the following deductions: health insurance at $20.00 weekly (before taxes); federal income tax at 15%; and state income tax of 3.5%. Calculate your weekly net pay.

Chapter **4** Review & Activities

Section Summaries

4-1 The basic skills for employment as a care professional include speaking, writing, reading, listening, math, and thinking skills.

4-1 A strong work ethic shows a personal commitment to do the best job possible.

4-1 Employers look for employees with leadership potential, people who will motivate others to accomplish goals.

4-1 The resources that care professionals must learn to use effectively are people, information, technology, energy, money, and equipment and supplies.

4-2 A résumé includes your career objective, work experience, skills, and education or training, along with basic contact information.

4-2 Interviewing successfully with an employer for a position relies on demonstrating workplace etiquette.

4-2 Your employer has a legal responsibility to protect you from unfair treatment on the job.

4-3 When calculating job compensation, consider benefits and wages.

4-3 Teamwork requires that coworkers have a positive attitude, respect one another, follow respectful ways in resolving conflicts, and behave ethically.

4-3 Advancement opportunities in the child care and older adult care industries primarily center on the employee's willingness to take initiative and seek additional training or education.

Check Your Knowledge

1. What is active listening?
2. Give examples showing the three thinking skills employers want their employees to demonstrate.
3. Name four traits you can display to show a positive work ethic.
4. List two ways to demonstrate leadership.
5. What are the key resources care professionals must use effectively?
6. Why is networking the most successful resource in searching for a job?
7. Why might a temporary employment agency be a good place to start for an entry-level position?
8. How should you prepare for and follow-up on a job interview?
9. List two employee responsibilities and two employer responsibilities in the workplace.
10. What kinds of employee benefits might an employer offer?

Thinking Critically

1. Analyze your personal behavior in terms of work ethic and leadership. What can you do to develop these skills while you are still in school?
2. Predict the potential benefits of professional development activities, including networking with other care professionals, joining professional organizations, and reading trade publications. Is it possible to be truly professional without engaging in such activities? Why or why not?

3. Evaluate the relationship of good physical and mental health to job success and achievement. Draw conclusions and share them with the class.

Practical Applications

1. **Basic Skills Applications.** Interview a care professional to obtain examples of ways he or she uses basic skills every day. Share the information you obtain with your class.

2. **Job Search Sources.** Circle all the positions for care professionals in the local newspaper. For each position, track the job title, business name (if given), skills required, education required, and pay rate (if given). Then search the Internet for similar job titles in nearby cities until you have found 15 listings. Draw conclusions from this exercise and then share them with the class.

3. **Professional Organizations.** Write a letter to a professional organization serving care professionals to obtain information on the purposes, activities, and publications of the organization. What are the costs for joining the organization and benefits of membership? What opportunities do members have for participating in the organization?

4. **Assessing Safety Concerns.** Research common safety concerns of care professionals. Create a list of questions to ask and observations to make before accepting a position.

5. **Mentor Review.** Volunteer at a local facility that offers services to children and older adults. Ask your mentor to evaluate how effectively you demonstrate productive work habits and attitudes.

Building Your PORTFOLIO

Interview Practice

Effective interviewing skills are essential to finding employment in child care and older adult care careers. Use the following steps to sharpen your interview skills.

Step 1: Research an early childhood or older adult care facility in your area. Identify a position in which you are interested to apply. Create a list of job interview questions the interviewer might ask. Also, make a list of questions to ask the interviewer about the workplace or the job.

Step 2: Write a résumé that summarizes your personal, educational, and employment information. Complete a sample employment application.

Step 3: With a partner, conduct a mock job interview. Be sure to reverse roles so you each have a chance to perform an interview. Videotape the interviews to share with your team.

Step 4: In teams, rate each of the videotaped interviews for your team members. Use the following rating scale: Poor = 1; Fair = 2; Good = 3; Great = 4. As a team, identify the strengths of each applicant and offer constructive ideas for improvement.

Step 5: In your portfolio, include a description of the position and facility you researched, your résumé, your completed sample employment application, and a summary of your interview ratings. If possible, include a copy of the videotape.

Chapter 5
Professional Skills

Section 5-1

Professional Communication

OBJECTIVES

- Explain the barriers to effective communication.
- Identify ways communication is used in the workplace.
- Explain how effective communication improves program functions.
- Identify effective ways to minimize and resolve conflict.
- Describe ways to use documentation in the workplace.

KEY TERMS

communication barriers
public relations

Communication is a process of giving and receiving information. In the human service professions, there is a wide variety of information to be shared between staff and the clients they serve. How well that information is communicated determines a program's level of success. This chapter will explore ways communication helps provide the foundation for a high-quality program.

Communication Barriers

Any obstacles that prevent people from sending or receiving information are **communication barriers**. When communication breaks down, there is a loss of trust and hurt feelings often result. Cultural and language differences, medical factors, and social factors, such as age and education, are often barriers to effective communication.

Cultural and Language Differences. A person's culture combines his or her ethnic background, customary beliefs, language, social practices, religious beliefs, and family values. When working with children and older adults, you will find many cultural and language differ-

ences. While a child may easily adapt to the care center, an older adult may desire to hold onto his or her cultural practices. Language may be the biggest cultural factor in communication breakdown. Remember, people from other cultures often communicate differently. What is readily accepted in one part of the world may be offensive in another part of the world—especially with nonverbal communication. Awareness of these differences can help prevent problems; it can also help you become a well-rounded professional.

Medical Factors. Medical factors that are communication barriers for children and older adults include vision or hearing loss, medical illnesses, and medication use. People of all ages

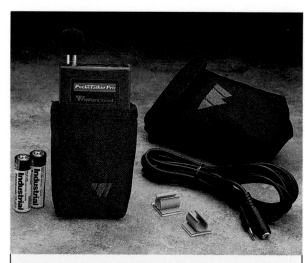

FIG. 5-1. Use every available technological aid to effectively communicate with those who have medical barriers to hearing. What is the value in using a "Pocket Talker" over other technological aids for hearing?

are susceptible to vision loss; however, this is very common with older adults. Medical illnesses, such as inner ear infections, often impact hearing. See Fig. 5-1. Some medications can cause confusion and alter a person's ability to communicate well.

Social Factors. Age, education, family, friends, and contact with care providers are all social factors that can influence a person's ability to communicate. People in each generation have their own way of communicating. People of similar ages are able to talk about events and activities that are understood by all in a particular age group. For example, most young children can probably talk about the habits of a particular cartoon character or television personality. Older adults may talk about a favorite news commentator.

Overcoming Communication Barriers

In working with children and older adults, there are a number of things you can do to open the doors of communication and avoid obstacles.

- Take the time to get to know the children and older adults in your care in order to establish trust. This takes time and patience, but it is well worth your efforts.

- Ask questions to stimulate conversation. Children and older adults enjoy sharing information. Use open-ended questions— ones that have to be answered with more than a yes or no—to obtain information from the children or older adults in your care.

- Human touch is often important when working with children and older adults. Giving a hug, holding a person's hand, or gently touching an arm shows children and older adults that you care about them. Be sure to ask those in your care for permission to touch them. For example, you might ask, "Is it okay if I give you a hug?" Be sure to respect their wishes if they say no.

- Try using humor or music to open the doors of communication. Using a humorous story or an energetic piece of music not only can eliminate communication barriers, but also can help start a social activity or physical-fitness activity.

Workplace Communication

Answering people's questions about your program and explaining your services to future and current clients is an ongoing process. Following are some of the ways in which communication takes place within human service careers.

Communicating Goals & Philosophy

As a human service professional, you must be able to communicate well whenever you interact with your supervisor, coworkers, children or adults in your care, clients' families, or anyone else. All of your communication skills are put to use when informing others about your program's mission and goals. People will want to know what your program offers to the community and to their loved ones. You will need to communicate the array of services you provide, as well as where and when these services are provided. The ages served, costs, and eligibility information must be shared. If you do not communicate clearly, those who use your program will be confused. In addition, those who might benefit from your program will not understand how it could help them. See Fig. 5-2.

Human service careers require very close partnerships between clients and a program's professional staff. For example, parents of young children will want to know what type of learning activities will take place and why. They will have questions about naps and how the staff manages children's behavior. Likewise, family members of older adults will want to know how the physical, social, and emotional needs of their loved ones are met. All parties will want to know how meals are served, how menus are developed, and how special dietary needs are met. Family members have a right to clear, understandable answers to all those questions.

FIG. 5-2. Communicating well with program participants and their families about program services enhances the effectiveness of the program. How are parents and family members likely to react when a care provider communicates well?

Public Relations

Communication with the general public about your program is called **public relations**. Getting a program's name out to those who might use its services and establishing a good reputation for services provided are both public relations goals.

Telephone. A telephone call is often a future client's first contact with a human service program. Therefore, it is very important to have someone well acquainted with the program accepting telephone calls. He or she should be trained in using courteous phone manners so a positive image of the program is conveyed. The person answering the phones should be able to describe your program's services and associated fees in a clear and simple way.

Brochures and Advertisements. A small pamphlet or brochure condenses all the most important information about a program's purpose and its services. Advertisements in newspapers or a telephone book do the same thing. All such information must be clearly written so clients can easily access services.

Public Presentations. To inform the public about their program's services, many human service professionals give speeches at local meetings. Dressing appropriately, having a well-prepared presentation, and using good audio-visuals contribute to effective communication.

Web Sites. Creating and maintaining an up-to-date Web site is both a cost-efficient and effective way to communicate a variety of information to a wide audience. Web sites are especially helpful for people who cannot contact a program during its hours of operation. Web sites should offer at least basic program details, such as hours, location, and fees. However, Web sites can also communicate information about discipline policies and family involvement, or even list Internet links to related information. See Fig. 5-3.

FIG. 5-3. Many educational and care centers provide information about their services over the Internet. If you were setting up a Web site for your care service, what details would you include and why?

Family Communications

Children and older adults benefit when human service professionals share information with family members and work with them as a team. Family members want to know how their loved ones are doing in the program, what they have accomplished, and whether they show signs of special needs. Care providers also need insight into how home life affects behavior. Through regular communication, a trusting relationship is built between family members and staff. Following are communication methods most commonly used.

Informal Conversations. Arrival and departure times are ideal for brief, informal conversations. At arrival, parents may share helpful information—for example, "Nikki's grandparents visited last night, so we let her stay up a little later than usual." At departure, early childhood staff can tell parents how their child's day went. You might say, "Jeremy tied his shoes without help today." During informal conversation, avoid making negative comments or discussing confidential matters others may overhear. Problems and private matters should be discussed during scheduled meetings when both the staff and the family members have more time and can be more focused.

Conferences and Scheduled Meetings. Formal conferences and meetings between family members and program staff should be scheduled on a regular basis, or at least twice a year. These conferences or meetings allow information to be shared about an individual's progress or special needs. They also give family members an opportunity to ask questions and discuss concerns. See Fig. 5-4. In some special cases, care professionals may call a short-notice "on demand meeting" between regularly scheduled meetings or conferences. These on demand meetings allow care providers and family members to address issues or problems early rather than waiting for a biannual meeting. The guidelines for conducting conferences or meetings include the following:

- Try to find a time that is convenient for the parents or family members.

- Let family members know that they will be able to bring up any questions or concerns they may have.

- Prepare for the meeting by reviewing records of the client's behavior and progress. Identify the topics you would like to discuss.

- Help family members feel at ease by greeting them in a friendly, respectful manner.

- Start by focusing on the client's strengths. Discuss areas in which the client is doing well or has shown improvement. Share specific examples to illustrate your points.

- Avoid labeling the client or criticizing the family members when bringing up problems or concerns. If you say, "Paige is a trouble-maker who has obviously been allowed to run wild," the parent will probably take offense. It is more effective to say, "Paige finds it difficult to sit and listen quietly during story time." Not only is this statement more positive, it is also more clear.

- Suggest ways that the family members and staff can work together to help the client improve.

- Listen carefully to what family members say. Make sure you understand their concerns. For example, one adult son told his father's care provider, "I am a little worried that dad is having some speech problems. He has been slurring his words together lately." Knowing this, the care provider is better able to respond to the son's true concern.

- Take the opportunity to learn more about the client by asking questions of the family members.

- End the discussion on a positive note. Be sure to thank the family members for coming.

Family Meetings. Many programs have weekly or monthly evening group meetings so family members can learn about program operations and have the opportunity to give their input. They often discuss program curriculum and activities, or cooperatively plan events. Family advisory boards also meet regularly to discuss program business that affects their children or loved ones.

Newsletters. Many child care and adult care programs send home weekly, semi-monthly, or monthly newsletters. This is a

good way to keep all families informed of the program's activities. A typical letter might include a list of learning experiences and special events planned for the coming week. It might also suggest activities for families, children, and older adults to enjoy at home.

Group Events. Social events help program families get to know each other. Sometimes they are organized around a theme or a special day. Other times they might be a fundraiser or a potluck dinner. Programs may also offer specialized group events, such as a support group for single parents of young children. Another group may be for grown children coping with a parent's illness, such as Alzheimer's disease, an illness that affects the memory of aging adults.

Written Messages. Sharing information in writing also plays a role in human service programs. A written note, whether on paper or as an e-mail message, helps professionals and families communicate information when a face-to-face conversation cannot take place. Sometimes a written note is preferable so a record of the communication can be put in a client's file.

FIG. 5-4. **A reciprocal relationship between parents or guardians and early childhood professionals enhances communication about a child's progress.** How should a care provider or teacher express the strengths and weaknesses in a child's progress?

Telephone Usage. Occasional telephone calls can help keep care providers and family members in touch. Leaving a voice message for family members is an easy way to share a brief, encouraging message. Likewise, leaving a message explaining how a bump or scrape occurred can prevent a family member from feeling uneasy. See Fig. 5-5.

Staff Communication & Teamwork

Communication and teamwork go hand-in-hand. Staff members who take the time to communicate with each other during the workday tend to have better working relationships. This style of cooperation shows consideration for all staff members. Communications that encourage teamwork include informal conversations, staff meetings, written communication, and technological communication.

Informal Conversations. Engaging in comfortable, courteous conversations helps staff

members develop a friendly rapport. When you arrive, take breaks, or leave for the day, exchanging greetings or chatting about recent events will help you and your coworkers build a sense of unity and teamwork.

Staff Meetings. A human service program cannot run smoothly without the cooperation of the whole staff. Each must do his or her fair share of the work by performing assigned tasks to the best of his or her ability, without stalling or complaining. Regular staff meetings are the most effective way to ensure ongoing communication. All staff members must understand their assignments and how tasks are being divided. They must also make sure they are in agreement about general matters, such as the goals of the program. Meetings also give staff a chance to share ideas and stay informed about new developments.

Written Communication. Few people can mentally keep track of all the details that are important to smooth program operation. Whether creating activity plans, contributing to a newsletter, recording concerns about a client, or updating each other on events, staff work better as a team if they write down details to keep everyone informed.

Using Technology to Communicate. In today's human service programs, it's not uncommon for one program to have several different locations. Staff must find creative ways to maintain communication despite their physical separation. Using e-mail and telephones for conference calls are ways that technology can improve program operation and staff communication. See Fig. 5-6.

Communicating About Sensitive Issues

Even the best of staff run into communication challenges from time to time. How they approach these sensitive issues affects how well they continue working together.

FIG. 5-5. Using the telephone or e-mail when face-to-face conversation can't take place is an effective way for care providers to connect with client's family members. How should care providers prepare themselves for making telephone calls to family members?

Respectful Discussion. You will not succeed in a job if you treat your supervisor in a disrespectful or rude manner. The same is true of your relationship with your coworkers. Treat them with professional respect, and ask that they treat you in the same way. If a coworker asks for feedback, offer helpful suggestions. Express your thoughts and feelings in a positive, nonjudgmental way. Avoid demeaning or attacking a person if you disagree with his or her point of view. Remember to share compliments when a coworker does an especially good job. A sincere word of praise goes a long way in establishing a good working relationship.

Cooperative Planning. The family members of those enrolled in a program also deserve your courtesy and respect. If you need to discuss a problem with them, be tactful. Ask for input on why the problem exists and how it might be solved. When you speak, address issues with a cooperative, rather than judgmental, tone. For instance, avoid saying, "You've done a terrible job of teaching your child manners." Instead, try saying, "I've noticed Jacob has a hard time sitting at the table during lunch. We believe he'll be safer if he sits down to eat. May we discuss some ways we can work together to help Jacob learn to sit while eating?" In an older adult care setting, a care provider may say to a family member, "When your mother is frustrated with something, she tends to lash out at people around her." This is more tactful than saying, "Your mother is violent."

Minimizing Conflict

There are times when staff members, or a staff member and a client's family member, do not agree. Minimizing, rather than exaggerating, conflict will lead to better cooperation. How you respond in words and actions determines if a problem will be solved or will grow out of proportion.

Suppose one of your coworkers said to you, "You are so irresponsible. You never put the art materials back where they belong. Because of

FIG. 5-6. Care providers must have a confidential method of writing and maintaining documents. How may password-protected data be stored to create more formal reports at a later date?

you, I will not be able to do my art activity today." Your feelings would probably be hurt. Comments like these do not encourage you to remedy the problem very quickly. On the other hand, suppose your coworker said, "It's frustrating when I can't find the art materials I need for activities. Can we all agree to make a greater effort to put them back in the right places?" In this case, you would probably be more willing to cooperatively solve the problem. Since your character was not attacked, the relationship between you and your coworker would likely remain friendly and respectful.

If your supervisor criticizes some aspect of your work, resist the urge to become angry or defensive. Listen carefully and try to understand the reasons behind the comments. If something is not clear to you, politely ask for further explanation. At the end of the conversation, agree on actions that will remedy the criticism. See Fig. 5-7.

Almost nothing ruins the positive atmosphere of a workplace faster than a disagreement

FIG. 5-7. Excellent communication skills are necessary to resolve conflicts. How can controlling your emotions be a benefit to resolving conflict?

between workers. If two employees are constantly snapping at each other, or have stopped speaking at all, everyone suffers. Here are some suggestions for minimizing conflict.

- Keep the lines of communication open.
- Resolve small differences right away, before they can grow into major conflicts.
- Keep discussions positive. Address issues, not personalities.
- Do not jump to conclusions. Give people a chance to explain their side of the story.

The ability to resolve conflict is important in every job. In human service programs, conflicts and problems are likely to arise every day. Some are large issues, such as how to calm parents when another two-year-old has bitten their child, or how to calm family members when their parent's walker has been taken by another older adult. Others are small, such as not having enough napkins for lunchtime.

Most issues require careful thinking and an efficient solution. Before trying to resolve a conflict, be sure you have the authority, knowledge, and experience to make the necessary decisions. If you do not, obtain assistance from a coworker or the director.

Documentation

In human service programs, information is documented and recorded so it can help staff provide high-quality service. The following shows how documentation is used in the workplace. Care providers will document information, such as conversations and observations. Information may relate to medical conditions or descriptions of daily behavior.

Recording Concerns. Taking time to document items of concern helps care providers determine how severe a concern is and how long the problem endures. If concerns persist, the documentation can be used as a basis for discussion with family members of enrolled clients.

Individualized Services. Documentation about a child's or older adult's abilities can guide staff in selecting activities and experiences geared to individual needs. The records can be helpful during activity or lesson planning as well as during conferences with family members.

Referral Records. There are times when staff members feel they must refer clients to specialized services. Whether it is a referral for speech services or nutrition supplements, documentation provides evidence of how staff members have responded to individual needs and concerns. Documentation also helps staff avoid duplicating a coworker's efforts on a client's behalf.

Recording Information

A number of different methods can be used to record vital documentation in early childhood and older adult care programs. Making sure that your written correspondence is accurate is key to documentation. Some methods for documenting information include:

Details to Document. When documenting information, always write down the full date of the recording. In addition, write the client's full name, age at the time of recording, and specific, objective information related to the purpose of the documentation. Sign your name so those who review the information know whom to contact for further information. See Fig. 5-8.

Written Notes. Some information that is short and specific can be simply recorded on paper to be put into a file for future reference. Highly computerized care programs may request staff to enter documentation into a computer database.

Checklists. In order to record broad concerns, such as a client's language use or motor skill capabilities, checklists are quick ways to record information for future reference.

FIG. 5-8. Documenting information accurately is an important skill for care providers. What are the consequences of inaccurate documentation?

Section 5-1 Knowledge Check

1. What are two barriers to effective communication? Give an example showing how to overcome each barrier you list.

2. Name three qualities that are important to dealing with sensitive issues.

3. Identify three ways that documentation is used in the workplace.

Mini-Lab

Investigate how to communicate with family members who do not speak English. Then, create signs or other visual aids that would assist these family members. For example, create a visual to assist with client sign-in. Evaluate your visuals with the class.

Section 5-2

Professional Ethics

OBJECTIVES

- Define professional ethics.
- Explain the importance of professional ethics.
- Describe the ethical responsibilities of human service professionals.

KEY TERMS

professional ethics
dress codes
continuing education
conferences
confidentiality

Because young children and older adults can be very vulnerable, it's especially important for families to trust that the human service professionals working with their loved ones have good character traits and values. When faced with dilemmas in child and adult care, a clear set of guiding principles can point you toward the right path. The backbone of trust is a staff with sound personal and professional ethics.

What Are Professional Ethics?

As you learned in Chapter 4, your internal guidelines for distinguishing right or wrong behavior are your ethics. In human service careers, ethics relates in particular to a provider's sense of fairness, kindness, and humane treatment for all people.

A sense of purpose is also important in human service careers. Providing daily care for children or older adults is hard work. Professionals with the talent and knowledge needed to make a positive difference in the lives of families develop a strong sense of ethical duty to help others. These human service professionals take pride in being able to meet these ethical obligations.

The standards of right and wrong that apply to your professional behavior are called your **professional ethics**. The way you conduct yourself on the job and carry out your responsibilities should be guided by professional ethics at all times. Ethical standards are like road signs. Professionals can look to these guidelines to help them choose the right paths.

Professional Ethics Statements

Many professional organizations create statements to help their members perform ethically. For programs that serve young children, The National Association for the Education of Young Children (NAEYC) has the most widely known ethics statement, called the "Code of Ethical Conduct." The code addresses four areas: responsibilities to children, to families, to colleagues, and to the community and society. See Fig. 5-9A. Fig. 9B offers excerpts from the Ethical Standards of Human Service Professionals.

FIG. 5-9A.

EXCERPTS FROM THE CODE OF ETHICAL CONDUCT NATIONAL ASSOCIATION FOR THE EDUCATION OF YOUNG CHILDREN

Ethical Responsibilities to Children

- Above all, we shall not harm children. We shall not participate in practices that are disrespectful, degrading, dangerous, exploitative, intimidating, psychologically damaging, or physically harmful to children...

- We shall involve all of those with relevant knowledge (including staff and parents) in decisions concerning a child...

- When, after appropriate efforts have been made with a child and the family, the child still does not appear to be benefiting from a program, we shall communicate our concern to the family in a positive way and offer them assistance in finding a more suitable setting...

- We shall be familiar with the symptoms of child abuse and neglect and know community procedures for addressing them...

Ethical Responsibilities to Families

- We shall not deny family members access to their child's classroom or program setting...

- We shall inform families of program philosophy, policies, and personnel qualifications, and explain why we teach as we do...

- Families shall be fully informed of any proposed research projects involving their children and shall have the opportunity to give or withhold consent...

- We shall not use our relationship with a family for private advantage or personal gain...

- We shall maintain confidentiality and shall respect the family's right to privacy...

Ethical Responsibilities to Colleagues

- When we have a concern about the professional behavior of a coworker, we shall first let that person know of our concern and attempt to resolve the matter...

- When we do not agree with program policies, we shall first attempt to effect change through constructive action within the organization...

- Employees who do not meet program standards shall be informed of areas of concern and, when possible, assisted in improving their performance...

- Hiring and promotion shall be based solely on a person's record of accomplishment and ability to carry out the responsibilities of the position...

Ethical Responsibilities to Community & Society

- We shall communicate openly and truthfully about the nature and extent of services that we provide...

- We shall cooperate with other professionals who work with children and their families...

- We shall not participate in practices which are in violation of laws and regulations that protect the children in our programs...

(Additional principles and ideals are found in the complete Code of Ethical Conduct and Statement of Commitment brochure by S. Feeney and K. Kipnis. Copyright ©1992 by the National Association for the Education of Young Children. Excerpts used by permission.)

FIG. 5-9B.

EXCERPTS FROM THE ETHICAL STANDARDS OF HUMAN SERVICE PROFESSIONALS

Responsibility to Clients

Human service professionals:
1. Negotiate with clients the purposes, goals, and nature of help relationship...
2. Respect the integrity and welfare of the client at all times...
3. Protect the client's right to privacy and confidentiality...
4. Act in an appropriate and professional manner if it is suspected that danger or harm may occur to the client or to others as a result of a client's behavior...
5. Protect the integrity, safety, and security of client records...
6. Are aware that in their relationships with clients power and status are unequal...
7. Are aware that sexual relationships with current clients are not in the best interest of the client and are prohibited...
8. Protect the client's right to self-determination...
9. Recognize and build on client strengths...

Responsibility to Community & Society

Human service professionals:
10. Are aware of local, state, and federal laws. They advocate change in...
11. Keep informed about current social issues as they affect the client...
12. Understand the complex interaction between individuals, families, and...
13. Act as advocates in addressing unmet client and community needs...
14. Represent qualifications to the public accurately...
15. Describe the effectiveness of programs, treatments, and/or techniques accurately...
16. Advocate for the rights of all members of society...
17. Provide services without discrimination or preference...
18. Are knowledgeable about the cultures and communities...
19. Are aware of own cultural backgrounds, beliefs, and values...

Responsibility to Colleagues

Human service professionals:
22. Avoid duplicating another professional's helping relationship with a client...
23. When a human service professional has a conflict with a colleague, he or she first seeks out the colleague in an attempt to manage the problem...
24. Respond appropriately to unethical behavior of colleagues...
25. Keep consultations confidential...

Responsibility to the Profession

Human service professionals:
26. Know the limit and scope of their professional knowledge...
27. See appropriate consultation and supervision to assist in decisions...
28. Act with integrity, honesty...
29. Promote cooperation...
30. Promote continuing development of their profession...

Responsibility to Employers

Human service professionals:
32. Adhere to commitments made to their employers...
33. Participate in efforts to establish and maintain employment conditions...

Responsibility to Self

Human service professionals:
35. Strive to personify those characteristics typically associated with the profession...
36. Foster self-awareness and personal growth in themselves...
37. Recognize a commitment to lifelong learning...

(Additional standards are found in the complete Ethical Standards of Human Service Professionals by the National Organization for Human Service Education. Used with permission.)

Certain ethical standards apply to every profession, whether or not the standards are part of a written code of conduct. What happened to Bob is an example of the results of a lack of professional ethics. One day Bob and another care provider at the center discussed several ideas for a musical presentation to be given on Family Night. Later, Bob's coworker described one of the ideas to the center director. Although Bob had originally suggested the idea, his coworker chose not to mention this. When the director complimented Bob's coworker for her creativity, she just smiled and thanked him. What do you think of these professional ethics? Would you want to work with this person?

Early childhood and adult care professionals who abide by ethical standards earn the respect of their supervisors, coworkers, parents, family members, and community members. They are able to respect themselves, too.

Ethical Responsibilities

Professionals must assume ethical responsibilities for their own growth, as well as for the well-being of their clients and the community at large. As a human service professional, you also have responsibilities to your employer.

Responsibilities to Self

In return for your pay and benefits, your employer has the right to expect certain things from you. One expectation is that you will perform the duties of your job to the best of your ability. You are also expected to follow all guidelines and rules, such as those found in your employee handbook. You must also meet certain basic expectations that apply to any job, whether they are spelled out in the handbook or not. Here are some examples.

Professional Attitude and Conduct. Ethical professionals maintain desirable character traits, such as honesty, dependability, and trustworthiness. Professionals with a strong work ethic are motivated to perform their job to the best of their ability. Supervisors and coworkers alike value a professional who shows initiative and dedication.

Dress Codes. Your appearance on the job also makes a statement. It shows how you feel about yourself and your job. Proper dress and grooming convey a professional image to your employer, coworkers, parents, family members, and program visitors. A professional appearance starts with good grooming. You should arrive at work clean, with teeth brushed and hair neatly combed. A well-groomed appearance provides children and older adults with a healthy role model. See Fig. 5-10. **Dress codes**, or rules for

FIG. 5-10. **Conducting yourself in a professional manner through attitude and appropriate attire gives a positive impression to your employer and your clients. How should you dress for work in child or adult care centers?**

workplace dress, vary from one program to another. In general, clothing should be clean, practical, and in good repair. There should be adequate coverage for modesty. If T-shirts are allowed, avoid those with inappropriate pictures or slogans. For example, a shirt advertising alcohol or cigarettes should not be worn in a human service program. Avoid jewelry that poses a safety hazard, such as a long necklace or hoop earrings that could be pulled out by a child or older adult reaching for help.

Continuing Education. The world changes quickly, resulting in new information and new processes. Keeping up with the latest developments requires continual learning. Through **continuing education,** people update their career knowledge and acquire new job skills. Continuing education takes different forms. Some are single events, and some are ongoing experiences. They may be free of charge or involve costs. Motivated human service professionals look for continuing education opportunities that fit their needs as well as their budgets. They might:

* Attend a class on new children's or older adult literature at a community college.

* Take classes that lead to a related degree.

* Learn first aid or CPR.

* Observe teachers or care providers in other programs.

* Attend a weekend workshop on guiding behavior, curriculum or activity planning, or administration.

* Travel to another country to visit early childhood, adult day care, and intergenerational programs.

Organization Membership and Participation. A simple and inexpensive way to continue education is to join organizations in the professional field and subscribe to their periodicals. These magazines are a good resource for new ideas and products. In addition, these organizations may offer educational workshops on both regional and national levels. See Chapter 4 for

FIG. 5-11. Many early childhood and adult care providers are members of professional organizations. How can they benefit from sharing current research results and up-to-date information?

more information on professional organizations and publications. See Fig. 5-11.

Conference Attendance. For continuing education, professionals attend conferences. Large gatherings at which members of a specific profession exchange information about the latest findings, developments, and practices in their field are called **conferences.** For example, the National Association for the Education of Young Children (NAEYC) hosts a yearly conference of about 30,000 early childhood professionals. At this conference, people attend workshops conducted by their peers. Experts speak on important topics. Businesses display the latest in early childhood care and education materials and equipment. Other groups that sponsor care provider conferences include the American Association of Family and Consumer Sciences (AAFCS) and The Children's Defense Fund (CDF), The National Council on Aging (NCOA), the American Society on Aging (ASA), and the Gerontological Society of America

(GSA). You can find out more about conference attendance by checking out the Web sites for these organizations.

Acquiring Credentials. Earning the Child Development Associate (CDA) credential is another type of continuing education. One of the requirements for receiving this credential is the completion of course credit in several subject areas. The subject areas are related to the six competencies listed on pages 14 to 25 of this text. Courses may be offered by colleges and universities or by organizations recognized for early childhood teacher preparation. Pursuing the CDA credential benefits candidates. It lets them measure their own skills and knowledge against a national standard. It gives them feedback from peers and authorities in the field, which they can use to grow as professionals. Because the CDA credential is a valued award, it provides incentive to learn new skills or fine-tune existing ones in order to be accredited. Credentials essential to caring for older adults can be acquired from the National Commission for Certifying Agencies (NCCA), the National Organization for Competency Assurance (NOCA), and The Rehabilitation Accreditation Commission (CARF). You can find out more about acquiring these credentials by contacting the Web sites of the various organizations.

Director's Credential. Many states offer a director's credential for managers of early childhood care and education programs. The programs require program directors to obtain formal education along with experience to earn the credential. Some states' child care licensing laws require a director's credential in order for an individual to be legally qualified to direct an early childhood program. Depending upon the type of adult day services program, the director may be required to have credentials and management experience in any of the following areas: nursing, gerontology, geriatrics, social work, or counseling.

Responsibilities to Clients

Human service professionals accept ethical responsibilities for those entrusted in their care. The following information discusses areas of critical importance for human service professionals.

Protection from Harm

A key responsibility for all early childhood and adult care professionals is to protect program participants from harm. This protection can take place in a number of ways, including taking medical and environmental precautions.

- **Medical Precautions.** Professionals have an obligation to help keep clients as healthy as possible. It is their responsibility to be aware of their client's special health needs and to know how to respond to them. They are ethically bound to obtain training that would help them respond appropriately to client's health needs.

- **Environmental Precautions.** Maintaining a safe environment protects clients from injury and limits safety hazards. Professionals diligently survey program facilities for safety problems. If hazards are spotted, staff members should remedy them as quickly as possible. See Fig. 5-12A & B.

Respect for Diversity

Americans are guaranteed basic civil rights. It is illegal to discriminate based on race, ability, religion, gender, or any other such difference. However, ethical professionals do more than avoid discrimination; they do all they can to respect and value diversity. They do their best to include foods, activities, and cultural practices that help all people to feel comfortable, accepted, and valued. In addition, staff may be responsible for translating program information into another language for those who use English as a second language.

FIG. 5-12A & B. Adult and child care centers take every precaution to make sure the care environment is safe for clients. How can each provider be sure to maintain a safe environment throughout the day?

Developmentally Appropriate Practices

Human service professionals do all they can to match program services with a client's individual needs and abilities. For example, many programs encourage participants to learn a second language. Staff members organize the environment and plan activities, taking into account each client's personal situation and experiences.

Confidentiality

For care providers, confidentiality is one of the most critical areas in which to be guided by ethical standards. **Confidentiality** is the belief that the privacy of others must always be maintained. Care providers, who often know many private family details, are bound by their professional ethics to maintain confidentiality if they are to maintain the trust and confidence of those they serve.

Maintaining confidentiality means keeping individual family information private. It also means keeping individual staff member and sensitive program information private. Human service providers make it a practice to share information only when family members give written permission. Professionals follow a program's written guidelines as to how confidentiality will be maintained and to whom information may be provided.

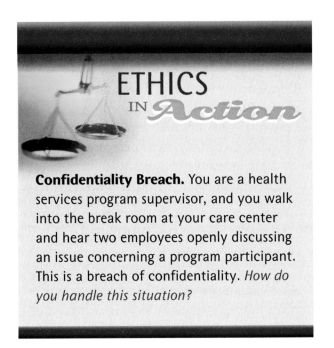

Confidentiality Breach. You are a health services program supervisor, and you walk into the break room at your care center and hear two employees openly discussing an issue concerning a program participant. This is a breach of confidentiality. *How do you handle this situation?*

Responsibilities to Families

Families are the foundation of young children and older adults. They support, nurture, and care for all family members. Whether serving young children or older adults, professionals should see their clients not simply as individuals, but as members of families. To ensure clients receive the valuable support that family members can provide, professionals make extra efforts to include them in program services and decisions. Following are ways this can be done.

Partnerships in Caring. Cooperative teamwork between family and program staff ensures that the needs of children and older adults will be fully met. Regular communication and decision making can take place during arrival and departure times or during scheduled family conferences.

Information Sharing. Information can be shared with clients and family members in a variety of ways. Making available program brochures, policy handbooks, newsletters, and reports on daily activities are all good methods of sharing information. Monthly family meetings allow families to contribute information to program staff as well.

Open Door Policies. Families have the right to know how their loved ones are at all times. While admittance to programs may be limited to the public in general, ethical human service programs maintain an open door policy that allows family members to visit at any time. Such a policy builds trust and decreases the chance that an unethical staff member would mistreat clients. See Fig. 5-13.

Family Involvement. Children and older adults in programs feel most comfortable and secure when their family members are encouraged to participate regularly. Such involvement can include evening family events or special daytime celebrations. Family members should feel welcome to volunteer time or special talents for these events.

Cooperative Care. There are times when clients need services beyond what the program staff can provide. For instance, a child may need speech therapy. In such cases, professionals refer families to other service programs to obtain the extra assistance their loved one needs.

FIG. 5-13. **People who trust their family members to care providers like to have as much information about a facility as possible.** How can the day care staff and clients benefit from an open door policy?

Bilingual Services. Families are best served when they receive program information in their primary language. Programs may need to have printed materials translated into several different languages. For programs, events, and activities in which oral communication is used, information should be presented in diverse languages whenever possible. For example, care providers should:

- Use the language best understood by children and older adults to explain safety practices and procedures.

- Provide health and nutrition information to parents and family members in a language best understood.

- Incorporate objects, music, and celebrations that encourage cultural understanding and multiple language use for children and older adults.

- Assist family members and parents in locating resources that support multiple language use.

- Maintain routines that include the use of multiple languages in daily activities.

Responsibilities to Coworkers

As a member of a child or older adult care team, you have a responsibility to cooperate with your coworkers to keep the program running smoothly. An effective team accomplishes more than any individual could alone. Your responsibilities to your coworkers include respect, courtesy, communication, and cooperative planning.

Respect and Courtesy. Professionals work more easily together when they treat each other with respect and common decency. Name-calling, judging, and belittling team members undermine staff morale and interfere with program services.

Ongoing Communication. To meet job expectations and to keep updated on program developments, professionals attend regular staff meetings. Such communication also helps team members avoid duplicating one another's efforts.

Cooperative Planning. To ensure that clients' overall needs are met, professionals create program activities and schedules together. They make special efforts to delegate job duties so that each member can put his or her unique strengths and talents to good use. See Fig. 5-14.

Responsibilities to Community & Society

As a human service professional, you have a number of responsibilities to your clients, your community, and society at large. These responsibilities include compliance with laws related to child and older adult care, cooperation with other professionals, and community outreach.

Compliance with Laws. Professionals are ethically required to follow laws that apply to their program. If their program is not in compliance, it is their responsibility to bring the problem to the attention of the program director. In severe cases, a professional might need to report legal violations to official authorities, such as a state's Department of Human Services.

Cooperation with Other Professions. In some situations, professionals from a variety of fields will work with a client. These professionals may need to share information in order to help the child. For instance, a child with behavior disorders may be visiting a child psychologist. With written permission from the parent, early childhood staff would cooperate with the psychologist as he or she provides treatment to the child. Cooperation might include sharing assessment information or allowing the psychologist to observe the child's behavior in the classroom.

Community Outreach. When families need extra help, such as with home heating or a child's nutrition, staff members refer families to community services, such as a utility support program or the local health department.

FIG. 5-14. **Working together on program planning allows care professionals to provide the best possible service to their clients.**

Section 5-2   Knowledge Check

1. Contrast ethics and professional ethics.
2. Cite specific issues that require professional confidentiality.
3. Explain the ethical responsibilities program staff members have to children, older adults, families, coworkers, and community and society.

Mini-Lab

Attend a family meeting of a local program in your community. Analyze how the meeting is conducted. In what ways are families made to feel welcome? How is acceptance of diversity communicated? How does the discussion leader find ways to let everyone contribute? What communication skills do you see put into practice?

Section 5-3

Advocacy

OBJECTIVES

- Describe a human service professional's advocacy responsibilities.
- Explain how individual rights are protected.
- Describe advocacy issues and the levels of advocacy involvement.
- Summarize how to contact legislators.

KEY TERMS

advocacy
advocates
constituents

A basic principle of democracy is the privilege to make your opinions known to those who create laws. Acting on behalf of the needs, rights, and well-being of their clients is the right and responsibility of every human service professional. In a human service, this action can take many forms. This section will discuss protecting individual rights and advocacy responsibilities.

What Is Advocacy?

The process of pleading a cause to influence change for the best interests of others is called **advocacy**. For example, organized advocacy efforts can influence change in public policy, allocation of resources, and social justice that affects the lives of all people. People who inform legislators (or policymakers) of their clients' needs and welfare are called **advocates**. Almost everyone has taken action on issues by which they are personally affected. Human service professionals have an ethical responsibility to take action on behalf of their client's basic needs and rights. What are some basic needs and rights of children and older adults?

Advocacy Responsibilities

Whenever conditions or circumstances need to be improved for clients or for program staff, advocacy efforts can be put into action. As a human service professional, you assume the responsibility of meeting the needs and rights of the children, older adults, and families in your care. You also have a responsibility to meet and support the needs of your coworkers. Issues for advocacy can vary widely. The common issues for children, older adults, and coworkers may include:

- Creating community awareness about the quality of services and rights for children and families.

- Influencing public policy to include stricter abuse laws.

- Promoting better licensing laws for early childhood and adult care and education facilities.

- Supporting legislation, such as child and adult care tax credits, to better meet the care and educational needs of children and older adults.

- Promoting such issues as better pay and working conditions for staff members.

Protecting Individual Rights

Part of your advocacy efforts as a human service professional will involve protecting the individual rights of your clients. All individuals have the right to be free from physical or emotional harm. They also have the right to be assured of privacy and protected from fraud. American society has created laws to protect such individual rights. You, as a human service professional, should be aware of these laws and should be able to use them in order to protect your clients, if necessary.

Legal Acts Offer Protection. In order to protect every person's rights, state and local legislatures create laws that insure fair treatment for all people. Several acts provide the basis for

laws by which human service professionals must abide. See Fig. 5-15.

Keeping Current on Legal Rights

Laws that apply to clients in human service programs change frequently, even from year to year. Professionals must always operate legally—keeping well informed of changes in laws and how these changes impact their programs.

Resources. Human service professionals are obligated to keep up-to-date on the legal rights of those they serve. Newspapers, radio, television, and the Internet are media sources early childhood and adult care professionals can use to keep current. In addition, licensing and accrediting agencies often distribute updates regarding new laws. Professional journals, magazines, and agency Web sites also provide quick references for new laws.

FIG. 5-15.

LEGAL ACTS FOR ADVOCACY

- Abuse & Neglect Act
- Americans with Disabilities Act
- Individuals with Disabilities Education Act
- Family Educational Rights & Privacy Acts
- Harassment Act
- Social Security Administration (Fraud) Act

Knowing the Facts

Part of advocacy is to thoroughly understand the facts about your cause. Before talking with others, you will want to carefully research all of the facts related to the issue. Be sure that your facts come from a variety of reliable sources of information. Although the Internet can be an effective source of information, there is also much unreliable information on the Internet. Reliable sources of information can include:

- Experts in the field related to the issue.
- Professional journals, government publications, and newspapers.
- Government agencies that focus on the issue, such as the Administration on Aging.
- Advocacy organizations. It is helpful to become aware of groups that support and oppose your position on the issue.
- Libraries, both public and university.

FIG. 5-16. **Early childhood or older adult care professionals often serve as advocates for those with special needs.** Investigate the role of advocates in various areas, such as special needs, child or elder abuse, and special legislation for families of young children.

Becoming an Advocate

It takes work to be an informed and influential advocate, but it is not as hard as many believe. You can make an advocacy effort once a year, once a month, or once a week, depending on how much time and determination you have. Your advocacy efforts can be short-term or long-term. They can be as quick as writing a letter to a legislator or as committed as serving on a task force or committee. See Fig. 5-16. The following shows how you can become an advocate at a low, medium, or high level.

Low-Level Influence. At a minimum, you need to keep informed about advocacy issues that impact your clients. Here are some ways you can be involved on a monthly basis at a low level:

- Listen to news reports that announce when bills are being considered at the state and national levels.
- Review newsletters and journals of professional organizations or professional advocacy groups so you know when to write letters or make telephone calls to decision makers who can impact human service programs.
- Talk with others about issues. Tell a friend or neighbor about the need for improved services for children and older adults.
- Get on the mailing lists of advocacy groups that deal with issues related to children and older adults.

Medium-Level Influence. In order to maintain a medium level of advocacy influence, you will need to work toward advocacy issues on a weekly basis. Here are some things you can do weekly to impact your client's needs:

- Maintain memberships in professional organizations. Professional organizations—such as the National Association for the Education of Young Children (NAEYC), the Administration on Aging (AoA), the League of Women

FIG. 5-17. Professional organizations often lead advocacy workshops for people interested in promoting laws that protect children, older adults, and their families. How could you be an advocate?

Voters, or AARP—often hold advocacy workshops that teach professionals how to promote good laws for children, older adults, and families.

- Write, call, or visit a local agency, such as the health department, that serves the needs of children and older adults.

- Write a letter or call your local, state, or federal legislators about issues related to early childhood and older adult care.

- Visit local, state, or federal legislators.

Specifically target senators and representatives in your voting district. Legislators welcome contact with their **constituents** (kuhn-STICH-oo-wuhnts), or the residents of their electoral districts.

High-Level Influence. In addition to taking the above actions on a monthly and weekly basis, your greatest level of influence will likely be with the voters in your area. Remember, it is the civic responsibility of all voters to make their viewpoints known. To achieve the greatest level of impact on issues related to children and older adults, write, call, or visit other voters in your area. When people are made aware of the specific needs of others, they tend to support the issues with their votes. See Fig. 5-17.

Contacting Legislators

An important measure for any advocate is to contact legislators who can influence policy change. Any contact with voters has the potential to influence a legislator's stand on various issues. A personal visit, either at a legislator's home state or Washington DC office, is the most effective way of contacting a legislator. It shows your commitment to an issue. If you want to visit a legislator in person, be sure to call his or

Intergenerational ***Interactions***

Advocates for Intergenerational Programs

As America begins to realize the benefits of intergenerational programs, groups and individuals are coming together in support of those programs. They understand that members of every generation—young and old alike—have special talents and abilities that can help meet the needs of other age groups.

- **The Brookdale Center on Aging** in New York City organized several intergenerational programs over the last ten years. Their Intergenerational *Program for Health Careers in Aging* introduces high school students to nursing homes and hospitals in an effort to educate young people on various jobs relating to older adults. Through the *Intergenerational Life History Project*, high school students visit homebound older adults and learn about 20th-century events from those who lived through them.

- **The Senior Corps**, a division of the Corporation for National and Community Service, sponsors a variety of Intergenerational Programs. This government organization, which operates throughout the country, is especially known for its *Foster Grandparent Program*. Foster Grandparents volunteer to assist children with special needs. They offer emotional support to abused children, tutor children with learning difficulties, mentor troubled teens, and care for children who are disabled or severely ill.

- **Generations Together**, an Intergenerational Studies Program conducted at the University of Pittsburgh, sponsors the *Youth in Services to Elders* (YIST) program. YIST encourages students to visit frail older adults, especially those who are clients of the Living-at-Home Program sponsored by the University of Pittsburgh Medical Center. During their visits, students and older adults may read or write letters, go for walks, watch movies, run errands, do chores, play games, and more.

Follow-Up

The advocates mentioned above are just a few of those that exist in America today. Research similar groups that operate in your state, county, or neighborhood, and describe how you may be able to contribute to or participate in their programs.

her office to make an appointment. You can locate addresses and telephone numbers for local, state, and federal legislators on the Internet.

Personally written letters and telephone calls are also effective means of contacting legislators who influence public policy. Use the following guidelines when writing to legislators:

- Always write with courtesy and respect.
- Neatly type or write your letter so it can be easily read.
- Use a formal writing style. To address your letter, always use the formal title "The Honorable" followed by the legislator's title and name. Be sure to use the correct address.
- Include your complete name and address in the letter.
- Write the clear purpose of your letter in the first paragraph. Address only one issue per letter. If you are writing in regard to a specific bill (or piece of legislation), be sure to include the number and title of the bill. Be sure to state your viewpoint on the bill.

- Use concise and clear information to support your viewpoint.
- Identify yourself as a constituent if you are in the legislator's electoral district.
- Finish your letter by requesting a direct response regarding the legislator's stand on the issue in your letter. For example, you might say, "I would appreciate hearing from you regarding this matter."
- Thank the legislator for his or her time and consideration of the matter.
- Follow up your letter with a telephone call to the legislator's office after a reasonable period of time. This will help confirm your stand on the issue.

Whether you choose to become a human service professional or a caring neighbor, there is much you can do in advocacy for the needs and rights of others. What role do you see yourself playing in advocacy for children and older adults?

Section 5-3 Knowledge Check

1. What is the human service professional's responsibility in advocacy?
2. List the levels of advocacy. Give an example of what you can do at each level.
3. What is the most effective means of contacting a legislator?

Mini-Lab

Investigate an early childhood or older adult advocacy issue. Create a poster or a display-case feature to inform others in your school or community about this issue.

Review & Activities

Section Summaries

5-1 Communication improves staff performance.

5-1 A variety of methods of communication should be used.

5-1 Recording information improves communication.

5-2 Personal ethics affect job performance.

5-2 Ethics standards guide professional behavior.

5-3 Laws protect individual rights.

5-3 A variety of resources can be used in advocacy efforts.

5-3 Advocacy is targeted toward decision makers at the local, state, and national level.

Check Your Knowledge

1. What are the basic areas of communication?
2. What are some barriers to communication?
3. Explain communication methods of public relations.
4. How are records used by human service professionals?
5. Describe characteristics of an ethical professional.
6. List two ways in which human service professionals can continue their education.
7. Give an example of a way in which a human service professional might be inclusive of diversity.
8. What might be some consequences of a breach in confidentiality?

9. Why is it especially important for human service professionals to be aware of laws protecting individuals?
10. List four reliable resources to use for advocacy efforts.

Thinking Critically

1. Analyze how stereotypes cause communication barriers. What common stereotypes do adults have about children? About older adults? How might each stereotype affect communication with the child or older adult?
2. Predict the consequences a staff member's poor attitude would have on communications with clients, clients' families, and human services staff. If you were the coworker of a staff member with a poor attitude, what could you do to improve communications?

3. Consider the types of personal and family information care providers may know about their clients. Draw conclusions about the consequences of violating ethical confidentiality.

4. Describe advocacy opportunities you might have as a human services professional. Why are human services professionals in a unique position to serve as advocates? Do these professionals have more responsibility than others to serve as advocates? Justify your response.

Practical Applications

1. **Investigating Legal Issues.** Investigate legal issues for child and adult care providers. Discuss the ethical implications for care providers. What do care providers need to know to protect their clients and themselves?

2. **Comparing Web Sites.** Locate five Web sites for human services. Note the features that make each Web site effective or ineffective. Create a checklist for developing an effective human services Web site.

3. **Identifying Ethical Issues.** Interview a human services provider to identify ten ethical issues that might be encountered when providing human services for children or older adults. For each issue identified, describe appropriate ethical behavior.

4. **Advocacy Investigation.** Locate a newspaper or magazine article about advocacy for children, older adults, families, human services clients, or human services staff. Make a brief presentation to the class summarizing the article.

Building Your PORTFOLIO

Learning to Communicate Effectively

Your future employer will want to evaluate your professional communication skills. Many of the human services professional's daily communications are written.

Step 1: Interview a human services professional to learn what types of written communication are used regularly. Examples: notes, e-mail messages, meeting agendas, announcements, newsletters, health reports, incident reports, and activity plans. If possible, collect samples of each type. Ask what guidelines are followed for each type of written communication.

Step 2: Research techniques for clear business writing using library and Internet sources.

Step 3: Create your own samples of at least three different types of written communication used regularly by human services professionals.

Step 4: Write or keyboard your samples as appropriate. Carefully proofread each sample and make corrections before adding them to your portfolio.

Chapter 6

Health & Safety

Section 6-1

Health & Safety for Children

OBJECTIVES

- Describe a healthy environment in a child care setting.
- Explain the practices used to check for illnesses.
- Identify children's special health conditions.
- Identify effective health and safety policies and procedures.
- Explain how to eliminate safety hazards.
- List the supplies in a first aid kit.

KEY TERMS

pathogens
immunization
universal precautions
biohazardous
hypothermia
frostbite
heat exhaustion
screenings
safety policy
risk-management plan

Parents of children enrolled in early childhood programs trust that staff will do everything they can to keep their children safe and healthy. They expect the early childhood staff to respond wisely if a health or safety problem arises. This section will prepare you for that responsibility.

Promoting Children's Health

Everyone wants children to develop to their full potential. To achieve this goal, it is important to ensure children's health and safety during the early years. Illness or injury can interfere with children's normal development, ranging from poor bone growth to impaired brain development. Healthy children have the foundation they need for early learning. They have energy and have good appetites. Their eyes and noses are clear, and they are free of coughs and congestion. However, even the healthiest children experience occasional mild illness. One reason is that a child's immune system is still developing. The immune system

helps resist disease. Until the immune system develops and children master good health habits, early childhood staff must take extra steps to keep children healthy.

Limiting Contagious Disease

Children are subject to many infectious diseases. The disease-causing organisms are called **pathogens**, or germs. Bacteria and viruses are two kinds of pathogens.

Some infectious diseases are passed from person to person. They include colds, influenza, chicken pox, and strep throat. Some conditions, such as diaper rash or an ear infection, are not contagious. See Fig. 6-1.

FIG. 6-1. Care providers must do their best to ensure the health of children in their classroom. What should care providers do when children come to the center with symptoms of illness?

Infectious diseases spread easily among children in group care. Coughing, sneezing, and physical contact allow illness to pass easily. Everything touched—toys, drinking glasses, infant teething rings, bedding, food, books, and other people—becomes a possible source of illness. Some pathogens are found in feces, urine, and blood. Contact with these sources can spread disease, too. For example, changing diapers and caring for injuries pose a risk when not done properly.

Enrollment Records. Health records, which list results of health checks and screenings, are a protection for everyone involved in a child's care. These records include a doctor's report of good health and may include a negative tuberculosis test. Health reports may also include information about known conditions, diseases, or other problems. Records of **immunizations**—vaccines that protect children from certain diseases—should be included. See Fig. 6-2. Obtain children's records from parents or

guardians. These records should include details about a child's developmental growth, allergies, medications, and medical problems or injuries that affect development. See page 164 for more information on health checks.

Emergency Forms. Every child and staff member should have emergency forms on file. They list the telephone numbers and addresses of people to contact in case of emergency and those people *not* to contact. Every child's doctor and dentist are also noted. Signed emergency treatment waivers allow the staff to obtain emergency care for children, if necessary.

Using Universal Precautions

Universal precautions are infection-control guidelines staff must follow to protect themselves from infectious disease and limit its spread. The Occupational Safety and Health Administration (OSHA) requires these precautions. Because some pathogens are present in blood and other bodily fluids—such as urine, feces, vomit, or draining wounds—universal precautions must be followed routinely to prevent direct contact.

Hand Washing. The best way to teach children and staff members good health practices, such as hand washing, is through classroom activities and routines. Monitor children and guide them as they wash. Posters, signs, and bulletin boards educate and remind everyone about good health practices. Be a good role model by following the hand-washing guidelines. The feature on page 162 shows the proper method for thorough hand washing.

Environmental Disinfection. Cleaning and sanitizing or disinfecting with a solution, such as bleach and water, limits germs. Use a daily fresh disinfecting solution of ¾ cup of ultra liquid bleach to one gallon of water for disinfecting diapering areas, toys, cribs, walls, and floors. Toys that are mouthed by infants should be disinfected daily. Toys used by older children should be disinfected weekly or when soiled.

FIG. 6-2.

Recommended Immunizations for Children

	Birth	1 Mo.	2 Mo.	4 Mo.	6 Mo.	12 Mo.	15 Mo.	18 Mo.	4-6 Years
Hep B	1	2			3				
Hib			1	2	3	4			
DTaP			1	2	3		4		5
IPV			1	2	3				4
PVC			1	2	3	4			
MMR						1			2
Var						1			
Hep A									1 2

Hep B—Hepatitis B
Hib—Meningitis, pneumonia, infections (Hemophilus influenza type b)
DTaP—Diptheria, tetanus, and pertussis (whooping cough)
IPV—Inactivated polio vaccine
PVC—Pneumococcal (NOO-muh-KAH-kuhl) conjugate
MMR—Measles, mumps, rubella
Var—Chicken Pox (varicella zoster virus)
Hep A—Hepatitix A (2 doses at least 6 months apart; recommended in certain areas for children over 2 years)
Adapted from the Centers for Disease Control and Prevention immunization schedule.

Timing for certain immunizations may vary according to doctor's advice. A short bar means the vaccine should be given at that age. The longer bar indicated gives an age range over which a vaccine can be given. The numbers inside the bars indicate the sequence in which the vaccine doses are given. Parents will need to provide documentation showing their children have received the necessary immunizations when enrolling at an early childhood center.

How To...

Wash Hands Effectively

The best way to limit the spread of contagious diseases is by frequent and thorough hand washing. Children and staff should wash their hands upon arrival, before and after preparing or eating meals and snacks, after handling pets, and after coughing, sneezing, and toileting. Staff members must also wash their hands before and after diapering. Everyone should wash his or her hands after messy activities, such as sand or water play, finger painting, and using clay and dough. Use warm water, liquid soap, and paper towels.

1. Turn on the water and wet your hands and forearms. Warm water at 110°F is recommended.

2. Apply liquid soap and build up a good lather.

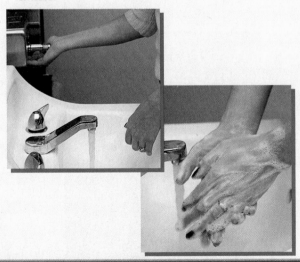

3. Rub your soaped hands for 20 seconds. Wash the backs of hands, wrists, between fingers, and under fingernails. Clean fingernails with a brush.

4. Rinse well.

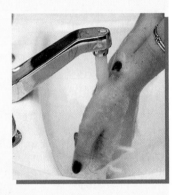

5. Dry hands with a paper towel.
6. Turn off the water faucet using a paper towel, not your clean hands.

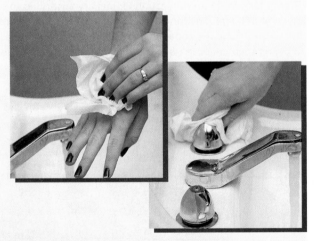

APPLY IT!

In teams, practice the above hand-washing procedure. Critique each other on effectiveness of following the guidelines.

When using disinfecting solution, be sure to rinse items thoroughly in clear water, and then air dry. Store all cleaning supplies in a locked cabinet. A daily fresh sanitizing solution of one tablespoon of ultra liquid bleach per gallon of water is good for sanitizing hard surfaces, such as meal service tables. Wear disposable gloves when handling blood spills or objects with blood on them. Then disinfect the area thoroughly.

Wearing Gloves. Wear fresh, disposable latex or vinyl gloves whenever you may come into contact with bodily fluids, such as during diapering, toileting, or treating an injury. Remove gloves by pulling them off inside out. Wear gloves only once. To complete the process, thoroughly wash your hands.

Disposal of Biohazardous Materials. Materials that come into contact with bodily fluids are called **biohazardous**. Diapers, diaper wipes, used latex gloves, and blood-soaked clothes are examples of potentially hazardous materials. Biohazardous materials should be double-bagged and securely tied. Label each bag as biohazardous waste. Contaminated clothing should be double-bagged and sent home with parents. Keep it out of children's reach. If contaminated items are to be washed—not discarded—they must be washed separately.

Limiting Weather-Related Illness

Diseases are not the only threat to health. Overexposure to extreme weather can cause illness, too. As an early childhood professional, you will need to protect children from the following types of extreme weather:

- **Hypothermia** (HY-poh-THUHR-mee-uh) results when the body's temperature gets dangerously low. It can occur if children are out too long in cold weather. See Fig. 6-3A.

- **Frostbite**, the freezing of body tissue, occurs if parts of the body—especially feet, hands, face, and ears—are not well protected. Even if dressed in warm and waterproof clothing,

children may still get frostbite if they are outside for long periods in severely cold weather. Signs of frostbite include numbness and white or grayish-yellow skin.

- **Heat exhaustion** is a hot-weather concern. It results in dizziness and fatigue caused by the loss of fluid and salt through profuse sweating. Children with symptoms of heat exhaustion should drink fluids and rest in a cool place. Prevent heat exhaustion by not allowing children to play outdoors for long periods during very hot weather. Play areas should be shaded if possible. Encourage children to drink water frequently to replace water lost through perspiration. See Fig. 6-3B.

- **Heatstroke** is another hot-weather concern. Symptoms of heatstroke include a lack of sweating, extreme body temperatures, and the possibility of collapsing. Care providers can help prevent heatstroke by following the same preventative measures as for heat exhaustion.

- **Sunburn** can be a problem during any season. When playing outdoors, children should

FIG. 6-3A. **Making sure children are dressed properly for outdoor play, regardless of the weather, is the responsibility of all care providers.** How would you make sure that children are protected from the cold on a cold, winter day?

FIG. 6-3B. **Protecting children from sunburn is a care provider's responsibility.** How would you make sure that children are protected from the heat on a warm, sunny day?

wear sunscreen with an SPF level of 30. Parents should supply the sunscreen for their children.

- **Air pollution** can pose risks for those with allergies, asthma, or other breathing problems. During an air-pollution alert, keep children indoors until the alert is cancelled.

Handling Illness & Injuries

Even in the best of environments, illness occurs. Early care professionals work to limit the spread of illness and care for ill children appropriately. They also record health information to comply with health codes and licensing requirements.

Health Checks & Screenings

Routine health checks help staff spot children's health problems early, when an illness is most treatable and can be kept from spreading. Health checks take place when children arrive. Staff members note children's appearance, attitudes, and behaviors. They check for physical signs of illness. A rash, blisters, watery eyes, harsh coughing, inflamed throat, fever, or discharge from the nose or mouth could signal illnesses, such as colds, influenza, or pink eye. Staff members may check children's hair for lice. Unusual behavior, such as tiredness, crankiness, and whining, may also signal illness.

Examinations given to a group of children to look for one specific health problem are called **screenings**. Those children with an identified problem are referred for special treatment.

Vision and hearing screenings usually start at age three—earlier if problems are suspected. Some children are checked for diseases they may have inherited, such as blood diseases. Lead poisoning, which causes serious illness and brain damage, is detected through screening, too.

Reporting Illness and Informing Parents. Certain contagious diseases, such as chicken pox, should be reported to the public health department for tracking. Children's parents should be informed of outbreaks of infectious disease as well. Send home letters that identify:

- The illness or condition.
- Associated symptoms.
- Time that elapses before symptoms become apparent.
- Typical length of the illness and suggested treatment.
- When the child can safely return to the classroom.

FIG. 6-4. Most early childhood centers require that children who are running a fever must stay home until they've been fever-free for 24 hours. Why is this guideline important?

Isolation and Restricting Attendance. Those with a contagious illness may have to be temporarily absent from child care. Restricting attendance protects others from illness. Programs establish guidelines so that parents and staff know when attendance is not acceptable. The guidelines also specify when people may return to the center after illness, such as being fever-free for 24 hours. A child who becomes ill while in child care should rest in the isolation room until taken home. See Fig. 6-4.

Medicine Dispensing Procedures. State licensing laws may restrict dispensing medicine in child care settings. However, programs that do administer medicine follow a system so children receive the correct dosage. Parents complete and sign a medication permission form. On the form they indicate the child's name, the exact time, amount, method of dosage, and any side effects the medication may have on the child. Parents should also include the prescribing physician's name. When staff members give the medicine, they enter the information on a log and sign the entry.

Label and store all medications properly. Store nonrefrigerated medicines in locked, dry storage areas out of children's reach. Store refrigerated medicines in a labeled and locked container in the refrigerator.

Treating Minor Injuries

Often injuries are minor and can be quickly treated. For bumps and bruises an ice pack minimizes swelling; a scraped knee may require cleaning with soap and water and a bandage. First aid training helps staff treat minor injuries.

Basic supplies, such as blankets, towels, and a first aid kit, should be on hand. First aid kits should include a first aid book, bandages, gauze pads and strips, adhesive tape, thermometer, flashlight, tongue depressors, cotton balls, blunt scissors, liquid soap, disposable latex or vinyl gloves, and tweezers. In case of accidental poisoning, call your local Poison Control Center. See Fig. 6-5.

FIG. 6-5. Maintaining a well-equipped first aid kit is essential for all early childhood and older adult programs. How often should supplies be replenished?

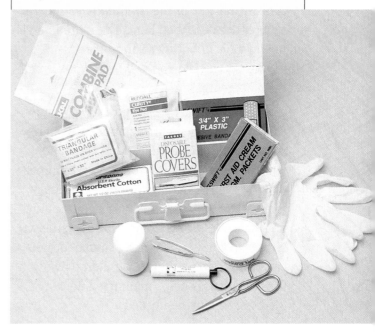

Treating Serious Injuries

If a child requires professional medical treatment, the teacher should stay with the child and administer any appropriate first aid while someone else calls for emergency assistance. Then call the child's parents and obtain the medical treatment waiver from the child's file. If parents do not arrive in time, a teacher should go to the hospital with the child. See Section 6-3 for more information on skills care providers need for handling serious emergencies.

Special Health Concerns

Some children have health conditions that require special attention. Information about care and medication should be noted on enrollment applications and discussed with parents. When caring for children with health problems, professionals respond to the child's individual needs. They are sensitive to the child's feelings and find ways to avoid setting the child apart as "different."

Conditions That Impact Child Health

Every special health condition has its own set of concerns. A few of the conditions you might encounter are described here. The more knowledge you have about these and other conditions, the better able you will be to handle children competently.

- **Asthma** (AZ-muh) is a respiratory condition characterized by recurring attacks of shortness of breath. Coughing, wheezing, and whistling breathing are common symptoms. Asthma attacks may last for a few hours or for weeks. Factors that trigger an attack are not the same for everyone. Dust, weather changes, strenuous exercise, smoke, or pets can cause asthma. Keeping children away from the causes helps minimize attacks. Medication may be needed.

FIG. 6-6. Keeping early childhood centers clean and dust-free helps eliminate possible allergens from the environment.

- **Allergies** are an unusual reaction to a substance that most people can tolerate. The substances cause a reaction when eaten, breathed in, or touched. Allergic reactions include nasal congestion, coughing, wheezing, asthma, frequent sneezing, a rash, eye irritation, upset stomach, and diarrhea. Many substances—including foods, animal fur, insect stings, dust, pollen, and mold—can trigger allergic reactions. Some allergic reactions are treated with medication. You can help prevent allergic reactions by keeping children from trigger substances and by maintaining cleanliness standards. Follow parents' directions for treatment of allergic reactions. If an allergic reaction is severe, call the child's physician right away. See Fig. 6-6.

- **Giardiasis** (jee-ar-DEE-uhsis) is a contagious disease caused by a parasite and results in diarrhea. It can be passed among children when care providers do not clean children's or their own hands after diapering or when an infected person touches toys. Proper diapering and hand washing are the best ways to prevent the spread of giardiasis. Since infants and toddlers constantly mouth objects, daily toy sanitation helps avoid spreading the illness.

- **Head lice** are small insects that live close to the scalp on human hair. Lice are usually identified when lice eggs, called nits, are found. Nits are typically spotted at the back of the neck, behind the ears, and on the top of the head. Signs of lice include itching at the roots of the hair and small red bite marks on the scalp. Head lice are easily treated. Staff members should alert parents and other staff members as soon as an outbreak of head lice occurs. Doctors and public health departments can provide advice on treatment.

- **Epilepsy** is a disorder in which the electrical rhythms of the central nervous system are disturbed, resulting in seizures. Medication is often prescribed for epilepsy. Consult with parents to learn how to respond in case of a seizure.

- **Diabetes** (dy-uh-BEET-eez) is a condition in which the body does not produce enough of a chemical called insulin. Diabetes is usually controlled through medication and diet.

- **Sickle-cell anemia** is an inherited blood disorder accompanied by pain in the arms, hands, feet, legs, and abdomen. Infection or injury can make these attacks more likely to occur.

- **Drug exposure**, either prenatally or during nursing, affects children's health and overall development. The drugs a mother ingests and transfers to her child may affect the child's nervous system, resulting in physical, emotional, and social problems. Also see Chapter 1.

- **Human Immunodeficiency Virus (HIV)** is a virus that attacks and slowly weakens the body's immune system. Over time the affected person has frequent illnesses that a healthy person's immune system would easily fight off. This cycle of repeated illness from infectious disease is called Acquired Immune-Deficiency Syndrome (AIDS). People with AIDS die from diseases that others usually survive, such as pneumonia and influenza. At this time, there is no known cure for AIDS.

Enrollment of Children with Health Conditions

The Americans with Disabilities Act (ADA) protects children's rights to be enrolled in child care whenever reasonably possible. When staff members learn of a child's special condition, confidentiality is critical. Information about children's health is limited to the main classroom teacher and the director of the program. Staff members who want to discuss the case with the child's doctor must get written permission from the parents. Staff should work cooperatively with parents to receive specialized training they may need to provide children with the best care possible. You can find out more about the ADA law and child care on the Internet. See Fig. 6-7.

FIG. 6-7. Care providers often meet with the parents of special needs children to help determine the best program for the child. How do early childhood staff, parents, and special needs children benefit from such meetings?

Ensuring Children's Safety

The most important safety precaution in group care is adequate and continuous supervision of children. They should never be left unattended or cared for in dangerous conditions. Children also need teachers who model good safety practices.

Children learn to practice safety during classroom activities. Field trips, such as visits to the fire station, emphasize the importance of being careful. Children can help teachers with safety inspections. Here are simple safety rules children can learn:

- Walk indoors. Running is for outside.
- Give broken toys to a teacher.

- Settle conflicts with words, not by hitting, biting, pushing, or throwing toys.
- Stay with the teacher when on walks or a field trip.
- Obey safety rules when using art supplies, cooking utensils, and woodworking tools.
- Tell a teacher right away if a stranger comes into the classroom or play yard.
- Tell a parent or teacher if anyone touches you on a private area of your body.

Safety Risks for Children

Children are exposed to hazards indoors and outdoors. Staff members must make sure the furniture, toys, and play structures are safe. See Fig. 6-8. Here are ways to ensure safety:

- Avoid toys with long cords or strings to avoid strangulation.
- Use only nontoxic items in the science projects. Remember that some plants can be poisonous. Avoid plants, such as English ivy and daffodil bulbs.
- Provide only round-tipped scissors.
- Take special care with electricity, particularly electric appliances and electric or battery-operated toys. Make sure wires are not frayed and batteries are not leaking. Cover all unused electric outlets.
- Label potential poisons and lock them out of children's reach. This includes cleaning preparations, aerosol sprays, drain cleaners, and medicine.

FIG. 6-8. **A primary responsibility of care providers is to keep children safe. Teaching children to use safety scissors properly is just one precaution.** What other ways can care providers keep children safe?

- Place decals at children's eye level on low windows and sliding glass doors. This helps children be aware of the glass and keeps them from running into it.

- Bolt tall toy shelves to the wall to prevent them from falling onto a child.

- Make sure water temperature in restroom is warm, not hot, to prevent burns.

- Do not allow children in kitchen and garage areas.

- Select toys that are appropriate for the ages and abilities of children in your classroom.

- Read labels and catalog descriptions for age recommendations before purchasing toys.

- Avoid sharp-edged toys. Toys should not have glass, sharp points, or metal edges.

- Make sure that plastic toys are shatterproof and nonflammable.

- Only use painted toys and art supplies that are labeled nontoxic.

- Toys, and any removable parts from toys, must not be small enough to swallow or inhale. For children under three, toys or parts of toys that fit completely into a "no-choke testing tube" should not be used. No-choke testing tubes can be purchased at toy stores. If you do not have one, you can use a toilet-paper roll.

Developing a Safety Policy

To ensure safe conditions, program directors develop a **safety policy**. The policy states the rules and procedures that protect children and staff. Staff must receive training on the policy. A safety policy addresses:

- Facility safety.
- Toy safety.
- Rules for children's conduct.
- Positive methods of discipline.
- Transportation safety.
- Safety inspections.

- Emergency procedures.
- Evacuation procedures.
- Dealing with strangers.

Risk-Management Plans. When emergency procedures are established in writing, it is called a **risk-management plan**. Creating and following such a plan helps staff and children remain calm and respond quickly to any emergency. Risk-management plans may contain procedures to follow for emergencies, such as weather, fire, bomb threats, or other violent threats. The plan includes telephone numbers for the fire, police, and weather stations; hospital; ambulance service; child abuse hotline; and poison control center. Parents and family members must be informed about the risk-management plan and what they should do in an emergency.

Fire Evacuation Drills. Fire evacuation diagrams, with arrows toward exits, must be posted in all classrooms. Evacuation plans will vary depending upon the facility. Staff members should be trained on using fire extinguishers located in each classroom, the kitchen, and laundry area. Hold fire drills monthly. In the event of an actual fire, sound the alarm at the first sight of smoke or flames.

Severe Weather Drills. Weather emergencies include electrical storms, tornadoes, hurricanes, blizzards, and floods. Safety procedures vary. The American Red Cross, the local fire department, or weather station can give you recommended responses. Here are some general rules that apply to weather emergencies: See Fig. 6-9.

- Keep battery-operated radios and flashlights readily accessible.

- Post directions to rooms designated as shelter areas.

- Take shelter at the first sound of an alarm and remain there until the all-clear signal is given.

- Take attendance immediately after reaching shelter so you can locate missing children.

Disaster Drills. Disasters, such as earthquakes or explosions, require an evacuation

FIG. 6-9. Regular drills help children and care providers react calmly when severe weather strikes. **How might children respond if they are not trained how to react in weather emergencies?**

plan so children and staff can seek shelter quickly. In cooperation with civil defense personnel, identify locations in your building that would offer the best protection. Post those locations for all to see. See Section 6-3 for more information on evacuations.

Injury & Accident Prevention

Prevention means taking action to keep something from happening. No child care program is completely free of accidents. With prevention, however, the number and severity of incidents can be limited.

Care providers reduce the risk of mishaps by anticipating problem situations. Alert teachers know that a safe toy for a four-year-old may be hazardous for a one-year-old. Teachers should never assume children will use toys and equipment in appropriate ways. They should ask themselves, "How else might a child use this item?"

Keen observation is important for accident prevention. Always be alert to safety hazards—items, conditions, or situations that put children in danger.

Safety Inspections. Indoor and outdoor play areas should be inspected daily for safety hazards. Toys, equipment, and facilities should be checked for wear and damage. Such hazards as torn carpeting and exposed wiring should be reported for immediate repair. Quickly dispose of litter, especially glass. Frequently conduct safety inspections, using a checklist.

Vehicle Inspections. Child care facilities must transport children safely, whether during field trips or daily trips to or from school. Safety is ensured by:

- Conducting vehicle safety inspections.
- Making sure all drivers are legally licensed to drive the vehicle.
- Equipping vehicles with seat belts and car seats.
- Providing adequate adult supervision.
- Having a first aid kit in each vehicle.
- Making sure all vehicles are equipped with a working two-way radio, flashlight, fire extinguisher, and city map with the location of hospitals clearly identified.

Field Trip Safety. Field trips are safer when staff choose safe sites to visit. Field trip vehicles should be parked in a safe, off-street area as children enter and exit them. Each child should wear a name tag identifying the facility's name and telephone number. Inviting parents along increases supervision. Counting the number of children before leaving on the field trip, and counting them several times during the trip, is

FIG. 6-10. **Field trips provide wonderful learning opportunities for children; however, careful planning and extra supervision are needed to keep children safe.**

helpful for keeping track of the children. A first aid kit should be carried on field trips as well as permission forms for emergency treatment should a child be injured. See Fig. 6-10.

Safety Documentation

In following a center's safety policy, staff members need to be familiar with the forms that they have to fill out as they work with children. These forms apply to:

- **Injuries.** All injuries, no matter how minor, must be recorded on an accident report form and an accident log immediately after a child is treated. Use the accident report form to record specific information. Include the date, child's name, and time of injury; names of witnesses to the injury; the classroom location; equipment or products involved; the cause of the injury; the type of injury; who gave the first aid and what they did; and any action taken by a doctor, dentist, or emergency personnel. This form is placed in the child's file. See Fig. 6-11.

- **Suspected Abuse.** Any suspected cases of child abuse or neglect must be documented and reported. Chapter 8 includes more about this subject.

FIG. 6-11. An important role for care providers is to record all accidents and injuries. Give two reasons why documenting accidents and injuries is important.

- **Releasing Children.** Children may leave a program's care only with their custodial parent or legal guardian. However, parents may sign a waiver giving release permission to someone else. In most programs, parents or guardians must sign the children in and out of the center. Special care must also be taken in cases of divorce, separation, or other special circumstances where it is necessary to know who has legal access to a child. Before a child can be released to that person, staff must see photo identification.

- **Emergency Treatment.** An emergency treatment waiver form is maintained for each child. This statement, signed by a parent or legal guardian, gives the program permission to secure emergency medical treatment for a sick or injured child. Also on the form are parent work and home telephone numbers, additional people to contact when the parent or guardian is unavailable, and the name and telephone number of the child's doctor and dentist.

Section **6-1** Knowledge Check

1. What are the proper hand-washing steps?
2. Explain the importance of following universal precautions. Give an example of when you would use these precautions.
3. Name four types of documentation used when caring for children.

Mini-Lab

Write a newsletter for parents telling ways to promote children's health and safety. Use print and Internet resources for your research.

Section 6-2

Health & Safety for Older Adults

OBJECTIVES

- Identify ways to promote and maintain good health and wellness practices for older adults.
- Determine how stress can trigger illness during older years.
- Identify safety practices for older adults in adult day centers.

KEY TERMS

pediatrician
geriatrican
disparities
polypharmacy
stress
cardiopulmonary
  resuscitation
  (CPR)

"Prevention is worth a pound of cure; wellness is worth a ton of prevention." Maintaining health and wellness means following a plan that helps people in good health to stay healthy. Practicing good health is a process that includes nutrition awareness, stress management, physical fitness, being aware of the surrounding environment, safety, and getting regular medical screenings.

Maintaining Health & Wellness

Practicing good health starts from birth and continues throughout a person's life. It's important for people to have health care providers with whom they feel comfortable. The physician that provides care for children is called a **pediatrician**. A **geriatrician** provides care for older adults. These physicians keep track of all medical records and histories to help make diagnoses and treat illnesses.

Health & Wellness Practices

Good health and wellness practices concern everyone. As people age they should have the opportunity to improve their quality of life by promoting their own healthy lifestyles. See Fig. 6-12. Sponsored by the Department of Health and Human Services, *Healthy People 2010* is a full set of health objectives for the United States to achieve by the year 2010. *Healthy People 2010* builds on the foundation set by the 1979 Surgeon General's Report—*Healthy People and Healthy People 2000*. The goals of *Healthy People 2010* are to:

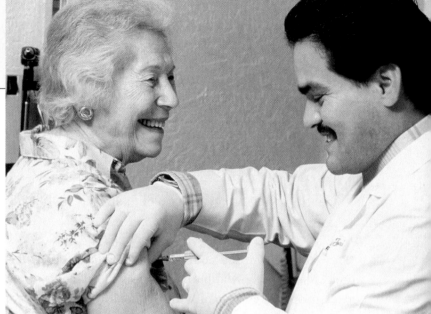

FIG. 6-12. **Immunizations from infectious diseases can help improve the quality of life for older adults.** What permissions and precautions might be necessary before older adults receive immunizations?

- **Goal 1. Increase the quality and years of healthy life.** This goal is to help people of all ages to increase life expectancy and improve their quality of living during those years.

- **Goal 2. Eliminate health disparities.** This second goal is to eliminate health **disparities**, or inconsistencies in health care, among different groups in the population.

The objectives of *Healthy People 2010* cover 28 areas, including cancer, diabetes, food safety, immunization and infectious diseases, nutrition and obesity, respiratory diseases, substance abuse, and access to quality health care. Each of the areas has one or more objectives. For example, the objective of the food safety area is to reduce foodborne illnesses. Some key practices that help all people, including older adults, are using universal precautions and proper sanitation, getting regular immunizations, and using medications properly.

Using Universal Precautions

Like child care professionals, all adult care providers who may come in contact with blood or other body fluids are required by OSHA to practice universal precautions. (See Section 5-1 for detailed information on universal precautions.) Universal precautions include:

- Using proper hand-washing procedures. See page 162 for information on proper hand washing.

- Wearing latex or vinyl gloves when contact with body fluids occurs, such as when treating injuries.

- Disinfecting the environment, such as cleaning recreational items, tables and other surfaces, and restrooms. Use a bleach solution for disinfections. See page 160.

- Disposing of biohazardous materials, such as urine-soaked clothing, by double-bagging the items and securely tying the bags.

Immunizations & Quality of Life

When discussing good health practices with older adults, it is important to point out how their quality of life can be improved. Older adults can improve their quality of life through the promotion of a healthful lifestyle, self-reliance, and independent living. Regular health screenings are part of a healthy lifestyle. Older adults should also receive proper immunizations. Immunizations start at infancy and continue throughout a person's life. See Fig. 6-13 for more information on immunizations for adults.

FIG. 6-13.

IMMUNIZATIONS FOR OLDER ADULTS

Tetanus, Diphtheria (Td)	After completing a primary series of three tetanus shots in childhood, all adults should have a tetanus booster at 10-year intervals throughout life. They should not wait until they have an accident, such as a puncture wound, to get a tetanus booster.
Influenza Vaccine	Adults 50 years of age and older, including those in nursing homes, should have the influenza vaccine each year in the fall or winter, unless prohibited by certain chronic health conditions.
Pneumococcal Vaccine (PPV)	Health professionals recommend that adults age 65 and older receive a pneumonia vaccine. Some older adults may need more than one vaccination if they were vaccinated before age 65. People who are less than 65 years of age and who have chronic health problems should consult with a doctor.
Measles, Mumps, Rubella (MMR)	Adults born after 1956 should receive one dose of the MMR vaccine. Some adults may need a second dose and should check with their doctors.
Hepatitis B (Hep B)	Adults who are at risk of exposure to hepatitis B (through blood or blood-contaminated body fluids) should receive this vaccine. Any at-risk adults should check with their doctors.
Varicella (VAR)	Health professionals recommend that adults who have not had chicken pox receive two doses of this vaccine.

Source: Adapted from the Centers for Disease Control and Prevention Adolescent/Adult Immunization Recommendations.

Prescriptions & OTC Drugs

Older adults tend to take more medications than younger people. Chances are they take one or more prescription drugs and over-the-counter (OTC) medicines. Older adults often take more medication than needed because they're trying to stay healthy. These medications may react with each other and cause bigger health problems. All physicians who treat older adults should know all of the medications that they take, including OTC drugs. Combining medications is known as polypharmacy. **Polypharmacy** refers to problems that can occur when more medications are taken than needed and is a major concern for older adults. See Fig. 6-14.

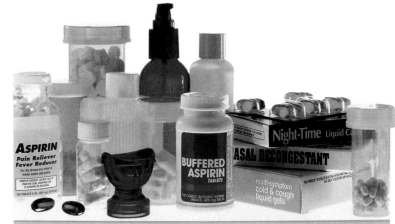

FIG. 6-14. **Polypharmacy can be a serious problem for older adults who may take a number of prescription medications and OTC medications. As a care provider for older adults, what should you observe about your clients' behavior that may indicate a problem?**

Intergenerational *Interactions*

Helping Children & Older Adults Cope with Disasters

Regardless of where you live, you probably have a disaster plan in place. Perhaps your home or neighborhood has a shelter to protect you from natural disasters like tornadoes, hurricanes, and floods, or you've prepared a plan to escape nonweather disasters like house fires. Even when we think we're prepared for potential disasters, the balance of everyday life still can be upset by unexpected turmoil. All age groups have difficulty dealing with disaster aftermath, but children and older adults often have an even harder time coping. Of course physical injuries are the most urgent emergencies; however, it's also important to protect the emotional health of children and older adults following a disaster. Here are some tips you may use to ensure the emotional well-being of disaster victims.

1. **Listen to Fears.** Small children and older adults, especially those who have little social interaction with people outside their homes or shelters, can become fearful. By listening to their fears and reassuring them about their safety, you can ease their worries.

2. **Resume Routines.** Sticking to regular eating, sleeping, and working schedules can help establish a sense of normalcy among children and older adults. Routines can also help reduce the feelings of anxiety brought on by disorder and unrest.

3. **Include All Generations When Making Plans.** When children and older adults are left out of decision-making processes, they may feel helpless in moving forward. By including these age groups in planning, they can gain a sense of security about their future.

4. **Consider Professional Help.** If children and older adults show ongoing signs of shock, denial, and anxiousness after a disaster, they may need counseling. By talking to a professional who listens without judgment, children and older adults can minimize harmful post-trauma symptoms.

5. **Monitor Media Exposure.** Media coverage following a disaster can be helpful to older adults who don't have contact with many people outside their home. However, for children and some older adults, media coverage can be overwhelming and frightening. If you determine how TV, radio, and newspaper coverage are affecting the child or older adult, you can then limit access to media coverage as needed.

Follow-Up

Make a list of additional ways you could help children and older adults cope with disaster. Then, to assist each of you in helping disaster victims, share your tips with your classmates.

FIG. 6-15. **Providing the right nutritious food choices is essential for older adults to maintain their health.** How might meals be handled for those older adults who have specific diet restrictions?

Issues Related to Illness

Illness in older adults can be caused by a variety of things. Some of these factors include stress, poor nutrition practices, and a lack of wellness education.

Stress. If stress is not handled properly, it can cause illness in people at any age and is particularly hazardous as people get older. **Stress** is the tension people feel when they face a situation that is different, new, unpleasant, or threatening. Some stress is good and helps people meet life's challenges, as long as they manage it properly. However, too much unpleasant stress is unhealthy and can lead to illness, depression, and other serious problems. Different factors can cause stress in older adults. Living alone, having financial worries, or having too much or too little leisure time causes some older adults stress. Lack of transportation or caring for a spouse with an illness or disability also causes stress in older adults.

Nutrition Practices. As people age, they go through biological, psychological, and social changes. The nutrition practices of older adults affect their health in all developmental areas. Some older adults may not be able to prepare nutritious meals to meet the demands of their bodies. Living on lower, fixed incomes also prevents many older adults from buying nutritious foods. See Section 10-2 for more on nutrition for older adults. See Fig. 6-15.

Wellness Education. Good health requires that people practice lifelong wellness principles, such as good nutrition, regular exercise and activities, and social interaction. Wellness education includes a variety of activities and programs that encourage health and independence. To help older adults stay active, wellness programs often include organized trips or tours to the theater or ballet, museums, historic sites, shopping malls, or sports events. Wellness programs also include transportation services. These services may also provide people to accompany older adults on their trips to the doctor, adult day programs, or community centers. Older adults can also enroll in different lifelong education classes including painting, creative writing, and fitness programs. See Fig. 6-16.

FIG. 6-16. **Helping older adults with wellness issues is part of the responsibility of adult day care providers.** Investigate wellness issues that are of concern for older adults.

homes longer as they age. Here are some likely safety hazards that often impact older adults:

- **Falls** are the most common home accidents for older adults. People can fall from ladders or stairs, and they can trip or slip on floors or sidewalks.

- **Fires and burns** are the next common type of home accident. Burns and asphyxiation (as-fihk-see-A-shuhn) from smoke or toxic fumes are the major health risks associated with fires. Young children and older adults are often victims of fire.

- **Suffocation** from ingesting or inhaling food particles is the most common cause of death to older adults at home.

Safety Practices for Older Adults

Older adults must practice safety at home and at adult day programs. It is important for care providers to know basic first aid practices and how to use first aid supplies. Adult care professionals must know emergency techniques and how to assist others.

Safety Practices for Home

Making the home safe is most important because home is the place where people spend most of their time. In many cases, care providers can help older adults and their family members make the home safer. Home modifications can help older adults practice independent living activities—such as, bathing, cooking, and climbing stairs—in an easy and safe manner. See Fig. 6-17. These modifications help accommodate lifestyle and increase comfort and overall safety. They also allow people to live in their

FIG. 6-17. **Making minor repairs may be all that is necessary to keep an older adult safe at home.** What other precautions should be taken to keep older adults safe at home?

Independence Skills

Preventing Falls

The number of accidents due to falls increases as people get older. Many older adults suffer from injuries or die as a result of falling. Here are some tips for preventing falls.

1. Check the arrangement of furniture. Clear walking paths of all furniture, electrical cords, and the telephone cords. Make sure lighting is adequate. Consider placing night-lights in wall sockets in all hallways and rooms.

2. Check for fixtures that allow for extra support. Grab bars placed in bathrooms and rails placed along stairways and halls provide anchors for support.

3. Check the placement of items in cabinets. Frequently used items should be placed within easy reach to avoid the need for stools and ladders.

4. Check for rugs that can cause tripping and surfaces that can cause slipping. Secure loose rugs with double-sided sticky tape or remove them. Place non-slip mats or non-slip strips in showers and tubs.

5. Check the medicine cabinet for medications that are old or outdated. Some medications cause drowsiness or dizziness so their effects should be monitored.

6. Encourage older adults to get regular eye exams and remind them to wear their glasses if prescribed. A physician may also prescribe a regular exercise program to improve balance and increase strength and coordination to help prevent falls.

7. Help older adults select shoes that are low-heeled and well fitting. Shoe soles should not be slick.

Try It!
Volunteer to help an older adult check his or her environment for hazards that could cause him or her to fall. List the changes made and share your list with the class.

- **Poisonings** are usually associated with young children, but frequently affect older adults, too. Drugs, medicine, poisonous foods, and carbon monoxide are common dangers for older adults.

- **Firearms, drowning, and electrical shock** are common causes of accidental deaths and injuries in and around the home.

You can avoid many of the accidents and deaths by following a home-safety checklist. You can get a home-safety checklist from your local center for emergency services, health department, or Cooperative Extension Agency.

Safety Practices for Adult Day Centers

The design of adult day centers should comply with ADA laws and accommodate individuals with disabilities. The facility and the outside environment should be safe, clean, and accessible to all participants. It should also meet Occupational Safety and Health Administration (OSHA) guidelines. See Fig. 6-18.

First Aid Principles & Supplies

First aid is the care that is first given to an injured or sick person after an accident or illness. When working with older adults, you will be required to take a course in first aid. You can receive first aid training from the American Red Cross. In addition, you can receive **cardiopulmonary resuscitation** (CAR-dee-oh-PULL-muh-NAIR-ee ree-SUH-suhTAY-shun) (CPR) training through the American Heart Association. CPR is a life-saving technique used when the heartbeat has stopped.

The first principle of first aid is immediate action. Your first line of defense is to have emergency phone numbers for the doctor, hospital, emergency center, ambulance, police, fire department, poison control center, and the victim's relatives near the phone. Another important piece of first aid is the first aid kit. This kit can contain many items, depending on the environment where it is needed. Most workplace environments will require you to have a first aid kit. It is very important that you check the contents of the first aid kit periodically and replace missing items. You should note the expiration dates on the items that are kept in the kit. See Section 6-3 for more information on CPR.

Emergency Plans & Drills

When you are working with older adults, it is a good idea to understand their physical conditions and adhere to the basic safety plans. You can obtain an emergency plan by contacting the Office of Emergency Services (OES) in your area. If you are working in an area that is unfamiliar, you should find out from the OES what types of disasters are most likely to happen in that area. Request information on how to prepare for each type of disaster. Also, find out how to best assist older adults in emergency situations, such as hurricanes, tornadoes, earthquakes, and blizzards. You can also obtain information on preparing for emergencies from the American Red Cross. See Fig. 6-19.

FIG. 6-18.

MODIFICATION & REPAIRS THAT PREVENT ACCIDENTS

Problem	Solution
Difficulty getting in and out of the restroom.	Install grab bars or transfer benches.
Slipping in the restroom.	Place nonskid strips or decals on the floor.
Difficulty turning faucet handles or doorknobs.	Replace knobs with lever handles.
Unable to access day center.	Install ramps.
Inadequate heating or ventilation.	Install insulation, storm windows, and air conditioning.
Problems climbing stairs.	Install handrails for support.

Disaster Plans & Drills

Older adults should understand the day center's disaster plan. Explain and share the emergency evacuation plan with them and answer their questions. You may need to walk them through the escape routes from different areas of the facility. It is a good idea to have each of the older adults that you work with to participate in a first aid and CPR training.

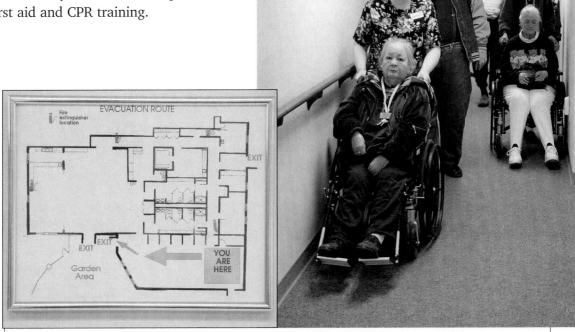

FIG. 6-19. Emergency plans and drills must be tailored to the clients in the care center. Why must care providers know the abilities of each older adult in order to respond in a life-saving manner?

Section 6-2 Knowledge Check

1. How can maintaining a wellness plan help older adults stay in good health?

2. What are some of the reasons why older adults experience stress?

3. Identify ways to prevent the most common accidents that affect older adults.

Mini-Lab

Alone or with your classmates, complete a standard course in first aid through the American Red Cross or the American Heart Association.

Section **6-3**

Health & Safety for Staff

OBJECTIVES

- Describe procedures to maintain the health and safety of all staff members.
- Identify procedures to limit the health and safety risks to staff members.
- Summarize the emergency skills training needed by staff members.

Human service programs must do more than protect their clients' health and safety. They must also protect the health and safety of the human service staff, too. This section will discuss procedures and training to help ensure staff member health and safety.

KEY TERMS

**foodservice sanitation certificate
toxins
Heimlich maneuver
automated external defibrillation (AED)**

Ensuring Staff Health & Safety

The Occupational Safety and Health Administration (OSHA) provides guidelines to which child and adult day centers must adhere. These guidelines for safety and health program management help employers prevent occupational injuries and illness. Under the Occupational Safety and Health Act, OSHA has the authority to mandate these guidelines.

All staff members are required to submit a physician's report verifying their good health. In addition, each staff member must receive a negative result on a tuberculosis test. To limit their vulnerability to contagious disease, staff should get regular immunizations, such as influenza, tetanus-diphtheria, and Hepatitis B.

In order to help maintain the health and safety of center participants, staff members at

child or adult day centers should obtain a first aid certificate and a CPR certificate. In addition, many states require people who work with children and older adults to be fingerprinted. Their fingerprints are then put through a criminal background check. Those who do not pass the criminal background check are not hired to work with children or older adults. See Fig. 6-20.

Sick-Leave Policies. Employers with generous sick-leave policies encourage their staff to stay home when they have a contagious disease. Most sick-leave policies allow staff to save unused sick days. In addition to sick leave, the Family and Medical Leave Act of 1993 allows employees to have up to 12 weeks of unpaid, job-protected leave. During this time, employees can keep their health benefits, but probably will need to pay for them. Employees are required to have documentation and supervisory approval to be granted the 12 weeks of unpaid leave.

Staff Substitutes. Centers should keep a list of qualified staff substitutes who can provide good care for clients even when regular staff must be absent. When a staff member is absent from work, it is the supervisor's responsibility to find another worker to fill the position. In some adult day centers, volunteer staff members assist the paid staff. When paid staff members are absent, the center director can draw from a pool of volunteers to fulfill the job duties.

Certifying Foodservice Staff. Most foodservice staff in child and adult day centers are certified to handle food by the local health department foodservice unit. To reduce chances of illness caused by mishandled or tainted food, foodservice staff must be regularly trained in proper food-handling and sanitation practices. Managers may be required to obtain a **foodservice sanitation certificate** showing that they passed a state-administered test covering proper

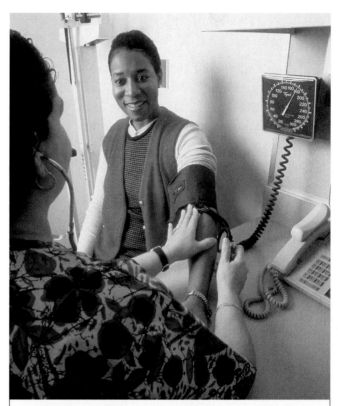

FIG. 6-20. **Care providers need to have routine health exams and immunizations to be certain they are healthy and capable of caring for their clients.** Why should care providers be immunized against contagious diseases?

Protection Plans. To protect staff members from exposure to contagious diseases passed through blood, programs must have and follow a written plan. According to OSHA, the plans must contain the following:

- **Exposure Determination.** A list of job titles or duties that put staff in contact with blood or blood-containing fluids, such as first aid treatment or diapering.
- **Methods of Compliance.** A statement of how staff will follow the plan, in terms of limiting exposure to blood, following universal precautions, and cleaning and sanitizing or disinfecting.
- **Hepatitis B Vaccination.** Employers must offer vaccinations within ten days of employment at no cost to staff.

foodservice practices. Foodservice staff should also follow the *Healthy People 2010* Food Safety Guidelines. These guidelines outline five basic food-safety practices:

- **Clean.** Use universal precautions for hand washing. Sanitize all food preparation surfaces and cooking utensils.
- **Separate.** Do not cross-contaminate foods. Keep different types of foods separate during preparation. Clean and sanitize the workspace before preparing another type of food.
- **Cook.** Prepare foods to the proper temperature, according to Food Code guidelines provided by the USDA and the FDA.
- **Chill.** Refrigerate foods promptly at 41°F or below, according to Food Code guidelines.
- **Serve.** Hot foods should be served at 140°F or above and cold foods at 41°F or below.

Avoiding Workplace Risks

Day center staff can experience a variety of workplace risks. Good programs take steps to reduce the risk of staff members becoming ill or injured while performing their jobs.

Requiring staff to consistently follow universal precautions reduces their exposure to contagious disease and harmful substances, called **toxins**, that are in certain cleaning, sanitation, or pest-control products. Toxins can cause different illnesses, from rashes to flu-like illness. See Section 6-1 for more information on universal precautions.

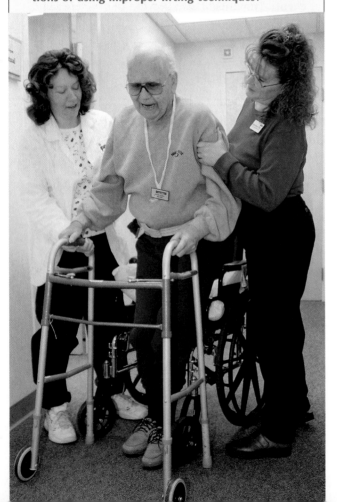

FIG. 6-21. **Using proper lifting techniques allows care providers to lift older adults without injury to themselves or their client.** What are the implications of using improper lifting techniques?

Proper Lifting Procedures

Because staff members may be required to lift or move very young or very old clients, they must be trained in proper lifting techniques. This training ensures that staff can do their job without neck and back injuries.

When moving or lifting children or older adults, you should encourage them to assist you as much as possible. When they help you, it encourages independence. To get the full cooperation of children and older adults, explain what you are trying to do and ask for their help. With older adults, be sure their privacy is maintained. When lifting people, be careful to lift them without dragging them. Dragging can cause the fragile skin of older adults to tear. See Fig. 6-21. Use the following principles when lifting or moving an older adult:

1. **Stand Properly.** Stand with your feet apart, knees slightly flexed, and one foot forward. Keep your head and trunk upright and in proper alignment.

2. **Keep Your Balance.** To save energy and keep your balance, hold the weight as close to your own center of gravity as possible.

3. **Know Your Limits.** Do not attempt to lift someone alone especially if you have any doubts about your ability to do so.

4. **Lift with Your Legs.** Keep your legs positioned so that they supply most of the force for shifting your trunk. Shift weight from one leg to another during the lifting procedure. Do not attempt to lift with your back alone. Bend your knees and hips, rather than your back.

5. **Use Your Whole Body.** Your whole body must work together as a unit as you complete Steps 1 through 4 when lifting another person. When lifting with another person, use a counting system (1, 2, 3, lift).

6. **Work as a Team.** When several people are moving a person, the person who is lifting the heaviest part, or who is pushing should give direction. Avoid jerky movements.

Emergency-Skills Training

Because children and older adults are more at risk for injury, center staff must be able to respond to emergencies. If a participant requires medical treatment, a staff member should be on hand to give appropriate first aid, while someone else calls for emergency medical assistance. Occasionally a participant's injury can even be life threatening. Staff should have emergency-skills training to respond to these situations.

Choking. Choking happens to both children and older adults. An important factor in identifying choking, however, is inability to speak and discoloration of the face. A choking victim can become red, pale, or somewhat bluish in color. Choking victims need immediate attention. An important technique to remedy choking in conscious adults and children older than one year of age is the **Heimlich maneuver** (HIME-lick muh-NOO-vuhr). See Fig. 6-22A. With this technique, pressure on the diaphragm is used to dislodge an object that is blocking air through the windpipe or throat. A diagram that shows and explains how to use the Heimlich maneuver should be posted in the eating area, and staff members should be trained to use the procedure. This maneuver should not be used on infants because of the possibility of internal injury. With conscious infants, trained staff members use a first aid procedure called back blows and chest compressions.

Rescue Breathing. When a person stops breathing but has a heartbeat, it is important for care providers to breathe for them. This is called rescue breathing. During rescue breathing, the victim's head is tilted back, the chin is lifted, and the nose is pinched shut. The rescuer then seals his or her mouth over the victim's and gives a breath about every five seconds.

Staff members must be certified to perform rescue breathing.

Cardiopulmonary Resuscitation (CPR). Staff must be certified in CPR before they can apply the technique. CPR is used when no heartbeat or pulse is detected for 10-12 seconds. Gentle puffs of air are given to the person along with compression of the chest to help the heart circulate blood. CPR can be used for suffocation, drug overdose, electrical shock, choking, drowning, and heart failure. CPR can keep a person alive until emergency medical professionals arrive. The American Red Cross provides excellent first aid and CPR training that can be used with infants, children, and adults. See Fig. 6-22B.

Automated External Defibrillation (AED). Many states are now requiring that early childhood and adult care providers be trained in automated external defibrillation. This procedure is used when there has been a disruption in a person's regular heart rhythm. Disease or an injury can cause sudden cardiac arrest. **Automated external defibrillation**, or AED, requires an electrical shock that reestablishes a

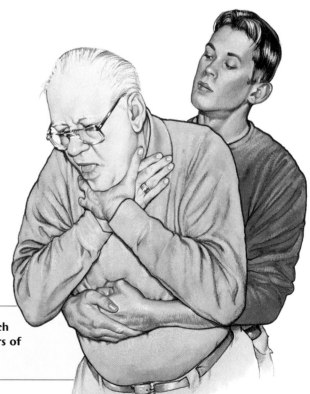

FIG. 6-22A. **Certification in the Heimlich Maneuver is required for care providers of older adults and children.**

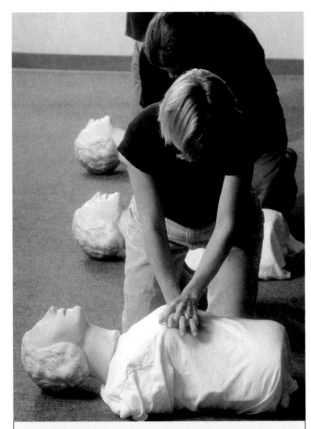

FIG. 6-22B. Certification in CPR and AED are essential for all care providers. What other emergency skills should a care provider learn in order to more fully care for the participants in his or her care?

normal heart rhythm. Early CPR will help circulate oxygen-containing blood to vital body organs while an AED is prepared for use. An automated external defibrillator is a machine that analyzes heart rhythm and tells the care provider to deliver a shock to a cardiac-arrest victim. The AED will also tell the care provider when no shock is advised. Care providers can obtain AED training and certification from the American Red Cross. See Fig. 6-22C.

Accidental Poisoning. Poisoning is a serious medical emergency. Figure 6-23 contains a list of some poisonous substances children and older adults may encounter. Signs that may indicate poisoning include:

- Burns around or in the mouth and throat.
- Vomiting from swallowing poisons.

- Burns or rash on the skin from direct contact with poisons or chemicals.
- Burning or irritation of the eyes or blindness caused by poisons or chemicals coming in contact with the eyes.
- Choking, coughing, headache, nausea, or dizziness from inhaling fumes, sprays, or poisonous gases.

If poisoning is suspected, quickly try to determine the cause. Immediately call a poison control center and follow its directions. Be prepared to give the following information when you call:

- Symptoms the person displays.
- The person's age and weight.
- Substance that poisoned the person, if you know.
- When and how much poison was ingested, if it was swallowed.
- The list of ingredients on the product container, if possible.

Handling Emergency Evacuations

When an emergency requires that care providers evacuate children or older adults from the care facility, care providers must act swiftly and calmly. Regular emergency drills will help care providers, children, and older adults to know what to do in case of a real emergency.

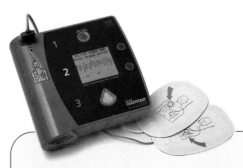

FIG. 6-22C. An automated external defibrillator (AED) is a machine that provides an electrical shock that reestablishes a normal heart rhythm. Why is an AED used only when the heart has stopped beating?

FIG. 6-23.

POISONOUS SUBSTANCES

Plants	• English ivy, daffodil bulbs, rhubarb leaves, holly berries, poison ivy and oak. • Poisoning occurs through the skin and by swallowing the substance.
Medicine	• Aspirin, sleeping pills, tranquilizers, vitamins, and cold and allergy preparations. • Poisoning occurs by swallowing.
Cleaning Products	• Ammonia, laundry detergent, bleach, drain and toilet bowl cleaners, disinfectants, and furniture polish. • Poisoning occurs through inhalation, contact with skin and eyes, and by swallowing the substance.
Personal Care Products	• Shampoo, soap, nail polish and polish remover, perfumes and aftershave lotions, mouthwash, rubbing alcohol, and sunscreens and lotions. • Poisoning occurs through eye contact, inhalation, and swallowing.
Miscellaneous Products	• Insecticides, insect repellant, paint thinner, paint, and rodent poison. • Poisoning occurs through contact with skin and eyes, inhalation, and by swallowing.

Here are some tips for care providers in handling emergency evacuations:

- Immediately get children or older adults out of the building via the closest emergency exit and to a safe place when an emergency occurs that requires evacuation. Do not stop to get coats, shoes, purses, or medicines. Do not even finish diapering a baby if you need to evacuate.

- Designate one care provider to grab the sign-in sheet so that children and older adults can be accounted for once in a safe place.

- Put all infants into one evacuation crib that is on wheels to speed evacuation. Infants should always be cared for on the main floor of a facility for ease in evacuation.

- Toddlers and other children may need to be carried to safety by care providers. Older adults with mobility problems may need to be put into wheelchairs for swift evacuation.

Regardless of the emergency, the important thing for care providers is to get everyone in their care to a safe place. You can obtain more information about how to handle specific emergencies from the American Red Cross or your local Office of Emergency Services (OES).

Section Knowledge Check

1. List at least three health and safety requirements for child and adult care staff.

2. Describe the procedure for properly lifting or moving an older adult.

3. What circumstances could require staff to implement emergency skills?

Mini-Lab

Alone or with a partner, take a CPR course and an AED course from the American Red Cross.

6
Review & Activities

Section Summaries

6-1 Staff can limit the spread of contagious disease.

6-1 Universal precautions are the best protection against contagious disease.

6-1 Safety policies and procedures require staff to identify and reduce risks of injury.

6-2 Good health practices include: nutrition awareness, physical fitness, environmental awareness, and regular medical screening.

6-2 Polypharmacy is the process of taking and mixing various types of over-the-counter and prescription medications.

6-2 To maintain good health throughout the lifespan it is important to practice lifelong wellness principles.

6-2 First aid is the initial care for an injured or sick person.

6-3 OSHA is a branch of the federal government that sets guidelines to ensure safety and health program management.

6-3 Emergency-skills training helps staff respond immediately during emergencies.

6-3 Four basic food safety practices include: wash hands and surfaces; do not cross-contaminate; cook foods to proper temperature; and refrigerate leftover foods promptly.

6-3 Care providers should have at minimum a first aid certificate, CPR certificate, fingerprint processing, proof of current good health (signed by a physician), and a tuberculosis test.

Check Your Knowledge

1. In what ways can the spread of contagious disease be limited?
2. What are the proper solutions for sanitizing and disinfecting materials?
3. What types of immunizations help maintain health?
4. Describe special health conditions human service professionals might encounter.
5. What should be included in a risk-management plan?
6. What health and wellness practices are needed by older adults?
7. Why is polypharmacy a major health concern for older adults?
8. What factors contribute to the health and safety of staff members?
9. Contrast rescue breathing and CPR. When is each used?
10. What are the signs of accidental poisoning?

Thinking Critically

1. Draw conclusions regarding perspectives that may differ from your own regarding immunizations. Should parents be able to decide not to immunize their children against contagious diseases? Why or why not?

2. Consider the effects of stereotyping on special needs children. How might special needs children be stereotyped by other children and adults? What can human services workers do to eradicate negative stereotypes about these children?

3. Compare and contrast safety precautions appropriate for young children and older adults. How are safety precautions for young children and older adults similar? How do they differ?

4. Take a stand regarding the need to protect the health and safety of care providers. How important is it for care providers to protect their own health and safety?

Practical Applications

1. **Health Check.** Obtain a copy of the health-check procedures from a local child care facility. Under a human service professional's guidance conduct a health check for several children or older adults.

2. **Safety Checklist.** Develop a safety checklist for use in evaluating an older adult's living space. Use the checklist to evaluate the residence of an older adult you know.

3. **Emergency Preparedness.** Investigate the Web site for the American Red Cross. Locate resources to help care providers prepare for emergencies, such as hurricanes, earthquakes, floods, tornadoes, terrorism, and other disasters.

Building Your PORTFOLIO

Developing a Safety Policy

Employers will want to know that you can plan effectively to maintain the safety of the young children or older adults in your care. Use the following steps to develop a safety plan.

Step 1: Collect safety policies from several local human service program directors. Review the policies and list the types of information that are usually included.

Step 2: Develop a safety policy for a child care facility, an adult day care, or an intergenerational facility. Be sure to include information on the topics addressed in this chapter.

Step 3: Research suggested contents for a first aid kit for a child care facility or an adult care facility. Make a list of suggested contents. If possible assemble a first aid kit for one of these facilities.

Step 4: Interview a human service provider to obtain information on the health and safety training provided for staff. Based on the information obtained, create a training schedule for the coming year.

Step 5: In your portfolio, include your safety policy, list of suggested contents for a first aid kit, and training schedule for human service staff members.

Chapter 7

Observation Skills

Section 7-1
Observing Children

Section 7-2
Observing Older Adults

Section 7-1

Observing Children

OBJECTIVES

- Explain why care providers observe and record children's behavior.
- Identify specific types of observation.
- Summarize behaviors that show children's development.
- Describe items to include in a child's portfolio that will reflect development.

KEY TERMS

objective observations
subjective description
naturalistic observation
participant observer
anecdotal record
running record
frequency count
checklist
rating scale

Firsthand observation of children gives care providers insight into children's behavior. It helps them assess children's development, so they can plan experiences to respond to and nurture that development. It takes practice to become a skilled observer, but the knowledge you gain through observations will help you make sound judgments.

Why Observe Children?

Those who work with children never stop observing. Child care staff systematically record details of observations and put these details to use in different ways. The reasons why early childhood staff observe and record children's behavior include to:

- **Know individual children better.** Observations help care providers learn about each child's abilities, interests, and level of development.

- **Identify special needs.** Observation records help determine whether a child needs special services or programs, such as speech therapy, counseling, or a gifted program.

- **Address specific problems.** Observing children helps care providers respond wisely and sensitively to problem behaviors.

- **Guide curriculum development.** Motivating learning experiences are planned based on children's observed play, interests, and abilities.

- **Document progress and assess skill development.** Care providers and parents want to know how children are progressing in their development. When observation records are kept, development can be tracked. This information helps guide activity planning.

- **Evaluate the program.** Observations help staff determine if all the program goals are being met effectively and efficiently.

FIG. 7-1. **As an early childhood professional, you will have an opportunity to observe the development of children in a number of settings.** How can early childhood professionals benefit from observing children?

- **Learn about child development.** Even the most experienced early childhood staff members gain a deeper understanding of children from firsthand observation. See Fig. 7-1.

Becoming a Skilled Observer

It may seem easy to watch children at play, but developing a keen eye for detail requires effort and practice. Concentration and a good attention span result in better observations. Learning how to observe without interfering takes skill, too. This section includes ways to build your observation skills.

Observer Conduct

Whenever you observe children, your goal is to see what would naturally happen if you were not present. Observers should do their best not to detract or influence the activity they observe. It is important to be quiet, courteous, and respectful to children and staff you observe. When there is not a separate observation booth or room, follow these guidelines for observer conduct:

- Sit in a low chair.
- Position yourself off to the side but where you can still observe easily.
- Wear simple, appropriate clothing.
- Do not start a conversation with children or maintain prolonged eye contact.
- If a child asks what you are doing, give a brief but honest answer. You might say, "I am writing down how children play so I can remember it later."
- Do not interfere in what is going on unless a child is in immediate danger and no other adult is available.

FIG. 7-2. **As part of maintaining confidentiality, do not share your observation notes with coworkers other than your director. You might consider maintaining your observations in a password-protected computer file.** Why is maintaining confidentiality important?

ETHICS IN Action

Breaking Confidence. While waiting for children to leave at the end of the day, you hear a staff member sharing confidential information about a child in the program with an adult who is not the child's parent. She elaborates on how the child often misbehaves and requires too much adult attention. She goes on to say the child is the troublemaker of the class because he never sits still during circle time. *How would you react to your staff member sharing such information? How would the parents of the "trouble-making" child feel about their child being discussed publicly? What would you do to remedy the situation? What would you say and to whom?*

Ethics & Confidentiality

To ensure that the privacy of a child and family is protected, observation records must remain confidential. Do not leave them in open view for others to see. If the records will be shared with people other than the child's program staff, a custodial parent or legal guardian must give written permission. If observations are used in research, consider using false names or initials to identify children who have been observed. See Fig. 7-2.

Making Objective Observations

Observations are not useful unless they reflect what really happens. It is important for observers to keep facts separate from personal opinions, preferences, or bias. **Objective observations**

record facts rather than personal opinion or bias. An objective observation might say: "Shannon walked into the room with her head held down. She was dragging her sweater on the ground behind her." A **subjective description**, on the other hand, is an observation based on personal judgments and might state: "Shannon was depressed as she came into the room."

While you observe, your job is to record facts. Later, you can think about your impressions of what took place. Was Shannon depressed, or was she tired, ill, lonely, or disappointed? Do you have enough information to decide? Others may want to read what you have recorded and draw their own conclusions.

Objective observations require you to record only what you actually see happen, not what you hear about secondhand. Do not record that a child hit another unless you actually saw it happen. You may, however, report that a child told you someone was hit. The difference is small but very important. See Fig. 7-3.

FIG. 7-3. **Make clear unbiased observation statements when recording your observations of children.** What may be the consequences of making subjective rather than objective observation statements?

Recorded observations should include the following:

- Your name so that others will know who made the observation.
- The date and the beginning and ending time.
- A list of children involved and their ages. Also note any adults involved.
- Identification and brief description of the setting.
- Specific behaviors and events in the order they happen.

Interpreting Observations

Observations are of little use if they are just filed away and never used. When reviewed and interpreted, however, they give information that can be helpful. To interpret something is to explain its meaning. When interpreting observations, early childhood staff look for *patterns* and try to draw conclusions about the causes and meaning of behavior.

Interpretations must always be made with care. Experienced professionals resist drawing conclusions based on one observation. Instead, they review a series of observations. These may have been collected over several days, weeks, or months. Professionals base their interpretations on facts, experience, and training. They do not base them on personal likes and dislikes. Care providers also make interpretations in light of a child's individual culture and past experiences. Behavior that is respectful in one family or culture may not be acceptable in another. Wise care providers realize that their interpretation is only an educated guess, so before interpreting facts, they consult with a child's family for clearer understanding.

Observation Style

Observing is a purposeful, structured task. It can be done in several ways. Researchers sometimes place children in special experimental situations to see how they react. However, early childhood staff are more likely to observe children in their regular daily setting.

Naturalistic Observation

Care providers in the classroom commonly use a style of observation called **naturalistic observation**. It means the observer watches children and records their natural behaviors as they occur.

With this style the observer is called a **participant observer**, someone who interacts with children while observing. The participant observer still talks to the children and leads them in activities. During the activities, he or she notices details about the children's behavior and writes these details on index cards or a note pad.

FIG. 7-4. Some observations are done while you participate in activities with children. What are the pros and cons of this style of observation?

Anecdotal Record

Date: 9/23   **Time:** 11:15 a.m.
Setting: Dramatic Play Center   **Observed by:** Karen
Child: Courtney, age four

Observation: After Courtney played alone in the dramatic play center, she started to leave. All of the dress-up clothes she had used were on the floor. When reminded of the rule for putting things away, Courtney walked away. After a second reminder, Courtney said, "I don't have to." Miss Winn responded, "You'll miss out on snack time. When you pick up the clothes, you can join us."

FIG. 7-5.

The naturalistic style of observing is convenient, but it also has drawbacks. When you interact with children, you become a part of the situation you are observing. This makes it impossible to step back and see the situation as an outsider. In addition, thinking about what you are doing can distract you from what you are observing. Finally, you may not have time to record your observations right away or in as much detail as you would like.

For these reasons, it might be better if someone who is strictly an observer makes these observations. This person might be one of the classroom staff, who is temporarily assigned to observe rather than participate. It might also be a child care student, like you, who is visiting the classroom for the purpose of recording observations. See Fig. 7-4.

Sometimes the observer actually sits in another room and watches children through a one-way window. This is a special type of window that the observer can see through but that looks like a mirror to the children on the other side. More often, the observer has no choice but to sit in the same room with the children. In that case, the observer must take care to stay in the background as much as possible.

Observation Methods

Care providers use several systematic methods for recording observations. The method you choose depends on your purpose for observing. Some commonly used methods are described and illustrated here. Note that the examples in the illustrations are incomplete. They are intended to give you an idea about what these records are like.

Anecdotal Record. A written description that focuses on a particular incident is called an **anecdotal record** (ANN-ik-DOH-tul). Care providers might use an anecdotal record to observe how a child interacts with classroom materials and how his or her development is enhanced by these experiences. The record includes where and when the incident took place, who was involved, and what was said and done. For instance, you might write an anecdotal record about the interaction among several children in the dramatic play area on a certain day. You would describe everything the children do and say, including tone of voice, facial expressions, and body language. See Fig. 7-5.

Intergenerational Interactions

Observing Intergenerational Activities

As you just learned, observing child care and older adult care programs is very important. The same is true in building a successful intergenerational program. Without evaluating the participants and their activities, program planners would not learn how to organize a program to benefit all generations. Careful observation helps program planners:

- **Develop Programs.** Observing older adults interacting with children helps program planners decide which activities interest the participants. If children and older adults enjoy reading together, program planners can set aside more time for that particular activity.

- **Match Participants.** Everybody has different interests. By observing intergenerational activity participants, planners can determine which older adults and children may get along better than others. For example, older adults who love the outdoors may enjoy teaming with teens interested in landscaping careers.

- **Identify Problems.** Typically, there are few problems associated with intergenerational programs; however, it's important to quickly identify any that do exist. For instance, an older adult who tires easily may not be well suited for an activity involving a tireless toddler. Before the older adult's patience wears thin, the observer can pair the youngster

with an older adult who enjoys active children.

- **Document Progress.** The purpose of all intergenerational programs is to improve the quality of life for those who participate. By closely observing older adults and children, care providers can see even the smallest improvements in program participants. Perhaps an older adult smiles more frequently since being introduced to a toddler. A teen may take more interest in studying history after talking to an older adult who lived through the Great Depression. Without observation, subtle progress may be overlooked.

Follow-Up

Create a list of ways an intergenerational program planner could observe activities. Then determine what can be learned through those types of observation.

Running Record. With a **running record**, the observer creates a sequential record of anything that happens during a specific period of time. The time period may be as short as ten minutes or may last all day. The observer may write down everything that happens during the time period or may observe and record at specific intervals within the time period. For example, a staff member may want to identify a toddler's developmental abilities. The staff member decides to observe for ten minutes. During this time, the staff member writes what the toddler is doing each minute. When completed, the notes provide insight into the child's current skills. See Fig. 7-6.

Frequency Count. A record of how many times a particular behavior or situation occurs during a specific period of time is called a **frequency count**. A tally sheet is used for recording this information. The observation may focus on one child or include several children. Repeating the frequency count at a later date can help you see whether the behavior is occurring more or less often than before. For example, to find out how often hitting incidents occurred on the playground, a preschool teacher made five observations during the day. Each observation period was three minutes long. No notes were made; only a tally mark indicated each hitting episode. Totaling the tally marks gave an indication of how serious the problem was. Later, after further investigation and corrective measures, another frequency count showed that the number of hitting incidents had decreased. See Fig. 7-7.

FIG. 7-6.

 Running Record

Date: 2/5   **Time Segment:** 10:00-10:10 a.m.
Gender: male   **Age:** 2 1/2
Child Observed: Nathan   **Observed by:** Sue

Time	Observation
10:00-10:01 a.m.	Nathan walked over to the sand and water table. He picked up a cup and dipped some water and poured it out. Nathan repeated this action two more times.
10:01-10:02 a.m.	Nathan switched from dipping water to dipping sand. After spilling out the first cup of sand, Nathan looked inside the cup and said, "Sand stuck." He put the cup back into the sand.
10:02-10:03 a.m.	Nathan crawled over to the block center. He took a block from a little girl who was already playing in the center. The little girl cried. Nathan gave the block back.
10:03-10:04 a.m.	Nathan walked over to the shelving where blocks are stored and took several blocks off the shelf. He stacked the blocks on the floor and then knocked them over. He stacked the blocks again.

FIG. 7-7.

Frequency Count

Purpose: To see how many picture books were used during free play

Date: 10/17   **Time:** 2:00-2:30 p.m.

Setting: Language area   **Observed by:** Naomi

Child's Name and Age	Frequency (Number of Books)
Gretchen (4 yrs. 2 mos.)	II
Alex (4 yrs. 5 mos.)	
Cassie (3 yrs. 11 mos.)	IIII

Checklist. A **checklist** is simply a list of specific information for which a care provider is looking. It can be used to study the environment, but more often a checklist identifies behavior or skills that children are expected to develop. When the child demonstrates a behavior or skill, such as drinking from a cup, the care provider either makes a check mark or writes the date next to the appropriate item on the list. Additional space may be provided for comments or descriptions. Some care providers update each child's checklist weekly. Others may do so only twice a year. Checklists are useful for parent-teacher conferences because they can give parents a picture of how their child is developing.

Rating Scale. In a **rating scale**, the observer records a verbal or numerical evaluation of listed items. The listed items might focus on children's abilities or behaviors. The items might also focus on the characteristics of the center's environment. For example, the observer might rate a child's skill in performing a certain task on a scale of 1 to 5. As with checklists, rating scales are often used periodically throughout the year to give an overall picture of a child's development. Care providers may develop checklists and rating scales for their specific use. These items also can be purchased from suppliers of educational materials, many of which can be found on the Internet. See Fig. 7-8.

Assessing Children's Development

As you have read, people observe children for different reasons. Some reasons to observe are to identify a child's skills, needs, and rate of progress. To determine a child's overall development, you should observe him or her in a variety of situations over time. Take care to collect details about all areas of development, including physical, intellectual, social, and emotional.

FIG. 7-8.

◆ Rating Scale

Child's name: JaNelle   **Age:** 3 yrs. 2 mos.
Date: 4/16   **Time:** 9:00-9:30 a.m.
Observed by: Celia   **Setting:** Preschool Lab

Skill Observed: Language Skills

Skill	Always	Sometimes	Never
Speaks clearly enough to be understood		✔	
Uses past tense verbs correctly			✔
Uses correct word order when asking questions		✔	
Joins in conversations with other children		✔	

Observation records should be filed for later reference. Several easy systems can be used for keeping observations organized. All records that pertain to individual children should be placed together under each child's name. Some care providers keep a file folder for each child. Others place observation records in an accordion file or tabbed ring binder. Care providers should review the records periodically to make sure they are collecting adequate information about each child in the program.

Records that deal with certain situations can be organized and filed in some systematic manner. For example, a study of how often children use a particular toy on the playground might be filed under "active play."

Some of the basic things early childhood professionals look for in children's overall development are listed as follows. See Fig. 7-9.

Collecting Samples of Children's Work

Observation is one way to gather details about children's development. Another is collecting samples of their work and storing it for reference. These collections of work—often called portfolios or authentic assessment—can be shared during conferences to show parents examples of their child's progress. Children's art projects show their creativity and their ability to use their small muscles to handle art tools. Audiotapes of stories told to a care provider prove children's language, vocabulary, and ability to apply concepts. Videotapes of children during dress-up play allow observers to witness imagination and emerging social skills. Photos of children's block buildings show their understanding of size, shape, and spatial concepts.

FIG. 7-9.

OBSERVING DEVELOPMENT

Physical Development	• Signs of health: smooth, soft skin; clear, bright eyes; clear nose, not runny or stopped up and blocking breathing; clean teeth; firm, clean gums. • Changes in napping, toileting, or eating habits. • Evidence of large and fine motor skills. • Evidence of eye-hand coordination (when using blocks and puzzles, for example).
Intellectual Development	• Problem-solving ability. • Ability to recognize shapes, colors, numbers, sizes, and spatial relationships. • Vocabulary development and the ability to communicate effectively. • Use of imagination and creativity.
Social Development	• Social skills, such as sharing, cooperation, and taking turns. • Ability to follow directions and accept responsibility. • Number and types of friendships maintained. • Small and large group play skills.
Emotional Development	• Evidence of identity and self-esteem. • Methods of dealing with frustration. • Evidence of trust and attachment to classroom adults. • Ability to express feelings constructively.

Section 7-1 Knowledge Check

1. What are the purposes of observing children's behavior?
2. What should be provided in an observation record?
3. How can an observer make records objective?

Mini-Lab

Use the running-record method to observe and record a young child's behavior for ten minutes while a classmate does the same. Compare your observations with your classmate's and look for patterns of things each of you noticed. What conclusions can you draw about recording behavior?

Section 7-2

Observing Older Adults

OBJECTIVES

- Identify reasons why older adults need to be observed in an adult day center.
- Determine ways to observe older adults in adult day centers.
- Outline procedures for observing older adults in day centers.

KEY TERMS

subjective reporting
objective reporting
agitated
Activity of Daily
    Living (ADL)
radial pulse

When working with older adults, you will need to observe them. Observation can give you insight into their development, social interactions, and behavior. Through observation, you can gain the necessary knowledge and skills to better work with older adults.

Why Observe Older Adults?

Older adults participating in older adult centers need to be observed to determine the types of activities that can be offered. These activities should help them maintain and build their skills. Through observation, you can design programs that will maintain older adults' participation and their quality of life. Your program design will also help recruit others to the center.

Developing skills to observe the older adult population is very important. As you prepare for careers in the field of gerontology, you will have many opportunities to observe older adults in various settings. You will learn that all older adults will not have the same physical func-

tional abilities. They may all be able to participate in the same activities, but they might have different levels for participation. For example, they all might be able to participate in leg exercises. Some will be able to lift their legs higher than other older adults will. Through observation, you can determine how to design activities that will benefit all participants.

Sensory Techniques for Observing

You need to use all of your sensory skills to successfully observe older adults. Watching and listening are probably the most important skills to have. Making eye contact and being an attentive listener will help you learn about older adults. Many of the older adults who attend adult day centers go to socialize and will welcome your attention. The socialization period is an excellent time to observe the participants. Using skilled sensory techniques, such as watching and listening, you let them know that you are attentive to their concerns. You should also use body language that shows you are listening. You can photograph and videotape their activities while you observe so that you remember specific details that happened during your observation. Be sure to obtain permission from older adults and their family members before videotaping. See Fig. 7-10.

Communication for Observation

When communicating, it is important that you identify in advance the topic that is to be discussed or observed, so that you can stay focused. When working with older adults, it is important to make certain that they clearly

FIG. 7-10. Observing older adults during group activity periods may help you observe changes in behavior in physical skill from one session to another. How can noticing these changes give you clues to the well-being of your client?

understand the intent of your communication in order to avoid confusion. It is a good idea to encourage them to repeat what they heard you say and give you the opportunity to confirm your intention. This process keeps you aware of what the observation is about, and it keeps you on task.

To effectively communicate with older adults, it is a good idea for you to use "I" statements. For example, "I think," "I feel," and "I want." These statements will help you to communicate effectively and sensitively with older adults. Remember to verify information with them and practice mutual respect.

Observation Methods

Observation methods are ways people watch, examine, and study an activity during a certain time. Written comments record details about behavior and a separate analysis containing the care provider's opinion about the behavior. The following information describes different observation methods.

Subjective Reporting

Subjective reporting is often viewed as an informal type of observation. With **subjective reporting**, observers include their own personal ideas, thoughts, feelings, and attitudes in their records. This type of reporting is unstructured and is generally used daily to record actions and behaviors of older adults. Journaling is one type of subjective reporting.

Journaling. Using a journal is one way of recording subjective reports from an observation. This method allows you to draw brief conclusions about what you observe. Journaling usually occurs immediately after an activity. Journaling allows you to give more details about the observation. A journal is often written in story form and is an excellent way to keep up with the facts you learn about older adults.

FIG. 7-11. **Journaling is a common method of subjective reporting at older adult day centers.** What may be the pros and cons of subjective reporting?

Because of the uniqueness of some older adults' physical conditions, writing the facts as stories allows you to write more-detailed information about their conditions. You can write in your journal in chronological order by activity. You can include details about older adults' levels of involvement. See Fig. 7-11.

Objective Reporting

The objective form of observation can give you more varied results. **Objective reporting** requires that the observer leave any personal judgments out of the observation. The most common way to use this method is to check items on a form as you observe participants. At the end of the observation, you can summarize the information and form generalizations. Objective reporting can be done as a summary of daily activities.

- **Frequency count.** Frequency of events can be important in an adult day center. If you are working in a center that uses a health model, it might be your job to observe and track how often a person has to take medication throughout the day. See Fig. 7-12. You

FIG. 7-12.

Frequency Count

Purpose: To verify client is taking medication on time
Date: 2/4
Observed By: Ron

Client Name & Age	Medication Frequency					
	Time Meds Taken	Time Meds Taken	Time Meds Taken	Time Meds Taken	Time Meds Taken	Time Meds Taken
Geneva (72 yrs.)	8:00 a.m.	12:00 p.m.	4:00 p.m.	NA	NA	NA
Nicholas (80 yrs.)	9:00 a.m.	NA	4:00 p.m.	NA	NA	NA
Niana (67 yrs.)	7:00 a.m.	11:30 a.m.	4:30 p.m.	NA	NA	NA
Clara (78 yrs.)	9:00 a.m.	NA	2:00 p.m.	NA	6:00 p.m.	NA

might also need to record how often their blood pressure is taken. By observing, counting, and recording the number of times the task is done, you can assist in making certain the participant follows the medication schedule. This is very important when working with older adults, specifically those who have medical concerns or challenges.

- **Interval recording.** When observing older adults, it is often helpful to record information at various intervals during the day. Many older adults have to have their vital signs taken throughout the day. Taking and recording older adults' vital signs could save their lives. For example, you might make sure that older people who are on blood pressure medication have their blood pressure taken before they take their medication. Interval recording helps staff to make an evaluation based on vital sign readings at particular times during the day.

- **Time sampling.** When working with older adults, you might use time sampling. If you are observing an older adult's behavior during an activity and it seems unusual, it is important to document it at that particular time. There are several reasons you should do this. An unusual behavior could be related to medication. For example, an older adult who is diabetic might have a drop in sugar level during an activity each morning at 11:30. You might notice the participant looks as if he or she might faint or becomes agitated with peers. When a person becomes **agitated**, he or she tends to get nervous or disturbed. If you document this situation each time it occurs, you can track and assess why the older adult's behavior might be changing during that time period. See Fig. 7-13.

- **Anecdotal records.** Anecdotal records are useful because they provide information that centers need for record keeping. For example,

FIG. 7-13.

Time Sampling

Date: 2/28/02   Time: 10:00-10:24 a.m.
Client Name: Nicholas   Gender: Male   Age: 71
Observer: Niana

Activity & Observer Comments

T1	10:00-10:02	Becomes agitated with card playing partners.
T2	10:02-10:04	Appears to be sleepy.
T3	10:04-10:06	Gets very aggressive with card playing partners.
T4	10:06-10:08	Gets up from the table and walks away from the group.
T5	10:08-10:10	Props against the wall.
T6	10:10-10:12	Talks to himself.
T7	10:12-10:14	Appears confused.
T8	10:14-10:16	Appears weak.
T9	10:16-10:18	Loses balance.
T10	10:18-10:20	Stumbles to the chair.
T11	10:20-10:22	Takes medication for diabetes just before lunch.
T12	10:22-10:24	Resting.

many older adults use one or more prescription medications and many over-the-counter (OTC) supplements. These medications and supplements should be recorded and kept in a file. Also, it is a good idea that older people keep a list of their medications with them, such as in their wallets or purses, at all times. Anecdotal records let center staff know when older adults have taken their medication.

Activity Safety. When observing a physical fitness activity, make sure each participant has enough space to move and carry out the activity. If you are leading a fitness session, you should be able to see each participant.

Summary of Daily Activities

There are different ways to create a summary of daily activities for each older adult at the center. One way is to complete a daily task report. In most cases, whether a center is a profit-making center or nonprofit center, daily task records are required for funding and for future program implementation. Weekly, quarterly, and yearly reports are required for the same reasons.

Activity of Daily Living (ADL)

An **Activity of Daily Living** worksheet asks for details about an older adult's impairment if he or she has one. The older adult's health care provider needs these details to make an accurate report. Medicare needs it to determine the impact of an illness or injury for reimbursement purposes. There are several standardized assessments, or evaluations, you can use to assess the functional ability of older adults. See Fig. 7-14. They include:

FIG. 7-14.

◆ Activities Of Daily Living

Client Name _____ **Date** _____

1. **TYPICAL MONTH.** Please state how many good, fair, and bad days you have each month. (Consider a month to be 30 continuous days.)
   a. GOOD DAYS – days when you do well and complete all living and home care activities. Total good days a month: _____
   b. FAIR DAYS – days when you function with serious difficulty and fail to complete some living and home care activities. Total fair days a month: _____
   c. BAD DAYS – days when you function very poorly and fail to complete most living and home care activities. Total bad days a month: _____
   d. PLEASE DESCRIBE YOUR TYPICAL MONTH IN TERMS OF GOOD, FAIR, AND BAD DAYS, AND GIVE EXAMPLES OF HOW BAD OR FAIR DAYS ARE WORSE.
   _____

2. Are there days when you don't go out because of your health? If yes, how many days a month does your health keep you in? _____ Please explain: _____

3. Compared with a year ago, are you functioning: Better? Worse? About the same? Please explain.
   _____

- A Health and Lifestyle Review (HLR) can be used to screen for vision, hearing, mobility, strength, and flexibility. This assessment tool can be obtained through the Internet by joining the HLR Consortium.

- Activity of Daily Living assessments can be used to determine the older adults' personal daily activity levels. These tools measure basic, personal activities—such as mobility, dressing, eating, bathing, and toileting. They measure how much help a person needs from others when performing daily tasks.

Measuring & Recording Vital Signs

Some participants are required to have vital-sign screenings and take medication at different intervals. This may occur during their visit at the day center and may require the assistance of a nurse. For example, a person who takes blood pressure medication is required to screen the blood pressure prior to taking the medication as part of medication management. It is the participant's responsibility to make arrangements with the care provider or nurse. The participant must bring a self-reporting chart to have results recorded. This process is very important because it gives a clear picture of the intervals, frequency, and results of the screenings over a period of time. The care provider or nurse should also keep a copy on file at the center. It will be the participant's responsibility to inform the nurse that he or she needs assistance with blood pressure screenings, glucose monitoring, or medication.

Blood-Pressure Screenings. For many older adults, regular blood-pressure screenings are crucial to maintaining health. If older adults

---

FIG. 7-15.

TAKING TEMPERATURES

Equipment: Ear thermometer, disposable cover for the probe.

1. Identify the participant. Call the participant by name.
2. Introduce yourself if necessary.
3. Explain the procedure to the participant.
4. Wash your hands. Provide privacy.
5. Place a cover over the probe on the thermometer.
6. Insert the probe in the participant's ear and hold in place.
7. When the temperature reading is complete, the probe emits a tone.
8. Read and record the participant's temperature in the proper place.
9. Press the button that ejects the probe cover. Discard the cover into the wastebasket.
10. Place the thermometer back into its base. Wash your hands.
11. Report any abnormal readings to the nurse.

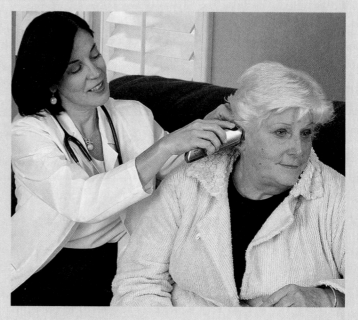

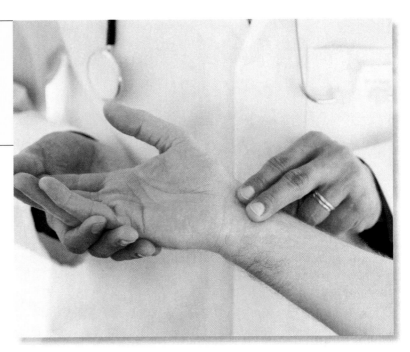

FIG. 7-16. **It is essential for care providers to immediately report to the nurse if a participant's pulse rate is less than 60 beats per minute or greater than 100 beats per minute.** Why is this essential for client health?

take medication to regulate blood pressure, regular screenings help health care professionals prescribe the proper doses of medication. Some older adults may require regular blood-pressure checks, or checks before and after exercise. It is essential that blood-pressure screenings be precise and accurate. See the feature on page 208 for more information on taking blood pressure.

Temperature Monitoring. Body temperature is an important source of information about a person's health condition. Body temperature can vary throughout the day depending upon activity involvement, body conditions like infections, or extreme weather conditions, such as very cold temperatures. See Fig. 7-15 for information on taking a person's temperature with a tympanic (in the ear) thermometer.

Pulse Monitoring. Taking pulse measurements gives an overall indication as to how well the circulatory system is functioning in older adults. The pulse rate can be affected by many factors including strong emotions, exercise, body temperature, and pain. Some medications taken by older adults can also slow the pulse rate. One of the quickest methods to observe and measure the pulse rate is by taking the pulse rate at the wrist, or **radial pulse**. Use the following steps:

1. Have your participant sit down in a private area and remain quiet while taking his or her pulse.

2. Wash your hands.

3. Locate the radial pulse in the participant's wrist using your middle two or three fingers. See Fig. 7-16.

4. Note the strength and regularity of the pulse on your observation record.

5. Begin counting the pulse beats and continue counting for one minute.

6. Record the pulse rate, force, and rhythm.

7. Report your readings to the day center nurse immediately if your participant's pulse rate is less than 60 beats per minute or greater than 100 beats per minute. These measurements may signal a problem. The center nurse will likely contact the participant's doctor.

Blood-Sugar Monitoring. A common occurrence in older adults is the onset of Type II diabetes (dy-uh-BEE-teez). Diabetes is characterized by low production and use of insulin by the body, overproduction of urine, and excessive amounts of glucose (sugar) in the blood and urine. Some older adults are able to control their blood glucose levels by following a prescribed

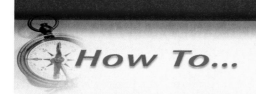

How To...

Measure Blood Pressure

Blood pressure is a measure of the force of the blood flow that is exerted against the walls of an artery. This measurement consists of the blood flow when the heart beats (systolic pressure), over the pressure of the blood flow when the heart is at rest (diastolic pressure). The blood pressure reading is measured in millimeters (mm) of mercury (Hg). For example, a normal reading might be 110/70 mm Hg. Here are the steps for measuring blood pressure:

1. Gather supplies: sphygmomanometer (sfyg-moh-MAN-ah-meh-tuhr), stethoscope, and alcohol wipes.

2. Identify the participant, introduce yourself, and wash your hands. Provide privacy.

3. Using alcohol wipes, clean the diaphragm and the earpieces of the stethoscope.

4. Ask the participant to sit still.

5. Place the participant's arm in a position level with the heart, with the palm of the hand facing up.

6. Uncover the participant's arm.

7. Squeeze the cuff on the sphygmomanometer to make sure there is no air in the cuff. Close the valve on the bulb.

8. Locate the participant's brachial (or arm) artery. Place the cuff on the participant's arm, at least one inch above the elbow, with the tube over the brachial artery. Make sure the cuff is evenly positioned around the arm and then tighten it so it fits snugly. See Fig. 7-HT.

9. Put the stethoscope around your neck and insert the earpieces in your ears.

10. Find the client's radial artery and feel the radial pulse.

11. Explain that the participant will feel tightness in the arm that may be uncomfortable. Begin inflating the cuff by pumping the bulb with your other hand.

12. Inflate the cuff an additional 30 mm after you no longer feel the participant's pulse.

13. Place the diaphragm of the stethoscope over the participant's brachial artery.

14. Turn the valve on the sphygmomanometer counterclockwise and begin to evenly deflate the cuff at a rate of 2 to 4 mm per second.

15. Note the reading on the scale when you first hear a sound. This is the participant's systolic reading.

16. As you continue to deflate the cuff, note the reading on the scale when you no longer hear sound. This is the diastolic reading.

17. Continue letting air out of the cuff until it is completely deflated. Remove the cuff and stethoscope from the participant's arm.

18. Record the client's blood pressure reading.

19. Clean the diaphragm and earpieces of the stethoscope with alcohol wipes.

20. Place all equipment back where it belongs.

21. Wash your hands.

22. Report abnormal blood pressure readings to the nurse at the care center.

APPLY IT!

With a partner, practice taking blood pressure readings under the direction of a health care professional. Practice until you take the readings accurately.

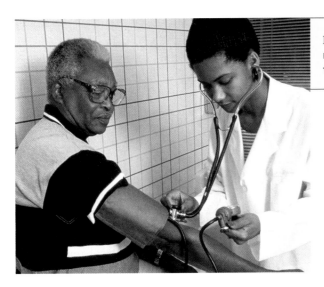

FIG. 7-HT. **Taking accurate blood pressure measurements can help older adults maintain their health.**

FIG. 7-17. **Many older adults have diabetes and must monitor their blood sugar regularly throughout the day.** What is the benefit of monitoring clients' blood sugar?

diet. Others require medication and a healthful diet to help control excessive blood glucose levels. In either case, regular monitoring of blood glucose levels is essential. Blood glucose levels are generally checked before meals and snacks. Those care center clients who are diabetic will likely have their own blood glucose monitors. See Fig. 7-17. These monitors require special test strips on which a drop of the client's blood is placed. The test strip is placed into the monitor. It will then give a blood glucose reading within a certain time, usually 60 seconds. Be sure to record the results of the test in your records. You may also need to duplicate the records for your client to keep track of at home.

Section **7-2** Knowledge Check

1. How can effective communication improve your ability to conduct an observation?
2. Why are frequency counts important when observing older adults?
3. Contrast subjective and objective reporting.

Mini-Lab

With a team member, write a case study to show the process of effective communication during observation.

Chapter **7**

Review & Activities

Section Summaries

7-1 Observing children gives care providers insight into children's development and behavior.

7-1 Care providers can use different observation methods, including anecdotal records, rating scales, running records, and checklists.

7-1 Collecting children's work samples is one way to show levels of development.

7-2 Care providers observe older adults to help build and maintain their skills.

7-2 Using your sensory skills when observing older adults leads to beneficial observations.

7-2 Frequency count, interval recording, and time sampling can be used to observe older adults.

7-2 Care providers can use objective or subjective reporting with older adults.

Check Your Knowledge

1. What are two benefits of observing children?
2. What is naturalistic observation?
3. Name one advantage and one disadvantage of the participant-observer approach.
4. Why should a nonparticipant observer stay in the background?
5. What type of information is included in an anecdotal record for children? Older adults?
6. Describe a frequency count for children and older adults.
7. What is the difference between a checklist and a rating scale?
8. What is meant by interpreting observations?
9. Give two reasons why sensory skills are important when observing older adults.

Thinking Critically

1. When observing children, consider why observer conduct should be strictly observed. Why is each of the guidelines important to follow?
2. What factors might cause human service professionals to interpret the same observation records differently? Is there usually only one "correct" interpretation of an observation? Why or why not?
3. In what ways are observing young children and older adults similar? In what ways do they differ?

Practical Applications

1. **Making an Anecdotal Record.** While observing young children or older adults, make an anecdotal record of a particular incident that occurs. Be sure to record the date, time, setting, observer, information about the person observed, and details of your observation.

2. **Creating a Rating Scale.** Create a rating scale that might be used in observing a child's skill in performing a certain task. Investigate the skill to determine what is age-appropriate for that particular skill. For example, what a preschooler's skill level should be in identifying alphabet letters. Be sure to include spaces for recording the child's name, age, date, time, observer, setting, and skill observed. Ratings might be *always*, *sometimes*, and *never*, or you could use a scale of one to five, indicating ratings from *poor* to *excellent*.

3. **Collecting and Analyzing Samples.** Collect samples of children's completed art projects, audiotapes of children's stories, videotapes of children during dress-up play, or snapshots of children's block building. Analyze the samples for evidence of the children's levels of development.

Building Your PORTFOLIO

Recording Observations

Professionals frequently make observations of the young children or older adults in their care. These observations may be made for many purposes.

Step 1: Interview a human service professional who works with young children or older adults. Collect samples of observation forms used for observing children or adults. Evaluate the forms collected. How easy would each form be to use? What changes would you suggest to improve the forms? Include two or three samples along with your evaluations in your portfolio.

Step 2: Develop two forms you could use in observing young children or older adults. Ask a human service professional to evaluate the forms and make suggestions for improvement. Based on the professional's input, revise the forms. Then use them to make observations. How well did the forms work? How could you improve the forms? Make any needed improvements and include copies in your portfolio.

Step 3: As you observe young children or older adults for the remainder of this course, collect samples of the observation records you create. From these, choose the best samples of your work. Put two or three of the best in your portfolio. Make sure they show your skill in making objective observations.

Chapter **8**

Abuse & Neglect

Section 8-1

Child Abuse & Neglect

Abuse is a hard topic to face, but many people in society harm children, sometimes their own. Child abuse and neglect are common conditions in today's society. Child abuse and neglect happen in all neighborhoods and to children of all races and economic backgrounds. Early childhood professionals are among the people who can help prevent child abuse and neglect. Because they see children daily, they are in a unique position to help children who suffer from abuse and neglect.

Types of Child Abuse

Child abuse occurs when an intentional injury is inflicted on a child. The injury may be physical, sexual, or emotional in nature. As an early childhood professional, you need to recognize the symptoms of each type of child abuse.

Physical Abuse. Physical abuse often results in visible injury to the child's body. Because children frequently injure themselves through their own activity, how can you tell the difference between abuse and a routine injury? Normal bruising often occurs on bony areas, such as the knees, shins, and forehead. Watch for severe injury, repeated injuries, and indica-

tions from the child that something out of the ordinary is occurring. See Fig. 8-1. Early childhood professionals should note any, or a combination, of the following symptoms:

- Unexplained bumps, bruises, burns, welts, cuts, or unexplained sensitivity on areas of the body that indicate abuse: face, neck, torso, back, buttocks, or thighs.
- Evidence of molestation, or forced physical or sexual contact.
- Evidence of repeated skin injuries or bone fractures.
- Reflexive fear, such as shielding self from a sudden blow.
- Evidence of malnutrition or dehydration.

FIG. 8-1. Early childhood professionals must be aware of severe signs that indicate a child is being physically abused. These signs show severe injuries that go beyond the types of injuries children get through normal play. What should you do if you if you notice signs of possible abuse?

Emotional Abuse. Emotional abuse occurs when an adult chronically says things that hurt a child. This language may be foul, vulgar, or demeaning. Children who are emotionally abused may suffer ridicule, torment, and unmerciful teasing by a parent or care provider. Emotional abuse may include demanding that a child perform tasks that are too difficult. Failing to provide a child with continuing affection and emotional support can be considered abusive. In addition, encouraging children to commit illegal acts, such as stealing, is also considered emotional abuse. Care providers may notice the following symptoms when a child is suffering emotional abuse:

- Displays low self-esteem or calls self names.
- Expresses sadness, depression, a sense of hopelessness, or displays extreme shyness.
- Lacks self-confidence.
- Acts out aggressively, has uncontrollable outbursts, or uses foul, demeaning language.
- Shows excessive fear of making mistakes.
- Displays unusual anxiety or fear.

- Displays stuttering or other speech difficulties that have not been present earlier.
- Appears to have trouble sleeping.
- Shows changes in appetite or regular complaints of an upset stomach.
- Displays unwillingness to try new things.
- Withdraws from activities and other children.

Sexual Abuse. When someone subjects a child to any sexual activity, sexual abuse occurs. Examples of this type of abuse include fondling, pornography, incest, and rape. This may also include genital exposure, touching personal body parts (both the child's and the adult's), and other inappropriate sexual contact. The blind trust children tend to have in adults also makes them vulnerable to sexual abuse. Abusers often use intimidation and fear to keep children from telling anyone about the abuse. For example, children may fear being physically hurt if they tell about the abuse. See Fig. 8-2. Children may display the following symptoms when experiencing sexual abuse:

- Unusual sexual knowledge for the child's age.

FIG. 8-2. After a referral from a care provider, social workers often use dolls when working with young children to determine sexual abuse.

- Soreness, sensitivity, or injury in genital region of the body.
- Very low self-esteem.
- Drawings with sexual themes or advanced sexual play with peers or dolls.

Child Neglect

Child neglect is the failure to provide a child with the basic necessities of life, including food, clothing, shelter, and medical care. Because young children cannot care for themselves, they need reliable attention from adults. A child who is neglected may be left without adult supervision for hours, days, or weeks at a time. Neglect puts a child's health and safety at risk.

Signs and Symptoms. If you notice a child's habitual lack of adequate cleanliness, nutrition, shelter, clothing, medical care, or dental care, you may be seeing signs of neglect. Neglected children may be deprived of sleep, so they behave especially tired in the early childhood setting. Some neglected children demand more individual attention than children who are not neglected. Others are quiet and shy and often wander aimlessly. Their concentration and attention spans may be poor, which can result in learning problems.

Responding to Child Abuse & Neglect

Children are put at great risk if suspicions of child abuse and neglect are ignored by those who care for them. Early childhood professionals and other caring adults must take action on children's behalf. If adults fail to work for the children's well-being, children will have little hope of overcoming harmful experiences.

Documenting & Reporting

All states have laws against child abuse and neglect. They also operate agencies staffed with social workers that investigate suspected child abuse and neglect.

Child-abuse and neglect laws in all states require those who work with children to report suspected abuse or neglect. These people are called mandated reporters. Early childhood staff must file a report even if neglect or abuse is only suspected, not absolutely proven. Reporting suspected abuse is required even when the adult is a parent or a fellow staff member. Because accusations of abuse and neglect are very serious, professionals must act in good faith by reporting only those conditions that cause genuine concern for a child's health or safety. See Fig. 8-3.

Documenting is what care providers do when making a confidential, written record of suspected abuse or neglect. It includes recording what the care provider sees and the comments the parents make. Conversations staff members have about their suspicions, including

FIG. 8-3. **Early childhood professionals are mandated reporters of child abuse.** **What other people are considered mandated reporters?**

dates and information shared, also must be recorded. If there are physical symptoms of abuse, use photos to record the injuries.

When reporting suspicious conditions, mandated reporters must follow the guidelines set by their state child-abuse and neglect laws. In some states, reports can be made anonymously. Procedures for reporting abuse usually require calling the police, a child-abuse hotline, or contacting the child-welfare agency. When calling in a report, you will need to report other facts besides the child's symptoms. Be prepared to provide the child's basic information, such as the child's full name, age and birth date, address, and parents' names and home and work telephone numbers.

Once a report is filed, it should be documented in the child's file for future reference. Be sure to include the details of the report. Note that any type of documentation can be used in a court of law should the suspected abuse or neglect be found true. See Fig. 8-4.

Parent Referrals

Although there are no excuses, certain factors seem to be associated with abuse. Parents and others who abuse or neglect children often suffer from low self-esteem. Many are very young parents or have poor coping skills. They may lack knowledge about parenting and appropriate care, which causes them to put unrealistic expectations on children. Some of these individuals were abused children themselves.

Many early childhood programs offer evening workshops for adults to deal with these issues. These programs address parenting topics, such as developmental stages of children, alternative forms of discipline, and ways to cope with stress.

Referring parents to support groups, such as Parents Anonymous, can help relieve stress and prevent further abuse. Parents can also be informed of community mental health agencies that offer affordable family therapy. These agencies can be found in your local telephone book under key headings, such as counseling, social services, or behavioral health services.

Some communities have a **crisis nursery** that provides 24-hour child care services to parents who feel they might hurt their child. While at the crisis nursery, a child can be safely cared for while the parent receives support services, such as emergency counseling.

Building Children's Resilience

Life events, such as child abuse and neglect, often make children feel powerless and out of control. Those understandable feelings undermine their coping abilities. When you discover that a child has problems, there are things you can do to help build a child's resilience. **Resilience** occurs when children learn to cope with and eventually recover from the hardships of abuse and neglect. See Fig. 8-5.

Children are known for bouncing back from trials and tribulations, but they do not often do

FIG. 8-4. **Hotline workers take down necessary information so that intervention can take place in cases of abuse.** What information should you have ready when reporting a case of abuse or neglect?

Impact of Prolonged Stress. Child abuse and neglect stresses children in physical ways that cannot be seen. Prolonged stress can impair brain development. For example:

- When children are frightened, stress hormones are released into their internal systems. These hormones prevent the brain from transferring information along the central nervous system.

- Violence can cause hidden stress in children. Children who regularly endure violence have difficulty controlling their actions. The part of the brain that controls social behaviors may not develop as it should when children are overstressed.

Warm, responsive child care helps offset the stress children endure as a result of child abuse or neglect. These children benefit when care providers create calm, predictable environments for children.

it alone. Research shows that resilient children have formed a deep and trusting relationship with at least one adult in their life. Extended family and care providers are often those adults who make the difference for an abused or neglected child. Here are some things that early childhood professionals can do to help build resilience in children:

- Give children individualized attention.

- Spend quality time with children to build their sense of self-worth.

- Respond warmly to children to help them relax. This also helps children maintain a hopeful attitude even during hard times of life.

- Talk with children and listen to them closely. Listening to children's thoughts, fears, and feelings helps them sort out their emotions. Respond meaningfully when children share information or ask questions.

- Give children some decision-making power and control over their daytime experiences. Self-confidence is built when care providers encourage children to be independent in developmentally appropriate ways.

- Provide children with a consistent daily routine. When children live in fear, classroom routines promote a sense of security and stability. Abused and neglected children need to rely on predictable people and places to help them feel safe and cared for during times of extreme stress.

FIG. 8-5. Early childhood professionals who provide individualized attention to children who have suffered abuse help build resilience in these children. What are ways to help build resilience in children?

Intergenerational *Interactions*

Preventing Abuse Among Children & Older Adults

Abuse knows no age boundaries; however, children and older adults are at a higher risk than other age groups. By knowing what to look for, you can help end and prevent abuse among the people in your life. Abuse can take many forms: physical abuse, emotional abuse, sexual abuse, neglect, and even financial abuse. Following are just some of the ways you can help prevent abuse among children and older adults.

- **Observe Children Closely.** Aside from cuts and bruises, children who are abused often show one or more of the following emotional symptoms: nervousness around adults, difficulty playing/relaxing, low concentration levels, aggressiveness, poor self-esteem, learning disabilities, relapse into babyish behavior, and more. All children may show one or more of these symptoms from time to time, but if you notice children displaying such symptoms frequently, contact your local Child Protective Service Agency.

- **Offer to Help Troubled Families.** Stress can push even the most gentle people to do unthinkable things. Care providers who spend long periods of time with a cranky baby or disabled older adult need to take time away from their care-giving roles to regroup and relax. If you notice a care provider reaching the end of his or her patience, offer to help or take over the care-giving role for a short time.

- **Keep Older Adults Social and Active.** Older adults who stay in touch with friends and participate in groups and functions outside their home, are less likely to be abused. Because they are in contact with multiple people, they are more likely to tell friends and loved ones if they are being mistreated. Likewise, the people with whom they spend time are apt to observe symptoms of abuse even if the older adults choose not to talk about it.

- **Help Older Adults Stay Organized.** By keeping their belongings orderly, older adults send the message to others that they are in control of their property. When older adults take care of their own surroundings and belongings, potential abusers will be discouraged from trying to steal from them.

Follow-Up

Think about the children and older adults in your life. Are any of them in danger of being abused? Have you noticed symptoms of abuse? If so, talk with your teacher or guardian about your observations to determine whether protective services should be involved.

Preventing Child Abuse & Neglect

Recognizing and reporting cases of suspected child abuse can put an end to existing abuse. Child care providers can also help prevent abuse and neglect from happening in the first place. One way of preventing abuse is to screen early childhood staff prior to employment by conducting a criminal background check. This check, which usually involves fingerprinting, identifies people who have been convicted of a crime against children. Of course, such a conviction would prevent employment in an early childhood program. There are other ways to prevent abuse as well. See Fig. 8-6.

Limiting Abuse Opportunities. Visibility and continuous supervision greatly reduce opportunities for abuse to occur. In early childhood programs, children should never be taken alone to a private room that can be locked by any staff member. Rooms with doors should have windows, so staff may be easily observed at any time. Training on child abuse and neglect, including how to spot it, report it, and prevent it, should be provided yearly to staff members.

Staff Protection. Regrettably, child abuse has occurred in low-quality child care programs, so some parents may be suspicious of staff members. Children need to be protected from

FIG. 8-6. Providing staff with effective training for spotting, reporting, and preventing child abuse is an essential part of continuing education for early childhood professionals. Why is staff training an important part of protecting staff against false accusations?

child abuse, but staff members also need to be protected from false accusation. To dismiss questions about your conduct with children, make sure you always supervise them with another adult present. This is especially important during nap time, toileting, outdoor play, and bus loading. Child care providers are safe from possible accusations when accompanied by another staff member. This way a witness can verify that appropriate behavior was used. False accusations should be documented and immediately reported to a supervisor.

Section **8-1** Knowledge Check

1. List three types of child abuse or neglect. Give two symptoms of each type.
2. Describe steps professionals should take in documenting and reporting suspected child abuse or neglect.
3. Explain what it means for a child to be resilient.

Mini-Lab

In teams, request an interview with your school's counselor, a community social worker, or police officer. Ask how this person handles issues of confidentiality in abuse and neglect cases. What tips can he or she share to prepare you to cope with the same responsibilities if you pursue a career with children?

Section 8-2

Elder Abuse & Neglect

OBJECTIVES

- Determine why older adults are vulnerable to abuse and neglect.
- Identify the signs of abuse among older adults.
- Identify the agencies that assist older adults who experience abuse.
- Describe a procedure to report abuse and neglect of older adults.

KEY WORDS

vulnerable
elder abuse
financial abuse
fraud
con artists
quackery
adult protective
services

Like children, older adults are easy targets of abuse and neglect by those who do not have their best interests in mind. As a professional who cares for older adults, you will need to identify and intervene in abuse and neglect cases. In addition, you will be responsible for preventing the abuse of older adults in care centers.

Vulnerability of Older Adults

Older adults who are not able to care for themselves without assistance are **vulnerable**, or unable to defend themselves against acts of unkindness or mistreatment. Vulnerable older adults become victims of abuse and neglect when they are mistreated or exploited by the people they depend on for assistance. Many of these older adults live alone, or they live in care centers. Many older adults who live in care centers are frail, which makes them even more vulnerable. They may become isolated from close family members and friends. This isolation makes the abuse easier to commit and more difficult for care providers to notice.

Adult day programs can increase the social interaction of older adults by providing a place for them to gather. This can also relieve some stress for their care providers. Both efforts decrease the likelihood of older-adult abuse. Adult day centers also put older adults in contact with more people, which increases the likelihood that abuse will be noticed. Adult day center staff members are trained to spot signs of abuse, and they have a responsibility to take actions to prevent the abuse. See Fig. 8-7.

Types of Elder Abuse

Each year, millions of older adults become victims of physical, emotional, sexual, and financial abuse. Abuse and neglect among the older population is complex. **Elder abuse** is any act that harms the health or welfare of an

FIG. 8-7. Older adults often feel vulnerable in a group of strangers when away from their own homes. How can adult day care providers help ease the sense of vulnerability?

older adult. Abuse can also take the form of neglect by older adults themselves or by their care providers. Older adults are abused and neglected in many ways and in many places. It can happen in the home, the community, and in short-term or long-term care facilities. Abusers can be family members, care providers, friends, or landlords. Authorities are often unaware of the abuse that is inflicted on the older-adult population because many incidents are not reported. Elder abuse can be viewed as an infliction of physical, emotional, or psychological harm, sexual or financial exploitation, or neglect.

Some programs help abused older adults. People who work in these programs must recognize who is at risk for abuse. Older adults most at risk are dependent on others, socially isolated, depressed, or disabled. Another risk factor is care provider stress. People's initial reaction to a suspected abuse case can range from concern, to fear, to anger. Adult care staff members must adhere to strict guidelines in responding to abuse.

These guidelines protect the older adults they serve as well as the staff members. These guidelines help staff members know that they not only have a responsibility to respond to abuse, but that they will be supported in the process if they do. Here are some signs that may indicate that an older adult is experiencing abuse:

Physical Abuse. When someone willfully causes pain or injury, they are committing physical abuse. This type of abuse includes slapping, bruising, molesting, or restraining older adults. Care providers who use enough force to cause unnecessary pain or injury can be considered abusive. Care providers who try to assist older adults, but use too much force, can still cause physical harm. See Fig. 8-8.

Emotional Abuse. People who inflict mental anguish commit emotional abuse. Examples of this abuse include humiliating, intimidating, or threatening others. Family members, care providers, or other people who emotionally abuse older adults act in ways that cause fear, mental anguish, or emotional pain or distress.

Sexual Abuse. When someone subjects another person to any unwanted sexual activity, sexual abuse occurs. Examples of this abuse include fondling, rape, pornography, or incest. Sexual abuse is about power and control on the part of the abuser. The abuser often uses fear

FIG. 8-8. Unfortunately, the physical abuse of older adults occurs more often than people care to think. How could you as a care provider help in the prevention of physical abuse of older adults?

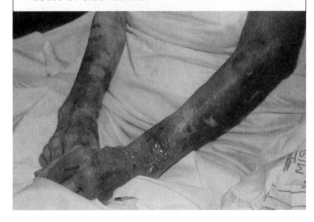

and intimidation to control the victim. Vulnerable older adults who are sexually abused may also experience emotional and physical abuse.

Financial Abuse. Some people use older adults to benefit themselves financially. The abuser uses the older adult's money or possessions without permission. He or she might commit forgery, or alter documents to get money. This exploitation of older adults is **financial abuse**. It involves taking unfair advantage of older adults' resources for others' personal gain by use of undue influence, harassment, pressure, trickery, or false representation. Older adults who are financially exploited might experience the following:

- Unapproved withdrawals from or loss of access to bank accounts.

- Inadequate care, even if money is available for proper care.

- Missing jewelry, clothing, or other valuables.

- Little or no cash to spend.

Watch for Signs of Abuse. Family members or care providers most often inflict abuse on older adults. Some of this abuse is not intentional. For example, abuse may occur when an older adult's care provider becomes "burned out" from the stress of performing daily tasks, such as bathing, for the older adult. As an adult day care services provider, watch for signs of burnout, such as anger, frustration, or depression, in other staff members to avoid incidents of abuse. If you notice any of these signs, refer the care provider to counseling services or a group, such as Families Anonymous.

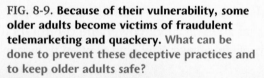
FIG. 8-9. **Because of their vulnerability, some older adults become victims of fraudulent telemarketing and quackery.** What can be done to prevent these deceptive practices and to keep older adults safe?

Fraud and Quackery. Older adults account for more than half of all victims of fraudulent telemarketing and other types of fraud. Older adults are often targets of scams because they tend to trust people, including strangers. Likewise, older adults are often victims of quackery because they tend to trust those who offer seemingly miracle cures to some of the health issues with which older adults deal. Older adults are also more likely to be home alone and willing to talk with callers or people who stop at their doors. Fraud and quackery can also be called consumer abuse. See Fig. 8-9.

- **Fraud.** The intentional misrepresentation of something or someone to another person for financial gain is called **fraud**. It is to be dishonest and cheat someone. There are different types of fraud. Scams that convince someone that he or she has won a prize and that sell phony travel packages are fraudulent. Some scams persuade older adults to invest in get-rich-quick scams and fake charities.

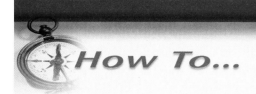

Protect Older Adults from Crime

Because of the vulnerability and frailty that come with age, many older adults become victims of crime. As a care provider, there are a number of ways you can teach older adults to protect themselves from crime. Encourage older adults to report a crime to the local police or prosecuting attorney's office. Suggest the following ideas to older adults:

Banking…

- Avoid carrying checks. Use direct deposit, if possible.
- Never withdraw money at a stranger's request.
- Store valuables in safe deposit boxes and keep the keys in a secret location.

In a Car…

- Keep the doors locked when driving.
- Keep the car in gear at stoplights.
- Keep the car in good running condition and make sure gas is always in the tank.
- If you break down, move the car to the right shoulder, raise the hood, and stay inside the locked car until help arrives. If the weather is warm, open the windows a small distance to allow air circulation.
- Lock valuables in the trunk.
- Always check inside the car before entering.

Walking…

- If assaulted, call for help, making as much noise as possible, or blow a whistle.
- Always walk with a friend and in well-lighted places.
- Plan your route.
- Walk with confidence.
- Carry your door key and identification in your pocket, not in a purse or wallet.

At Home…

- Lock all doors.
- Use timers to activate lights when away from home.
- Notify neighbors and cancel deliveries when leaving for a trip.
- Do not trust people who make unsolicited offers to repair your home.
- Photograph valuables and record their serial numbers.
- Do not hide keys in places where thieves are likely to look, such as under the door mat.
- Never give out information that would let a stranger know you're not going to be home.
- Do not enter the house if you think a stranger is inside.

APPLY IT!

Create a brochure to inform older adults about ways to protect themselves from crime.

FIG. 8-10.

POSSIBLE SIGNS OF ABUSE & NEGLECT

Many of the symptoms listed below can occur as a result of disease conditions or medications. The appearance of these symptoms should prompt further investigation to determine and remedy the cause.

Physical Abuse	• Bruises or grip marks around the arms or neck • Rope marks or welts on the wrists and/or ankles • Repeated, unexplained injuries • Dismissive attitude or statements about injuries • Refusal to go to same emergency department for repeated injuries
Emotional/ Psychological Abuse	• Uncommunicative and unresponsive • Unreasonably fearful or suspicious • Lack of interest in social contacts • Chronic physical or psychiatric health problems • Evasiveness
Sexual Abuse	• Unexplained vaginal or anal bleeding • Torn or bloody underwear • Bruised breasts • Venereal diseases or vaginal infections
Financial Abuse or Exploitation	• Life circumstances don't match with the size of the estate • Large withdrawals from bank accounts, switching accounts, unusual ATM activity • Signatures on checks don't match elder's signature
Neglect	• Sunken eyes or loss of weight • Extreme thirst • Bed sores

©2002 American Psychological Association

Some older adults lose their homes because of fraud. These older adults have been approached by people they trust to give up their homes and move into an independent living environment. People who are skilled at conducting these acts are known as **con artists**. They are so well trained that it is difficult to see through the scam. People who care about older adults can assist them by describing some tips for spotting scams.

- **Quackery.** Many older adults are most trusting of medical professionals. Older adults tend to believe in untraditional practices because they feel they can get quick relief for whatever is causing their discomfort or ill health. Most quacks tend to be in a health practice. **Quackery** is being dishonest about medical claims, most often misrepresenting a medicine or device.

The abuse and neglect of older people happens every day. If you see signs of abuse, you must report it to the authorities immediately. As a responsible citizen, it is your duty to report abuse and neglect acts. There are clear signs of abuse and neglect with which you should be familiar. See Fig. 8-10.

Elder Neglect

Neglect is the failure of a care provider to provide goods or services necessary to avoid physical harm, mental anguish, or mental illness. Neglect can include abandonment and denial of food or health-related services.

Passive Neglect. If a person who provides services for an older adult unintentionally fails to carry out the duty, the person has committed passive neglect. The failure to carry out the act is usually because the care provider is overwhelmed with the responsibility or does not know how to carry out the task.

Active Neglect. Care providers who purposefully fail to carry out their tasks commit active neglect. Active neglect also might include failure to use available funds to help care for the older adult. See Fig. 8-11.

Self-Neglect. Older adults might neglect themselves, either intentionally or unintentionally. The older adult might be grieving the loss of a spouse or friend. This grief might cause depression. Depression might cause older adults to lack the desire to maintain their health and strength. Some older adults may not remember whether they took their medication or ate a meal. The older adult might not be able to prepare a nutritious meal or purchase needed medication. It is very helpful for care providers to be familiar with the signs of self-neglect. See Fig. 8-12.

FIG. 8-12. Some older adults become depressed at the loss of their independence and physical abilities. Some may refuse to eat or get necessary exercise or therapy. How can a care provider help older adults overcome self-neglect?

Services for Abuse Victims

The Older Americans Act makes prevision for the protection of older adults against abuse and neglect. There are elder abuse and neglect programs in all states. The best way to get information about agencies that help older people is to call your local Area Agency on Aging. Agencies to whom you can report abuse and neglect cases list their numbers in local telephone directories. Other agencies that have information about elder abuse and neglect include:

- The Administration on Aging (AoA).

- U.S. Department of Health and Human Services.

- National Center on Elder Abuse.

FIG. 8-11. Some people exploit trusting older adults by charging them for services they have not performed or for overcharging for services, such as shopping or housecleaning. How can older adults be protected from such exploitation?

- Adult Protective Services.
- Eldercare Locator.
- National Organization for Victim Assistance.
- AARP—Criminal Justice Services.

Reporting Abuse & Neglect

Abuse and neglect of older adults is a major concern for people who work with older adults. In most cases, these are criminal acts. When cases of abuse and neglect are properly reported, those who commit the acts can be prosecuted and tried in court. See Fig. 8-13.

Legislatures in all states have created some form of elder-abuse-prevention laws. The laws vary in each state, but all states have a standard reporting system for abuse and neglect. **Adult protective services** agencies receive and investigate reports of suspected abuse and neglect. However, most cases of abuse and neglect of older adults go unreported. In some instances, people abuse older adults without realizing it because of cultural differences, lack of understanding, or physical conditions of the older

FIG. 8-13. **Reporting cases of abuse is mandated for all care providers.**

adult. Older adults are more likely to be abused because of their limited social interaction, increased stress of their care providers, and their increased dependence on others.

All people deserve to be treated with respect. No one should be subject to violent, humiliating, or neglectful acts. The Older Americans Act gives federal funds to the National Center on Elder Abuse to provide training on abuse awareness and reporting. This program protects the health, safety, and welfare of people 60 years of age and older. Some of these older adults might not be able to protect themselves from abuse, neglect, exploitation, or abandonment. Older adults do not report abuse of themselves for many reasons, including:

- Fear of retaliation.
- Fear of being put in an institution.
- Shame that a family member mistreats them.
- Belief that the police and social agencies can not really help them or that they will not believe them.
- Unsure of whom to call.
- Fear of getting involved.

It is important to know the signs of abuse to report it responsibly. The protective services program includes two types of reporting—voluntary and mandatory.

Voluntary Reporting. If you suspect abuse of any kind, including neglect or abandonment, you may file a report with any Area Agency on Aging. You can also call the state elder-abuse hotline. Both programs take reports 24 hours a day. You can file the report for any older adult in the community, not just those in care facilities. You do not have to give your name when you make the report. You also have legal protection. No one can file a lawsuit against you because you reported abuse.

Mandated Reporting. Care providers are mandated to report suspected abuse and abuse of older adults. Reports are generally made to a local social service office. If the abuse involves serious injury, sexual abuse, or suspicious death, you must also call the police and the department of aging. You will be required to fill out an incident report and identify the details of the suspected abuse. If you fail to report abuse, you can be terminated from your job or be charged with a crime. Any report can also be used in a court of law.

Helping Victims Recover

Victims of abuse need help to recover. You can help victims recover by doing the following:

* Let them know you support them and that you care. Knowing someone is concerned helps victims regain confidence. See Fig. 8-14.

* Let the victims know you want to listen to their fears.

* Listen to them but don't question them about the abuse or give opinions.

* Offer to take them to the doctor, the police, or victim services.

* Let them know about available services, such as counseling.

* Help the older adult with household chores, such as shopping and preparing meals.

As victims start their recovery period, they go through various stages of emotional reactions. These emotional reactions include: shock and denial, anger, guilt, powerlessness, and depres-

FIG. 8-14. Reassuring an older adult who has suffered abuse of any kind helps to restore the self-esteem and overall morale of the older adult. What other ways show caring and comfort?

sion. It is normal for victims to experience these emotions. Remember that each person moves through the stages at his or her own pace. Working through these stages helps victims put their lives back together. However, if victims seem unable to move through the stages of grief, they may need counseling to recover. See Chapter 2 for more information on the stages of grief.

Section Knowledge Check

1. What makes older adults vulnerable to abuse and neglect?
2. Identify five signs of abuse often observed among older adults.
3. Identify seven agencies to which you can report elder abuse and neglect.

Mini-Lab

Assume that you are the director of a non-profit adult day center. Determine a plan for reporting abuse and neglect of older adults who participate in the center. Find out what the sexual abuse and neglect law is in your state. Identify the agencies that investigate and follow up on abuse and neglect cases.

Review & Activities

Section Summaries

8-1 Child neglect and abuse interfere with children's development.

8-1 Care providers must be able to recognize signs of child neglect and abuse.

8-1 Care providers must report suspected child neglect or abuse.

8-1 Confidential records document cases of suspected child neglect or abuse.

8-1 Care providers can refer parents to services to help prevent or respond to child neglect and abuse.

8-1 Children who experience child neglect or abuse can be resilient with others' help.

8-2 The adult protective services agencies receive and investigate reports of suspected abuse and neglect of older adults.

8-2 Day center staff members must follow procedures and report signs of abuse.

8-2 Older adults are more vulnerable to abuse than other adults because of social isolation.

8-2 Social interactions in adult day centers and relieving care-provider stress help decrease abuse of older adults.

Check Your Knowledge

1. Define child neglect and child abuse.
2. What are signs of abuse or neglect of children that care providers should notice?
3. What does it mean to be a mandated reporter?
4. Name three ways to help build a child's resilience.
5. What are two ways to protect staff from false accusations of abuse?
6. Explain the purpose of criminal background checks for early childhood or older adult staff.
7. How does the vulnerability of older adults impact abuse and neglect?
8. What are types of abuse in older adults? Give an example of each type of abuse.
9. List at least three agencies that supply services for older-adult abuse victims.
10. Contrast voluntary and mandatory reporting of abuse.

Thinking Critically

1. It is hard to believe that any adult would intentionally neglect or abuse a young child or older adult. Why do you think some adults abuse young children or older adults?
2. Consider your feelings about reporting child or elder abuse. What personal concerns do you have about reporting abuse? How would you feel if your suspicions were confirmed? How would you feel if your suspicions were proven wrong?
3. Why might a young child falsely accuse an adult of child abuse? How would you feel if you were falsely accused of abusing a child? What would you do?
4. What factors do you believe motivate people who abuse the elderly financially? What factors do you believe motivate people who deceive older adults? What suggestions do you have for protecting the elderly from these types of abuse?

Practical Applications

1. **Reviewing Neglect and Abuse Articles.** Collect newspaper and magazine articles describing neglect or abuse of young children or older adults. Analyze each article. What symptoms of neglect or abuse were identified in each case? Who reported the neglect or abuse? Has the case been resolved? If so, how? What was done to protect the child or older adult? How was the abuser punished? What insights did you gain from studying these accounts of neglect or abuse?

2. **Researching State Laws.** Research your state's laws regarding child or elder neglect and abuse. What requirements for reporting suspected neglect or abuse are outlined? What are the consequences of failure to report suspected neglect or abuse? What are the provisions for protecting the abused child or older adult? What range of punishment is provided for the abuser?

3. **Identifying and Reporting Abuse and Neglect.** Interview a human service professional to learn more about identifying signs of neglect or abuse. What procedures for reporting suspected neglect or abuse are observed at the human service professional's facility? Take notes and share your findings with your class. If possible, obtain copies of forms used for documenting suspicions of abuse or neglect.

4. **Identifying Community Resources.** Identify resources in your community that are designed to help neglected or abused children or older adults or their abusers. Research the services provided by each of these resources. Create a directory of the services available.

Building Your PORTFOLIO

Preventing Abuse & Neglect

Every care provider has a personal responsibility to prevent abuse and neglect of the young children or older adults in their care. They are also required to report suspected neglect and abuse by others.

Step 1: Obtain information regarding requirements for criminal-background checks of people working with young children or older adults in your state. Are the background checks required in your state as vigorous as those required in other states? If not, what improvements would you suggest? Write a position paper outlining your findings and your recommendations. Include the position paper in your portfolio.

Step 2: Interview the director of a facility that provides care for young children or older adults. What guidelines does the facility observe to limit opportunities for abuse of the young children or older adults at the facility? How are staff members protected from false accusations? Write a summary of your interview for your portfolio.

Step 3: Obtain a copy of the form used for reporting suspected neglect or abuse at a facility that provides care for young children or adults. Using a case situation, complete the form. Include the completed form in your portfolio.

Chapter 9
Schedules & Routines

Section 9-1
Schedules & Routines for Children

Section 9-2
Schedules & Routines for Older Adults

Section 9-1

Schedules & Routines for Children

OBJECTIVES

- Explain what a schedule is and how one is developed.
- Describe common routines incorporated into a daily schedule.
- Explain why and how transitions are used.
- Identify the need for safety checks as part of the care provider's regular routine.

KEY TERMS

schedule
self-directed
routine
transition
transition techniques
chore board
job jar
choice time

In any early childhood program, many different experiences take place in one day, for children as well as staff. When a day goes smoothly, it is the result of thorough planning by the staff. This section will explain the basics of that planning process.

Daily Schedule Needs

When you carefully plan a day, you help ensure that children will be happily engaged in beneficial activities. A structured day helps children behave appropriately. Staff also benefit from a well-planned day because they can perform their duties in a relaxed, enjoyable setting. In addition, having a well-planned day provides enough structure so that care providers can cope well with emergencies.

Schedule Considerations

A **schedule** is a plan for how time will be used. No single schedule works for every child care program. Although some patterns may be similar, each schedule is planned according to the program's characteristics. All of the following affect schedules:

- **Program type.** The main goals of a program determine how a schedule is arranged. A program emphasizing active investigation and independent learning provides ample time for small-group, self-chosen activities. If creativity is emphasized, scheduling of art and music may be given a high priority.

- **Length of the program.** A full-day child care program includes a longer schedule than a half-day program allows. A full-day schedule allows for more varied activities. See Fig. 9-1.

- **Children's ages.** Infants and toddlers have very different needs than older preschoolers. Older preschoolers typically have longer attention spans and need shorter rest periods. Younger children need more assistance

FIG. 9-1. **The hours for early childhood center operation are often scheduled to meet parent work schedules.** Why is it important to consider parent needs when scheduling hours of service?

with self-help skills. Those factors affect the amount of time needed for activities.

- **Size of the program and class grouping.** A large program requires several groups of children, so meal-service times must be staggered. Serving meals to smaller groups helps create a relaxed mealtime routine. As a general rule, the larger the group of children a care provider has to supervise, the more time needed for each activity in the schedule.

- **The facility.** A small center may have multipurpose rooms that require rotation of activities and careful scheduling of different classrooms for efficient use.

Balancing a Schedule

A schedule plans events in the order they will occur and indicates how long each event will last. Schedules bring order to life. In an early childhood program, the schedule is the guideline that assists children with routine activities. It tells how the hours will be spent from the time children arrive until they leave at the end of the day.

A predictable daily schedule creates a secure, stable environment for children and staff. It becomes something familiar on which to rely. A schedule helps guide children's behavior so they are less likely to get sidetracked by distractions. A schedule allows children to become **self-directed**, meaning they learn to cooperate in class activities in an independent, cooperative fashion. Fig. 9-2 gives an example of a daily schedule. How might you adapt this schedule to meet the needs of infants and toddlers? School-age children?

Pacing the Day

Good care providers plan schedules so children's days can be interesting and engaging. They are also sure not to overstimulate or overwhelm children. For example, effective care providers avoid introducing activities for holidays and other special days too soon since these activities can be a high source of stress for children. The pace of the daily schedule should not be too hurried or too boring. Daily schedules require a delicate balance of activities, taking into consideration the following factors. Care providers take care to track their time during the day, either mentally or with a watch. Tracking time helps make sure the pace of the day is appropriate.

Include All Developmental Areas. So children reach their full potential, a daily schedule allows for experiences that address all their developmental areas. Staff should plan activity times to nurture children's intellectual, physical, social, and emotional growth.

Provide Active and Quiet Play. Young children have lots of energy, so they need daily opportunities for active play. Building with blocks or playing dress-up fulfills children's need for active play. So children do not become

FIG. 9-2.

SAMPLE SCHEDULE

Time	Activity
7:30 to 9:30 a.m.	**Families Greeted/Self-Directed Play.** Children play at indoor and outdoor learning centers.
9:30 to 9:50 a.m.	**Snack.** Children wash hands and eat nutritious foods.
9:50 to 11:40 a.m.	**Morning Meeting/Project Work/Activity Time.** Children and care providers discuss ideas for activities for the day. Children explore activity areas within the indoor or outdoor classroom. Activities may include art, science, math, dramatic play, language arts, creative movement, water/sand play, woodworking, block play, and table games.
11:40 a.m. to 12:00 p.m.	**Music Time.** Children sing songs while taking turns washing hands for lunch. This activity serves as a transition to lunchtime.
12:00 to 12:40 p.m.	**Lunchtime.** Children eat in small groups to promote conversation about the day's experiences.
12:40 to 1:00 p.m.	**Transition to Rest or Quiet Time.** Toileting, hand washing, and tooth brushing after lunch followed by a story, quiet play, or a movie prior to rest time helps children settle down. Older children who do not need naps often enjoy the movie and time for quiet relaxation.
1:00 to 2:30 p.m.	**Rest Time with Calming Music.** Early risers play quietly.
2:30 to 5:00 p.m.	**Gradual Wake Up, Toileting and Hand Washing, Snack, Self-Directed Play.** Children play indoors or outdoors. Children help clean up the center by sorting toys and straightening areas at the end of the day.

exhausted, balance active play with quieter pursuits, such as playing board games or playing with puzzles. See Fig. 9-3.

Give Individual Attention. Opportunities for individual attention contribute to children's emotional and social growth. When children receive friendly, individual attention from care providers, attachment and respectful relationships are formed. Children know staff care when they make time to respond to them individually. Playing, reading a story, or singing songs together provides children with individual attention.

FIG. 9-3. **Scheduling time for active and quiet activities provides children a balance of activities throughout the day.** Why do children need a balance of activities?

FIG. 9-4.

STAFF RESPONSIBILITIES IN DAILY ROUTINES

Routines	Staff Responsibilities
Arrival	• Check in the children and perform health check. • Greet parents. • Help children separate from parents. • Bridge home to school with conversation. • Store belongings. • Provide chances for independent play.
Health & Hygiene	• Plan for hand washing for children and staff. • Plan time to brush teeth and assist children with brushing teeth and storing toothbrush. • Help children learn the location of tissues, assist them with nose blowing, and teach them to wash their hands after blowing. • Respond to children's personal schedules for toileting and diapering, encourage children's self-help skills, teach health routines, and properly dispose of soiled items.
Dressing	• Encourage self-help skills for dressing. • Dress for outdoor play. • Teach responsibility for belongings. • Dress after soiling and toileting accidents.
Play Time	• Provide a choice of developmentally appropriate activities. • Provide appropriate supervision.
Mealtimes	• Consider age appropriateness when planning. • Make mealtimes pleasant. • Encourage age-appropriate self-help skills by helping to set tables and using utensils and lunch kits. • Record number of meals served.
Nap Times	• Lower lights, read a story, and pass out stuffed toys for easier resting. • Arrange nap mats or cots, get blankets and pillows. • Ease children into sleep: use music, stories, mobiles, and back rubs.
Departure	• Reunite family. • Share information with parents. • Help children get their belongings and projects to take home. • Put away toys.

Provide Large- and Small-Group Activities. Young children learn best in small groups. However, they also enjoy the sense of community that comes from large-group activities. Children should have chances to participate in both small- and large-group activities each day. Morning meetings, music time, and story time work well as large group activities. Art and science activities and playing with blocks are good small-group activities.

Provide Indoor and Outdoor Play. Children need chances for fast-paced active play as well as more reserved, quiet indoor play. A daily schedule that balances indoor and outdoor play meets both needs and allows children to develop large and small muscle control. Children enjoy nature experiences that outdoor play provides. Fresh air and sunlight promote children's mental and physical health.

Daily Routines

Schedules provide the structure and order for daily classroom activities. Clear, predictable routines put the schedule into action. A **routine** is a regular, expected procedure that is followed to accomplish something. It provides orderliness and discourages conflict, which helps save valuable learning time. Predictable routines contribute to a calm, dependable classroom atmosphere. A routine may be short, such as washing hands, or long, such as eating lunch. When routines are consistent, children learn what to expect in a daily schedule and when to expect it. See Fig. 9-4.

Encouraging Self-Help

Clearly stated routines help children understand what is expected of them. As they adapt to routines, such as getting coats on for outdoor play, children gain confidence and become more independent and organized. See Figs. 9-5 and 9-6.

To be effective, routines respond to children's age and developmental abilities. Care providers need to know each child's abilities and identify children with special needs. Children with special needs might need more flexibility in their routine. Flexibility gives them more time to

learn self-help skills. When that is done, children's independent self-help skills, such as hand washing, putting on shoes, or brushing teeth, develop and improve.

ETHICS IN Action

Employee Absenteeism. Many employers report that employee absenteeism has the greatest negative impact on workplace schedules and routines. Assume you are the director at an early childhood program. You notice that one of your early-morning teacher aides has been consistently absent on Monday mornings for the last three weeks. This is especially hard on the children as they start their week at the early childhood program. *How would you handle this situation with your employee?*

FIG. 9-5. Encouraging children to clean up their own messes is part of learning self-help skills. What are some other ways to encourage self-help skills?

An Arrival Routine in Preschool

Fig. 9-6A. **Sign In.** In many programs the arrival routine begins with some technique for taking attendance. When parents accompany children, they might sign an attendance sheet or log in on a computer.

Fig. 9-6C. **Storing Items.** Include time during arrival to store personal belongings. Cubbies can hold small items. Jackets and coats might hang on hooks. Children learn independence as they perform these tasks on their own.

Health Check. As children enter the classroom, make an informal health check. Pay attention to the appearance of children to spot any problems.

Fig. 9-6B. **Greeting.** Arrival time is happy and positive when a friendly greeting comes from a staff member. Bend or kneel at the child's level and smile warmly. Use the items children bring, such as a favorite stuffed animal, to start conversations. You can show interest and respect by asking questions and listening attentively. Your interest also helps children adjust to the child care setting each day.

Fig. 9-6D. **Group Meeting Time.** An arrival routine can end with care providers and children gathered in a group to discuss the upcoming day's activities. Telling children the schedule for the day, and having the schedule posted in picture form at children's eye level, helps them feel secure at the center. A good way to begin this conversation time is to sing a familiar greeting song. For children who speak other languages, this serves as a good time to talk, sing, or read stories in other languages. It also helps the children learn about different cultures.

Handling Transitions

A **transition** is a short activity or technique used to guide children smoothly from one activity, routine, or event to another. Transition activities provide children with something to focus on so they make it from one place to another without becoming distracted. As transitions become familiar, they help children adjust to the child care routine. Smooth transitions prevent crowding and keep the classroom atmosphere relaxed but organized.

Transition Times. Transitions take place throughout the day, particularly when children move between learning activities and daily routines. A transition takes place as children leave a large group to play in small-group activities. Transition time can be hand washing before sitting at a table to eat a snack or lunch. After children come inside from outdoor play, a transition takes place as they use the toilet before engaging in an indoor activity. Children picking up toys between activities or at the end of the day are other examples of transition times.

Transition Techniques. Signals or short activities that prompt children to move from one place or routine to another are called **transition techniques**. They often include sounds and visual cues that alert children to what is coming next. Transitions help guide children's behavior without repeating detailed directions. Here are some examples of transition techniques:

- Sing a simple tune when it is time to pick up toys.
- Jingle chimes to gather the group in a circle for music.
- Flicker the lights off and on to signal story time. See Fig. 9-7.
- Play a recording of a drumbeat to lead children to outdoor play.
- Ask children to move like gorillas, rabbits, or robots as they go to wash hands.
- Use puppets, fingerplays, or props to focus children's interest during group-discussion times.

FIG. 9-7. Transitions are essential to help children move from one activity to another. Evaluate various transition techniques for their appropriateness in helping children adjust to the early childhood setting.

- Add surprise to capture curiosity. At music time, use cards with the title of a different children's song on each. Children randomly pick a card, and the class sings the chosen song.
- Play thinking games. Rather than moving children in one large group, play games to move them in smaller groups. Ask children wearing red shirts to leave first, then children with blue shirts, and so on. Many themes can be used, such as patterns on clothing or first letters in children's names. See Fig. 9-8 for more transition techniques.

FIG. 9-8.

TRANSITION TECHNIQUES

- A **chore board** allows children to select a classroom chore to perform. A picture of a different cleanup activity, such as washing paintbrushes or putting away tricycles, is identified on each section of the board. The board is laid flat on the floor. A child tosses a beanbag onto the board and then completes the task indicated by the beanbag's position on the board.

- A **job jar**—a container filled with pieces of paper that show pictures of activities— serves the same purpose as a chore board. Each child draws a piece of paper from the jar and completes the job indicated. Some care providers include special "jobs," such as "hug a friend."

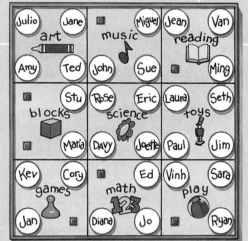

- **Choice time** is a transition technique that lets children decide which activity they would like to participate in next. Care providers handle choice time in a variety of ways. Most begin by gathering children into a group. Then each child is given a nametag, often with a photo on it for easier identification. Care providers then provide a poster board or peg-board that has sections squared off and pictures of different classroom play areas in each section. Children make a choice by placing their nametag in their desired play area, such as art or block building.

Section 9-1 Knowledge Check

1. Explain why the arrival routine sets the tone for the day.
2. What should be included in a daily schedule? Give examples of typical daily routines.
3. Explain three different transition techniques.

Mini-Lab

Observe at two of the following types of early childhood programs: a family day care, a small preschool (one room), or a large child care center (several classrooms). While observing, take notes on routines and transitions that are used. Contrast the use of routines and transitions in each program. Then prepare a written summary of your observations.

Section 9-2

Schedules & Routines for Older Adults

The types of adult day care programs will determine the most appropriate schedules and routines to operate that center. Older adults participate in programs and activities based on their needs. Schedules guide daily routines and encourage older adults to participate in center programs and activities. Schedules and routines also help staff members to plan and implement programs that are appropriate for older adults.

Creating a Schedule

An adult day care program's schedules and routines will vary according to the types of services that are offered and the funding source or sponsor. A **schedule** is a plan that shows task assignments for each staff member. The schedule helps make the services run smoothly. **Routines** are tasks that are performed daily, weekly, or monthly. These routines outline activities and services for center operations. Listing these tasks helps staff members to know what their duties are on a daily basis.

There are just as many types of schedules and routines as there are adult day care programs in America today. According to the

National Adult Day Services Association, adult day care programs generally operate programs during normal business hours five days a week. However, some programs offer evening and weekend services.

Program Needs Impact Schedules

Program requirements can impact the scheduling of activities because of varying needs of participants. Older adults who have physical limitations need help with daily tasks, such as getting their food trays and eating. This kind of assistance requires extra staff time. The time to carry out these tasks must be scheduled so that it will not impact the time to carry out other

FIG. 9-9. One of the first items of consideration for an adult day center is to determine the hours of operation that will best suit the needs of the community. Why might a center need nontraditional hours of operation?

the number of staff members and their roles, tasks, and qualifications and schedules staff members to meet the needs of all older adult participants.

Each day care service program serves a certain number of older adults. This number is used to determine the number of staff members who must be on duty. Generally, one staff member is assigned to no more than six older adults at one time. The schedule shows the names of staff members who are on duty during the day and their assignments. See Fig. 9-10.

An adult day care program needs to have care providers to assist older adults in specific areas. Some staff members can serve in more than one position. The following list shows some possibilities:

- **Nurse.** If the program uses the medical model, it will be necessary to have a nurse on duty during all hours when older adults are present. A nurse might also be a program coordinator.

activities. Since the needs of each participant may vary, it is important to identify and list all needs. The staff assignments are then posted on the daily schedule. See Fig. 9-9.

It is a good idea to list all services that are offered at the center on the schedule. The schedule identifies the number of staff members needed to carry out activities. It also helps to identify the need for full- or part-time staff members.

Staffing Needs Impact Schedules

The program director creates a work schedule for the day care center staff. In order to determine how many people are needed to work and when they are needed, the program director may conduct a needs survey. The director reviews information from each older adult's intake form as part of the survey. This information tells the director about each participant's interests and needs. Then the director reviews

FIG. 9-10. Coordinating medical and social services into the daily routine can impact the planning of activities for the remainder of the day. Individual participants may have differing needs requiring some individual scheduling.

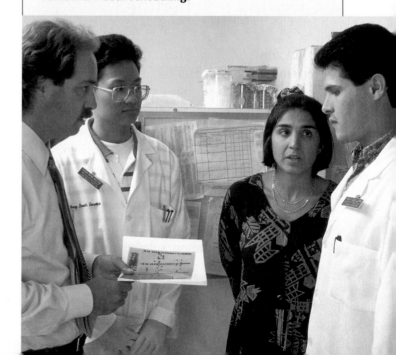

Intergenerational *Interactions*

Scheduling Intergenerational Activities

In scheduling intergenerational activities, care providers need to take the needs of children and older adults into account. The following points should help care providers schedule activities that are rewarding for all generations.

- **Age and Attention Span.** Because older adults can usually adapt to activities as needed, most sessions should be planned around the age of the participating children. For instance, preschoolers have very short attention spans. The planner will want to schedule activities that do not take much time.

- **Number of Participants.** When scheduling intergenerational activities, it is important to maintain a participant-to-staff ratio that ensures safety. A large group of participants playing a parachute game will require more staff than a small group of pairs working on separate art projects. The scheduler will also need to select activities according to the number of participants.

- **Past Experience.** Children who have had little or no interaction with older adults may be fearful of spending one-on-one time painting a picture with older adults. However, those same children may feel very comfortable learning a new song in a large intergenerational group. The same may be true for older adults who have not been around children very often.

- **Activity Location.** People of all generations feel uncomfortable in settings that are unfamiliar or scary to them. Children may be scared at older adult facilities that care for severely ill people. Oxygen tanks, wheelchairs, and other medical equipment may be frightening to young children. Activities should be scheduled in neutral settings, such as multi-purpose rooms.

- **Back-Up Plan.** Regardless of the amount of time and energy a scheduler devotes to planning an intergenerational activity, there is always a chance that the activity may not interest the participants. For that reason, a scheduler should plan a back-up activity to keep participants involved.

Follow-Up

Make a list of 20 activities that could be scheduled for an intergenerational group of ten preschoolers and ten healthy older adults meeting in a community gym. Assume that everyone in the group has intergenerational experience.

FIG. 9-11. Care providers may be assigned to schedule meetings that allow participants to feel there are others who share their special kinds of needs. For example, a care provider may schedule a group of older adults who have diabetes to meet with a nutritionist.

- **Program coordinator.** A program coordinator can be a social worker, a geriatric care manager, or another type of health professional. It is best if the coordinator has a background in services for older adults. A **geriatric care manager**, or a social worker, is a human service professional. He or she has assessment training and experience and monitors services for older adults.

- **Personal care technician.** The individual who provides personal care help with exercise, meal assistance, and medication reminders is the personal care technician. This staff member assists older adults with walking and exercising, personal care, health care, and taking medication. The personal care technician could be a home health aide, certified nursing assistant, or nurse's aide.

- **Family life educator.** The staff member that helps older adults with their finances is the family life educator. These staff members help

older adults and their families with Medicare, Medicaid, and private health insurance. They also run group sessions in the adult day care service program for older adults and their families. The session topics may focus on making decisions about nutritional needs, housing, clothing, and effective communication. See Fig. 9-11.

Personal Care Procedures

All day care programs should provide for personal care procedures and should adhere to national care standards. Adult day care programs should schedule activities to ensure:

- Privacy and confidentiality.
- Personal dignity.
- Social, emotional, and physical health and well-being.
- Activity choices and opportunities to participate and maintain independence.
- Respect for culture beliefs.

Program directors should make every effort to adhere to the program's values and principles when planning and scheduling tasks for staff. The center should have a list of all participants who need assistance for personal care. A staff member is assigned to each participant who needs assistance to make certain that he or she gets to the appropriate activity at the appropriate time. A schedule of each person's routine will help ensure that his or her daily routine is achieved. See Fig. 9-12.

Special Needs

Individuals who have physical restrictions should be given adequate time to carry out tasks in their personal care plans. Staff members should have the necessary training and time to assist these individuals with respect and dignity. The Americans with Disabilities Act (ADA) should guide the services for people with special needs.

activities of daily living are specially trained to help impaired older adults. For example, a physical therapist might help an older adult with muscle-strengthening exercises to increase his or her ability to get out of a chair. See Fig. 9-13.

Instrumental Activities of Daily Living (IADLs). IADLs include six home-management activities: preparing meals; shopping for personal items; managing money; using the telephone; doing heavy homework, such as mowing the lawn; and doing light housework, such as dusting or washing dishes. Many times older adults participate in adult day service programs in order to take advantage of the social service programs, such as referrals to other agencies that provide assistance. Case managers and family life educators are helpful in finding people help for home-management activities.

FIG. 9-12. **Care providers may need to assist some older adults with personal care.** What are some ways to assist older adults with personal care?

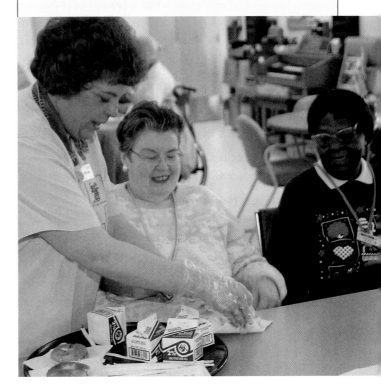

FIG. 9-13. **Providing individual or group physical therapy sessions is often included in the daily schedule. Staff must be scheduled to perform these duties and must work in a timely fashion to avoid interrupting the routines of other staff workers.**

Activities of Daily Living (ADL). Studies show that one-quarter of the elderly population requires assistance with activities of daily living (ADLs). As the population gets older, the number of people in need will increase. Activities of daily living are tasks that people need to perform in order to maintain a quality life. There are seven personal care activities that are included in the ADL category. They are: eating, toileting, dressing, bathing, walking, getting in and out of bed or chair, and getting outside. Care providers who give assistance with the

Administering Medications. Some older adults participate in adult day care programs for reasons that may include getting their vital signs checked. For example, many older adults have high blood pressure and need regular monitoring. In some cases, their medical providers suggest that they take and record their blood pressure daily. People with chronic blood pressure problems are often checked before taking their medications. In most adult day care programs, the participants are required to take their own medication. However, if needed, a certified health care worker should provide assistance. For example, if a person is blind and needs to take a medication before a meal, a health care worker should verify the correct medication and make certain that it is taken appropriately. Therefore, it is important for the director to know why people participate in the programs and activities at an adult day care program. This information helps the director develop programs and activities as well as make staff assignments. See Fig. 9-14.

Daily Routines

The average adult day care program offers a wide range of routine services. These services typically include:

- Providing social service activities, such as making referrals for other needed services in the community.

- Providing a nutritious mid-morning snack, lunch, and afternoon snack.

- Offering nursing care for taking vital signs and medication monitoring as directed by a physician or wound-dressing changes (as needed).

- Assisting with activities of daily living that include, but are not limited to, feeding and toileting as needed by individual participants.

- Conducting physical activities appropriate for each individual's abilities.

- Providing opportunities to develop peer relationships and friendships.

FIG. 9-14. Most older adults are responsible for monitoring when to take their medications when at an adult day center. What exceptions might there be to this rule?

- Providing social, recreational, and entertainment activities. See Fig. 9-15.

Work Plans

A work plan is necessary for care providers to focus on the specific tasks that must be carried out. It serves as a road map to achieving your goals. For example, it helps care providers to outline their activities to meet their clients' needs for a specific time period. Care providers should review their plan of work regularly to make certain that they are accomplishing their daily goals.

Tasks. In adult day service programs, care providers are faced with many duties in their

FIG. 9-15.

DAILY ROUTINES IN ADULT DAY SERVICE PROGRAMS

Routines	Staff Responsibilities
Arrival	• Sign in with the receptionist. • Include meal participation. • Give tour of facility to newcomers and family members. • Arrange for special needs, such as storage of medication. • Take vital signs.
Activities	• Prepare areas for activities (social and therapeutic). • Assist older adult to specific area (if needed). • Take tours (off-campus activities). • Provide personal care (hair salon, hair cuts, pedicure). • Arrange for transportation for medical treatments, such as dialysis.
Mealtimes	• Prepare meals for serving. • Assist those who need help. • Conduct nutritional tips at each meal.
Departure	• Check for belongings. • Assist those who need it to their mode of transportation.

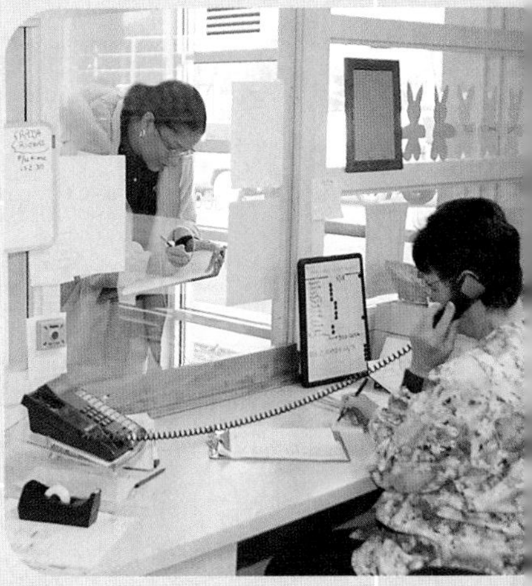

work plans. Tasks are those identified activities that have to be achieved in order for care providers to carry out activities that are listed on their plan of work. They need to be aware of what they have to do at all times. Therefore, it will be important that care providers list their activities that are outlined on their plan of work.

Responsibilities. In order to carry out a plan of work, care providers have to make certain that they achieve their tasks. Responsibilities are those tasks on the work plan for which care providers are legally responsible to carry out. The work plan is a very important document that helps care providers be responsible professionals in working with people at various life stages.

Section 9-2 Knowledge Check

1. How can maintaining a schedule and routine help to have a quality program?
2. What are the typical activities of daily living?
3. What are staff responsibilities in daily routines?

Mini-Lab

Assume that you are the director for an adult day care program that uses a social-medical model for services. Use the key principles for personal care to outline a care provider's schedule to assist an older adult who has some physical restrictions and needs assistance during an 8-hour day program.

Chapter 9 Review & Activities

Section Summaries

9-1 Different programs have schedules that suit their specific needs.

9-1 All children's developmental needs should be considered when creating a schedule.

9-1 Routines are established for arrival, toileting, naps, dressing for outdoor play, meals, and departure.

9-1 Care providers can use transitions to make the schedule operate smoothly.

9-2 A schedule is a document that outlines the tasks for staff members and the activities for older adults.

9-2 The number of staff and their roles, tasks, and qualifications should be considered when making a schedule.

9-2 Care providers work to assist older adults with activities of daily living while maintaining the independence and dignity of each participant.

9-2 A work plan is a document that allows you to outline activities according to tasks that need to be accomplished by a specific time period. It helps workers to keep focused on specific tasks to be achieved.

Check Your Knowledge

1. What is a schedule and why is it useful?
2. List factors that should be balanced in a daily schedule.
3. What is a routine?
4. What is a transition?
5. Explain how each of these transitions techniques can be used in early childhood classrooms: signals, music, chore boards, job jars, and choice time.
6. Contrast activities of daily living with instrumental activities of daily living.
7. List the instrumental activities of daily living.
8. What are the general daily routines at an adult day center? Give an example of staff responsibilities for each.
9. What is a plan of work?

Thinking Critically

1. How can carefully planned schedules and routines contribute to a sense of security and well-being for both young children and older adults?

2. Why is it important to encourage self-help through the routines provided for young children?

3. Contrast planning schedules for young children and older adults. Would it be more difficult to plan schedules for young children or for older adults? Why?

4. Contrast the safety needs of young children and older adults. How are they similar and different?

Practical Applications

1. **Job Shadow.** Shadow a few care providers at an early childhood or adult care facility to learn more about their responsibilities in carrying out the facility's schedule. Write a summary of each person's responsibilities.

2. **Personal Care Routines.** Investigate the care providers' role in assisting older adults with personal care routines. Name at least two personal care routines and describe the care providers' role.

3. **Medical Routines.** Summarize medical routines at one or more early childhood or adult care facilities. Ask about medical records and screening. What local or state guidelines do the centers follow?

Building Your PORTFOLIO

Schedules & Routines

Planning schedules and routines to meet the needs of young children or older adults at a care facility is an important skill. Routines ensure that daily needs of participants are met.

Step 1: Study several resources describing procedures for planning schedules and routines for young children or older adults. Using these resources create a list of guidelines for planning schedules and routines to include in your portfolio.

Step 2: Collect sample schedules from several early childhood facilities or adult day care facilities. Analyze the key quality characteristics of each schedule. What are the similarities and differences? Include the schedules and your analyses in your portfolio.

Step 3: Observe or participate in the routines and transitions of an early childhood or adult care facility for several hours. Draw conclusions about the effectiveness of these routines. Place a copy of your conclusions in your portfolio.

Step 4: Identify the needs to be considered in developing a schedule for a particular child or adult care facility. Create a schedule and routine for the facility. Ask a child or adult care professional at the facility to evaluate your work and make suggestions for improvement. Based on the professional's suggestions, revise the schedule. Include a copy of the revised schedule in your portfolio.

Chapter 10
Meeting Nutritional Needs

Section 10-1
Child Nutrition

Section 10-2
Nutrition for Aging

Section 10-1

Child Nutrition

- Explain the impact of nutrition on early childhood development.
- Identify nutrients required for good nutrition.
- Plan balanced menus for young children.
- Describe proper food safety and sanitation practices.
- Identify meal-service guidelines.

KEY TERMS

nutrients
nutrition
fiber
amino acids
complete protein
incomplete protein
deficiency
Food Guide Pyramid
perishable
health department inspector

Exposure to a variety of foods helps children develop positive attitudes toward eating properly. In turn, eating properly enhances children's well-being. Those who are responsible for children need to understand how proper nutrition improves the lives of young children.

Basics of Good Nutrition

Nutrients are the substances in food that the body uses to function, grow, repair tissue, and produce energy. **Nutrition** is the process through which the body uses the nutrients in food.

Some nutrients provide energy for activities, such as running or playing a game, and for essential body processes, such as pumping blood and digesting food. Other nutrients help keep the body working smoothly. With the right balance of many different nutrients, the body can produce the energy it needs. It functions properly and has resistance to illness.

Good nutrition is especially important in the early years. It provides the foundation for children's normal physical growth. Proper early growth and development are critical to having a long, healthful life. Nutrition affects intellectual development as well. To function properly, the brain must regularly receive important chemicals from nutrients. Most of the brain's growth occurs in the first two years of life. Research has shown that well-nourished children learn better. Their ability to combat fatigue and everyday stress is enhanced.

Nutrition Requirements for Children

For good health, the body needs six types of nutrients: carbohydrates, proteins, fats, vitamins, minerals, and water. Each plays a unique role in developing a healthy body. See Fig. 10-1.

- **Carbohydrates** (car-boh-HI-draytes). The body's main source of energy comes from carbohydrates. There are two types of carbo-

FIG. 10-1. Children need to eat healthful foods that provide each of the basic nutrients. These nutrients help children grow and develop and provide energy. What are the consequences of poor nutrition for young children?

hydrates: simple carbohydrates which are sugars and complex carbohydrates which are starches. Simple carbohydrates, such as those found in candies and desserts, should be limited. Complex carbohydrates—such as those found in vegetables and breads and cereals, rice, and pasta—are also rich sources of other nutrients. They also help the body make the best use of proteins and fats. Many complex carbohydrates also contain **fiber**, a plant material that doesn't break down when the body digests food. Fiber helps the body eliminate waste and is an important part of healthful eating.

- **Proteins.** These nutrients help the body build, maintain, and repair body cells. They are necessary for growth and to fight off disease. Proteins are made of chemical compounds called **amino acids**. The body makes all but nine amino acids which are called *essential amino acids* because they must be supplied by the food people eat. Meat, poultry, fish, eggs, and dairy products provide

complete protein—protein that contains the essential amino acids. Individually, proteins from plant sources provide **incomplete protein**—protein that doesn't contain all of the essential amino acids. Complete protein can also be formed by eating the right combination of foods from plant sources. Simply combine dry beans, dry peas, or peanut butter with grains, nuts, or seeds. For example, peanut butter and whole wheat bread together provide complete protein.

- **Fats.** Providing energy and carrying some vitamins that regulate body processes are the functions of fats. They are also needed for healthy skin. Fats are obtained from foods, such as meat, vegetable oils, whole dairy products, egg yolks, nuts, margarine, mayonnaise, and salad dressing.

- **Vitamins.** These nutrients help keep the body working properly and help other nutrients do their jobs. They include vitamins A, C, D, E, and K, as well as the B-complex vitamins (a group of several nutrients which includes folate). Each vitamin has specific jobs to do. For example, vitamin A protects the eyes, contributes to healthy skin, and helps provide resistance to disease. Vitamin D combines with the minerals calcium and phosphorus to build and maintain strong bones and teeth. Vitamins are found in varying amounts in a wide variety of foods including grain products, fruits, vegetables, dairy products, meat, fish, poultry, eggs, dry beans and peas, and nuts.

- **Minerals.** Helping regulate body processes is the function of minerals. They also become a part of the body's bones, tissues, and fluids. Many different minerals—including calcium, phosphorus, iron, potassium, and sodium—carry out specific functions in the human body. For example, iron helps build red blood cells and sodium helps maintain the fluid balance in the body. Eating a wide variety of foods—including milk and milk products, meat, poultry, fish, and eggs, whole grains, and vegetables and fruits—helps the body

FIG. 10-2. Water is essential to good health. Children, just like adults, must have adequate amounts of water to maintain good health. **Why is water important?**

get all of these important minerals and the other nutrients it needs.

• **Water.** Water is essential for life. You can live for several days or even weeks without food, but only about three days without water. Water is present in every cell of the body. It delivers nutrients throughout the body, serves as the body's cooling system, and helps the body eliminate waste. See Fig. 10-2.

Balanced Nutrition

As you have seen, many different nutrients play a role in maintaining good health. These nutrients work as a team. The body needs specific amounts of each. If children are lacking in one or more nutrients, especially over long periods of time, they can develop serious health problems. For instance, a **deficiency** (severe shortage) of vitamin D can lead to rickets, a disease in which bones soften and may become deformed. A deficiency of iron can cause a type of anemia. Children with this condition are tired, pale, and weak and have poor appetites. Getting too much of some nutrients, such as fat, sugar, and sodium, can also lead to child obesity and health problems in later life.

To maintain good health, children need a variety of nutritious foods daily. These foods should be chosen with care to ensure that they provide the right balance of nutrients.

Food Guide Pyramid. One way to plan balanced, nutritious meals and snacks is with the help of the **Food Guide Pyramid**—a guide to daily food choices based on the recommendations of nutrition experts. The Food Guide Pyramid organizes food into five main groups, according to the nutrients they contain. Children and adults need foods from each of the following groups every day:

• Bread, Cereal, Rice, and Pasta Group.
• Vegetable Group.
• Fruit Group.
• Milk, Yogurt, and Cheese Group.
• Meat, Poultry, Fish, Dry Beans, Eggs, and Nuts Group.

These food groups are shown in the pyramid diagram in Figure 10-3. The small tip of the pyramid represents Fats, Oils, and Sweets. Large amounts of foods in this category are not essential for good health and should be used sparingly. The amounts required are easily obtained through eating foods from the five main groups. Children under age two, however, experience rapid growth and brain development. They need the fat in foods for growth. Milk should be whole, not low-fat, for children at this age. Following food guidelines, such as the Food Guide Pyramid, is essential in promoting children's good health.

FIG. 10-3.

FOOD Guide PYRAMID
for Young Children

A Daily Guide for 2- to 6-Year-Olds

Fats & Sweets — Eat LESS

MILK Group 2 servings

MEAT Group 2 servings

VEGETABLE Group 3 servings

FRUIT Group 2 servings

GRAIN Group 6 servings

U.S. DEPARTMENT OF AGRICULTURE
CENTER FOR NUTRITION POLICY AND PROMOTION

USDA is an equal opportunity provider and employer.

FOOD IS FUN and learning about food is fun, too. Eating foods from the Food Guide Pyramid and being physically active will help you grow healthy and strong.

U.S. Department of Agriculture
Center for Nutrition Policy and Promotion
March 1999
Program Aid 1648

WHAT COUNTS AS ONE SERVING?

GRAIN GROUP
1 slice of bread
½ cup of cooked rice or pasta
½ cup of cooked cereal
1 ounce of ready-to-eat cereal

VEGETABLE GROUP
½ cup of chopped raw or cooked vegetables
1 cup of raw leafy vegetables

FRUIT GROUP
1 piece of fruit or melon wedge
¾ cup of juice
½ cup of canned fruit
¼ cup of dried fruit

MILK GROUP
1 cup of milk or yogurt
2 ounces of cheese

MEAT GROUP
2 to 3 ounces of cooked lean meat, poultry, or fish

½ cup of cooked dry beans, or
1 egg counts as 1 ounce of lean meat.
2 tablespoons of peanut butter count as 1 ounce of meat.

FATS AND SWEETS
Limit calories from these.

Four- to 6-year-olds can eat these serving sizes. Offer 2- to 3-year-olds less, except for milk.
Two- to 6-year-old children need a total of 2 servings from the milk group each day.

EAT a variety of FOODS AND ENJOY!

Servings for Children

The five main food groups are equally important to health; however, they are not needed in equal amounts. The Food Guide Pyramid shows a range of recommended daily servings for each group. Generally, young children should have at least the lowest number of servings in the range. The needs for older children usually fall in the middle of the range. The needs of adults vary depending on their daily activities.

Serving sizes for young children are smaller than those for adults. Young children have smaller stomachs that cannot hold as much food at one time. For example, a preschooler might be served half of an apple for lunch instead of a whole apple. Some nutritionists recommend serving about 1 tablespoon of each food choice per year of a child's age. A serving of vegetables for a three-year-old might be about 3 tablespoons. One exception is milk. Children need the same amount of milk or milk equivalent per day as most adults—at least 2 cups. This amount can be divided into several small portions and may include foods such as milk, yogurt, and pudding.

A child should not be forced to eat large portions at mealtime. Offer small amounts at first, and then let the child have more if he or she is still hungry. Between meals, offer nutritious snacks that keep up children's energy and provide additional servings from the food groups.

Menu Planning

The type of meal service provided by a child care program depends on the hours of operation and the age of the children. A full-day program might provide breakfast, lunch, and one or two snacks. If a program is open later hours, an evening meal may also be provided. Half-day preschools might only provide a snack.

When programs provide full food service, they usually employ a person to plan menus and food budgets, purchase food, and prepare meals. This person may be a nutritionist or dietitian. In other programs, care providers may take on some or all of the responsibility for planning, preparing, and serving meals and snacks. See Fig. 10-4.

Meet Nutrition Requirements

When planning menus for a child care program, three important questions must be considered: Will the meal or snack be nutritious yet within the budget? Will it be easy and safe for children to eat? Will it appeal to children?

FIG. 10-4. **Planning nutritious meals and snacks is part of the responsibility of early childhood professionals.**

SAMPLE MENU

Breakfast: Sliced Banana, Corn Flakes, Milk

Midmorning Snack: Pineapple Juice, Whole-Wheat Toast

Lunch: Baked Chicken, Mashed Potatoes, Carrot Sticks, Roll, Milk

Afternoon Snack: Milk, Bean and Cheese Burrito

FIG. 10-5.

MEAL PATTERNS FOR CHILDREN

Breakfast	Children 1-3 years	Children 4-5 years	Children 6-12 years
Milk, fluid	½ cup	¾ cup	1 cup
Juice or **Fruit** or **Vegetable**	¼ cup	½ cup	½ cup
Bread and/or **cereal**			
Enriched or whole-grain bread	½ slice	1 slice	1 slice
Cereal: Cold dry or	¼ cup[1]	½ cup	¾ cup[2]
Hot cooked	¼ cup	½ cup	½ cup
Mid-morning or Mid-afternoon snack (supplement)			
(Select 2 of these 4 components.)			
Milk, fluid	½ cup	½ cup	1 cup
Meat or meat alternative	½ oz.	½ oz.	1 oz.
Juice or **Fruit** or **Vegetable**	½ cup	½ cup	¾ cup
Bread and/or **cereal**			
Enriched or whole-grain bread	½ slice	½ slice	1 slice
Cereal: Cold dry or	¼ cup[1]	½ cup	¾ cup[2]
Hot cooked	¼ cup	½ cup	½ cup
Lunch/Supper			
Milk, fluid	½ cup	¾ cup	1 cup
Meat or meat alternative			
Meat, **Poultry**, or **Fish**, cooked (lean meat without bone)	1 oz.	2 oz.	2 oz.
Cheese	1 oz.	2 oz.	2 oz.
Egg	1	1	1
Cooked dry beans and peas	¼ cup	¼ cup	½ cup
Peanut butter or other nut or seed butters	2 Tbsp.	2 Tbsp.	4 Tbsp.
Nuts and/or seeds	½ oz.[3]	¾ oz.[3]	1 oz.[3]
Vegetable and/or **fruit** (two or more)	¼ cup	½ cup	¾ cup
Bread or bread alternative, enriched or whole-grain	½ slice	½ slice	1 slice

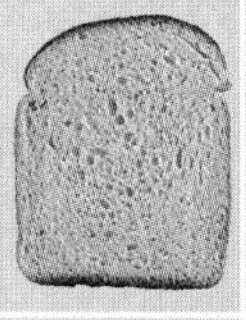

[1] ¼ cup (volume) or ⅓ ounce (weight), whichever is less.

[2] ¾ cup (volume) or 1 ounce (weight), whichever is less.

[3] This portion can meet only one-half of the total serving of the meat/meat alternate requirement for lunch or supper. Nuts or seeds must be combined with another meat/meat alternate to fulfill the requirement. For determining combinations, 1 ounce of nuts or seeds is equal to 1 ounce of cooked lean meat, poultry, or fish. Caution: Children under five years of age are at the highest risk of choking. The USDA recommends that any nuts or seeds be served to them in a prepared food and be ground or finely chopped.

Metric Conversions (approximate): 1 Tbsp.=15 mL; ¼ cup=50 mL; ⅓ cup=75 mL; ⅜ cup=90 mL; ½ cup=125 mL; ¾ cup=175 mL; 1 cup=250 mL; ⅓ oz.=9 g; ½ oz.=14 g; ¾ oz.=21 g; 1 oz.=28 g.

FIG. 10-6. Care providers need to keep the cultural and ethnic diversity of the children in mind as they prepare menus for weekly meals. How can regional differences impact diverse meal planning?

Answering yes to all those questions takes creative planning. Including bright colors and different shapes on the plate makes for attractive meals and snacks. For even more interest, serve foods with different textures—soft and creamy, hard and crunchy, chewy, or crisp. Children's taste buds are sensitive, so foods should be only lightly seasoned.

Preparing foods in a variety of ways encourages new food choices. For instance, broccoli may be part of a salad for one meal. The next time it is served, it may be steamed as a side dish or eaten raw with a dip as a snack. A sample child care menu is shown on page 253. How well do you think it fulfills the goals of nutrition, ease of eating, and appeal to young children?

Child and Adult Care Food Program. A child nutrition program that many early childhood programs participate in is the Child and Adult Care Food Program (CACFP). This is a federally funded program that helps provide healthful meals and snacks in child and adult care facilities. To participate and receive funding from CACFP, programs must serve meals that meet federal nutrition guidelines. The meal pattern established by the CACFP is shown in Fig. 10-5.

Cultural and Ethnic Diversity. Menus should include foods children are familiar with in their home. This requires planning meals and snacks that include foods from diverse cultures and ethnicities. Introducing such foods broadens all children's food preferences. Adding ethnic foods—such as bagels, tortillas, lavosh (Armenian bread), scones, or wontons—during snack time is a good start. Lunches that include different pastas, various types of rice and beans, breads, fruits, and vegetables go a long way in making all children feel welcome in a program. See Fig. 10-6.

Accommodate Special Needs. Some children may be unable to eat certain foods because of allergies or other medical problems. In addition, religious beliefs may call for avoiding certain foods or food combinations. Be sure to ask parents about any such restrictions that may apply to their child. Keep a convenient record of these restrictions to consult when planning meals. Consult with the staff member who plans meals to determine appropriate alternatives for children with special needs. Working together, staff members can provide dietary modifications for those with special diet needs. For example, if a child is allergic to strawberries, you might offer the children blueberries or orange slices for a fruit item.

Allergy Identification. Enrollment applications should ask parents to list children's allergies. They should include allergies to food or other substances. When a new child joins the class, care providers should review his or her application to identify allergies. If a food allergy is noted, the care provider should alert fellow staff, including meal planners and food servers. If a child has an allergic reaction that requires emergency treatment, call for medical assistance immediately.

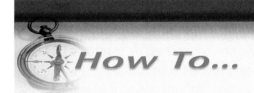
How To...

Encourage Good Eating Patterns

Eating habits learned in early childhood continue into adulthood. If children learn to choose wisely and moderately from the food groups, they will live more healthful lives. To encourage good eating patterns, conduct nutrition education activities for children and parents. This ensures that healthful eating will be reinforced at home. Preschoolers can understand these basic nutrition concepts:

- Food is fuel for the body. It helps people grow and gives them energy.
- People should eat a variety of foods every day to remain healthy.
- People need to drink eight glasses of water every day.
- Food comes from plants and animals.
- People eat different parts of plants, including stems, roots, leaves, and seeds.
- Most food is grown on the farm and then taken to a supermarket.
- People can grow their own food in gardens.
- People from different parts of the world eat different foods.
- Food can be cooked in many different ways.
- When preparing food, hands must be clean before and during cooking.

Nutrition concepts are taught to children through simple food or cooking activities. The younger the child, the more simple the activity should be. Two-year-olds can spread peanut butter on crackers. As children develop, they can prepare muffins or vegetable soup. Conduct food activities at a child-size table with an easily cleaned surface. Talk about food safety skills, as well as the smell, taste, and appearance of the food.

Link many activities to nutrition education. After reading "Goldilocks and the Three Bears," ask children to prepare porridge (oatmeal) for that morning's snack. Field trips to a farm, orchard, supermarket, or restaurant highlight food choices. Use songs, finger plays, games, poems, flannel board stories, and puppet shows to teach good eating habits.

As parents learn about nutrition, they will provide healthful meals at home. They will also be more likely to set a good example for healthful eating. Following are ways to educate parents on nutrition:

- Ask parents to join the class for a meal, cooking project, or food-related field trip.
- Include nutritious snack or meal recipes in center newsletters.
- Host a potluck meal featuring healthful foods.
- Invite parents of various cultures to share ethnic recipes and cooking techniques.

Some parents may need extra assistance with nutrition. These parents may be referred to a federally funded nutrition program called the Women, Infants, and Children (WIC) Program. This program provides nutrition advice and low-cost food, including infant formula. It is available to low-income pregnant and breast-feeding women, infants, and children up to five years old.

APPLY IT!

Plan and carry out a food-related activity for preschool children. The activity should incorporate all of the information found in this section, including nutrition and proper sanitation. Evaluate the results of your activity.

Serving Meals & Snacks

Care providers who plan menus for early childhood programs should read food labels so they choose products with high nutritional value. Here are tips for making sure the foods served are nutritious:

- Choose fruit and vegetable juices that are 100 percent juice, with no added sweetener.

- Serve fruits and vegetables raw when possible. Valuable nutrients can be lost during cooking. When you do cook fruits and vegetables, choose such methods as microwave cooking, steaming, or simmering in a small amount of water. Avoid overcooking.

- Choose low-fat dairy products for children older than age two.

- Serve only lean meats. To reduce fat, bake or broil meats instead of frying.

- Choose whole-grain breads, crackers, and cereals. Whole-grain products provide fiber, which helps keep the digestive tract working normally.

- Encourage children to drink small amounts of water frequently throughout the day. Of course, water is also present in juices and milk, but the best source is plain, natural water from the tap or drinking fountain.

Serve Easy-to-Eat Foods. Young children are just learning to use eating utensils. Offer eating utensils that are appropriate for the age of the children. Younger toddlers may need sipper cups with lids or straw. Older toddlers might be able to use sturdy cups with handles. In order to make eating easier, include some finger foods, such as carrot sticks or apple slices. Serve children's food in small, bite-size pieces. Large chunks of meat, vegetables, or fruit may be difficult for them to chew and could cause choking. Children may need to be reminded to eat slowly and chew food thoroughly. See Fig. 10-7A.

FIG. 10-7A.

FIG. 10-7B. **Foods for children, such as fruit and vegetable slices, should be easy to handle and eat. Children can easily choke on other foods, such as those above.**

Foods to Avoid. Avoid serving young children nuts, popcorn, grapes, hot dogs, and hard candies. These foods can be inhaled easily and cause choking. For some children, foods such as nuts can also cause allergic reactions. In case of choking, use the Heimlich maneuver (explained in Chapter 6). A poster showing how to perform the Heimlich maneuver should be displayed in every eating area. See Fig. 10-7B.

Building Social Skills. Snacks and meals should be served under pleasant, relaxing conditions. Care providers should carefully role model good manners, so children can learn to develop them. Care providers can guide children in proper meal conversation, so they learn how to behave respectfully at home or when eating out.

Food Safety & Sanitation

Part of taking good care of children is ensuring that they receive nutritious foods that are safe to eat as well as handled in clean, sanitary ways. Safe food-handling standards have been established by the United States Department of Agriculture (USDA) and the Food and Drug Administration (FDA). Use the Internet to locate the most recent edition of the Food Code.

Food Safety

Food that is spoiled or tainted with bacteria can cause serious illness in children and adults. Anyone preparing to serve food must be trained in food safety and sanitation practices.

In addition to cleanliness, proper temperatures for storing and serving food are necessary. Many foods are **perishable,** which means they will spoil if not refrigerated or frozen. That is because bacteria multiply rapidly at room temperature. Cold temperatures limit the growth of bacteria. High temperatures used in cooking food destroy many harmful bacteria. See Fig. 10-8.

Limiting Food Hazards. To maintain proper food temperatures, follow these guidelines:

• Store food in properly cooled refrigerators and freezers. Keep refrigerator temperatures between 32°F and 41°F. Keep the freezer at 0°F or lower.

• Never let frozen food thaw at room temperature. Instead, thaw it in the refrigerator. You may also use a microwave oven to defrost the food, as long as you cook it right away. Refrigerated foods, especially protein foods, should be out of the refrigerator no longer than a total of four hours which includes preparation and serving time.

• Be sure food is cooked thoroughly. Meats should be cooked to a minimum internal temperature of 155°F. Poultry should be cooked to a minimum internal temperature of 165°F. Refrigerated or frozen leftovers should be thoroughly reheated to an internal temperature of 165°F. Once you begin to cook the food, continue until it reaches proper temperature and is completely done.

• When serving a meal or snack, keep hot foods hot at 140°F or above and cold foods cold at 41°F or below. Otherwise, bacteria will grow rapidly as the food reaches room temperature.

• After a meal, discard table leftovers. Freeze or refrigerate any kitchen leftovers promptly. If perishable food has been left sitting out for more than one-half hour, discard it.

Keeping Records. State laws usually require child care programs to be monitored regularly by the local health department. A **health department inspector** periodically observes and evaluates a program's health practices including the foodservice area. Health inspectors make sure that meal-service personnel follow and practice proper food safety and sanitation procedures. Records of health department inspections must be maintained in an office file. See Chapter 5 for more information on keeping records.

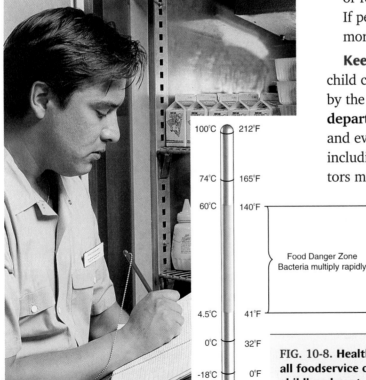

100°C	212°F
74°C	165°F
60°C	140°F
	Food Danger Zone Bacteria multiply rapidly
4.5°C	41°F
0°C	32°F
-18°C	0°F

FIG. 10-8. Health inspectors make regular visits to all foodservice operations, including those in early childhood centers. Why are regular health inspections important?

FIG. 10-9. Cleanliness is vital in preparing, storing, and serving foods. Sanitizing tables on which food will be served (or has been served) is important to prevent foodborne illness. Why is hand washing and using hair restraints important for all foodhandlers?

Sanitation

Sanitation means practicing cleanliness to prevent the spread of illness and disease. Harmful bacteria and other disease-carrying agents can easily spread from unclean hands or equipment to food. Strict cleaning routines and consistent use of proper sanitary precautions help keep food safe for eating. See Fig. 10-9.

Foodhandlers must wear hair restraints while preparing food. If a foodhandler has a wound, he or she must wear disposable gloves until it is healed. Foodhandlers must take care not to cough or sneeze on the food. They also must wash their hands thoroughly at the following times:

- Before beginning food preparation.
- After coughing, sneezing, or blowing their nose.
- After using the restroom.
- After handling raw meat, poultry, fish, or eggs.

Clean, sanitary cooking equipment also contributes to food safety. Equipment that touched raw food, such as cutting boards and knives, must be scrubbed in hot, soapy water before being used for other foods. All dishes and utensils must be sanitized after each use and cleaning. This is usually done in dishwashers, using very hot (170°F) water to kill bacteria. Eating areas and food-preparation areas must be cleaned with a sanitizing solution before and after each use. Sanitizing solution can consist of one tablespoon of ultra bleach per gallon of water. Food must be served on clean dishes, never the same dishes that were touched by raw food.

Section **10-1** Knowledge Check

1. What are basic nutrient requirements for young children?
2. What qualities make up a safe, appealing meal for young children?
3. What are the safety and sanitation methods for keeping food safe to eat?

Mini-Lab

Using the Food Guide Pyramid, plan nutritious meals and snacks for an early childhood program for a week. If possible, prepare at least one meal and snack for your on-site early childhood program. Be sure to explain how you would meet any cultural or special needs.

Section **10-2**

Nutrition for Older Adults

OBJECTIVES

- Identify the nutritional needs of older adults.
- Summarize the guidelines for effective meal planning for older adults.
- Explain how to effectively make food purchases, label food properly, and handle food safely.
- Describe how illness and medications impact nutrition for older adults.
- Summarize the key components of food assistance programs.

KEY TERMS

antioxidants
anemia
osteoporosis
nutrient dense
shelf life
Elderly Nutrition
  Program (ENP)
Meals on Wheels
congregate meals

As you learned in Section 1 of this chapter, nutrients come from many sources, and they function to keep the human body healthy. Good nutrition means eating a balanced variety of nutritious foods and drinking the recommended daily amount of water. Practicing good nutrition helps people to have and to maintain wellness. Proper nutrition and regular exercise are the keys to having a healthy body. When experts determine nutritional plans for people, they must consider their physiologic, economic, and cultural issues.

Nutritional Needs for Older Adults

As people age, they have the same general nutrient requirements (with some exceptions) as they did when they were younger. For good health, older adults need foods from each of the six classes of nutrients: carbohydrates, proteins, fats, vitamins, minerals, and water. Here are some ways that each of these nutrients plays a role in helping older adults maintain good health.

Carbohydrates. As you learned in Section 10-1, carbohydrates are the body's main source of energy. Older adults should obtain 55 to 60 percent of their calories from complex carbohydrate sources. Complex carbohydrates—such as dry beans and peas, fruits, vegetables, and all grains—are rich in nutrients and high in dietary fiber. Dietary fiber helps eliminate body wastes and may help older adults maintain blood sugar and blood fat levels. Fiber may also be helpful in preventing heart disease and certain colon disorders. Foods that are high in complex carbohydrates are often lower in cost and fit well into the older adult's budget.

Protein. Essential for building, maintaining, and repairing body cells, protein foods are necessary for good health. Lack of protein can interfere with healing, the older adult's ability to fight off illness, and can reduce the strength of body muscles. Older adults need the same amount of protein as they did when they were younger—about five ounces per day. Good sources of protein are found in meats, poultry, fish, eggs, dairy products, dry beans and peas, and peanut butter. Some older adults do not eat enough protein because many protein foods may be difficult to chew or may be too expensive on a limited budget. See Fig. 10-10. Here are some ways that care providers can help encourage older adults to get enough protein:

- Suggest choosing soft protein foods, such as eggs or ground meats.

- Suggest lower-cost protein sources, such as dry beans and peas, eggs, and peanut butter.

- Promote using small amounts of protein foods in casseroles to make them go further.

- Encourage older adults to get their teeth and gums checked by a dentist. Sometimes dental problems get in the way of older adults eating protein foods.

Fats. Older and young adults alike have the same requirements for fats. Providing energy, carrying vitamins that regulate body processes,

FIG. 10-11. **Foods packed with vitamins and minerals help regulate body processes for all people, including older adults.**

FIG. 10-10. **Inexpensive sources of protein help older adults meet their nutritional needs.** What other sources of protein are healthful for older adults?

and maintaining healthy skin are just some of the functions of fats. The intake of fats should be limited to 30 percent of a person's calorie intake per day. Some older adults may need to limit their intake of saturated fats and cholesterol for health reasons. Food sources of fat include: vegetable oils (such as olive or peanut oil), nuts, egg yolks, butter and margarine, whole milk and dairy products, and salad dressings.

Vitamins. These nutrients regulate body processes and help other nutrients do their jobs. Older adults need to have an adequate intake of vitamins. Vitamins C, D, A, E, B_{12}, and folic acid (a B vitamin) require special attention from older adults to make sure their intake is adequate. See Fig. 10-11. As people age, their ability to absorb these nutrients decreases. Therefore, it is essential to eat foods rich in these nutrients. Vitamins C, E, and A are called the antioxidant vitamins. **Antioxidants** appear to play an important role in some age-related concerns, such as arthritis and eye problems. Here are some good sources of these nutrients:

- **Vitamin C.** Foods rich in vitamin C include oranges, grapefruit, cantaloupe, strawberries, broccoli, and baked potatoes. Vitamin C helps the body absorb iron (a mineral) from plant food sources which in turn helps develop red blood cells.

- **Vitamin D.** Foods rich in vitamin D include milk and dairy products and cereals with added vitamin D. The human body will also make vitamin D when the skin is exposed to sunshine for short periods of time several days per week. Vitamin D is necessary for preventing bone loss. Many older adults do not eat enough foods that are rich in vitamin D. Care providers should encourage older adults to increase their intake of milk products by eating foods such as milk-based soups and puddings.

- **Vitamin A.** Vitamin A is necessary to maintain sight and is also an antioxidant vitamin. This vitamin helps the eyes adjust to low light levels and is important for a healthy immune system. Beta carotene (bay-tuh KAR-uh-teen)—a yellow pigment found in foods—is converted into vitamin A by the body. Good sources of vitamin A and beta carotene include: dark green leafy vegetables; dark yellow vegetables, such as carrots and winter squash; and fish, liver, and eggs.

- **Vitamin E.** Also an antioxidant vitamin, vitamin E research indicates that this nutrient may be helpful in enhancing the immune systems of all older adults. Vitamin E may be helpful in lowering the risk of cardiovascular (KAR-dee-oh-VAS-kyuh-luhr) disease and heart attack. Sources of vitamin E include dark green leafy vegetables, nuts, wheat germ, and vegetable oils.

- **Vitamin B_{12} and folic acid.** These vitamins work together with vitamin D to help the body make red blood cells. When older adults do not get enough of these vitamins, they may develop **anemia**—a condition in which there are not enough red blood cells in the body to carry oxygen. Good sources of folic acid include: yeast breads, dark green leafy vegetables, dry beans and peas, and some cereals with added folic acid. Good sources of vitamin B_{12} include dairy products, meat, poultry, and fish.

Minerals. Like vitamins, minerals are essential for regulating body processes and building and maintaining body tissues. With the exceptions of calcium, iron, and zinc, the mineral needs for older adults do not appear to change throughout life. The following information offers details about the mineral needs of older adults:

- **Calcium.** Used for building and maintaining bones and teeth, calcium is a nutrient that requires special attention by older adults and their care providers. Women over age 65 require at least 1000 to 1500 milligrams of calcium per day. Men over age 65 need at least 1000 milligrams per day. Proper intake of calcium combined with vitamin D helps reduce bone loss in older adults. Although women are more prone to this disease, both older men and women are at risk for devel-

FIG. 10-12. It's easy to forget that water is a nutrient and essential for good health. How can lack of adequate water impact older adults?

oping **osteoporosis**, a disease in which bones become brittle and weak and can fracture easily. For this reason, older adults need to eat calcium-rich foods, such as milk and milk products, broccoli, and foods with calcium added, such as juices.

- **Iron.** Although older women need less iron than younger women, iron deficiency can still be a problem for older adults. In order to ensure adequate dietary iron, older adults should eat whole-grain foods, dry beans and peas, cereals with added iron, lean meat, liver, and fish. Eating foods that contain vitamin C—such as melons and citrus fruits— helps the bodies of older adults better absorb iron.

- **Zinc.** Many older adults lack enough zinc in their diets. Some medications may limit how well the body absorbs zinc. Fighting infections and building and repairing body tissues are some of the functions of zinc in the body. Zinc also helps the body use carbohydrates, proteins, and fats. Good sources of zinc include: meat, poultry, fish, and eggs.

Water. For many older adults, dehydration (dee-hi-DRAY-shuhn) can be a serious problem. Older adults may not sense thirst as they did when they were younger. They should drink a minimum of eight cups of fluid daily. The best source of fluid is water; however, other sources include fruit juice, soup, and milk. See Fig. 10-12.

Nutrition Principles

Although the general nutrient needs do not change, many older adults need fewer calories than they did in their younger years. Activity level and calorie intake go hand-in-hand. Older adults who are less active are more likely to gain weight. Therefore, increasing activity levels or taking in fewer calories can help older adults maintain a healthy body weight as they age.

When calories are limited, older adults must be careful to eat foods that are packed with

FIG. 10-13. **Because they often need fewer calories, older adults need smaller portions of nutrient-dense foods. Creative use of nutrient-dense foods helps to maintain the health and weight of older adults.**

nutrients. Foods that are **nutrient dense** provide a large amount of nutrients in relation to the number of calories. For example, a serving of broccoli has high amounts of vitamins A and C with few calories. Whereas, a doughnut is high in calories and fat, but low in other essential nutrients. Nutrient-dense foods include: cheese, dry beans and peas, fruits and vegetables, eggs, fish, poultry, and meat. See Fig. 10-13.

Guidelines for Healthful Eating

Recent research at Tufts University suggests a modified Food Guide Pyramid that accurately recommends calories and nutrients needed for healthy adults 70 years of age and older. These guidelines help older adults avoid some of the common dietary deficiencies they might experience as they age. See Fig. 10-14. This modified Pyramid recommends that older adults:

- Eat at least the minimum number of servings from each food group in the Food Guide Pyramid. However, include only sparingly amounts of foods from the Pyramid tip, since they are calorie-dense choices that offer few other nutrients.

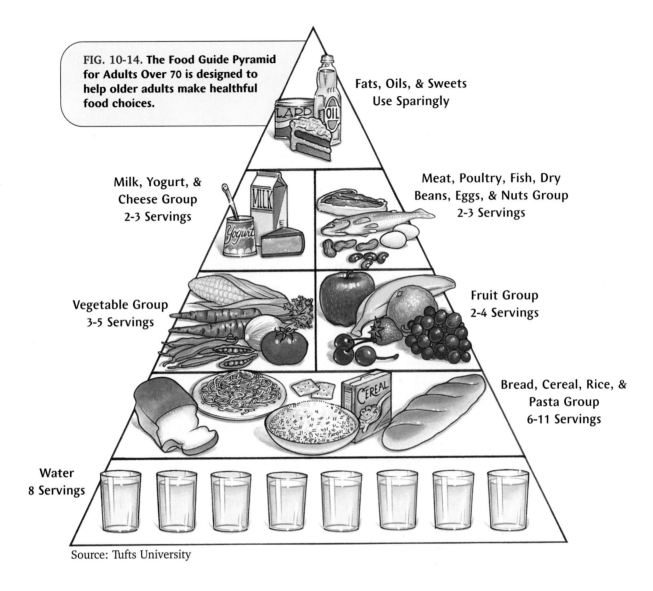

FIG. 10-14. The Food Guide Pyramid for Adults Over 70 is designed to help older adults make healthful food choices.

Fats, Oils, & Sweets
Use Sparingly

Milk, Yogurt, & Cheese Group
2-3 Servings

Meat, Poultry, Fish, Dry Beans, Eggs, & Nuts Group
2-3 Servings

Vegetable Group
3-5 Servings

Fruit Group
2-4 Servings

Bread, Cereal, Rice, & Pasta Group
6-11 Servings

Water
8 Servings

Source: Tufts University

- Eat a variety of foods that are good sources of protein, vitamins, minerals, and fiber. It is important to eat nutrient-dense foods.

- Eat at least three servings of calcium-rich foods.

- Eat fiber-rich foods, including whole grains, fruits, vegetables, dry beans, and nuts.

- Eat foods with added vitamin B_{12}, calcium, and vitamin D. Older adults or their care providers should consult a doctor or dietitian to determine if a dietary supplement is needed.

- Drink at least eight cups of water each day. Because older adults take more medications and are more at risk for dehydration and constipation, older adults need more water.

Dietary Deficiencies & Disorders

Dietary deficiencies and disorders in older adults can be contributed to the lack of vitamins, such as vitamin D, and inadequate amounts of food that can cause malnutrition. Many things contribute to the risk of malnutrition in older adults. For example, chronic diseases—such as arthritis—may lead to physical limitations and chronic diseases—such as Alzheimer's disease—that lead to cognitive limitations. Dental problems may be a concern for some older adults so they avoid eating foods that must be chewed well, such as vegetable salad and certain meats. Depression may also lead to severe weight loss. Changes in the senses of smell and taste, which can result from aging or from medications, can cause a decrease in food intake or a disinterest in food that older adults have once enjoyed.

Dietary Modifications. The Food Guide Pyramid can be helpful in making the proper modifications for eating a healthful diet. Although many older adults will eat a normal diet, dietary modifications may be necessary when some older adults have health concerns that require changes. These diet changes are used to improve the health of older adults. Here are some possible diet modifications you may be required to use with older adults:

- **Liquid diet.** When older adults are ill or have difficulty chewing, a liquid diet may be prescribed by a doctor. Liquids may include fruit juices, broth, cream soups, gelatin, sherbet, strained vegetable juice, milk, and milk- and soy-based supplements.

- **Soft diet.** When older adults are recovering from illness, they may need a soft diet. Soft diets consist of soft-textured foods that are easy to digest. Food examples include soft-cooked eggs, chopped meats, potatoes and other soft vegetables and fruits, and some cereals. Note that foods should not be fried or highly seasoned. See Fig. 10-15.

- **Diabetic diets.** Considered a modification of a normal diet, diabetic diets are individually designed to meet the nutritional needs of people who have diabetes, including children and older adults. In diabetes, the body produces little or no insulin, a hormone that helps the body utilize foods that contain glucose (sugar) and carbohydrates. Diabetic diets use exchange lists, or groups of foods that have similar food values. This makes it easier for people with diabetes to substitute one food for another within a group. For example, a person with diabetes might exchange a slice of bread for a serving of mashed potatoes.

- **Low-calorie diets.** These nutritionally adequate diets are useful for people who need to lose weight. Low-calorie diets are used with a doctor's supervision and often involve a nutritionist in meal planning. Limiting calories, using low-fat products and reducing sugar intake is helpful for weight reduction. Once overweight older adults lose the required amount of weight, they will need to follow calorie-controlled diets to maintain their desired body weights.

- **Low-fat diets.** Low-fat diets are useful for older adults who may have such diseases as heart disease or gallbladder disease. Low-fat meal plans include lean meats and lots of low-fat grains, fruits, vegetables, and dairy products. Since low-fat diets limit fat, they are often lower in calories. In order to meet calorie requirements, older adults may need to eat more of these low-fat foods.

- **Low-sodium diets.** When older adults experience swelling related to heart problems or kidney problems, they may need to follow a diet that limits sodium, or salt. They may need to limit or totally avoid foods such as ham, olives, sauerkraut, salted crackers, and pretzels. Instead, older adults should eat fresh prepared meats and vegetables. The older adults in your care may need to avoid adding salt to cooked foods.

FIG. 10-15. Some older adults may require a soft diet due to various health conditions. What are some other soft, nutritious foods you could serve to older adults with this need?

Intergenerational *Interactions*

Intergenerational Kitchen Connections

The kitchen is often known as the favorite room of the house. It can be a source of wonderful smells, tastes, and memories. It's also a room that holds no age boundaries. Whether you're two or 102, you can still enjoy cooking. That's right, even a two-year-old can help in the kitchen by pouring cold ingredients into bowls.

- **Form a Bond.** Research shows that the kitchen is the best room in the house for building relationships. In the kitchen, children and older adults can work together toward a common goal. Whether they are baking cookies or making a meal, the teamwork that goes into the food preparation helps children connect with their older teammates. It also helps children learn the lifelong lesson of working well with others.

- **Apply School Lessons.** The kitchen makes a great classroom. Cooking not only helps children learn about nutrition and healthful eating habits, but also reinforces lessons learned in school. Reading a recipe helps children boost language skills, and measuring allows them to apply math lessons. Young children can even learn about telling time by setting a timer.

- **Share Customs.** Older adults enjoy sharing foods from their culture, while teaching children that people of differing races all share similar traits. Children enjoy tasting different foods and hearing about the backgrounds of older adults. This time spent together also helps children realize how valuable and fun it can be to continue traditions.

- **Enforce Safety.** Cooking can be fun for all generations, but it's important to put safety first in the kitchen. Older adults must supervise young children around sharp utensils and hot surfaces. All generations must be reminded not to leave cooking food unattended. To ensure food is safe to eat, keep fresh meat and dairy items refrigerated or frozen until ready to use. Promptly refrigerate leftovers, and wash hands and utensils after touching raw meats.

Follow-Up

Create an intergenerational cookbook for children and older adults. Visit, telephone, or write to older adults in your community. Ask them to share their favorite recipes with you. Gather the recipes together to make an intergenerational cookbook. As an extra touch, you may wish to ask the older adults to tell you why certain recipes are their favorites, or share a memory they associate with various dishes.

Meal Planning for Older Adults

Planning meals for older adults can be very challenging because older adults need different types of diets. In planning meals, most people follow the Dietary Guidelines for Americans. See Fig. 10-16. In planning and preparing food, keep in mind the principles of good nutrition. You will also want to know the types of foods that the older adults in your care like to eat. Find out the ethnicity of the people who will be eating the food and ask about how to prepare these foods. A healthful meal plan begins with the menu and the recipes and includes safe preparation of food.

- Follow dietary needs outlined in older adults' enrollment records.
- Use recipes that require little fat, cholesterol, sodium, or sugar.
- Use low-fat cooking methods, such as broiling, baking, and steaming, instead of frying.

- Use standard recipes that provide a consistent, nutritious product with every use.
- Choose healthful, ready-prepared food products that meet specific nutrition needs.
- Prepare tasty menu items with good visual appeal and fragrant aromas.

Child and Adult Care Food Program (CACFP). Many older adult day centers participate in the CACFP program that is sponsored by the USDA. In order to receive funding from CACFP, the meals each program serves must meet federal guidelines. See Fig. 10-17.

Purchasing Food

When purchasing food always use the menu as a guide. Make sure your food order is within the planned budget. It is best to organize the food list into categories, so you can keep track of what you need to purchase while shopping. Make certain that you purchase quality food by evaluating food sources. To appraise a food source, read the label on each item and purchase the most nutritious foods. Also, read the label to find the expiration date. Do not purchase items that are expired or are very close to

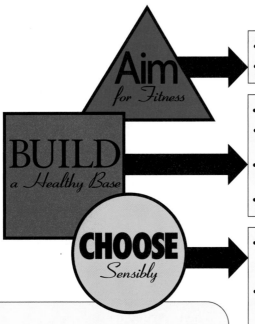

Aim *for Fitness*

- **Aim for a healthy weight.**
- **Be physically active each day.**

BUILD *a Healthy Base*

- **Let the Pyramid guide your food choices.**
- **Choose a variety of grains daily, especially whole grains.**
- **Choose a variety of fruits and vegetables daily.**
- **Keep food safe to eat.**

CHOOSE *Sensibly*

- **Choose a diet that is low in saturated fat and cholesterol and moderate in total fat.**
- **Choose beverages and foods to moderate your intake of sugars.**
- **Choose and prepare foods with less salt.**

FIG. 10-16. The Dietary Guidelines for Americans should be used with special attention given to portion sizes for older adults. Why is portion size a concern for older adults?

FIG. 10-17.

MEAL PATTERNS FOR OLDER ADULTS

Breakfast	Number of Servings	Serving Size
Milk, fluid	1 milk	1 cup
Juice, or **Fruit**, or **Vegetable**	1 fruit/vegetable	½ cup[1]
Grains and/or **Bread**[2]		
Whole-grain bread or cornbread, biscuit, roll, or muffin	1 grain	2 slices or 1 serving
Cold dry cereal		1½ cups dry cereal
Hot cooked cereal		1 cup hot cereal
Pasta		1 cup pasta

Lunch/Supper	Number of Servings	Serving Size
Milk, fluid	1 milk (lunch only)	1 cup
Juice, or **Fruit**, or **Vegetable**	2 fruits/vegetables	1 cup[1]
Grains or **Bread**[2]	1 grain	2 slices or 1 serving
Meat or **Meat Alternate**		
Lean meat, poultry, fish, or cheese	1 meat/meat alternate	2 oz.[3]
Egg		1
Cooked dry beans or peas		½ cup
Peanut butter or other nut seed butter		4 Tbsp.[4]
Yogurt		8 oz.[5]

Snack	Number of Servings	Serving Size
(Select 2 of these 4 components.)		
Milk, fluid	1 milk	1 cup
Juice, or **Fruit**, or **Vegetable**	1 fruit/vegetable	½ cup[1]
Grains and/or **Bread**[2]	1 grain	1 slice or 1 serving
Meat or **Meat Alternate**	1 meat/meat alternate	1 oz.[3]

[1] Fruit or vegetable juice must be full-strength.
[2] Breads and grains must be made from whole-grain or enriched meal or flour. Cereal must be whole-grain or enriched, or fortified.
[3] A serving consists of the edible portion of cooked lean meat, poultry, or fish.
[4] Nuts and seeds may meet only one-half of the total meat/meat alternate serving and must be combined with another meat/meat alternate to fulfill the requirement.
[5] Yogurt may be plain or flavored, unsweetened or sweetened.

expiration. Make every effort to select items that are fat free or low fat and low sodium for those older adults with dietary restrictions.

Labeling Foods

Labeling items is important and useful when working with any age group, specifically older adults. By labeling food containers, foodhandlers and care providers will be better able to track the shelf life of the items. The **shelf life** is the length of time the product remains healthful and safe to eat.

When labeling foods for older adults, make certain that the labeling procedure is understood by everyone. Foodservice operations use

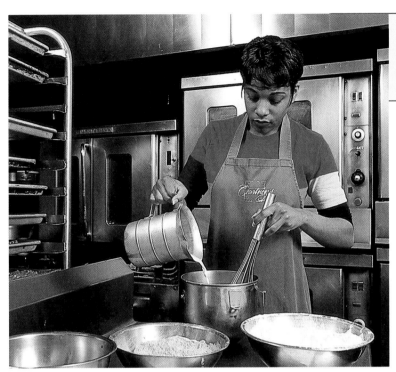

FIG. 10-18. **Modern technology helps foodservice staff members at adult care facilities modify foods to meet the dietary needs of clients.**

the First-In, First-Out (FIFO) procedure. Foods are marked with the date they are received or purchased and then used in the order received or purchased. As foods are purchased, older items are moved to the front of the storage area and newer items are placed in back. The FIFO method can be used in the foodservice facility of adult day service programs or in an older adult's home. The labels should be clear and easy to read. All foodhandlers and care providers should know the labeling system to ensure older adults have food that is safe to eat.

Preparing Food

Foods are prepared in different ways, depending on cultural and regional influences, food availability, and the nutritional needs of older adults. The most important goal is to prepare healthful food. See Fig. 10-18.

Following a menu that is based on the culture of the older adults you work with can assist you in preparing meals that they will enjoy. Research the background of the older adults in the program to find out the types of foods that they like. After you get that information, suggest ways of preparing the foods to make them more healthful for older adults.

Computer-based programs are often used to assist in diet modification. Also, these programs can be used in planning appropriate meals for older adults based on their needs. They are written so that care providers can input information about their clients' special health conditions, ages, gender, etc., to determine the diet modifications to be made for specific individuals.

Cooking, Storing & Handling Food

Older people are at greater risk than younger people of becoming seriously ill due to improper handling, cooking, and storage of food. Because older adults have changes in sight, smell, and taste, they may not notice food that has spoiled. Older adults are more likely to eat tainted food which causes them to become ill. Always use precautions when preparing food to avoid the spread of bacteria. Cooking utensils should be cleaned and sanitized daily. Dishtowels and aprons should be washed and dried daily in the laundry. Foods should be cooked to proper temperatures following the USDA and FDA Food Code guidelines. Store leftovers immediately in the refrigerator in shallow containers so that foods cool to proper temperature quickly. Foods must be cooled to 41°F or less within four hours.

Factors Affecting Food Intake

Older adults can have physical or medical problems that affect their food intake. They experience changes in their sensory systems. Not being able to see, smell, or taste the foods they are eating could have an impact on the diet of older adults. Dental problems also can prevent older adults from eating properly. Dentures or dental problems influence how well older adults chew food. These problems might cause them to eat less than they should.

Physical Changes

Several physical changes accompany aging. These changes impact the nutritional needs of older adults. Because of these changes, care providers must be sure that older adults eat well and drink enough fluids throughout the day. Changes include:

- **Change in flavor perception.** Around age 70, the taste buds begin to decline. They respond more to bitter and sour flavors and respond less to sweet and salty flavors. The decline in the sense of smell also impacts flavor perception.

- **Reduction in gastrointestinal motility.** Due to the weakening of the intestinal walls, older adults may have problems with motility, which leads to constipation. Older adults may experience digestion problems because the stomach also makes less hydrochloric acid. This leads to less absorption of nutrients, such as vitamin B_{12}.

- **Decline in lean body mass.** With aging, muscles, bone, internal organs, and body metabolism decline.

- **Changes in kidney and bladder control.** Due to changes in kidney and bladder function, older adults may have to urinate more often as they age. Older adults may also respond less to thirst signals. These two changes can lead to dehydration.

- **Decline in bone mass.** Beginning at age 40, bone mass decreases up to five percent per decade of age. As bone mass decreases, older adults are more at risk for bone fractures.

Illness

Many illnesses can affect the eating habits of older adults. When older adults feel bad, they may lose their appetites. It is best to suggest that they see their physician immediately. Not eating a proper diet can cause other health problems. Therefore, immediate attention to loss of appetite could avoid other health problems. Illness or disability may influence whether older adults need assistance with feeding or whether they need help keeping track of medication and food combinations.

FIG. 10-19. Assistance with feeding is sometimes needed in older adult day centers. Why is it important to remain respectful while assisting older adults with feeding?

Assistance with Feeding. Some older adults need assistance with feeding. See Fig. 10-19. When assisting them, make every effort to maintain their privacy and to treat them with dignity. They are vulnerable when they have to depend on someone to help them with their food. For example, if an older adult is blind, he or she cannot see the food on the plate. Communicate with the older adult to let him or her know what is on the plate, how it is prepared, and where the utensils are on the table. Some older adults cannot use their hands and will need you to give them food. In this case, let the older adult know what you are doing at all times. Show respect by allowing the person time to eat and talking with him or her between bites.

Medication and Food Combinations. Two-thirds of adults 65 years and older use one or more medications each day, and about one-fourth of them take three medications daily. When two or more medications mix in the body, they may interact with each other and produce uncomfortable or even dangerous side effects. In some cases, medications interact with various foods and cause dangerous side effects. Reactions can vary depending upon the older adult. Care providers need to be aware of possible food-drug interactions for the people in their care. Care providers can check with a doctor or pharmacist (FAR-muh-sist) for drug interactions with certain foods or nutrients.

Food Assistance Programs

Nutritional programs provide food to older adults who gather at nutritional sites, to homebound older adults, and to at-risk older adults. There is an emergency program that provides food to people who have no means to purchase food. Some programs deliver food to older adults' homes. Others provide emergency service by distributing hot meals at central places in a community. Some sites also provide groceries or funds to purchase food.

Medication Combinations. Not all medication combinations are bad. Taking a mixture of medications can be dangerous, however, unless under a doctor's care. For example, taking aspirin along with a blood-thinning medication thins the blood more and could cause severe bleeding should an older person become injured. Or, eating certain foods with some medications impacts absorption. Care providers should check with an older adult's physician about food and medication combinations. They can also help older adults balance medication and food by doing the following:

- Find out all the medications an older adult takes. Let the appropriate health care specialist know of any changes.
- Keep track of side effects. New symptoms may not be from old age but from the medications.
- Learn about the medications. Find out as much as you can by asking questions and reading the package inserts. Always follow package directions.
- Encourage older adults to follow the proper diet at home, so their medications will be absorbed correctly.

The Elderly Nutrition Program

The **Elderly Nutrition Program (ENP)** helps older adults build a foundation for health. Workers help older adults improve their diets and lifestyle choices and increase their physical activity. ENP is closely linked to other parts of the nation's emerging home- and community-based long-term care system. ENP receives many referrals from other agencies that serve older adults. The ENP provides:

- Nutrient-dense meals.

- Nutritious, satisfying meals in community settings, such as senior centers. The meals are usually served at noon, five days a week. See Fig. 10-20.

- Nutrition counseling to help manage nutrition-related chronic diseases.

- Links to other supportive and health-related services, such as physical activity or fitness classes and health screenings.

- Nutritious, satisfying home-delivered meals to homebound older adults. The meals are usually delivered at noon, five days a week. The program that delivers the meals is known as **Meals on Wheels**. Nutrition and health promotion education is also offered. This education helps promote healthful behaviors. This program is usually maintained by the Area Agency on Aging. Some of the meals are delivered to a local place where older adults meet to eat together. See Fig. 10-21.

All adults ages 60 and over and their spouses of any age can receive ENP services, if there is funding. Older adults who have the greatest economic or social need are the first to receive the service. Particular consideration is given to low-income, minority older adults.

In addition, the ENP program will give priority to adults who are at risk of losing their independence, such as:

- Disabled people under age 60 who reside in housing facilities occupied primarily by the older adults where **congregate meals** are served. Congregate meals are meals served in congregate, or group, settings. This nutrition program allows older adults to eat together in a central place. The program is usually sponsored by a neighborhood senior center. The hot meals provide for one-third of the nutrient requirements for people 60 years of age and older.

- Disabled people who reside at home and accompany older persons to meals.

FIG. 10-20. **Some communities have senior centers at which a nutritious meal is served to older adults, usually at noon on weekdays.** How can the Elderly Nutrition Program impact the health of older adults in your community?

Native Americans, Alaskan Natives, and Native Hawaiians have lower life expectancies and higher rates of illness at younger ages. Tribal organizations can set the age at which older people in their communities may participate in ENP services.

The ENP is authorized under the Older Americans Act (OAA) and is administered by the Administration on Aging (AoA). The AoA gives State Units on Aging (SUAs) Title III-C grants. These grants provide money for meals five days per week and related nutrition services in group centers or home settings.

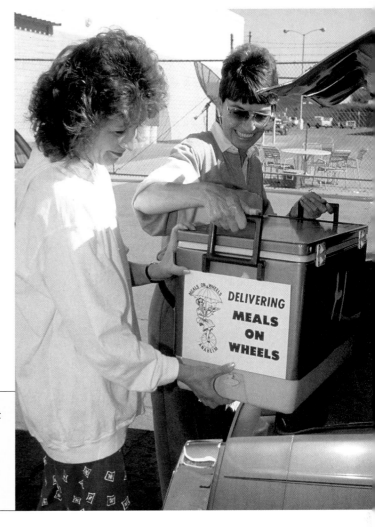

FIG. 10-21. **Meals on Wheels is a service that delivers a hot meal, usually at noon, to homebound people who cannot adequately prepare nutritious meals for themselves. Some services may also include a snack-type meal for later in the day.**

Section **10-2** Knowledge Check

1. What factors impact nutrition for older adults?
2. Why are food purchasing, food labeling, and proper food handling important when planning and preparing meals for older adults?
3. Describe three food assistance programs for older adults.

Mini-Lab

In teams, plan nutritious meals for older adults in an adult day program. Prepare foods to retain the most nutrients and then serve the foods to older adults. Consider any technology you can use that will aid in dietary modifications. Remember to analyze the factors that affect the eating practices of older adults. Evaluate your experience.

Chapter **10**
Review & Activities

Section Summaries

10-1 Good nutrition is important to physical, intellectual, and emotional development.

10-1 The body needs these nutrients: carbohydrates, proteins, fats, vitamins, minerals, and water.

10-1 Use the Food Guide Pyramid to plan meals and snacks that provide the right nutrition.

10-1 Children's meals should be nutritious and have variety and appeal.

10-1 Proper food safety and sanitation practices prevent food-related illness.

10-2 The nutritional needs of adults change as they age.

10-2 Care providers should consider the Dietary Guidelines and the Food Guide Pyramid when preparing meals.

10-2 The Child and Adult Care Food Program guidelines must be followed in order to receive funding from this agency.

10-2 Creating a meal plan, reading food labels, and labeling and storing food properly are important to overall nutrition.

10-2 Meals on Wheels and congregate meals are part of the Elderly Nutrition Program that helps promote healthful diets for older adults.

Check Your Knowledge

1. Name the food groups in the Food Guide Pyramid.
2. Why is it important to include cultural and ethnic foods in meal planning?
3. Give three examples of foods that could cause young children to choke.
4. When serving meals, why is it important to keep hot foods hot and cold foods cold?
5. What is the function of carbohydrates?
6. What is the function of proteins?
7. Contrast the Food Guide Pyramid with the Food Guide Pyramid for Older Adults.
8. Identify two ways you can assist an older adult with eating.
9. List three foodservice sanitation procedures.
10. List three nutrients that benefit the older adult population.

Thinking Critically

1. Draw conclusions about the challenges you could face in planning meals and snacks for children. What challenges might you have planning meals for older adults?
2. How can serving foods attractively influence their acceptance by young children or older adults?

3. What can care providers do to encourage good eating habits in the young children or older adults in their care? What can care providers do to encourage independent eating in children and independent meal preparation in older adults?

4. Analyze ways that care providers can help older adults avoid food and drug interactions.

Practical Applications

1. **Menu and Recipe Collection.** Start a collection of ideas for making food fun for young children or older adults. Use these ideas to plan a day's menus. Share your menus with a group of young children or older adults. Document their reactions.

2. **Cultural Food Research.** Research the foods and meal patterns of another cultural or ethnic group. Collect recipes and plan a day's menus using the Food Guide Pyramid and the results of your research.

3. **Special Food Needs.** Research the effects of special needs, such as food allergies, disabilities, illness, developmental level or changes, or environment, in meeting the nutritional needs of young children or adults. Create a visual of key points. Make an oral report to the class summarizing your findings.

4. **Written Report.** Research one of the nutrition programs designed to serve young children or older adults—Women, Infants, and Children (WIC) Program, Food Stamp Program, Meals on Wheels, or congregate meals. How do these food-related activities enhance the participants' development and social interactions? Write a report summarizing your findings. Include a bibliography documenting the resources you used.

Building Your PORTFOLIO

Meeting Nutritional Needs

Meeting the nutritional needs of the young children or older adults in your care is an important responsibility. This involves knowing the nutritional needs of the age group(s) you work with, planning and serving appetizing meals and snacks, understanding the factors that affect what people eat, maintaining strict standards of food safety and sanitation, and recommending food assistance programs when needed.

Step 1: Using current nutrition information, plan a day's meals and snacks for young children and older adults in a care facility. Use a computerized nutritional analysis program to evaluate and revise your menus. Include the menus in your portfolio.

Step 2: Interview a nutritionist responsible for planning menus for a local early childhood or adult care facility. How does he or she accommodate the special food needs of children or older adults in the facility? Write a summary of what you learned for your portfolio.

Step 3: Obtain a copy of food safety and sanitation guidelines that must be followed by care facilities from your state or local health agency. Using these guidelines, develop a checklist for limiting food hazards, keeping records, and sanitizing equipment in an early childhood or adult care facility. Include the checklist in your portfolio.

Chapter 11

Guiding Behavior

Section 11-1
Building Social Skills

Section 11-2
Guiding Children

Section 11-3
Guiding Older Adults

Section 11-1

Building Social Skills

OBJECTIVES	KEY TERMS

OBJECTIVES

- Describe social competence.
- Identify effective social skills.
- Describe ways to foster social development.
- Explain how communication skills and parenting styles affect social development.
- Explain how culture may influence social skills.

KEY TERMS

social competence
empathy
compassion

People do not live in isolation. Therefore, starting and maintaining social relationships is a basic human need. Children first develop caring attachments with parents. Then children form attachments with siblings and extended family, such as grandparents. As people grow, they develop relationships with many others in the community.

Social Competence Goals

Social competence is a person's ability to get along with others in acceptable and appropriate ways. It is important to nurture positive social traits in young children. Positive social traits include kindness, courtesy, adapting to peers, and respect for others. Those traits then foster specific social skills, such as cooperation, sharing, and conflict resolution.

Social Skills

The foundation of social skills is respect for self and others. Respect helps people view life from another person's point of view. As people learn to see things from another's view, there is a greater chance they will develop socially

acceptable ways of behaving throughout life. Following are ways to build social skills:

- **Model respect, acceptance, and positive social skills.** Treat children the way you want to be treated. Demonstrate behavior that is caring and nonabusive and that builds self-esteem and responsibility. Plan activities that value people of different cultures, age groups, genders, and abilities.

- **Encourage empathy and compassion.** The ability to understand another person's feelings is called **empathy**. The ability to respond sensitively to others' feelings and experiences is called **compassion**. Even very young children can comfort someone who is sad by offering a hug. Explaining situations, discussing feelings, and displaying empathy help build empathy and compassion in children.

Boosting Brain Power

Group Activities and Brain Development.
Participating in group activities nurtures brain development and thinking strategies, too. As children play with others and discuss thoughts and ideas with peers and adults, they stretch their mental abilities. They learn to better understand someone else's point of view. As they try to motivate others to cooperate with their ideas, children develop language skills. During play activities, they learn negotiation and compromise. Children expand their thinking by building on their play partner's ideas. When adults are play partners, children gradually learn more about how the world works and how to productively participate in it.

- **Encourage cooperation and teamwork.** The ability to work well with others helps people be successful throughout life. Care providers should give children opportunities to practice social skills. Group projects, such as gardening, building with blocks, and creating art murals together, nurture cooperation and teamwork. Contributing to classroom routines, such as setting tables for meals or watering plants, builds pride in teamwork.

Teaching children to respectfully solve problems together encourages a cooperative attitude. See Fig. 11-1.

- **Require self-control.** To work well with others, each person must be able to control his or her own actions. Intense feelings, such as anger, disappointment, frustration, or jealousy, must be managed appropriately. To get along well with others, everyone must address problems respectfully. Using physical or verbal aggression, such as hitting or yelling, is not a productive way to solve problems.

Fostering Social Development. A variety of activities encourage social development. Create an environment that encourages group activities and fosters friendships. Card and board games, sandbox play, and group storytelling encourage cooperative interactions. Care providers should coach social skills. If someone has trouble entering a group activity, care providers might suggest ways to join. For instance, if a child is watching dress-up play and would like to join, a care provider may quietly suggest the child say, "I'd like to play, too. What part can I play?"

FIG. 11-1. Children learn cooperation and teamwork when they share their toys and activities. What social interactions do you observe in this photo?

Social Communication Skills

In order to nurture and understand social communication, care providers must observe and carefully respond. Infants communicate through sounds, such as cooing or crying. They also use body language. Sensitive care providers learn the meanings of each child's different sounds and motions. For example, when an infant is tired of being held, the infant may show disinterest by turning its face away from the holder's face.

Listening to and speaking with infants builds the foundation for social attachment. Talk to babies frequently, using short sentences and exaggerated facial expressions. Talk more with toddlers as they become more verbal. Children begin more complex verbal communication in the preschool years. Language rapidly develops after age two, allowing children's social attachments to expand.

Expressing Feelings. Children experience a wide array of feelings. Their moods change quickly. One minute they may be angry, scared, or frustrated; and the next forgiving, calm, and happy. Learning to manage feelings appropriately is important for a child's lifelong happiness. When children are upset, it helps when care providers respond with understanding. Using active listening helps children learn to identify feelings and find appropriate ways to express them. For example, if a child's painting is ruined by a spill, a sensitive active-listening message would be, "You're really upset because the paint spilled on the picture. You really worked hard on that picture." Responses like these encourage children to maintain self-control within a social environment.

Parenting Styles. The children in the child care center come from very different families. Their parents will probably have very different parenting styles that can affect how children interact with others. It will also affect how you communicate with the parents. The different types of parenting styles include:

FIG. 11-2. As children get older, many parents choose to let the children help in setting the rules and the consequences for breaking the rules. How do cultural values impact parenting styles? Why is it important for care providers to understand cultural values?

- **Authoritarian style.** Parents who use the authoritarian style are strong leaders. They make the decisions concerning their children and expect children to accept their judgment. They believe in setting standards for behavior, and expect their children to meet them. When rules are broken, these parents act quickly and firmly. Children of these parents feel secure with their parents in charge.

- **Democratic style.** Parents in a democratic household believe that children deserve a say in matters that affect them. They allow their children to help set the rules and the penalties for breaking them. The children are given a certain amount of choice, as long as they stay within the rules. Children in these families are confident and move easily toward independence. See Fig. 11-2.

- **Permissive style.** Parents who are permissive give their children all the decision making they can handle, offering guidance as needed. Parents who use this style have fewer rules, but the children understand the expectations. These parents also let children experience natural consequences for behavior, instead of imposing penalties. Children in these families learn to solve problems creatively and learn from their experiences.

Few parents follow one style exclusively. Parents may also change their parenting style as children age. No one parenting style is better than another; only when one is carried to the extreme can it be harmful to a child.

Cultural Sensitivity. A family's beliefs, customs, and culture impact a child's behavior. For example, families differ in how they express and talk about feelings, and to whom. Some families prefer not to speak about family issues with care providers; others are eager to do so. Appropriate nonverbal communication also varies from culture to culture. Some cultures view direct eye contact between children and adults as offensive and disrespectful. However, other cultures insist on eye contact to show that a person is listening. Take time to learn about the values and beliefs of the families who use your program's services, so you can practice effective communication skills. When cultural differences are openly discussed among care providers and families, cultural practices are taken into account and respected.

Handling Guidance in Multigenerational Homes. Some children grow up in homes where

ETHICS IN Action

Promoting Cultural Acceptance. Several two-year-olds with varying cultural backgrounds enroll in an early childhood program. The director wants this to be a positive experience for the children, the children's families, and the early childhood staff. The director wants the center to promote cultural acceptance and diversity. *How should the director prepare everyone on the staff for this experience?*

children, parents, and grandparents all live together. Multigenerational homes provide children with much love and attention and a sense of belonging. However, it also means many people contribute to childrearing decisions. Care providers should encourage these families to cooperatively discuss how they should raise the children. They should agree on behavior expectations, consequences for misbehavior, and who has final say in behavior guidance.

Section **11-1** Knowledge Check

1. Define social competence.
2. List three ways to build social skills in children.
3. Explain how culture affects communication.

Mini-Lab

Imagine a child walks by and accidentally hits the base of the block building made by another child. The latter child begins to sob and screams, "I hate you! You did that on purpose!" With a partner, take turns explaining three ways you would respond to this situation. Explain your reasons for each response.

Section 11-2

Guiding Children

One of the joys of working with children is that a care provider is never quite sure what children will do next. While that makes for exciting workdays, children's unpredictable behavior also requires staff to be versatile and skilled in child guidance.

Positive Child Guidance

To skillfully guide children's behavior, early childhood professionals must think before they speak and act. Guiding behavior is a skill that comes with practice. To help you develop your skills, listen to and observe experienced care providers in action. They can show you how to build children's self-esteem and teach them to behave well with others.

Goals of Child Guidance

Children need guidance so they can learn to share, take turns, and resolve conflicts peacefully. Positive guidance helps children develop positive traits, such as kindness, courtesy, and respect for themselves and others. Guidance serves the following purposes:

- Protects each child's physical safety.
- Supports children's self-esteem and emotional well-being.
- Ensures respect for all children's rights and feelings.
- Teaches appropriate use of classroom materials and property.
- Maintains a good learning atmosphere for everyone.
- Promotes independence and the ability to make good decisions.
- Nurtures a sense of responsibility and accountability.
- Encourages self-control and **self-discipline**—the ability to guide your own behavior.

Child Guidance Basics

Children cannot learn to behave appropriately if they do not understand which behaviors are appropriate. Care providers' expectations must be simple, clear, understandable, and age-appropriate. Expectations and rules vary from one program to another. It is important that staff members agree on the expectations and consistently enforce them.

A long list of rules is overwhelming to children. When children help make classroom rules, they will more likely follow them. The rules that are chosen should be important ones that are developmentally appropriate. When developing rules with children, first agree on basic general rules. Then set up guidelines that will assist children with routine activities and learning areas. For instance, the rules for finger painting might be "Wear a smock, clean up spills right away, and paint on your own paper."

Children will understand and follow rules better if you phrase them simply. Be positive and specific. A rule for arrival time might be "Hang your coat on the hook in your cubby." This is much clearer than saying, "Don't leave coats lying around everywhere." Positive guidance also tells children what they can do instead of what they cannot do. See Fig. 11-3.

Explain the reasons for rules. You might say, "We walk indoors. If we run indoors, someone could fall and get hurt." The younger the child, the simpler the explanation should be. To help children remember the rules, display them on a poster in each learning center. Use pictures to clearly illustrate the rules.

Preventing Problems

Many potential behavior problems can be prevented through careful planning. By structuring the schedule and the environment to minimize boredom, frustration, and conflict, you can reduce misbehavior. Specifically:

- **Plan a balanced schedule.** Provide for both quiet time and active play. Children who are either overly tired or full of energy find it hard to behave appropriately. Remember to consider children with disabilities when planning active and quiet play. Some children with disabilities may need to rest more than other children. See Fig. 11-4.

- **Follow a consistent schedule with smooth transitions and routines.** Children find security in a predictable schedule. Prepare activities and routines that do not make children wait a long time for a turn. Effective transitions help children move between activities

FIG. 11-3.

POSITIVE MESSAGES

Say This . . .	Instead of This . . .
Hold on tightly.	Do not fall.
You may run outside.	Stop acting hyper.
Chairs are made for sitting.	Quit acting like you live in a zoo.
When you use your regular voice, I'll get your ball for you.	Do not whine like a baby.
Turn the pages gently.	Stop crumpling the pages.
Use your quiet voice.	No yelling!
When the blocks are on the shelf, we will go outside.	Quit dawdling.

FIG. 11-4. **Balanced schedules allow time for both active and quiet play.** What are the benefits of each type of play?

smoothly. See Chapter 9 for more information on schedules and routines. Also, be sure to start off the day on a positive note. Find appropriate techniques to help children adjust to the child care setting. A comforting hug and kind words as a child separates from his or her parent helps alleviate the child's stress.

- **Plan a wide variety and choice of interesting activities.** Children who are constructively occupied are less likely to misbehave. The chapters in Unit 6 will help you plan an interesting curriculum.

- **Plan activities appropriate for abilities.** To avoid frustration, boredom, and misbehavior, plan open-ended activities, or those without an expected result for multiple age groups. Activities should help create a positive and pleasant atmosphere, not a stress-filled atmosphere.

- **Provide enough equipment.** Children play more cooperatively when an adequate amount of toys and equipment is available.

- **Arrange the physical environment to promote children's success.** When toy shelves are within children's reach, they can easily obey rules about putting toys away. Store materials not meant for use by children out of sight.

- **Provide individual attention.** Plan times when children can interact with care providers one-on-one or in small groups. This prevents children from misbehaving to get a care provider's attention.

- **Consider each child's special circumstances.** Some children may come from homes that are less stable. This lack of stability might affect a child's behavior. Other situations, such as family crises, may have a negative effect on behavior.

Expectations & Limits

Expectations and limits for children's behavior should be clear, simple, and specific. Young children learn to abide by expectations and limits by watching adults. To encourage good behavior, provide children with a positive example to follow. Obey classroom rules, just as you expect of the children. Role model desirable social skills as you interact with children and

Independence Skills

Helping Children Resolve Conflict

Two children fighting over a toy is a common conflict in child care centers. Steps for resolving a conflict over a toy include:

1. **Assess the situation.** If aggressive behavior is taking place, immediately step in and stop the aggression.

2. **Help children identify the problem.** Help children tell their feelings about wanting the toy. Restate what each child says. For example, you might say, "James is angry because you took the toy from him."

3. **Ask children to think of several possible solutions.** You may have to make suggestions for younger children, such as, "Let's take turns. Andy, you play with the toy for a few minutes, then James can play with the toy." A timer may be used to signal the end of a turn. Older children can be asked to offer their own solutions.

4. **Help children arrive at a solution that is acceptable to everyone.** Once a solution has been reached, you need to allow the children to follow through with the solution, stepping in only if the conflict continues.

5. **Have the children evaluate how well they solved their problem.** If their problem is not solved, repeat the problem-solving steps.

6. **Provide positive reinforcement.** When children resolve conflicts well, let them know that they have done a good job.

Try It!
The next time you experience two children fighting over a toy, assess the situation and try the steps outlined for resolving conflict. Did the steps work? Share what you learned from the experience with your teacher or a classmate.

adults. For instance, if you would like children to say "please" and "thank you," make a habit of doing so yourself.

Clear expectations are often communicated by teaching children the functions of play materials, such as, "crayons are used for coloring on paper, not on walls."

Expectations and limits are also communicated using I-messages. **I-messages** include a specific description of behavior, how it affects you, and your feelings about it. For example, suppose that at mealtime, bowls of food are being passed around the table. The care

provider is just about to serve himself some peaches when a four-year-old grabs the bowl from his hands. Obviously, the care provider wants to discourage the child's disrespectful behavior. A care provider who nurtures positive behavior would respond with an I-message: "When you grab the bowl away from me without asking, it hurts my feelings. Think of a better way to get the peaches." The I-message does not attack the child's character. Instead, it helps the child see why the behavior is a problem. It also gives the child a chance to choose a more respectful behavior.

Handling Inappropriate Behavior

Many factors can contribute to misbehavior. Children who misbehave are not usually trying to anger care providers. They may be bored, frustrated, hungry, tired, or ill. If they are experiencing problems at home, such as fighting between parents or a parent's alcoholism, they may misbehave as a way of asking for more adult attention. This does not mean that misbehavior should be excused. However, if you are aware of these factors, you can guide behavior more effectively.

When you respond to misbehavior, choose your words and actions carefully. It is not necessary to hurt, frighten, threaten, or demean a child who has misbehaved. You simply want the child to understand that the misbehavior is unacceptable and cannot continue. You also want the child to feel like a worthwhile person who is capable of doing better in the future. In short, your goal is to discourage the misbehavior without discouraging the child. See Fig. 11-5. The following sections discuss ways to respond to inappropriate behavior:

Ignore Minor Misbehavior. Sometimes children misbehave just to get attention. For example, a child might continually stand and talk during circle time. The best response may be to ignore the misbehavior, as long as it is not harmful to anyone. If minor misbehavior gets positive attention—such as through yelling, using demeaning sarcasm, or embarrassing the children—it may increase rather than decrease.

Offer Choices. To encourage independence and build children's self-discipline, frequently offer developmentally appropriate choices. Allowing children to make age-appropriate decisions prevents needless power struggles with care providers. Only offer real choices. If a child is getting ready to go outdoors on a cold day, asking "Would you like to put on your coat?" is not appropriate. Instead, say, "Here's your coat. Which arm is going in the sleeve first?" Giving children a choice shows that you respect their opinions and independence, and that builds self-esteem.

Coach Appropriate Behaviors. Young children are forgetful and easily distracted. They need reminders to follow classroom rules. You might say, "Where do we put the costumes when we're finished playing with them?" or "Did you remember to wash your hands before coming to the table?" Coaching encourages children's progress and expresses confidence in their ability to behave correctly. A smile, a pat on the back, or a hug recognizes children's efforts. Children are encouraged when care providers acknowledge hard work, such as saying to a struggling child, "I'm proud of the time you've put into putting away the toys." Care providers should also recognize and reinforce motivation, initiative, and assertiveness.

FIG. 11-5. When you respond to inappropriate behavior, use a calm and direct tone. Get down to the children's eye level. Why are shouting and speaking harshly inappropriate behaviors for a care provider?

Handling Biting. Children who do not have full command of language may resort to biting. This most often occurs among toddlers and two-year-olds. Children bite for many reasons. Biting may be a response to teething pain, an experiment in cause and effect, a way to get a desired toy, a method of expressing anger and frustration, or a bid for a care provider's attention. A care provider has to observe closely and consider the circumstances around the biting to best determine the cause. Prevention, in terms of plentiful toys and care provider attention, is always the best way to approach biting issues. However, if biting occurs, here is a way to respond:

- Separate the children first. Attend to the hurt child first. If a child's skin is broken, put on latex or vinyl gloves. Show compassion and empathy. Tenderly comfort the bitten child, and wash the injury with soap and water, even if the skin is not broken.
- Deal with the child who did the biting once you have cared for the injured child. Move the child from other children. Make eye contact and in a firm, but calm, voice say, "Biting hurts people. We use our teeth only for food. It is unacceptable to bite." Make sure your facial expressions match your serious concern. Depending on the child's age, prompt him or her on better ways of getting needs met. If a child bites because of teething pain, chilled teething rings provide temporary relief.
- Record the incident and the circumstances under which it occurred. At the end of the day, inform both families of the incident. Seek input from the parents of the child who bites and ask if this occurs at home and, if so, how it is handled.

Distraction and Redirection. With very young children, such as infants, distraction is the best method of reducing dangerous behavior. For instance, distraction is used when a care provider jingles keys to shift a baby's attention from pulling a plug out of an electric socket. **Redirection** is more often used with preschoolers. Redirection involves steering a child's disruptive behavior to a different, more acceptable activity that still meets the child's basic needs. For instance, a care provider would interrupt children throwing blocks by saying, "Remember, blocks are for building, not throwing. If you want to play a throwing game, you may toss these bean bags into the bucket." In this instance, the care provider recognized the children's desire for an active game and provided a safe alternative to throwing blocks.

Establish Behavior Consequences

Allowing children to experience the consequences of their actions is one strategy care providers use to guide behavior. **Consequences** are events that occur as the result of a particular behavior. Consequences may be positive or negative. When children realize their actions may have negative consequences, they are motivated to control their own behavior.

Care providers should select consequences that are suitable for the child's age and developmental level. Make sure they are reasonable, respectful, and related to the appropriate or inappropriate behavior.

Positive Reinforcement. A consequence that rewards a particular behavior, making it more likely to be repeated, is **positive reinforcement.**

Praise, attention, and smiles are all examples of positive reinforcement. Praise and encouragement should be specific and genuine, such as, "Great job of putting all the blocks on the shelf. You didn't leave a single one on the floor!"

Natural Consequences. Sometimes the natural results of an action are enough to discourage the repeated misbehavior. For instance, if a child drops a drawing on the floor and does not pick it up, the drawing will be walked on and torn. Natural consequences can be effective but should be used only if they do not endanger the child or others.

Logical Consequences. By promoting responsibility, logical consequences teach a child to correct a mishap. For instance, if a book is torn, teach the child to repair it with tape. Or if a child spills milk, teach the child how to clean it up. Use the following guidelines for enforcing consequences:

- Speak privately to the child. Do not embarrass the child by making him or her, and the misbehavior, the center of attention.

- Give the child a chance to correct the behavior, then identify a consequence: "You may play with the puzzle as long as you keep the pieces on the table. If you continue to throw the pieces on the floor, the puzzle will be put away."

- Once you state consequences, take action right away, so the child understands the consequences are in response to the misdeed.

- Be consistent. If you enforce rules only some of the time, children can become confused.

- If the child cries or sulks, remain calm but firm. Giving in only teaches the child to use the same tactics again.

- Express your trust in the child to behave more appropriately in the future.

Withdrawal of Privileges. Another approach is to deny a child a privilege for a short time. The privilege being taken away should directly relate to the misbehavior, so the child understands the reason for its withdrawal. For example, if children throw sand, they may be denied access to the sandbox. Establish a definite time: "You may not play in the sandbox until this afternoon." Then direct the children to another activity where they may start fresh.

Cool-Down Moments. A child who continues to be very disruptive may be given a **cool-down moment.** This is a short period of time in which the child must sit apart from the other children and activities. Care providers should explain to a child why he or she needs a few cool-down moments. Cool-down moments should be no longer than three to five minutes. They are meant to help the child calm down and regain self-control. When the cool-down moment is over, the child is better able to listen to the care provider's directions. Be sure that the same care provider who takes the child to the cool-down area also brings the child back to classroom activities for consistency. The care provider can reinforce that he or she likes the child, but did not like the misbehavior. See Fig. 11-6.

FIG. 11-6. Cool down moments allow a child to regain self-control after disruptive behavior. Why are cool-down moments short?

Guidance Challenges

Conflict is a natural and common occurrence among children. Learning how to resolve conflicts in a positive manner—without physical or verbal aggression—is a major challenge of childhood. Resolving conflicts involves many social skills: communication, negotiation, cooperation, and the ability to stand up for your own rights while respecting the rights of others. A supportive care provider can help children acquire these skills.

Avoid Labels

A child who is labeled "troublemaker" or "bully" tends to confirm the label by giving adults just what they expect. In addition, such negative labels as "stupid" and "clumsy" create stereotypes, which are hurtful and damage self-esteem. Labels do not need to be spoken to have an effect. The labels assigned a child affect your tone of voice, your facial expression, and how you react to misbehavior. Children pick up on these subtle differences.

Conflict Resolution

As an early childhood professional, what should you do when conflict occurs? The answer depends on the situation. If a child is being physically harmed or endangered, immediately take action. Stop the child who is doing the hurting, and then comfort the one who is hurt. If the situation poses no immediate danger, simply move closer and remain observant. This lets children know that you are aware of what is going on. If children seem to need help resolving conflict, provide only as much guidance as necessary. See Fig. 11-7. Try these ideas:

- Encourage each child to express his or her point of view. Ask such questions as "What happened next?" and "How did you feel about that?"

- If children find it difficult to express their feelings, you may need to coach them: "Maybe you feel mad because Sonia took the tricycle away from you. It's okay to tell her that it makes you mad."

- Coach children through problem-solving steps. Teaching children how to resolve conflicts on their own takes more time than solving the problem for them. In the long run, however, it is much better for the children. Only as a last resort should a care provider solve a problem. If children cannot resolve the conflict, a care provider might say, "This is a tough one. I'll help you decide this time." See page 284 for more information on resolving conflicts with problem solving.

FIG. 11-7. **When conflicts arise, use mediation as needed to encourage both children to express their views.** Why might you need to coach children on effectively expressing their feelings?

Documenting Concerns

Some children have more difficulties than others. If a child's behavior problems last for weeks or months, they require special attention. To determine if there is a pattern or specific cause for a problem, care providers should make frequent, objective observations. A child's behavior should be recorded to see how often problems occur and when. Unresolved behavior problems require a parent conference. Be careful not to use negative labels or sound as though you are placing blame. Speak clearly, courteously, and concisely. Explain that you are concerned about the child's behavior and want to work together to find a solution. Make sure that parents have realistic expectations of their child. For example, some parents may expect their young toddler to sit quietly at the table, although that is not a developmentally appropriate behavior for a toddler. See Fig. 11-8.

You may want to ask some questions: Have there been behavior problems at home? If so, when did they begin? How do you handle them? Is there something in the child's life that might be upsetting? Some problems require parents to seek help. Give them referrals to appropriate agencies.

FIG. 11-8. If you observe a child having unusual outbursts of anger or crying, be sure to document your concerns. What should you do if the behavior continues?

Section *11-2* Knowledge Check

1. Identify four ways to build social skills in children.
2. Contrast effective and ineffective guidance techniques.
3. Name two behavior challenges and how to deal with them.

Mini-Lab

Observe a classroom at a local child development center. Determine the care providers' developmentally appropriate practices that promote self-discipline in children. Summarize your observations and present them to your class.

Section **11-3**

Guiding Older Adults

- Describe the process of talking with older adults.
- Describe how healthy development and well-being impact behavior.
- Identify the principles of conflict management.
- Determine an action plan for positive guidance.

KEY TERMS

small talk
search talk
fight talk
spite talk
conflict-management
    plan
action plan

When working with older adults, you may find yourself helping them to work out conflicts with their peers as well as younger people. You might find it difficult to serve as a mediator between an older person and a younger person. The best way to serve as a mediator is to use effective communication and the principles of conflict management.

Effective Communication

Communicating with older adults can be meaningful and rewarding. You can learn much about the world by interacting with them. Older adults want to communicate. They want to talk about what happened in their younger years and compare it with today's activities. Working with older people takes practice and patience. You must take the time to set a foundation for understanding.

Effective communication is an important skill. Communication involves speaking and listening skills. By communicating effectively with older adults, you can establish a relationship with them, build their self-esteem, and help them maintain their dignity.

Talking with Older Adults

People age differently and this can have an impact on communication with older adults. Every person may have his or her own way of initiating conversation. Some individuals will pleasantly initiate conversation by using small talk and search talk. Other older adults, due to health problems or other social issues, may start conversations on a negative tone by using controlling talk, such as fight talk or spite talk. As a care provider, you will need to differentiate between the types of conversation and understand the reasons behind each participant's way of talking.

- **Small talk.** Be willing to chat with older adults. **Small talk** is light, casual conversation. Older adults may ask you simple questions, such as "How is your family?" or "How

FIG. 11-9. Brushing up on your small talk skills is important in your job as a care provider for older adults. **What is the importance of small talk?**

is the weather?" This is their way of getting a conversation started. See Fig. 11-9.

- **Search talk.** Sometimes older adults will use **search talk**, or talk that occurs when a person is trying to find the right words to say in a conversation. The person says words until he or she finds the right ones.

- **Fight talk.** When some older adults think that they are not being heard or understood, they use **fight talk** as a defensive way of talking. In most cases, fight talk among older adults can be a way of letting you know that they want respect. Older adults might also use fight talk when they think they are being exploited or think someone has taken advantage of them. Care providers need to understand that the speaker feels insulted and is only using fight talk as a defense. They should respectfully let older adults know that they do not have the right to speak disrespectfully to others.

- **Spite talk.** In some instances, older adults use **spite talk** to make their views known. They might say something that is resentful, even though they know that it is not respectful. However, like any other age group, older adults might strike out in words to get back at someone. Spite talk is not an effective way to communicate. This way of communicating can make the care provider feel guilty. At the same time, it is a way that the older person may use to get attention.

To communicate effectively with older adults, you need appropriate communication techniques that include active listening, speaking clearly, and being aware of nonverbal language. Figure 11-10 offers some effective techniques for carrying out effective verbal and nonverbal communication skills.

Listening to Older Adults

The most important communication skill in working with older adults is listening. Use active-listening skills, such as the following:

- Maintain eye contact with the older adult and avoid distractions and interruptions.

- Listen to the entire message and watch for the nonverbal messages.

- Ask questions to clarify the older adult's thoughts, feelings, or experiences. When you listen actively, you seek information by asking open-ended questions in order for the speaker to fill in the answer.

- Show empathy to older adults. Notice feelings that the older adult may be expressing, such as sadness or anger. See Fig. 11-11.

FIG. 11-10.

EFFECTIVE VERBAL & NONVERBAL COMMUNICATION

Verbal	• Use "I"-messages to avoid coming across as negative or judgmental.
	• Speak at a moderate pace, not too slow or too fast.
	• Speak clearly, making sure all your words are understood.
	• Use correct grammar and avoid slang expressions that older adults will not understand.
	• Be respectful and polite as you speak.
Nonverbal	• Use direct eye contact. It helps you to show older adults that you care.
	• Use facial expressions to convey emotion.
	• Stand or sit facing the older adult to whom you are talking. Use good posture to show confidence and interest.
	• Make sure your verbal and nonverbal messages match. Your tone of voice, facial expressions, and gestures should say the same thing.

When you first start working with older adults, you might think it is time-consuming to talk with them or listen to them. Understanding the developmental stages of older adults will help you to communicate with them more effectively. See Chapters 2 and 23 for more information on adult development.

Healthy Development & Well-Being

Healthy development and well-being can affect a person's behavior. For example, an older person who has good health care and feels good may interact positively with others. In contrast, an older adult who has no access to medical care may not feel good and act gruff with peers. Care providers can understand older adults' behavior by knowing about each older adult's level of well-being and sensitive issues for each older adult. They should also learn how to respond to the issues in a social setting, such as the adult day care center. For example, if an older adult has personal problems, try to approach the older adult privately to discuss them.

FIG. 11-11. **Providing comfort and assurance to older adults with hurt feelings may be part of your job as a care provider.** Why should care providers give comfort and assurance without judging the older adult's feelings?

Intergenerational *Interactions*

Building Self-Esteem

When children and older adults work, play, and communicate with each other, increased self-worth is the reward for all. Programs that build self-esteem among generations include:

- **Older Adults Tutor Children.** When older adults help children and teens with schoolwork, the young people improve their grades and the older adults experience a greater sense of purpose. One tutoring program—the *Retired and Senior Volunteer Program*—pairs older adults with kindergarten through third-grade students in seven elementary schools around Middlesex County, MA. During a two-hour session each older adult tutors four children for 30 minutes each.

- **Adult Day Care Joins Child Day Care.** The *ONE* Intergenerational Center in Van Nuys, CA, offers a very unique adult day care and child day care combination. During the day, older adults from the *ONE* adult day care center can participate in the *J.O.Y.* (Joining Older & Younger) program, which links them to children from the *ONE* child care center. All generations experience improved self-esteem through *J.O.Y.*, which enables older adults to rock infants, create art projects with toddlers, and more.

- **Children Tutor Older Adults.** Older adults can also learn from children and teens. Expanding upon the pen-pal idea, Senior Services of Seattle/King County, WA, introduces *Computer Pals*. This program connects older adults and students via e-mail. Older adults benefit from learning computer skills, and young people boost self-esteem by helping an older adult discover new technology.

- **Youth Provide Companionship.** The *Youth and Elders Program* sponsored by Rainbow Bridge of Denver, CO, introduces school students to older adult nursing home residents. Young participants gain improved self-esteem in providing companionship to older adults. Likewise, the older adults experience a greater sense of self-worth through sharing life experiences with the students. Both generations gain respect for one another.

Follow-Up

Use the telephone book to find older adult care centers in your area. Speak to the facility director about ways you and your classmates can contribute to the lives of the center's residents, and about ways they can help you. Consider a pen-pal program in which you exchange weekly letters with a center resident.

Working with Noncompliant Older Adults.
A noncompliant older adult may be defined as a person that is not following orders prescribed for his or her individual needs. Medication non-compliance is most common and can take many forms that include errors of omission, unintentional and intentional overdosing, errors in dosing frequency, medications taken for the wrong purpose, or incorrect administration of medications. It may be unintentional or intentional. Noncompliance may result from impaired daily functioning due to causes, such as depression, anxiety, isolation, or undiagnosed Alzheimer's disease. In addition, older adults may be non-compliant for reasons such as:

- Lack of money to pay for medications.
- Lack of understanding to follow complicated routines.
- Lack of knowledge about the purpose or importance of a prescribed routine.
- Having cognitive, functional, or sensory impairments.
- Having unpleasant reactions to medications.

As you work with old older adults you can take an active role in assisting them in designing a plan that will help them to be compliant. For example, you can suggest that they purchase a medication organizer with the date and time to take specific medications.

Emotional Needs

Everyone has emotional needs, including love, friendship, and understanding. Older adults also have a need to maintain their dignity—or their sense of worthiness or esteem. When needs such as these go unmet, it can affect the behavior of older adults. Like anyone else, older adults can suffer from hurt feelings that can lead to a loss of self-esteem. Most conflicts among older adults start because of hurt feelings. When guiding the behavior of older adults, it is necessary to communicate effectively to avoid misunderstandings that could result in hurt feelings. The stronger the feelings, the more difficult it is solve the problem. Take the necessary time to listen carefully to what each person has to say about his or her feelings to successfully solve problems. Care providers should remember to never judge an older adult's feelings.

Mental and Emotional Disorders. Adults in their later years will have a greater chance of experiencing some mental and emotional disorders, such as anxiety, which are treatable just as they are in younger people. Older adults that experience anxiety likely experienced anxiety when they were younger. The causes of anxiety among older adults are different than those in young people. During later years, stress and vulnerabilities unique to the aging process—such as chronic physical problems, cognitive impairments, and significant emotional losses—bring anxiety. The loss of a loved one or loss of physical capabilities can cause great stress and lead to problems with adjusting to life changes. Some older adults feel stress due to some illnesses they have. Some other mental and emotional disorders related to aging include:

- Alzheimer's disease—a disease that destroys brain cells and memory—leads to intellectual, emotional, and behavioral impairments that get progressively worse.
- Sleep problems increase with age, and about one-half of those over age 80 complain of sleep difficulty due to conditions such as anxiety or arthritis pain.
- Drug abuse among older adults typically takes the form of prescription medication abuse. The drug-abuse problem among aging adults is often a result of having too many medications prescribed for them.

As people age there may be emotional disorders associated with aging. It will be important that you understand that some disorders are associated with the aging process. You will be better able to assist older adults if you are aware of age-related disorders. See Fig. 11-12.

Factors That Create Negative Stress Affect Behavior. Change is a big cause of stress in people's lives, and change is a fact of life even for older adults. Factors that cause stress for older adults include: retirement or change in income, the death of someone, an injury or illness, or change in residence, which could include loss of independence. Stress also affects the body, which in turn can affect behavior. While stress itself usually does not cause illness, it may contribute negatively to high blood pressure, headaches, digestive problems, or asthma. Physical signs of stress include:

- Cold hands and feet.
- Headache, backache, or stiff neck.
- Fatigue or nervousness.
- Change in eating or sleeping habits.

Managing Stress During Later Years. Positive thinking is one of the most effective weapons people of any age can use against stress. Older adults experience stress for various reasons including anxiety. Anxiety can be relieved by participating in activities that take the mind off of situations that cause stress, such as:

- Volunteering for community projects, such as Habitat for Humanity.
- Hobbies, sports, or home projects.
- Using prescription and over-the-counter drugs only as a health care provider or pharmacist recommends.
- Never combining drugs with alcohol—it's a deadly combination. Drugs can stay longer in older bodies than in younger ones. Encourage older adults to use all medications with care and according to instructions.
- Participating in fitness activities and eating nutritionally balanced meals.

As you work with older adults, influence them to seek help to control stress. Sources include health care providers, professional counselors, self-help groups, health departments and mental health centers, stress-management workshops, or older adult support groups.

FIG. 11-12. Learning to summarize conversations is an important skill for care providers. In what situations might you summarize what an older adult says to you?

Basic Needs

Care providers should make certain that each person's basic needs are determined and met. Basic needs include food, shelter, and security. Older adults should be allowed to verbalize their needs to care providers. Care providers need to listen, noting the tone of voice and facial expression of the older adults as they speak. These nonverbal signals help care providers understand the older adults' needs and how urgent they are. Listening and summarizing adults' basic needs help nurture mutual respect and trust.

Conflict Management

In any situation, conflicts can occur. Care providers should be prepared to solve conflicts as they arise. Effective communication helps resolve problems, but it takes time. To communicate effectively, you must know the problem.

FIG. 11-13.

PRINCIPLES OF CONFLICT MANAGEMENT

- Identify the problem.
- Design a fair conflict-resolution plan.
- Anticipate what could go wrong during negotiations.
- Work together in a positive manner.
- Set ground rules for mutual respect and trust.
- Focus only on one issue at a time.
- Avoid imposing a solution to rush the resolution.
- Allow enough time to solve the problem effectively and evaluate the process.

To resolve the problem, everyone must understand it and agree on a solution. Care providers can help foster a solution by first gathering information about the problem and then suggesting ways to solve it.

Using the principles of conflict management can be helpful in resolving problems. See Fig. 11-13.

Every situation is different and each conflict needs a plan. Guidelines should be followed in developing a conflict-management plan. Creating a **conflict-management plan** involves using problem solving to help older adults identify their needs and goals in regard to dealing with conflict. Everyone involved in the conflict should be involved in developing the plan. Older adults will be more accepting of a plan if they take part in developing it. Avoid rushing to a solution, which might frustrate the older adults. After the plan has been developed, everyone must agree to it. Although a plan may be effective, expect to modify it as new incidents occur. Guiding older adults through conflict resolution helps them to feel in charge. They can use the same process in setting ground rules on their own or for a group resolution.

Signs of Conflict

The indicator of conflict is body language. For example, some people use their fingers to point and shake at others when communicating. The finger pointing and frowning are most noticeable when a person feels out of control. When people understand each other, they use less aggressive body language.

Normal Conflict

Some normal conflict may occur each day. Most of the time, the older adults will be able to solve the problems on their own. Many times conflicts are a result of ineffective communication. Communication breakdowns can cause hurt feelings. If care providers have been trained in effective communication, they should guide older adults in identifying their feelings. If the provider is not trained, it is very important to not guide the older adult in expressing "hurt" feelings. It is better to refer the older adult to a person who is trained in conflict management, such as a counselor. See Fig. 11-14.

Avoiding Conflicts

The best tool for avoiding conflict is effective communication. By using your knowledge of communication, you can observe and identify older adults' behavior changes. Your effective speaking skills will help you speak so that older adults can understand you. As a skilled listener, you will hear and respond in a positive way.

Allowing people to give constructive feedback is important in avoiding conflicts. Feedback helps older adults feel respected. It also helps you confront problem situations early, before doing much, if any, emotional harm.

FIG. 11-14. **Conflict may arise in almost any group situation. Stay calm and guide the individuals through conflict resolution by having them communicate their feelings in a respectful way.**

Observing Behavior

As you guide older adults in conflict management, you can watch for behavior changes. Evaluate whether the conflict resolution plan was successful. Remember to document all observations and give feedback to the older adults. Be sure to document clients' identities while observing their daily activities. If you note any unusual behavior or major changes in daily behavior, be sure to report it to your supervisor. See Chapter 7 about types of observations.

Plan for Positive Guidance

An action plan helps care providers document the conflict-management process. The **action plan** provides written feedback, summarizes everyone's comments, and documents the solutions. It helps guide older adults in future similar situations. An action plan also helps care providers coach older adults on appropriate behaviors. Coaching is another way to foster mutual respect and trust among older adults.

Section **11-3** Knowledge Check

1. Contrast small talk with fight talk.
2. Give an example of an effective verbal and nonverbal way to communicate with older adults.
3. How do health issues impact the behavior of older adults?

Mini-Lab

Assume that you are a mediator between an older adult and a high school student. Using the principles of conflict management, develop an action plan that will best assist in resolving their conflict. Share your plan with the class.

Chapter **11**

Review & Activities

Section Summaries

11-1 Care providers can foster social development with good planning.

11-1 Care providers must be skilled at communicating with children.

11-1 Cultural sensitivity is required when communicating.

11-2 Guidance is needed for children's physical safety and emotional well-being.

11-2 Positive child guidance helps children learn acceptable behavior without inflicting physical or emotional harm.

11-2 Care providers must have realistic expectations for children's behavior.

11-2 Clearly stated rules help children behave appropriately.

11-2 Care providers can encourage good behavior by preventing problem situations.

11-3 Effective communication with older adults includes speaking, listening, and summarizing information.

11-3 Care providers can solve problems among older adults by using conflict management.

11-3 Healthy development and well-being can affect older adults' behavior.

11-3 An action plan for positive guidance outlines constructive suggestions that lead to positive outcomes.

Check Your Knowledge

1. How can positive child guidance lead to self-discipline?
2. What are the dangers of labeling children?
3. Name three guidelines for phrasing rules effectively for children.
4. Why should children be involved in creating classroom rules?
5. How does positive reinforcement affect behavior?
6. Why is consistency so important when enforcing consequences?
7. Describe three ways a care provider might react when conflict occurs with children or older adults.
8. Differentiate between the types of talk older adults might use to start a conversation.
9. What are characteristics of nonverbal communication?
10. Name the principles of conflict management.

Thinking Critically

1. What message does a care provider send if he or she hurts, frightens, threatens, or demeans a child or older adult? Why is it important to avoid labeling people?
2. Draw conclusions about how collaboration with a parent or family member can help solve problem behavior in children or older adults.
3. Contrast guiding older adults and young children. Draw conclusions about what skills you can use to guide both groups.

Chapter **11** Review & Activities

Practical Applications

1. **Responding to Crisis.** Research ways to respond to family crises or child abuse. Use library or Internet sources, or interview a child care director or social worker. Create a presentation for your class on appropriate ways to respond. Discuss the impact of crises on children, their families, and children's behavior. Provide contact information for child protective services, the Red Cross, and other assistance organizations.

2. **Conflict Resolution.** Observe the behavior of young children or older adults. Document situations in which conflict occurred. For each situation, write a dialogue showing how a staff member might mediate or provide positive guidance to resolve the conflict. Create a flowchart of your observations and share it with your class.

3. **Listening Skills.** Practice using good listening skills when talking to a young child or older adult. To encourage a relaxed conversation, ask the child or older adult to share stories of his or her family or culture. How did using good listening skills aid you in communicating effectively? Write a paragraph summarizing your experience.

4. **Research.** Using print and Internet resources, investigate ways in which nonverbal communication is used in different cultures. Explain how cultural differences in nonverbal communication will impact early childhood and adult care programs.

Building Your PORTFOLIO

Behavior Guidance Skills

Effective communication is an important part of guiding behavior for both children and older adults. Your future employer will evaluate how well you communicate when guiding behavior.

Step 1: Research the social communication skills used in three different cultures. Include information about cultural values and how people in each culture use body language and express feelings. Create a chart summarizing your findings to include in your portfolio. Be sure to include how this information will be useful in guiding behavior.

Step 2: Observe an early childhood or adult day care professional for at least one hour. Document examples illustrating how behavior problems and conflicts are handled. Identify the appropriate verbal and nonverbal guidance techniques the care provider used. Analyze your observation record and answer the following questions: What appropriate techniques were used when guiding children and older adults? Were these methods positive or negative? How were they appropriate for the person and the situation? Did the professional treat the child or older adult with respect? Explain. Were any conflicts resolved? Explain. Include your observation record and analysis in your portfolio.

Chapter 12
Appropriate Environments

Section 12-1
Sensory-Appropriate Indoor Environments

Section 12-2
Sensory-Appropriate Outdoor Environments

Section 12-1

Sensory-Appropriate Indoor Environments

Many children and older adults spend time in care facilities on a daily basis. The indoor environment should create a warm and inviting atmosphere for children and older adults. As a professional care provider, you will be involved in making the care facility a place where children or older adults can feel at home.

Indoor Environments for Children

Early childhood programs need caring professionals to create places where children will grow and develop safely. Most importantly, children need a warm and engaging environment that is fun to explore with friends. Early childhood staff must be able to maintain environments that are interesting, yet not over-stimulating. That's a big challenge, but this section will illustrate ways you can meet it.

Program Environments

There are many details to consider when designing early childhood classrooms. For example, state licensing laws are used to guide the design process. In addition, **accreditation criteria** list desirable features that are considered part of high-quality early childhood programs. These criteria are put together by various professional organizations, such as the National Association for the Education of Young Children (NAEYC). In addition to these resources, consider the following factors when planning environments that serve children and families.

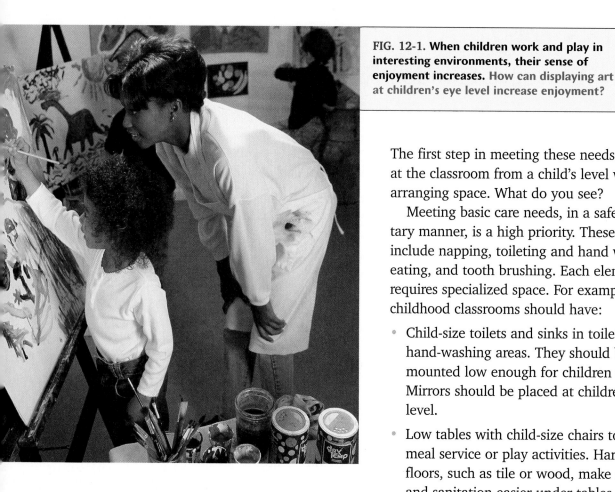

FIG. 12-1. When children work and play in interesting environments, their sense of enjoyment increases. How can displaying art at children's eye level increase enjoyment?

Program Services & Goals

Program services, including hours of operation, determine the range of areas in an environment. For example, a part-day program doesn't need the space for napping that a full-day program needs. Kitchen size will also vary with the number of meals served daily.

The environmental design impacts a staff's ability to meet program goals, too. For instance, an area that offers plentiful storage at children's height helps nurture children's independence. Likewise, a program supporting strong self-esteem displays children's art at eye level. See Fig. 12-1.

Developmental Needs

All areas of child development need to be considered when designing space for children. Since developmental abilities of children vary, classrooms must be set up to meet these needs.

The first step in meeting these needs is to look at the classroom from a child's level when arranging space. What do you see?

Meeting basic care needs, in a safe and sanitary manner, is a high priority. These needs include napping, toileting and hand washing, eating, and tooth brushing. Each element requires specialized space. For example, early childhood classrooms should have:

- Child-size toilets and sinks in toileting and hand-washing areas. They should be mounted low enough for children to reach. Mirrors should be placed at children's eye level.

- Low tables with child-size chairs to use for meal service or play activities. Hard-surfaced floors, such as tile or wood, make cleanup and sanitation easier under tables.

- Storage for cots in full-day programs.

- A separate **isolation room** for children who become ill. This gives children a cozy, comfortable place to rest until their parents arrive and helps prevent the spread of illness.

Most early childhood centers are set up to meet the needs of preschool children. Special considerations must be made when planning the space needs for infants, toddlers, school-age, and special needs children.

Infant and Toddler Program Needs. Infant and toddler and preschool environments differ. Diaper changing areas require proper ventilation, easy access to diaper disposal, and easily washed flooring surrounding the area. Changing tables must be the proper height to limit caregiver back injuries. Hand-washing sinks should be close by to limit the spread of disease. Low windows allow toddlers to see the outside world. A warm room adds to children's comfort. Since times for eating, sleeping, and playing may vary for each infant, separate areas for napping must be available throughout the day. See Fig. 12-2.

School-Age Program Needs. After a long day at school, the school-age child may be ready for either action or time to rest. Peer relationships are very important to school-age children. Their environment needs lots of room for group games and interaction. School-age children also need designated space away from younger children. Privacy is especially important to this group. A semi-secluded area allows these children to relax with a good book, listen to music, or chat with friends. Private storage for their belongings is also important. Space should be planned for activities that interest school-age children, such as:

- Hobby areas for activities, such as woodworking or sewing.
- Homework areas that are quiet and well lit.
- Computer areas for playing computer games or exploring the Internet.
- A play yard built for the size and abilities of school-age children.

Adapting for Children with Special Needs. Early childhood programs also serve children with special needs. An environment should be planned with features that allow easy access to children with special needs. For example, early childhood classrooms should have:

- Wider classroom pathways to accommodate wheelchairs and devices that aid walking.
- Ramps that provide access to classrooms.
- At least one toilet stall is needed to accommodate wheelchairs or walking devices. Stalls should be at least 69 inches deep and have grab bars mounted between 18 and 27 inches from the floor.
- At least one restroom sink and mirror should be accessible.
- Accessible tables in eating and activity areas with clear floor space for wheelchairs.

FIG. 12-2. **A higher staff-to-child ratio and specialized equipment are needed in infant/toddler programs in contrast with the needs of preschool programs. What flooring surfaces are best suited to infant/toddler rooms?**

Environmental Risks. Many materials found in the everyday environment can put children at risk of injury or serious illness. Locked storage should be out of children's reach. This is critical so children do not come into contact with harmful substances. Such items would include, but are not limited to:

- Household cleaning products.
- Pesticides.
- Asbestos.
- Old lead-based paint.
- Combustible items, such as hair spray or spray paint.

By working closely with families, early childhood professionals can meet the needs of children with special needs, too. Understanding the specific needs of each child allows the classroom staff to make further plans and adaptations to meet the child's needs.

Staff Space Needs

Staff members also need environments that help them do their jobs effectively and efficiently. A good working environment helps keep staff morale high. In turn, their attitudes toward the children are more likely to be positive. See Fig. 12-3.

Storage Needs for Children

Children arrive each day with an assortment of belongings. They may bring coats, hats, extra sets of clothing, and special items to share in class. Cubbies hold children's personal items. A cubby resembles a small locker, but without doors. Placing cubbies near an entrance makes them convenient and encourages children to be responsible for their possessions. See Fig. 12-4.

FIG. 12-3.

SPACE NEEDS FOR STAFF

Director's Office	Directors need a private office for conducting confidential business and storing important files and records. The director's office is usually placed near the entrance for viewing who enters and leaves the center.
Staff Training Room	A training room allows the director to provide on-site professional development for staff. The same room can be used to conduct parent advisory board meetings or parent education programs.
Teaching Staff Workroom	Teachers and classroom aides need storage space for instructional materials, such as art supplies. A staff lounge for work breaks is also helpful. Staff members also need space for storing personal belongings and teaching materials.
Kitchen Staff Work Area	The kitchen staff needs space and equipment for food preparation and storage.
Custodial Staff Rooms	Custodians keep cleaning equipment and supplies in a locked closet, since many cleaning supplies can be **toxic** (poisonous) to children.

Family-Friendly Environments

An entrance that is inviting and convenient for parents and children helps get every day off to a better start. Space is needed for parents to sign children in and out on a daily attendance sheet. Display space in this area is useful for posting items, such as parenting articles, notices, menus, and newsletters.

Many programs have an observation space for parents or child development students to use. These classroom and observation spaces are equipped with audio equipment which allows observers to hear children's discussions. The observation space has a one-way window that allows observers to watch children without interrupting activities. See Fig. 12-5.

FIG. 12-5. One-way observation windows help parents and early childhood students or staff observe children without interrupting classroom activities.

The Classroom Climate

Early childhood classrooms must meet children's needs for stability, curiosity, and delight in anything sensory. **Sensory** means experienced through the senses—sight, smell, sound, taste, and touch. Keeping sensory environments interesting requires balancing basic room arrangements with appealing items that are easily changed. The classroom sound level should be neither too loud nor too quiet. Instead, a continuous hum of activity should dominate the room as children learn through play. A sensory-effective classroom engages children without overwhelming them with too much change.

Creating Atmosphere

Elements—such as sound, color, lighting, patterns, and textures—have a large impact on the behavior of children. Creative staff members can use these elements to enhance the classroom atmosphere.

Sound. Rooms with a consistently high noise level fatigue children. This hinders their ability to concentrate and learn. To soften the noise level, designers use features such as carpeting,

FIG. 12-4. Cubbies are used to store children's belongings. Why should cubbies be placed near the entrance of a facility?

FIG. 12-6. **The atmosphere in an early childhood classroom should be warm, welcoming, and provide children with a variety of sensory experiences.** What could you do to ensure a pleasant environment for children?

upholstered furniture, and lined draperies. Tabletop water fountains also filter noise and produce sounds children enjoy. Using elevated play lofts, or sunken play spaces, also helps limit excess noise.

Color. The use of color in early childhood settings also affects children's activity level and behaviors. For example, the colors red and orange increase children's activity level and appetites. Cool shades of blue and green promote relaxation. Of course, children enjoy color variety, but too many colors at once will impact their ability to focus. Natural colors, such as the tans of wood furnishings, help calm children. Walls painted with a warm white color are perfect for showcasing children's artwork. Shelving on light-colored walls provides an interesting way to showcase children's three-dimensional creations.

Lighting. Healthful lighting conditions must also be considered when creating children's spaces. Because children spend so much time indoors, harsh fluorescent lighting can cause

fatigue and eye strain. Research shows that adequate amounts of daily sunlight play an important role in good mental health. Good design can help meet this need. All classrooms should have windows at children's eye level. Creative use of skylights and mirrors also helps reflect sunlight on play and learning spaces.

Pattern and Texture. The use of soft textures and muted patterns helps create a cozy, homelike atmosphere. A variety of textures may be featured in pillows, rugs, or wall hangings. Fabrics from around the world can be used on a rotating basis to help children understand the diversity in other cultures. Hanging plants, floor plants, or terrariums all help to create a homelike atmosphere. Aquariums with tropical fish fascinate children. The colored patterns of the fish and the rhythms of their movement capture children's attention and help them relax. See Fig. 12-6.

How To...

Plan a Learning Center

A typical child care classroom is a large rectangular room. Deciding how to arrange the learning centers within the room can be a challenge. You want each area to be distinct from the others, yet for safety reasons they all need to be visible to supervising teachers. When space is limited, combining or rotating learning centers works well.

- **Create Boundaries.** When learning centers are well marked, children understand the limits for play. Most areas need at least three boundaries. For instance, a block center can be placed in a corner of the room. The two walls make automatic boundaries. A block storage unit can serve as a third "wall." Colored tape on the floor can also divide play spaces. A piano might separate the music area from the art center.

- **Arrange for Privacy.** Learning centers can be arranged so that children have a degree of privacy when needed. Lofts—platforms raised a few feet off the ground—allow children to get away from loud activities when they feel like being alone or with a friend. Books, puppets, and puzzles are well-suited to lofts.

- **Create an Effective Traffic Pattern.** When planning learning centers, consider the direction, or **traffic pattern**, children take as they go from one learning center to another. Well-planned traffic patterns limit congestion as children enter or leave a learning center. They also help children move more easily during routines, such as hand washing before meals or getting ready for a nap.

APPLY IT!

Plan the arrangement of learning centers for an early childhood classroom. Draw your plans to scale on graph paper. Include dimensions of equipment, furniture, and shelving. Be sure to draw in the traffic patterns.

Learning Centers

The well-planned classroom is divided into learning centers. **Learning centers** are clearly-defined spaces for specific types of play and investigation. Each learning center is organized around a specific type of curriculum, or learning area. Areas for block play, art, science, or dramatic play are each suited to the age and number of children who will use them.

Learning centers provide an organized way to arrange space and manage the activity. Specifically, they:

- Direct children to activities and focus their attention.
- Allow children to learn by doing, while working at their own pace.
- Provide opportunities for independent and small group play.
- Distribute children throughout the classroom.
- Minimize conflicts and noise in any one area.

A program may not be able to offer every type of learning center at one time. Budget and space can be limiting. Most programs, however, do try to include certain learning centers as a core. These include centers for art, language arts, dramatic play, music, science, math, blocks, and active play. Other learning centers, such as woodworking and computers, can be added as space and resources allow.

A learning center should engage children's participation. It should also allow children to see where to get and return the materials they use. This promotes independence and encourages decision making.

Indoor Environments for Older Adults

Indoor environments for adult care centers should be warm and inviting. These environments should have space for programs that help older adults maintain their physical, social, cognitive, and sensory skills. These programs help older adults maintain their functional skills for independent living. See Fig. 12-7.

Activities for adult day programs are usually provided during daytime hours. The facility should have sufficient space for a full range of program activities and services for older adults. It should be safe and sanitary, and accessible to all participants. Facility design, construction, and maintenance should meet all local, state, and federal health and safety requirements.

Adult day programs will differ from state to state. The National Adult Day Services Association (NADSA) provides voluntary standards and guidelines for states that choose to regulate adult day services. The funding source for these

FIG. 12-7. Adult day care centers provide opportunities for older adults to socialize and participate in worthwhile activities. What are some ways that participating in adult day care programs benefits older adults?

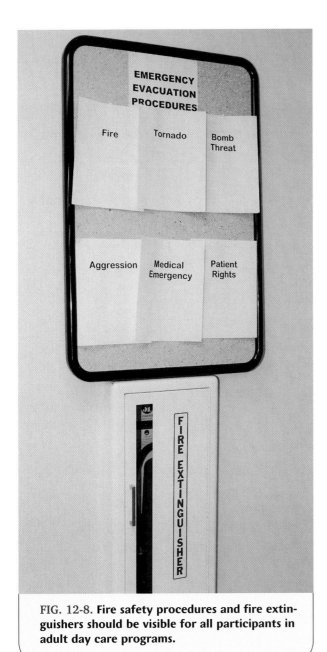

FIG. 12-8. Fire safety procedures and fire extinguishers should be visible for all participants in adult day care programs.

There are specific space requirements that are necessary when planning adult day programs. These requirements include:

- At least 35 square feet of program space for each adult day care participant.

- Intergenerational programs that house programs for children and adults should have a minimum of 120 square feet or 20 square feet per person.

- Adaptable space for large and small groups, and individual activities and services.

- Secure storage space for participants' personal belongings, such as their coats and hats.

- Locked storage for medications.

- At least one toilet for every 12 participants. In addition, there should be at least one wheelchair-accessible stall in each restroom.

- A separate area for those who require rest during the day or in case someone becomes ill. This area must have a sufficient number of reclining chairs or beds to meet these needs.

- At least one room for health care professionals to use as a treatment or examination room.

- An office area, which allows staff to work effectively and allows confidential discussions.

- At least two routes to exit the facility. At least one route should be located near a door or stairway with an unobstructed path to the outside of the building.

- Floors with non-slip surfaces or carpets on stairs, ramps, and walkways.

- Freedom from hazards, such as high steps, steep grades, or exposed electrical cords.

- Fire safety procedures posted for everyone to see. These procedures call for fire drills and inspection and maintenance of fire extinguishers. See Fig. 12-8.

- Visible and accessible first aid kits.

programs also determines the types of activities that are offered and who may participate. Outside the NADSA standards, there are not any national standards regarding the operation of adult care centers.

Most facilities have to meet certain standards to operate programs. For example, the Americans with Disabilities Act (ADA) sets accessibility requirements for people with disabilities. In addition, state and local governments often have set occupancy limits for adult centers.

FIG. 12-9.

ATMOSPHERE IN ADULT CARE CENTERS

Lighting	• Correct lighting levels help older adults see more clearly. Some people see better under strong clear light, while others function better with softer, dimmer lighting. • Center staff can adjust the lighting based on individual needs.
Color	• As people age, their sight not only worsens, but the colors they see change, usually taking on a more yellow cast. • Coordinate colors to help aging people use their sight effectively. For example, a brown door against an off-white wall is easier to see. • Avoid high-contrast colors, such as red and yellow, because these colors tend to be blinding. • Use color contrast in carpeting on stairs where older adults have to take a step. For example, color strips on the edges of steps alert the older person to step up or down. • Also avoid pattern designs in carpet that look like an object or appear to be moving. Older people may fear stepping over a carpet pattern or could lose their balance as they avoid the pattern.
Surface Textures	• Floor coverings made of non-slip materials are essential. • Handrails with grasp bars help older adults who have difficulty with balance. Grasp bars are usually 1.5 in. in diameter. • Countertops should be smooth and easy to clean.
Furniture	• Arrange furniture to encourage conversation. At least four people should be able to participate in a conversation at one time. • Tables should be adjustable to allow for wheelchair use.
Informational Signs	• Signs should be easily seen and give directions to various activities and locations to help older adults find their way independently. • Symbols, such as arrows, may be useful for older people who have visual problems. • Place two signs, one above the other—one for people who walk and the other for wheelchair users.

Indoor Living Areas

Adult centers have many rooms where activities take place. Upon arrival, the older adult should enter a living room, or gathering room. This room should have durable lighting, be color coordinated, be free of unsecured rugs, have directional signs to various areas, and include functional furniture. **Functional furniture** is practical, durable, and easy to care for.

Examples include a sofa, chairs, end tables, lamps, bookcases, and a television. The room atmosphere helps make the participants feel welcome and "at home." The gathering room is also a place where older adults meet with family members. Elements—such as color, lighting, texture, and furniture design—help make a facility safe and usable for aging persons and their families. See Fig. 12-9.

FIG. 12-10. Participating in sensory activities helps older adults maintain physical and cognitive skills.

Indoor Activity Areas

There are many areas for indoor activities in an adult day center. These activities help older adults maintain their cognitive, sensory, social, and physical independence skills in a leisurely way. When people enjoy themselves together in a relaxed environment, friendships can grow.

Activity classrooms should be large and spacious to accommodate various cognitive, sensory, social, and physical activities. Movable furniture allows participants to rearrange the room for various activities. The space might be used for activities, such as dancing, musicals, plays, or activities. Floor-to-ceiling shelving units are used to store equipment used for activities. Lockable cabinets are used for storing art supplies and musical instruments. Activity areas can include the following:

Kitchen and Dining Areas. The facility should be equipped with a kitchen/dining area. There should be plenty of counter space for food preparation in the kitchen. The kitchen should connect to the dining area, but be out of view. The dining area should be a large area with tables that seat no more than six older adults. Enough space should be allowed for people in wheelchairs and room to assist individuals who have special needs.

Physical Activity Areas. An effective, planned fitness program helps keep older adults in good health. The space for physical fitness activities includes a well-ventilated room that accommodates wheelchairs and provides floor space for chair exercise. Some of the activities include age-appropriate exercises to improve balance and coordination, strength, flexibility, and aerobic fitness. This multipurpose room may also be used for activities, such as movies and dancing.

Cognitive and Sensory Activity Area. As people age, they may fear losing their independence, their mental focus, and their sense of self and identity. These fears are often real and not imaginary. In an effort to maintain or strengthen these skills, adult day centers have many activities, such as arts and crafts, reading, and playing musical instruments. See Fig. 12-10. Spaces for cognitive and sensory activities may include:

- **A library.** In the library, individuals may check out books or just sit and read. Space can be set apart for individuals with visual impairments to listen to books on tape and have discussions afterward. Also, an area to show movies can be part of the library. Movies often trigger discussion and help stimulate memories in older adults.

- **A game room.** Interactive games that are challenging and rewarding can be held in the game room or multipurpose room. Older adults enjoy playing games, such as dominoes, checkers, and cards, which help to stimulate the memory.

FIG. 12-11A. Accessible space for children and older adults is required for intergenerational environments. In what ways might intergenerational care benefit all generations?

• **A music room.** A special music room or a part of the multipurpose room can be set up for older adults who play musical instruments or those who want to take lessons. Music can help decrease anxiety, loneliness, and depression. See Fig. 12-11A.

Social Activity Areas. These areas are designed to be fun and meet the social, recreational, and rehabilitative needs of older adults. Space for activities, such as singing, dancing, playing cards, dominoes, checkers, and chess, should all accommodate the needs of older adults. Social activity areas are equipped with tables and chairs that are easily moved for other activities.

Intergenerational Environments

An intergenerational environment should provide space that encourages interaction between two or more generations. It should be an open space where people of all ages can meet and feel comfortable. The family-living type environment should illustrate both a verbal and visual picture of interactions that attract many generations. The environment should be beautiful enough to instill pride, joy, and peace

FIG. 12-11B. Quiet space for children and older adults to participate in one-on-one activities, such as games, is important for both generations.

among generations. A circular design helps bring people together and encourage sharing. The intergenerational environment should facilitate mentoring and affordable projects, such as cooking and gardening. Along with visual appeal, intergenerational environments must meet the minimum space requirements set by state licensing agencies. Other qualities for indoor intergenerational environments include:

- Separate space for children and older adults along with a common area for intergenerational interaction. See Fig. 12-11B.

- Furnishings and other materials that meet the needs of all participants.

- Sounds that promote well-being. This includes noisy and quiet areas.

- Sensory activities that have a significant purpose. For example, indoor environments may include a kitchen in which children and older adults can experience ethnic cooking.

In addition, intergenerational environments must meet the same state standards for lighting, health, safety, sanitation, and storage as separate facilities for children and older adults.

Section *12-1* Knowledge Check

1. Contrast appropriate environments for children with those for older adults.

2. What elements enhance the atmosphere of environments for children and older adults?

3. What guidelines should be kept in mind when creating and arranging learning centers?

Mini-Lab

Create a room arrangement for either an early childhood classroom or an adult care activity room. Draw your plans on graph paper. Write a summary that includes a description of your arrangement, safety features, features for special needs, and atmosphere.

Section 12-2

Sensory-Appropriate Outdoor Environments

OBJECTIVES

- Identify licensing laws and accreditation criteria that apply to play yards and recreational areas.
- Explain how outdoor areas can be designed to meet the developmental needs and abilities of young children and older adults, including those with disabilities.
- Describe the role outdoor design plays in health, recreation, and overall learning for children and older adults.
- Describe the variety and purpose of play areas recommended for an outdoor environment.
- Identify outdoor sensory experiences that benefit children and older adults.
- Evaluate an outdoor environment for safety for children and older adults.

KEY TERMS

nontoxic
fall zones
therapeutic
dehydrated

Children and older adults often spend more time indoors than outdoors. Safe and appealing outdoor spaces help capture the interest of children and adults. This can lead to better health and enjoyment of nature and outdoor activities.

Outdoor Environments for Children

Children and adults alike have an inborn sense of wonder about the outdoor world. The fun and excitement of outdoor life is good for the mind and body. Outdoor play areas today are rich in natural green space, trees, native flowers and shrubs, and exposure to natural elements, such as dirt, sand, fresh air, and wind and water.

Color, texture, and aroma are introduced into outdoor play areas by including trees, shrubs, and other types of **nontoxic** (not poisonous) plants. Children can learn about animals and insects that make trees, shrubs, and plants their homes. When birdhouses and feeders are hung, children can observe bird habits and natural cycles, such as nesting time and migration. While outside, children can see and hear the effects of moving air on leaves and branches. Hanging wind chimes or colorful windsocks from trees shows air movement. Trees and shrubs also provide much-needed cool shade.

FIG. 12-12A & B. The ADA requires that play yard components be accessible to all children, including those with disabilities.

When seasons change, plants and trees show the effects of weather and climate. Aromas from trees and shrubs, such as pines and lilacs, offer more sensory experiences. Herbs and flowers have aromas that attract butterflies and hummingbirds.

As well as providing for beauty, these outdoor areas should be made accessible to all program participants. The Americans with Disabilities Act (ADA) is a civil rights law that offers specific guidelines for providing safe, accessible play yards for all participants.

ADA Playground Requirements

The ADA law states minimum accessibility requirements for new or altered play areas. These requirements ensure that children with disabilities are able to access a variety of com-

ponents in a play area. The ADA law describes accessible routes, ramps, landings and wheelchair accessible platforms, transfer systems, and accessible play opportunities. The ADA accessibility guidelines for play areas are very complex. When planning, building, or renovating play areas, be sure to obtain the complete ADA requirements. The following information gives an overview of the ADA requirements.

Accessible Routes. Specifically designed pathways that provide access to children with disabilities—such as those who use wheelchairs or other mobility devices—are called accessible routes. These routes must connect all entry and exit points to accessible play components. There are two types of accessible routes—ground level and elevated. See Fig. 12-12A & B.

FIG. 12-13. **Landings on elevated play equipment are essential for children with mobility problems.** What purpose do landings serve?

Ramps, Landings, and Transfer Systems. In providing access to elevated play components, ramps, landings, and transfer systems must meet specific requirements. Note that wheelchair parking and play space are required with play yard components and must be considered when planning ramps, landings, and transfer systems. A minimum parking space size of 30 by 48 inches must also allow for a connecting circulation path that is at least 36 inches wide.

• **Ramps.** Each elevated ramp run must have a 36-inch minimum clear width, a 12-inch maximum rise, and a slope of 1 inch for every foot of ramp run. The "rise" of a ramp is the amount of vertical distance a slanted surface ascends or descends. The "run" is the length of a continuous sloped surface. Handrails are required on both sides of ramps that connect to elevated play components. The handrail gripping surface must be .95-1.55 inches around. The handrail height can be a maximum of 20-28 inches above the ramp surface.

• **Landings and platforms.** The level surfaces at the top and bottom of each ramp run are called landings or platforms. Landings must be as wide as the ramps they connect to and must be at least 60 inches in length. If ramps change direction, the minimum landing size must be 60 inches in order to accommodate a turn. The turning space for wheelchairs and mobility devices must be 60 inches within a T-shaped area. Note that wheelchair turning space and parking space should not overlap. Barriers are required along landing

• Ground-level routes connect play components at ground level. These routes must have a minimum of 60 inches clear width.

• Elevated accessible routes connect elevated play components. These routes must connect at least 50 percent of the entry and exit points of elevated play components. Ramps, landings, and transfer points are common methods for providing access to elevated play components.

or platform edges to keep wheelchairs from falling off. When the space between the barrier and ramp/landing is greater than 1 inch, a curb is required along both edges. Curbs must extend a minimum of 2 inches above the ramp surface. See Fig. 12-13.

- **Transfer systems.** In order to provide access to elevated play components without wheelchairs or mobility devices, a transfer system is used. Transfer systems consist of transfer platforms, transfer steps, and transfer supports. A transfer platform is a landing that allows a wheelchair or mobility device user to lift onto a play structure and leave the mobility device on the ground. Transfer platforms are a minimum of 24 inches wide, 14 inches deep, and a height of 11-18 inches. Transfer steps are used to access different levels of play components. They are a minimum of 24 inches wide, 14 inches deep, and a maximum of 8 inches high. Transfer supports assist people when transferring to the entry or seat of a play component. Transfer supports include handrails, handgrips, and custom-designed handholds.

Accessible Play Opportunities. In order to make play areas more usable for children with disabilities, additional considerations should be made. These considerations include:

- Maneuvering space that allows a 180-degree turn in a wheelchair must be provided on the same level as elevated play components. Maneuvering space is also required to access ground-level equipment, such as swings.

- Vertical knee clearance minimum of 24 inches high, 30 inches wide, and 17 inches deep is required for equipment, such as play tables.

- The top of the playing surfaces must be a maximum of 30 inches above the accessible surface.

- Reach ranges that are appropriate for children who use wheelchairs to access play components. The recommended forward or side reach ranges are: 20-26 inches for 3- to

Avoid Dehydration. During warm season outdoor activities, children and older adults can overheat, become thirsty, and even become dehydrated. These conditions can lead to serious illness, such as heat stroke. To prevent heat-related health problems:

- Encourage frequent drinking-water breaks. If there is not an outdoor drinking fountain, provide a thermos of cool water and disposable drinking cups.
- Encourage children and older adults to stay in the shade and out of the sun.

4-year-olds; 18-40 inches for 5- to 8-year-olds; and 16-44 inches for 9- to 12-year-olds. Reach heights vary depending on how the equipment is accessed.

Outdoor Play Areas

Good outdoor play environments nurture children in all areas and stages of development. Good design also responds to varying abilities, including those of children with special needs. For example, sand and water play offered in raised tables allows for independent use by children in wheelchairs. For safety and developmental needs, infants and toddlers need a separate play yard built for their size and limited mobility. On the other extreme, school-age children require more complex play areas to challenge their more advanced motor skills. State licensing laws and the ADA act set standards for outdoor play yards. Accreditation

FIG. 12-14.

TYPES OF OUTDOOR PLAY AREAS

Hard Surface Areas	Grassy Areas	Climbing & Sliding Areas
Hard surfaces are needed for tricycle and wagon paths, and for games with balls, balance beams, or hoops. For safety, shock-absorbent rubber	Soft, grassy areas are ideal for playing group games, nature discovery, or reading stories. Small grassy slopes allow for sledding in winter, or rolling in summer.	Large spaces must be allowed for climbers and low slides. These items should be no higher than 4 ft. off the ground and must have at least 9 in. of shock-absorbing mate-

criteria, such as those of the National Academy of Early Childhood Programs, also address play yard features.

Play yards need a variety of areas and surfaces to allow for different types of play. Such play variety ensures children's development of fine and gross motors skills. See Fig. 12-14 on types of play areas.

Outdoor Environments for Older Adults

As with children, the outdoor environment for older adults must be safe, secure, and suit-able for recreational activities. The area must be large enough for activities and outdoor furniture, such as chairs, swings, gazeboes, decks, patios, and benches. The outdoor areas must be enclosed by a wall or fence. They may also be located in a courtyard that is surrounded by and directly accessible to the care facility. In addition to ADA accessibility requirements, outdoor activity environments should also:

- Provide the recommended square footage of outdoor space required by state laws.

- Provide a percentage of required outdoor space with shade trees, outdoor umbrellas, and covered patios or decks.

- Include required outside lighting at all outdoor entrances and activity areas.

Sensory-Rich Areas	Art Areas	Dramatic Play Areas
Sensory-rich areas, such as sand and water areas or gardens, are attractive to children. Sand can be packed in many ways, while playing with water cools and relaxes children. Outdoor water play may include a shallow stream or pool. Vegetable and flower gardens let children explore the natural world, such as worms, butterflies, and plants with a variety of textures. Choose nontoxic plants for children.	Art areas can be created on concrete walkways. Colorful wall murals can be made with chalk or water-soluble, nontoxic paint. Children can also sit at picnic tables to draw on paper with markers, crayons, and watercolor paints.	Playhouses or small stage areas encourage dramatic play outdoors. Children like to "play house" outdoors, too. They also enjoy pretending to be firefighters and police officers. 

- Provide safe parking for the arrival and departure of participants and workers.
- Provide signs for outdoor safety zones with help from local authorities.

Outdoor Activities

The activities can be rewarding and **therapeutic** (thair-uh-PYOO-tihk), or assist with healing. A trained activity coordinator can work with older adults to develop individualized walking plans that benefit health. Every person's activity plan should be approved by his or her healthcare specialist. This type of therapy can help with heart, circulatory problems, tight joints, and emotional health.

Gardening can be helpful therapy for many disabilities and illnesses that impact older adults. It can be used to help people who are physically or mentally impaired. Gardening and nature activities also help people who have had strokes or accidents rebuild their physical skills. Walking through a garden also improves mobility and endurance.

Outdoor Safety

Outdoor safety for children and older adults requires careful planning and maintenance. Shaded areas with drinking fountains help keep children and older adults from becoming

Intergenerational
Interactions

an intergenerational garden, consider:

1. **Location.** The garden location is critical. You will want a space large enough to plant the quantity and variety of plants chosen, as well as ensure the garden will receive plenty of sunshine and rain.

2. **Soil.** Soil that crumbles easily in your hand is ideal for growing most plants. You may need to add sand, clay, or compost to get the desired texture. Likewise, if the soil in your community is not fertile, you may need to add fertilizer. To ensure you apply the correct type of fertilizer and soil additives, visit a lawn and garden center near you.

3. **Climate.** Weather patterns in your area will dictate which plants will grow well in your garden. Some plants grow well in dry climates, while others prefer moist conditions.

4. **Tools.** While some gardening tasks, like weeding, can be completed with bare hands, you will want a few tools to make the job easier. A hoe is ideal for creating furrows for planting seeds and for removing weeds. A shovel is a necessity for planting seedlings. Children and older adults can use a small,

Larger plants, bushes, or trees may require full-size shovels for planting. You may want to use a tiller each year to cultivate the soil before planting.

5. **Water.** Make sure your garden is near a water source. Most plants require approximately one inch of water per week.

6. **Plants.** Last but not least, you will want to choose plants to teach children the value of gardening. Explain vegetables provide an inexpensive, fresh food source. Flowers offer beauty and fragrance that may also attract birds, butterflies, and bees. Herbs can be used for decorating or seasoning food or making tea. Pumpkins and gourds provide fall decorating fun.

Follow-Up

Use the above information to plan an intergenerational gardening experience to educate and entertain children and older adults. Summarize your ideas for this experience in a report.

dehydrated, from losing water or body fluids. Constant staff supervision is required when children and older adults participate in water activities, such as swimming and fishing. Fences around these outdoor areas help reduce safety risks.

Equipment and surface materials should be routinely checked for breakage, splintering, rusting, or jagged edges that could cause injury. Solid buildings, such as playhouses and decks, should be placed over concrete or asphalt. This helps keep wildlife, such as skunks, from building homes beneath the structures. Daily safety checks should be performed for all outdoor activity areas to ensure safety for children and older adults.

Outdoor Storage

To maintain the condition of outdoor recreation materials, and to reduce theft or vandalism, lockable outdoor storage is used. Storage areas should have adequate floor space for wheeled toys and garden chairs. Wall shelving for items such as sand toys and hand-held gar-

FIG. 12-15. Outdoor storage can be used to store equipment for intergenerational centers when indoor storage is lacking.

dening tools should be secure and easily reached. Outdoor storage can be placed near activity areas when the main building doesn't have enough storage space. See Fig. 12-15.

Section **12-2**   Knowledge Check

1. How can outdoor environments be designed to offer a variety of sensory experiences for children and older adults?

2. Name three outdoor activity areas that accommodate children and older adults.

3. How would you determine if a program's outdoor area was engaging as well as safe?

Mini-Lab

Create a plan for a vegetable garden that allows full garden access to children with special needs and older adults. Include space measurements, the height of raised garden beds, and how pathway surfaces will be covered. Determine the type, amount, and cost of supplies needed to create the garden.

Chapter 12 Review & Activities

Section Summaries

12-1 The needs of children and older adults who use a space influence how it should be arranged.

12-1 Environments must respond to children's ages and varying stages of development.

12-1 Environments should accommodate the space needs of children and older adults.

12-1 Classroom space is organized into learning centers that respond to the varying ages, abilities, and interests of children.

12-1 Adult care centers should provide space for activities that help older adults maintain cognitive, sensory, social, and physical independence skills.

12-1 Intergenerational environments should meet the needs of both children and older adults.

12-2 Play and recreational area design must comply with state licensing laws and ADA accessibility standards.

12-2 Outdoor areas must be designed with the ages, needs, and abilities of children and older adults in mind.

12-2 Outdoor activity benefits the health, recreation, and learning of children and older adults.

12-2 Sensory features in outdoor activity areas enhance children's learning and the enjoyment of older adults.

12-2 Outdoor environments should offer a variety of safe and engaging activities.

12-2 Safety checks for outdoor environments must be conducted daily to spot hazards.

Check Your Knowledge

1. What factors guide the design of indoor environments for early childhood and adult care programs?

2. How can a well-planned environment help children learn through their senses?

3. What are four ways to make an early childhood or adult care center feel more homelike?

4. Why do child and adult care facilities need an isolation room?

5. Why is a well-designed environment important for meeting the needs of program staff?

6. How do parents and staff members use a one-way observation window?

7. Describe five learning centers or activity areas and their purposes.

8. Contrast the environmental features needed for infant/toddler and school-age programs.

9. How can facility design encourage interaction between children and older adults?

10. List outdoor safety features that protect children and older adults.

Thinking Critically

1. Draw conclusions about how classroom design and arrangement can help children engage in self-directed learning.
2. Analyze environmental factors to consider if space were to be used by children as well as older adults. How could an environment be enhanced to reflect the diversity of those using the space?
3. Describe how you would supervise children and older adults at an outdoor intergenerational care environment in order to keep them safe.

Practical Applications

1. **Sensory Environment Checklist.** Develop a checklist to record the number of indoor sensory experiences offered in a program that serves children or older adults. Visit a local early childhood, older adult, or intergenerational care program. Record your observations using the checklist.

2. **Internet Investigation.** Search at least three Internet sites related to requirements for intergenerational care environments. Summarize your findings and share them with the class.

3. **Environment Planning.** Assume you are the director of a one-room intergenerational care center. How would you allocate space for children, older adults, and a common area used for both? Draw your plans to scale on graph paper. Indicate space allocations, how each area might be equipped to be accessible to children or older adults, and traffic patterns. Explain which factors influenced your decisions.

Building Your PORTFOLIO

Creating Care Environments

Your future employer will want to evaluate your knowledge in regard to the development and maintenance of the care environment.

Step 1: Think about the following questions. Keyboard your answers for your career portfolio.

- How should a care center environment benefit children and/or older adults?
- What physical standards must care centers meet?
- What role should you play in the development and maintenance of the care environment?

Step 2: Choose one of the learning or adult care activity centers from your Section 12-1 Mini Lab room arrangement plan. Carry out your plans for this center. Set up the physical environment. Include safety features, traffic patterns, items of visual interest, and the characteristics for meeting special needs.

Step 3: Take photographs of your learning or adult activity center arrangement. Write a summary describing your plan and how it will benefit children and/or older adults.

Step 4: Prepare your responses for a presentation in your career portfolio. Mount your photo(s) and keyboard your summary before adding them to your portfolio.

Chapter **13**

Appropriate Equipment & Supplies

Section 13-1
Early Childhood Equipment & Supplies

Section 13-2
Adult Care Center Equipment & Supplies

Section 13-1·

Early Childhood Equipment & Supplies

Classrooms that are carefully equipped allow children to participate in a wide variety of activities. Choosing equipment and supplies that meet children's varying abilities and styles of learning helps them to be successful during learning and play. Wise selection helps create a welcoming atmosphere that promises comfort and enjoyment. Such an environment does not come about by chance. It is the result of careful staff planning.

Supporting Program Goals

A facility with well-chosen, adequate equipment and supplies helps staff meet program goals. It also helps meet all areas of children's development. Items that fit children's abilities are called **developmentally appropriate**. For example, encouraging children's self-help skills is an example of a program goal. Wisely chosen supplies can support that goal, such as child-sized smocks available on low hooks in the painting area help children learn to be responsible and protect clothing during play. The following practices help to promote program goals in the early childhood classroom:

- **Self-esteem.** Provide toys and equipment that match the children's age and developmental level. Enable children to make choices. Use bulletin boards and display cases to exhibit children's work.

- **Social skills.** Provide culturally diverse toys and activities that encourage children to play and work together with respect.

- **Problem-solving ability.** Supply toys and materials that can be used in many creative ways. For example, blocks can be used to build intricate structures. Children may need to figure out how to make a block tower stand tall without falling over.

- **Language skills.** Provide toys, such as puppets, to encourage language use.
- **Large-muscle development.** Provide equipment and activities that require the use of the whole body, such as balls or balance beams.
- **Small-muscle coordination.** Provide supplies, such as connecting blocks or safety scissors and paper, to encourage small-motor development.

Plan for Basic Needs

Your knowledge concerning the developmental needs of children can help you select equipment and supplies. What a preschooler needs is quite different from a school-age child's needs. A preschooler will be frustrated if activities and toys are not age appropriate. A school-age child will not be comfortable in a preschool setting. Staff should be careful to address the basic needs of all children in their care.

Storage for Children's Belongings. Children arrive each day with an assortment of belongings, such as coats, extra clothes for toileting accidents, and items for show and tell. Each child needs a personal cubby identified by his or her name and photo and possibly a symbol or color. Parents can also tape a family photo inside the cubby to help children feel more at home. Children's labeled toothbrushes or diapers should be stored in a sanitary, organized fashion in their rest room.

Napping. Full-day programs provide cots and sheets for naptime. Stacking cots on a rolling cart makes it easier to move them into the classroom. See Fig. 13-1.

Meal Service. Infants and young toddlers eat in special feeding chairs that keep them secure in their seats. Bibs help protect the clothing of these children while they learn to eat. For older preschoolers, meal service is provided on low tables that can be used for play activities during the rest of the day. Chairs that fit small children should be available, and utensils should accommodate their smaller hands and mouths. Using age-appropriate equipment will help children learn to eat independently. See Chapter 10 for more information on feeding children.

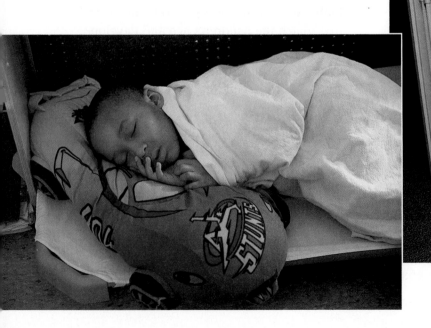

FIG. 13-1. Sanitary cots with sheets are provided for naptime in full-day programs. A rolling cart helps store the cots when not in use and assists in moving them to the classroom for naptime.

FIG. 13-2. **A blend of commercial and homemade toys encourages creativity in young children.** What types of homemade toys do you think would be most fun and beneficial for children?

First Aid and Emergency Supplies. Each classroom and each transportation vehicle needs a first aid kit and emergency supplies, such as a flashlight, battery-operated radio, and fire extinguisher. The first aid kits should be stored out of reach of children. Portable first aid kits should be on hand when children play outdoors and take walks. See Chapter 6 for more information on first aid and safety.

Indoor Equipment & Supplies

Use good judgment, knowledge of children, and creativity when selecting equipment. Good choices promote learning. Poor choices can create safety hazards and increase behavior problems. When selecting toys and equipment, the following guidelines will be helpful:

- Supply items that are safe and appropriate for children's ages and abilities. When care providers plan for children's developmental abilities, children are more likely to experience success. Injuries are reduced when staff avoid toys that could choke young children or puncture older ones.

- Provide a variety of materials. Children need variety and novelty to keep their interest and to allow them to develop at their own pace. Include items to develop physical, intellectual, social, and emotional skills. Rotate items regularly, maintaining a balance between familiar items and new ones.

- Include sensory materials that encourage hands-on play. Children need items at which to look, touch, listen, smell, and sometimes even taste.

- Materials should reflect diverse cultures. Children's books, puppets, dolls, musical recordings and instruments, dress-up clothes, pretend cookware, and posters should reflect the practices of different ethnic groups.

- Provide enough materials so children can comfortably share. Having too few materials frustrates children and sets the stage for conflicts. The younger the children, the more important it is to have duplicate toys.

- Provide a balance of commercially purchased and homemade toys. Creativity is encouraged when children learn they are not dependent on costly items to have fun. Teachers can make easy games with stickers and tagboard. Children can help make doll clothes. See Fig. 13-2.

- Include items adaptable to special needs. Materials in a classroom should respond to the varying needs and abilities of those enrolled. For instance, puzzles with knobbed pieces help children succeed despite small-muscle coordination challenges. Sensory play items can be stored in a raised table that allows a child in a wheelchair to use them.

Supplying Learning Centers

As you learned in Chapter 12, learning centers allow children to focus on specific types of play and learning. They are engaging and

ETHICS IN Action

Sanitizing Ethics. One of your coworkers is assigned to sanitize surfaces at the end of the day. She is supposed to use an approved sanitizing solution. However, you have noticed that instead of cleaning she is merely using a spray that masks odors. It may be your imagination, but you believe that you can smell urine on the sofas in the living area. *Should you approach your coworker with your concerns, tell the supervisor what you have observed, or just keep quiet about your observation? Why?*

pinwheels; wind chimes; magnifying glasses; balance scales; and magnets. See Fig. 13-3.

Woodworking Area. Supply a woodworking bench, child-size quality tools, carpenter's apron, safety goggles, scrap wood, nails, and screws.

Block Center. Provide shelving; wooden unit blocks (for a classroom of 20 preschoolers, 400 blocks of various shapes); toy vehicles; plastic zoo, circus, forest, and farm animals; and a train set.

Cooking Center. Supply aprons and hats and basic cooking items, such as unbreakable bowls, measuring cups, cookie sheets, and muffin pans.

Dramatic Play and Puppetry Center. Provide pretend home furniture, such as table with chair, refrigerator, and range; dress-up clothes; and dolls, stuffed animals, and puppets.

Language and Relaxation Area. Include a library bookstand with books; relaxing seating,

increase children's attention span when a rich variety is offered. Teachers create learning centers for their specific age group. For instance, a woodworking center is appropriate for preschoolers, but not for infants. Following are suggestions for supplying typical learning centers:

Art Center. Provide an easel with paints and brushes; smocks; storage shelves for supplies; scissors; crayons; markers; a variety of paper and scrap materials for cutting, painting or pasting; paint drying rack; play dough and modeling tools; art cart; and a locked storage cabinet for teacher supplies.

Sensory Play Area. Include a water and sand table, which can also be filled with other sensory items, such as cotton balls; plastic animals; tools, such as plastic buckets, shovels, sand and water wheels, plastic measuring cups, funnels, and sifters, for sand or water play; science discovery items, such as mineral, rock, shell, and other nature collections; bug cages; color paddles; aquarium, terrarium, and other plants;

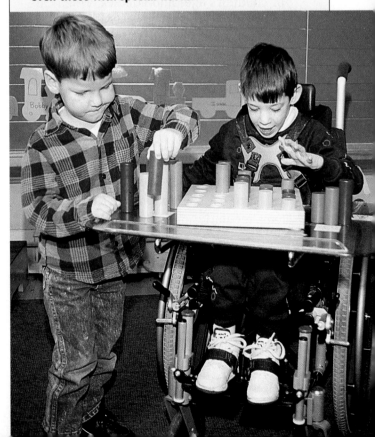

FIG. 13-3. Equipment and supplies in all learning centers must be able to be used by all children, even those with special needs.

FIG. 13-4. All equipment and toys for a center should be evaluated for safety, quality, and age-appropriateness before purchase and use. What are two questions you should ask yourself when evaluating toys to use with young children?

such as a love seat, rocking chair, glider, large pillows, or bean-bag chairs; and a tape recorder with books on tape (headphones optional).

Music Center. Supply multicultural musical instruments; basic rhythm instruments, such as tambourines, finger cymbals, triangles, and drums; compact disc player and disks or record player and records; cassette player and audiotapes; items for dancing and creative movement, such as scarves, streamers, tutus, grass skirts, and magic wands.

Media Stations. Include a computer and printer, computer table, and computer games; a VCR and videotapes; tape recorders and blank cassette tapes; and a handheld camcorder.

Manipulatives Center. Include items that help build small motor skills, such as stringing beads, peg boards, and snap-together toys; items that build concepts related to color, size, and shape, such as colored table blocks for

Disinfecting Play Equipment. Indoor and outdoor play equipment must be disinfected on a regular basis. Toys that are frequently handled (such as toys that infants mouth) should be disinfected daily. Toys used by older children or those out of diapers can be disinfected weekly. Use a fresh daily disinfecting solution of ¾-cup liquid ultra bleach to one gallon of water.

stacking and making patterns; items for counting, such as teddy-bear counters and number bingo; age-appropriate board games; and matching games such as memory, concentration, color bingo, and shape bingo.

Large Movement Area. Provide bean bags, streamers, balance beam, low climber over padding, parachute, expandable fabric tunnels, classroom slide, scooters, balls of all sizes from beach balls to sponge balls, plastic bowling-ball set, hula hoops, flags, wheel toys, and a thick mat for rough-and-tumble play.

Evaluating Quality

Careful thought pays when choosing equipment and toys. Selections will be better when you ask questions like these before making selections:

• Is the item safe? Metal, wood, and plastic edges should be rounded rather than sharp. Paint should be nontoxic. Some paints and other finishes contain ingredients that are toxic, especially to young children who may chew on the toys or equipment. See Fig. 13-4.

FIG. 13-5. **Separate play yards should be provided for toddlers and preschoolers and school-age children.** Why should all play yards be ADA compliant?

- Will the item withstand heavy or rough use by large groups of children? Is it durable?
- Will the toy be easy to clean? Can it be **sanitized**, or cleaned in a way that will kill the organisms that can cause illness?
- Can children of different ages use the toy?
- Does the toy encourage cooperative play, rather than aggressive, or even violent, play?
- Can more than one child use the item at a time?
- Does your classroom have storage space for the item?
- Can the item be used in more than one way? Will it encourage creativity?
- Does the item encourage children's active involvement, rather than passive observation? Will it hold a child's interest?
- Will children learn basic concepts while playing with the toy? Will it support program goals? Will it reinforce curriculum themes and objectives?
- Will the toy allow for sensory learning?
- Will both girls and boys enjoy the toy? Is the toy free of racial, cultural, and gender stereotypes?
- Are children likely to have fun with the toy?

Outdoor Equipment & Supplies

Because children have a wide range of physical and intellectual needs, separate outdoor play yards are necessary for infants and toddlers, preschoolers, and school-age children. (Some states do allow preschool and school-age children to use the same play yard.) Separate outdoor play areas protect the safety of each age group. They also prevent conflicts between children of widely varying abilities. Any outdoor play area should be inspected daily for safety and needed repairs, fenced, accessible to all, have a drinking fountain, and offer some shade.

Equipping Play Areas

Items offered in outdoor areas vary among programs. If a center believes the play yard should be an outdoor classroom, rather than just a recess area, it often includes areas for art activities or dramatic play. Outdoor play areas generally allow 75 square feet of play area per child. The following are suggestions for equipping typical outdoor play areas. Keep in mind that the suggested items must be adjusted to the size and needs of the group they serve and the available storage. See Fig. 13-5.

- **Climbers:** Ramps, slides, swinging bridge, and firefighter poles.
- **Swings:** Individual swings or porch-style swings for multiple seating.
- **Sand play equipment:** Sandbox or table with buckets, shovels, scoops, plastic dishes, molds, measuring cups, and plastic zoo, farm, or dinosaur animals.
- **Wheel toys:** Scooters, wagons, tricycles, push-pull toys, and large strollers for infants and toddlers.
- **Balls:** Rimball with basketballs, soccer balls, soft foam balls, T-balls, and other types of balls.
- **Garden toys:** Flower or vegetable garden space, water source, hose, watering cans, and gardening tools.
- **Dramatic play toys:** Play house, log cabin, tree house, tepees, and tents. Include equipment and supplies that might go with each of these items.

Safe Play Yard Equipment. Teeter-totters, merry-go-rounds, swinging exercise rings, trampolines, and high slides have been associated with many injuries to preschoolers. These and other similar items should not be included in the play yard. Be sure to arrange play yard equipment to allow for large fall zones around climbers, slides, and swings. In addition, adequate depth of padding, such as sand, pea gravel, or shredded tires, should be under climbing equipment to absorb shocks from falls. State licensing standards provide requirements for fall zones and surface padding. The arrangement should also allow for care providers to easily view and supervise all children while they play.

- **Multipurpose area:** Grassy open area for activities, such as running, racing, tumbling, large-group games, sledding, snow play, flying kites, and playing with pinwheels and streamers. Also include paved areas for riding tricycles and using other wheeled toys.

Section 13-1 Knowledge Check

1. How should a center be equipped to meet program goals?
2. What equipment and supplies are needed to meet children's basic needs?
3. What are some ways to include multicultural items in the center?

Mini-Lab

Visit a local toy store and randomly select three toys from the shelves that are designed for preschool children. Using the questions listed in this chapter's "Evaluating Quality" section, record how each toy does or does not meet the criteria for inclusion in a preschool classroom.

Section **13-2**

Adult Care Center Equipment & Supplies

OBJECTIVES

- Describe the equipment used in indoor and outdoor areas in an adult day center.
- Describe how a daily cleaning procedure is conducted in an adult day center.

KEY TERMS

consumable supplies
inventory
lap pool

Equipment in an adult center should promote a homelike atmosphere. It should accommodate all older adults, including those with physical restrictions. Care providers should follow their state's medical guidelines when selecting and arranging equipment.

Equipment & Supplies

Equipment and supplies at an adult day center should promote the goals of the program. For example, if the program uses a social-medical model, it will need equipment that promotes social activities. Most older adults want to have their vital signs screened at some point during their participation. Most programs provide equipment that supports medical services, such as blood pressure and diabetic screening.

Equipment and supplies at adult day centers should be educational and fun for all older adults. Everyone should have access to different types of equipment. When older adults have various materials to choose from, they can engage in activities that interest them. The center is responsible for providing supplies that older adults need. Centers should provide consumable supplies for older adults. **Consumable supplies** are supplies that can be consumed, or used up. Items such as pipe cleaners, food for activities, and paper are consumable items. They are used immediately and do not have to be counted in an **inventory**, or a detailed record of the quantity of supplies on hand. Adults can use consumable supplies for projects they can take home, such as crafts or baked goods.

Indoor Equipment & Supplies

Older adults choose day centers because of the programs they provide. Programs are designed to address skills at all levels. Program designers also plan for the equipment that older adults use. These professionals analyze the components of a stimulating environment, and then create the space. Developmentally appropriate equipment is equipment that helps develop and maintain older adults' skills. Programs provide directions and classes for using this equipment. These classes are important in helping older adults maintain their cognitive skills. Classes are skill-based and give older adults immediate enjoyment and satisfaction. In addition to being educational, classes should be ethnically appropriate. See Fig. 13-6.

Educational Areas

Educational areas are areas where learning activities take place. These activities help older adults with different abilities maintain and build their skills. The equipment in these areas supports the different activities. The equipment includes computers, photo cameras and video cameras, and sound systems.

- The computer area contains a computer and software for classes. The classes range from basic to advanced. The basic classes help older adults become familiar with the computer. The advanced classes help older adults learn technical skills, such as word processing, editing, and printing letters.

- The library area contains a variety of books and resources for older adults. It is a place where older adults can relax and read. Some library areas may also be equipped with computers with Internet access.

- The media area contains cameras and other photography equipment for classes. Photography classes allow older adults to take their own pictures. They can also develop them, if they choose. Older adults can use video cameras to record activities, such as social trips, family outings, or other special events. They may also use different forms of media to make scrapbooks.

- The music area includes musical instruments, such as pianos or keyboards, stereos, tape recorders, and CD players. Older adults can play, listen, and record music to enjoy with each other or their visiting family. Recordings are used to stimulate the memory.

FIG. 13-6. Many adult day centers are equipped with educational and entertainment equipment and supplies. How can these items help older adults maintain their cognitive skills?

Fitness Area

Adult day care centers should have fitness areas so older adults can maintain their strength and flexibility. The fitness area should be staffed by a fitness professional and paraprofessionals. These staff members direct and assist older adults with their fitness programs. The center should provide state-of-the-art equipment that is designed with older adults in mind. Those with disabilities should also be able to use the equipment. The fitness area should have exercise chairs, weights, and floor mats. These items help older adults feel comfortable and prevent injuries. Before starting a fitness program, older adults should consult with their health care specialists for approval. The fitness professional should help older adults develop a program that accommodates any special needs they might have.

Kitchen & Dining Area

The kitchen area should follow center standards and those of the Occupational Safety and Health Administration (OSHA).

The food preparation area should be separate from the dishwashing and garbage area. The

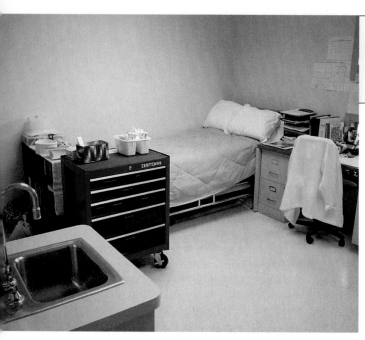

FIG. 13-7. **Older adults may use the clinical area of an adult day center when they are sick, especially tired, and need a place to rest away from the group.**

counter space should be free of food, and the counter accessories should be washed and sanitized daily. The refrigerator temperature should follow the guidelines of the manufacturer and the Food Code guidelines established by the Food and Drug Administration (FDA) and the U.S. Department of Health and Human Services. The sanitation and disinfecting rules for the kitchen should be posted visibly in the kitchen area. This helps staff members to easily see and follow them.

The dining room should be an attractive, inviting space. The tables and chairs should be arranged to accommodate wheelchairs, scooters, and other personal modes of transportation. Centers should provide utensils that older adults find easy to use. This is especially important for those with physical limitations or other health problems.

Rest Rooms

Rest rooms in an adult day care center should comply with the Americans with Disabilities Act (ADA). Signs with symbols indicating men's and women's rest rooms should be placed on the doors. The rest rooms should have handgrips on or near the toilets. Having handgrips allows older adults to be independent when using the rest room. Some rest rooms contain a seating area. Chairs should be placed in the seating area of these rest rooms so older adults can sit and take personal time, if needed.

Clinical Area

Adult day care centers that operate using the social-medical model also provide a clinical area. Older adults use the clinical area when they are sick and need a place to rest. The clinical area contains a bed or recliner, a first aid kit, a blood pressure device, and weight scale. The rest area should meet OSHA standards and the standards of other agencies that provide the center's support, license, or provide accreditation. The supplies and equipment in the clinical area should be cleaned and sanitized regularly. Sanitizing solution for hard, nonporous surfaces can be made from one tablespoon of liquid ultra bleach to one gallon of water. The manufacturer of the equipment should provide cleaning and maintenance guidelines. See Fig. 13-7.

Storage Area

Adult day centers have many storage areas. The kitchen should have a storage area to store dry cooking products. A closet or cabinet should provide storage for janitorial and cleaning supplies. This storage area should only contain cleaning products. The center should also provide a storage area for older adults' personal belongings. Another storage area should contain the supplies needed for program activities. All storage areas should follow OSHA standards.

Intergenerational *Interactions*

Equipment for Children & Older Adults

Some very successful intergenerational programs include activities as simple as older adults reading to young children. Those types of programs definitely bring generations together, but programs that include more activities are generally more successful. In order to plan more activities, programs often use equipment that all generations can enjoy.

- **Computers.** A great way to join together older adults and young people is the use of computers. They can use e-mail to communicate with each other, search the Internet to find out more about subjects that interest them, and play games to pass the time.

- **Audio-Visual Equipment.** Televisions and VCRs enable children and older adults to enjoy films for all ages. Programs may also use stereo equipment to play musical chairs, host a square dance, or teach dance lessons.

- **Art and Craft Materials.** These materials give children and older adults a chance to work with their hands and make something special. Some materials that a program may use include paper and paint, pottery clay and turntables, or yarn and crochet needles.

- **Fitness Equipment.** Items like bicycles and exercise mats help ensure physical fitness for people of all ages. Larger programs may even have the space and funding to offer walking tracks and swimming pools.

- **Games.** Everyone enjoys games. Some intergenerational games may include cards, board games, table tennis, badminton, shuffleboard, pinball, chess, checkers, and more.

- **Furniture.** Certain types of furniture can also help bring generations closer together. Couches, love seats, and double rockers invite children and older adults to sit together and listen to music, read, play with puppets, or just talk.

- **Outdoor Equipment.** Children and older adults can use a variety of outdoor equipment to interact while enjoying fresh air and sunshine. Programs may supply porch swings for quiet relaxing, tools for flower or vegetable gardening, birdfeeders for bird watching and sleds for winter fun.

Follow-Up

The equipment mentioned above is just a small sampling of supplies that intergenerational programs can use to bring generations together. Using this list as a starting point, name 10 additional items that children, teens, and older adults may enjoy. Explain the reasons for your selections.

Outdoor Equipment & Supplies

Adult day centers also provide outdoor areas for older adults. These areas can include places for older adults to engage in activities or to simply sit and enjoy nature. Some suggestions for outdoor areas include the following:

Relaxation Area. When older adults would like to reflect in peace, they can use the outdoor relaxation area. This area should be equipped with a bench, outdoor chairs, or swings. A fountain with running water is also a pleasant item in this area.

Reading Area. Outdoor areas can also include a reading area. This area allows older adults to read in a quiet, nature setting. When planning a reading area, be sure to find one that is not too shady. It should be in a well-lighted area so that older adults will not have difficulty reading. Staff members can keep books or other reading materials available in the reading area. Some examples include daily newspapers, novels, biographical books, or books about fishing or cooking.

Nature Area. In the nature area, trails provide a place for older adults to walk, enjoy garden plants and flowers, feed the birds, and

relax. Benches and chairs should be supplied along walking paths so that older adults can sit and rest when they want. A supply of birdseed should be kept for those who want to fill the birdfeeders. Walking and observing nature can be very therapeutic for older adults. Nature trails need daily care. They should be kept free of weeds, branches, and any other objects that will get in the way of older adults with walkers and wheelchairs. See Fig. 13-8.

Outdoor Fitness Areas

The outdoor fitness area at an adult day care center should have many purposes. Ideally, it is an intergenerational outdoor fitness area that encourages interaction. The equipment for this area should be nonthreatening to older adults. It should also attract younger people. The area could include a **lap pool**, a pool designed for people to swim in a small area. Water aerobics also can be taught in the lap pool.

The outdoor fitness area could also include a playing field for contact sports. The field should have adequate lighting to encourage evening events. The playing field could host intergenerational activities.

Adult day care centers can partner with other groups to provide a successful outdoor program. The center staff could solicit a partnership with a local school to assist in developing, implementing, and evaluating activities at the adult day care center. See Fig. 13-9.

Maintaining Outdoor Equipment

In most cases, outdoor equipment requires more maintenance than indoor equipment. Equipment that is left outdoors should be weatherized regularly to keep it in good working order. If possible, it should be kept in an enclosed storage area. Staff members should check the equipment for damage after each use.

FIG. 13-8. Nature trails for walking and relaxing help older adults maintain their fitness.

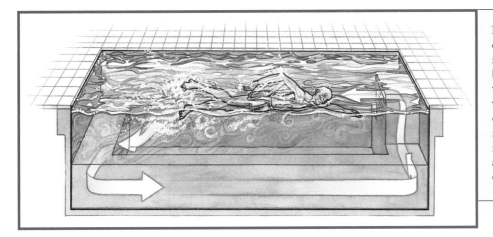

FIG. 13-9. **Lap pools are designed for swimming in small areas. Lap pools have a stream of water that keeps the body forced back while the older adults swim as if swimming laps in a full-size pool.** Why are water activities healthful for older adults?

Cleaning Equipment & Supplies

Equipment at adult day care centers should be cleaned daily. At times the equipment might have to be cleaned throughout the day. When cleaning the equipment, staff members need to be sure to pay special attention to the equipment manufacturer's instructions.

Daily Cleaning Procedures

Care providers clean equipment and supplies throughout the day while older adults are at the center. The director should create cleaning procedures for the staff to follow. By following the procedures, care providers ensure that the facility and equipment are free of clutter, soils, and spills. A written procedure should be posted for staff members. It should outline the times of a day to clean the equipment and replenish the supplies.

At the end of each workday, staff members should conduct a thorough cleaning. This includes washing and sanitizing all seating areas and work surfaces with an approved sanitizing solution. Center staff can use a solution made of bleach and water. See Chapter 6 for more information on sanitizing solutions.

Staff members should also follow a procedure for cleaning outdoor areas and equipment, such as gardening tools. Outdoor areas should be cleaned at least twice a week. In some seasons, more cleaning might be necessary.

Section **13-2**   Knowledge Check

1. What equipment is used in an educational area of an adult day center?
2. Describe a daily cleaning procedure in an adult day center.
3. What sanitizing solution is used on nonporous surfaces in the clinical area?

Mini-Lab

In teams, develop plans for a volunteer program to help conduct indoor or outdoor activities at an adult day care center.

Chapter 13 Review & Activities

Section Summaries

13-1 Basic principles guide the planning for how space is used in a child care facility.

13-1 Program goals and children's basic needs should be considered when purchasing equipment and supplies.

13-1 Equipment and supplies should be selected according to children's ages, stages of development, and varying abilities.

13-1 Well-supplied learning centers increase children's learning and creativity.

13-1 Toys and materials must be carefully chosen.

13-2 Developmentally appropriate equipment is selected according to the skill levels and needs of participants of the adult day center.

13-2 Daily routine cleaning procedures should involve keeping the facility and equipment tidy and free of clutter, soils, and spills.

13-2 There should be a written procedure that outlines suggested times of a day to do routine spot check on equipment and to replenish supplies.

13-2 A thorough cleaning should include washing down all seating areas and work surfaces with an approved formula.

Check Your Knowledge

1. How can equipment or supplies support program goals?
2. What criteria should equipment and supplies meet?
3. List five typical learning centers and describe how to supply them.
4. List five guidelines for choosing toys and materials.
5. What equipment and supplies should be in an outdoor play yard?
6. What equipment and supplies might be found in a social-medical model adult day program?
7. List three examples of equipment that might be found in the support areas of an adult day facility.
8. What is a lap pool? How is it helpful for older adults?
9. Contrast indoor cleaning procedures with outdoor cleaning procedures.

Thinking Critically

1. Analyze how the equipment for meeting young children's basic needs changes from infancy to school age.
2. How might the developmental changes in older adults influence equipment selection for an adult day care center?

Practical Applications

1. **Special Needs Equipment.** Study a catalog of equipment for children with special needs. For five typical learning centers, list adaptive equipment available to meet children's special needs.

2. **Playground Research.** Research outdoor playground equipment for young children. Use print and Internet resources for your research. Develop safety guidelines for equipping a safe play yard for young children.

3. **Checklist Evaluation.** Obtain a copy of your state's guidelines for equipping an adult day care center. Develop a checklist for evaluating an adult day care center.

Building Your PORTFOLIO

Choosing Equipment & Supplies

Choosing appropriate equipment and supplies is likely to be part of your job responsibilities. Equipment should support program goals, provide for basic needs, and provide for a variety of indoor and outdoor activities.

Step 1: Obtain a list of program goals for a child care or adult care facility. Study equipment catalogs and identify five pieces of equipment that would support each goal. Include the list of goals and the equipment you chose in your portfolio.

Step 2: Identify the basic needs of the children or older adults in a specific care facility. Visit the facility and list equipment and supplies provided to meet each basic need. Suggest one additional item that might be added to help meet each basic need. Include your suggestions in your portfolio.

Step 3: Research the first aid and emergency supplies recommended for a child or adult care facility. Using a supply catalog, select a first aid kit and emergency supplies for a specific situation. Describe the situation, include pictures of your selections, and figure the costs for your portfolio.

Step 4: Research the procedures for cleaning or maintaining a specific area or piece of equipment in a child or adult care facility. Develop an illustrated chart that might be used to train staff for your portfolio.

Chapter 14
Quality Early Childhood Programs

Section 14-1
Program Types

Section 14-2
Managing Program Services

Section 14-1

Program Types

KEY TERMS

philosophy
program goals
for-profit
nonprofit
program sponsors
nanny
au pair
license exempt
registration

Early childhood program is the broad term that describes any situation in which children have supervision, care, education, or special lessons by qualified people outside of their home. The demand for such programs has grown over the last few decades. This section will introduce you to a wide variety of early childhood programs.

Program Philosophy & Goals

The defining feature of any early childhood program is its program philosophy. A program's **philosophy** describes general beliefs, concepts, and attitudes the program has about how children learn. In addition, it describes how the program should serve and educate children and involve parents. See Fig. 14-1.

Program goals identify basic skills, concepts, and attitudes to develop and encourage in children. They also address the range of services to be provided. For example, program goals might expect children to:

- Gain high self-esteem and a positive attitude.
- Learn self-help skills and responsibility.
- Develop positive social skills, such as cooperation and sharing.

- Develop large and small motor skills.
- Improve communication skills, such as listening, speaking, reading, and writing.
- Develop curiosity, creative thinking, and problem-solving ability.
- Learn to respect, accept, and understand the rights and feelings of others.

Program goals for families of the children might include:

- Opportunities for classroom participation.
- Use of a child development lending resource library.
- Access to a toy-lending library.
- Options for parenting education workshops.
- Involvement in special family events.

Child Care Center

Mission Statement: Purpose & Services

The Child Care Center provides high-quality, developmental child care services for children ages 2-8 years. The Center, which is NAEYC accredited, serves as a model program for the community and the early childhood profession.

Service Philosophy

The Child Care Center staff believe children and parents are to be respected and treated with courtesy, dignity, patience, and compassion. While in our care each child is nurtured physically, socially, emotionally, and intellectually. Our well-trained teachers and care providers regard early childhood experiences with the respect and commitment they deserve. The staff work to share this attitude with the parents.

We believe children who feel loved can love others. We believe children who are guided with patience and gentleness learn to trust.

FIG. 14-1. **All early childhood programs must have a written program philosophy. Why is having a philosophy important?**

Sample Program Philosophy

The following beliefs guide program development in one specific child care center:

- Children need many sensory, concrete, and hands-on learning experiences.
- Children have different learning styles, rates of learning, and developmental levels.
- The classroom design should encourage curiosity, exploration, and investigation.
- Children need independent activities and group activities.
- The interests and needs of children should guide the changes in learning activities.
- Activities should encourage physical, intellectual, social, and emotional development.
- Activities should encourage problem solving and creativity.
- Parent involvement enhances children's overall development.

Profit and Nonprofit Programs. Programs that are designed to bring in more income than they spend on their services are called **for-profit**. This extra money goes to the owners or investors, sometimes known as stockholders. Some for-profit programs are owned by individuals. Others are national child care chains, such as KinderCare®. Some programs operate on a **nonprofit** basis. This means there are no stockholders who receive money from the program's income. Money earned by a nonprofit program goes back into the budget or into savings for future use. Staff members in nonprofit programs receive salaries just as those in for-profit ones do. See Fig. 14-2.

Program Quality

Whatever type of care a family uses, they want it to be high quality. When working in human services, you will be responsible for quality programming in all of these areas.

- Program philosophy and goals.
- Knowledge of child development; appropriate guidance.
- Basic health, safety, and nutrition; appropriate environment.
- Developmentally appropriate curriculum and practices.
- Activities, records, reports, and evaluations.
- Organized daily schedule.
- Family involvement.
- Ongoing staff training.

FIG. 14-2. A variety of for-profit and nonprofit centers exist throughout the country. What are the pros and cons of each type of center?

Program Options

Early childhood programs have both similarities and differences. All programs aim to provide a safe and healthy learning environment for children. However, **program sponsors**, the specific groups that fund or manage an early childhood program, vary in their operating purposes. Sponsors range from faith-based groups to social service agencies and colleges. Sponsors' program philosophies and goals vary according to their individual purposes.

Child Care Centers. Child care centers enroll children whose parents must work or attend school. Child care centers are typically open from 6:00 a.m. to 6:00 p.m. To accommodate parents' or care givers' schedules, some even operate evenings or 24 hours a day. Good child care centers provide learning activities, meals, snacks, and naptime. Centers may serve children from six weeks to twelve years of age. Centers vary in size, with enrollments ranging up to 400 children.

Family Child Care Homes. These programs are private child care services offered by individuals in their own homes. Such homes usually enroll three to eight children of varying ages. When care providers in family child care homes take in infants, fewer children can be cared for in these homes. Homes that serve more than eight children are called family child care group homes. Check the licensing laws in your state for specific licensing guidelines for family child care homes. See Fig. 14-3.

Before and After School Child Care. These programs provide care for school-age children before and after school. Some programs operate in schools. Other programs transport children to and from school to care for them at another site. Schools sometimes manage the programs, but often contract with other agencies, such as the YWCA, to operate them.

Preschools and Nursery Schools. These programs provide educational services to children from three to five years of age. These schools usually operate two and one-half hours per day, in the morning or afternoon. Preschools and nursery schools emphasize learning skills and social development.

FIG. 14-3. Family child care homes provide one option for parents in their need for child care. What are the benefits of family child care homes?

FIG. 14-4. **Both children and older adults benefit from intergenerational care.** Name several benefits of intergenerational care.

Public School Pre-Kindergartens. Early on, some children show characteristics that might cause them problems at school. Influencing factors include poverty, delayed development, poor language skills, premature birth, or prenatal drug exposure. Pre-kindergarten programs help prevent school failure. They usually serve three- to five-year-olds. They provide activities that prepare children for success in elementary school and beyond. Public pre-kindergartens usually run half-days and are free of charge. Most operate only during the school year. Parent involvement, including teacher home visits, is heavily stressed.

Employer-Sponsored Centers. Child care programs offered by businesses to employees are called employer-sponsored programs. The center may be on or very near the work site. The employer may operate the center itself or contract with a child care management firm to operate it for them. How can these centers benefit employers?

In-Home Child Care. Some parents or guardians employ someone to provide child care in their own homes. Sometimes a **nanny** lives with the family and receives free rent and food as part of his or her wages. Other times the nanny goes to the child's home each day. Another option for child care is an **au pair** (oh PARE). An au pair is a person who comes from one country to live with a family in another country. Au pairs exchange housework and child care for room and board.

Intergenerational Care Centers. These programs offer daytime care for young children and older adults. Young and old participate regularly in activities. The children benefit from the older adults' care and wisdom, and the older adults benefit from the children's energy and enthusiasm. This interaction helps children develop and older adults maintain zest for life-long wellness and learning. See Fig. 14-4.

Child Care for Mildly Ill Children. Staffed with early childhood professionals and nurses, these programs care for mildly ill children while they get better. Only children whose illnesses are not or are no longer contagious can attend. Program activities are slower paced and provide more rest time than a regular child care center.

Back-Up Child Care Centers. Sometimes an employer has a worker whose regular child care option is interrupted. For instance, a working parent may have a nanny or a family child care home provider who becomes too ill to provide child care for a few days. To help employees avoid missing work on those days, employers use the services of a back-up child care center. These programs specialize in providing short-term child care until a working parent can go back to the regular care provider. Unlike in most programs, the children who attend a back-up child care center vary greatly from day to day.

Head Start Preschools and Child Care. Head Start was created in 1964 as part of President Johnson's War on Poverty. Its purpose is to prepare economically disadvantaged preschoolers for school success. It offers education, health, dental, and nutrition services. Head Start requires active parent participation. For children under age four, Head Start employs home visitors to teach parents how to educate and care for children. Some Head Start programs operate for half days. Others operate full days to accommodate the child care needs of working parents. See Fig. 14-5.

Montessori Preschools. These programs are based on the teachings of Maria Montessori. Montessori schools use educational materials designed to help children master specific tasks in a step-by-step sequence. They encourage independent learning, learning-by-doing, and learning through the senses. For example, during a cooking activity, children may learn all about the ingredients in bread. Then the children would mix and bake the bread and use their senses to smell the bread and taste it. Teachers must receive formal instruction in the Montessori method before they can teach in Montessori schools. Some of these programs operate half-days; others operate full days.

Some Montessori programs serve infants through third graders. However, most serve three- to five-year-olds.

Preschool for Children with Special Needs. Usually sponsored through public schools, these programs serve children with special needs from birth to five years of age. Full- or part-day classes may include children who have birth defects or disabilities, such as cerebral palsy, autism, behavioral disorders, Down syndrome, or vision or hearing impairments. Teachers need special certification or courses in order to work in these programs.

Child Care for Children with Special Needs. Most child care centers try to include children with special needs in their regular programs. However, some children have disabilities that are very complicated. They, too, need safe and developmentally appropriate child care. To provide such care, some social service agencies, such as Easter Seals, operate child care programs designed to meet the specific needs of children with disabilities.

Crisis Nurseries. Crisis nurseries help to prevent child abuse. Overstressed parents who feel at risk of abusing their children may use a crisis nursery. These programs operate on a 24-hour basis. Children stay at the crisis nursery until the parents feel once again capable of caring for them in a safe manner. Some nurseries care for children for up to three days while parents seek counseling. The United Way or other social service agencies often fund crisis nurseries.

Parent Cooperatives. When parents jointly create a preschool or child care center, it is called a parent cooperative. In a cooperative, the parents hire a teacher,

FIG. 14-5. **Head Start programs help prepare economically disadvantaged children for school success.**

Locate Early Childhood Programs

You may not realize it, but there are probably a wide variety of early childhood programs in your own community. Locating all these programs can be difficult. Following are some ways to discover what programs are offered in your own community.

1. Refer to your telephone book's yellow pages. Early childhood programs may be listed under a variety of headings, so don't give up if you don't find the right one immediately. Some yellow pages list programs under the heading day care, child care, preschool, or day nurseries.

2. Locate your local child care program licensing office. Some states call it the Department of Human Services; others call it the Department of Children and Family Services. Once you locate the licensing office, call to ask if it provides a listing of local programs.

3. Contact your local United Way office or Cooperative Extension office. Both agencies work to support and improve community programs. Ask for a listing of programs near you.

4. Call a local child care resource and referral agency. An agency such as this, generally keeps a current listing of all early childhood programs in the community.

5. Contact your local public school district office. Ask for a listing of their pre-kindergarten classrooms or early childhood programs for children with special needs.

APPLY IT!

Create a resource pamphlet that contains information about various early childhood programs in your community.

---

determine the goals, and set the rules and procedures to be followed. Child care professionals, teachers, and parents work together to influence philosophy and goals. Cooperatives require parents to work in the program a few hours every month. They may assist teachers and do administrative work.

Laboratory Schools. Some universities, colleges, and high schools provide child care or a preschool for students, employees, or community members. These programs often serve as training sites for child development students and those preparing for careers with children. See Fig. 14-6.

Licensing & Registration Laws

Whether serving children, older adults, or both, each state has its own set of licensing laws for program operation. State licensing laws identify programs that must meet minimum requirements for legal operation. Licensing laws vary from state to state and are usually approved by a state's legislature. The legislature assigns a specific state agency to enforce licensing laws. The name of the agency office varies from state to state. However, it is often called the Department of Human Service or the Department of Children and Family Services.

FIG. 14-6. **Laboratory schools not only provide care for children of college students and faculty, but also serve as training sites for students training in careers with children.**

In some states, certain types of programs are **license exempt**. That means they are not required to obtain a license to operate legally. For example, in some states early childhood programs that are associated with a parochial school that is part of a place of worship can be license exempt. In addition, family child care homes that care for fewer than three children may also be license exempt in some states. Offices that license programs can tell you which programs are license exempt in your state.

Meeting a state's licensing laws for operation is a mandatory requirement, not a program choice. Once a license to operate has been granted, a program must renew its license regularly to prove ongoing compliance with laws. Some states require license renewal yearly; others every three years. See Fig. 14-7.

Some states require **registration**, rather than a formal program license. Registration requires a care provider to notify city or state officials in writing of the program's name, address, telephone number, and intention to provide services. States vary in these requirements and procedures.

Early Childhood Program Licenses

Some early childhood programs may be license exempt, such as a pre-kindergarten operated by a public school. However, most other early childhood programs, such as child care centers or nursery schools, require licensing. There are usually separate licensing laws that apply to center-based programs and family child care homes. There may also be separate laws for daytime and nighttime care. Some states require family child care homes to be registered, not licensed.

State licensing standards vary widely. However, they usually address minimum requirements for the following areas of program operation.

- Health, safety, and nutrition requirements.
- Maximum group size of children by age.
- Staff-to-client ratio, meaning number of staff to number of children.
- Square footage of space per child for indoor and outdoor areas.
- Minimum staff qualifications and in-service training requirements.
- Minimum amount of equipment and supplies for each classroom.

FIG. 14-7. **The director's responsibilities include making sure the program meets state licensing standards.**

FIG. 14-8.

SAMPLES OF NAEYC ACCREDITATION CRITERIA

Teacher/Child Interactions	• Have frequent interactions; respond effectively to children; nurture self-esteem. • Convey respect and affection verbally and physically. • Have nonbiased interactions; encourage positive social behaviors.
Curriculum	• Provide written statement of philosophy and goals. • Offer nonbiased and inclusive activities. • Provide developmentally appropriate activities. • Plan daily routines and a balance of activities; provide smooth transitions between activities.
Teacher/Family Relationships	• Provide families with written information about the program's philosophy, goals, and overall services; offer frequent communication. • Use cooperative planning based on children's developmental needs. • Invite parents to visit at any time.
Staff Qualifications and Professional Development	• Specify age requirements for entry-level positions. • Identify educational qualifications for job position and age-group assignment. • List prior experience requirements. • Offer ongoing staff training on work-related topics.
Administration	• Makes sure operating policies exist; informs staff of all policies and procedures. • Provides job descriptions and salary scales that are based on professional qualifications, ensures personnel policies are fair and nonbiased. • Maintains required licensing records and employee, governance, financial, and insurance records.
Staffing	• Employs sufficient staff for each age group of children in compliance with criteria requirements. • Makes sure each staff member has a clear, primary responsibility to a specific group of children. • Ensures substitutes maintain staff-to-child ratios in event of staff absence.

Accreditation Criteria

Accreditation criteria refer to a set of standards that represent high quality, developmentally appropriate programs. Accreditation is awarded from a professional organization that assures others that the program operates according to recognized professional practices.

The best-known accreditation program for early childhood settings is the National Academy of Early Childhood Programs, sponsored by the National Association for the Education of Young Children (NAEYC). Family child care homes seek accreditation through the National Association for Family Child Care.

Early Childhood Program Accreditation

Complying with accreditation criteria is voluntary. Programs that are committed to high-quality services work hard to meet as many accreditation criteria as possible. To ensure that programs maintain high quality, they must be reaccredited, usually every three years. Fig. 14-8 provides the basic areas of NAEYC accreditation. You can find out more information about NAEYC accreditation on the Internet.

SAMPLES OF NAEYC ACCREDITATION CRITERIA (Cont'd)

Physical Environment	• Ensures indoor and outdoor environment is safe, clean, attractive, and avoids overcrowding. • Clearly defines activity areas to allow for individual, small-group, and large-group play; maintains minimum indoor space of 35 square feet per child of usable play space and a minimum of 75 square feet per child for outdoor play. • Ensures outdoor spaces have a variety of surfaces and equipment for play variety. • Offers sufficient quantity of age-appropriate equipment and supplies that are available and stored for easy access by children; provides space for storing children's personal belongings, staff breaks and staff storage, adult rest rooms.
Health and Safety	• Ensures children and staff are free of contagious illness; maintains health records for children and staff. • Specifies in written policies when ill children must be excluded. • Supervises children at all times; practices prevention precautions consistently. • Reports suspected incidents of child abuse or neglect. • Plans exist for responding to emergencies; ensures at least one person skilled in pediatric first aid and CPR is present at all times. • Maintains facility, equipment, and supplies in good repair and cleans and/or sanitizes as required.
Nutrition and Food Service	• Meets nutrition requirements for children's meals and snacks; promotes healthful eating habits. • Stores, prepares, and serves food in compliance with health and sanitation requirements.
Evaluation	• Evaluates staff performance yearly. • Conducts program evaluation yearly, including feedback from staff and parents. • Records individual child development and learning to use as a basis for curriculum and activity planning.

Section 14-1 Knowledge Check

1. Give two samples of program philosophy statements.
2. List four appropriate goals for an early childhood program.
3. Contrast licensing and accreditation.

Mini-Lab

Begin a resource file of brochures, parent handbooks, and child enrollment applications from different early childhood programs. Research program Web sites listed in the brochures.

Section **14-2**

Managing Program Services

OBJECTIVES

- Describe the role of the director in managing program services.
- Identify director management and supervision duties.
- Identify the qualifications of early childhood staff members.
- Summarize the key factors of program governance.
- Explain financial management for early childhood care programs.
- Explain the ways directors conduct public relations.

KEY TERMS

job descriptions
organizational chart
reference checks
inventory record
board
program governance
advisory board
governing board
financial
    management
public relations

As you have learned, there are a wide variety of early childhood programs. Regardless of sponsorship, in order to provide quality services, programs must be well staffed and well managed. As you might imagine, the following program features require persistent attention to detail.

Program Leadership

A successful program relies on good leadership. Early childhood programs employ directors as administrators and managers. They are usually responsible to a board of directors or an owner; however, some directors own their own programs.

Director as Role Model. The director sets the tone for the entire staff's professional performance. The director demonstrates commitment to the program's philosophy and goals to the staff. Staff members then see the director put respect, cooperation, and teamwork into action.

Directors also lead staff by regular communication, often through weekly staff meetings.

Implementing Philosophy and Goals. Directors work with teachers to plan, apply, and evaluate learning programs and activities based on the program's goals and philosophy. They also work with other staff, such as food service staff, to meet other program goals like good nutrition. Every year, directors should re-evaluate program philosophy and goals. They also look at future needs and trends in early childhood programs. Based on these needs and trends, directors motivate staff to adjust or improve the program's services.

Recruiting & Supervising Staff

Staff performance influences program quality, so it makes sense for directors to maintain the best staff possible. They recruit, interview, and hire the best qualified employees. Age, education, and work-experience requirements for employees vary according to positions. See Fig. 14-9. Most directors hire the following staff members:

- **Assistant director:** Assists the director in administrative duties.
- **Teaching staff and substitutes:** Care for and teach children in classrooms.
- **Foodservice staff:** Purchase and prepare food for meals and snacks.
- **Transportation staff:** Drive school-age children to and from school.
- **Custodial and grounds crew:** Maintain the facility, outdoor drive, and play yards.
- **Health care staff:** Perform health checks, especially in infant rooms.
- **Family involvement coordinator:** Plans and conducts family activities.
- **Curriculum coordinator:** Makes plans for, and purchases, educational materials.

FIG. 14-9. Early childhood program directors are responsible for recruiting and supervising all of the program staff. What key requirements are necessary for each staff position?

Staff Qualifications

Quality programs have a specific plan for staffing. They describe responsibilities for each staff member to offer program services in an effective manner. The number of staff, and their qualifications, is determined by a program's purpose, services, and size. Licensing and accreditation criteria also influence program staffing.

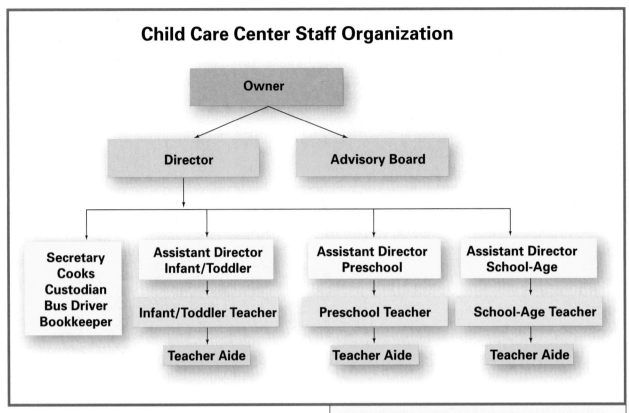

Child Care Center Staff Organization

- Owner
  - Director
    - Secretary
      Cooks
      Custodian
      Bus Driver
      Bookkeeper
    - Assistant Director Infant/Toddler
      - Infant/Toddler Teacher
        - Teacher Aide
    - Assistant Director Preschool
      - Preschool Teacher
        - Teacher Aide
    - Assistant Director School-Age
      - School-Age Teacher
        - Teacher Aide
  - Advisory Board

FIG. 14-10. **A staff organizational chart assists center employees in knowing to whom they report in regard to work issues.**

All staff positions have a **job description**. This is a written list of duties and responsibilities for each staff member. Job descriptions describe how much decision-making authority a position holds. For instance, a director's job description would allow him or her to hire or terminate employees. A teacher's job description would not include that responsibility.

An organized staffing plan identifies supervisors for specific positions. Such a plan is called an **organizational chart**. An organizational chart helps staff know to whom they report. For instance, it helps staff know whom they should inform about problems, solutions, or suggestions for program activities. It also reveals who will evaluate their work performance. See Fig. 14-10.

So program services can be well managed, directors create work schedules and inform each staff member of his or her specific work hours. Work hours for positions vary. For instance, a cook or van driver would work different hours than a custodian or classroom teacher.

Screening Staff

Directors are responsible for employing program staff. Before hiring, directors screen potential staff to make sure they hire only the best qualified employees. Directors review employment applications to make sure candidates meet minimum requirements for state licensing laws and, if applicable, accreditation criteria. They review each applicant's work history, educational background, and résumé. **Reference checks** are made by contacting people that know the applicant's character, job performance, and employment skills. Many states also require directors to conduct criminal background checks on potential employees. Such checks would identify persons who had been convicted of a crime, specifically one involving abuse or neglect.

FIG. 14-11. **Part of the director's job responsibility is to evaluate employees on a yearly basis.** How can a performance evaluation benefit the employee and the director?

Staff Development

Directors provide the following useful tools to help staff members perform their jobs to the best of their abilities:

Personnel Policies and Handbooks. Handbooks provide basic program information to introduce new staff to the policies and procedures they will be expected to follow. These materials provide employee job descriptions as well as conditions for employment. They outline requirements for continued employment as well as causes for dismissal.

In-Service Training. Directors must ensure that staff members receive yearly job training. Required training topics include identifying and reporting suspected child abuse and neglect, providing positive child guidance, and limiting the spread of illnesses.

Continuing Education. Motivated staff members will often seek ways to further their job-related education. Directors encourage continuing education by paying part of an employee's conference attendance expenses or the cost of a seminar or college course.

Performance Evaluation. Directors should evaluate every staff member's performance yearly. This evaluation gives valuable feedback on strengths and on skills that need improvement. Evaluations should be objective and based on direct observation of an employee's performance. Directors should make sure that all evaluations remain confidential in employees' personnel files. See Fig. 14-11.

Quality Facilities

A quality facility creates a nurturing environment for all. Its design should support the program philosophy and goals. For instance, if a program's philosophy states children should learn in small groups, the facility should meet this need. One way would be to provide learning areas created for four to six children to use at a time.

Good facilities are comfortable and useful for staff, clients, and clients' family members. Good storage allows staff to have supplies within easy reach, whether they are changing a child's diaper or conducting an art activity. Children need areas to learn, relax, and feel at home. Parents feel welcome in spaces that encourage them to sit and linger.

Licensing laws set minimum standards that facilities must meet. For instance, good facilities are clean and safe, and offer several ways to escape from fire or severe weather. Accreditation criteria require that physical environments be well designed and equipped for those who use them.

Impact of Gossip. Staff gossip can take many forms. It may be two or more staff members speaking negatively to one another about a particular coworker. It can involve spreading rumors about someone or sharing information that will reflect poorly on someone's performance or character. When staff members are allowed to gossip about each other or about clients, it becomes difficult for everyone in the program to maintain a positive attitude. Trust and teamwork are undermined. *How would you handle the situation if you overheard two coworkers gossiping about one of the families in your early childhood program?*

Maintenance & Upkeep

Human service facilities house a large number of people for long hours each day. All that traffic poses a constant challenge. Facilities must remain in good shape so that quality services can be provided. Daily maintenance and upkeep applies to the whole environment, including facility, equipment, and supplies. Everything, from toys to floors, requires regular cleaning, sanitizing, and repairing, if necessary.

Year-round facilities need routine care and upkeep indoors and out. For instance, buildings may need painting every five years. During the summer, playgrounds must be mowed and air conditioners repaired. During the winter, snow must be removed and furnaces maintained.

Quality Equipment & Supplies

Programs are required to have adequate equipment and supplies available. Those requirements are listed in licensing laws and accreditation criteria. Of course, potentially hazardous equipment and supplies should be stored away from children in a locked storage area.

When purchased, equipment and supplies should be listed on a sheet, called an **inventory record**. An organized inventory should include the following: item, date of purchase, place of purchase, cost, and warranty date, if any.

Inventory records have several uses. Staff can easily see what resources they have available. It allows a program director to see what materials are on hand, as well as what new materials need to be purchased. An inventory also allows staff to determine if broken appliances are still under warranty. If program theft occurs, an inventory helps police and insurance agents determine the extent of loss.

Regular safety checks of equipment and supplies must be conducted. Damaged or broken items should be repaired or discarded. Such actions should be noted on the inventory record.

Following are questions a program director asks to determine if a piece of equipment or a supply would promote quality:

- Is it easily maintained in terms of health and safety?
- Can it be used by a variety of ages or classrooms?
- Would it help staff meet program goals?
- Is it adaptable to children with special needs?
- Is it nonbiased and culturally sensitive?
- Will the cost, including shipping and installation, fit into the program budget?
- Does it require special storage?
- Does it come fully assembled?
- Will the piece fit in the space set aside for it?

FIG. 14-12. Governing boards work with program directors and staff to make decisions on items, such as program policies and procedures, finances, and enrollment.

Program Governance

In many programs, directors do not manage programs on their own. It is a cooperative effort between the program sponsor and a director. Another group of individuals, who support the program's purpose, but are not employed by the program, also influence program operation. That group of people is called a **board**. When a director and a board make decisions about a program's policies and procedures, the process is called **program governance**. The board helps make a variety of decisions, including budget, finances, and fundraising; enrollment policies; employing staff; and setting fees for services. See Fig. 14-12.

Organizational Structure

Not all programs require boards. It depends on the wishes of the program's sponsors. Programs that operate on a nonprofit basis usually have boards. Program sponsors, such as social service agencies, are more likely to have a board, too.

Some boards have members who are elected, either by program clients or board members themselves. Other boards merely ask for volunteers. People who serve on boards are not paid. They usually serve on the board because they want to make sure the program succeeds.

Advisory Boards and Governing Boards. Some boards only give directors recommendations on decisions to be made. This is called an **advisory board**. Other boards have full decision-making power, meaning they tell directors what actions to take. This is a **governing board**, because they have final authority for decisions. Whether it is an advisory or governing board, all boards assign leadership positions to lead work. Typical positions are president, vice president, treasurer, and secretary.

Board Responsibilities. Boards meet regularly to discuss program developments. They help plan activities that promote a positive image of the program to the community. Boards help ensure that many different people have input into a program's operation. They make sure policies and procedures are fair to staff and clients. They also help ensure that those policies and procedures apply fairly to everyone.

Board Committees. To conduct their work well and in a timely manner, boards divide into separate work groups called committees. Assignment to a committee gives a board member a clear idea of how he or she can serve the program. So they can perform well, committee members should be given a written job description. Typical committees include finance, fundraising, personnel, and public relations.

Governance Handbooks

Governance materials are written statements that help guide program operation. Handbooks help guide decision making for directors and

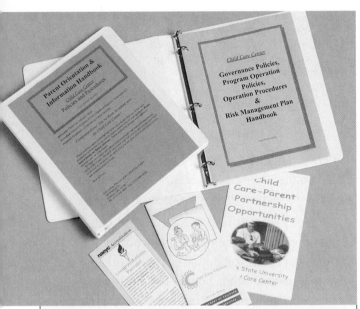

FIG. 14-13. Written policies that help guide program operation are the responsibility of the program director and the boards. Why are these handbooks valuable for staff and participants?

boards. They also help staff and clients understand program procedures so they can be followed more easily. See Fig. 14-13.

- **Constitution and by-laws.** This document states the program's purpose and establishes conduct rules for the board. For instance, it states how often board meetings should be held. It spells out term limits for board members. Committees are also established.

- **Governance handbook.** All of a program's policies and procedures are listed in this in-depth handbook, from enrollment to staffing. It details emergency routines staff must follow, such as medical emergencies or evacuation in case of fire or severe weather.

- **Parent or family handbooks.** These handbooks describe routine polices, such as eligibility criteria for program services and hours of operation. Parent handbooks also address a wide variety of topics, such as discipline styles, curriculum development, illness policies, and health and immunization policies.

- **Personnel handbook.** This states personnel policies, such as employment qualifications,

job descriptions, evaluation procedures, dress code, salary range and fringe benefits, and causes for suspension or termination of employment.

Administration

As you have learned, many people influence how a program runs. Those people who have a say in program operations make up a program's administration. Sponsors, or those who provide funding for a program, usually have the final say in administration decisions. However, wise sponsors utilize a team of people to guide good program operation.

For instance, board members can contribute legal, accounting, or public relations advice to sponsors and directors depending upon their special skills. Directors may ask board members to help recruit and interview job applicants. Directors can help sponsors determine if program goals are being met. Sponsors and board members can plan events to recognize the hard work of program staff. The list of cooperative efforts is endless. That cooperation allows programs to be creative as well as effective.

Managing Client Services

Early childhood programs frequently interact with the public. To serve children and families well, directors must have skills in managing public and client relations.

Program Enrollment. Directors advertise program services. The director's job is to attract and maintain a steady enrollment according to the program's licensed capacity. Once children are enrolled in a program, it is up to the director to maintain good relationships with the family to meet the child's needs and the family's expectations.

Parent Handbook. Parent handbooks give families an understanding of program policies and procedures. Well-written handbooks are a

How To...

Plan & Conduct Board Meetings

It is usually a board president and director's job to cooperatively plan a board meeting. Use the following guidelines to plan and conduct effective meetings.

- Select a date and time for the meeting and reserve a meeting room.

- Create an agenda of items to be discussed at the meeting.

- At least one week in advance, send board members a meeting notice, including: meeting date, beginning and ending time, location, telephone number or e-mail address for attendance confirmation, agenda, and directions for parking.

- A half hour before the meeting, arrange meeting room's lighting, temperature, seating, and place nametags and an attendance sheet on a table.

- The board president calls the meeting to order and follows parliamentary procedures (an accepted way of conducting all forms of meetings).

- The secretary reads or refers to the minutes (recorded notes) from the last board meet-

ing and accepts corrections or clarifications that may be needed.

- Throughout the meeting, the board secretary records minutes, which include the information shared and decisions made during the meeting.

- The president leads agenda discussion. This often includes committee members making progress reports on committee work.

- If a motion is made (a decision recommended by a board member) and voted on, the secretary records the person who made the motion, another board member who supported it, the discussion of the board members, and the results of the final vote.

- At the end of the meeting, the president accepts a board member's motion to adjourn. The time is noted by the secretary in the minutes.

- Within one week, typed minutes of the meeting should be distributed to each board member and filed in the program office for future reference.

APPLY IT!

Make arrangements to attend a board meeting for an early childhood program in your community. Write a summary of the meeting you attended.

---

handy reference for parents. Handbooks address many topics. However, most often they include information on hours of operation, billing policies, children's health and immunization requirements, daily schedules and routines, courses or classes, guidance policies, illness policies, and ideas for celebrating birthdays at child care. Most states require programs to inform parents of these policies in writing.

Family Involvement. Directors have frequent opportunities to talk with parents as parents drop off and pick up their children. In addition, directors use newsletters, postings on parent bulletin boards, and e-mail to communicate with families. They make sure parent-teacher conferences and family events are conducted. Many directors invite family members to serve on advisory boards so they have input on program operation. All parents should feel welcome to visit the program at any time. See Fig. 14-14.

Community Referrals. Many families have needs that cannot be met by an early childhood program. Good directors are well acquainted with community services, and they can refer families to help. Referrals may be in response to a child's disability, a housing problem, health insurance coverage for a child, or a question about applying for a state's child care subsidy program.

Financial Management

Balancing income and expenses to ensure that a program's doors remain open to children and families is called **financial management**. Good management allows a program to meet the costs of daily operation.

Financial management requires preparation of a yearly budget. A budget is a detailed listing of program expenses for services and an

FIG. 14-15. **Directors need to place information about their centers in places where potential clients will get the information.** If you were looking for information about child care facilities, where might you look?

account of how much money the program expects to receive for services. A budget should be reviewed monthly and requires an organized bookkeeping system. The director is responsible for making sure income meets or exceeds expenses. Otherwise, programs cannot continue to offer services.

Managing Income. A program earns income by charging an hourly or weekly fee for its services. Directors make sure the fees cover the cost of the services they provide. If the fees are too low, directors find other ways to bring in money. The program might host a fundraising event or write an application to receive money from a government grant or a private funding agency.

Managing Expenses. Costs that are a result of program operation are called expenses. Program expenses include building costs; monthly utilities, such as gas, water, electricity, and telephone; indoor and outdoor facility upkeep and repair; staff wages and staff training costs; vehicle purchase and routine care; equipment and supplies for all program services; and printing and postage fees.

FIG. 14-14. **Maintaining involvement with children and their families is an important role for program directors.** What types of events promote family involvement?

Public Relations

Directors recruit a qualified staff, maintain full enrollment, and increase donations by building a good reputation for their programs. They do all they can to present a positive image of the program to the community. These efforts are called **public relations**. See Fig. 14-15.

Community Outreach. Directors should be actively involved in the community. This involvement can be serving on local boards or helping to plan and conduct community events with other agencies. Directors place information about their programs where potential clients might see it. For instance, they place advertising posters at a doctor's office or laundromat. Directors also make sure their programs are listed with a local child care resource and referral agency that helps parents find care to match their needs.

Being a Reliable Source of Information. By keeping current on new child-related laws and research, directors can inform local government, city offices, and media of valuable information.

When a program director and staff are known to share accurate and current information about children and families, community members respect their program.

Professional Organization Membership. Active participation in professional organizations also conveys a positive image to the community. For instance, local chapters of the National Association for the Education of Young Children hold an annual Week of the Young Child. During this week, many different program directors and staff plan activities to raise community awareness of children's needs.

Quality Assurance

Maintaining quality standards is an ongoing process. Programs routinely undergo a variety of inspections and evaluations to confirm that quality is achieved. An outside person or agency often conducts inspections. This assures an objective evaluation of quality. Inspections often check to see if a program meets specific laws for operation. A health department inspects the cleanliness and sanitation of food service. The fire marshal inspects a facility to make sure it is free of fire hazards. A city building inspector makes sure a facility's plumbing, electricity, or other building features meet legal requirements for installation and upkeep. See Fig. 14-16.

An audit—or a review of a program's records, practices, and procedures—also assures quality. Programs whose meal service is partially funded by the federal Child and Adult Care Food Program are audited. The review assures that programs serve appropriate meals and maintain proper financial records, such as grocery store receipts listing food purchases.

Programs hire accountants to audit their financial records, such as budgets, bill payments and receipts of income. Sometimes state or federal agencies audit programs to make sure they are following fair employment practices. For instance, records may be reviewed to

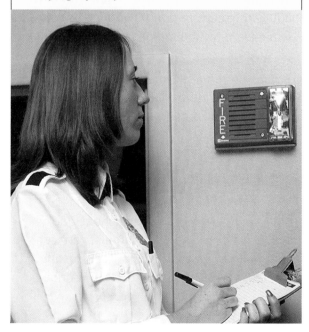

FIG. 14-16. Program inspections, such as fire and health, are crucial to running a quality program. What other criteria might be used to judge quality?

Intergenerational *Interactions*

The Friendship Center

The *Friendship Center* intergenerational child care facility joins older adults from the nearby *Health Village* retirement center with children ages two and one-half to five years. The center, said to be the first of its kind in Northwest New Jersey, opened in 1992. Within a year of opening, the center was running at full capacity and receiving top ratings for the quality of its child care. Today the center continues to operate at full capacity—caring for 42 children at all times. The children and older adult volunteers enjoy many intergenerational activities, including:

- **Pen Pals.** Each *Friendship Center* child keeps in touch with an older adult who resides at the nearby *Health Village* retirement center. The children and older adults enjoy frequent letters and look forward to seeing each other at special events and holiday celebrations.

- **Foreign Language.** Older adult volunteers help *Friendship Center* staff members teach Spanish to 4- and 5-year-olds. This program not only helps children expand communication abilities, but also helps them gain respect and understanding for a different culture.

- **Health Care Visits.** Monthly visits to the nearby *Clarence Sickles Health Care Center and Day Break* adult day care center help children understand and appreciate older adults.

- **Music.** Once each week an older adult plays the piano for group music time. The music program introduces children to a variety of songs and strives to increase children's appreciation for music.

- **Nature Trail.** Older adults take *Friendship Center* children on walks around the nearby Health Village nature trail. These periodic walks introduce children to a variety of plants and wildlife throughout the changing seasons.

- **Wood Shop.** Offered to 4- and 5-year-olds, the wood shop program is held at the *Health Village Wood Shop*. Children team with older adults to complete a woodworking project, while learning about tools and safety.

Aside from the rewarding intergenerational programs hosted at *Friendship Center*, children also enjoy many traditional day care activities like arts and crafts, dance, field trips, and reading.

Follow-Up

Using the Internet or local telephone book, research another intergenerational care center in your area. Write a report contrasting this center with *Friendship Center* described above.

see if staff members are provided with work breaks or correct overtime pay as required by law. Programs may also be reviewed to make sure they are not violating child labor laws.

Reporting Licensing Violations

Human service staff must know and follow the licensing laws that apply to their programs. Most staff members do so each and every day. However, sometimes licensing laws are not followed. That means a licensing violation has occurred.

The first people to become aware of violations are often staff. Therefore, reporting a licensing violation requires immediate staff action. As a professional, if you observe a licensing violation, you should write down the date, time, location, and situation surrounding the violation. Any information you record should remain confidential and only be shared with those legally involved.

Some violations must be immediately reported to authorities outside the program, such as violations involving child abuse or neglect. However, most often a violation concern should first be brought to the program director's attention. Then, all those involved in the violation should cooperatively create a corrective plan of action to restore licensing compliance.

FIG. 14-17. Reporting a licensing violation requires immediate action on the part of the early childhood staff. Why is confidentiality important when reporting violations?

If a program continues violating licensing requirements, despite efforts to remedy the problem, further action is needed. An agent from the licensing office should be notified by telephone or in writing. That person will then investigate the violation and decide upon further action. In most states, staff can report concerns to licensing agents anonymously. This protects staff members from punishment for making a formal report. See Fig. 14-17.

Section **14-2** Knowledge Check

1. What staff members are employed in an early childhood program?
2. List possible expenses included in an early childhood program budget.
3. Identify key factors involved in assuring quality in early childhood programs.

Mini-Lab

With a classmate, stage a mock interview for a potential program director. Record the questions you ask and the answers the director candidate supplies. Would you hire this person as your program director? Why or why not?

Chapter **14**
Review & Activities

Section Summaries

14-1 There are many types of early childhood programs.

14-1 Programs vary in terms of philosophy and goals.

14-1 Program sponsors determine philosophy and goals.

14-1 There are for-profit as well as nonprofit programs.

14-1 Licensing laws vary from state to state.

14-1 Accreditation identifies high-quality programs.

14-2 Directors provide leadership in early childhood programs.

14-2 Directors manage a variety of program staff.

14-2 Directors provide staff development.

14-2 Quality facilities support program goals and staff performance.

14-2 Inspections and audits assure quality.

14-2 Client services and public relations are director responsibilities.

14-2 Governing boards help manage quality programs.

14-2 Program sponsors, boards, and directors cooperatively administer programs.

Check Your Knowledge

1. What is a program philosophy?
2. Give an example of a program belief that is part of a program philosophy.
3. What is a program goal? Give an example of a program goal.
4. What is a laboratory school?
5. What are the responsibilities of a program director?
6. Cite two methods a director could use to communicate with clients.
7. What is one purpose of public relations?
8. List five criteria included in an accreditation for early childhood programs.
9. Identify factors that influence program quality.

Thinking Critically

1. When should the early childhood program's philosophy and goals be determined? Why?
2. Contrast factors parents should consider when deciding between a Montessori program and a family child care home.
3. Draw conclusions about how public relations influence the success of an early childhood program.

Practical Applications

1. **Implementing Program Goals and Philosophy.** Interview a local early childhood program director to learn the program's goals and philosophy. How might these affect the activities provided to children enrolled in the program?

2. **Creating Organizational Charts and Job Descriptions.** Identify the personnel in a local early childhood program. Using this information, create an organizational chart to illustrate the hierarchical relationships between positions. Create a job description for each position.

3. **Locating Continuing Education Opportunities.** Research the continuing education opportunities for early childhood professionals in your community. From a local early childhood program director, obtain a list of agencies to contact. Contact each agency to obtain a copy of its training schedule.

Building Your PORTFOLIO

Planning An Early Childhood Program

Program planning includes determining program type, philosophy, goals; recruiting and supervising staff; and managing client services, finances, and public relations.

Step 1: Assume that you are planning a new early childhood program. Decide what type program it will be. Write a description of the program and the reasons you chose that type of program. Write a program philosophy as described in the text. Then create a list of program goals that identifies skills to encourage in children. Define the services to be provided.

Step 2: Create an organizational chart for your early childhood program, and write job descriptions for each position.

Step 3: Create a personnel handbook that provides basic program information to introduce new staff to the policies and procedures they will be expected to follow.

Step 4: Create a parent handbook to communicate program policies and procedures to parents. Include the information described in Section 2.

Step 5: Create a budget for your program, itemizing expected income and expenses.

Step 6: Create a public relations plan for the program.

Step 7: In your portfolio, include the items you created in Steps 1-6.

Chapter 15

Quality Adult Care Programs

Section 15-1

Older Adult Activity Programs

OBJECTIVES

- Explain how philosophy and goals impact the quality of older adult activity programs.
- Summarize the types of quality activities offered at older adult activity programs.
- Describe three types of older adult activity facilities and how they are supplied and maintained.
- Explain how older adult activity programs are licensed, accredited, and staffed.
- Describe how older adult activity programs are operated and governed.
- Explain factors that influence the management of participant services and quality assurance.

KEY TERMS

multipurpose senior center
recreational programs
Material Safety Data Sheets (MSDS)
gerontology
geriatrics

As the population grows, older adults and their families will have an increasing need for programs created specifically for them. Adult activity centers promote and protect the well-being of older adults cared for in licensed community care facilities. These programs follow essential health and safety requirements. Also, they organize and manage local resources to meet the needs of participants.

Philosophy & Goals

The philosophy of the older adult activity programs is to encourage socialization, education, and well-being of older adults. The goal is to increase the self-esteem of older adults by planning and coordinating lifelong cultural, physical, and intellectual programs for older adults. The philosophy and goals of an older adult activity program will determine the types of services offered.

Types of Quality Programs

Because older adults learn differently, they take an active role in deciding the topics they want to learn and how they are taught. Most older adults want to interact with younger people. They also enjoy their relationships with peers. Therefore, many programs are intergenerational. Older adults and younger people learn from one another and are able to share their experiences.

Intergenerational Activities. Programs involving two or more groups of people at different age levels provide opportunities for the groups to interact. For example, younger people can assist older adults in using the computer to learn about health needs and practices, retirement benefits, and other topics. Or, older adults might tutor young people in reading or math. Some programs offer options for older adults to travel with their grandchildren. These activities help to stimulate thinking and build friendships between older and younger people.

Arts and Humanities. Programs for the arts and humanities help enrich the cultural experiences of participants. Often, older adult volunteers help plan program activities or participate in events at theaters, museums, and other places. See Fig. 15-1.

Fitness and Nutrition. Programs in fitness and nutrition help meet the needs of participants from many cultures and with different health concerns. Fitness programs may include dance and exercise options from other cultures followed by a nutritious meal to complement

the event. For example, at an intergenerational rodeo, everyone dresses in western attire, learns line dances, and eats a nutritious western-style lunch.

Financial Planning. Programs in financial planning can include a class to teach older adults how to invest on a fixed income or ways to manage money better. Programs may include a financial planner suggesting ways to invest, informing the group of changes in retirement benefits, and explaining Medicaid and Medicare benefits.

Employee Assistance Services. Some older adults who take part in adult activity programs also have jobs. Employee assistance services may provide counseling services for older workers. These services may also refer older adult workers to agencies that can assist with financial planning, mental or emotional problems, workplace discrimination, or legal issues.

Volunteer Services. Individuals from the community volunteer to carry out programs and activities of interest. For example, a local artist might volunteer to teach a weekly pottery class.

Travels and Tours. Many older adults go on education and travel tours sponsored by various organizations. Some tours are sponsored by local colleges and universities. Groups like Elderhostel™, an educational and travel organization for people 55 and older, offer lifelong learning options that enrich people's lives. Other activities may involve touring local historical sites or watching video presentations of exotic trips. Older adults interested in these programs can contact a local area agency on aging.

FIG. 15-1. Participating in arts and humanities events appeals to many older adults. How are some of the needs of older adults met through the arts and humanities?

FIG. 15-2. **Quality programs offer many opportunities for older adults to share their experience and wisdom with others.** In what ways could you benefit from sharing with older adults?

Factors Indicating Quality

Many indicators can help show the quality of a program. Programs of high quality do the following:

- Build self-esteem to eliminate isolation and loneliness; encourage positive social behavior.

- Provide opportunities to learn and develop a sense of self-worth and purpose; encourage participants to make a difference in the lives of others and their community; help participants overcome stereotypes about other generations.

- Help older adults and young people develop skills to listen effectively to each other.

- Encourage participants to build friendships across the "generation gap" and teach them that each generation has needs.

- Provide older adults with opportunities to share their wisdom and experience, increasing their sense of fulfillment by contributing to others and erasing stereotypes about youth. See Fig. 15-2.

Service Providers

Businesses, community agencies, the general public, corporations, and industries usually sponsor, or fund, adult activity programs. Some funds may come through grants from foundations that support projects related to aging issues. The Administration on Aging (AoA) and the Department of Health and Human Services provide leadership, technical assistance, and support to the National Aging Network. This network includes state units on aging, tribal and native organizations, plus thousands of service providers, adult care centers, and volunteers.

Types of Facilities

Adult day care for older adults can be held in a variety of facilities throughout the country. These facilities include:

Multipurpose Senior Centers. A **multipurpose senior center** is a community-based facility usually sponsored by the city and county department on aging. As community-based agencies, these centers have resources and expertise to assess the needs of older adults. These centers began as part of the Older Americans Act of 1965.

Recreational Programs. Usually funded by city governments, **recreational programs** encourage a warm, friendly atmosphere where people meet other people of a similar age. They have the opportunity to establish friendships, share hobbies or problems, read newspapers or books, watch TV programs or videotapes, and participate in musical events. These centers usually provide a variety of games like puzzles, chess, and checkers for people to play. Older adults may organize a reading club for the pleasure of reading and listening to poetry or stories. Trips to the theater, opera, or ballet are often organized for interested persons.

Nutrition Centers. These programs provide nutritious meals and companionship. Individuals gather at these facilities for approximately two hours to receive a nutritious meal. Places of worship, parks and recreation centers, or social services agencies usually serve these meals. For people with disabilities who cannot get to the meal site, this program delivers meals. An Older Americans Act program, this service is usually administered by a local area agency on aging.

Facility Maintenance & Upkeep

In most cases either the city government or nonprofit organizations maintain adult day care facilities. Each program must adhere to the maintenance standards of the sponsoring organization(s). In addition, these programs must also comply with standards set by the city fire codes, local health department, Occupational Safety and Health Act (OSHA), the Americans with Disabilities Act (ADA), and the Older Americans Act (OAA).

Material Safety Data Sheets (MSDS) are a key component of these safety regulations. MSDS provide information about a substance's ingredients, properties, hazards, and precautions for use, as well as first aid advice and places to contact for more information. Current laws require manufacturers to prepare up-to-date MSDS for all hazardous substances, such as cleaning fluids and other chemicals. MSDS must be provided at no charge to all people who purchase these substances. Suppliers must periodically update their MSDS. Employers are required to inform employees where these sheets are located.

Quality Equipment & Supplies

In accordance with the program's goals, funding agencies' requirements, and accreditation standards, the activity center must provide equipment and supplies that meet program goals. The types of equipment and supplies depend on the participants' activity plans. For example, if a per-

son needs physical therapy, a physical therapist will assess the area(s) that need strengthening, such as the legs. He or she will select equipment, such as a ball, that the older adult can manipulate to strengthen the leg muscles.

Licensing & Registration Laws

All facilities must meet state standards for operating a facility. The Administration on Aging (AoA) and the aging network continue working to improve the quality and array of services offered by multipurpose senior centers. The AoA funds education and training materials for program managers that are published by the National Council on Aging, Inc. (NCOA). These tools guide senior center managers in program development, assessing program quality, and identifying areas of improvement. See Fig. 15-3.

FIG. 15-3. **Licensing and registration are required in every state for adult day care centers. Accreditation is optional.** Why would it be to a program's benefit to also acquire accreditation?

Intergenerational *Interactions*

Condell Day Center for Intergenerational Care

The 27,000-square-foot Condell Day Center in Libertyville, IL, provides day care services for children ages six weeks to six years and adults over the age of 55. The facility features playrooms, activity rooms, a gymnasium, solarium, and garden. With all of these areas designed for interaction, it is no wonder the center is so successful in building relationships among children and older adults. The center focuses on fun and includes the following activities:

- **Individual Interaction.** While many centers offer group intergenerational programs, the Condell Day Center encourages one-on-one contact. A child and older adult may shake hands, read books, do puzzles, play checkers, color together, and more.

- **Positive Role Models.** Children who do not have the benefit of being near older friends and relatives on a regular basis need role models. When they have fun with older adults at the center, children begin to respect and understand older adults.

- **Painless Days.** Older adults interacting with children quickly forget their aches and pains. When they come to the center, they play. They have fun. While enjoying the company of energetic children, older adults often stop worrying about their problems and illnesses.

- **Unconditional Love.** Children and older adults often don't have a chance to share feelings and thoughts with busy middle generations. Interaction at the center gives them a chance to be recognized. Children enjoy showing off a little, while older adults clap their hands and cheer for the youngsters. Children also enjoy listening to the stories that older adults share.

- **Fitness.** This center also encourages health and fitness. In joint exercise programs, children stand and do exercises, while older adults remain seated and do similar movements. These programs help all generations maintain strength and flexibility.

- **Educational Games.** Mental fitness is just as important as physical fitness. Intergenerational games, such as alphabet matching games, help children learn the alphabet and keep older adults mentally alert.

Follow-Up

Write a report on how the above activities could improve the lives of children and older adults. In your report include additional activities that the Condell Day Center may want to offer.

Accreditation

Accreditation shows that a center meets the high standards set by the accrediting organization and demonstrates that a center provides quality programs for older adults. Accreditation can be obtained through the National Institute of Senior Centers (NISC). In addition, accreditation can also be acquired from The Rehabilitation Accreditation Commission (CARF). This is a nonprofit group that accredits programs and services for adult day services and many others.

Program Governance & Leadership

Usually the older adult activity program adheres to the policies and leadership of the funding organization. If it is a nonprofit program, it must follow the state guidelines for nonprofit organizations. If the program is accredited, it must also follow the accreditation organization guidelines. The board of directors and executive director oversee how these programs follow the policies and guidelines usually through an annual inspection and audit of reports. In many cases, the executive director takes the order from the board of directors to make certain the task is done at the appropriate time.

FIG. 15-4.

Organizational Structure for Activity Model Centers

Advisory Board/Owner

Director

Secretary

Recreation Therapy

Social Services

Nutrition

Transportation

Arts & Crafts
Music & Drama
Dance & Fitness
Adult Education
Current Events

Community
Outreach
Referrals
Counseling

Lunch

To and From
the Center

Supplementary Services

Volunteers

Income Tax Service
Consumer Protection
Vision Screening
Hearing Screening

Activities
Transportation
Community Outreach
Companionship
Field Trips

Organizational Structure

Regardless of which type of group sponsors a program, it is a good business practice to have an organizational structure. A common organizational structure includes an advisory board to assist and guide the staff. As a condition of giving financial support to a program, all funding sources require programs to have a governing body to oversee the program operations. See Fig. 15-4. Although each program is different, an organizational structure for older adult activity programs (senior centers) usually consists of the following:

- **Advisory Board.** Older adult day programs generally have an advisory board that includes a chairperson, treasurer, and secretary. In addition, the board will include at least three directors who make note of changes in laws and program governance and funding. They also supply expertise and advice in various areas, such as fundraising and managing volunteers. Participant family members are often on the board.

- **Director.** The program must have a director, who is usually a full-time staff person. Directors are paid employees who show commitment and responsibility for the daily operation of the facility. This person supervises program coordinators and volunteers. The director also oversees the facility operations, manages finances, and makes sure the program meets state and accreditation standards.

- **Program Coordinator.** A program coordinator must make certain the programs—such as the arts, fitness, or travel—are planned and carried out according to the program goals.

- **Secretary.** A secretary may be a part-time employee. The secretary's responsibility is to answer the telephone and serve as receptionist. This person may be a volunteer, depending on the center and the funding. A knowledgeable and friendly secretary is an important asset to the center. He or she is usually the first person with whom participants and their families have contact.

Director & Board Interaction

The director attends board meetings to keep the members informed about the program operation. The board serves as the director's supervisor. It receives written reports from program coordinators and answers all inquires from the sponsoring organizations. For example, the board may answer questions about statistics required by the state, such as the number of people using the facility or the number of people using the congregate meal program. The board also deals with program evaluations and employee issues.

Governance Handbooks

The program must have a governance handbook that serves as an operational procedure manual for the program. These handbooks include daily operating procedures, employment policies, grievance procedures, employee conduct and dress code, employee evaluations, workplace safety, and procedures for reporting problems. Most funding sources require written documents to show the operational policies and procedures. These handbooks are also useful in training new staff members about the way the program is run.

Staff Requirements

People from the community volunteer to work in many senior centers. Volunteers often assist with activities of their choice. The activity assignments are based on the personal interests, skills, and time availability of the volunteers. Without these volunteers, it would be impossible for many senior centers to operate. The volunteers are supervised by paid staff members.

Staff Qualifications

The director is a paid employee with a background in management and business practices. It is helpful for the director to have knowledge of gerontology and geriatrics services. **Gerontology** (jer-uhn-TAH-luh-jee) is the study of the aging process. **Geriatrics** (jer-ee-A-trihks) is a field of medicine that focuses on preventing or managing common diseases for older adults.

Screening of Staff

The board of directors or advisory committee will want to have the best staff possible to operate the senior activity center. If it is a city-sponsored program, the governing body must follow the guidelines of the city government for selecting and hiring staff. Nonprofit organizations use similar guidelines for screening applicants. Generally, potential staff must meet educational requirements, must enjoy working with older adults, and must have knowledge about aging.

Staff Development

All leaders and staff need continuing education in the area of program planning and development in order to stay current. The director should get training to learn about the latest trends and information in older adult care. The director in turn trains other staff members and volunteers so that the program as a whole stays up to date.

Personnel Policies and Handbooks. Personnel policies and handbooks are used as a training tool. The director uses the book to inform the staff members and volunteers. Issues, such as personnel policies, how the center handles sexual harassment, sick leave, and vacation time, are covered in these handbooks.

In-Service Training. In-service training should be conducted at least once a month to keep everyone informed of the latest policies and current trends. For example, in-service training issues may include changes in laws, funding changes, new services, or the development of new programs. In addition, recertification of first aid and CPR training or annual hazardous chemical communications may be addressed. See Fig. 15-5.

Continuing Education. The director may opt to obtain personal credentials, such as certification for managers. Most states offer some type of credentials, such as Senior Center Program Manager, Senior Center Manager, and Aging Services Administrator.

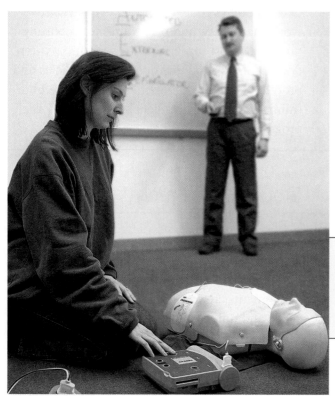

FIG. 15-5. **In-service training, such as learning automated external defibrillation (AED), is an important part of staff development at adult day centers.** What other training might be necessary for the adult day care staff?

Managing Stress. Overwhelming emotional stress can impair a person's ability to perform his or her job safely, effectively, and lead to a condition called burn out. Stress can result from very demanding participants or from the struggle to meet both work and family responsibilities. Directors often provide stress-management training for staff. This training helps staff members learn to manage their stress. Stress-management training focuses on:

- Recognizing situations that cause stress on the job and at home.
- Identifying and finding ways to deal with stress that could ultimately lead to health problems.
- Providing time management and relaxation techniques.

Staff Supervision

The director supervises the program staff and volunteers. Depending on the size of the program, the director can appoint others to serve in supervisory roles, such as coordinator of volunteers. The board of directors serves as the supervisor of the director.

Evaluating Performance. Regular evaluations should be done according to the policy and procedures established by the governing board and the director. All staff members, including volunteers, should be informed of the evaluation procedures. Some programs use peer evaluations. Others also survey the participants who use the program. Staff should use the evaluation as a tool for improvement. Evaluations help show where staff members' strengths lie, as well as areas that need more work.

Managing Participant Services

The director is responsible for advertising and recruiting participants. This task may be delegated to other members of the team. Participants may be recruited through agencies, businesses, newsletters, the area agency on aging mailings, or direct-mail advertising. In addition to recruiting and advertising, the director is also responsible for financial management, program planning, and quality assurance.

Financial Management

Most senior centers are nonprofit and spend as much money as they take in. Some for-profit senior centers generate income. The profits come through travel, transportation, or meal charges. As in any other business, it is essential to have a system for budgeting, reporting, and distributing income. Regular financial statements show how funds are distributed according to the budgets. The board of directors is primarily responsible to oversee the financial management of the program. The board must have an acceptable accounting system to ensure responsible use of funds. It generally evaluates the budget on a monthly basis.

- **Income.** The finances necessary to operate the adult day center can be obtained in a number of ways. Income may be generated from participant fees for services. Other income may come from fundraising events, Administration on Aging grants, state and federal funding, United Way funding, and private donations.
- **Expenses.** Expenses may include staff payroll, equipment and supply purchases, and facility rent and maintenance costs.

Programs Provided

Programs are designed to meet the educational and physical needs of older adults. Many older adults meet friends at the center to participate in events as shown in Fig. 15-6.

FIG. 15-6.

ACTIVITY PROGRAMS FOR OLDER ADULTS

Program	Activities	
Physical Fitness	Line dancing Chair exercises Lightweight resistance activity Walking indoors and outdoors	Treadmill walking Water aerobics or water exercises or therapy Swimming classes
Games	Puzzles Board games Card games	Horseshoes Shuffle board
Community Beautification Project	Container gardening Community gardening	Herb gardening Flower arranging
Travel & Tours	City-guided tours Historical sites	Art museum tours Musical tours (opera, concerts, etc.)
Continuing Education	Financial management Book reviews Trusts and wills	

Quality Assurance

It is important to encourage further training and certifications for personnel. The program leaders align goals and objectives of the program, provide yearly reviews by the board of directors or advisory committee members, and make changes as needed. Every effort must be made to obtain and maintain accreditation through The Rehabilitation Accreditation Commission (CARF) and the National Adult Day Services Association (NADSA).

Section **15-1** Knowledge Check

1. How do philosophy and goals impact adult activity center quality?
2. Contrast licensing and accreditation of adult activity centers.
3. What are the director's responsibilities in managing participant services?

Mini-Lab

Interview a director from a senior center. Discuss the organizational structure of the program including business operations, such as managing participant services, financial management, and program planning. Write a summary of your interview to share with the class.

Section 15-2

Social-Medical & Medical Model Programs

OBJECTIVES

- Identify the primary goal of social-medical and medical model adult day care programs.
- Describe the two adult day care program models.
- Identify factors that indicate program quality.
- Determine the staff requirements for the social-medical and medical model adult day care programs.
- Determine the process of managing participant services in a medical model adult day center.

KEY TERMS

respite care
shareholders

The social-medical model and the medical model programs offer additional services from adult activity centers. Social-medical activity programs provide planned programs that include a variety of health, social, and support services in a protective environment during daytime hours. Medical model programs primarily deal with managing the health care of participants in a protective daytime environment. Both programs meet the needs of older adult participants.

Older Adult Day Care Centers

With the substantial increase in America's older adult population, it is no surprise that the fastest growing area of community-based care is that of older adult day care centers. While more families are now able to care for their older adults at home, these families often need help in caring for their loved ones.

Programs at adult day care centers are service oriented and consumer focused as shown in the program philosophy, goals, and mission statement. Programs are designed to meet the needs of each participant, individually, to the extent of the services provided by the facility. One service might offer **respite care**. This is temporary relief care for family members who care for a relative who is unable to function independently but does not require 24-hour nursing care. The center provides a safe group environment with coordinated health and social services to promote maintaining or improving self-care. These programs have a full range of health care, social and recreational services, and activities for persons who are physically frail. The services are coordinated and individual care plans are developed as part of the older adult's daily program.

Types of Quality Programs

Quality older adult programs provide daily activities that meet the social, recreational, and personal care requirements for older men and women of different ages and functional levels. Activities that adhere to or exceed state and national standards or guidelines are conducted in a safe and secure environment with qualified, well-trained staff and volunteers.

Programs concentrate on the participants' physical, emotional, and mental care. An active fitness program is important because it helps to increase strength, flexibility, and balance, and it improves mood. The combination of nursing, personal care, and health care services helps improve the participants' overall health. See Fig. 15-7. Programs can help monitor and help treat chronic and acute illnesses, including high blood pressure. Quality programs may include the following services:

- Nursing care and meal services.
- Therapy activities and social events.
- Transportation to appointments and social events.
- Physical fitness, exercise, and rehabilitation programs.
- Individual and family counseling.

Factors Indicating Quality. Centers that observe recommended standards are considered high-quality programs. In order to obtain certification or a license, a program must maintain and periodically evaluate specific quality standards, such as:

- Following or exceeding state and national standards and guidelines for care facilities.
- Assessing older adults, prior to admission, to determine their range of needs and abilities.
- Offering an environment that is safe and secure for older adults.
- Meeting the social, recreational, and rehabilitative needs of older adults through an active day program.
- Creating care plans for individual participants and monitoring progress on a regular basis.
- Offering an activity schedule that gives choices and covers the full day with activities geared to individual interests and functional abilities.
- Making referrals to other helpful services in the community.
- Offering a supportive environment that takes into account physical and cognitive functions.
- Using set standards for service and clear guidelines for termination of service based upon how well the older adult functions.
- Having a program philosophy that offers choice to both participants and care providers.
- Offering a complete range of services, such as transportation, health screening or monitoring, meals and snacks, personal care, or educational activities.

FIG. 15-7. Social-medical and medical model programs provide many services to meet the basic needs of older adults.

FIG. 15-8.

FUNDING SPONSORS FOR ADULT DAY CARE SERVICES

Funding Sources	Types
Government	• Federal grants (funds that the federal government allocates to support specific programs for a set period of time). • Medicare Part B (covers out-patient rehabilitation by licensed physical, occupational, or speech therapists or other specified personnel). • Medicaid (some states use a medical waiver to cover all adult day care services provided for qualified low-income older adults). • Title III—Older Americans Act, Part B—supportive services, Part C—nutrition services (covers a portion of the cost of transportation, social, recreational, educational, and nutrition services).
Private	• Fee for services (paid by the participant, insurance companies, or managed care insurance companies).
Private For-Profit	• Marriott™ Senior Program
Private Non-profit	• University laboratories • Places of worship • YMCA/YWCA
Foundations	• Robert Wood Johnson • AT&T™ • IBM™

• Utilizing qualified staff and volunteers with solid activity-based training. Organizations, such as the National Adult Day Services Association (NADSA), have curriculums for such training.

Licensing Factors Indicating Quality.
The National Adult Day Services Association (NADSA) provides educational materials that can help centers meet licensing guidelines. Most facilities seek a license in order to be recognized as a high-quality program. Each state offers a license to operate an adult day care center, and the criteria differ from state to state. Factors indicating a quality program include:

• Qualified staff who provide a full range of services.

• A focus on the specific needs of older people of different cultural backgrounds, physical limitations, and age groups.

• Designated space for providing adult day services is accessible to all participants.

• Involvement of older adults in planning programs and activities and determining the benefits of the activities.

• An evaluation plan to determine the quality of the services. The results can be used to improve services.

• An organized system that shows lines of responsibilities and methods of reporting results of the services offered.

• Newsletters and reports that describe the services offered and the program performance to a variety of people, such as potential participants, agencies that fund programs, and state and local governments.

Service Providers

Service providers may include the owner of an adult day care center and the representatives, agents, and employees of the facility. If a corporation or a nonprofit organization owns the center, the providers may include people who have ownership of the business or control over the corporation and the officers, director, and **shareholders**. Shareholders are people who have funds invested in the center. These funds are necessary in order for the adult day care center to operate and provide services. Funding sources include local governments, private nonprofit organizations, or places of worship. Some of the groups that provide funds to adult day centers are listed on page 377. See Fig. 15-8.

Types of Facilities

Adult day care services offer respite for families who care for a relative who is unable to function independently. However, older adults can also choose this service independent of family members for social and health-monitoring reasons. Participants may have:

- Physical limitations or disabilities.
- Social or psychological health needs.
- Assistance needs with everyday activities .
- Rehabilitation needs after a hospital stay.

These facilities provide a safe group environment with coordinated health and social services to help families provide care for their loved ones. These models of center-based care may prevent, postpone, or reduce the need for long-term, residential care. Both the social-medical model and medical model older adult day care programs may be offered within the same center.

Social-Medical Model. Planned activities for a variety of social, health, and support services are offered through social-medical programs. These programs offer care to meet each participant's needs.

- **Level of care.** All-day service offers daytime care for older adults with rehabilitative or physical or mental health needs. This type of service may include monitoring health conditions or physical and recreational therapy. Medication management may involve working with older adults to create a manageable plan for taking medication. The purpose is to help older adults maintain their functional level.

Medical Model. Medical model programs offer medical supervision and health-related care on a daily basis. Trained staff dispense medicine and monitor medical conditions. Therapy services, such as speech or physical therapy, are usually available.

- **Level of care.** Assistance with personal care and other additional services are offered at some medical model programs. Older adults who have recently been discharged from a hospital might be referred to a medical model center for additional care and rehabilitation services.

FIG. 15-9. Material Safety Data Sheets must be on file in adult day facilities when certain hazardous materials are found in the facility. Why are cleaning supplies considered hazardous materials?

Facility Maintenance & Upkeep

The rules for facility maintenance and upkeep are outlined in each state's standards for operation. The licensing body requires each center to keep a copy of the entire license showing clearly the responsibilities of its membership for the maintenance and upkeep of the property. The local government also requires programs to follow specific standards from the fire department and health department. See Fig. 15-9.

Quality Equipment & Supplies

Equipment and supplies for the day center should meet the program goals. Directors must plan carefully in order to provide participants with the proper equipment and supplies based on participants' needs and the licensing standards for the center. For example, if an older adult needs physical therapy and is required to build leg strength, the center must have the proper equipment to offer the service. If the center cannot offer the needed service, the center will have to hire an independent contractor to come as needed to perform the specific task.

If the center is to dispense medication to participants during their stay at the center, the center is responsible for making certain that the participant either brings the medication or the medication is available at the center.

Licensing & Registration Laws

The Department of Social Services or Department of Human Services, Bureau or Department of Licensing provides licensing of adult day centers at the state level. Each center has to apply for the license by filling out an application and submitting an application fee. The fee is usually a small, nonrefundable amount. The application for license usually has sections that seek the following types of information:

FIG. 15-10. **Approving a center's annual budget is part of the responsibility of the director and the board of directors.** What other responsibilities does the governing board perform?

- **Directions and guidelines.** Outlines steps in filling out the application and provides information about application fees.
- **Center information.** Includes the center's name, location, mailing address, and telephone number.
- **Type of license.** Initial application or renewal application.
- **Program information.** Type of center (social-medical or medical).
- **Center operations.** Description of who is served, their ages, and when services are offered during the day.
- **Organizational structure.** Includes type of ownership of the center (individual, partnership, place of worship, university, corporation), officers of the board, list of owners, ownership status (profit or nonprofit), and tax-identification number. See Fig. 15-10.

- **Funding sources.** Includes Medicaid, Medicare, social services departments, rehabilitation agencies, or private pay.

- **Personal references.** Includes names, addresses, and telephone numbers of at least three non-related persons who are able to relate to the licensing body the applicant's ability to operate an adult day care center.

- **Certification by owner/director.** This section lists information about the applicant's background, including whether or not violations or criminal acts have been committed that would keep the applicant from operating a center. The authorized official's signature, title, and date must be obtained.

The licensing is based on each state's adult day care center *minimum* standards. The standards outline health and safety practices for operating adult day care services. Most standards are based on staffing patterns and ratios, and facility management; and many are dementia or Alzheimer's disease care or respite care programs.

Program Governance & Leadership

The leadership and program governance will vary based on how each center is structured, operated, or funded. The center must have a governing body that is responsible for the policies and activities of the center. The governing body should have at least two meetings a year. The duties of the governing body include:

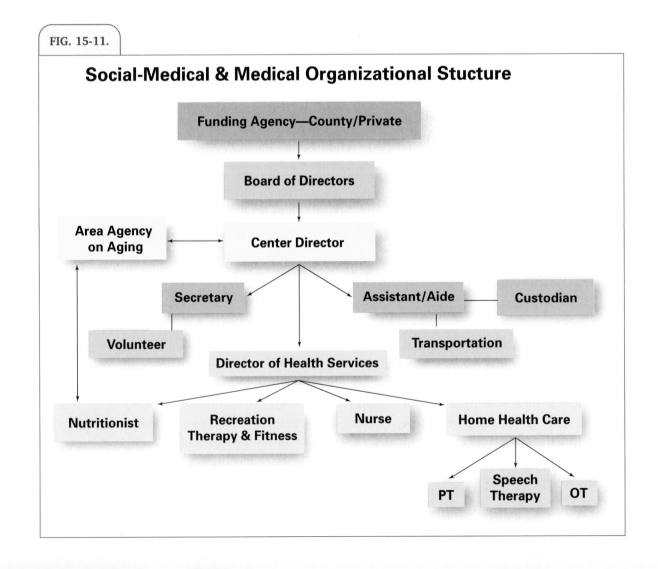

FIG. 15-11.

Social-Medical & Medical Organizational Stucture

- Ensuring that the center agrees to and conforms to the governing body's policies.

- Ensuring that the center agrees to and conforms to all relevant federal and state laws and regulations.

- Reviewing and approving the center's annual budget.

- Ensuring that the center is housed, maintained, staffed, and equipped appropriately, considering the nature of the program.

- Designating a person to act as administrator and delegating sufficient authority to the person to manage the center.

- Formulating and reviewing written annual policies concerning the center's philosophy, goals, services, personnel practices, and financial management.

- Evaluating the administrator's performance annually.

- Having the authority to dismiss the administrator.

- Meeting with designated representatives of the licensing and accreditation agencies and the program officer whenever required.

- Informing the licensing and accreditation agencies and program officer in writing prior to initiating any substantial changes in the program, services, or physical set-up of the facility.

- Maintaining governance handbooks that outline all policies and procedures.

Organizational Structure

The organizational structure will vary depending on how the center is funded. In most cases, the area agency on aging will be involved in all programs and services that operate for older adults. This agency serves as a clearinghouse for services to support community-based adult day centers, senior centers, and nutrition programs. See Fig. 15-11.

Staff Requirements

Requirements for staff depend on the types of services provided by the center. For most centers, a staff ratio of 1 to 5, excluding the director, or as required by the state, serves as a good baseline for both social-medical and medical model centers. Both the paid and volunteer staff count in the staffing ratio for an adult day center. The director should not be counted because most of his or her time is spent planning, implementing, and evaluating the program's services. Administrative records of staff must include:

- Position title and job description.

- Copies of licenses or certifications of professional qualification.

- Educational background.

- Employment background, history including the previous year's work record, and references.

- Work performance evaluation.

- Orientation and in-service documentation.

- Documentation of any communicable disease as well as a physician's written release to return to the employment market.

- Documentation of current training in first aid and CPR.

Care Management Team. The members of the care management team work together to form a quality plan of care for the participant. A plan of care may include the number of hours a participant is at the day center, any medications to be administered, or fitness or therapy programs needed. The team includes a physician, geriatric social worker or geriatric family life specialist, center staff, and family care provider. Each person on the team plays a major role in the care plan for the older adult. See Fig. 15-12.

FIG. 15-12.

ADULT DAY CARE PROGRAM STAFFING

Position	Qualification	Description
Director (full-time)	Gerontology trained; continuing education.	• Manages the adult day program or facility. • Trains and supervises faculty.
Nurse (full-time)	LPN or RN.	• Oversees medication and health care plan.
Secretary (full-time)	Clerical skills.	• Receptionist, keeps records, tracks supplies, and does data entry.
Custodian (full-time)	Skills in janitorial services.	• Keeps facility clean; may serve as bus driver.
Aides (full-time)	Training; continuing education.	• Assist participants with daily activities.
Volunteers	Orientation sessions.	• Work in a position free of charge.
Recreation Therapist (contractual)	State license.	• Plans activities based on the care plan of each older adult. Carries out plans.
Registered Dietitian (contractual)	Certified.	• Plans meals according to participant care plan.
Social Worker (full-time)	State license.	• Provides health, maintenance, and social day care services to participants. • Conducts home assessments, coordinates admission process, counsels participants and families, leads support groups, and acts as community liaison.
Physical, Occupational, or Speech Therapists (contractual)	State license.	• Design and carry out participant care plan.

Director & Staff Qualifications

State regulations and the people served dictate the staff qualifications. It is absolutely necessary that the adult day center be staffed with a sufficient number of qualified people to ensure that the planned programs and activities can be provided. The National Adult Day Services Association (NADSA) standards address staff qualifications. The center should not depend solely on volunteers and participants to carry out the necessary duties of the social-medical and medical adult day care center.

As a program employee, the director should be trained in the area of gerontology or geriatrics services. The director should have skills and talents to be creative in planning programs that meet the needs of the participants. The director must market the program to the public and make referrals to other agencies.

Some programs make an effort to recruit older people to staff centers so they can serve as role models to the participants. Younger volunteers, specifically student interns, must have a written plan to follow during their time at the center. They must participate in an orientation and training about the philosophy, policies, and procedures of the center. Other training topics include the center's confidentiality policy, the needs of the older adults, and appropriate methods of meeting needs.

Staff Development

Staff development is an important part of adult day care programs. The director should provide orientation for all new staff members, including part-time staff and volunteers. The training must include a review of the personnel polices and handbooks that outline the center's philosophy and goals.

Periodic training must be given to provide current information related to services and practices. Related topics for staff development must include:

- Stress-management training.
- Effective communication training.
- Cultural sensitivity and ethics training.
- CPR and first aid training.
- Medical emergencies, emergency, and safety procedure training.
- Program's policies and procedures.
- Participants' rights.
- Detecting and reporting suspected abuse and neglect. See Fig. 15-13.
- Reporting critical incidents.
- Managing aggressive behavior.

Staff Supervision

Staff supervision is critical to the success of adult day care centers. Poorly trained staff that lack an understanding of later life development have a high turnover rate. Staff cannot be successful without good supervisors. Staff members must have an understanding of the tasks to be performed. It is equally important for them to understand the staff evaluation process.

Evaluating Performance. In order to judge staff effectiveness, supervisors should evaluate

employee and volunteer performance regularly. Evaluations should be used as a learning tool rather than as a means of criticizing a staff member's performance. Results of the performance evaluation should be worked into an improvement plan for the next evaluation period. The evaluations must remain confidential.

Supplementary Services

An adult day care program usually will not include medical care, diagnosis, or treatment. However, some community-based multipurpose adult day centers schedule supplementary services for older adults and their family members. Services may include the following:

- Dental care, both preventative and care for dental problems.
- Podiatry services to care for foot problems.

FIG. 15-13. **Training in detecting and reporting abuse and neglect of older adults is important for the adult day center staff.**

- Vision and hearing screening services to determine the need for items such as eyeglasses, hearing aids, or cataract removal.
- Legal aid for issues such as wills, housing issues, or financial concerns.
- Consumer protection against fraudulent practices.
- Financial support services, such as tax preparation, housing repairs or modifications, fuel assistance, food stamps, or security income.

Managing Participant Services

Managing the participants and the center operation is an important task involving record keeping and reporting. Programs should have written procedures and criteria for admission and a written orientation program for participants admitted to the center. The written information should include:

- The center's responsibilities to the participant.
- Cost, if any, for services.
- Information about the types of activities and programs the center offers.
- Nondiscrimination provisions—participants must not be turned away for service due to age, gender, race, or disability.
- Participants' rights and responsibilities.
- Grievance and appeal procedures for participants.
- Referral system for other services.
- The participants and staff members must sign and date a statement verifying the service plan.

Participants' records are confidential. The program must have written procedures for the maintenance and the security of records. All records must be maintained in a safe file that is accessible only to staff members who have the authority to handle the records.

FIG. 15-14. **Strict adherence to schedules and quality is essential for meeting the needs of older adults.**

Procedures & Schedules

Written records are also necessary for accepting and making referrals. A system for scheduling potential participants must be established. It is helpful to provide participants with an application packet including the necessary paperwork for services provided. A participant packet may include:

- Intake referral—referrals made for a participant after an interview.
- Application—a document that accesses important information about the participant.
- Assessment—information about a participant's needs.
- Trial participation—temporary time period to determine if the program's services are right for the participant.
- Full participation—unlimited time period for a participant to participate in the program's services.
- Maintenance—upkeep of facility and services.
- Transition—to make changes in services.
- Discharge—to exit a service.

Financial Management

Every program must keep records of all income and expenditures. An accountant or other qualified person should set up a record system that will be acceptable for the purpose of audits. Records are important not only for businesslike management of the program, but also for an accurate report of cost per participant and reporting to the state.

Quality Assurance

Certification is a way to make certain that programs maintain high standards, as well as a way to promote the program to the general public. In order to maintain its license or accreditation status, the program must maintain the quality of its services. Licensing and accrediting organizations use established criteria to access centers and ensure that high-quality services are provided by centers. Once a center receives a license or accreditation, the credentialing criteria must be maintained in order to renew the credentials. See Fig. 15-14. The minimum standards address the:

- Legal authority of regulations and licensing authority that are listed for each state.
- Description of the types of programs offered at the center.

- Definitions of terms used to describe a position or task, such as administrator, owner, or manager.
- Procedures to follow in operating a center.
- Description of the licensing authority, approval, and documentation of the authority to operate.
- Administration and governing board responsibilities.
- Management responsibilities for administrative files, program descriptions, participants' rights, record keeping, and confidentiality and security of participants' records and personnel files.
- Human resource staff plan and personnel action, orientation, annual training, number and qualification of staff, and volunteers or student interns.
- Direct-service management of the admission process, participant plan of care, and reporting process including behavior management.
- Discharge, foodservice, and transportation information.
- Physical environment, general safety and emergency practices.

Quality assurance can be a long list of criteria used to judge service quality. Centers should follow the system the governing body makes to accurately measure the quality of services.

Section 15-2 Knowledge Check

1. What activities are carried out in a medical model day center?
2. Name two licensing factors that indicate program quality.
3. Describe the types of care providers and their responsibilities.

Mini-Lab

Assume that you are a director of an adult day care center. Investigate the continuing education programs you would need to participate in to maintain current services for older adults.

Chapter **15**
Review & Activities

Chapter Summary

15-1 Older adult activity centers promote and protect the health and safety of older adults in their care.

15-1 Program accreditation promotes high standards and demonstrates that a center provides quality programs for older adults.

15-1 To ensure quality, advisory boards align program goals and objectives, encourage staff training and certification, and obtain or maintain accreditation.

15-1 Businesses, community agencies, the general public, corporations, and industries usually sponsor adult activity centers.

15-2 Quality adult day care programs provide daily activities that meet the social, recreational, health monitoring, and personal care needs of older adults at differing functional levels.

15-2 The social-medical and medical model programs offer health monitoring services in addition to social, recreational, and personal care services.

15-2 A care management team may include a physician, a geriatric social worker or family life specialist, center staff, and family care provider.

15-2 Quality programs meet or exceed the standards of state and national licensing laws.

15-2 Rules for facility maintenance and upkeep are set by each state and include fire prevention and health standards.

15-2 Program governance and leadership varies based on the organizational structure and funding source of each center.

Check Your Knowledge

1. What roles do volunteers serve in the older adult activity center?
2. Why should the philosophy and goals of the program be aligned with participants' activity plans?
3. Why should continuing education for staff members be encouraged?
4. What are the benefits of program accreditation?
5. What is the accreditation organization for adult day care centers?
6. What are the staffing requirements of the social-medical and medical model programs?
7. Name at least five factors that indicate program quality.
8. Contrast social-medical and medical model programs.
9. What is the major purpose of a care management team?
10. What responsibilities are involved in managing social-medical and medical model participant services?

Thinking Critically

1. Draw conclusions about how older adult activity center staff might facilitate intergenerational participation, communication, and friendships.
2. Draw conclusions about how older adults can be encouraged to participate in older adult activity center programs.
3. Contrast the services of adult activity centers and the social-medical model centers.

Practical Applications

1. **Funding Source Presentation.** Research one of the sources of funding for adult care programs. What procedures must be followed to obtain funding from this source? What requirements must be met? How much competition is there for the funding? How much funding is available? What standards must be met and maintained? What reports must be provided to the funding agency? Make a presentation of your findings to your class.

2. **Licensing and Accreditation Report.** Research the procedures for obtaining a license or accreditation for an adult care program. Write a report describing the licensing or accrediting agency, the steps in obtaining the license or accreditation, and the standards that must be maintained.

3. **Attending a Meeting.** Arrange to attend a board of directors meeting or an in-service training session at a local adult care facility. Write a summary of what you learned.

Building Your PORTFOLIO

Evaluating Adult Care Programs

Learning to evaluate the quality of adult care programs will make it easier to maintain quality standards as an adult care provider.

Step 1: Develop a directory of adult care programs in your community. List each center's name, address, telephone number, and director. Include information regarding licensing and accreditation, funding source, staff, client services, and program. Place a copy of the directory in your portfolio.

Step 2: Visit an adult care program. Obtain information regarding the type of facility, organizational structure, funding, licensing and accreditation, staff, business operation, participant services, and program goals and activities. What signs of quality did you observe? Include a copy of your evaluation in your portfolio.

Step 3: After volunteering at a local older adult care program, ask the director to evaluate your performance and help you develop an improvement plan. Include copies of the evaluation and improvement plan in your portfolio.

Chapter 16
Intergenerational Care Programs

Section 16-1
Intergenerational Care Program Basics

Section 16-2
Managing Intergenerational Programs

Section **16-1**

Intergenerational Care Program Basics

OBJECTIVES

- Define intergenerational care.
- Identify goals and philosophy of intergenerational care programs.
- Summarize the benefits of intergenerational care for children and older adults.
- Identify intergenerational services.

KEY TERMS

partnership
integrated services
support services

Today, both young children and older adults sometimes need care and supervision outside of the home. Some parents enroll children in early childhood programs because the parents work during the day. Others use them so children can experience enriching activities. For the very same reasons, family members responsible for the care and supervision of older adults use community programs for those age 55 and older. In order to meet the similar but unique needs of young children and older adults, many communities offer intergenerational care programs.

Intergenerational Goals & Philosophy

Through careful planning, intergenerational programs offer frequent opportunities for old and young to interact in meaningful ways. The following concepts provide the foundation for planning intergenerational programs.

- Children and older adults deserve high-quality, developmentally appropriate services.
- Lifespan developmental stages are important.
- Family members should have active involvement in the program.
- Generations benefit from being together. Intergenerational activities offer opportunities to learn and grow together.

- Intergenerational activities address cultural heritage, traditions, and personal histories.
- Mixing of ages, rather than age separation, reflects real life.
- Society benefits from strong relationships between young and old.
- Intergenerational activities promote an inclusive sense of community. See Fig. 16-1.

Intergenerational Programs

There are many different creative ways to bring young children and older adults together. Program types vary in terms of:

- **Program sponsor's goals.** Goals may include care and education.

FIG. 16-1. **Intergenerational program philosophies promote an inclusive sense of community.** What are some ways that children and older adults benefit from intergenerational interactions?

facility. Integrated programs have one administration. It is responsible for all participant services. Staff members understand the developmental needs of all ages served. They plan and conduct a variety of daily intergenerational activities. In order to promote frequent interactions, the facility design must be accessible to all participants. Integrated programs offer greater opportunities for formal and spontaneous interactions between the generations. See pages 87-88 for more information on types of intergenerational programs.

Intergenerational Care Benefits

Intergenerational programs offer many benefits. Children and older adults benefit from regular and meaningful interactions.

Benefits for Children. Children benefit from positive personal relationships, unconditional acceptance, and emotional support from older adults. See Fig. 16-2 on page 392. They can develop positive attitudes about growing older and gain an understanding about physical limitations. Other benefits include:

- Having a realistic view of the aging process.
- Having more attention, encouragement, and nurturing.
- Improving social skills and behaviors.
- Increasing in knowledge, skills, and guidance from older adults.

Benefits for Older Adults. Older adults can benefit greatly by sharing past experiences with younger people. Benefits include:

- Chances to share time, talents, and culture.
- Maintenance of old skills and development of new skills.
- Motivation to remain actively engaged in life.

- **Program's purpose.** Intergenerational programs serve to unite the young and old in a variety of situations. For example, older adults might serve children as mentors.
- **Facility design.** Some intergenerational programs operate in the same facility to meet the needs of all generations. Some may have separate facilities with a common area.
- **Frequency of intergenerational contact.** Intergenerational activities may be daily, weekly, monthly, or may be spontaneous.
- **Nature of activities offered.** Activities may be purely social or social and educational.

Partnerships. When separate programs plan activities to bring participants together, the programs have formed a **partnership**. Partnerships may be formed between early childhood and adult day care programs. Activities may take place in either facility. The administration for each program is completely separate. Skilled staff from each program work together to plan and conduct intergenerational activities.

Integrated Services. When programs simultaneously care for young children and older adults, they have **integrated services**. The services for all participants are housed in the same

Intergenerational Interactions

Sharing Oral Histories

When older adults talk about events that have happened during their lives, everyone benefits. Children gain an appreciation for the way life was before CDs, dishwashers, and the Internet. At the same time, older adults get a chance to talk to an interested audience. Oral histories can be shared in various ways, such as written reports, poetry, dance, music, theater, murals, quilts, and drawings. The following programs help educate children and teens, while allowing older adults to revisit past times.

- **The World War II Veterans Project** at the *Brookdale Center on Aging* introduces high school and college students to WWII veterans. The program is designed to help students understand the war era from both the military and home front perspectives.

- **The Intergenerational Oral History Program**, sponsored by the *Institute for Global Education & Service Learning*, can be used for in-school and after-school programs. Students partner with older adults in their communities to learn how to research, conduct interviews, and write biographies. Once students make contact with the older adults, they often form relationships that extend beyond the oral history project.

- **Latino Legacy: A Community Oral History Project** helps Denver Public School students gain an understanding of their community from older adults who have lived their lives in the area. This project also helps them gain an ethnic perspective on historical events.

Students use audio and video equipment to record oral history interviews with older adults. From the tapes, students write, proofread, edit, and publish oral histories.

- **The Bay Creek Oral History Project** included people ages 12 to 95. Sponsored by the *Bay Creek Neighborhood Association*, this Wisconsin-based project recorded the living history of the area. Individual and group interview sessions, photos, and music from various eras were included in a one-hour videotape. Upon completion, all participants received a copy of the tape.

Follow-Up

Conduct an oral history with an older adult in your area. First, contact an older adult and set up a time for the interview. Prior to the interview, ask the older adult to gather old photos, music, and articles to be shared with you or your class. Write a report on the older adult's history and share it with your class. Be sure to give a copy of the report to the older adult you interviewed.

FIG. 16-2. Children gain an increased sense of self-esteem from interacting with caring older adults. What are some other ways that children benefit from these relationships?

Support Services

Support services are programs that provide interaction between two or more groups for a specific cause. These programs provide rewarding experiences that motivate the growth and development of all involved. Support services for intergenerational programs include:

- **Intergenerational mentoring.** Older adults can serve as mentors to children (ages five to eighteen) in various types of projects, such as music and art.

- **Call-a-friend project.** Children (ages five to eighteen) can serve as telephone pals to older adults who are homebound and who could benefit from frequent telephone calls. On the other hand, older adults can serve as telephone pals to children, helping them with reading or homework over the telephone.

Networking Services

Networking services help intergenerational programs cut down on the duplication of projects and services that are often offered by other community agencies. This uses fewer community resources. Also, networking provides an opportunity for neighbors to come together to work on a common project. The project can bring diverse groups of people together.

Section **16-1** Knowledge Check

1. What is intergenerational care?
2. How does intergenerational care differ from other forms of early childhood and older adult care?
3. Contrast support services and networking services.

Mini-Lab

Create a list of questions to ask an older adult in an intergenerational care program. Using the questions for reference, interview an older adult about his or her experiences. What does she like or dislike about intergenerational care? What does he see as the benefits and drawbacks?

Section 16-2

Managing Intergenerational Programs

- Describe the staffing needs of intergenerational programs.
- Explain the qualifications and training guidelines for successful intergenerational staff.
- Describe an effective program schedule.
- Summarize how intergenerational activities are planned.
- List appropriate intergenerational activities.

KEY TERMS

intergenerational coordinator

cross-training

proactive

Programs that meet the dual needs of children and older adults require special knowledge, skill, and attention to detail. The following key program features should be considered when planning intergenerational care programs.

Staffing Intergenerational Programs

The staffing of an intergenerational program will vary depending on the program type. Intergenerational partnerships have a separate staff for each program who work together to plan and implement activities. Staffing for child care programs must comply with state regulations that apply to early childhood program licensing laws. Staffing for older adult programs complies with state adult day care service or older adult living facilities laws. In both cases, laws specify minimum requirements for staff-to-client ratio. In some intergenerational programs, there is one trained staff person that specifically plans, coordinates, and leads activities for children and older adults. This person is referred to as an **intergenerational coordinator**. In addition to this coordinator, programs may also employ nurses, occupational therapists, or other specialized professionals.

Staff Qualifications & Training

In intergenerational partnerships, each program's staff meets the needs of a specific age group, either young children or older adults. Individual state licensing laws identify staff qualification and training requirements for staff of each type of care. See Fig. 16-3.

FIG. 16-3. **Intergenerational staff members must meet the state licensing laws that apply to both early childhood and older adult care.** Why is this an important requirement?

Scheduling Intergenerational Programs

Schedules for intergenerational programs must meet all participants' developmental needs. Balanced schedules give ample time for activities, but must also allow for daily routines that are a necessary part of providing quality care. Keep the following in mind when creating intergenerational care schedules:

* Arrivals and departures should foster communication between families and staff.
* The pace of the day should be leisurely.
* Transition times should provide adequate time for participants to move to other activities.
* Participants should be able to choose to participate in a variety of activities.
* Participants should be able to choose solitary, small-group, or large-group activities.
* Daily routines should include time for group meetings, meal service, and naps or rest time.
* Flexibility should be built in for medication schedules and therapeutic appointments.
* Plan for formal and spontaneous interactions, such as outdoor time for older adults corresponding with the outside play time for children.

Some states have licensing laws that apply to either early childhood programs or adult care programs that sponsor intergenerational activities. Child care or adult care staff may have to learn specific ways to encourage relationships between the young and old.

Integrated service programs must meet the state licensing laws that apply to both early childhood care and older adult care. Such programs employ some staff members that specialize in providing care for a specific age group. However, all staff must receive **cross-training** about the needs and development of younger and older age groups. Training should be ongoing and offer opportunities for staff feedback and team building. All staff would need to know:

* Early childhood development and older adult development.
* How to support brain development and function across the lifespan.
* How to plan activities that encourage development and interactions across all age groups.

Scheduling Activities

Intergenerational activities should occur often. Frequent interactions allow sincere and caring relationships to develop between young and old. These activities should be co-planned and based on staff and participant feedback to be rewarding for all. The co-planning should include staff who can plan developmentally appropriate activities for both children and older adults.

Depending on a program's goals and philosophy, the frequency of activities will vary from daily to monthly. However, integrated programs often plan two or more intergenerational activities per day. Those interactions depend on the interest and choices of the participants.

Special Considerations

Before engaging in intergenerational activities, all participants should be oriented to the program to help them feel comfortable in the environment. Preparations can be in the form of discussions about the other age groups, sensitivity training for children about issues facing older adults, and icebreaker activities.

The program site must be prepared to accommodate disabled participants. The Americans with Disabilities Act requires all public facilities to make provisions for persons who have physical disabilities and vision or hearing loss.

Motor Skills and Capabilities. Program staff members plan activities that can be adapted to a wide variety of client skills and abilities. Planning adaptable activities requires creative problem-solving skills. Activity equipment and tools must be designed so that clients of varying abilities can use them. See Fig. 16-4.

Mobility Equipment Usage. How clients move around will affect how activities can be implemented and where they can be conducted. Facilities should be free of trip hazards for those using walkers or crutches. Traffic pathways must be wide enough for wheelchairs. Activity and meal-service tables must accommodate clients' mobility equipment.

Special Needs of Children. Whenever activities are planned, the unique needs of every child in a group must be taken into account. Based on the nature of the special needs, staff must ensure that all children can be included in safe and meaningful ways.

Special Needs of Older Adults. Older adults' needs may not be any different from the average person's. However, if an older adult has physical limitations, accommodations should be

FIG. 16-4. **Accommodations should be made to meet the needs of both generations when planning intergenerational activities.** What accommodations might need to be made for children and older adults?

made. Considerations should be made to have adequate lighting; chairs should be firm and at an acceptable height.

Staff-to-Client Ratio. State licensing laws often require staff members who supervise a specific group of children to remain present during all intergenerational activities. State laws also require programs to maintain specific staff-to-client ratios during intergenerational activities. These ratios vary from state to state.

Intergenerational Activities

There are a wide variety of activities children and older adults enjoy together. Some may take just a few minutes, such as watching fish in an

FIG. 16-5. Spending time together outdoors leads to additional learning on the part of the generations. How can children and older adults benefit from a walk in the park?

aquarium. Others activities, such as art projects, may take 30 minutes or longer. The amount of time participants spend in activities varies according to their abilities, personal interest, and attention span. Activities may be planned for small groups or one-to-one. Following are a variety of activities planned in good intergenerational care programs.

Storytelling. Storytelling helps develop the language skills of both young and old. Such activities can take many forms. Older adults can tell traditional stories, folk tales, or stories from their personal lives. They can read books to children, or they can listen to audiotapes with them. Puppetry, dress-up play, dollhouse play, nursery rhymes, or finger plays are all activities that allow participants to share ideas and develop a love of language and reading.

Show and Tell. Group gatherings set the stage for conversations between old and young. Children usually sit in a circle on the floor dur-

ing such gatherings. If their muscles are flexible enough, some older adults sit on the floor with them. However, most adults sit in a circle behind the children in more comfortable seating. During group gatherings, children love to share treasures from home. Older adults often like to share collections or examples of their hobbies. Sharing across the generations builds strong attachments and true friendships.

Taking Walks Together. Taking leisurely walks together allows opportunities for all kinds of learning. Local wildlife, such as birds, can be watched. Parks can be investigated. See Fig. 16-5.

Field Trips. Community connections are encouraged during field trips. Older adults offer extra hands to keep young children safe. They also can help children understand field trip experiences better. A library, museum, fire station, or post office can be overwhelming for some children. An older adult can give the children guidance and answer their questions. Figure 16-6 lists many other ways older adults and young children can spend time together.

FIG. 16-7. Some older adults may choose to participate in quiet activities while children nap during intergenerational programs.

FIG. 16-6.

ACTIVITIES FOR ALL AGES

Age Groups	Activities	
Infants & Toddlers with Older Adults	• Feeding • Holding • Rocking	• Reading • Playing with Puppets or Stuffed Toys
Preschoolers with Older Adults	• Reading and Writing • Arts and Crafts • Computer Play • Puppetry • Dramatic Play • Music and Singing • Woodworking	• Hobby Sharing • Snacks and Mealtimes • Special Celebrations • Games • Blocks and Vehicle Play • Special Visitors
K-3 with Older Adults	• Arts and Crafts • Music • Dance • Physical Fitness • Writing Stories • Pen Pals • Cooking and Nutrition	• Birthday Celebrations • Memory Kits • Show and Tell • Hand Massage • Living Histories • Exploring Cultural/Family Traditions

Meals. Some programs have children and adults eating together daily. Other programs rotate a few children from a classroom each day to eat with older adults in a cafeteria. Still other programs have adults and children eat in separate places and at different times. Whatever the program decides, it is important that older adults have the choice of eating alone or with only older peers when they desire.

Naps and Rest Time. Naps and rest time vary depending on program location. If an intergenerational program offers 24-hour nursing home care, participants may be able to go rest whenever they feel the need. In daytime programs, naps and rest times are usually scheduled, with children and adults resting in separate areas. See Fig. 16-7.

Exercise. Casual exercise, such as walking or gardening, often takes place with children and older adults together. However, more strenuous adult exercise that requires exercise equipment takes place away from children. This ensures privacy for older adults and keeps children safe.

Medical and Therapeutic Treatment. Whether given to a child or older adult, major medical or therapeutic treatments are provided in private rooms or areas. Such treatment might include physical therapy to help a participant regain motor control after a stroke.

Evaluating Intergenerational Programs

Quality counts in any program. The foundation of quality includes a written statement of program goals and philosophy. Meeting relevant licensing laws is also important. The following items are important to examine when evaluating a program's quality:

- Written family permission for loved ones to participate in intergenerational activities.
- Health screening results are maintained for all participants and staff.

- Adequate supervision is provided at all times.
- Well-trained staff that meets the needs of all participants.
- Daily schedules that meet the needs of all participants.
- Written activity plans available for families to review.
- Good sanitation practices that limit the spread of illness.
- The facility's space meets the abilities and developmental needs of children and older adults. See Fig. 16-8.

Evaluation Methods

An effective intergenerational program is constantly evaluating itself. These regular evaluations should be simple and easy to conduct. See Chapter 7 for more information on evaluation. Standard evaluation forms include:

- **Checklist.** A form that lists all compliance requirements for the program site. Space should be provided for the date, the category, and any comments.
- **Daily journals.** A daily record that includes information about daily activities.
- **Random survey.** Sent to participants and agencies, random surveys ask for feedback on services rendered at the center.
- **Focus groups.** Children and older adults give their feedback on the activities through a group interview.

Supervising Intergenerational Programs

The supervisor of intergenerational programs must have multiple skills, including a knowledge of child and adult development, in order to carry out several functions. The supervisor must be able to manage people. This involves knowing the needs of people and how to motivate them while maintaining a positive attitude.

FIG. 16-8. Evaluating the quality of a program is essential for the family members of the program participants. What characteristics indicate program quality?

Also, he or she must have strong leadership skills, including effective communication and knowing how to take disciplinary action without causing mental distress to another person.

Effective supervisors must be **proactive**, which means being a problem solver and knowing how to continue to develop the program for participants. When working with and for people in various age groups, the leader must have a high-performance team to satisfy the different age ranges as well as personalities. The whole care team must be involved in the decision-

Section 16-2 • Managing Intergenerational Programs 399

making process as it relates to planning, implementing, and evaluating effective intergenerational programs. The supervisor's responsibilities include:

- Recruiting, hiring, and orienting staff, including activity leaders and volunteers.
- Conducting meetings, training staff, and giving clear directions. See Fig. 16-9.
- Working with youth, older adults, and staff to design and implement the program.
- Providing links to the community.
- Activating advisory committees that include a diverse group representative of all participants and the community.
- Coordinating administrative details, such as payroll, ordering supplies, invoicing, and data collection for state and federal reports.
- Providing leadership to staff.
- Conducting ongoing evaluations.

Successful intergenerational programs allow for both freedom and flexibility. There must be

FIG. 16-9. Hiring qualified staff is just one of the responsibilities of an effective intergenerational program supervisor. What other responsibilities are required of the program supervisor?

clear, formal agreements with staff, volunteers, and community partners. Staff members must have a proper orientation about the center and its services. Paid staff and volunteers will be loyal if they feel that they are needed. It is very important that they are involved in planning activities and are recognized for their dedication and service.

Section 16-2 Knowledge Check

1. What are the specific staffing needs for an intergenerational program?
2. What consideration must be made for older adults in intergenerational programs?
3. What skills must a supervisor have in order for an intergenerational program to be successful?

Mini-Lab

Using print and Internet resources, investigate and give examples of goals and objectives for intergenerational programs.

Chapter **16**
Review & Activities

Section Summaries

16-1 Intergenerational care has program goals and philosophy.

16-1 There are different types of intergenerational programs.

16-1 Children and adults benefit from intergenerational activities in many ways.

16-2 Intergenerational programs have unique staffing needs.

16-2 Cross-training is important for intergenerational care staff.

16-2 The supervisor of an intergenerational program must have multiple skills.

16-2 Staff members working in intergenerational centers must have training in both gerontology and child development.

Check Your Knowledge

1. What is intergenerational care?
2. How do children benefit from intergenerational programs?
3. How do older adults benefit from intergenerational programs?
4. What is meant by cross-training for intergenerational care staff?
5. What should be considered when developing an intergenerational care schedule?
6. List five types of activities old and young can do together.
7. How should intergenerational care programs be evaluated?
8. What is an intergenerational coordinator?
9. What skills are needed to work in an intergenerational care program?

Chapter **16** Review & Activities

Thinking Critically

1. Analyze which type of intergenerational program would suit your interests, skills, and abilities. Why?
2. Who do you think benefits more from intergenerational care—the children or the older adults? Why?

Practical Applications

1. **Research.** Research the support services for intergenerational programs in your area. Put together an information sheet for older adults in your community.

2. **Network Proposal.** Suggest three opportunities for networking services for children and older adults in your community. Write a one-page proposal describing your networking idea.

3. **Certification Requirements.** Research staffing and certification requirements for adult care and child care in your state. Write a one-page paper describing how requirements in your state would affect staffing an intergenerational care program. Analyze conflicting requirements and possible barriers to intergenerational programs.

4. **Activity Plans.** Create and implement an appropriate intergenerational activity. Evaluate the effectiveness of your activity upon completion.

5. **Program Evaluations.** Investigate and compare various methods of evaluation used in intergenerational programs. Share the results with your class.

Building Your PORTFOLIO

Building Intergenerational Skills & Abilities

Working in an intergenerational care program requires special skills and abilities. By learning how intergenerational care programs work, you will be increasing your employment possibilities and developing your leadership skills as well.

Step 1: Develop a plan for an oral history project that could be carried out in your community. Share your plan with a local historian. Ask for suggestions to improve your plan. Use the suggestions to revise your plan. Include your revised plan in your portfolio.

Step 2: Plan an intergenerational activity. Show the activity to someone who works with an intergenerational program or with children and older adults. What suggestions does this person have for improving the activity? If possible, carry out the activity. Include a copy of the activity and a summary of the results in your portfolio.

Step 3: Develop a checklist or survey for evaluating the effectiveness of an intergenerational program. Show the evaluation instrument to your teacher or to an intergenerational care program director for suggestions. Revise the instrument and include a copy in your portfolio.

Chapter 17

Family Involvement in Care

Section 17-1
Services & Referrals

Section 17-2
Legal Issues

Section 17-3
Family Care Management

Section 17-1

Services & Referrals

OBJECTIVES

- Explain how family involvement helps participants.
- Explain an open door policy.
- Identify needs and opportunities for parental or family involvement in the child or older adult care setting.
- Explain types of family referrals.
- Determine appropriate ways to make necessary and useful service referrals.

KEY TERMS

open door policy
support groups
referrals
community service directory

Good relationships with families help early childhood and adult care providers give high quality care. Information family members share allows care providers to appropriately meet the needs of all participants. Family members should be involved in planning, applying, and evaluating services that dependent family members need. You, as a care provider, should involve family members in the total services that you provide. This section will explore ways to build good partnerships between families and staff.

Family Involvement in Early Childhood Centers

The first step in building good partnerships with participants' families is to welcome them warmly. Frequent, positive interactions help build supportive relationships. This makes communication easier. Meeting the participants' needs is a team effort, and family members are critical team members.

Family members need to feel included in every area of the early childhood operation. In many cases, family members want to be involved, but they may not know how to do so. Or the staff may not know how to involve them. When care providers practice effective communication techniques that promote parental involvement, they encourage family members to use their knowledge and skills in the program. Family members can serve in many areas of early childhood programs. For example, they may provide a service for an activity or share information that is helpful to the staff.

Early Childhood Open Door Policy

An **open door policy** means that all family members approved by the child's legal guardian can visit the program anytime. Open door policies allow families to visit the center without special permission.

This kind of policy builds trust. An open door policy encourages families to visit often. It also gives them many chances to be active in program activities. During visits, family members are better able to check on service quality. An open door policy reassures families that programs have nothing to hide. See Fig. 17-1.

Family Involvement Opportunities

Since every family is different, programs plan various ways for families to be involved. Families can be involved in child and adult day centers according to their own interests and schedules. Here are some ways to include families in program services.

- **Conferences and scheduled meetings.** Once or twice a year, care providers schedule

FIG. 17-1. Trust is built when families are encouraged to drop in at the early childhood center at any time of the day. How do open door policies benefit early childhood centers and the families that use them?

Security Systems. For safety and to prevent children and older adults from wandering, many program facilities remain locked at all times. For instance, some programs have a computerized security system. Families gain entrance to the facility by entering a code into a keyboard. Other programs ask families to ring a doorbell so staff members can let them in the door. Both systems work well as long as approved family members can enter the facility at any time.

a 30- to 60-minute visit with parents to privately discuss children's development and behavior. This time is ideal for making decisions together on the care and guidance of each child. Likewise, meetings may be scheduled with the family of older adults to discuss the older adult's needs.

- **Family member chaperones on field trips.** Programs can almost always use extra hands when taking children on field trips. Family members can share the field trip experience with each other and with their children.

- **Sibling and family member visits.** Family members often feel better knowing where their loved ones are. Allowing siblings and other family members to visit builds a sense of community for everyone.

- **Family night events.** Many family members work during the day, so they need nighttime chances for program involvement. Potluck meals allow families to get to know one another and share their unique cultural foods. In addition, programs may host magicians, storytellers, or musicians for a fun way to share in program activities. See Fig. 17-2.

- **Weekend family events.** Many programs like to bring families together to explore the community. Weekend events held at zoos, family theaters, or museums are great group events.

- **Activity volunteers.** Volunteers are needed to assist in planning and running activities on a daily basis. Family volunteers can substitute for staff members at older adult facilities. This gives families time to see what types of activities are appropriate for their loved one's age and abilities.

- **Advisory board involvement.** Family members are more supportive of programs that give them a say in how the programs run. Having families serve on early childhood and older adult advisory boards allows them to influence program quality. They also can offer specialized help, such as advice on managing program finances.

- **Committee involvement.** Programs form committees to handle specific projects. For instance, some programs form a committee to plan play yard improvements or a fundraiser.

- **Support groups.** People with similar needs can often help each other by sharing information or advice. Some programs create **support groups** for this purpose. Support groups meet regularly to discuss common concerns and needs. For instance, support groups may exist for single parents, for grandparents raising grandchildren, or for parents raising children with special needs.

Referring Families to Services

Many families need services beyond those offered by early childhood programs. Staff well informed of community services can connect families to the assistance they need. This is called providing **referrals**. Staff members must be aware of the participants' needs and requests in order to make helpful referrals.

Types of Referrals

Staff members make referrals after identifying specific needs or in response to a family question. Referrals are often made to those who specialize in specific types of care, such as pediatricians or speech therapists. The following are typical referrals made by care providers:

- **Nutrition education.** Referrals to nutrition education programs can help promote good health. In some cases, referrals are made for problems, such as under nourishment, obesity, or eating problems. See Fig. 17-3.

- **Family therapy.** When families are under stress, they can benefit from family therapy. Referrals for family therapy may be made in

FIG. 17-2. Family night activities involve the care providers along with the children and all of their family members. Why are family night activities beneficial for all involved?

FIG. 17-3. **Supporting the total health of the children may include referring families to a nutrition education program. Maintaining healthful eating habits at home is a continuation of care outside the center.**

Family Involvement in Older Adult Care

Family members of older adults in care programs often volunteer at the care facility. Older adults who want to keep active identify jobs for which they are well suited. They tend to be dedicated to helping those who are not able to help themselves. For example, if a man who has had a stroke has physical therapy at an adult care program, his wife can assist him or serve in other areas. If a husband whose wife is suffering from Alzheimer's disease feels the need for extra support, he might start a support group for family members of loved ones with Alzheimer's.

response to a concern about suspected neglect or abuse. Families may need extra help in learning how to solve conflict without violence.

• **Financial assistance.** Families with limited income, or those who experience a job loss, may require income assistance. Program staff can refer these families to financial assistance programs. For instance, many states provide monetary help to low-income families to help pay the cost of quality child care.

• **Child development services.** If children have delayed development, they may benefit from extra help. For instance, a physical therapist can help a child with delayed motor skills to develop muscle strength and motor coordination appropriate for his or her age.

• **Medical referrals.** Families often need help with finding medical care. A family may need a referral for required immunizations. Parents of a child who has trouble listening and following directions may be referred to a hearing specialist. See Fig. 17-4.

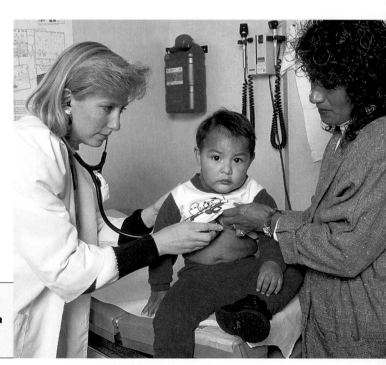

FIG. 17-4. **A center director may refer a family to a health care professional when a child has a continuing health problem.**

Intergenerational *Interactions*

Family Night Activities

With the demands of school, homework, and after-school activities, it is sometimes easy to lose track of what other members of your family are doing. When you set aside some time each week for family night activities, it gives you a chance to regroup, have fun, and talk. The following are just a few family night activities that you may want to try. Do not forget to include the older adults in your life.

- **Plan a Picnic.** If weather allows, picnics can be a great way to enjoy time together outdoors. However, picnics don't have to take place outside. Make some sandwiches. Grab a bag of chips. Lay a blanket out on the living room floor.

- **Solve a Puzzle.** Jigsaw puzzles are fun for one, but even more fun for a group of people. Puzzles give everyone a chance to help solve the picture.

- **Bake Cookies.** Get your favorite recipe and mix up a batch of fun and cookies. When everyone helps, the treats taste even sweeter.

- **Help the Needy.** Whether you volunteer at a homeless shelter or help an older neighbor rake leaves, helping the needy is a great way to feel good about yourself and your family.

- **Ride Bikes or Take a Walk.** Exercising together gives you a chance to talk about what's going on in your lives and get in shape.

- **Make Sundaes.** Select your favorite ice cream and pile on the toppings. Share your sundaes to see who made the best one.

- **Make Pizza.** Whether you purchase the crust or make it from scratch, when everyone adds their favorite topping, you're sure to bake up a winner.

- **Play a Game.** There are many games that the whole family can play. Pick one and have fun.

- **Make a Time Capsule.** Each member of the family, old and young alike, can select an item that will remind him or her of this period in time. Bury the capsule in your yard, or hide it in the back of the closet. Dig it up in five or ten years and enjoy the memories.

Follow-Up

See how many more fun family activities you can add to the list. Tell your classmates what types of activities you would like to do with your family or the older adults in your life.

In adult day programs, there are many chances for family-member involvement. Volunteers can:

- Assist in planning and running daily activities.
- Serve on an advisory committee or advisory board for the program.
- Sponsor specific events, such as an afternoon of singing or playing games.
- Lead family support groups for family care providers. See Fig. 17-5.

Older Adult Care Open Door Policy

Most older adult day centers have open door policies and welcome family participation. Neighborhood residents are also welcome. Many times family members want to make a surprise visit to see the daily operation and quality of services. Many adult day programs are located in neighborhoods. The area residents see the program as a service to people who live in their neighborhoods.

FIG. 17-5. Family members are welcome to participate in the care of older adults at adult day centers. How does this benefit family members?

Referring Families to Services

Older adults usually attend adult day centers for social or therapeutic reasons. In addition, many of the older adults seek other types of services. Program staff must be aware of the participants' needs and requests and be able to make appropriate referrals.

Types of Referrals

The types of referrals made for older adults include nutrition education, blood pressure follow-up, hearing and vision screenings, and legal advice. These referrals are usually made to a geriatric specialist in the specific area. Professionals who specialize in aging often give the best evaluation for older adult needs.

- **Nutrition education.** With nutrition education, older adults and their families learn to cope with issues associated with physical changes. They also learn to use the Food Guide Pyramid for people age 70 and older.
- **Occupational therapy.** Fitness is a major concern for older adults. Occupational therapists can assess range of motion for older adults and provide specific exercises for mobility limitation, handgrip strength, and memory stimulation. The goal is to help older adults function in their environments.
- **Financial assistance.** Retired people may need financial help, as they often live on a fixed income. Many adult programs provide services to help them adjust to living on a fixed income. Program staff can also help older adults access and manage services for which they are now eligible, such as Medicare, Medicaid, supplemental insurance, and Social Security benefits. See Fig. 17-6.

Community Service Directory

In order to give families timely referrals, many early childhood and adult care programs create a **community service directory**. The

FIG. 17-6. The adult day center can refer its clients to special agencies for assistance with their finances.

directory is a quick reference guide for staff members in making referrals. It consists of a detailed list of helpful referral agencies or organizations. The following details are listed for every service in the directory:

- **Agency description.** The full name of the agency and its specific services are described.

- **Eligibility requirements.** Those who may use an agency's services are listed. Eligibility requirements, such as geographic areas, age ranges, and income levels, are also included.

- **Contact information and application procedure.** An agency telephone number, e-mail address, and fax number are listed. Information on whom to contact and how to apply for services is also provided.

- **Location.** The specific agency address is listed. If the application office and the location where services are provided are different, the address for each is recorded.

- **Cost for services.** Referral agencies vary on how they charge for services. Some bill all people the same; others charge different rates according to a family's income level. Directories list an agency's current costs and information on how charges are made.

Section **17-1** Knowledge Check

1. What is an open door policy?
2. In what ways can families be involved in programs?
3. What are referrals?

Mini-Lab

Locate a program that sponsors a support group in your area. Request permission to observe at the next meeting. Take notes on the meeting. Write a summary of the meeting including: the meeting purpose, who led the meeting, the discussion topics, and ways the support group members participated.

Section **17-2**

Legal Issues

OBJECTIVES

- Identify family involvement in legal issues that apply to early childhood and adult care programs.
- Describe legal enrollment practices.
- Summarize the purpose of complying with laws and regulations.
- Explain how staff should respond to program violations that affect participants and their families.
- Identify legal concerns that many impaired children and older adults encounter.
- Identify the steps family members should take to assist children or older impaired adults.

KEY TERMS

fee agreement
   contract
durable power of
   attorney
advanced directive
living will

Early childhood and adult care programs are subject to many types of laws and regulations, including city, county, state, and federal requirements. It is important for care providers to be aware of the basic legal issues related to family involvement in care and education programs.

Legal Duties for Early Childhood

In order for early childhood programs to operate within the law, program directors and staff must be aware of the legal duties of their positions. This helps ensure that children are better served and are well protected.

Early Childhood Enrollment

From the time of their application to acceptance and ongoing enrollment in the program, laws protect the rights and interests of children and their families. Program staff must keep in mind the following legal issues when performing their duties.

- **Enrollment application legalities.** Each state's licensing laws specify the minimum amount of information to be included in a program's application form. Required information typically includes a child's name, birth date, age, home address, and contact information. The legal parent or guardian must be named along with his or her address and contact information for home and work. Application records include health reports, immunization records, and state required medical tests for communicable diseases, such as tuberculosis. Signed permission forms are usually required from parents or legal guardians if children are to participate in field trips, research studies, or activities that will be photographed or videotaped.

- **Nonbiased enrollment practices.** Programs must offer enrollment services on an equal opportunity basis. Programs that receive government funds cannot reject a potential client for reasons of gender, religion, income, race, or other protected statuses. In addition, the ADA law ensures the enrollment rights of those with special needs. If enrollment ends for any client, programs must provide at least one week's notice and must document suitable reasons for discontinuing enrollment. See Fig. 17-7.

- **Ensuring privacy and confidentiality.** All children and their families have rights to privacy. Information from their files, or about their behavior while in the program, may only be shared with specific supervising staff. Before information about a child can be shared verbally or in writing with nonprogram staff, written permission from a legal parent or guardian must be obtained. A court of law can also require a program to share confidential records.

- **Fee agreement contracts.** In order for families to know what they will need to pay for services, programs develop **fee agreement contracts.** The written contract states the days and hours of a child's attendance, costs for services, and payment procedures. These contracts also specify consequences if bills are paid late. Programs keep the signed fee agreement in enrollment files.

Compliance with Laws

Protecting the legal rights of participants and their families requires daily staff attention. When employed in an early childhood program,

FIG. 17-7. **The ADA law ensures enrollment rights to make sure that children with special needs have equal access to care.** Investigate other requirements of the ADA law in regard to caring for children with special needs.

it will be your legal responsibility to respond if laws are being ignored or incorrectly followed.

First, decide if you can take corrective action on your own. If you cannot solve violations on your own, alert your supervisor. Verbally inform him or her and then provide your concerns in writing. Be clear and specific about the problem and state why it raises concerns. Work cooperatively with the staff to solve problems.

If you have continuing concerns about unresolved problems, you are ethically required to report them to the proper legal authorities. The following violations would require reporting:

- Failure to maintain legal records or their confidentiality. Illegal financial practices, such as fraud.

- Biased, discriminatory practices.

- Licensing and accreditation violations.

- Health, safety, and fire code violations. See Fig. 17-8.

- Suspected abuse and neglect.

FIG. 17-8. Staff members can make some corrective actions themselves; however, law violations must be reported to their supervisors.
What is the procedure for reporting a violation?

Legal Duties of Adult Care Providers

As they age, many people face legal concerns, such as accessing bank accounts or determining durable power of attorney. When people become impaired, they may not be able to carry out some of these tasks. They will need to have their adult children, another family member, or other trusted adult act on their behalf. The adult day program should have some knowledge of older adults' situations. This way they can assist participants and families and make effective referrals. The family members should inform the administration of an older adult day program about who can act on behalf of an impaired older adult. Some of the legal concerns that families should consider include:

Bank Account Access. When bank account access is necessary for the care of an older adult, the older adult can make an adult child or other family member a joint owner of the bank account(s). This allows the family member to act for the older person in an emergency. The older adult can also appoint that person as joint renter or agent for his or her safe deposit box.

Durable Power of Attorney. A **durable power of attorney** is a document that gives one or more people the authority to handle finances, property, or other personal matters in case a dependent family member becomes unable to take care of his or her business. Without this document, the court will need to appoint an adult child or family member to manage the dependent family member's affairs.

Advanced Directives. Many older adults choose to prepare an **advanced directive**. This document states how an individual wants his or her medical decisions made if he or she becomes unable to make decisions. Note that advanced directives are not required. If prepared, they can be canceled at any time. Before deciding to prepare this document, an older adult should discuss his or her medical care desires with a doctor and an attorney. There are two common types of advanced directives: a living will and a durable power of attorney for health care.

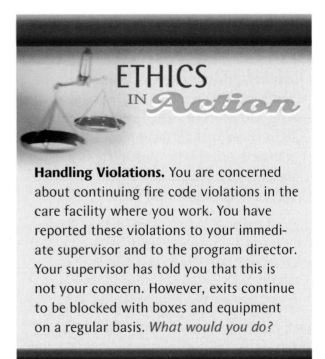

ETHICS IN *Action*

Handling Violations. You are concerned about continuing fire code violations in the care facility where you work. You have reported these violations to your immediate supervisor and to the program director. Your supervisor has told you that this is not your concern. However, exits continue to be blocked with boxes and equipment on a regular basis. *What would you do?*

- **Living will.** This document, a **living will**, allows a person to state the type of medical care he or she wants (or does not want) if unable to make a decision while still alive.
- **Durable power of attorney for health care.** This is a signed, dated, and witnessed document that names another person—such as a spouse, adult child, or close friend—to make medical decisions for a person should he or she become unable to make them. See Fig. 17-9.

Legal Assistance Programs. Due to the growing number of legal issues impacting older adults, some adult day care programs offer legal aid services. These services are usually coordinated with other legal aid services or organizations. Attorneys who understand the laws affecting older adults are able to serve them. Elder law services include:

- Preservation or transfer of assets seeking to avoid spousal impoverishment when one spouse enters a nursing home.
- Medicare, Medicaid, and public aid claims and appeals.
- Social Security and disability claims and appeals and supplemental, and long-term health insurance issues.
- Disability planning, including preparation of durable powers of attorney and living wills, financial management, and guardianship.
- Probate, or proving a will is valid in court.
- Long-term care placements in nursing homes and life-care communities.
- Elder abuse and fraud recovery.
- The Patient's Bill of Rights.

An elder law attorney who understands the aging process and its challenges can better help a client evaluate his or her needs. An elder law attorney is often aware of social support systems that can help older adult clients.

Adult Care Administration

The adult day care program's administration must make certain that the program follows all state standards for operation. This is especially important for programs that depend on Medicaid reimbursement for services provided.

Employment & Enrollment Practices

An agency that sponsors an adult day care program outlines the employment and enrollment practices. For example, each state has specific standards for older adult day services. Each program has to follow the certification standards in order to provide services and especially for cost reimbursement. Older adult care activity programs, or senior centers, do not have these strict guidelines. These programs provide recreational and leisure activities and are mostly operated by volunteers. However, they do adhere to fire department codes and safety practices set by OSHA.

FIG. 17-9. A durable power of attorney for health care names another person to make medical decisions for someone who is unable to make them.

FIG. 17-10.

INFORMATION FOR INDIVIDUAL RECORDS

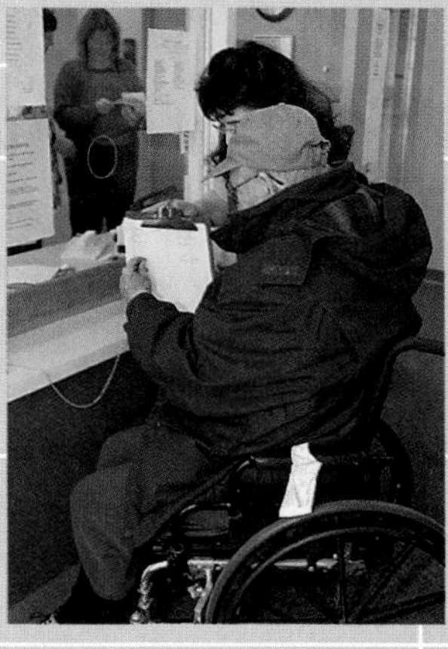

Information	Description
Fact Sheet	Name; address; telephone number and directions to the home; date of birth; emergency contact information; information about the home situation; and date of adult day care admission and initial arrangements regarding attendance and payment.
Medical	Physician's initial physical examination report including any later recommendations for care, including diet, medication, and limitation on activities.
Accident/Illness	Record any accident or illness that occurs at the center including date, what was done by staff, or where the person was sent for treatment.
Attendance	Record the person's attendance and the activities in which he or she participates. Note group leader comments on person's behavior and progress monthly.
Home Situation and Referrals	Record significant information about the person's home situation that may have a bearing on his or her well-being. Also include referrals to services.

Compliance with Laws

In adult day care programs offering medical and health services, records document what is done for the number of people served and the cost for the services. Everything must be accounted for, including income, free services, equipment, and expenditures. Many of these programs receive Medicare, Medicaid, or insurance reimbursements for which detailed documents are needed.

Information about the range of services provided for each participant is documented. Records are especially important to cases in which care providers must report progress and other details necessary for further treatment. Records should be kept simple. Keep only information that is really useful, such as the type of information shown in Fig. 17-10.

Section 17-2 Knowledge Check

1. Name four legal responsibilities of child and adult care providers.
2. What items must be included in a program's enrollment application?
3. What types of program violations should be reported to authorities?

Mini-Lab

Create a reference sheet of offices responsible for enforcing early childhood and adult care laws and regulations in your area. Include at least the licensing office, health department, and fire marshal's office. Record their office addresses, telephone numbers, fax numbers, and, if applicable, e-mail addresses.

Section *17-3*

Family Care Management

KEY TERMS

family care management
family care manager
daily care plan
interpersonal relationships

Today, family members are recognized as important members of the care-giving team. In most families, there is one person who makes sure that the dependent person gets the services he or she needs.

Family Care Management Basics

Family care management is the process through which family members and service providers work together as a team to manage the care of a dependent family member. The dependent family member is also an active member of the care team. Other members of the care team may include: one or more doctors, dietitians, therapists, or social workers. Family members have always played a major role in planning and obtaining services for dependent family members. However, they have not always been given credit for their hard work on the care team.

The **family care manager** is the person who best understands the wants and needs of the dependent family member and speaks on his or her behalf. The family care manager plans, coordinates, and evaluates services with the care team for the dependent family member. When selecting an adult day program, the dependent family member and the family care manager work closely with the program staff to determine the appropriate daily care plan. A **daily care plan** gives a description of the person and his or her care needs. It outlines goals to provide as much independence as possible for the person needing care. For example, the daily care plan will describe ways for an older adult to meet the activities of daily living (ADLs) and instrumental activities of daily living (IADLs). Specific needs—such as medical care or speech therapy—may also be part of the daily care plan.

Family Care Manager Roles

The role of family care manager is to help determine the care needs for the dependent family member. The family care manager makes regular visits to the adult day program to gain and offer helpful information for carrying out the care plan goals. These goals can be met both at home and through the adult day program.

The family care manager can be a resource for the program. As an active member of the care team, family care managers can express the needs of the dependent family members to those who can access services. See Fig. 17-11. Here are some additional roles of the family care manager:

- **Identify resources.** The family care manager best knows the loved one's needs and may be most able to identify resource needs. For example, an older adult may need help with basic activities of daily living, vision or hearing assistance, or mobility.

- **Activate existing resources.** Family care managers persist in getting resources for dependent family members. For example,

FIG. 17-11. **The family care manager plays an active role on the care team.** What information can the family care manager share with the team that will influence the care of dependent family members?

he or she may pursue further medical treatments, Meals-on-Wheels, or home health services. In addition, the family care manager may make sure an older adult receives: monetary benefits, such as Social Security or disability insurance; therapies, such as speech or physical therapy; or equipment needs, such as hearing devices, eye glasses, walkers, or wheelchairs.

- **Network with other groups.** Family care managers network with other outside groups and organizations to obtain specific services. For example, the family care manager might contact the Alzheimer's Association for current research information on the disease or a dialysis clinic for services close to an older adult's home.

- **Coordinate legal and financial affairs.** The family care manager maintains all important legal and financial papers, such as wills, Social Security papers, deeds, and bank accounts.

Interpersonal Family Relationships

It is very important for family members to maintain mutual respect for each other. It is also important that the family care manager and all family members clearly understand the needs of the older person. **Interpersonal relationships** are positive, caring, and respectful relationships. See Fig. 17-12. These relationships involve effective communication and conflict resolution skills. The stress of caring for dependent family members can cause conflicts. Keeping a clear list of duties for the care of dependent family members is essential to reducing conflict among family members who share in the care. Most of the responsibilities fall on the family care manager.

It is helpful for all family members to participate in an organized family support group. Adult day programs usually offer family support groups as part of the services for family members. When family members feel overwhelmed with providing care, it is wise for them to take time out from the care-providing situation.

Assigning Roles

Assigning care roles is a very important task for the family care manager. When each family member takes on a small role in caring for a loved one, the stress of providing care lessens. The family care manager outlines the activity needs of the dependent family member and shares them with other family members. To avoid conflicts, it is a good idea to have a family meeting to discuss the roles each family member can take in caring for the dependent member. For example, one family member may care for the medical needs—such as doctor appointments or picking up prescriptions—while another takes care of transportation needs or social needs. Other tasks may include: preparing meals, house cleaning, doing laundry, mowing the lawn, or shoveling snow. Even children can help provide care for an older adult. After assigning roles, the family care manager gives a copy of the list to all family members. A copy of this list is often given to the adult day program staff to

FIG. 17-12. Close family ties are important for those who care for older adults. Why is a positive attitude important when caring for an older adult family member?

show the type of home support given to the older adult.

In addition to the family, friends can be involved in assisting with care of the older adults. Friends are also key to having a strong care support system.

Section **17-3** Knowledge Check

1. What is family care management?
2. What are the roles of a family care manager?
3. Determine how family members assign roles to carry out tasks for a dependent family member.

Mini-Lab

Working in teams, create a learning situation for a family meeting in which family members come together to outline roles for providing care for an older adult family member. The family care manager will lead the family meeting. Write a summary of your team's plan.

Chapter **17**

Review & Activities

Section Summaries

17-1 An open door policy is essential to including families in programs.

17-1 Human service professionals provide families with many types of referrals.

17-1 A community service directory helps staff make accurate, timely referrals.

17-2 Program staff are required to meet a variety of legal responsibilities.

17-2 Compliance with laws requires daily staff attention.

17-2 Staff must report identified problems to supervisors.

17-2 Unresolved program violations should be reported to legal authorities.

17-3 Family care management involves family members and care providers working together to provide care for dependent family members.

17-3 Family care managers assign caretaking roles to other family members to assist in the care of a dependent family member.

Check Your Knowledge

1. What is an open door policy?
2. In what ways can families be involved in programs?
3. Give examples of appropriate weekend family events for an early childhood program.
4. If a child is underweight, what kind of referral would be suitable for him or her?
5. What is a community service directory?
6. What should be included in a community service directory?
7. Name two types of legal issues related to early childhood family involvement of which staff must be aware.
8. What would be included in a fee agreement contract?
9. Contrast a living will and a durable power of attorney for health care.
10. Summarize the role of the family care manager.

Thinking Critically

1. What are the benefits of family involvement in programs that provide care for children or older adults?
2. Analyze ways to approach a family to suggest referral to a community agency.
3. Draw conclusions about the importance of understanding the legal issues of family involvement in care.
4. Analyze ways to establish healthy relationships with each child's or older adult's family.

Practical Applications

1. **Research Activity.** Research a community agency that serves families of young children or older adults. Obtain the following information about the agency: name, description, eligibility requirements, contact and application procedures, location, and cost for services. If possible, visit the agency to obtain firsthand information about its services.

2. **Observing Laws.** Research a law that must be observed by early childhood or adult care programs in your locale. What are the basic requirements of the law? What are the consequences of failure to observe the law? Write a report outlining your findings.

3. **Event Plans.** Plan an event that would involve the families of young children or older adults. Through this event, implement strategies that enhance cooperation among the center, teacher, community, and family. Describe the event and explain how the families will be involved.

Building Your PORTFOLIO

Developing a Family Involvement Plan

Showing you value family involvement in the program is one way to impress a prospective employer.

Step 1: Develop a year-long monthly schedule of family involvement opportunities that might be provided at an early childhood or adult day program. Gather ideas from program descriptions or interviews with facility directors. Also, get ideas from families of young children or older adults.

Step 2: Develop a community service directory listing services the families of young children or older adults might need. Include each agency's name, description, eligibility requirements, contact and application procedure, location, and cost for services.

Step 3: Interview the director of an early childhood or adult care program to learn more about the laws that affect care facilities. What are the most common legal issues? What are the legal responsibilities of the individual provider? Based on your interview, write a list of legal guidelines for care providers.

Step 4: Ask the director of an early childhood or adult care program or your teacher to evaluate your family involvement plan and make suggestions for improvement. Revise your plan and include it in your portfolio.

Chapter 18
Caring for Infants

Section 18-1
Development & Care

Section 18-2
Managing Infant Programs

Section 18-1

Development & Care

Infancy is often defined as the time between birth and 12 months of age. Like all children, infants progress through developmental stages. The remarkable changes that take place make up the most concentrated period of accelerated growth and development in a person's life. Good health services, sound nutrition, and loving care allow infants to have the best possible start in life.

Prenatal Development

The foundation for lifelong development starts at conception. Once conceived, humans undergo their most rapid period of physical development. Changes that occur during the nine months of pregnancy are referred to as prenatal development. Prenatal development includes three distinct stages: the zygote stage, the embryo stage, and the fetus stage. Figure 18-1 provides important changes that occur during each stage of prenatal development.

As with all life stages, the progress of prenatal development varies slightly from one person to another. Factors that contribute to healthy prenatal and lifelong development include good maternal nutritional and mental health. Adequate exercise, sleep, and added vitamins and minerals allow a pregnant woman to adequately nourish the rapid growth of a child.

There are many factors that can delay, hinder, or interfere with typical prenatal development, including those that are genetic, or inherited. Avoiding risk factors, such as the following, provides children with a good start in life.

- Poor maternal physical condition.
- Malnutrition of the pregnant woman.

FIG. 18-1.

STAGES OF PRENATAL DEVELOPMENT

First Trimester	
Month	**Developmental Characteristics**
First Month (Stage of the Zygote)	• Size of a pinhead at two weeks. • Egg attaches to uterus lining. • Internal organs and circulatory system begin to form. The heart begins to beat. • Small bumps indicate the beginning of arms and legs. 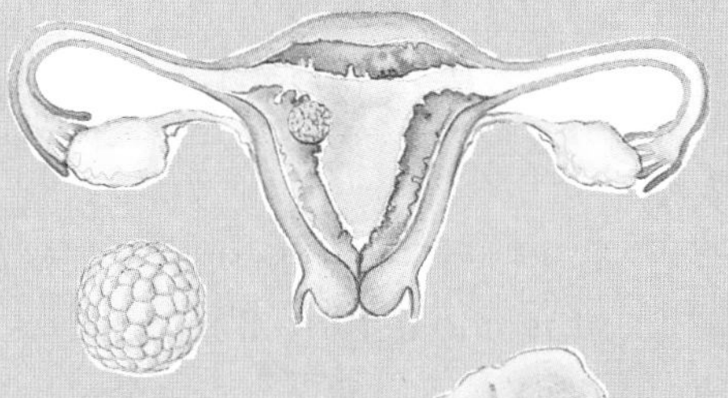
Second Month (Stage of the Embryo)	• About ¼ inch long as month begins. • Face, eyes, ears, and limbs take shape. • Bones begin to form. 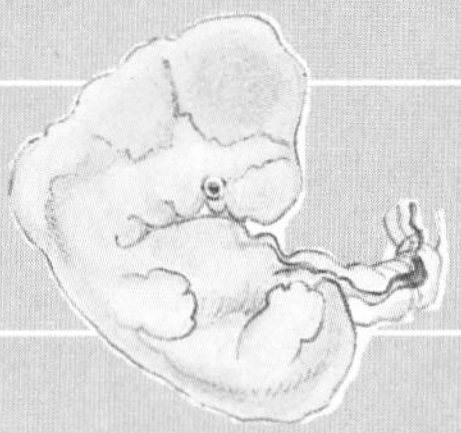
Third Month (Stage of the Fetus Begins)	• About 1 inch long as month begins. • Nostrils, mouth, lips, teeth buds, and eyelids form. • Fingers and toes almost complete. • All organs present, although immature. 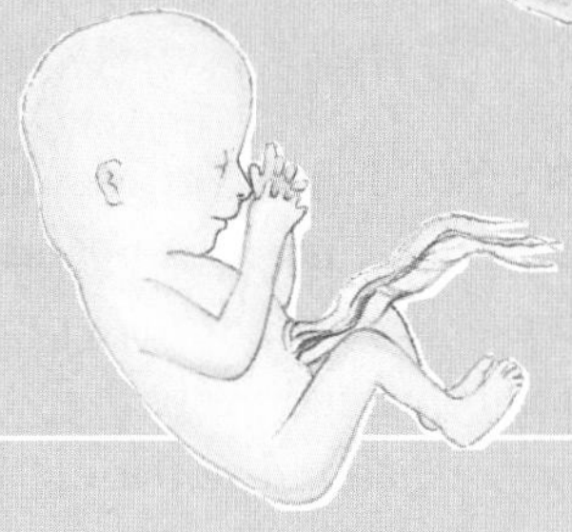

Second Trimester	
Fourth Month	• About 3 inches long, one ounce as month begins. • Can suck its thumb, swallow, hiccup, and move around. • Facial features become clearer.
Fifth Month	• About 6½-7 inches long, about 4-5 ounces as month begins. • Hair, eyelashes, and eyebrows appear. • Teeth continue to develop. • Organs are maturing. • Becomes more active.
Sixth Month	• About 8-10 inches long, about 8-12 ounces as month begins. • Fat deposits under skin, but fetus appears wrinkled. • Breathing movements begin.

STAGES OF PRENATAL DEVELOPMENT (Cont'd.)

Third Trimester		
Month	**Developmental Characteristics**	
Seventh Month	• About 10-12 inches long, about 1½-2 pounds as month begins. • Periods of activity followed by periods of rest and quiet.	
Eighth Month	• About 14-16 inches long, about 2½-3 pounds as month begins. • Weight gain continues rapidly. • May react to loud noises with a reflex jerking action. • Moves into a head-down position.	
Ninth Month	• About 17-18 inches long, 5-6 pounds as month begins. • Weight gain continues until the week before birth. • Skin becomes smooth as fat deposits continue. • Movements decrease as the fetus has less room to move around. • Acquires disease-fighting antibodies from the mother's blood. • Descends into pelvis, ready for birth.	

• Mental health problems of the pregnant woman, including depression or disabling stress.

• Physical injury of the mother during pregnancy.

• Pregnancy during adolescent development.

• Maternal smoking, or exposure to second-hand smoke.

• Drug use, whether medical prescriptions, alcohol, or other drugs.

Early Brain Development

The first year of life is an especially important time for brain development. During this time, the foundation for all future development is formed. As you recall from Chapter 1, the brain coordinates all human growth. Learning pathways are created in the brain when infants are responded to appropriately. Children's brain function develops best in a secure environment. Consistent, calm care providers are most important to a secure environment.

Infancy is a time when the brain is very responsive to positive experiences. Different sensory experiences stimulate the brain. The brain then organizes and makes sense of the world. Interesting and repeated experiences strengthen infants' learning power. An infant's brain is also vulnerable to negative experiences. Physical or emotional harm can interrupt normal brain function. Such harm can delay or limit an infant's learning potential in all developmental areas.

Physical Development

Rapid growth and development require energy. To help sustain them, very young infants sleep up to 17 hours a day and need frequent feedings. Generally, infants weigh between six and ten pounds at birth. They are usually about 20 inches long. By the end of their first year, most infants weigh about 22 pounds and are 30 inches long. Of course, inherited qualities from a mother and father influence this growth.

An infant's head grows rapidly. Open spaces in the bones of the infant's skull, called fontanels, allow for the growth of the brain. The bones of the skull gradually grow together, and the open spaces are usually closed by 18 months of age. At six months, baby teeth begin to appear. By two years of age, all 20 baby teeth are usually present.

FIG. 18-2. **All newborns have involuntary reflexes.** What reflexes are shown here? Why are these reflexes necessary during the early months?

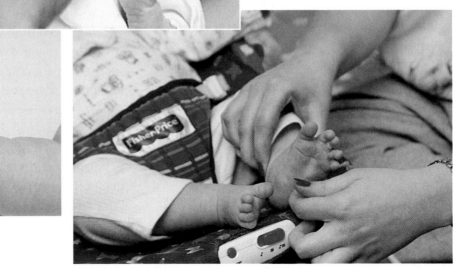

Fontanels. The largest fontanel on an infant's skull is located on the top of the head. It is often called the soft spot. Until the bones of the skull cover the soft spot, the possibility of injury to the brain is present. Although the overlying skin is tough, any sharp or hard blow to the head could cause internal injuries. Care providers need to be especially cautious about protecting an infant's head while the soft spot exists.

All humans are born with **reflexes**, or instinctive, involuntary reactions to a stimulus, such as a noise or touch. Infants have certain reflexes that function during the first months of life. After that, intellectual and physical growth allow for voluntary action. See Fig. 18-2. Infants have the following reflexes:

- **Startle reflex.** The infant throws out the arms and legs in response to a loud sound or sudden movement.

- **Rooting reflex.** The infant turns toward a touch on the cheek or lips and begins to suck.

- **Grasping reflex.** The infant automatically closes a hand when the palm is touched.

- **Babinski reflex.** The toes of the infant fan out when the bottom of the foot is stroked.

- **Other reflexes.** Infants make a walking motion when held up with the feet touching the floor and appear to swim when held horizontally in water.

Sensory Development

At birth, infants are equipped with all of their senses. They can see, hear, taste, feel, and smell. Newborns hear well enough to discern the voices of those who spend the most time with them. Vision is not clear at birth, but it improves within weeks. Soon, infants prefer looking at a human face, or picture of a face, that is held about 12 inches from their eyes. They enjoy brightly colored objects and patterns with contrasting colors. Care providers can place infants under floor mobiles to promote sensory development. Infants also sense differences in taste. They prefer sweet over plain tastes. Within the first two weeks of life, an infant knows the unique scent of its mother. Infants feel differences in texture. In fact, some infants are so sensitive that they cry if dressed in clothing of a texture they dislike.

Motor Development

At birth, infants are completely dependent on others. They cannot lift or hold up their own heads, roll over, sit up, or stand. Physical strength and movement improve quickly, however. Muscular development eventually gives infants mobility, allowing them to move from one place to another. Figure 18-3 lists major motor developments during the first year of life.

As infants progress physically and intellectually, they acquire **perceptual motor skills**—skills that require the coordination of vision, intellect, and movement. Climbing up a step is a perceptual motor skill. The child must see the step, judge the height, and lift his or her hands and knees. A related skill is **eye-hand coordination**—the ability to move the hands and fingers precisely in relation to what is seen. Infants begin to develop eye-hand coordination around three or four months of age. They can see a toy, reach for it, and grasp it successfully. Care providers can influence motor development by encouraging infants to move, reach, and grasp.

FIG. 18-3.

MOTOR DEVELOPMENT DURING INFANCY

Age	Motor Development
Two months	Lifts head and chest when lying on stomach.
Four months	Sits erect in arms of adult; reaches for objects.
Six months	Grasps objects; rolls self over.
Eight months	Thrusts arms and legs out and squirms to push self forward; pulls self up.
Ten months	Crawls on hands and knees; walks with help of adult.
Twelve months	Stands, sometimes walks alone; picks up small objects between thumb and forefinger; begins self-feeding.

Intellectual Development

The work of cognitive theorist Jean Piaget has provided much insight into how children learn to think. He identified four periods that people go through as they develop intellectually from infancy through adulthood. The first one, the sensorimotor period, applies to infants.

Piaget used the term **sensorimotor period** (sents-ree-MOH-tur) to describe the time frame during which infants develop their intellect. During this period, from birth to age two, infants and one-year-olds learn by using their senses and motor abilities to gain information about the world. They learn by touching, tasting, smelling, and hearing. For instance, the principle of cause and effect is learned when an infant sees that pulling a string on a toy will make the toy move. If the child moves forward while pulling the string, the toy follows. This and similar types of learning usually begin between seven and eight months of age.

At around nine months, Piaget found, most children acquire an intellectual ability called **object permanence**. This is the understanding that an object continues to exist even when out of sight. Children discover that although a person or object disappears from view, it will be back. Before object permanence develops, you can cover a child's toy with a scarf and the child's interest shifts to something else. After object permanence develops, the child deliberately removes the scarf to find the toy.

As intellect increases, children begin to analyze, make associations, and form predictions. At one year, for example, an infant can learn that the rattle of keys in the front door lock means that mom or dad has come home. Care providers and the environment greatly influence a child's intellectual development. Care providers ensure that infants have a safe environment with developmentally appropriate materials available to explore.

Language Development

Language plays a large role in developing intellectual abilities. Children understand language long before they can speak it well themselves. By six months of age, children can understand some spoken words, such as "mommy" and "daddy." By one year, children can usually speak several words. By 18 months, two-word sentences are common; by age two, complete sentences can be formed.

Even very young infants benefit when you talk to them. Although they do not understand the words, they soon make **vocalizations**—sounds that imitate adult language. When adults respond, infants begin to learn that their wants and needs can be expressed through language. Eventually, they learn specific ideas. Understandable spoken language is not far behind.

ETHICS IN Action

Developmental Delays. Your observations over a period of weeks have led you to believe that one of the infants in your care is lagging behind others of the same age in motor development. While the other infants are pulling up or crawling, one seems content to lie quietly wherever you place him. He makes no attempt to move on his own. When you express concern to his mother, she reacts angrily and tells you that you are not a doctor and that there is nothing wrong with her child. *What would you do?*

Emotional Development

Infants experience emotions, such as fear, discomfort, and happiness. As children develop, feelings become more specific. Excitement, joy, frustration, and anger are evident. These emotions are much easier to identify and manage after an infant learns language skills.

Bonding & Attachment

Throughout a baby's first year of life, an important emotional development called bonding is taking place. Bonding is forming a strong attachment to, and preference for, a specific person. This is usually a parent or parents. Secondary bonding can take place with other care providers. A sign that bonding has occurred is **attachment behavior**. The infant shows signs of pleasure when a preferred person appears and signs of distress when that person leaves. Infants who smile and gurgle with delight when their care providers enter the room and cry or fuss when these individuals leave are testimony to sound attachment. See Fig. 18-4.

Bonding is necessary for development of good self-esteem. According to theorist Erik Erikson, children develop a sense of trust or mistrust based on the quality of early experiences with care providers. If the needs for food, warmth, and comfort are met, infants will develop a sense of trust. If these needs are not satisfied, they develop a sense of mistrust. They see the world as a threatening and unpredictable place. The earlier children develop trust in others and in their environment, the better their emotional health. Responsive and reliable care providers influence the development of trust. When children experience warmth and caring, they are more likely to be resilient throughout life.

FIG. 18-4. Infants often develop attachment to their secondary care providers at the infant care center. How can this attachment benefit infants and care providers?

Personality Development

Personality development also begins during infancy. Inherited traits form the basis for personality, which is also influenced by experiences with the environment. Reactions from care providers affect personality. Interactions with people and the environment, however, do not completely explain how personality develops.

From birth, every child has a different way of approaching the world. A person's inborn style of reacting to the environment is known as **temperament**. Temperament has a strong impact on personality.

Identifying Temperament. Doctors Stella Chess and Alexander Thomas identified three categories of temperament: easy, slow-to-warm-up, and difficult.

- **Easy children.** Easy children adjust quickly to changes in their routines. They respond to stimulation, tend to be sociable, and smile frequently. They have few problems with eating or sleeping. Their relaxed outlook on life often makes them easy to care for.

- **Slow-to-warm-up children.** Slow-to-warm-up children can also be outgoing and sociable, but they usually need more time to adjust to new people and new situations. Often these children are prematurely labeled as shy. Slow-to-warm-up children require notice of change. They may hesitate to begin new activities. With time and experience, this hesitance lessens. It is important not to force slow-to-warm-up children into any activity they are hesitant to do.

- **Difficult children.** Difficult children can be more challenging, but they are not bad. They require more patience from care providers. Difficult children often have digestive and sleeping problems. They do not adjust well to changes in routine. They can be negative, and they need lots of support when trying something new. Difficult children easily become over-stimulated and frustrated, often causing them to withdraw from contact. These children may have a high activity level. They experience emotions intensely and sometimes unpredictably.

Although no child is completely one temperament or the other, children do exhibit a general pattern of behavior that is consistent with one category more than another. Knowledge of temperament does not allow you to change a child, but it helps you better understand behavior. This will help you to better plan for each child's need for active play, quiet activity, and rest.

Intergenerational *Interactions*

Older Adults Interacting with Young Children

Interactions between older adults and young children may occur in several types of settings. Regardless of the setting, the goals of such programs remain basically the same—to encourage understanding and respect between older adults and young children. Evaluation, orientation, and training are all key to creating successful interactions.

1. **Consider Backgrounds.** Prior to introducing older adults to infants and toddlers, it's important to talk to the older adults about their experience with small children. If older adults are inexperienced or feel uncomfortable around small children, they may be best suited for group interaction instead of one-on-one communication. Check the backgrounds of children. Children with little or no experience around older adults may feel more comfortable in a group setting until they get to know more about older adults.

2. **Evaluate Physical Health.** Even wheelchair users can participate in intergenerational programs. However, it's important to talk with frail or disabled persons to make sure they are interested in taking part. They may be more at ease simply watching others participate in intergenerational activities.

3. **Consider Emotional Health.** Older adults and children with mental or emotional limitations can gain a great deal through intergenerational activities. For instance, depressed individuals or those with low self-esteem gain a sense of self-worth by connecting with others—especially others from different generations. However, in order to ensure the safety of all participants, a doctor should screen people with mental disabilities before they are allowed to participate in intergenerational activities.

4. **Provide Training and Direction.** Prior to introducing young children to older adults, both groups should be prepared. Young children and older adults should be told in advance that another group will be joining them. Children should be told about the physical limitations of the older adults they will meet. Older adults should be reminded about the energy levels of small children.

Follow-Up

Team up with a partner to discuss the four keys to creating a successful intergenerational program. Tell the class which point you believe to be the most important and why.

Social Development

The foundations of social development—the ability to form relationships with others—are laid during infancy. Piaget believed that during the first year of life, children's thinking is **egocentric** (ee-go-SEN-trick). They see everything only from their own point of view. During infancy, for example, children do not play cooperatively with each other. They may show interest in another infant but only as they would another object. They do not perceive the infant as another person. It is impossible for them to understand how anyone else thinks or feels.

It takes several years of social experiences to help children grow beyond egocentrism. Emotional development is linked to this process. Care providers influence children's social development. When infants learn to trust care providers, they learn to value a social relationship. They discover that they can depend on others for assistance. They become secure in their relationships. Positive social skills are further developed when such routines as feeding, diapering, and bathing are pleasant experiences. See Fig. 18-5.

An infant's fear of unfamiliar people, usually expressed by crying, is called **stranger anxiety**.

FIG. 18-5. **A child's temperament strongly influences his or her personality. How can understanding a child's temperament be helpful to care providers?**

It becomes common as object permanence develops, usually around nine months of age. By then, children distinguish between strangers and familiar loved ones.

Children usually grow beyond stranger anxiety by 12 or 15 months of age. Because of this fear, parents are advised to avoid placing children in a new child care setting when they are between the ages of 8 and 15 months.

Section 18-1   Knowledge Check

1. Summarize the stages of prenatal development and factors that influence this development.
2. Explain the influences on the physical, emotional, social, and intellectual development of infants.
3. What is stranger anxiety?

Mini-Lab

Observe the relationship between infants and their care providers at a local program. Look for bonding and interactions during routine care, such as feeding, diaper changing, and playtime. Record incidences of infant attachment behaviors, such as infants smiling.

Section 18-2

Managing Infant Programs

OBJECTIVES

- Describe the responsibilities of infant care providers.
- Plan ways to respond to infant development.
- Identify components of infant programs.
- Suggest ways to communicate effectively with parents.

KEY TERMS

staff turnover
on demand
care provider report
  form
parent report form

Many families today are headed by single parents or dual-earner couples. Seeking outside help with infant care is often a necessity. The result is a great demand for high-quality infant care services. One of this country's biggest challenges is recruiting and training enough talented people to meet the growing need for quality infant care.

Staff Responsibilities

Caring for infants requires a wide variety of skills and personal qualities. Success as an infant care provider starts with understanding the basics of infant development. Care providers must be warm, gentle, and responsive to development. They must be able to relate to and understand infants' needs and feelings. They must understand each child's unique temperament and respect each family's cultural beliefs and traditions.

Attention to Emerging Skills. Good infant care providers take interest in infants' emerging skills. Care providers praise each new accom-

plishment of an infant with enthusiasm. In addition, they are able to spot delays in development that may need extra attention.

Interpreting Infant Cues. Skilled care providers can interpret the cues infants give them. They can distinguish a "hungry" cry from a "change-me" cry and attend to both quickly. Infant cries for help or attention are quickly met with comforting arms and reassuring words.

Observing and Recording Behavior. Infant care providers must be careful and exact about observing and recording behavior. This is time consuming, but necessary for monitoring children's well-being and development.

Management Responsibilities

Infant care requires a surprising amount of paperwork. Detailed records must be maintained daily. This paperwork requires good organizational skills and attention to detail. Activities planned for and conducted with children must be recorded. Copies of communications with fellow staff, parents, or social workers must be maintained in confidential files.

Infant care providers must also manage classroom resources. Regular inspection records and an inventory of equipment and supplies, and their condition, must be maintained. Such tasks remind staff to request additional supplies or to repair or replace broken toys or equipment.

Teams of individuals provide infant care, often with a lead provider and an assistant. In this approach, specific staff are assigned as primary providers of care for individual children. This requires staff members to co-plan, delegate, and share responsibilities with others.

Program Components

Infant care programs must follow rules established by state licensing laws. Infant programs must be well managed to provide quality care.

Infants thrive on adult attention. They also keep care providers very busy. For these reasons, there are fewer children per care provider in an infant care program than in a program for older children. In addition, the maximum number of infants in the group is smaller than with older children. A typical group may have six to eight infants with two or three care providers. State requirements vary. See Fig. 18-6.

To promote bonding and attachment, each child is often assigned one primary care provider to respond to all of the child's basic needs. Managers of infant programs must work hard to limit frequent staff turnover. **Staff turnover** is the rate at which employees leave their jobs, creating the need for hiring new employees. When staff turnover is high, infants do not have a

Floor Safety. Infants spend much time on the floor. To ensure floor safety, care providers should:

- Provide disposable booties for visitors to wear over street shoes to avoid tracking dirt on the floor.
- Vacuum carpeting daily or as needed.
- Routinely inspect floors for sharp objects.
- Store purses and briefcases out of reach.
- Put on electrical outlet protective caps. Keep electrical cords away from play space.
- Make sure all shelving is securely stable, so an infant cannot pull it over.
- Never use space heaters on the floor.

chance to bond with one care provider. Infants need familiar and predictable care. Too much change is upsetting to them and can hinder their emotional and social development.

Infant and preschool programs differ in the way daily routines are managed. In a preschool program, a schedule is set and maintained by the teachers. For instance, all the children eat lunch at a specific time. In infant care, routines should be conducted **on demand**, or according to each child's individual needs. Each requires food, sleep, diapering, and play activities at different times. Infant care providers must be alert for each infant's signals and give proper care.

Infants are especially vulnerable to illness because their immune systems are not fully developed. Their tendency to put items in their mouths increases their chances of illness. Throughout the day, staff members should clean and sanitize toys and equipment and frequently wash their hands and the infants'.

FIG. 18-6. The ratio of care providers to infants is lower than with older children, but may vary from state to state. Why do you think the staff ratios are lower for infants?

Staff & Parent Communication

Establishing a friendly relationship with parents is a must for care providers. Parents and care providers should meet daily to discuss the infant's overall health and well-being. Share important information with parents by providing them with a copy of the daily **care provider report form**, a form used to organize and record the routine care provided. This form includes information such as:

- The amount of liquid and solid food served.
- The number of diapers changed and the consistency of bowel movements.
- The length and quality of naps.
- Any accidents and the treatment provided.
- Any signs of illness and any medicine given.
- The infant's overall mood and activity level.

Parents, in turn, can fill out a **parent report form** each morning. This form details the infant's activities and behavior before arrival at the center. Having this information can help staff members provide the best care possible.

Care providers can effectively communicate with parents in other ways. They can show parents photos of their children at play. Parents should be encouraged to visit and participate frequently. Care providers can share parenting information from articles, videotapes, or books. Together, parents and providers can think of new experiences to offer infants. Regular contact with parents is one way of providing stability between the home and infant care center.

Nurturing Development

During infancy, humans experience their fastest rate of growth and development. New skills and abilities emerge daily as children progress through developmental stages. Development in one area affects development in another. Good care providers can determine the developmental differences of children at various ages. Quality infant programs address children's changing developmental needs.

As a care provider, you can encourage an infant's overall development. You should get to know each individual infant. If you feel an infant is lagging in an area of development, provide activities to help the child develop and refine skills. When typical growth and development are significantly delayed, refer the family to special services.

During the first year of life, muscle growth and coordination are major goals for physical development. Infants are developing perceptual motor skills, which require them to coordinate vision, intellect, and movement. Care providers plan an environment that allows the infants to develop these skills at their own rate. See Fig. 18-7.

FIG. 18-7.

CARE PROVIDER RESPONSE TO PHYSICAL DEVELOPMENT

Physical Development		
Age	Emerging Development	Care Provider Responses
Birth to 4 Months	• Muscle growth. • Motor coordination. • Improved vision and perceptual motor skills. • Awareness of body parts.	Near crib, place brightly colored pictures or family portrait. Hang mobiles over crib. Encourage gazing by holding objects about 8 to 12 inches from the baby's face. Play vision-tracking games by moving objects slowly from side to side. During routines, such as changing clothes, bathing, or diapering, name baby's hands, feet, and facial features.
4 to 8 Months	• Increased muscle strength. • Muscle control. • Motor coordination.	Provide toys infants can use to bang, hit, shake, and squeeze. Offer toys with handles that can be easily grasped. As babies begin to roll over by themselves, provide open space on carpeting. Provide toys that roll, such as soft sponge balls, so infants crawl for them. Encourage crawling and creeping by placing toys just outside of baby's reach. Let them crawl on materials of different textures.
8 to 12 Months	• Learning to stand and balance. • May take steps. • Picking up items with thumb and forefinger. • Improved perceptual motor skills.	"Dance" together by holding onto both of baby's hands. Provide low, soft chairs or sofas to allow baby to practice walking skills. Sturdy handrails mounted securely to walls encourage cruising. Provide open space as baby tries to walk. Allow infants to go barefoot for better footing. Avoid walkers that can interfere with muscle and joint development. Allow babies to feed themselves small pieces of healthful cereal. Provide stacking and nesting toys.

Nurturing Intellectual Development

Intellectual development occurs as infants notice details of their environment and try to make sense of them. Experiences with care providers, especially verbal and nonverbal interactions, help infants understand their world.

Emerging Development. During infancy, babies show language and communication skills. Their first language skill is babbling, which they will later use to form words. Babies also learn cause and effect and object permanence, two crucial skills in development. Some infants in child care have parents who are not native English speakers. Care providers also need to understand bilingual language development.

Care Provider Reponses. Care providers can respond in many ways to nurture intellectual development. Care providers can:

- Use the same sounds in response to an infant's vocalization.

- Use language frequently. Explain what you are doing: "We turn on the water. We fill up the tub." Comment on things the baby is seeing or hearing, such as "That's a red bird."

- Use three- or four-word sentences.

- Use facial expressions and a lively tone of voice to convey word meanings. Name your feelings as you talk, so infants understand how the words, facial expressions, tone of voice, and feelings are connected. Keep in mind that different cultures express feelings in different ways. Infants from other cultures may not express their feelings in ways that you may expect.

- Look at pictures and read books together. Name the objects in pictures as you point to them. Let the infant turn the pages.

- Play with puppets and stuffed animals.

- Sing to infants. Repeat songs often, so infants become familiar with the tune and the words.

- Carry infants around frequently until they are old enough to sit up or crawl on their own. This gives them new views of their surroundings. Vary the direction that infant chairs face so that babies can see what is happening in the room. Infants also enjoy outdoor sights

and sounds. Take them on frequent strolls and name objects outside.

- Play games, such as peek-a-boo or hide and seek with objects.

- Offer toys with different shapes, colors, and textures. Provide toys infants can manipulate and investigate, such as plastic blocks, nesting toys, and stacking rings. Noise-making toys teach cause and effect. Provide interesting objects to look at, touch, taste, smell, and listen to, as well as grasp, push, pull, and kick. See Fig. 18-8A & B.

Nurturing Emotional Development

The foundation for lifelong emotional well-being begins at birth. Nurturing infants' emotional development helps children grow into confident, well-balanced adults.

Emerging Development. Safe, secure environments and nurturing care providers help infants' emotional development. Infants form bonds with care providers, express attachment behaviors, and express their feelings.

Care Provider Responses. Care providers are responsible for nurturing infants' emotional development. Some ways to promote healthy development include:

- A primary care provider should provide feeding, diapering, dressing, and all other basic routines for an infant. This encourages care provider and infant bonding.

- Respond immediately to crying infants.

- Hold, cuddle, and rock infants frequently to nurture the feelings of caring, closeness, and security. To show affection and interest to infants, talk to them, read or tell them stories, and play with them.

- Vary the music tempo and volume to help calm anxious, fussy, or crying infants.

- Plan challenging activities, but within infant's developmental capabilities.

- Be enthusiastic when infants develop new skills. Praise builds a sense of self-esteem.

FIG. 18-8A. As infants in your care "work" at play, they increase muscle control and coordination. What other activities encourage motor skill development?

FIG. 18-8B. **As a care provider, you play an important role in the language development of infants in your care.** What are some ways you can encourage language skills for infants?

Care Provider Responses. Care providers help infants to develop socially. To encourage development, good care providers can:

- Make feedings social times. Hold infants when feeding and talk quietly to them. When feeding from a high chair or eating at the table, allow time for friendly conversation.

- Talk to the infant while diapering.

- When the infant smiles, smile back.

- Snuggle in a soft chair together to read a book. Talk about what you see.

- Play give-and-take games, such as pat-a-cake. Hand objects back and forth to each other. Reinforce imitation by playing copycat.

- Establish a regular pattern of routines and rituals to give infants a sense of comfort and security. See Fig. 18-8C & D.

Nurturing Social Development

Learning how to respond and behave appropriately with others begins during infancy. Infants' first steps toward social development begin with their care providers. From that beginning, children are gradually prepared for social experiences that will develop with peers and during their preschool years.

Emerging Development. Infants' social development begins with a special relationship with a primary care provider. This relationship, when consistent and interactive, provides infants with opportunities to learn about others.

FIG. 18-8D. **Playing games like pat-a-cake with an infant helps build social skills and self-esteem.** What other activities might help build social skills for infants?

FIG. 18-8C. **Holding, cuddling, and rocking infants help build attachment and feelings of security in the infant.**

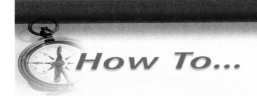

How To...

Introduce Babies to Different Cultures

Because infants learn from their environment, you can inspire appreciation for cultural variety even at this early age. Simply add a multicultural twist to the usual items and practices found in the program.

- Do not limit room decorations to the traditional pink and blue. Choose brightly colored curtains, floor pillows, and wall hangings made of batik and other ethnic fabrics.

- Babies are fascinated by pictures of other babies. Find drawings or pictures showing infants of varied ethnic backgrounds. Laminate them and then put them up at children's eye level and above the changing table for infants to view.

- Many mail-order music catalogs offer lullabies from around the world. The soothing voices and melodies of different lands can add variety and culture to nap routines.

- Read books that include diverse people and settings.

- Provide dolls of different ethnic backgrounds and other ethnic toys.

APPLY IT!

Create a list of cultural items you would include in an infant room. Record the names of any books or musical recordings you wish to include. Collect catalogs that sell cultural items you would purchase for an infant room.

Section 18-2 Knowledge Check

1. Identify staff responsibilities in infant programs.
2. List three ways to respond to an infant's intellectual development.
3. How do infant care providers effectively communicate with parents?

Mini-Lab

Investigate the business management skills that are necessary for planning and operating an infant care program. Write a summary of your findings to share with the class.

Section Summaries

18-1 Infants are born with certain reflexes.

18-1 Senses are quickly refined during infancy.

18-1 Greater mobility comes as infants develop motor skills.

18-1 Intellectual development takes place when babies are allowed to explore their environment with senses and motor skills.

18-1 Development of trust is needed for emotional health.

18-1 Children are born with different temperaments.

18-2 The demand for high-quality infant care programs and qualified infant care providers is increasing.

18-2 Good infant care providers are thoroughly knowledgeable about all areas of development. They are also enthusiastic, understanding, patient, warm, gentle, caring, responsive, good observers, good planners, and well organized.

18-2 Care providers plan a variety of activities to nurture infants' physical, intellectual, emotional, and social development.

18-2 Care must be taken to ensure that the environment provided for infants is safe and healthful.

18-2 Infants' daily routines should be conducted according to their individual needs, rather than a group schedule.

Check Your Knowledge

1. What is infancy?
2. Describe four reflexes present at birth.
3. What qualities describe the sensorimotor period of development?
4. Define and give an example of object permanence.
5. Briefly describe the three types of temperaments.
6. List responses a care provider can give to an infant who is crying.
7. Cite three ways to help infants develop language.
8. What is staff turnover? How is it related to infants' emotional development?
9. How does the staff-to-child ratio for an infant program differ from that for older children? Why?
10. Give three suggestions that can help care providers maintain a good relationship with the parents of the infants in their care.

Thinking Critically

1. Draw conclusions about the qualities a program director should look for when selecting an infant care provider.
2. How should a care provider react if an infant cries and becomes fearful when the parent leaves the child with the care provider?
3. Draw conclusions about what factors determine developmental differences in infants.

Practical Applications

1. **Chart Development.** Explain how infants progress through developmental stages. Develop a chart for observing each area of an infant's development. Include a heading listing factors that can affect the development of infants.

2. **Planning for Special Needs.** Assume you have an infant in your care who does not babble at age 10 months. The other infants in your care can babble or speak a few words. What types of activities would you plan to encourage speech development in the baby who is lagging behind? Consult a speech therapist or child care director for ideas. Write a summary of your plan and present it to your class.

3. **Infant Observation.** Observe an infant care provider at a local child care facility. Determine the developmental differences between infants, and note the differences in your records. Note ways the care provider nurtures the development of the infants in his or her care. Suggest three additional ways the care provider might nurture the infants' physical, intellectual, emotional, or social development.

4. **Interview.** In teams, make an appointment to interview a nurse at a hospital nursery. During the interview, ask questions regarding infant development during the first 48 hours. What medical tests are run before an infant goes home? If possible, discuss the development of low-birth-weight infants in contrast to full-term infants.

Building Your PORTFOLIO

Planning an Infant Care Program

Adequate planning helps to ensure a quality infant care program. By starting now, you can learn the elements of planning that will contribute to your success as a child care provider.

Step 1: Write an advertisement describing the qualities desired in an infant care provider.

Step 2: Write a description of an infant care program that incorporates the rules established by your state's licensing laws. Include the number of infants to be cared for, the size of the group, the number of care providers, and their responsibilities. Also include copies of the forms that will be used to facilitate staff and parent communication.

Step 3: Plan the layout and design of the infant room. Draw the layout of the room to scale using graph paper or a computer-aided design program. Select furnishings, equipment, and accessories for the room from catalogs or Web sites. Include storage areas for materials. Include pictures of your selections in your portfolio.

Step 4: Share your plan with the director of a facility that provides infant care. Ask the director to review your advertisement, program description, and infant room layout and design and make suggestions for improvement. Revise your plans and include them in your portfolio.

Chapter **19**
Caring for Toddlers

Section 19-1
Development & Care

Section 19-2
Managing Toddler Programs

Section 19-1

Development & Care

OBJECTIVES

- Explain the signs of and influences on the physical, emotional, social, and intellectual development of toddlers.
- Identify the characteristics of the preoperational period.
- Describe an environment that promotes healthy emotional development.
- Summarize the impact of play on social development.
- Identify ways to promote responsibility in toddlers.

KEY TERMS

self-help skills
attention span
symbolic thinking
preoperational
  period
concepts
assimilation
accommodation
autonomy
solitary play
parallel play

An exciting time for learning takes place during the toddler stage. Toddler is the term given to a child between the ages of 12 and 36 months. Children at these ages are ready to absorb all the information they can. Toddlers are in a transition stage. No longer infants, they eagerly increase their skills to become more independent.

Physical Development

Watch a 15-month-old walk and you will see why children this age are called toddlers. Learning to stand erect, they often appear a bit bowlegged. Their stomachs stick out, and they toddle from side to side. By 18 months, toddler balance is much improved. Once they reach age two, their bodies begin to slim down and take on the appearance of more mature children.

After infancy, growth in height and weight slows for toddlers. Because less fuel is needed for growth, toddlers' appetites decrease. Teeth come in rapidly between 18 and 24 months of age. Body proportions gradually change along with height and weight. An infant's head is rela-

tively large compared with the rest of the body, and the arms and legs are short. As children grow, they achieve more mature proportions. Figure 19-1 shows approximate heights and weights for children from ages one to three. Remember, these numbers do vary from child to child.

Motor Development

Toddlers' motor development and coordination advance quickly. Improved large motor skills—skills that use the larger muscles of the back, legs, shoulders, and arms—let children achieve new physical abilities. Learning to walk gives them greater independence.

FIG. 19-1.

AVERAGE HEIGHTS AND WEIGHTS OF TODDLERS

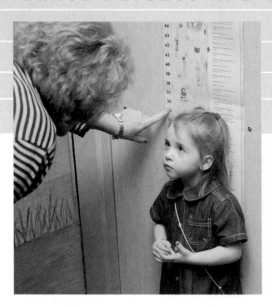

Age	Height	Weight
One year	30 in.	22 lbs.
Two years	34 in.	28 lbs.
Three years	38 in.	32 lbs.

Between 12 and 18 months, children begin to climb. At first, climbing up stairs is easier than climbing down. By age two, however, this skill is mastered. Older toddlers love to climb over, on top of, and through items in their way. Their skills in running, hopping, and jumping increase.

Between 18 and 24 months of age, children begin to push themselves on wheeled toys. By the end of their second year, they are able to pedal a tricycle or other vehicles with pedals.

Toddlers also are refining their small motor skills, those that require use of muscles in the fingers, wrists, and ankles. These skills contribute to improved eye-hand coordination and other perceptual motor skills. Children learn to stack blocks, string beads, and put together simple puzzles. Children 12- to 18-months old can stack two to four blocks and join a two-piece puzzle. Between 18 and 36 months, they can put together six-piece puzzles and stack about eight blocks.

Self-Help Skills

Greater physical control allows toddlers to develop more **self-help skills**. These are skills that allow children to help take care of their personal needs. Self-help skills for toddlers include getting dressed, washing hands, eating with utensils, brushing teeth, and putting away toys. Toddlers can also assist in household chores, such as dusting. Using self-help skills helps toddlers feel competent. That feeling leads to pride and confidence. See Fig. 19-2.

FIG. 19-2. **Learning self-help skills helps build a toddler's self-esteem.** Identify a self-help skill and develop a plan for the best way to teach that skill to toddlers.

How To...

Toilet Train Older Toddlers

For toilet training to be successful, the child must have achieved control of the muscles of elimination. Training that starts too early will be unsuccessful and frustrating for both the child and the adult. Parents and care providers should cooperatively toilet train at home and child care.

Children usually learn toileting skills during the end of the toddler stage. Awareness of bodily functions is one sign of readiness. Children may gesture to show when their diaper needs to be changed. Their facial expressions may show awareness that elimination is about to occur. Some child care centers have toddler-size toilets. If these are not provided, special child-size seats or chairs may be used.

When children are developmentally ready, the learning process usually takes only a few weeks or even days. However, newly trained children usually do not stay dry during naps. Provide diapers or a rubber mat as long as necessary. Even during waking hours, occasional accidents occur. Accept these in a calm, matter-of-fact way. Use the following steps when toilet training a toddler:

- Dress the child in elastic-waist, pull-down pants for easy removal.
- Be alert for signs that children need to use the toilet, such as tugging at their pants.

- Remind children of feelings that signal it is time to use the toilet.
- Take children to the toilet as frequently as needed. If care providers and parents are consistent, children eventually associate the toilet with needing to eliminate.
- If a child does not urinate or have a bowel movement within five minutes of sitting on the toilet, allow the child to resume play. Never leave a child on a toilet for an extended time.
- Always use sanitary procedures when toileting or diapering. After using the toilet, have children wash their hands. Show children how to wash their hands effectively.

APPLY IT!

Interview a toddler care provider to find out his or her experiences with toilet training. What toddler fears about toileting did the care provider encounter? How did he or she help reduce those fears? Did the care provider use children's books to help with the toileting process? If so, which ones? Record what you learned about successful toileting to share with the class.

Independent Toileting. At about age two, most children are ready to begin toilet training. Toddlers can recognize the bodily sensations that precede elimination and understand the use and purpose of a toilet, or potty chair. Girls tend to master toileting skills earlier than boys.

Care providers can assist toddlers with toileting by providing easy access to toilets and hand-washing sinks. They can also help toddlers with buttons and zippers, but should be aware that some toddlers prefer to dress independently.

Climbing Hazards. Toddlers cannot tell where it is safe to practice their climbing skills. Children may create "stairs" from pieces of furniture, from chairs and tables, or from drawers and cabinets. Eliminate chances for climbing hazards whenever possible. Indoors and out, offer safe climbing alternatives. Stable climbing equipment should have handrails toddlers can reach.

Intellectual Development

Discovery is a big part of intellectual development. Toddlers learn by doing and by using their senses. They need many hands-on experiences. Toddlers continue to grow intellectually through sensorimotor development. They have a keen sense of wonder and are fascinated by the simplest things. Toddlers need freedom and time to explore a safe environment to satisfy their curiosity. Children become enthusiastic learners when care providers patiently respond to multiple questions, such as "Why?" and "What's that?"

Toddlers learn in other ways, too. They use trial and error, repetition, and imitation. They closely observe adults and copy their behavior. They adopt attitudes that adults have. Care providers that toddlers attach to are powerful role models.

Attention & Memory

Toddlers develop an increased **attention span**, which is the time spent focused on one activity. It generally increases with age. A child's interest in an activity and the activity's developmental level can also affect attention span.

Children continue activities that are challenging without being boring or frustrating. These positive experiences encourage learning.

Increased memory also helps intellectual development. Memory is the ability to recall images and information. Without memory there would be no learning. Memory begins to develop in infancy and grows rapidly during the first two years. Toddlers begin to have memory of actual events. Two-year-olds can remember a parent who has been absent for several weeks. They can repeat favorite rhymes and stories and tell about experiences after returning from a walk.

Symbolic Thinking

With increased attention span and memory, children develop a more advanced thought process—**symbolic thinking**. With symbolic thinking, children understand that one thing can stand for something else. They learn to use images, art, and language as symbols to represent objects, events, and concepts. See Fig. 19-3.

FIG. 19-3. Children in early childhood programs use symbolic thinking as they play. How can playing "dress-up" help encourage this type of thinking?

Symbolic thinking occurs during Piaget's second period of intellectual development—the **preoperational period**. This period covers ages two to seven. In this period children start to think symbolically and imaginatively. Because they can think symbolically, older toddlers enjoy make-believe play. It is not unusual to see a two-year-old holding "conversations" with the use of a wooden block "telephone" or sitting inside a cardboard box that has become a vehicle.

Imagination and creativity are natural products of symbolic thought. With symbolic thinking, children can create their own ideas. This is a significant milestone in a child's development.

Language Development

Vocabulary and language skills advance greatly from ages one to three. Toddlers acquire up to 50 words. Babbling continues as children learn the meaning of their native language.

Eighteen-month-olds can respond with "yes" or "no" to questions. They identify parts of the body by pointing to them when named. They follow simple commands, such as "Hand me the ball." Nonverbal signals using the hands, arms, head, or face—gesturing—begin at this age.

Many two-year-olds have a vocabulary of 50 to 300 words. They can name familiar objects. More understandable speech includes three- to four-word sentences. They can follow increasingly complex directions, such as "Put the ball inside the box."

Conceptual Development

The ability to understand **concepts**—general ideas formed from other information—increases rapidly with emerging language skills. Concept development and language development build on each other. The more concepts children encounter, the more words they need to label them. The more words children understand, the more concepts they are able to identify and label.

ETHICS IN Action

Toilet Training. One of your coworkers dislikes changing diapers. She is determined to toilet train the toddlers in her care as quickly as possible. She makes the toddlers sit on the toilet every thirty minutes to prevent accidents, leaves toddlers sitting on the toilet for long periods, and punishes those who have accidents. She told you that you should do the same. *What will you do?*

When first labeling concepts, children use broad generalities. To them, one word has many meanings. As their experiences increase, they gradually learn that concepts have limits. Piaget explained how children absorb information and attempt to make sense of it. He used two terms—assimilation and accommodation—to describe this skill.

- With **assimilation** (uh-sih-muh-LAY-shuhn) children take in new information and try to make it fit with what they already know and understand. For example, a child might see a red cup on the table. Although the cup might be new, the child understands that it is similar in shape to other cups. It also is on the table, where cups usually are. The child assumes that the cup holds a drink because what the child observes fits in with the information the child already has about cups.

- With **accommodation** (uh-kah-muh-DAY-shuhn) children change their thinking to make the new information fit. Intellectual development involves balancing new information with existing concepts to achieve better understandings. For instance, at first, two-year-olds may think all four-legged animals are called dogs. Given time and experience, they learn to see other important features that distinguish four-legged animals from each other. Through accommodation, children alter their concepts to make better sense of new information.

Toddlers learn to notice many similarities and differences. They match and sort items that look alike. They begin to recognize shapes and sizes. For example, many toddlers can work a puzzle with four pieces. This ability is critical to learning to read letters. See Fig. 19-4.

Toddlers also begin to understand opposites. They start to see the relationship between hot and cold, hard and soft, and up and down. Cause and effect also fascinates toddlers. When playing hide-and-seek, toddlers are more logical than random. They think about where and how to look for a hidden person or object. This problem solving reveals complex intellectual abilities.

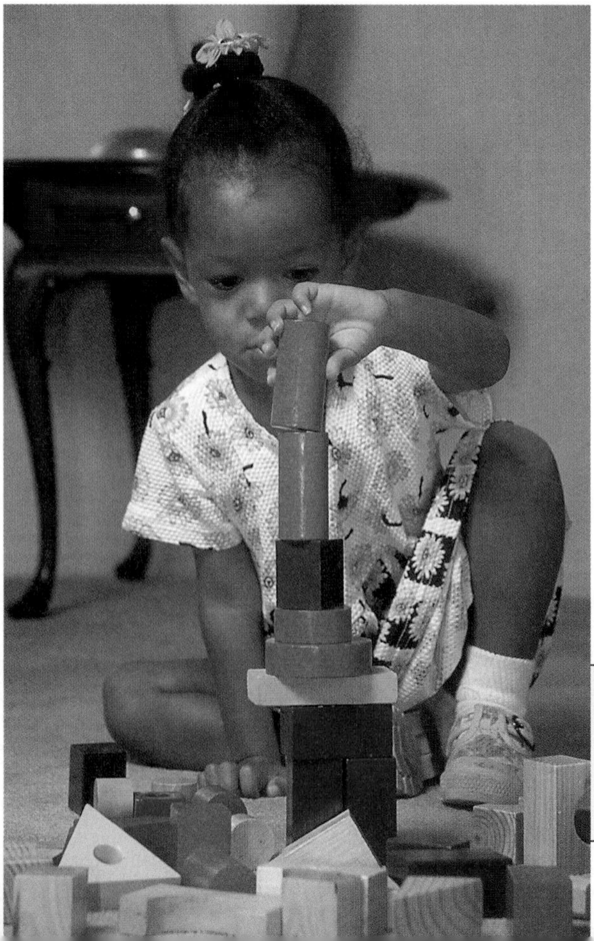

Emotional Development

Toddlers are beginning to develop emotional control. They are still prone to impulsiveness and quick mood swings. Toddlers may be happy one minute and screaming the next. Working with toddlers is easier when you understand child development and know that a stage will pass.

When the basic needs of toddlers are met, they are very pleasant and cooperative. Sudden shifts in mood and behavior are more a result of individual temperament. Problems may stem from frustration. Toddlers struggle to learn and do more, but not all their abilities are yet present. When their grasp of language is inadequate, toddlers resort to whining and crying. As language improves, toddlers are better able to communicate their wants, needs, and feelings. They gradually learn to appropriately identify and express their feelings. Language advances help children gain greater control over their behavior.

Independence & Autonomy

According to Erik Erikson, toddlers develop a sense of **autonomy** (aw-TAHN-uh-mee), or independence. They start to see themselves as separate from loved ones. Toddlers assert their independence and make their own decisions. They frequently exclaim "No!" They often resist cooperating in routines, such as eating and bathing. Toddlers are sensitive about being shown, helped, or directed. They frequently do the opposite of what a care provider wants. With patience and by offering reasonable choices, care providers help toddlers move toward autonomy.

FIG. 19-4. As conceptual development occurs in toddlers, they begin to sort items by size, shape, and color. What activities can help toddlers with conceptual development?

Emerging Fears

Having specific fears is common for toddlers. Their fears may include such things as storms, birds, clowns, or being alone in a room. Fear arises for several reasons. Healthy fear contributes to children's safety. Children should be afraid of jumping from a high wall or petting a wild animal. However, some fears are needless. Fears often develop from lack of experience. For a young child who has never been in a wading pool, stepping into water may cause fear. Some fears stem from misconceptions. Others are learned from other children and adults.

When fears arise, care providers should stay close to the toddler. This will usually calm the child. Children overcome fears when care providers are patient. It often helps to talk about their fears. If a toddler fears storms, explain that rain is needed for flowers to grow. If an older child fears climbing, gradually introduce the child to different heights on climbing structures. Pushing children to overcome fears all at once usually backfires. It results in more fearful children. Most fears pass with time and experience if handled in an understanding manner. See Fig. 19-5.

Importance of Security

A toddler's sense of security is a primary emotional need. Stable routines help fulfill this need. Toddlers are more secure and relaxed when their daily schedule and environment are reliable and predictable. They feel free to explore and pursue learning through trial and error.

The importance of reliable and consistent care for toddlers cannot be overemphasized. Attachment to and having relationships with specific people sets the foundation for children's future emotional and social development. Children experience greater trust and security when caring and dependable adults provide their care.

Social Development

Social development progresses slowly for toddlers. It takes time for them to develop social relationships with their peers and new adults.

Beginning at age two, children can take part in groups of up to eight children for short time periods. They may enjoy group singing for five minutes or listening to a short story with others. Their main social interactions, however, continue to be with parents, siblings, and other care providers. Toddlers are most at ease sharing time with a care provider and two or three children.

Children begin making friends at age two. They often show kindness when someone is hurt or crying. At this age, children like to snuggle with a buddy in a cozy space. Children develop friendships after the age of three.

FIG. 19-5. **With reassuring care providers, toddlers begin to overcome their fears.** What is the difference between a healthy fear and an unhealthy fear?

FIG. 19-6. **Young toddlers begin to play next to each other but with little interaction.** What is the care provider's role in encouraging social interaction?

Play & Social Development

Throughout the early childhood years, play is the best method of learning. Through play, toddlers stretch their abilities and expand concepts. They spend hours poking, prodding, and manipulating objects. They engage in delightful conversations with care providers.

From 18 to 24 months, children still engage mostly in **solitary play**. They play alone, rather than with other children. They are interested in other children, but more out of curiosity than a desire to form friendships. Between 24 and about 36 months of age, children engage in **parallel play**. You will see them playing near each other, but not with each other. Two children of this age might investigate a toy together at the same time, but each acts independently of the other. A small group of toddlers might all play with the same adult at once. The interaction, however, is taking place primarily between the adult and each separate child, not among the children.

As they approach three, children begin to interact more with other children, but for limited time periods. Parallel play continues to be their main style of interaction. See Fig. 19-6.

Independence & Responsibility

Even at this early age, a sense of responsibility develops. You can foster independence and responsibility by promoting the use of self-help skills. Setting limits also help toddlers become responsible. Toddlers understand very simple limits and rules. Rules should relate primarily to safety. Very brief explanations for rules help children understand their purpose.

Toddlers can also learn social skills, such as using table manners, sharing, and cooperating. Care providers should give toddlers plenty of chances to develop these skills. The best way for care providers to teach positive social behavior is to model appropriate behavior.

Section **19-1**   Knowledge Check

1. Explain the development of motor skills in toddlers.
2. What is symbolic thought?
3. What is the best way to help toddlers cope with their fears?

Mini-Lab

Imagine you are a two-year-old in a new situation, such as a first visit to a child care center or meeting a large dog. Write a paragraph describing your fears and anxieties from a child's point of view.

Section 19-2
Managing Toddler Programs

OBJECTIVES

- Identify key features of toddler programs.
- Plan a safe, healthy, and developmentally appropriate environment for toddlers.
- Describe how to nurture toddlers' overall development.
- Suggest ways to handle common challenges of the toddler years.

KEY TERMS

receptive language
productive language
separation anxiety
negativism
temper tantrum

Toddlers emerge from infancy with a sense of competence and a spirit of adventure. They delight in new accomplishments. They need sensitive adult guidance so they can safely and successfully explore their expanding world.

Daily Routines

In toddler programs, routines provide structure for daily events. Children choose from several individual or small-group activities. Some activities come directly from children's play with classroom materials. Others are planned and led by care providers or teachers. Typical daily routines followed in toddler rooms include:

- Arrival.
- Playtime in learning centers, including outdoor play.
- Diapering, toileting, and hand washing.
- Meals and snacks.
- Napping.
- Story time and music.
- Departure.

Following a consistent schedule and routine helps toddlers feel secure. When handled well, routines allow children to develop self-help skills, such as using a fork during meals.

Nurturing Development

Programs for toddlers must be designed around their growth and developmental needs. To better understand and meet these needs, many programs ask parents for information about their child's development. This information helps the program provide individualized care and activities that nurture all areas of development. The information may be collected on a form or through an interview. The parents provide information about the child's:

Safety First

Eliminating Hazards. Lock up all toxic substances, such as medicines and cleaning agents. Also lock the classroom refrigerator. Children can suffocate from crawling into a refrigerator and becoming trapped when the door closes behind them. Continue to keep small objects that could cause choking—such as buttons, hard candy, or balloons—out of toddlers' reach. Choose toys with safety in mind. Check them daily for loose or broken parts. Use safety caps on electrical outlets, nonslip rugs, and secure shelves that will not fall over on children.

- Extent of vocabulary and the primary language spoken at home.
- Toileting, small motor and large motor skills.
- Napping habits.
- Typical behavior and recent experiences that might affect behavior. Type of experiences with other children.

Managing Classroom Atmosphere

Age ranges in toddler classrooms vary. Some programs put one- and two-year-olds in the same classroom. Others have a separate classroom for each age level. Although state requirements vary, an ideal program might have eight toddlers and two adults per classroom.

Early childhood programs strive to promote positive physical, emotional, social, and intellectual development of all children. Toddler spaces are designed to help them develop new abilities and gain independence.

- **Furniture and toys.** Toddlers need age-appropriate furniture and toys. Serve snacks and meals at low tables with small chairs. Toddlers should nap on small cots. Play equipment, such as wheeled toys and low climbing equipment, help children practice their increasing physical skills.
- **Security items.** A secure, homelike atmosphere with soft sofas and rockers allows toddlers to relax with a book or cuddle with a teacher. Pillows, stuffed toys, or beanbag chairs help create a comfortable environment.
- **Learning centers.** Toddler classrooms are divided into learning centers, as discussed in Chapter 13. The equipment should fit a toddler's size and abilities. Most toddler rooms have a manipulative center instead of a math center. This area is stocked with items—such as pop beads, puzzles, and snap toys—that require eye-hand coordination and small motor skills.

Nurturing Physical Development

Large motor skills develop quickly in toddlers. Children just learning to walk enjoy noisy push and pull toys. Smaller wheeled toys and wagons are good choices. Older toddlers need plenty of chances to run, jump, and climb. Promote coordination skills with low swings, climbers, or obstacle courses. Toddlers also like balls that they can safely kick, roll, or toss.

Care providers should supply manipulative toys, such as nesting cups, simple puzzles, sewing cards, snap beads, small blocks for stacking, and large beads for stringing. Inexpensive household objects can also be used as manipulative toys. For example, let toddlers practice twisting and untwisting the covers on plastic jars. They can also use metal tongs to put cotton balls into empty oatmeal boxes. For active outdoor play during warm months, squirting water from empty dish detergent bottles strengthens muscles while providing fun.

Creative activities also encourage small motor skills. Toddlers enjoy scribbling, finger painting, painting with brushes, cutting with scissors, and molding dough. See Fig. 19-7. For

FIG. 19-7. Finger painting is an enjoyable, creative experience for toddlers. Why do you think finger painting appeals to toddlers?

practical experience with self-help skills, let children practice working zippers, buttons, and snaps. Sandboxes and sensory tables provide opportunities for learning to pour and scoop.

Nurturing Intellectual Development

Toddlers continue to learn best by using their senses. They develop an understanding of concepts by experimenting with hands-on materials. Care providers promote concept development in environments where experimenting is encouraged, such as with:

- **Matching games.** When toddlers begin to notice like and unlike qualities, they are ready to play matching games. Begin with basic colors and shapes. Provide safe objects to sort, such as large colorful table blocks.

- **Blocks.** Blocks of all kinds stimulate learning through trial and error. Toddlers can explore concepts related to balance, size, shape, and weight. Light cardboard and plastic floor blocks are best for beginning builders.

- **Nature experiences.** Nature items trigger curiosity. Let children handle pinecones, flowers, leaves, and seashells. Have them use

a magnifying glass to capture interest. An aquarium at toddlers' eye level can be exciting and physically relaxing. See Fig. 19-8.

- **Sensory activities.** Include items and activities that allow toddlers to use all their senses—sight, smell, touch, taste, and hearing. Encourage sensory learning with things such as: shaving cream mixed with food coloring; sensory tables filled with corn meal or colored water and ice; or eating colorful and tasty snacks.

Toddlers learn by watching and doing. Do not be distressed if a child spends a lot of time watching others play. He or she may be gathering new information before participating.

Language Development. Language plays a large role in intellectual development. Toddlers understand much more language than they can speak. The ability to understand spoken words is called **receptive language**. The ability to use words to express oneself is called **productive language**. Toddlers have more receptive language than productive language. Nurture all language by modeling. Use language to:

- Label, describe, count, and explain objects that are part of everyday life.

FIG. 19-8. Sensory experiences, such as viewing an aquarium, allow toddlers to gather information about their world. How can sensory experiences encourage language development?

- Read books, tell stories, and invent dialogue for puppets and dolls.
- Call the children by their names and have them address staff members by name, too.

Although your sentences should be short and simple, avoid "baby talk." Gradually make your language more complex, using more adverbs and adjectives. Be aware of children whose parents do not speak English. Understanding bilingual language development will help you encourage children to speak instead of becoming fearful of using words.

Nurturing Emotional Development

Toddlers can undergo difficult emotional times. They are experiencing new feelings that they may not understand. They are coping with fears. They are struggling with the unfamiliar practice of self-control.

As they help children adjust to the care environment, effective care providers assist with emotional development. They help toddlers identify their feelings—both positive and negative—and deal with them in appropriate ways. To help toddlers deal with fears, for instance, teachers show empathy, understanding, and gently encourage children to overcome their fears. Many children's books are written for just this purpose. See Fig. 19-9.

Building self-esteem is another high priority. Care providers can plan positive experiences that give toddlers chances to succeed. Encouraging self-help skills and offering developmentally appropriate toys and tasks help toddlers feel good about their accomplishments.

Most importantly, care providers who are warm, loving, and comforting can help children become emotionally secure as they adjust to early childhood care routines.

Toddlers face a number of emotional issues, such as separation from loved ones or learning to grow beyond negativism and temper tantrums.

Separation Anxiety. A child's fear of separation from familiar people is called **separation anxiety**. It may occur when a child first begins child care. Separation anxiety also occurs in times of stress, such as when a sibling is born. It is a sign of positive emotional development. It shows development of a strong emotional bond to parents or care providers. Separation anxiety usually lasts a few weeks. Patient care providers help children learn to cope.

Negativism. Toddlers often show **negativism** by refusing to do what is asked or doing just the opposite. Saying "No!" is a way for toddlers to rebel. Negativism does not mean a child is "bad" or will grow up to be defiant. It is simply a healthy sign of growing independence. To reduce negativism, give toddlers many chances to make choices and practice self-help skills.

Temper Tantrums. A **temper tantrum** is an episode in which a child shows anger or frustration in an aggressive or destructive way. See Fig. 19-10. Toddlers do not yet have the coping skills to handle frustration. A tantrum may occur when a want or privilege has been denied. During a temper tantrum, children may scream, kick, or hold their breath. Care

Boosting Brain Power

Bilingual Language Acquisition. **Toddlers who are exposed to two languages at the same time tend to learn both languages. This is called *simultaneous acquisition.* Children learn languages more easily when they engage in meaningful activities that require using language. Care providers can take an active role in encouraging bilingual development by modeling the use of language. For example, care providers might use both English and Spanish terms when naming colors or shapes.**

FIG. 19-9.

RESPONDING TO TODDLERS' FEARS

Don't...	Do...
• Make fun of fears. • Become angry or scold the child. • Shower the child with too much sympathy—"You poor thing. That big mean dog scared you!" You will just convince the child that there really is something to fear. • Try to explain too much. Toddlers will not understand. • Force the toddler to confront the fear.	• Stay calm and confident. • Avoid the fearful object or situation, if possible. If a child is afraid of a dog on your daily walk, explore a different route. • Distract the child. Try singing a song or talk about an activity the child enjoys. • Help the child act out whatever is causing the fear.

providers offer age-appropriate activities so toddlers experience success with minimal frustration. They give reasonable choices and let toddlers do as much as possible for themselves. If a tantrum occurs:

- React calmly. Some children need to be held and comforted until they calm down. Others simply want to be left alone.

- Keep an eye on the child at all times. Tell the child you understand the child's anger. Naming feelings helps children recognize and deal with them. Then offer a tissue to signal it is time to end the tantrum.

- Provide a place to rest. Some children become exhausted from tantrums.

- Communicate with parents. Notify the parents at the end of the day. Ask how tantrums are handled at home. Be aware that different cultures express emotions differently. Allow the parents to give you input on how to effectively deal with the tantrums. Frequent tantrums could be a sign of emotional difficulties or other problems, such as illness.

Nurturing Social Development

During the toddler stage, children move from solitary play to parallel play. As children approach age three, they begin to interact with one another in cooperative play. Carefully arrange the environment for cooperative play. With toy wagons, for instance, you encourage children to cooperate by pulling each other.

Toddlers can understand simple rules for behavior. As they get older, these rules can become more specific. Always state rules positively. Say, "When you're angry with people, tell them," instead of "Don't hit people when you're angry." Guide them by telling them what to do.

FIG. 19-10. **Toddlers may show anger and frustration by having a full-blown temper tantrum.** As a care provider, what is your role in minimizing and coping with temper tantrums?

Intergenerational *Interactions*

The Importance of Pets

Anyone who has ever loved pets knows the value of their unconditional love. A pet loves you regardless of your grades, popularity, appearance, and age. Even people who don't have their own pets love to watch and touch animals. That is why animals can be so helpful in joining generations and healing people of all ages.

- **One Geisinger Health Systems Intergenerational Program** links animals and local high school students with nursing homes, assisted living facilities, and senior centers. Through the pet therapy program, students learn to train dogs to provide companionship and comfort to older adults. This program not only soothes older adults, but also educates young people on aging.

- **The Humane Society of the Willamette Valley** in Salem, OR, reaches out to all generations. Through one intergenerational program sponsored by the humane society, elementary school students take animals to a local retirement center. The animals enjoy people of all ages, and the children learn to appreciate and respect animals and older adults.

- **Pet Express** programs join elementary school students and their pets with older adults. Provided by *Alternative Solutions*, a training guide and video can help you set up a *Pet Express* program in your community. The guide encourages programs to set up

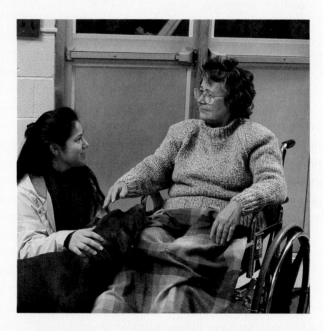

weekly or monthly intergenerational pet visits. It also talks about the importance of intergenerational holiday pet visits. For example, children and their pets could dress in costume on Halloween, then visit their local assisted living center.

Follow-Up

Write a report on why you think intergenerational pet programs benefit young people, older adults, and pets. Then consider consulting a local humane society or a local retirement home about starting a program in your area.

Toddlers are just beginning to learn to share. Introduce sharing while children are playing in small groups in a learning center. Toddlers share more easily in groups of two or three. Care providers should also model sharing. Toddlers who see adults cooperating are more likely to behave the same way.

Disputes are bound to occur among toddlers. When conflicts arise, care providers can distract, divert attention, or redirect the child to a different, acceptable activity. Conflicts that include hitting—and even biting—can occur among toddlers. Children who bite or hit usually do it out of frustration or anger. They may want a toy but have not learned to express their feelings in words. Others seem to do it for attention. Biting may be an attempt to relieve teething pain. In other cases, children are simply copying another child's behavior. If a child has acted aggressively, follow these steps:

1. If one child does bite or hit another, first attend to the victim with comfort and first aid if necessary. Directing your attention first to the aggressive child teaches that biting or hitting is a good way to get attention.

2. Firmly tell the aggressive child that hurting others is not permitted. If necessary, remove the aggressor from the group for a time.

3. At the end of the day, talk with parents about the problem. Agree cooperatively on how to respond to aggression.

FIG. 19-11. **Toddlers need to learn acceptable ways to resolve conflict.** What is the care provider's role in helping children learn conflict-resolution skills?

As with any discipline problem, observation may give you clues to a solution. Certain situations may lead to conflict. If so, take steps to reduce or eliminate those situations. See Fig. 19-11. Perhaps there is too much pressure to share when the child is not developmentally ready. The child may need to be redirected to quiet, solitary activities at certain times of day. Children who are ill, tired, or hungry are also more prone to conflict. If your solution does not work, try an alternative solution.

Section **19-2** Knowledge Check

1. Explain the factors that influence program design for toddlers.

2. What types of self-help skills can toddlers master?

3. Why is separation anxiety a healthy sign of emotional development?

Mini-Lab

With a partner, write a skit showing a care provider resolving a conflict after one two-year-old has bitten another. Have the teacher demonstrate effective as well as ineffective tactics. Have the rest of the class critique the care provider's responses and suggest improvements.

Section Summaries

19-1 The rate of physical growth for toddlers slows.

19-1 Care providers should design spaces that encourage healthy development.

19-1 Symbolic thinking, creativity, and imagination are important intellectual developments that begin at this age.

19-1 Toddlers strive to develop autonomy.

19-1 Toddlers engage in solitary and parallel play.

19-1 Toddlers can begin to understand simple rules and develop a sense of responsibility.

19-2 Consistent daily routines help toddlers feel secure. Emphasize self-help skills.

19-2 Toilet training can begin when children show signs of being developmentally ready.

19-2 A developmental history form or interview helps teachers meet each child's individual needs.

19-2 Teachers plan activities that nurture physical, intellectual, emotional, and social development in toddlers.

19-2 Teachers must learn to deal with problems common to children this age, such as fears, separation anxiety, negativism, temper tantrums, and aggression.

Check Your Knowledge

1. During which time do most children become ready for toilet training?
2. What is attention span?
3. Contrast assimilation and accommodation. Give an example of each.
4. What is autonomy? Describe the behavior of a child who is working toward autonomy.
5. What can be done to help give toddlers a sense of security?
6. What is a good group size and number of care providers for a toddler classroom?
7. Contrast the equipment needed in infant and toddler programs.
8. Name three items of information that may be part of a developmental history form or interview.
9. Identify three activities that help children develop large muscles.
10. Explain how children progress through developmental stages.

Thinking Critically

1. Analyze the developmental differences in infants and toddlers.
2. Draw conclusions about why safety is an important issue when caring for toddlers.
3. What might be the consequences of responding to toddlers' behavior (fears, negativism, separation anxiety, or temper tantrums) inappropriately?

Practical Applications

1. **Toddler Observation.** Observe the development of a toddler. Note signs of physical, intellectual, emotional, and social development. Practice creating parent reports by summarizing your findings. If you notice any characteristics of disabilities or special needs, include your observation along with a referral to a local intervention program.

2. **Evaluating Schedules.** Obtain a copy of the schedule used in toddler rooms at a local child care facility. Evaluate the extent to which you believe the schedule would meet the needs of most toddlers. Write a summary of your evaluation and suggestions for improving the schedule.

3. **Developmental History.** Develop a form for collecting information from a toddler's parents regarding their child's developmental history.

Building Your PORTFOLIO

Planning a Toddler Program

Planning is the key to a successful toddler program. Learning how to meet the needs of active toddlers will contribute to your success as a child care provider.

Step 1: Write an advertisement describing the qualities desired in a toddler care provider.

Step 2: Write a description of a toddler care program that incorporates the rules established by your state's licensing laws. Include the number of toddlers to be cared for, the size of the group, the number of care providers, and their responsibilities. Also include copies of the forms that will be used to facilitate staff and parent communication.

Step 3: Plan the layout and design of the toddler room to scale, using graph paper or a computer-aided design program. Select furnishings, equipment, and accessories for the room from catalogs or Web sites. Include pictures of your selections in your portfolio. Include items that can help accommodate children with special needs.

Step 4: Share your plan with a toddler care provider. Ask him or her to review your work for Steps 1, 2, and 3 and make suggestions for improvement. Ask about a typical budget for a child care center and evaluate whether your plan fits a typical budget. Revise your plans and put them in your portfolio.

Chapter 20
Caring for Preschoolers

Section 20-1
Development & Care

Section 20-2
Managing Preschool Programs

Development & Care

OBJECTIVES

- Explain the influences and signs of the physical, intellectual, emotional, and social development of preschoolers.
- Describe the key points of children's understanding in Piaget's preoperational period.
- Explain Vygotsky's sociocultural theory.

Children three, four, and five years old are referred to as preschoolers. They are eager and ready to learn and interact with others in larger group settings, such as child care and school.

KEY TERMS

**centration
seriation
rote counting
one-to-one
   correspondence
rational counting
conservation
native language
bilingual
cooperative play
sociocultural theory**

Physical Development

Physical growth during the preschool years is slow and gradual, which keeps the appetite small. Figure 20-1 on page 460 shows the average heights and weights of children at different preschool ages. Because preschoolers consume such small amounts, it is essential to make sure that what they eat is healthful. Adequate vitamins, minerals, and other nutrients are needed. Regular and adequate sleep routines nourish the body, too.

As preschoolers grow, their bodies appear less babylike. Body fat is reduced, and most growth occurs in the muscles and bones. Posture becomes erect. The neck lengthens, the shoulders widen and flatten, and the once protruding stomach flattens as well. Legs become proportionally longer.

Motor Development

Preschoolers play energetically, as new physical and motor abilities rapidly emerge. Both small and large motor skills gradually become refined and complex. By age five, preschoolers can run fast and can walk on a balance beam. Three-year-olds ride tricycles. Five-year-olds can usually ride bicycles. At three, children move and sway to music. By five, they can learn specific rhythms and dances. A three-year-old can throw a ball. A five-year-old can also catch a ball.

FIG. 20-1.

AVERAGE HEIGHTS & WEIGHTS OF PRESCHOOLERS

Age	Weight	Height
Three years	32 lbs.	38 in.
Four years	36 lbs.	41 in.
Five years	41 lbs.	44 in.

FIG. 20-2. Motor control emerges rapidly during the preschool years. How can care providers encourage motor control and development?

Preschoolers master greater control of their bodies, so they can move in a variety of ways. They hop, gallop, and run. They zigzag while running and change directions with increasing ease. Climbing is a favorite activity of preschoolers. The older they become, the more challenging the structures they try to climb. See Fig. 20-2.

Perceptual Motor Development

Preschoolers become more skilled in eye-hand coordination and small motor skills. Three-year-olds learn to use crayons and paintbrushes to create pictures. By five, they can draw and paint letters and shapes, too. These are important first steps in learning to read and write. Other activities that develop perceptual motor skills include simple cooking tasks. For example, they can help spread peanut butter on crackers.

Intellectual Development

During the preschool years, children's intellectual abilities also become more refined. Attention span lengthens. Curiosity leads them to observe, analyze, problem solve, and note cause and effect. Preschoolers' memory and ability to anticipate events increase. As a result, they can make more complex decisions and improve their game-playing skills.

Preoperational Stage of Development

Although Piaget's preoperational period begins during the toddler years, by the time children are preschoolers, the characteristics of this period are much more evident. With the increasing ability to think symbolically, children readily understand new concepts.

Classification and Centration. Preschoolers begin to learn classification—they can group objects into categories according to similarities. For example, they can separate a mixed set of

Recognizing Varied Learning Styles. Dr. Howard Gardner's theory of multiple intelligences stresses that individual children have preferred learning styles. Some children learn best by watching a skill and then performing it. Others learn best by listening and following directions. Still others prefer to learn through movement and music. Skilled care providers plan activities that allow children to learn and express themselves in a variety of ways. For instance, after a field trip, a small group of children may write a story about their trip. See Chapter 24 for more information on learning styles.

before children can see the relationship between the sizes of all ten blocks.

Numbers and Counting. Children in this period begin to understand numbers and counting. Often two-year-olds are capable of **rote counting**—simply reciting numbers in order. They do not understand that each number represents a specific amount. When counting by rote, preschoolers may count some objects more than once. Likewise, they might not count some objects at all. **One-to-one correspondence** is counting each item once. Children must comprehend this math concept before they can count accurately. When one-to-one correspondence is grasped, rational counting is possible. **Rational counting** is the understanding that the last number counted in a group represents the entire number of objects. Preschool children also have difficulty understanding time. They can understand the difference between "now" and "later," but not the passage of time according to a clock or calendar. See Fig. 20-3.

cards with pictures of cats and dogs into two smaller groups of just cats and just dogs. Preoperational thought, however, limits children's focus to one characteristic at a time. Piaget called this **centration**. Younger preschool children, for example, can sort objects by color alone. They can find all the red items in a group of toy cars, trucks, and airplanes. Not until children are almost six can they pick out only the red cars. Considering two qualities at once is very hard for preschoolers.

Seriation. Around age five, children learn **seriation**, the ability to organize objects according to increasing or decreasing size. As with classification, their understanding is very limited. If you give a three-year-old ten blocks and say, "Line these up from biggest to smallest," the child may put a large block beside one of the smallest ones. It will be several more years

FIG. 20-3. During the preschool years, children learn basic math concepts of rote counting, one-to-one correspondence, and rational counting. Plan three activities to help promote the understanding of numbers and counting in preschoolers.

Conservation. Preschoolers' understanding is limited by what they see, making some concepts difficult to grasp. When determining amounts, they cannot consider varying features, such as size, shape, and volume. Suppose you had a tall, thin glass that held 12 ounces of water. You know that if the 12 ounces of water is poured into a short, wide glass, the amount of water—12 ounces—remains the same. Children in the preoperational stage cannot understand that the amount of water stays constant, regardless of the shape of its container. Preschoolers assume the shorter glass holds less water, and the taller glass holds more. Piaget termed the understanding that an object's physical weight and properties remain the same even when its appearance changes as **conservation**. School-age children grasp the concept, but most preschoolers do not.

Language Development

The human brain is specially designed to learn language. With proper brain development, children learn language from their environment. Adults reinforce language development by praising them for first making sounds, then words, and finally sentences.

With reinforcement, language blossoms during the preschool years. Preschoolers also notice that writing on paper, such as in books, magazines, or in family recipe books, represents specific language. The average three-year-old has a vocabulary of 300 words. Four-year-olds speak about 1,500 different words. By age five, an average child speaks 2,200 words. As with most age groups, preschool children understand more words than they can speak. Their language becomes more expressive. Children use facial expressions, tone of voice, and a variety of gestures to show meaning.

With good examples, children develop their language ability more quickly. Talking and reading to children daily helps them expand their language use and grasp its meaning. For instance, a three-year-old may simply say, "My ball." An adult can encourage more complex language by saying, "Yes, that is your big, red ball. Show me how you can bounce the ball." Care providers should encourage children to ask questions and tell stories or jokes.

Grammar and Pronunciation. Gradually, children learn rules for grammar and pronunciation. With experience, they also learn exceptions to rules. For example, three-year-olds first notice that plurals are formed by adding "s" onto the ends of words. This leads them to make incorrect plurals, such as saying "foots" or "gooses." As they casually hear correct language during conversation, they gradually become aware of the exceptions to plural rules. They will learn that in English "feet" is used instead of "foots," and "geese" is used instead of "gooses." When children are first developing language, focus on content rather than on grammar or speech mechanics. See Fig. 20-4.

Stuttering. During the preschool years, most children speak clearly. However, you can expect that children may say some sounds incorrectly.

FIG. 20-4. **Reading to preschoolers helps encourage vocabulary development.** What other activities encourage language development in preschool children?

Some preschoolers have problems with stuttering. They may leave long pauses between words or repeat a sound or word many times before continuing a sentence. This is not "true" stuttering. It is the natural result when thinking ability exceeds speaking ability. It does not mean a child has a special need or disability. Once speaking abilities catch up with thinking abilities, this speech pattern usually subsides. By not emphasizing it, care providers preserve a child's self-esteem. If children stutter past age six or seven, they are usually referred to a speech therapist for evaluation.

Bilingual Development

There are times when the language spoken at child care is different from a child's **native language**, meaning the language spoken in a child's home. Such situations provide chances for children to become **bilingual**, or able to speak more than one language.

Because of unique early brain development, preschoolers can master multiple languages more easily than adults. When a language is used in meaningful ways, children learn to use different languages in their appropriate setting. They quickly learn that there are two or more ways of saying things.

When children speak a different native language, care providers should make it a point to learn certain words and phrases in the child's language. It helps them respond to children warmly and appropriately. Whenever possible, care providers should speak to the child in both English and the native language, such as during meal times and activities. To encourage bilingual development:

- **Use names correctly.** Names are often linked to culture, making some difficult to pronounce and spell for those who are not familiar with them. Names are a vital part of identity. Greet children at arrival time by name, making sure that you pronounce their names correctly.

- **Use cultural greeting songs.** Add variety to the greeting songs each morning by learning

FIG. 20-5. **Sensitive care providers offer opportunities for children to learn and speak a second language.** What are some ways that care providers can encourage the use of a second language in the preschool classroom?

some songs in children's native languages. Parents can be a helpful resource.

- **Label learning centers.** Identify the learning centers with labels in English and the children's native languages. See Fig. 20-5.

- **Use languages at snack time.** During snack time, use both languages for discussion. Include favorite foods from children's diverse cultures.

- **Play ethnic music at nap time.** Nap time can be a time to play lullabies in English and other languages.

- **Use native language at departure time.** At departure, speak with parents and say goodbye in the children's native languages.

Emotional Development

Preschoolers experience an increasing range of emotions, including loneliness, disappointment, anticipation, and sympathy. With increasing language skills, preschoolers are able to identify feelings and vent their emotions appropriately with words, rather than by hitting or pushing. Preschoolers may still have a variety of fears. Most of these will pass with time and experience.

Though often self-centered, preschool children begin to develop empathy and compassion. This is the ability to recognize and understand the feelings of others. Preschoolers learn to regret actions that hurt others. They begin to help others without expecting a reward. This emotional development paves the way for making friends and fostering further socialization.

Identity & Self Esteem

During the preschool age, feelings of self-esteem become more distinct. Preschoolers' self-esteem comes from their pride in performing the physical and intellectual skills. They often ask for attention when climbing, running, or hopping, or after naming colors, counting, or reciting the alphabet. "Teacher, see what I can do!" is frequently heard in a child care center.

Self-esteem also increases as preschoolers develop their self-help skills. They like to take care of themselves and their personal needs. You will often hear preschoolers say, "I want to do it myself." Three-year-olds can begin lacing shoes. With practice, five-year-olds can tie them. By four, children can dress themselves, eat neatly, and use proper manners.

As the list of accomplishments grows for preschoolers, the resulting feelings of independence and self-worth excite children. According to Erikson, these feelings give rise to a sense of initiative (ih-NIH-shuh-tiv)—or motivation to accomplish more. Children feel proud about what they learn to do and try to accomplish more to increase the good feelings. As a result,

preschoolers are very willing to be helpful. They especially like contributing to the group. In the classroom, they can pick up toys, set the table, feed animals, or help pass out name cards.

Gender Identity and Roles. Preschoolers learn who they are as males and females by watching adults and mimicking some of their behaviors. For example, a little girl might hand a parent tools while he or she fixes the family car or set the table while her dad or mom prepares a meal. A little boy might help a parent mow the lawn or bake cookies. Care providers are careful to show the full potential of both genders in the work setting and at home. They promote diversity by including children in all activities, according to their interests and abilities. This action helps promote self-esteem as children learn and grow as males and females.

Building Resilience. As during other developmental stages, care providers can promote children's resilience. Consistent, reliable routines help preschoolers feel relaxed and secure. Stable relationships and a strong attachment to one care provider builds children's self-esteem and confidence, despite adversity. See Section 8-1 for more information on building resilience.

Social Development

Before the preschool years, most social interactions for children are with adults. By age three, peers increase in importance. When given many chances to play, children become skilled in forming relationships.

Forming Friendships

Three-year-olds like to play in small groups of two or three. By five, children enjoy playing in groups of five to eight. Through play, preschoolers develop social skills. They learn to get along and trade with each other. They learn to reach compromise to please playmates. They can also bargain for what they want. Preschoolers

How To...

Include the Family in Bilingual Development

Children more easily develop native and non-native language skills when care providers and family work cooperatively. To include families in their child's bilingual development, care providers can:

- Meet with parents before a child's first day. Determine the extent of their language skills. Determine if parents need program information translated into their native language.

- Encourage parents to develop a second language to enhance their children's second language skills. If interested, refer parents to affordable community resources.

- Inquire how languages are used in the home. Is native language used in public settings and in the home? Which language mastery does the family prefer?

- Ask and take notes on how parents would like their child's language development to be handled in child care.

- Communicate with children to some extent in their native language. This helps children feel more relaxed and welcome. Ask parents of non-English-speaking children to complete a home language survey. The survey provides translations and phonetic spellings of common native language words and phrases. The survey list should include not only basic words, such as "hello," "doll," "toy," and "good-bye," but also important phrases, such as "Do you feel sick?" "Do you need to use the toilet?" and "Are you hungry?"

- Include families of non-English-speaking children in the classroom as often as possible. Encourage them to share native customs, children's books, cultural toys, songs, and traditional recipes.

- Encourage parents to form friendships with other parents who use the program. Encourage them to arrange weekend play dates for their child by inviting other program children to their home or neighborhood park.

- Provide translators at evening parenting workshops, so those using a second language can be more involved in discussions.

- When signs are created for facilities, use bilingual labeling.

APPLY IT!

In teams, develop a plan for encouraging the development of a second language for children in a preschool classroom. What environmental changes would encourage bilingual development for children and their families?

become more comfortable joining in activities. They learn to capture other children's interests with play ideas. This enables them to engage in **cooperative play**—playing together and agreeing on play activities and themes.

By four, children can form close friendships with one or two other children, whom they may call their "best friends." By age five, children form close-knit groups of preferred playmates.

They can be extremely blunt in their rejection of anyone who is not in their "group."

Preschoolers often "bribe" other children into friendship. A child might offer to let another child play with a favorite toy on the condition that they become best friends. These friendships are usually temporary. Preschoolers may have a different "best friend" every day of the week. After age six, friendships become more stable. See Fig. 20-6.

FIG. 20-6. **During the preschool years, children begin forming closer friendships with one or two other children.** What is the care provider's role in encouraging friendships?

Dealing with Conflict

When conflicts arise between preschoolers, it is often over toys or personal property. Children in group care often need to be reminded of which toys belong to the program and which belong to others. When children bring personal items from home, care providers ask them to bring only items that are easily shared, such as books and tapes. Children who have trouble sharing are asked to keep personal items in their cubbies.

Around four or five years of age, some children engage in name-calling. They may direct silly, crude, or hurtful names at others. Some of this can be ignored. If it becomes too frequent, however, care providers should firmly tell children that name-calling is not allowed because it hurts people's feelings. When dealing with conflict, care providers should help the children recognize and accept their feelings by naming them for the child.

Influence of Social Play. According to Vygotsky, cooperative play has a great influence on children's intellectual and social development. His **sociocultural theory** states that children learn their culture's beliefs, customs, and skills through social interactions with skilled peers and adults. When children talk to people with a strong command of language, children expand their language skills. In addition, children increase their thinking and problem-solving skills. As children cooperatively play with others who are socially competent, they learn to act according to their culture's specific rules.

Section 20-1 Knowledge Check

1. Explain how preschool children progress through developmental stages.

2. List four ways to include families in children's bilingual development.

3. In what ways did Vygotsky believe cooperative play fostered development?

Mini-Lab

While staying within hearing range but as much out of sight as possible, observe the roles children play. Listen carefully to what they say. How do the youngest play and interact in this area? How is the play of the older children different? Summarize your findings.

Section 20-2

Managing Preschool Programs

OBJECTIVES

- Identify features of preschool programs.
- Describe how to broaden preschoolers' skills.
- Explain how preschoolers develop literacy.
- Cite ways to encourage cooperative learning.
- Suggest ways to introduce children to community participation.

KEY TERMS

literacy
cooperative learning

Growth in the preschool years is dramatic and exciting. As preschoolers become more mobile, as their vocabulary grows, and as they learn to play with others, their overall development and learning capacity advance by leaps and bounds. This section will explore some of the highlights of that development.

Broadening Experiences

Children's preschool abilities build on the achievements of all previous developmental stages. Programs must offer preschoolers many chances to refine their skills so children may reach their full learning potential. As their skills quickly develop, they require more freedom to make independent choices during play and learning times. As with services for other ages, safety, nutrition, and good sanitation are also important parts of the preschool program.

Managing Daily Schedules and Routines. Regular routines are important to preschoolers, just as they are to younger children. Include routines in a balanced schedule, as described in Chapter 9. Depending on the length of day, schedules and routines should include:

- Arrival.
- Meals, including breakfast, morning snack, lunch, afternoon snack, supper, and evening snack.
- Personal hygiene, such as hand washing, toileting, and tooth brushing.
- Morning group meetings to plan the day's events.
- Group times for large-group experiences, such as story time and music. Activity times for individual and small-group learning and extended periods of free play time for self-chosen activities either indoors or outdoors.
- Monthly or quarterly field trips that relate to classroom curriculum.
- Toy clean-up times. Nap or rest time.
- End of day group activity and departure.

Evacuation Pathways. There are times when adults and children must evacuate classrooms and facilities for safety reasons, such as severe weather, fire, earthquake, or a civil defense emergency. Evacuation directions help everyone find safe shelter. Near every entrance and exit of a facility, post boldly labeled escape directions. Clear evacuation pathways should be identified for each type of emergency. Some programs color-code pathways for different emergencies. For fire emergencies, there should be primary and secondary escape routes posted. Laminate the evacuation sheets so they remain in good, readable condition. Update evacuation directions as necessary.

Nurturing Physical Development

The preschool years are a time of refinement in all areas of growth. Observable changes take place in terms of children's increased physical size. Using more complex small motor and large motor coordination skills allows preschoolers to enjoy a wider variety of games and physical activities. Preschoolers like to challenge their emerging abilities while using safe climbing equipment. They enjoy vigorous large muscle play, whether indoors or out.

Small muscle development, such as coordination of small finger muscles, allows preschoolers to do more complicated art activities. Their refined coordination paves the way for intricate large block buildings or constructions with small manipulative blocks. The ability to hold crayons and markers leads children to the ability to handle a pencil for future writing. These increasing physical skills then aid in intellectual development.

Nurturing Intellectual Development

As the brain develops, preschoolers are able to grasp increasingly complex thinking skills. The ability to speak and listen to language is mastered during the toddler years. Once this is achieved, preschoolers' greater intellectual capacity allows them to recognize and understand abstract symbols that represent spoken words. That process includes the beginning steps toward achieving the ability to read and write language, often referred to as **literacy** skills.

Emerging Literacy. Preschoolers develop literacy skills rapidly. They enjoy communicating with others. They increasingly see the need to put all their expanding language skills to good use. Care providers can foster emergent literacy of preschoolers in the following ways:

- Offer many daily opportunities for listening and speaking. For example, encourage creative use of language through music, storytelling, and puppetry.

- Read books to groups of children and individuals several times a day. Let children look at books, or listen to books on tape, independently during activity times. See Fig. 20-7.

- Give children easy access to literacy tools, such as crayons, pencils, books, or paper. Plan activities that allow children to make and illustrate their own books.

- Show children how literacy relates to real life, such as when reading a recipe during cooking or reading directions to put together a new toy.

- Include printed materials in learning centers—such as toy traffic signs and cars in the block center, menus in a pretend restaurant, or a telephone book in a pretend home.

- Allow children to see written words used in meaningful ways, such as writing thank-you cards to field-trip hosts or labels on common items, such as tables and chairs.

FIG. 20-7. **Preschoolers are taking their first strides toward literacy.** What activities encourage literacy development?

Nurturing Emotional Development

Preschoolers begin to handle their emotions more maturely. Greater language mastery helps them deal more effectively with frustrations. More and more they use their words to cope with emotions, rather than having emotional outbursts.

Preschool children often face new emotional realities. For instance, during these years children first encounter a feeling of jealousy when a new sibling is born. During short separations from parents, they learn to cope with a momentary sense of loss. Many preschoolers must learn to cope with the sorrow when a close family member or pet dies.

Care providers support children's emotional development by giving them many opportunities to express their emotions and ideas. Such communication can take place during pretend play or during mealtime conversations. When children experience conflict, care providers support children's emotional development by coaching them through the positive steps for problem solving and resolving conflict. See Chapter 11 for more information on conflict resolution.

Nurturing Social Development

Toddlers most often engage in solitary and parallel play. As you learned in Section 20-1, preschoolers venture into play that includes playing together and agreeing on play activities and themes, or cooperative play. Through cooperative play, preschoolers refine social skills, such as listening and sharing ideas with others. During cooperative play, they are more inclined to make plans with peers by taking turns and creating play themes together. The give-and-take of these play experiences increases children's social skills and stimulates greater peer learning.

Cooperative Learning. A preschooler's ability to cooperatively investigate a specific topic of interest with other children expands greatly and is called **cooperative learning**. As a result of greater experience with peers and a greater command of language, children can work well in groups. To encourage preschoolers' cooperative-learning skills, care providers can:

ETHICS IN Action

Cultural Sensitivity. The new preschooler in your care recently moved to America with his parents who are employed by an international company in your community. The child's ethnic clothing and unfamiliar accent were novelties to the other children at first. In the past few days, however, you have heard some of the children make fun of the new child, saying that he should learn how to talk right and dress right. Something should be done about it. *What would you do?*

Intergenerational Interactions

Building Birdhouses

Birds are beautiful and fascinating creatures. That's why bird watching is a favorite pastime for people of all ages. To attract birds, children, teens, and older adults can make birdhouses or nesting boxes out of simple materials, such as gourds, twigs, or wood. To make wood birdhouses or nesting boxes, you can purchase a kit from a local arts and crafts store or locate instructions on the Internet. Here are some general guidelines to remember when making birdhouses:

- Choose the type of birdhouse or nesting habitat for the species of bird you want to attract. Some birds, such as robins, like cup-shaped nests. Others like nesting habitats with a closed cavity, such as a birdhouse that they can go inside.

- Build the right size birdhouse. In the same way that people come in various shapes and sizes, so do birds. Various bird species will require different-size birdhouses and entrance holes. Locate birdhouse plans and kits for the various species that live in your area.

- Select woods, such as cedar, to build birdhouses with good insulating properties. Woods like cedar are naturally weather-resistant and blend in well with the environment. Avoid using treated lumber or exterior-grade plywood for building birdhouses. These building materials are treated with chemicals that may be toxic to birds.

- Paint *only* the outside of a birdhouse with exterior grade latex paint. Painting the inside of a birdhouse could leave residue that is toxic to the birds. Use light paint colors that blend in with the environment, such as gray or green.

- Mount birdhouses on specially designed metal or wood posts about six to ten feet off the ground. You can also hang certain types of birdhouses in trees, but that will depend on the species for which the house was built. For example, do not hang bluebird houses in trees because there will be too much competition for the house from other species.

- Protect birds in the birdhouses from other predators, such as squirrels. You can purchase sheet metal guards or make your own protective guard to use with birdhouses that are mounted on wood posts. Attach the guard to the post under the birdhouse.

Follow-Up

Use print or Internet resources to locate simple plans for building a wood birdhouse. The plans should be simple enough to use with children and older adults.

- Create more detailed, elaborate learning centers that encourage group play. Introduce a wider variety of play materials that require more advanced thinking skills.

- Provide more intricate play materials that require more refined perceptual motor skills. Include more toys that require cooperative play, such as board games. See Fig. 20-8.

- Plan projects that require teamwork, such as making murals or cardboard cities. Encourage children to suggest topics to investigate.

- Conduct activities that allow children to plan together and make decisions, such as creating and putting on a play.

Community Participation. With their expanding ability to grasp new concepts and information, preschoolers enjoy learning about the community. They benefit from seeing how many different people it takes to make communities operate. Learning about the many jobs and services a community needs helps children see how they can participate in communities when they become adults. To encourage preschoolers' community participation, care providers can:

- Offer field trips to introduce children to the diversity in their communities.

- Use community resources to expand the curriculum. For instance, visit the local humane society when studying pets.

FIG. 20-8. **Cooperative learning can take place as preschoolers relate better with peers and develop a strong command of language.** What can a care provider do to encourage cooperative learning?

- Invite community members to share their skills and knowledge with children.

- Include children in community service projects, such as picking up litter or donating toys.

- Draw children's attention to basic rules communities set for behavior. Help them identify rules and laws that protect everyone's safety and well-being.

Section **20-2** Knowledge Check

1. What routines should be part of a preschool program?
2. Name ways care providers can encourage emergent literacy.
3. List ways to engage preschoolers in cooperative learning.

Mini-Lab

List items to include in a preschool classroom and identify sources to obtain them. Sources may include cultural stores and centers, thrift shops, and catalogs. Room areas include: dress-up clothing; housekeeping corner; doll and puppet area; books; music and musical instruments. Share your findings with the class.

Chapter

20 Review & Activities

Section Summaries

20-1 Growth rate is slow and gradual during the preschool years.

20-1 Motor and perceptual motor skills improve during the preschool years.

20-1 Piaget described preschoolers' intellectual development as the preoperational period.

20-1 Preschoolers rapidly expand vocabulary and expressive language skills.

20-1 Preschoolers have better control over their emotions. They may still have a variety of fears.

20-1 Self-help skills and other physical and intellectual accomplishments enhance preschoolers' self-esteem.

20-1 Social development includes the ability to make friends, keep friends, and deal with peer conflicts.

20-2 Daily routines continue to be important in preschool programs.

20-2 Preschoolers are developing literacy skills.

20-2 Preschoolers are more capable of cooperative learning.

20-2 Preschoolers benefit from greater community participation.

Check Your Knowledge

1. Describe the characteristics of the preoperational period of intellectual development.
2. How should you handle children's grammar and pronunciation mistakes?
3. Describe the type of stuttering that is common in many preschoolers. What is usually the cause of their stuttering?
4. What is empathy?
5. What is initiative? Why does Erikson believe preschoolers strive to develop initiative?
6. Describe the relationship between children's self-esteem and their physical and intellectual accomplishments.
7. What is cooperative play?
8. What are ways to introduce preschoolers to community participation?
9. What are literacy tools for preschoolers?
10. What are ways to include print in a preschool program?

Thinking Critically

1. Contrast the advantages and disadvantages of growing up bilingual.
2. Should early childhood facilities hire both male and female care providers? Why?
3. Draw conclusions about the importance of providing a variety of activities for preschoolers.

Practical Applications

1. **Observation.** Observe a group of preschoolers at play. Note differences in their levels of physical, intellectual, emotional, and social development. Write a summary of your observations. Explain the influences on each area of development.

2. **Program Schedules.** Obtain a copy of the preschool program schedule from a local child care facility. Compare this schedule with the toddler program schedule you obtained earlier. Note differences between the two schedules and identify activities and routines that specifically meet the needs of preschool children. Present your findings in an oral report to your class.

3. **Activity Planning.** Plan one dramatic play activity that would help preschoolers develop in each of the following areas: literacy, cooperative learning, and community participation. If possible, use one of the activities with a group of preschoolers. Write a paragraph describing the results.

4. **Motor Development.** Plan several developmentally appropriate small motor, large motor, and sensory activities for preschoolers. If possible, conduct the activities with a small group of children. Evaluate your activities and write a paragraph describing how the activities could be improved.

Building Your PORTFOLIO

Planning a Preschool Program

Learning to plan a preschool program that broadens children's experiences will contribute to your success as a child care provider.

Step 1: Write an advertisement describing the qualities desired in a preschool care provider.

Step 2: Write a description of a preschool program that incorporates the rules established by your state's licensing laws. Include the number of preschoolers to be cared for, the number of care providers and their responsibilities, and your budget. Include a list of activities that will be used to foster literacy, cooperative learning, and community participation. Include ways to accommodate children with special needs.

Step 3: Plan the layout and design of the preschool room to scale. Select furnishings, equipment, and accessories for the room from catalogs or Web sites. Be sure the items you choose fit within your budget. Include pictures of your selections in your portfolio. Also include an emergency evacuation plan.

Step 4: Share your plan with the director of a facility that includes a preschool program. Ask the director to review your work for Steps 1, 2, and 3 and make suggestions for improvement. Revise your plans and include them in your portfolio.

Section 21-1

Development & Care

- Describe the overall development of school-age children.
- Explain how improved motor and perceptual motor skills influence school-age children's activities.
- Analyze the impact of puberty, self-esteem, competition, fear, stress, and rules on school-age children.
- Contrast friendship among preschoolers to that of school-age children.

KEY TERMS

growth plateau
puberty
hormones
depth perception
concrete operations
    period
industry
inferiority
egocentric
diversity

To work well with school-age children, you need to understand their unique development and challenges. Children ages six to 12 are considered school-age children. Because children change so much during these years, this book breaks down the ages for discussion. This chapter refers to children ages six to 10 as school-age children. References to older children apply to children ages 11 and 12 years of age.

Physical Development

Younger school-age children are in a **growth plateau**, which means their growth is slow and steady. They continue to build muscles and bone, giving them a longer, leaner appearance.

Figure 21-1 shows approximate heights and weights for children ages six to eight. Throughout this period, boys are a little heavier than girls. By age eight, however, girls catch up with boys in weight.

At ages five or six, children begin losing their baby teeth. Gaps left by missing teeth may temporarily affect speech, causing some children to lisp. The letters "s" and "z" may sound like "th."

By age 10, these children have many of their adult teeth.

Signs of Puberty. Around age 12 (slightly younger for girls), children undergo a surge of growth. Older children begin **puberty**—the transition stage when children undergo a series of physical changes and begin to look like adult men and women. Puberty is triggered by an increase in **hormones**, or chemical substances carried in the blood that impact growth and development. Puberty leads to adulthood. Girls may begin puberty at younger ages than boys, usually six months to a year earlier. Here are some changes that come with puberty:

FIG. 21-1.

AVERAGE HEIGHTS & WEIGHTS OF SIX- TO EIGHT-YEAR-OLDS

Age	Height	Weight
Six years	46 in.	45 lbs.
Seven years	48 in.	50 lbs.
Eight years	50 in.	55 lbs.

- Hormone changes cause girls to begin to menstruate, usually between ages 10 and 14.

- Body fat increases in girls, so they may weigh slightly more than boys. This is normal and healthy for girls during puberty. It is also not unusual for girls to surpass boys in height. Once boys are well into puberty, their height and weight surpass that of girls.

- Boys develop more muscle, which adds weight. Facial hair appears. Male hormone production causes boys' voices to gradually lower.

- The high level of hormone production can cause mood swings in both boys and girls.

Motor Development

School-age children perfect the skills they need for body control. Large muscles now work in unison, improving coordination. By age 10, all types of large motor movement, such as gal-

loping and leaping, are possible. School-age children often like to challenge their bodies with daring feats of climbing and other risky activities.

Control over small muscles is most often fully achieved by age seven or eight. The ability to control muscles in the wrists, hands, and fingers enables children to develop their handwriting or play a musical instrument.

Both genders experience increased muscle strength and coordination and improved perceptual motor skills. They become more skilled in team games and sports. These activities require quick movements, coordination of the body, and **depth perception**—the ability to judge distance and see objects in perspective. With perceptual motor development comes many new skills. Younger school-age children can learn to skate, play T-ball, and snow ski. By ages eight to ten, many can play hockey, dodge ball, and baseball. See Fig. 21-2.

FIG. 21-2. **School-age children experience an increase in muscle strength and coordination.** What activities might a care provider offer to promote physical skill development?

FIG. 21-3.

EXPANDING LANGUAGE & LITERACY SKILLS

Age	Skill Development
Six to Seven Years	• Learns to print capital and small letters. • Learns short vowel sounds and common consonant and vowel blends. • Reads a simple book alone. • Recognizes common word endings, such as -er and -ing.
Eight to Nine Years	• Prints all letters and begins to learn script (handwriting). • Reads aloud fluently. • Writes a simple story alone. • Begins to use a dictionary.
Ten Years and Older	• Writes in script automatically. • Reads for information and writes a simple factual report. • Begins to use indexes, appendices, and footnotes to find information. • Learns to use prefixes and suffixes to identify meanings of words.

Intellectual Development

The ability to create, analyze, and evaluate ideas progresses rapidly during the school-age years. According to Piaget, school-age children are no longer bound to learning through their senses like preschool children. They are now at Piaget's developmental stage of **concrete operations period**. During concrete operations, children (ages seven to 11) learn to think logically. They use valid reasoning to think things through and relate logic to actual objects and experiences. For example, during concrete operations:

• Children can grasp the principle of conservation, or considering several variables at one time. This allows them to classify and order different categories of objects. These are skills used in math and science. In this period, children can understand and calculate the passage of time.

• This age group still benefits from active learning with hands-on materials. However, increasingly they think abstractly. For instance, school-age children can remember the past, consider the present, and anticipate and plan for the future.

• Curiosity about a wide variety of topics is characteristic of school-age children. By age 10, they have mastered the basic language skills of speaking, reading, comprehending, and writing. They understand basic math concepts and can apply them in solving problems. Their abilities help school performance and allow children to pursue hobbies, such as woodworking or crafts. See Fig. 21-3.

Emotional Development

School-age children have a wide array of emotions. Increased language skills allow them to express their emotions frequently and more clearly. School-age children understand the viewpoints of others better; however, they do not always agree with others. True discussions and debates begin to surface.

With improved empathy, these children better recognize, understand, and sympathize with the feelings of others. School-age children can be very sensitive and sentimental. Their compassion inspires them to want to make a difference in the world.

Self-Esteem Development

By age six, most children have established a clear gender and role identity. They have developed strong ties to their families and cultural backgrounds. All of this helps children form a stable and secure self-concept.

According to Erikson, school-age children strive to develop a sense of **industry**. This is the desire to perform skills, succeed at tasks, and make social contributions. School-age children want to put their energy to use. Erikson claimed that if school-age children do not feel productive, they will develop a sense of **inferiority**, a feeling of not having met expected standards. Feeling inferior greatly damages self-esteem. School-age children develop self-confidence and pride when they achieve new physical accomplishments. They need successful experiences with peers—through games, sports activities, and group projects—to prevent feelings of inferiority from developing. See Fig. 21-4.

Competition

School-age children begin to compare themselves to other people. As they grow, these children encounter more competition in sports and school. Comparing their skills to those of others is only natural. Trying to measure is challenging, but it can also be disappointing.

Many people see healthy competition as good for children. It motivates them to do their best and helps them assess their individual abilities as compared to the group. Competition can refine skills and talents. Participating in a team rewards children for cooperating with others and recognizing their contributions.

Excessive emphasis on competition—the idea that winning is more important than

FIG. 21-4. As school-age children mature emotionally, they develop compassion for others and the world around them. What role do teachers and care providers play in helping school-age children develop emotionally?

FIG. 21-5. Healthy competition can help motivate school-age children to do their best work. What type of competition may be unhealthy? Why?

Responding to Bullying. Some children with low self-esteem become bullies, who taunt and threaten their classmates. Deep down, they lack confidence and fear they will not be liked. To prove—especially to themselves—that they are superior, they intimidate other children. Care providers need to treat bullies firmly, but with compassion. Make it clear that bullying behavior is not acceptable. Establish and follow through with developmentally appropriate consequences. Teach positive conflict resolution skills that are nonviolent. Talk with parents to learn how they handle bullying. At the same time, look for chances to praise and encourage the positive social qualities of these children.

enjoying the activity—can be harmful. Some children may focus more on their weaknesses than on their strengths. This also damages self-esteem. Children may avoid participating in activities for fear of failure, thereby hindering their development. To avoid these situations, many care providers emphasize cooperative games over competitive games. Confidence builds when children identify their strengths and take pride in them. See Fig. 21-5.

Typical Fears

When children reach school age, they usually let go of the specific preschool fears. They are not as likely to be afraid of things like dogs and storms. Instead, their increased reasoning skills allow for more abstract fears that are every bit as troubling. For example:

- School-age children may fear not belonging to a group. They often worry that they will not have friends. They may fear being different and not being accepted.

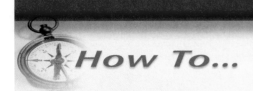

How To...

Prepare School-Age Children for Peer Pressure

As stronger peer relationships are formed, school-age children are more likely to feel peer pressure when making choices. This especially happens when they try to decide between right and wrong. There are times when the behavior and beliefs of school-age children will be highly influenced by peers. Sometimes this is good, sometimes not. Parents, family members, care providers, and teachers can help children comply with appropriate expectations, despite peer pressure. Following are helpful methods:

• Regularly take time to listen to school-age children, their hopes, and their concerns. Provide meaningful and respectful feedback during talks.

• Express trust in children's ability to make good independent decisions. Remind them that they can think for themselves and still be liked.

• Guide children to anticipate positive and negative consequences for behavior.

• Help children to value friends who do not pressure them to engage in questionable activities.

• Build self-esteem so children are not desperate to find love and attention from others.

• Maintain a calm environment where children feel safe and loved.

• Remind children that some secrets are too dangerous to keep. Encourage them to seek help from a trusted adult when someone scares them or makes them uncomfortable.

APPLY IT!

Interview one or more school-age children regarding their concerns about peer pressure.

• They may fear being teased and criticized. School-age children may imagine that others talk about them behind their back.

• Many school-age children fear failure. They dislike the thought of disappointing parents, care providers, and other respected adults.

Because school-age children are less **egocentric**—only seeing things from their own point of view—they worry about events they cannot control, such as war, earthquakes, or homelessness. Fears are very real to school-age children. Adults should take them seriously and not make fun of

them. Giving children a chance to talk about their fears is helpful.

School-Age Stressors. Stress is present at every stage of life. Children show stress in many ways. They may develop fatigue, apathy, and even depression. Some children become easily angered, aggressive, and disobedient. Symptoms, such as fingernail biting, also signal stress. Care providers should watch for these signals and consult with parents and mental health professionals when necessary. Stressors for school-age children include the following:

FIG. 21-6. **School-age children become stressed when they do not have enough leisure time to spend with family and friends.** How can teachers and care providers help school-age children achieve a good balance between school and home?

- Hours of energy needed to develop new intellectual and physical skills.
- New fears or excessive emphasis on competition with others.
- Rejection by peers.
- Less relaxation and leisure time at home with family and friends. See Fig. 21-6.
- Family and personal problems or changes, such as new siblings or divorce.

Social Development

School-age children handle friendships differently than preschoolers. Their friendships are more lasting and meaningful. Feelings and beliefs are shared. Children form friendships because they sincerely appreciate the characteristics of another person, not because of convenience or personal gain. Younger school-age children have many friends of both genders. By ages seven or eight, children prefer friends of the same gender.

School-age friendships remain fairly stable, despite periodic conflicts. Squabbling seems to be just another part of being friends. Socially competent school-age children know how to maintain friendships.

Among school-age friendships an attitude of "us versus them" sometimes exists. School-age children do have the capacity for great sensitivity. However, their growing concern for peer acceptance can lead them to be cruel to those not considered "friends."

Younger school-age children are very concerned about rules. They continue to obey them to earn rewards and avoid punishment. They also begin to see that rules are needed for people to live together peacefully. Awareness of rules and their purposes allows children to participate more in group games. Playing fairly takes on great importance to school-age children. See Fig. 21-7.

Diversity Awareness. The qualities people have that make them different from one another is called **diversity**. School-age children are aware of differences and similarities. They see differences in gender, race, culture, and

FIG. 21-7. School "buddies" can become lifelong friends. How can care providers encourage school-age children to build and maintain good friendships?

FIG. 21-8. A diverse classroom environment helps school-age children develop compassion and acceptance. How can you as a care provider model compassion and acceptance?

physical and mental abilities. They need role models who hold positive attitudes about diversity. Diversity should be discussed openly and honestly. Programs that include children from many economic, social, and cultural backgrounds help children accept and celebrate diversity. A diverse environment helps school-age children become compassionate, tolerant, and accepting. See Fig. 21-8.

Section 21-1 Knowledge Check

1. Describe growth patterns during puberty.
2. Explain how children progress through language development.
3. What are possible stressors for school-age children?

Mini-Lab

In newspapers and magazines, find articles and advertisements related to the stress and pressures school-age children face today. Discuss which types of stress are inevitable, which can be reduced, and which are completely avoidable.

Section 21-2

Managing School-Age Programs

- Explain the need for school-age child care programs.
- Describe an appropriate environment for school-age children.
- Discuss considerations in planning schedules, routines, and activities for school-age children.
- Identify ways to nurture overall development of school-age children.

KEY TERMS

latchkey children
special activities

You might think of the school-age years as the last act in the stage drama of childhood. Much has yet to be learned and resolved before the curtain falls. When it rises again, the main characters will be on the verge of adulthood. When children get what they need from skillful care providers, they can eventually manage adulthood with confidence and competence.

School-Age Programs

Millions of children who need care outside of school hours are left without adult supervision. Children who stay home alone before and after school are sometimes called **latchkey children**. This is because they carry a door key to let themselves in when no one else is at home. Children who are unsupervised can become bored and aimless. Even worse, in the event of an accident or emergency, they may confront real danger.

The need for school-age care programs is great. Such programs offer children a safe place to interact and learn until they can go home with an adult family member. These programs also bring peace of mind to parents who know their children are in a safe place.

Most of the children in school-age programs are between ages six and 10. However, some may be as old as 12. A typical program operates before school, from 6:00 a.m. to 9:00 a.m., and after school, from 2:00 p.m. to 6:00 p.m. On school holidays and during the summer, programs must be open all day.

Many school-age programs are part of a child care center. A bus or van takes children from the center to school in the morning and returns them in the afternoon. Increasingly, elementary schools are offering after-school care programs.

Ideally, a school-age group includes no more than about 20 children, although some states do allow more. Many states require only one care provider per 20 children. However, one care provider for every 10 children is most desirable. School-age children deserve a reasonable chance to receive personal attention. Being able to share the day's events with an adult helps them build self-esteem and cope with the pressures they often face.

After-school care enhances the growth and development of school-age children, but in a less structured manner than in the classroom. Quality programs provide school-age children chances for fun and for learning. They are safe but not stifling, stimulating but not stressful.

Environment

Classrooms in good school-age programs are casual and comfortable. A relaxed atmosphere helps children get the day off to a good start. It also helps them unwind after a long and sometimes stressful day at school.

A well-planned classroom includes learning centers that offer many interesting activities. There are also private areas, where children can read quietly, listen to music, or talk with a friend. Furnishings include soft sofas or beanbag chairs and tables or desks for doing homework.

Learning centers for school-age children should not simply be larger versions of those created for preschoolers. Some learning center titles may be the same, but materials and activities must be designed for children ages six to 12. An arts and crafts area may include materials for drawing, painting, pasting, weaving, jewelry making, and photography. See Fig. 21-9.

FIG. 21-9. School-age children have diverse interests and hobbies. What learning center activities should be provided for school-age children?

Ideally, programs provide indoor and outdoor areas for active play. On-site programs usually have access to the school gymnasium, playing fields, and sports equipment.

Daily Routines

Like everyone else, school-age children need some predictable daily routines. However, they also need variety and choices. As children get older, they must learn to make good use of their time, rather than having all their activities planned for them. Thus, programs for school-age children strike a balance between routines and the freedom of unstructured time.

Daily routines include arrival and departure time, both in the morning and in the afternoon. The arrival routine includes a greeting and a health check. See Chapter 6 for more information on health checks. Younger children may enjoy a song to begin the day.

After arrival, most programs schedule a planning time. Children hear about the activity options for the day, so they can make choices. One or more group activities may be offered, such as woodworking instruction and a soccer game. In addition, blocks of time are set aside for children to do activities they enjoy, such as playing checkers with a friend, reading for pleasure, or climbing on outdoor play equipment. Leisure time is especially necessary in the afternoon, after children have spent the day in school.

Meals are a large part of daily routines. Breakfast gets the day off to a good start. A healthful snack in the afternoon satisfies a child's hunger after school and helps meet nutritional needs. During the summer and on holidays, most programs serve breakfast, lunch, and two snacks. Meal routines should be calm and leisurely. To build skills and a sense of

FIG. 21-10. A healthful snack is part of the daily routine in after-school care programs. What types of healthful snacks may appeal to school-age children?

responsibility, children can help prepare food, set tables, and clear dishes. See Fig. 21-10.

All-day programs generally provide a rest time, especially for children six and seven years old. Grooming and hygiene are other regular routines.

Planning Activities

When it comes to planning activities, school-age programs share some qualities with programs for younger ages. Care providers must plan for all areas of development, instead of focusing on just one or two. The program should provide a reasonable balance between quiet, active, indoor, outdoor, large-group, and small-group experiences.

Care providers in school-age programs spend less time directing specific activities. Preschool care providers might plan for young children to make collage pictures of farm animals. School-age children would find this too restrictive. They need the freedom not only to decide

FIG. 21-11. **School-age children enjoy participating in a variety of after-school activities, including martial arts.**

whether to make a collage, but also to determine the type of collage to make and how to make it.

Care providers of school-age children provide stimulating options. Creative care providers enjoy sharing their own hobbies, such as cooking, computers, or dance. They discover new interests along with the children. They expand on the activities that children find most appealing.

Another planning challenge a care provider for school-age program faces is a classroom with a wide age range of children. The needs, interests, and abilities of a six-year-old are much different from those of a 12-year-old. Accommodating all ages can be a challenge. Sometimes organizing groups of younger and older children works best. However, children also benefit from mixed-age groupings. Younger children look up to older ones and enjoy learning from them. Older chil-

dren gain a sense of responsibility by watching out for younger ones and helping to plan activities for them. Many experiences, such as a nature walk, can interest both younger and older children, if care providers are sensitive to the needs of each age group.

Community Participation. During school vacations, when children attend all-day child care programs, field trips can stimulate interest and provide new experiences. Explore your community for good resources. Museums, aquariums, and zoos are natural choices. Children may also enjoy visiting an ethnic restaurant, an airport or train station, a utility company, a recycling center, a bank, a plant nursery, or a bicycle shop. Of course, a trip to a park, swimming pool, or other recreational facility is always welcome. Be sure to invite parents to attend field trips whenever possible. Taking field trips to parents' workplaces is also a good way to encourage parent involvement in the program.

Clubs and Special Activities. Some programs for school-age children form clubs around a special theme. Clubs foster interests and build friendships. Clubs for children may include creative writing, photography, collecting trading cards, drama, or art. A survey of children's interests can help you decide which clubs to offer. Many programs also offer **special activities**, such as gymnastics, swimming lessons, or organized sports. Usually, parents must pay an extra charge for these activities. Like clubs, special activities allow children to apply skills, expand interests, and form friendships. See Fig. 21-11.

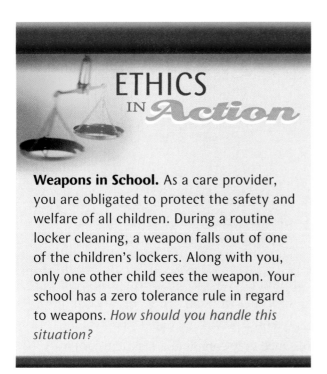

Weapons in School. As a care provider, you are obligated to protect the safety and welfare of all children. During a routine locker cleaning, a weapon falls out of one of the children's lockers. Along with you, only one other child sees the weapon. Your school has a zero tolerance rule in regard to weapons. *How should you handle this situation?*

Nurturing Development

School-age children do not need the constant supervision required for younger children. However, care providers must still keep up with their developmental needs. Care providers must also recognize and report to parents any delays in development. Children this age need chances to be active and to investigate their world. They need support from caring adults as they mature and expand their horizons.

- **Physical development.** Children need opportunities to participate in physical activities. This helps with physical fitness. Large motor skills are needed when children play tag and other active games, hold relay races, or play team sports, such as T-ball and volleyball. Noncompetitive activities also aid development. Children enjoy jumping rope, skating, using outdoor play equipment, and engaging in creative movement. Small motor skills and eye-hand coordination are strengthened through arts and crafts, such as needlework, pottery, basket weaving, woodworking, and model building. See Fig. 21-12.

- **Intellectual development.** School-age programs can provide enjoyable, interesting ways for children to use their minds. These children like group games that challenge them to think and solve problems. Many popular card, board, and computer games are fun and stimulate thinking skills. Microscopes, magnets, magnifiers, and prisms can encourage children to explore the natural world. Children's reference books help them to identify native trees, flowers, butterflies, and birds. Nurture language skills

FIG. 21-12. Physical fitness is important for school-age children. Identify at least five types of fitness activities, both group and individual, that would be appropriate for school-age children.

Independence Skills

Helping Children with Homework

School-age children often have homework to complete after school. Sharing a few study skills with them can help them develop positive lifelong study habits.

1. Have the children begin by listing all the homework tasks they need to complete. Depending on the age of the child, there may be a printed assignment sheet from the teacher or an assignment notebook with homework notes written by the student. Check each day to see that it is being used.

2. Once the tasks are listed, have children prioritize their list by identifying the most important task or tasks with which they will need the most help to complete.

3. Next, have the children gather all necessary supplies and materials they will need. These may include pens, pencils, paper, books, crayons, markers, or other items.

4. Tell the children to start first on the task they identified as the most important task or the one with which they need the most help.

5. Assist children by answering questions or checking work for them. Teach them how to check their own math answers.

6. Once they complete a task, have them mark it off their list.

7. Create a system of communicating with parents about homework completion. Let parents know each day what needs to be done.

Try It!

Help one child complete his or her homework at least once a week for a grading period. Did the child's grades improve during that period of time? Is the child able to implement study skills independently? Present your findings in an oral report to your class.

---

by creating quiet areas for leisure reading. Provide a library of paperback books for children to exchange. Be aware of students who are not native language speakers. Provide various language experiences at different levels for these children.

- **Creative development.** Encourage children to apply creativity and imagination to all areas of life and learning. Let them experiment with art materials and help decorate

the classroom. Encourage them to make new types of structures with building blocks. Give them opportunities to write stories, poems, songs, and plays. Older children might put on a puppet show for the younger ones, using a script they write themselves and puppets they make.

- **Emotional development.** It is not always easy for school-age children to sort through their emotions. Care providers should be

Boosting **Brain Power**

Musical Training Builds Math Skills.
Researchers have found that children who learn to play a musical instrument also perform math tasks better. This is because portions of the brain that process the knowledge needed to play an instrument also process mathematical information. Learning to read music and regular practice playing an instrument build and reinforce the information pathways that allow the brain to make sense of both music and math.

assuming greater responsibilities. Chances to do so build their self-esteem. Younger school-age children may be given a choice of snacks from a selection of nutritious foods. An older child may be responsible for organizing books in the reading area. Encouraging pride in children's cultural background is another way to boost self-esteem. Invite children to share foods, celebrations, history, and other aspects of their cultural heritage. Children who are secure in their cultural identity tend to be more accepting of other cultural groups.

• **Social development.** Cooperative projects are a good way to help children develop social skills. Children might work together to paint a mural, construct a large papier-mâché

available to listen to school-age children's thoughts, feelings, and fears. They may help children recognize their emotions by naming them for the children. In particular, care providers can be a valuable resource for children who are confused about peer relationships. Sensitive care providers give school-age children opportunities to examine their emotions. One way is through drama and other creative activities. School-age children may also like keeping a diary or recording their feelings on a tape recorder. (Ensure privacy when this is done.) Care providers can supply many good books dealing with school-age emotions. Children from different cultures might express feelings in different ways. When selecting books, consider the different cultures of the children and try to offer books that accurately portray different ethnic groups. See Fig. 21-13.

• **Building self-esteem.** School-age children are capable of making more decisions and

FIG. 21-13. The use of drama is one way for school-age children to express emotion. What other types of creative activities would benefit the emotional development of school-age children?

Intergenerational *Interactions*

Adopt-a-Grandparent Program

Many young people take for granted the chance to sit, talk, and play with their grandparents. However, for children who do not have a grandparent living near them, programs that allow children to "adopt" grandparents are a great way for them to form relationships with older adults. Older adults also benefit from these types of programs. Fortunately for all generations, there are many adopt-a-grandparent programs operating throughout America.

- **Elders Without Walls** offers an electronic adopt-a-grandparent program. While visiting the Elders Without Walls Web site, potential "grandchildren" can select an e-mail Pen-Pal. Pen-Pals are retirement home residents who want to communicate with children of all ages. Through regular communication with these older adults, foster grandchildren may exchange information about hobbies, background, or interests.

- **University of Georgia** students enjoy meeting two hours each week at area nursing homes or at the *Athens Council on Aging*. Through this adopt-a-grandparent program, students may develop a relationship with one special older adult or enjoy group activities, such as dancing.

- **Students of Quail Valley Middle School** near Houston, Texas, volunteered over 10,000 hours to the *Mariner Health of First Colony* from 1998 to 2001. For one hour each Friday of the school year, volunteer

students are divided into groups. Each group visits with two adopted grandparents. Some students enjoy the time they spend with the older adults so much that they continue visiting with their "grandparents" throughout the summer. The program teaches students to respect older adults and to enjoy getting involved in community activities.

Follow-Up

Write a one-page report on an ideal adopt-a-grandparent program. You may research an actual program, or make up qualities that you think are necessary to create the perfect program. Discuss how children and older adults benefit from the program.

dinosaur, or prepare a meal together. Planning parties is also a good exercise in cooperation and teamwork. Field trips can expand children's awareness of their community, as can special classroom visitors. Include parents as guest speakers—not only can they share information about their work, but they will also enjoy visiting their child's classroom.

- **Guiding behavior.** The principles of positive guidance discussed in Chapter 11 apply to all age groups. However, care providers must take the child's level of development into account. School-age children need fewer restrictions than preschoolers. They also have greater expectations for responsible behavior. All children, for example, can be taught to respect the property of others. Older children can see how this principle requires them to take care of the program's equipment so that all can enjoy it. As children move toward independence, they may still test the limits set for them. Care providers must establish clear, firm boundaries for acceptable behavior. School-age children are more likely to follow rules when they help create them. Discussing and voting on rules teaches children to consider the needs

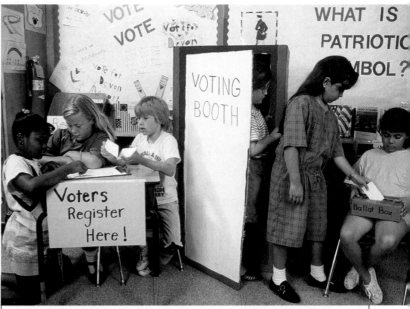

FIG. 21-14. School-age children are more likely to follow classroom rules when they help set them. What does this teach school-age children about teamwork and cooperation?

and wishes of others. They also learn to negotiate and compromise to reach an agreement. Care providers should show respect for the children and always speak courteously to them when discussing rules. In this way, care providers can model appropriate discussions while building students' self-esteem. See Fig. 21-14.

Section 21-2 Knowledge Check

1. Who are latchkey children?
2. Describe the characteristics of an appropriate environment for school-age children.
3. What types of clubs do school-age children enjoy?

Mini-Lab

Interview a school-age child who attends a child care program. Ask the child what he or she likes and dislikes about the experience. Record suggestions the child has for program improvements.

Section Summaries

21-1 Younger school-age children are in a growth plateau. Older school-age children are approaching, or experiencing, a growth spurt and the beginning of puberty.

21-1 Motor and perceptual motor skills develop rapidly during the school-age years.

21-1 School-age children are in the concrete operations period of intellectual development.

21-1 Competition, fears, stress, and puberty affect emotional development.

21-1 School-age children form deep and meaningful friendships.

21-2 Programs for school-age children provide care during times when children are not in school and parents cannot be with them.

21-2 School-age children need less supervision and structure than do preschoolers.

21-2 Quality programs provide a safe, interesting, and relaxed environment for school-age children.

21-2 School-age children need a reasonable amount of freedom to choose their own activities.

21-2 Field trips, clubs, and other special activities can add interest to the program.

21-2 Physical, intellectual, emotional, and social development are nurtured in school-age child care programs.

Check Your Knowledge

1. Briefly describe the motor development of school-age children and how it influences the activities they enjoy.

2. Explain Erikson's beliefs about the relationship between industry and inferiority.

3. Describe both the positive and negative effects of competition on emotional development.

4. How and why do school-age children's fears differ from preschoolers'? Give examples.

5. What happens when care programs for school-age children are not available? Why is this a problem?

6. What is an ideal group size and number of care providers for a school-age program?

7. How do learning centers for school-age children differ from those for preschoolers?

8. What can care providers do to counteract the negative influence of peer pressure?

Thinking Critically

1. What are advantages and disadvantages of self-care versus program care for school-age children? Answer from three viewpoints: parent, child, and child care services provider.

2. Explain influences on the physical, emotional, social, and intellectual development of school-age children. How does puberty influence development?

3. Draw conclusions about ways classrooms and routines for school-age children should differ from those designed for preschoolers.

Practical Applications

1. **Observation.** Observe a group of school-age children in a care program. Determine differences in age, physical growth, motor development, intellectual development, emotional development, and social development. Do you notice any characteristics indicative of special needs in the children? Write a summary of your observations.

2. **Contrasting Programs.** Obtain a copy of the school-age program schedule from a local care facility or on-site school-age child care program. Compare this schedule with the preschool program schedule you obtained earlier. In a brief report, note differences between the two schedules and identify activities and routines that specifically meet the needs of school-age children.

3. **Activity Planning.** Plan three activities that would be appropriate for school-age children. The activities should be culturally diverse and anti-bias in nature. Include at least one activity that would encourage community participation or foster special interests. Be sure to include accommodations for children with special needs. If possible, use one of the activities with a group of school-age children. Present your results in an oral report to your class.

Building Your PORTFOLIO

Planning a School–Age Program

Learning to plan a school-age program that broadens children's experiences will contribute to your success as a child care provider.

Step 1: Write an advertisement describing the qualities desired in a school-age care provider.

Step 2: Write a description of a school-age program that incorporates the rules established by your state's licensing laws. Include the number of school-age children to be cared for, the size and ages of the group, the number of care providers, and their responsibilities. Determine a reasonable budget for your program. List activities that will be provided, including those that encourage community participation and special interests.

Step 3: Plan the layout and design of the school-age room. Draw the layout of the room to scale. Select furnishings, equipment, and accessories for the room from catalogs or Web sites. Make sure you stay within the budget you set. Include pictures of your selections in your portfolio.

Step 4: Share your plan with the director of a facility that includes a school-age care program. Ask the director to review your work for Steps 1, 2, and 3 and make suggestions for improvement. Revise your plans and put them in your portfolio.

Chapter 22
Caring for Special Needs Children

Section 22-1
Development & Care

Section 22-2
Managing Inclusive Programs

Section 22-1

Development & Care

The unique development and abilities of children vary. In any classroom, some children may be developmentally ahead, and some may lag behind. Some children with special needs require extra attention. Sensitive care providers respond to them with these needs in mind. They plan activities so all children can participate to the best of their abilities.

Defining Special Needs

The term **special needs** refers to circumstances that cause a child's physical, cognitive, and behavioral development to vary significantly from the norm. Some children with special needs have disabilities, such as vision problems, limited mobility, mental retardation, or learning difficulties. Other children who learn and develop more quickly than others may be gifted. As an example, a child who is physically disabled may be a gifted writer or artist.

It is important to think of children with special needs as children first and as people with disabilities second. Like all children, those with

special needs have the same basic desire to be loved, accepted, and respected. Each requires a secure, nurturing, and stimulating environment.

Laws Impacting Special Needs

As a means to help parents, care providers, and other advocates ensure that children with disabilities have their needs met, certain laws exist that offer safeguards in obtaining a free and appropriate education. The key laws concerning children with special needs include:

- **Individuals with Disabilities Education Act (IDEA).** IDEA guarantees free special education and related services to all children with disabilities ages three to 21. An individualized program of goal-oriented instruction is designed to meet the needs of each child. Parents must be included in the planning process. Related services may include speech, physical, or occupational therapies.

- **Americans with Disabilities Act (ADA).** This civil rights law prohibits discrimination on the basis of a disability in public services, accommodations, and employment. The ADA law requires that all children be eligible for child care services, despite their special needs. This law provides for equal access to public and private services and facilities. For example, a ramp may need to be installed for wheelchair access to a child care center.

- **Rehabilitation Act, Section 504.** Like the ADA law, this law prohibits discrimination against persons with disabilities. This law states that people with disabilities should have an equal chance to be successful. The services and protections of this law extend beyond IDEA. For example, eligibility for services covers people from birth to death and is not related to specific categories of disabilities.

Specific Disabilities

In order for children with special needs to participate more fully, sometimes changes are made in a classroom. Such changes are called **accommodations**. The information that follows identifies characteristics and accommodations for those with special needs or disabilities.

Hearing Impairments

Difficulty in hearing ranges from mild impairment to total deafness. Hearing problems interfere with language development and other areas of learning. Social relationships can be more challenging for those who have hearing problems. Here are some ways that children with hearing impairments communicate:

ETHICS IN Action

Meeting Special Needs. Your center director informs you that a new child will be joining your class. The child has cerebral palsy and is unable to talk or walk. Upon his arrival, the other children ask questions about why he cannot walk, why he drools, and why his hands are curled. After the other children's parents arrive, they ask you how you will meet all the needs of the children when you have one who requires so much attention. *What do you say?*

- **Hearing aids.** Some children have limited to almost full hearing with the use of hearing aids. Care providers should ask parents to teach them how to handle the device properly. Hearing aids have limitations. A child who uses one cannot be expected to hear a care provider who is at the other end of the room. Hearing aids make all sounds louder. Care providers should reduce distracting background noise whenever possible.

- **Sign language.** Some hearing-impaired children use *American Sign Language* to communicate with others. Care providers should become familiar with sign language to communicate with the hearing-impaired child. The program may also provide an interpreter skilled in sign language to help with a child's communication skills. Children with hearing impairments who sign often enjoy being able to teach others how to sign.

- **Lip-reading.** When a child lip-reads, make sure you face the child when you speak. Communicate with the child at eye level and face the light if possible. Lipstick helps draw attention to a female care provider's lips. Male teachers should be clean-shaven so that lips can be easily seen. Lip movement should be distinct but natural. Children who read lips should sit directly in the front of the care provider during group activities. Facial expressions and frequent gestures help convey meaning.

- **Visual helps.** Props, pictures, and hands-on experiences help children with hearing impairments learn concepts. You might illustrate a story's plot as you read it, for example. During music time, let a child with a hearing impairment feel the vibration of the musical instrument. Clapping along with music lets the child sense a song's rhythm. Use visual cues—such as turning the lights on and off— to signal transitions between activities. See Fig. 22-1.

Vision Impairments

Vision impairments range from mild loss to total blindness. Children with severe vision impairment need a consistent physical arrangement in the classroom. They often memorize room set-up to help identify clear pathways.

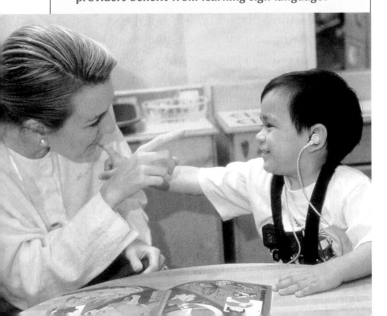

FIG. 22-1. A hearing-impaired child may use various methods of communicating, such as lip-reading or American Sign Language. How can all care providers benefit from learning sign language?

High-contrast color tape along the edges of the furniture gives visual cues to children with minimal vision loss. Always provide consistent storage for all classroom materials. Cubbies can be marked with bows, feathers, or large buttons. To help children with severe vision loss, use plastic labels with raised print or Braille labels. Braille is the system of writing for the blind that uses characters made of raised dots.

Encourage children to use their other senses to move around the classroom. For example, point out that paints and clay make the art center smell different from other areas of the room. Mark different parts of the room with items that can be felt, heard, or smelled.

Vision impairments interfere with learning by limiting cognitive associations. Impaired vision can also diminish curiosity. Children who cannot see new things have less reason to explore. Physical and intellectual growth may be hindered as a result. Care providers must use the child's other senses to motivate learning.

To adapt activities, use words and hands-on experiences as much as possible. For example, during a garden activity, let the child touch and smell the soil and the seeds. Guide the child's hand as you dig with the spade, while describing what is happening. Let the child hear and feel the drops from the watering can. In the classroom, provide toys of many different shapes, textures, and weights, especially ones that move or make sounds. Provide safe, open areas for small and large motor activities, such as creating a mural or running outdoors.

Many books and games are available in large-print versions to benefit children with impaired vision. Care providers can enlarge some classroom materials for easier viewing. Children who are blind can listen to recorded stories or music.

Physical & Motor Impairments

Some children have physical conditions that affect their large or small motor abilities. They may use crutches, a walker, or a wheelchair to get around. They may have poor muscle control or be missing part of an arm. All of these conditions create challenges, but none should prevent a child from participating in a program.

The first step in making accommodations is to ensure that the building is accessible. If a child uses a wheelchair, doors and pathways need to be wide enough for easy access. See Chapter 12 on ADA guidelines. If a child has limited use of his or her hands, faucets in hand-washing areas must be easy to operate. Remember that the goal is to provide all children in the classroom with the same level of independence. See Fig. 22-2.

Classroom routines, play equipment, and activities may also need adaptations. Many solutions do not require much time or expense—just some creative thinking. For example, you may need to provide:

- Double-handled cups to use at mealtime.

FIG. 22-2. When planning an early childhood center, plans should include accessibility requirements for children who are confined to wheelchairs and other mobility devices. What environmental qualities would make the center user-friendly for children?

- Puzzle pieces fitted with large knobs for easier handling. Or, suction cups that attach to the bottom of toys can help hold them steady.
- Raised sandboxes to accommodate children in wheelchairs, and beanbags attached to long pieces of string to make them easier to retrieve when playing target games.
- Chairs with seat straps for children who cannot easily sit.

Cognitive Impairments

Like physical impairments, cognitive disabilities may be mild, moderate, or severe. Children who are cognitively challenged develop intellectual abilities more slowly than others. Their intellectual skills can be altered. These children may have shorter-than-average attention spans. Motor skills and eye-hand coordination are often affected. Some show less emotional control and have fewer social skills than other children.

Children with cognitive impairments may be placed in a classroom according to their developmental abilities, not their chronological ages. These children respond well when given short, clear directions. You may need to break down activities into simple steps. You also may need to guide these children more closely. Demonstrate and repeat activities as often as needed. Give children many chances for success.

Learning Disabilities. A disorder that affects the way the brain processes information is called a **learning disability**. It is not the same as a mental impairment. In fact, many children with learning disabilities have above-average intelligence. However, because they cannot interpret and use information in a typical way, learning may be hindered. Learning disabilities can be caused by errors in fetal brain development, alcohol and drug use during pregnancy, problems during birth, or toxins in the environment. Many specific types of learning disabilities exist. Here are some examples:

- **Speech and written language disorders.** Children may have difficulty understanding spoken and written language or may have difficulty speaking. A disorder called **aphasia** (uh-FAY-zhee-uh) is a language impairment that affects a child's use of speech and understanding of language.

- **Reading disorder.** With the reading disorder **dyslexia** (dihs-LEK-see-uh), a child may have trouble learning to recognize letters of the alphabet and difficulty reading. With dyslexia, the letters may appear backwards or jumbled or seem to move around on the page.

- **Math disorder.** A disorder related to math skills is called **dyscalcula** (dihs-KAL-kew-luh). The child may be unable to count objects or recognize basic shapes. See Fig. 22-3.

- **Reasoning and memory disorders.** These disorders are often caused by severe head injuries. Children with a reasoning disorder may have difficulty organizing learned facts or organizing and integrating thoughts. Children with a memory disorder may have trouble remembering instructions and what they have learned.

Mental Retardation. Mental retardation may be characterized by less than average intelligence and limited adaptive skills, such as self-care skills and social skills. Mental retardation is a permanent condition. It appears some time during early childhood and must be carefully diagnosed by a team of people, such as a psychologist, physician, learning specialist, and the child's parents. When parents suspect their child may have a problem, they often seek outside assessment before the child starts preschool or elementary school. Children with mental retardation have varying levels of skills.

Professionals trained to identify learning disorders and those that help children overcome them are called **learning specialists.** They can help children learn to use different ways of gathering, organizing, and interpreting information. Counselors can help children deal with behavioral and self-esteem problems associated with learning disabilities. Care providers work closely with parents and specialists to determine what techniques best meet the child's needs.

FIG. 22-3. Parents or care providers may notice that a child has a learning difficulty at an early age. What are the future benefits of early diagnosis of learning disabilities?

Behavioral & Emotional Disorders

All children occasionally have trouble relating to others or coping with their emotions. Their behavior may be aggressive or overly active at times. With some children, however, emotional or behavioral problems are frequent and extreme. Their behavior interferes with learning. These children may be diagnosed with a behavioral or emotional disorder. Here are some examples:

- **Attention deficit hyperactivity disorder.** A disorder of the central nervous system that is caused by a lack of certain brain chemicals is called **attention deficit hyperactivity disorder (ADHD).** Some children with ADHD have difficulty paying attention and following instructions. Others are aggressive, impulsive, and overly active. Some show a combination of these symptoms. ADHD is *not* a learning disability; however, sometimes children with a learning disability may have ADHD. Children with ADHD may be treated with certain medications.

- **Autism.** Typically affecting communication and social interaction, **autism** is a brain disorder that impacts normal development. Children with autism may show a wide range of symptoms and disabilities. Children with autism can vary in language skills and intelligence. The symptoms may include repeated actions, such as rocking, head banging, and rigidly following daily routines. Autistic children may be very sensitive to touch, sound, light, or smell. Some people with autism display exceptional skills in one particular area, such as art, music, or completing complex puzzles. Diagnosing autism is not easy. Several conditions can mimic autism. The parents and pediatrician must rule out these other disorders before a team of specialists begins the process of identifying autism. By age three, specialists must observe clear evidence of poor social relationships, underdeveloped communication skills, and repetitive behaviors, interests, and activities. Early intervention and special education can help autistic children to learn, communicate, and have productive social relationships.

Children may have other behavioral and emotional disorders. For example, children may be withdrawn, depressed, anxious, unusually fearful, or violent.

Children with behavioral and emotional disorders require professional help. Medication may be prescribed by a medical doctor to control the symptoms. Psychological therapy can also be helpful. The classroom atmosphere should be a calm, consistent, and nurturing one. Care providers should also make sure they understand the child's culture and assist the child in expressing feelings in culturally appropriate ways.

Health Conditions

Some children have health conditions—such as asthma, epilepsy, or diabetes—that may affect how they participate in activities. Some health conditions require medications to be administered while a child is in group care. Care providers may want to discuss a child's health profile with the parents and the child's doctor.

Accommodating Health Conditions. Accommodating children's individual health conditions sometimes requires care providers to make adjustments in how activities are conducted. Accommodation may require a provider to be prepared to cope with an unpredictable health emergency. A child highly allergic to bee stings needs to be included on outdoor walks. However, an alert provider would avoid walking in areas where bees may visit. If applicable, the provider would include the child's bee sting medication in a first aid kit taken along during the walk. See Fig. 22-4.

Gifted & Talented Children

Gifted children are those who have extraordinary talent in one or more areas. Some children are intellectually gifted. Others excel in some form of artistic expression, such as music or art. Exceptional athletes have physical talents and abilities. Signs indicating giftedness include:

FIG. 22-4. Some children have health conditions, such as asthma, that require daily monitoring by care providers. The child's physician and parents must authorize medications. Why is it important for care providers to talk with parents daily about medications?

- A good memory and advanced vocabulary and language skills. Ease in grasping new concepts and ideas.

- Developmental skills—such as walking and talking—that are acquired earlier than usual in infancy than most peers.

- Creativity in inventing and problem solving.

- Intense curiosity and advanced attention span with an ability to concentrate on and persist in complex tasks. An unusual attention to detail.

- A preference for company of older playmates and adults.

- A good sense of humor.

- Talent for making plans and organizing tasks.

Gifted children need programs that challenge them at their advanced developmental levels. Otherwise they lose interest and do not bother to do their best. They may misbehave out of boredom. Care providers can respond to gifted children in many ways. For example:

- Plan enrichment activities that explore concepts in more depth.

- Plan group projects and involve gifted children in the planning and organizing.

- Include field trips and special visitors to help satisfy a gifted child's intellect, as well as stimulate and motivate other children.

FIG. 22-5. **Some children are gifted or talented with certain abilities in one or more areas while at the same time they lose interest in other areas.** What should care providers do to accommodate the needs of children with special gifts and talents?

Because they pay close attention to detail, gifted children often take longer to complete projects to their satisfaction. Allow them large blocks of time to thoroughly investigate topics. Avoid rushing them through projects.

Children who excel in a particular area, such as dance or music, should be given adequate opportunity to develop their skills. If lessons or experiences outside the program are not available to the child, recruit a volunteer talented in that area. See Fig. 22-5.

Section 22-1   Knowledge Check

1. What laws impact the care and education of children with special needs?

2. List three types of specific disabilities you might encounter in an early childhood classroom.

3. What characteristics may indicate a child is gifted?

Mini-Lab

Take a tour of your school using a wheelchair or crutches. Include all areas, indoors and outdoors. What obstacles did you encounter? Record how you felt when you encountered each obstacle. List ways to eliminate the obstacles you found. Share your findings with your class.

Section **22-2**

Managing Inclusive Programs

The education of children with special needs has changed greatly in recent decades. In the past, children with special needs were automatically assigned to special education classes or special schools. For some, that remains the best option. However, people are recognizing the value of including children with special needs in regular classrooms.

Inclusive Programs

Research shows that children with special needs learn best when they learn from positive role models in the natural environment. The Individuals with Disabilities Education Act (IDEA) is a federal law that states that children with disabilities must be educated with children who are not disabled whenever possible. This is called **inclusion,** or integrating children with special needs into regular education classrooms. The Americans with Disabilities Act (ADA) further ensures equal access opportunities for people with disabilities in all public areas.

These laws mean that children with disabilities cannot legally be excluded from public child care programs. Private programs have the same obligation, unless the cost of including such children is financially impossible.

Providers can explore many resources to locate the items they need for serving children who have disabilities. The Easter Seals organization is one source of information, assistance, and referral. Volunteers, training programs, and special funding also may be available through community resources. See Fig. 22-6.

Supportive Care Providers

Successful inclusion begins with positive attitudes among care providers. Those who accept and respect children with special needs serve as

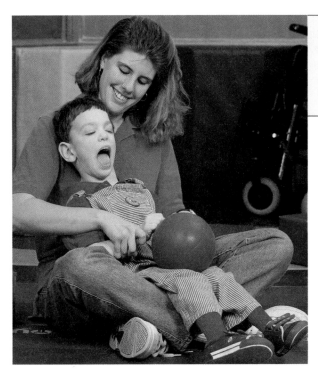

FIG. 22-6. **Successful inclusive programs begin with care providers and educators who understand special needs and focus on the abilities, rather than the disabilities, of children.** Investigate the requirements to be a special education teacher.

a model for others. Care provider attitudes set the tone for the classroom, helping to create a comfortable atmosphere for everyone. Effective care providers focus on abilities of these children, not their disabilities. They find out what children with disabilities can do and encourage them to work to their potential.

As much as possible, treat a child with special needs as any other. Expect no more or less than the child is capable of doing. Show patience and understanding. As with all children, avoid labeling. Children should not be defined by their disabilities.

Tolerance & Understanding

When children encounter something new, they are usually curious about it. They may also be fearful at first. Meeting someone who has a disability is no different. A person who wears leg braces, or someone whose speech is slurred because of a mental disability may seem strange and puzzling to many young children. Care providers can minimize these natural reactions by helping children better understand disabilities.

Care providers can promote understanding in many ways. Books are available to help children of various ages understand differences. Special puppet programs feature characters who talk about their disabilities. In one outreach project, dolls with special needs visit children without disabilities and their families for a weekend. The dolls come with letters that describe their special needs and suggest things the family can do to make their stay more pleasant.

In addition to learning about disabilities, children need to see that people who are different are part of everyday life. Display posters and pictures that show children of varying abilities playing together. Provide stories that affirm disabilities without making them the focus of the plot. In the dramatic play area, include dolls, puppets, and doll house figures that represent children with special needs. Invite adults with special needs to the program as guest speakers. Ask them to talk about their hobbies, talents, or careers. This helps children see that people with varying needs can lead independent and successful lives.

Goals of Inclusive Programs

Research shows that children with and without disabilities benefit from inclusion. Following are goals of inclusive programs:

- Provide all children with enriching experiences they might otherwise miss.

- Help all children value diversity. Encourage compassion, respect, and appreciation for all.

Intergenerational Interactions

Any Baby Can

Any Baby Can of San Antonio was founded in 1982. Serving 12 counties around San Antonio, the program is focused on helping chronically and critically ill or disabled children meet their full potential. To make the lives of these children and their families easier, *Any Baby Can* finds medical/nutritional, therapeutic, and educational resources for them. The program also helps families cope with the challenges of raising children with special needs. Among the program's many fine services is the *Family Friends* intergenerational volunteer program.

- **Crisis Assistance** helps families meet immediate needs—financial, medical equipment, medication, and supplies.

- **Information and Referral** puts families in touch with resources, organizations, and support groups that will help them manage care for the ill or disabled child in their lives.

- **Family Friends** at *Any Baby Can* started as a National Council on the Aging (NCOA) pilot program. The service still follows many NCOA guidelines as it links older adult volunteers with families of chronically ill or disabled children. Volunteers are asked to commit at least one year of service to the program. Once they are trained, each volunteer is matched with one or more families in need of assistance. In return, volunteers earn a small salary to cover meal and travel costs associated with volunteering.

- **Michael's Place** resource library provides materials to families and friends wishing to learn more about the illnesses or disabilities that affect the children in their lives.

- **The Parent Support Group** links parents and guardians with other adults who care for ill or disabled children. It offers adults a safe place to share feelings and receive support from others facing similar problems.

- **The Sibling Support Group**, like the Parent Support Group, enables brothers and sisters of ill and disabled children to share thoughts and feelings with those living in similar situations.

- **Family Counseling** to *Any Baby Can* clients is offered by the Counseling Psychology Department of Our Lady of the Lake University. Short-term therapy focuses on using the family's strengths and available resources to care for the ill or disabled child.

Follow-Up

Research an organization that focuses on helping children or older adults with life-threatening illnesses or disabilities. Write a report on the positive effects this organization has on victims and their families.

- Help all children recognize and cope with their strengths and limitations.

- Help children to be comfortable with, rather than fearful of, disabilities.

- Allow children with special needs to participate in an everyday setting.

- Provide ways parents of children with special needs can interact with other parents. Refer parents of all children to needed support services.

Staffing & Group Size

Depending on the type and extent of a child's disability, some individual instruction and assistance may be required. Some children may need extra help during basic care routines, such as dressing, feeding, or toileting. Others may need assistance moving throughout the classroom.

For these reasons, classroom size may be smaller. In addition, an extra care provider, assistant, or trained volunteer may be needed to give extra individualized help and guidance. To make sure a child is well cared for, many programs assign a **primary care provider** to a child with special needs. It is the primary care provider's responsibility to make sure the child participates in all routines and activities in a meaningful way. This person also assists the child with self-care tasks, such as toileting, diapering, and hand washing, if necessary.

Children with severe impairments may need to be assisted or taught by someone with specialized education and training. Many colleges have courses and degree programs relating to children with special needs. See Fig. 22-7.

Working with Parents

Parents of children with special needs are a valuable resource for care providers. They can provide specific information about a child's disability, individual needs, medications, habits,

FIG. 22-7. **Classroom group size may be smaller when children with special needs are included.** Why is it important for some children to have a primary care provider?

and day-to-day changes. In return, care providers must keep parents informed. Parents naturally want to know what the program is doing for their child and how their child is progressing. They also have a right to take part in decisions regarding their child's care and education. Encourage parents to observe the program on a regular basis. After observation times, a conference allows parents and care providers to ask questions and share insights.

Parents of children with special needs have many concerns. They may worry about their child being rejected by others or whether they are doing everything they can to help their child. These parents must make difficult decisions about care, educational programs, and medical treatment. Sensitive care providers are supportive as they listen and respond to parents' concerns. They also refer parents to appropriate sources of help and information. These might include parent support groups, local agencies, and national organizations, such as the March of Dimes or Easter Seals.

Serving Children with Special Needs

Like all children, those with special needs benefit from activities and experiences designed to nurture their physical, intellectual, emotional, and social development. When children are younger than age three, they may be enrolled in **early intervention programs**, which are sponsored by local public schools. In such programs, staff and parents cooperatively create an **Individualized Family Service Plan (IFSP)**. This is a plan created to make sure goals are set to meet a child's overall needs. It includes an assessment of a child's development, goals for development, and specific ways to promote and support a family's involvement.

For children with special needs who are age three or older, public school administrators, parents, teachers, and specialists work together to create an Individualized Education Program for each child. An **Individualized Education Program (IEP)** is a written document that outlines how to encourage development in a child who has special needs. It is required by the IDEA law and must include the following information:

- Current level of the child's abilities.
- Annual goals for the child's development.
- Short-term educational goals.
- Educational services to be provided.
- The procedure for determining whether the program's goals are being met.
- Degree to which the child will be included in a regular classroom. Some children may need to spend part of the day receiving special services from a therapist.

Adapting the Environment

The most enriching program will not benefit a child who cannot attend because of physical barriers. Making the physical environment **accessible**, or easily used by those with disabilities, is important. Care providers, children, parents, and others should work together to identify and remove barriers and safety hazards, so children with special needs can explore the environment safely. Chapter 12 provides many suggestions for creating accessible facilities.

Adapting the Curriculum

To make sure children are not isolated, avoid planning separate activities for children with special needs whenever possible. Creating separate activities emphasizes differences in the children, rather than similarities. Instead, plan activities in which all children can participate.

Handling Medical Emergencies. Children with conditions such as epilepsy or cerebral palsy may have seizures that require emergency medical assistance. In such an emergency, call 911 immediately. In some instances, a care provider may need to gently guide the child safely to the floor until emergency help arrives. A qualified staff person should administer first aid until emergency staff arrives. So treatment can be quickly and safely provided, keep multiple copies of a child's vital information in a handy file. The sheet should list the child's name, home address, parents' or guardians' day/evening phone numbers, and an additional contact person in case of emergency. It should also include the child's current age, weight, height, disability, current medications and dosages, and known allergies. Give medical personnel a copy of the sheet. Also provide a parent-signed emergency medical treatment waiver, in case the child is transported to a hospital for further care.

To accommodate individual children, modify the activity, the equipment, or the teaching method, as needed. For instance, all children enjoy and benefit from playing with puzzles. However, the degree of difficulty of the puzzle and how it is made can vary. A child with a mental impairment might work on a four-piece puzzle, while peers work on one with eight pieces. A child with poor small motor control may be able to do an eight-piece puzzle, but would need knobbed puzzle pieces that could be picked up and moved more easily. See Fig. 22-8.

Adapting Schedules & Routines

Routines, such as eating, dressing for outdoor play, toileting, and transitions, can be especially time-consuming for children with disabilities. Allow for extra time when planning the schedule. As with all children, encourage independence and self-help skills. Other children in the classroom may try to be helpful by doing things for the child who has a disability. Remind them that people like to do as much as possible for themselves.

Some children require special health care in their daily routine. This may include medicine, emergency treatment, or some form of therapy. Care providers should request specific written instructions from parents to meet these needs.

FIG. 22-8. **Adapting activities to meet the physical and intellectual needs of children is an important responsibility of care providers.**

Section 22-2 Knowledge Check

1. What is inclusion?
2. How do children benefit from an inclusive program?
3. What does it mean for a program to be accessible?

Mini-Lab

Find three children's books that feature characters with disabilities. Analyze the books for how the characters are portrayed and the roles they fulfill. Do the characters function independently and successfully? Record your feelings about the way in which persons with disabilities were characterized in each book.

Chapter 22 Review & Activities

Section Summaries

22-1 Special needs occur when development varies significantly from the norm.

22-1 A positive attitude calls for focusing on children's abilities, rather than their disabilities.

22-1 Care providers can help children understand disabilities and accept differences.

22-1 There are different types of disabilities and special needs.

22-1 Accommodations in the curriculum help children with special needs.

22-2 Including children with special needs in regular classrooms can benefit the children, their classmates, their parents, and their care providers.

22-2 Meeting special needs may require additional staff and smaller group sizes.

22-2 Environments must be accessible to those with special needs.

22-2 Adapting routines according to the needs of children with disabilities is sometimes required.

Check Your Knowledge

1. What are public school programs for children under age three who have special needs called?
2. How should care providers treat children with special needs as compared with other children?
3. How can a care provider make a classroom accessible for children in wheelchairs?
4. Why are primary care providers often assigned to special needs children?
5. In what way can parents of children with special needs help care providers? In what way can care providers help parents?
6. What is included in an Individualized Education Program?
7. What should be emphasized when adapting activities for children with limited vision?
8. What is the purpose of the Individuals with Disabilities Education Act?
9. What is the difference between a mental disability and a learning disability?
10. Should gifted children be given less time than others to complete projects? Explain.

Thinking Critically

1. Analyze why care providers should carefully examine their attitudes toward children with special needs. What can they do to improve their attitudes, if needed?
2. Draw conclusions about why it is important for parents and care providers to work together to meet the needs of children with special needs.

Practical Applications

1. **Observation.** Observe a child with a special need at a local child care facility. How did the child differ developmentally from other children the same age? What were the child's strengths? What challenges did the child encounter during your observation? What accommodations were being used? What additional accommodations might be helpful? How did the child's special needs affect his or her participation in activities at the child care facility? Write a summary of your observations.

2. **Interview.** Interview the parent of a child with disabilities, special health care needs, or signs of giftedness. What challenges has the parent faced in meeting the needs of his or her child? What are some of the influences the parent sees on the physical, emotional, social, and intellectual development of his or her child? Write a report summarizing your interview.

3. **Adapting Activities.** Show how an activity might be adapted to meet the needs of children with special needs. Explain how you would modify the activity, the equipment, or the teaching method, or all three. Demonstrate the activity and the adaptations to the class.

4. **Analyze a Classroom.** Tour a classroom at a local child care center. Walk through the classroom, noting the different centers, materials, and displays. What factors in the classroom might positively affect the growth and development of children with special needs? What factors might negatively affect children with special needs? Make a chart listing the positives and negatives of the classroom.

Building Your PORTFOLIO

Developing an Inclusive Early Childhood Program

Learning to meet the needs of children with special needs can increase your professional skills.

Step 1: Write a description of an inclusion program that incorporates the rules established by your state's licensing laws. Include the number of children with special needs along with the total number of children to be cared for, the number of care providers, and their responsibilities. Outline ways you will work with the parents of children with special needs. List local resources available to these parents. Also include copies of an IFSP and an IEP.

Step 2: Show how the room you designed for infants, toddlers, preschoolers, or school-age children could be adapted to meet the needs of a child with a specific disability. Write a description giving additional details.

Step 3: Show how you would adapt a schedule designed for infants, toddlers, preschoolers, or school-age children to meet the needs of children with disabilities, special health care needs, or signs of giftedness. Write a summary describing the changes and the reasons for each schedule change.

Step 4: Share your work in Steps 1, 2, and 3 with the director of an early childhood program or your teacher. Get suggestions for improvement. Revise your plans and put them in your portfolio.

Section 23-1
Physical Care

Section 23-2
Social, Emotional & Cognitive Care

Section 23-1

Physical Care

OBJECTIVES

- Identify changes in older adults that may lead to the need for care.
- Explain chronic health conditions and how these impact activities of daily living.
- Summarize the role of older adult care providers in meeting the physical needs of older adults.

KEY TERMS

chronic
functional ability
functionally
   dependent
learned helplessness

People are healthier and are living longer. Because of this, the number of older adults is growing. By 2030, one in five Americans will be older than 65 years of age. These older adults will use a variety of programs and services resulting in new jobs and career opportunities. Older adults are living longer, healthier lives. Yet, some have physical health and mental health problems. This chapter focuses on older adults who need help with physical or mental health care.

Physical Characteristics of Aging

Aging occurs throughout life. As people age, their bodies change. When you think about older adults, perhaps you think of gray hair and wrinkles. You may think of someone who walks at a slower pace. These changes do occur when people age, but they occur differently for each older person. For example, some people have gray hair at a very early age and others at an older age. Many people participate in activities when they are young that affect how they age. For example, sun exposure and smoking can increase wrinkles. It is important to remember that a person's health cannot be judged by appearance.

Health & Aging

One of the important questions to consider is which of the physical characteristics are part of the normal aging process and which changes are related to disease. This question is hard to answer because as people age they are more likely to develop certain types of diseases. For example, aging includes increased risk of cardiovascular disease. This disease is the leading cause of death in older adults. Aging is related to most cancers, diabetes, and arthritis. Older adults are more likely than young people to have high blood pressure, which can increase their risk of stroke. Still, aging itself is not a disease. The problems linked with aging are most often because of a disease, not because of aging. See Fig. 23-1.

FIG. 23-1. **Older adults who experience a chronic condition, such as arthritis, can learn effective ways to manage their conditions.** How can exercise benefit an older adult with arthritis?

Normal Aging. What can people expect to see as part of the "normal" aging process? In most people, aging includes gradual reductions in the functions of internal organs, such as the heart, kidneys, digestive system, and lungs, as well as vision and hearing. As they age, people can expect a gradual decrease in muscle mass and strength. They can also expect to see a decrease in bone density. Bone density refers to the strength and thickness of the bones. A condition called osteoporosis occurs when too much bone is lost. This puts a person at risk of breaking a bone. This can be very serious when the broken bone is the hip. Some older adults have fractures of the bones in their spine. This can lead to a hunched posture and shrinkage in height. Exercise and good health habits throughout life can help prevent much of this bone and muscle loss. Exercise also helps to maintain healthy lungs. Care providers should remember that aging is different for each older adult.

Health Concerns. Some people live to be 80 or 90 years of age without suffering from any major diseases. Others begin to experience health problems at a young age. Certain conditions, such as high blood pressure, obesity, and high cholesterol, may increase with age. These conditions can increase the risk of illness. For example, aging is related to weight gain, which may impair an older adult's health and increase the risk for diabetes. Older adults who become ill may take longer to recover because of reduced immune functioning. Older adults with reduced muscle strength may be at higher risk of falling. Those with significant loss of bone density are at higher risk of bone fractures.

Chronic Health Problems. The longer people live, the more likely it becomes that they will develop chronic health problems. **Chronic** means that there is no cure. The person with a chronic health problem must learn to live with and manage the illness as much as possible. More than 80 percent of people age 65 and older have at least one chronic health condition. Common chronic conditions include:

- **Arthritis.** This condition affects about half of the older population. Arthritis is characterized by inflammation of the body joints. It can cause mild to severe pain.

- **Heart disease.** Heart disease refers to problems with the heart's ability to pump blood. Evidence that someone has heart disease can occur suddenly, such as when someone has a heart attack. A heart attack occurs when a blood clot restricts blood flow in the heart.

- **High blood pressure.** High blood pressure is also called hypertension. Blood pressure refers to pressure on the walls of the blood vessels as the blood circulates. There are two measures of blood pressure: systolic and diastolic. Systolic measures the pressure when the heart muscle contracts. Diastolic measures pressure when the heart muscles relax. Blood pressure is "read" as the systolic blood pressure over the diastolic blood pressure.

Normal blood pressure is 120/80 or lower. Hypertension occurs when blood pressure is higher than 140/90.

- **Hearing problems.** Hearing loss affects about one-third of the older adult population. This can range from mild hearing loss to total hearing loss.

Yet, these health concerns do not tell us much about someone's overall health and well-being. Disease does not equal disability, and most people with chronic conditions are able to manage their health problems and function effectively in their day-to-day lives.

Besides the need to be aware of which type of disease an older adult has, care providers should be concerned with how an older adult manages the disease. For example, care providers should ask whether the chronic illness affects a person's ability to function independently. Is the older adult able to manage his or her daily tasks alone? Does the older adult require some assistance? If the older adult needs assistance, how much and what type of help does he or she need? What can the care provider do to help the older adult manage activities of daily living?

Who Needs Care?

Although people tend to talk about older persons as if they are all alike, older adults are a diverse group of people. Older adults can be as young as 60 or as old as 100 or more. They also have a wide range of physical health and mental health conditions and varied abilities. Many older adults are healthy, high functioning, and productive. Older adults have different roles. They can have jobs, care for grandchildren, and volunteer in their communities. Most older adults live alone or with their spouse. Very few older adults live in institutional settings, such as nursing homes. However, even though they might live in their own homes, older adults are more likely than younger persons to have

chronic health conditions that impair their functioning. When this occurs, they turn to care providers for assistance. See Fig. 23-2.

Some chronic health and mental health problems can affect a person's ability to care for him- or herself. **Functional ability** refers to the ability of older adults to take care of themselves and manage their environments. Disability refers to limitations in the ability to function. A disability is a physical or mental impairment that greatly limits one or more important life activities. Some older adults with disabilities are **functionally dependent**, which means they must rely on others for help with basic activities. For example, someone in a wheelchair may need help getting around in the house. This is called being functionally dependent in mobility. If the person in the wheelchair needs help get-

FIG. 23-2. A broken hip or hip replacement surgery may temporarily impair an older adult's ability to carry out the typical activities of daily living. In what ways might a care provider help an older adult regain his or her independence?

FIG. 23-3.

TASKS OF FUNCTIONAL ABILITY

Activities of Daily Living	Instrumental Activities of Daily Living
Bathing	Shopping
Dressing	Doing light housework
Toileting	Preparing meals
Transferring from bed to chair	Using the phone
Eating	Taking medication properly
	Managing money

ting in and out of bed, he or she is functionally dependent in "transferring." The most common problems that get in the way of carrying out typical daily activities are heart disease, a broken hip, and loss of vision.

Aging & Activities of Daily Living

Young adults and children sometimes think that *all* older adults have illnesses or need assistance. This is not true. Most older adults are healthy and active. However, aging is linked to greater dependency and the need for help with everyday tasks. This is because older adults are more likely to have illnesses that affect their ability to function.

Everyday self-care tasks are sometimes referred to as activities of daily living, or ADLs. A related set of tasks that an older adult performs to manage in the home are called instrumental activities of daily living, or IADLs. (See Chapters 7 and 9 for more information on ADLs and IADLs.) See Fig. 23-3. When a person needs assistance, he or she is said to have a disability or functional limitation.

About six percent of people between the ages of 65 and 69 need help with one or more ADLs. More than one-third of older adults ages 85 and older need help. Older adults may need help because they have a physical impairment. For example, a stroke may cause paralysis on one side of the body, limiting the older adult's ability to get dressed or bathe without help.

Cognitive problems may also cause disability. Some older adults have both physical and cognitive disabilities that impair their functioning.

Sensory Impairment

Sensory impairment refers to problems with the senses—seeing, hearing, smelling, tasting, and touching. Changes in the senses occur with the aging process. For example, hearing loss affects almost one-third of older adults. Hearing loss can increase social isolation. Hearing impairment can also affect balance and increase the risk of falling.

With normal aging, vision changes are common at a relatively young age. Starting at about age 40, people may have difficulty reading and seeing things that are close without glasses. They may also need better light than younger people need. Peripheral vision, or seeing things to the side of the visual field, may be reduced. Diseases of the eye are also more common in older people, such as cataracts, which cloud the eye. About 17 percent of older adults have cataracts. Macular degeneration (MAH-kyuh-luhr dih-jeh-nuh-RAY-shuhn), which causes loss of central vision and may lead to blindness, also affects older adults. About nine percent of older adults suffer from macular degeneration. Certain diseases, such as diabetes, can also lead to loss of vision. For people with diabetes, vision care and regular follow-up visits to a doctor are important to manage the disease.

Meeting Physical Needs

The role of care providers is to assist older adults who have functional limitations. Sometimes care providers need to do something for the older person. For example, the care provider may assist by feeding the older person. Sometimes the care provider might need to prepare older adults to perform a task independently. For example, the care provider might bring an older adult a lunch tray and make sure that it is set up so that the older person can eat independently. A care plan should tell which type of assistance is required. It also explains how the assistance should be offered.

Because each person is different and has different needs, the assistance will be different for each older adult. Care providers need to remember that each older adult's needs vary from day to day. Like all people, some days older adults have more energy, enthusiasm, and interest than at other times. On these days, they will need less assistance. Sensitive care providers understand

FIG. 23-5. **Finding appropriate equipment to assist older adults with physical limitations is an essential responsibility of care providers.**

that their assistance needs to be acceptable to the older adult and support his or her dignity and independence. The assistance should restrict the older adult as little as possible. See Fig. 23-4.

Promoting Independence

Care providers ensure that older adults maintain as much independence as possible. For example, it might take longer to help older adults perform a task independently, such as combing their hair. Yet supporting self-care efforts is often better than taking over and doing something quickly and efficiently. The term **learned helplessness** refers to people who lose their ability to do things because someone takes over. To promote independence, it is important to understand what people want and are able to do themselves, where they need help, and how best to provide that help in an acceptable way. At times, a care provider will need to offer encouragement. On some days, older adults can do the task, but it makes them tired, which might prevent them from participating in an activity that they would like. For example, someone may want help dressing to save his or her energy for a sing-along. There is a delicate balance between helping too much and not helping enough. See Fig. 23-5.

FIG. 23-4. **Preparing place settings is one of the instrumental activities of daily living that older adults need to achieve to maintain independence.** What other instrumental activities can be therapeutic for older adults?

Accommodating Physical Limitations

It is important for care providers to treat older adults with respect. Sometimes care providers are rushed. Even so, care providers should try to respect each older adult as an individual rather than thinking of the older adult only as someone to be cleaned, fed, or cared for. For example, if an older adult in a wheelchair needs to be taken to the dining room, it is important to discuss this with the older person first. You might bend down to be at eye level with the older adult and say, "It's time for lunch. Is it okay if I wheel you to the dining room?" Problems occur when a care provider, who is focused on getting the person to the dining room, comes up behind the older adult and starts to push the wheelchair. This can be frightening and confusing.

Dignity can also be enhanced by treating older adults as adults, helping them dress and groom appropriately, and listening to and respecting their opinions. The following sections include ways to accommodate older adults with physical limitations. See Fig. 23-6.

Decreased Mobility. Care providers often work with older adults who have decreased mobility. To show respect and promote independence, walk at the older adult's pace. Take breaks as needed. If needed, offer your arm for support. Some older adults need a support person on each side. If the person uses an assistive device, such as a cane, make sure that it is available. Avoid chairs that are too soft or low. These chairs make it difficult for older adults to stand after they sit down. Chairs should have arms that older adults can use to support themselves as they stand up.

Decreased Vision. Some older adults have vision impairments and need special assistance. Let these persons take your arm. Approach them and ask, "Would you like to take my arm?" Let them know where your arm is by telling them, "Here it is." Touch them lightly on their arm. Walk at the person's pace. Give verbal instructions as you walk. For example, let the older adult know if there is anything to walk around, such as a curb, a step, or a turn. Many older adults with vision impairments are used to being helped. Sometimes they will tell you how to best help them. Or, you may want to ask them, "How can I help you?"

Mental Confusion. When assisting older adults with mental confusion, be sure to let them know what you are doing. Sometimes simple coaching will be all that is needed. For example, if you are helping an older adult into the dining room, tell the older adult that you are going in to sit down for lunch. Explain to the older adult, "This is your seat. You can sit right here." If the older adult appears confused, gentle reminders may be needed. For example,

FIG. 23-6. **When assisting visually impaired older adults with meals, keep utensils and foods in the same place.** How might this help visually impaired older adults maintain their security?

Independence
Skills

Assistance with Dressing

Older adults may need assistance with dressing as their physical skills become more limited. Here are a few ways care providers can promote dressing assistance to encourage independence and reduce frustration for older adults.

1. Minimize the chore of selecting clothes by storing clothes that are out of season or eliminating clothes that are difficult to put on, such as those with little snaps or buttons.

2. Arrange all pieces of an outfit, including accessories, together when storing them.

3. Clearly label containers, shelves, and drawers with pictures or words to indicate their contents. Store clothes on low shelves or in low drawers, so they are easy to reach.

4. Use large buttons or large hook and eye combinations to make fastening clothes easier. Replace fasteners that are difficult to close with hook and loop tape when possible.

5. Select clothes with elastic waistbands made of machine washable cotton or cotton blend for the greatest comfort. Shoes should have nonskid soles and should fit well. If shoelaces are difficult to manage, look for shoes with hook and loop tape fasteners.

6. Keep in mind the physical limitations or disabilities of older adults. Tops that open down the front or that have shoulder openings are easier to put on than those that fasten in the back or pull over the head. Garments made in two pieces rather than one make for easier dressing.

7. Make sure garments are functional, clean, and attractive. Looking attractive improves the self-image of older adults.

Try It!

Offer to help an older adult simplify the dressing process by sorting and organizing his or her clothes. Check back with the older adult periodically to find out how the system is working. Keep a journal describing the experience and recording the responses.

---

you might say, "We're waiting for lunch to be served." Sometimes an older adult with a cognitive impairment will become frightened and combative. Remain calm. Avoid physical contact and try to reassure the person.

Meeting Personal Care Needs

Personal care can include helping older adults with such activities as dressing and grooming. These activities can include help with washing the older adult's hands and face, combing and

FIG. 23-7. Many senior center programs include library facilities. How can care providers help older adults use library resources?

handle on a comb or razor, an adaptive device can be placed over the handle to make it easier to hold. Patience and reassurance may be important to help the older adult build confidence in his or her abilities to perform personal care.

Assisting with Community Services

Older adults with functional impairment may benefit from participation in community services and programs. These can include services, such as group or home-delivered meals, transportation, and housecleaning. They can also include recreation programs, such as senior centers and parks and recreation programs. See Fig. 23-7.

Exercise. Many older adults enjoy physical exercise. Exercise provides health benefits, such as reducing stress and strengthening muscles. It also helps improve older adults' well-being. Identify a variety of services that older people might use. Contact the area agency on aging by phone or the Internet to locate the services. Determine the types of people who use the program, the program's hours of operation, and its enrollment procedures.

(when needed) washing hair, brushing teeth, selecting clothes, and dressing. Men may also need help shaving. Whenever possible the care provider will assist the older person. Sometimes, the care provider will actually need to do the task. At other times, the care provider may let the older adult try the task first; then if more help is needed the care provider can offer it.

Various assistive devices and modifications may help make the tasks easier. For example, if an older person has problems gripping a small

Section **23-1** Knowledge Check

1. List the characteristics of normal aging.
2. Name two health concerns of older adults.
3. Define functional ability.

Mini-Lab

Create a care plan for older adults with physical limitations. Summarize how you would assist the older adult in adjusting to the physical changes. Include techniques for promoting independence. Share your summary with the director of a local adult care center.

Section **23-2**

Social, Emotional & Cognitive Care

- Describe the social, emotional, mental, and cognitive care needs of older adults.
- Summarize theories associated with the social changes of aging.
- Identify ways to meet the social needs of older adults.
- Identify special emotional needs of older adults.
- Utilize care provider techniques promoting positive emotional health of older adults.
- Determine the impact of family support on the emotional well-being of older adults.

KEY TERMS

continuity theory
engagement
formal support
informal support
intergenerational
  support
cognitive ability
depression
anxiety
grief
assessment
consumer-directed
  care

In addition to helping with physical activities, care providers also need to be aware of the older adult's social, emotional, mental, and cognitive needs. Older adults also have emotional needs for love, happiness, joy, and a sense of well-being. Social needs are addressed by relationships with others. Emotions may be affected by social relationships. Care providers must understand how older adults emotionally cope with impairments, social relationships, support systems, and general approach to life.

Theories About Aging

A number of theories have been offered to explain changes in people as they age. The oldest of these is called disengagement theory. This theory was an effort to explain why older people stopped being active and involved in life. It held that with aging came a gradual withdrawal from activities. This theory was extremely negative. It said that this withdrawal helped prepare older people to die. This theory could be nicknamed "rocking chair theory."

Needless to say, this theory got a strong reaction from researchers and older people. Most people did not believe disengagement theory. One response was the introduction of activity theory. As the opposite of disengagement, this theory said that activity was good for older adults and led to higher satisfaction with life. Researchers found that this was true for some older adults, but not all.

A third approach was put forward. This approach is called continuity theory. The **continuity theory** holds that older adults continue to build on their lifetime of experiences, preferences, likes, and dislikes. People who were very active as younger adults are likely to value and enjoy more activity as older adults. Those who are fond of time spent alone in quiet activities continue to value those activities as they age. Continuity theory focuses on older adults as unique individuals who adapt to the changes due to aging by keeping, and if necessary modifying, the things that they have always done and enjoyed. See Fig. 23-8.

Although older adults continue to enjoy what they have enjoyed throughout their life, illness or disability may limit what they are able to do. If this happens, they may save their energy for the most meaningful and enjoyable activities. This may mean that they may have to give up some activities. Sometimes they will continue the activity with additional support. For example, someone who has always loved to travel may continue to do so but he or she may require more help. One example of this is an older adult who has recovered from a stroke and is able to get around at home. This person may choose to travel in a wheelchair with a care provider to save energy and still be able to see the sights.

Maslow's Hierarchy of Human Needs. All people have similar needs. These needs can impact social and emotional well-being. Care providers need to be attuned to the needs of older adults as they provide daily care. Abraham Maslow, a psychologist (see Chapter 2), identified five categories of human needs: physiological need for food, water, sleep, and shelter; need for safety; need for love and belonging; need for self-esteem; and the need for self-actualization, or to reach full potential in knowledge and wisdom. People strive to fulfill the higher needs as the more basic needs are met. Older adults may feel threatened when one or more needs that they have strived to fulfill in life change (such as due to the death of a spouse) or go unmet. Those who care for older adults must be aware of these needs in order to help them remain socially and emotionally engaged. See Fig. 23-9.

FIG. 23-8. **Participating in horticultural therapy results in renewed self-esteem and value for older adults. What are some other benefits of horticultural therapy?**

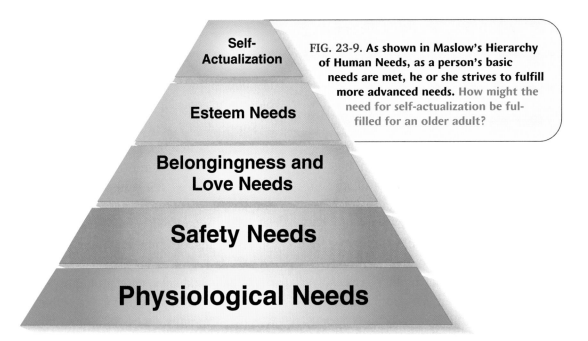

Self-
Actualization

Esteem Needs

Belongingness and
Love Needs

Safety Needs

Physiological Needs

FIG. 23-9. As shown in Maslow's Hierarchy of Human Needs, as a person's basic needs are met, he or she strives to fulfill more advanced needs. How might the need for self-actualization be fulfilled for an older adult?

Social & Emotional Engagement

Engagement refers to the extent to which an older person is involved and active with others and with activities in the environment. A person may be actively engaged with friends, a job, volunteer activities, hobbies, and leisure activities.

Providing care includes more than physical support for functional impairment. Providing care also involves caring for the older adult's emotional well-being and showing that you care. Most older adults are not socially isolated or lonely. Most live on their own, have spouses and friends, and enjoy activities. However, those who are ill or functionally impaired often find it more difficult to engage in social activities. Enjoyable social activities are good for people of all ages. When providing emotional support, care providers should remember:

- Loneliness and isolation are risk factors for poor health.

- Supportive social relationships have a positive effect on health.

- Social support can help reduce the effects of disease related to aging.

Individualized Support

Social and emotional support are positive, but it is important to know that people vary greatly in what type of support they like and feel comfortable having. Some people are outgoing and enjoy sharing their emotions. Others are quiet and private. Some older adults may be socially isolated because of health conditions that make it difficult to engage in social activities, or they may have sensory impairment, such as hearing loss. If the older adult has impaired hearing, it is important to look at the person when you are speaking. Speak slowly and distinctly and make sure that the person hears what you are saying.

Because everyone is different, care providers must understand how to connect with each older adult. As continuity theory shows, it is important to respect each older adult's preferences for social interaction and activity. Take your cues from the older adult. Ask the older adult if he or she would like to talk, participate in an activity, or have time alone. You could ask, "Would you like a little time to yourself?" or "What would you like to do this afternoon?" Active listening also helps you understand what the older person is saying. You might say, "You seem quite happy today. Did something special happen?" or "You are unusually quiet. Is anything wrong?"

Interacting with Older Adults

Sometimes older adults are concerned that they are burdening those who help them. It is important to let them know that you and others enjoy the relationship and that you, too, benefit from it. Reassure older adults that you enjoy the work and the time you spend with them. Sometimes, it is difficult for young people and older adults to understand each other's issues and concerns. Sharing your views and learning about the views, likes, dislikes, and concerns of an older adult can be enjoyable and educational for both you and the older adult. Sometimes, too, older adults are good listeners and are willing to share their years of wisdom and life experiences.

In addition to providing support, care providers can encourage older adults to engage in activities that are meaningful and enjoyable.

Some older adults need reassurance that such activities are important. The care provider can help by understanding what the older adult values and enjoys and finding ways to help the older adult participate in the activities.

Support of Friends. Friendship is important to people of all ages. Friends provide emotional support and opportunities to share and to compare experiences. For frail older persons, friends can also be a source of instrumental support, which includes helping with tasks such as shopping or transportation. Having a close friend to confide in seems to help older adults avoid depression and cope with problems. Friends are often involved in sharing leisure activities such as games, outings, or travel. Sometimes older adults' network of friends may shrink due to death or illness or loss of social roles through retirement. Participating in day care or senior programs may offer the older adult an opportunity to make new friends. See Fig. 23-10.

Family Support

Formal support refers to paying care providers to care for and support others. Most of the time, however, family members and friends provide care. This type of support is called informal support. **Informal support** is non-paid and includes helping provide for social and emotional needs, as well as assisting with ADLs and IADLs.

The family is the major source of social and emotional support for older adults. Most older adults are highly valued by their families. Frail older adults receive most of their support from family members. Older adults without available

FIG. 23-10. Regular social interactions with peers are important for emotional health. What are some ways that care providers can promote social interactions for older adults?

FIG. 23-11. Loneliness can be a common problem for older adults. A visit from family members brings meaningful social interaction to an older adult's life.

families are more likely to enter a nursing home. Although most older adults do not live with their children, some cultures are more likely to live in households with grandparents, parents, and young children. See Fig. 23-11.

Even when older adults and their children do not live together, they often provide help to each other. This help is called **intergenerational support**. Family members serve as care providers to older adults. Older adults often help younger family members in return. Sometimes they do this by providing money or property. Sometimes older adults help families care for young children. Many young people are attracted to work with older adults because of a valued relationship with an older family member, such as a grandparent.

Care providers cannot replace a loving family, but they can offer valuable social and emotional support. Actively listening, offering physical support, or giving a hug are other forms of support and encouragement.

Social Activities

Older adults often enjoy spending time in leisure activities. Leisure activities become more important when people retire and children leave home, giving them time to spend on activities. However, some older adults have illnesses that reduce their energy. Reduced energy and vigor may make them selective about the types of activities that they are able to manage and enjoy. The continuity theory tells us that older adults are more likely to enjoy activities that are

similar to what they have enjoyed at younger ages. This means that care providers should consider personal and cultural preferences when planning activities.

Ethnically Appropriate Activities. Adult day care programs should include activities that are associated with the ethnic backgrounds of people in their program. For example, many cultures participate in dancing. The type of dancing offered should depend on the preferences of the participants and their physical functioning. Line dancing, swing dancing, and two-step dancing are enjoyed in many cultures. Older adults build their physical skills while they engage in a cultural activity. Those who are not able to dance may still enjoy watching and listening to the dance music.

Two other ethnically appropriate activities for older adults who are able to do them are yoga and tai chi chuan (teye chee schwahn). Yoga is practiced mainly for health and vitality. It is a way of exercising, stretching, and freeing the body so it can be healthy. Tai chi chuan is an ancient Chinese form of exercise. Tai chi may help improve both health and peace of mind. The exercise is gentle and promotes coordination.

Intergenerational *Interactions*

Intergenerational Fun & Games

Games, especially those played among different age groups, teach children patience, imagination, problem solving, language, and social skills. Games also benefit older adults physically and emotionally. Play relaxes people and helps maintain mental alertness, memory, and problem-solving skills. Active games help improve strength, coordination, and reaction time.

- **Outdoor Games.** When weather cooperates, outdoor games can be among the most fun. Games—such as shuffleboard, horseshoes, bocce ball, and croquet—can be played at a slow pace and can be fun for a variety of ages.

- **Board Games.** Board games are entertaining when shared among generations. Any number of board games exist for children as young as three and older adults of 103 years or more. Select one and let the fun begin.

- **Electronic Games.** Hundreds of electronic games are available. You may play games on a computer or television, or you can play a handheld game. Most of these games are designed to quicken reaction time and eye-hand coordination. Plus, unlike many other types of games, electronic games often give children an opportunity to teach older adults something new about technology.

- **Card Games.** Many card games are suitable for all generations. A standard deck of cards allows the young and old to play rummy, hearts, war, go fish, and more.

Regardless of the game you choose, the object is the same—fun.

Follow-Up

Make a list of additional games that could be played among people of various age groups.

Skills-Appropriate Activities. Activities that develop, preserve, and stimulate the senses are skills appropriate. These activities help older adults maintain their quality of life. Stimulating games develop skills and bring social enjoyment at the same time. The games may even help older adults maintain their memory and concentration. At the same time, they help them build friendships.

One of the best things that care providers can do is to survey the older adults in their care about the things they enjoy and like to do. The older adults may include a wide range of activities from listening to radio programming to watching a sporting event to playing a musical instrument. Again, an older adult may like skiing. Even though older adults may no longer be able to ski, they might like to read magazines about skiing or watch ski events on television. The types of activities should not be restricted, even when the activities are not within the skill range of the older adults. After surveying the older adults, care providers should then plan activities with them to meet a variety of needs. After completing some of the activities, survey the older adults again to see if they enjoyed the activities.

Mental Health

As with physical health, most older adults enjoy good mental health. Mental health problems affect only a small portion of older adults. Some mental disorders that affect older persons are cognitive impairment, depression, and anxiety. Sometimes these mental health problems are linked to physical illness. Both physical and mental health problems affect older adults, their family members, and their care providers. Care providers need to understand cognitive impairment and how to work with older adults with cognitive and mental health problems. See Fig. 23-12.

Cognitive Impairment

Most older adults have healthy cognitive abilities. **Cognitive ability** refers to thinking and includes memory, learning, reasoning, and problem solving. Although most people think that memory loss is very common in older adults, *most* older adults' minds function very well. Unfortunately, as with physical impairment, a small number of older adults have diseases that affect their cognitive functioning.

FIG. 23-12. **An opportunity to tutor a young child brings a sense of self-worth to older adults.** What are some other ways that children can benefit from the experience and wisdom of older adults?

Alzheimer's Disease

About 10 percent of older adults age 65 and older have Alzheimer's disease or a related disorder. Over time, this disease causes cognitive impairment. Early in the disease, the older adults might have trouble performing complex tasks, such as managing finances. Eventually, they have problems performing simple tasks, such as eating. Alzheimer's disease is not common in the group of older adults called the young old. Older adults in this group are between the ages of 65 and 74. As older adults age, they are more likely to be diagnosed with Alzheimer's disease. Older adults—older than age 74—have a greater likelihood of getting Alzheimer's disease. Some experts think that almost half of older adults age 85 and older may have Alzheimer's or a related disease.

Some older adults may fear that normal slowing in cognitive ability is caused by Alzheimer's disease. For example, older adults may interpret memory lapses that could happen to anyone, such as losing keys or forgetting someone's name, as signs of Alzheimer's disease.

Mental ability may slow with age. Some increased forgetfulness also may be part of normal aging. Other problems, such as depression, stress, changes in medication, or physical illness, also can affect mental functioning. Normal age-related changes do not affect an older adult's ability to function. This is not true of Alzheimer's disease, which progresses over time and for which there is no cure.

Depression

Most older adults are not depressed. Yet, depression may be more likely in older adults who have experienced major illnesses, such as a stroke and Alzheimer's disease, and in older adults who are frail. Sometimes medication can alter moods, causing an older adult to become depressed. Depression is more than feeling sad, a problem that most of us experience at one time or another. **Depression** is having feelings of sadness, hopelessness, helplessness, and worthlessness over a period of time. Depression includes experiencing at least five of the following problems:

- Feeling and acting sad and blue.
- Loss of interest in activities.
- Sleeping too much or not being able to sleep well.
- Overeating or loss of appetite.
- Feelings of guilt and worthlessness.
- Agitation or extreme lack of emotion.
- Inability to concentrate.
- Thoughts of suicide.

To be considered depressed, the person must experience these problems for at least two

FIG. 23-13. Care professionals work with older adults and their families to complete assessments of daily living skills. How can you encourage older adults to accept care and services?

weeks. Depression may include anxiety, but a person may experience anxiety without depression. **Anxiety** is extreme or unrealistic worry about something for a prolonged period of time. Symptoms of anxiety may include fear, shortness of breath, uncontrollable worry, and nervousness.

Depression is different from grief. **Grief** is extreme sadness related to a loss, such as the death of a loved one. Grief may include some of the same problems and symptoms as depression. Through the process of grieving, the person attempts to overcome the loss. (See Chapter 2 for information on the stages of grief.) Sometimes providing an opportunity to talk about the loss is helpful. If an older adult wants to talk about the loss of a loved one, listen to the older adult. Talking will not make the older adult feel worse; it may help him or her to feel better. Active listening skills can be used to communicate your interest and support.

Comprehensive Assessment

If family members, friends, professionals, or older adults become concerned about functional ability, an assessment should be done. An **assessment** measures a person's ability to function and helps to identify the help and services that are needed. Such an assessment includes examining the person's ability to perform ADLs and IADLs. A test of the older adult's cognitive functioning is also part of assessment. Often an assessment is needed to develop a care plan. Care plans detail the types and levels of services that a person requires. An assessment allows care to be tailored to the specific needs of each older adult. The assessment shows how much help is needed. For example, some older adults only need to be reminded to carry out a task, such as paying a bill. Others may need someone to do the task for them. See Fig. 23-13.

An important aspect of assessment and care planning is to involve the older person. One of the greatest fears of older adults is to lose inde-pendence. Loss of independence can be threatening for older adults who have raised families, paid mortgages, worked, and enjoyed the status that goes with these activities. Therefore, consumer-directed care is important when creating a care plan. **Consumer-directed care** means that the older adult has the opportunity to make choices, based on his or her likes and dislikes. It also means that care and services should not be forced on the older adult.

Strengthening Cognitive Functions

All people need stimulation to function well. Boredom and isolation can affect how well people perform. This is true of older adults, too. Yet it appears that the type of stimulation that older adults need is different from the needs of younger people. Young people may thrive on a chaotic environment and may enjoy doing several things at once, such as listening to music while doing homework. Older people may have difficulty focusing on several tasks at once and may do better when they can concentrate on one thing at a time. Older people may also do better when they are not rushed. Aging affects the speed at which a person processes information. Sometimes slowing down helps improve performance.

The Care Provider's Role

Participation in activities that require thinking skills helps keep the mind sharp. Such activities should be enjoyable and rewarding to older adults and suit their preferences. Care providers can encourage older adults to participate in activities. They also support older adults' efforts to participate. There are many activities that stimulate thinking skills. Encourage participation in such activities, and remember to give older adults a choice of activities. These activities may include:

Independence Skills

Maintaining Cognitive Skills

As people age, the ability to remember things may become more difficult. Memory can be stimulated by activities such as the following:

1. Keeping a daily journal or diary.

2. Making to-do lists and checking off activities as they are completed.

3. Posting calendars with important dates marked.

4. Planning activities, such as trips or purchases, in detail.

5. Playing games, such as card games and board games.

6. Writing cards or letters.

7. Doing crossword puzzles, word searches, or other word games.

8. Having a specific place to put things that are used often, such as eyeglasses or keys, and always returning the items to the same place.

9. Using sticky notes in various colors, sizes, and shapes for reminder notes.

10. Using mnemonics for remembering short lists of things. For example, the letters *M.E.A.L.S.* might be a way to remember milk, eggs, aluminum foil, lettuce, and soup.

Try It!

Help one older adult who is having trouble remembering things by implementing one or more of the ideas listed. Check back with the adult periodically to find out if his/her ability to remember things has improved. Make a class list of the ideas that worked to improve memory.

- **Word games.** Activities such as crossword puzzles require older adults to think and problem solve which may help keep their minds focused and sharp.

- **Crafts.** There are a variety of different crafts that are enjoyable. Some are crafts that older adults have enjoyed over their lifetime. Older adults can offer suggestions about what they have done and enjoy doing. Sometimes the opportunity to try a new craft will introduce the older adult to something different. For example, much to his wife's surprise, a retired physician discovered that he enjoyed working with his hands on needlepoint projects. For the next 10 years, he kept his friends and family supplied with beautiful needlepoint items. Another example is Grandma Moses, who became a famous artist very late in life.

- **Reading choices.** Older adults may enjoy reading everything from novels to magazines. Older adult programs should offer a range of reading materials. Reading material can be

FIG. 23-14. Musical expression is another way for older adults to maintain mental alertness and enjoy a positive social experience.

available for older persons to read by themselves. Care providers can also structure time to read out loud to those who have visual problems or other problems that make if difficult for them to read themselves.

- **Music involvement.** Music offers the opportunity to participate by singing along, playing an instrument, clapping to the music, or just listening. Older adults often enjoy the music that was popular when they were young. Care providers can ask older people to identify their favorite music. See Fig. 23-14.

- **Card games.** Card games are enjoyable and also involve stimulating one's memory and thinking processes. Card games, such as bridge, can be very complex and challenging. Other card games can be enjoyed by people with a variety of abilities.

Supporting Older Adults with Special Needs. People not only have different preferences, but they also have different ability levels. Some older adults suffer a decrease in cognitive functioning because of an illness, such as Alzheimer's disease. These diseases may result in memory loss. Some people think that if the older adult tried harder, he or she could do better. Many family members believe this and grow frustrated with an older adult who repeats things or gets lost. It is important to understand that the behavior is related to the illness. Often the older adult is trying hard and still has difficulties. It helps to support older adults' efforts. Tell them that you know they are trying. Sometimes it helps to simplify things. When appropriate, keep important items where they can be found easily, use routines, and make lists. Each older adult is different, however. Sometimes it is worth experimenting and problem solving with the older adult to see what seems to work.

Section **23-2** Knowledge Check

1. Identify special emotional needs of older adults.
2. List the effects of Alzheimer's disease.
3. What is depression?

Mini-Lab

Contact a community service agency to locate an older adult in need of some assistance with whom you can visit and build a relationship. Utilize planning and leadership techniques to meet the recreational needs of the older adult. Carry out your plans. Keep a journal to document your experience.

Section Summaries

23-1 The way people have lived their lives is a primary factor that will determine their physical condition as they age.

23-1 All people will experience changes in their bodies as they age, but the changes will be more apparent for some people than others.

23-1 Basically, the physical needs of older adults are the same as other people; as they age, adjustments have to be made to accommodate the degree of changes.

23-1 The social needs of older adults vary depending on personal preferences.

23-2 Issues encountered by older adults are similar to those of other adults, such as finances and living conditions.

23-2 Theories about aging include disengagement theory, activity theory, and continuity theory.

23-2 Maslow's Hierarchy of Human Needs: physiological needs, the need for safety, the need for love and belonging, the need for self-esteem, and the need for self-actualization.

23-2 Reduced energy and vigor may make older adults who are ill or functionally impaired selective about the activities that they are able to manage and enjoy.

23-2 Some older adults experience mental disorders, such as depression and anxiety.

23-2 Alzheimer's disease is a major cognitive impairment that affects about 10 percent of older adults.

23-2 An assessment can measure a person's cognitive ability and ability to function.

23-2 Mental alertness is a process of using cognitive skills to keep mentally active.

Check Your Knowledge

1. Contrast the activities of daily living and instrumental activities of daily living.
2. Identify the various physical changes related to aging.
3. Contrast social and emotional needs of older adults.
4. How do family and friends meet the emotional and support needs of older adults?
5. How are health and aging related? Distinguish between changes related to normal aging and those related to disease.
6. What are some of the most common chronic health conditions associated with aging?
7. What should a care provider know about an older adult's functional ability?
8. Discuss the role of sensory impairment in an older adult's functional ability.
9. What steps might care providers take to promote an older adult's independence?
10. What is cognitive impairment? How might it affect an older adult's ability to function?

Thinking Critically

1. Draw conclusions about how changes in appearance, health, senses, and mobility affect an older adult's self-esteem.
2. Do you think our society has negative stereotypes about aging and older adults? Defend your answer.

Practical Applications

1. **Role-Play.** With a partner, role-play assisting older adults with physical limitations. Take turns being an older adult with a vision or hearing impairment. You can wear eyeglasses with petroleum jelly spread on the lenses to distort your vision. Earplugs should be inserted into the ears when role-playing an older adult with a hearing impairment. Try performing daily tasks, such as making change, eating lunch, walking around the room, or communicating with another student. Discuss your thoughts about physical limitations with your class.

2. **Activity Research.** Using print and Internet sources, research social activities for older adults in your community. Create a resource guide that could be distributed to them.

3. **Learning from Older Adults.** Spend an afternoon with an older adult. Ask the older adult to teach you about something that interests him or her. In return, teach the older adult about something that interests you.

4. **Conversation-Starter Research.** In preparation for talking with older adults, research the top songs from the 1920s to the 1960s. In addition, research games and historical facts to use as conversation starters in working with older adults. Prepare a file folder of information for each decade.

Building Your PORTFOLIO

Planning a Program for Older Adults

Caring for older adults can be an enriching experience for the giver and the receiver. Learning about the aging process will enable you to better meet the physical, social, emotional, and cognitive needs of older adults. By learning how to plan a program for older adults you will increase your skills as an adult care provider.

Step 1: Interview an older adult to identify the person's physical needs. What physical changes are of concern? What types of assistance are needed? Create a care plan to help the older adult adjust to physical changes and to provide assistance as needed. Include the care plan in your portfolio.

Step 2: Plan an activity that would meet the social needs of older adults. It might be a craft activity, a game, a party, or an outing. If possible, carry out the activity with one or more older adults. Write a description of the activity for your portfolio.

Step 3: Obtain a copy of the monthly schedule of activities at a local adult care facility. Identify activities that would promote physical, social, emotional, and cognitive health in older adults. Include your analysis of the activity schedule in your portfolio.

Chapter 24
Approaches to Teaching & Learning

Section 24-1

Teaching Children

OBJECTIVES

- Describe principles related to how children learn.
- Explain the role of play in children's learning.
- Describe the characteristics of different learning styles.
- Summarize the concept of multiple intelligences.
- Explain how grouping of children affects teaching.

KEY TERMS

manipulatives
intelligence quotient
multiple intelligences
facilitate
teachable moments
open-ended
    materials
close-ended
    materials

The better you understand children, the better able you are to help them grow and develop. Experiences you plan for children must take into account how they learn. This section will explore how to plan for activities with the learner in mind.

How Children Learn

Children learn differently than adults. They are not just miniature people. At birth, only about 25 percent of the brain's learning pathways are developed. Due to this, children's vocabularies remain limited for several years. Attention spans are short. Motor skills are still developing. Many concepts are not understood. For reasons like these, early childhood professionals must plan children's activities carefully. Keep the following principles in mind when planning:

- **Children learn best by doing.** They do not learn best by listening to explanations. Children need hands-on experiences. For this reason, teachers provide many **manipulatives**, or toys and materials that children can operate and change with their hands. Clay, dough, sand, and snap beads are examples. Manipulatives help children develop small motor skills as they learn concepts. Objects of many shapes, sizes, and colors also stimulate thinking.

- **Children learn best when using their senses.** Sensory experiences—seeing, touching, hearing, smelling, and tasting—capture children's attention and maintain their interest. Children learn about the world by exploring concepts with their senses.

- **Children often learn through trial and error.** Children actively explore and experiment when interacting with their environment. They learn what works and what does not work. Making mistakes and learning from them is a natural part of the learning process.

- **Children learn best when all areas of development are nurtured.** Children need activities that aim at intellectual, physical, emotional, and social development to become well-balanced adults. Remember that these areas are interrelated. Progress in one area usually means progress in another. See Fig. 24-1.

- **Children learn through positive reinforcement.** When a child builds a tall block building that remains standing, he or she learns about the principles of weight and gravity. Praise and recognition from care providers when children learn something new builds children's confidence. Experiencing success in new accomplishments encourages learning.

FIG. 24-1. Activities that allow children to experiment with their environment help children develop physically, intellectually, socially, and emotionally. Why is making mistakes part of the learning process?

- **Children acquire and experiment with new behaviors through imitation and role modeling.** The significant people in children's lives provide them with words and actions to learn. Children often model their behavior after their parents and care providers.

Learning Styles

Think about how you learn best. Suppose you need to learn a new soccer or basketball play. Would you rather hear an explanation, see a diagram, or try it yourself? You might want some combination of hearing, seeing, and doing. Someone else on your team may learn the same play differently than you do.

There is no single right way to learn. Everyone has his or her own style. Some children are more verbally expressive, others more quiet. Some children are visual learners. They learn best by observing others, looking at pictures in a book, or watching a video. Others learn through listening and language activities.

Some children like to jump in and experience a new activity, whereas others wait for step-by-step instruction. Individual and small-group learning is best for some children, especially if they are easily embarrassed in front of others. However, other children bloom in larger groups. They enjoy performing and participating with others. Sensitive teachers get to know children as individuals so they can gear activities to children's preferred learning styles.

Multiple Intelligences

At one time, there was thought to be just one type of human intelligence. It was believed that the relative intelligence of a person could be measured by a standardized test and scored to reveal a person's IQ, or **intelligence quotient** (the ratio between mental age and chronological age). These IQ tests assessed language, logic, and academic potential. However, they

Boosting Brain Power

The Impact of Sleep. Just as a well-functioning body needs food and water, it also needs the nightly nourishment that sleep provides. Research shows that children who receive adequate nightly sleep learn better. The brain's short-term memory, necessary for paying attention and participating in learning activities, doesn't perform well when a child is sleep deprived. The typical preschool child requires 11 to 12 hours of sleep daily.

others is called linguistic (lihn-GWIS-tihk) intelligence. Writers, speakers, and lawyers often have linguistic intelligence.

- **Logical-mathematical intelligence.** The ability to understand underlying principles of systems and logically manipulate numbers, quantities, and operations are all part of logical-mathematical intelligence. Scientists, mathematicians, and inventors often use this type of intelligence.

- **Spatial intelligence.** The ability to comprehend the spatial world in the mind is called spatial intelligence. Architects, sailors, pilots, and sculptors often use spatial intelligence.

- **Bodily-kinesthetic intelligence.** The ability to use the whole body, or body parts, to solve problems, make something, or put on some kind of production is called bodily-kinesthetic (kih-nuhs-THEH-tihk) intelligence. Athletes, dancers, and actors use this type of intelligence.

ignored other types of intelligence or talent, such as musical ability or physical competence.

In contrast, Dr. Howard Gardner, a professor of education, believes people vary in terms of intelligence and learning strengths. See Fig. 24-2. He believes individual intelligence varies, just as learning styles do. His theory is referred to as **multiple intelligences**.

Gardner believes children understand concepts better when care providers and teachers plan activities that allow children to engage their own unique intelligences. For instance, children highly skilled in language can learn about food and nutrition by talking to a cook or listening to a recording. Children who learn well through body movement can learn from planting a garden and then actually cooking food. Musically talented children enjoy singing songs that teach information and concepts. Gardner identified the following eight types of human intelligence:

- **Linguistic intelligence.** The ability to use language to express thoughts and understand

FIG. 24-2. **Howard Gardner, in his theory of multiple intelligences, believes that intelligence varies just as learning styles do.** What are the eight types of human intelligence in Gardner's theory?

FIG. 24-3. **The way children are grouped in a classroom impacts activity planning.** What is the impact of each type of grouping?

- **Musical intelligence.** The ability to think in music, to hear patterns, recognize them, remember them, and manipulate them is part of musical intelligence. Composers, singers, musicians, and orchestra conductors often use this type of intelligence.

- **Interpersonal intelligence.** The ability to understand, relate to, and work well with other people is interpersonal intelligence. Teachers, salespeople, public relations specialists, counselors, therapists, and politicians often use this type of intelligence.

- **Intrapersonal intelligence.** A keen knowledge of your abilities, strengths, and limitations are all part of intrapersonal intelligence. People with strong intrapersonal intelligence readily find help when they need support. Business owners and managers of organizations often use this type of intelligence when they delegate responsibilities to others.

- **Naturalist intelligence.** The ability to see differences between living things, such as

plants and animals, and other features of the natural world, such as pattern, shape, and color, is called naturalist intelligence. Ecologists, biologists, botanists, insect specialists, and others who work with the natural world use this type of intelligence.

Grouping & Peer Learning

When planning learning activities, care providers and teachers must think about the mixture of children in the class. The number of children, their age ranges, and their ability levels all affect teaching and learning. Grouping begins with how children are placed in classrooms. See Fig. 24-3.

- **Same-age grouping.** This grouping occurs when children of the same age are placed together.

- **Developmental grouping.** This grouping places children in classrooms according to ability.

- **Mixed-age grouping.** Children of a certain age range are put in the same classroom in mixed-age grouping. For example, three- to five-year-olds might be grouped together.

Each method has its pros and cons. When children of the same age or ability level make up the classroom, it is easier to plan activities that will be suitable for all. However, children miss the opportunity to relate to those of other ages and abilities. Mixed-aged grouping can be a challenge because care providers and teachers must consider a wide range of developmental needs. An inappropriate activity will leave older or younger children in the age range feeling left out or bored. On the other hand, mixed-age grouping gives older children the chance to relate positively with younger ones and increases their self-esteem. Younger children learn from slightly older peers, who can be role models for advanced skills.

Often care providers divide the class into smaller groups for specific activities. They determine group size according to how much per-

Use Computers Effectively with Children

Like other play materials, computers can benefit children. Small motor, verbal, and problem-solving skills and basic concepts can be developed through computer play. Computers can also help prevent bias toward children with special needs because some of these children perform as well as their peers on computer tasks. However, computers should not be overused. They should enrich learning, not replace active engagement with other typical play activities, such as art or music. Computer desks and chairs should be child-size and at the correct level to avoid neck or eye strain. Evaluate software programs and offer only the best. Following are guidelines for the effective use of computers with young children:

1. The software uses pictures, colorful graphics, and spoken instructions, rather than written ones, so that children will not need to ask for help.

2. Children control the level of difficulty, the pace, and the direction of the program.

3. The software offers variety; children can explore a number of topics on different levels.

4. Children receive quick feedback, so they stay interested.

5. The software appeals to children by using interesting sights and sounds.

6. The product is appropriate for a child's current level of development and skills.

7. The software engages children's interest by encouraging children to laugh, explore, and use their imagination.

8. The program allows children to experience success and feel empowered through learning.

APPLY IT!

Visit a computer store and ask to preview a selection of children's programs. Which ones offer more interactive learning? What makes them more interactive?

sonal attention an activity requires. During some parts of an activity, especially when children are learning new skills, care providers may divide the class into smaller groups to give more one-on-one attention to each child. Later, when children are more confident and competent in their abilities, the care provider may have them work in larger groups.

Some activities are better suited to a certain group size. Most outdoor games are more fun with more players. Some art and science projects, on the other hand, are best conducted in small groups.

Generally, groups should be small enough to prevent overcrowding. A child can feel overwhelmed or lost in a group that is too large. Some children misbehave under the same circumstances. Usually, the younger the child, the smaller the group size should be.

FIG. 24-4. Spontaneous learning opportunities are called teachable moments. Why is it important for care providers to be sensitive to a child's teachable moments?

Learning Through Play

Learning is play for many young children. Living and learning are inseparable. Many experiences are new to them, so learning is a continual process. Early childhood specialists agree that play has a major role in learning. Playful interactions with peers, adults, and materials in the environment add to a child's store of knowledge about the world. Through activities that involve play, children grow in all areas of development.

Because children learn through play, care providers need to handle play activities carefully. Care providers should **facilitate** play, or help bring it about without controlling it. This skill comes with experience. For example, a care provider or teacher who tells the children to make a train with the empty boxes controls play. A care provider or teacher who puts the boxes out and says, "What can be done with these?" facilitates play.

With the right attitude and actions, you can help children get the most out of play. Give chil-

dren some freedom to choose play materials and use them in ways that suit them. An open-minded approach to play gives children a chance to be creative and independent.

Effective care providers interact with children while they play. By interacting with children in play situations, they can spot opportunities for growth and learning. Care providers or teachers can assess children's language and motor skills and act as role models for language. They also can recognize **teachable moments**, unplanned opportunities for learning. With experience, they also become skilled at interpreting the thoughts and feelings children express through play. When care providers interact with children, they give children the opportunity to share their experiences from home. This sharing helps build a trusting relationship between the care provider and the child. See Fig. 24-4.

Some toys and play materials promote learning better than others. Even those that contribute to learning do so in different ways. When analyzed as teaching tools, play materials are said to be either open-ended or close-ended.

Effective teachers make sure that they offer both types during classroom activities.

Open-ended Materials. Items that can be used in a variety of ways, with no single correct outcome, are called **open-ended materials**. In other words, the child decides what to do with them. These materials allow children to creatively develop independence, language skills, decision-making and problem-solving skills, and imagination. Many art materials, such as paint and dough, are open-ended. Water, sand toys, and blocks can be used in an open-ended manner. Open-ended materials can usually be successfully adapted for the learning needs of mixed-age groups.

FIG. 24-5. Open-ended teaching materials have an expected result. How can children benefit from using open-ended teaching materials?

Close-ended Materials. Structured materials, or **close-ended materials**, are items that are to be used primarily in one way, with an expected result. These materials are less open to input from the child. They help children learn how to follow directions. They also help develop sensory perception and motor skills. Examples include puzzles, matching games, snap beads, stringing beads, and sewing cards. Close-ended materials provide a specific and known outcome. These types of materials stimulate and enhance the learning process. See Fig. 24-5.

Section **24-1** Knowledge Check

1. Contrast intelligence quotient with the theory of multiple intelligences.
2. Explain how children's learning styles might vary.
3. Give three examples of open-ended learning materials.

Mini-Lab

Observe two or three children of the same age playing together, such as three-year-olds. Then observe a small group of children of different ages playing together, such as three- and four-year-olds. In your notes, contrast the behavior, play skills, and dialogue. How do the two groups differ?

Section **24-2**

Curriculum Planning for Children

By nature, children are eager to explore and make discoveries. They need opportunities to grow and learn. Without them, development suffers. As a child care professional, an important part of your job is to promote child development through learning activities.

What Will You Teach?

The experiences and activities that support and guide children's learning is called the **curriculum.** In a good preschool program, activities do not just happen. Learning activities are carefully developed as part of the curriculum framework, giving children relevant educational experiences.

Early childhood classrooms require a **developmentally appropriate curriculum.** That means curriculum activities are geared to the specific abilities and levels of development in a group of children. If activities are geared too far below children's developmental levels, children become bored and restless. They may turn to disruptive behavior. If activities are too difficult, children become frustrated. They begin to believe they cannot learn and then self-esteem suffers. The ideal curriculum challenges children, yet enables ongoing success.

Building a Strong Curriculum

The key to a strong curriculum is well-planned activities. They should be stimulating and varied, not repetitive and boring. They should capture children's interest, giving them information and encouraging them to think.

A strong curriculum is balanced. In other words, it includes activities that address all areas of development, as well as different subject areas. The curriculum also integrates cultural diversity and bilingual development with the various subject areas. Typically, the curriculum is divided into subject areas that correspond to the learning centers in the classroom. The chapters in this unit describe learning centers that are typically included. Remember, however, that activities can also be created for any other learning centers a program might have.

Setting Goals & Objectives

Curriculum is planned to meet all program goals. For example, fostering creativity and imagination is a goal of many programs. To meet this goal, care providers and teachers plan activities in art, music, creative movement, dramatic play, and other subjects that encourage children's creative expression. See Fig. 24-6.

Once a curriculum topic and associated activities are selected, care providers keep in mind activity objectives. **Objectives** are outcomes for

ETHICS IN Action

Promoting Cultural Understanding. Care providers today are not as likely to use multicultural themes as a basis for units as they once were. Instead, they weave projects, toys, and props that promote understanding and appreciation of different cultures into the entire curriculum throughout the school year. To offer them as a novelty or one-time experience only marks them as foreign and different, not as part of a truly multicultural society. *Do you agree or disagree?*

children to achieve or experience through participation in a specific curriculum activity. Objectives support goals that relate to all areas of development, including social, intellectual, emotional, or physical development.

Dr. Benjamin Bloom, a developmental psychologist, established a ranking of educational objectives for cognitive development. The system ranks mental abilities, from very basic to more complex thinking skills. It is called **Bloom's Taxonomy** (tak-SAH-nuh-mee). By keeping Bloom's Taxonomy in mind, care providers set objectives and plan activities that will allow children to put all levels of thinking skills to use. Here are the key levels of Bloom's Taxonomy:

* **Level 1: Knowledge.** This level requires the ability to remember and recall information. The activity objectives include the following skills: list, name, remember, show, or recognize.

FIG. 24-6. Fostering creativity and imagination is a goal in many early childhood programs. What types of activities promote creativity and imagination?

- **Level 2: Comprehension.** Ability to understand information and explain or summarize it is required at this level. The skills in these activity objectives include: discuss, describe, restate, express, explain, or review.

- **Level 3: Application.** This level requires the ability to apply information in a new situation. The activity objectives include such skills as: collect, classify, sort, choose, show, or group.

- **Level 4: Analysis.** The ability to understand isolated parts of information and discovering relationships between them, such as the ability to identify similarities and differences, requires analysis. The activity objectives include skills, such as: explain, combine, describe, compare, contrast, distinguish, examine, organize, give reasons, or explain relationship.

- **Level 5: Synthesis.** The ability to combine ideas, information, or objects to create a new whole is called synthesis (SIN-thuh-suhs). The activity objectives include skills, such as: create, develop, invent, construct, design, assemble, or problem solve.

- **Level 6: Evaluation.** The ability to make judgments for a specific purpose is called evaluation. The activity objectives may include such skills as: choose, select, rate, recommend, judge, recommend, or state an opinion.

Approaches to Teaching

Care providers vary on how they make curriculum decisions. In some early childhood programs, all classrooms must follow the same curriculum and approach to teaching to meet the program philosophy and goals. Others allow care providers individual choice in planning for learning in their classrooms. In either case, care providers and teachers must be able to demonstrate developmentally appropriate teaching methods and techniques in their classrooms.

Care providers in charge of classrooms do most of the curriculum planning. Because early childhood classrooms have a variety of staff, such as care providers or teachers and teacher assistants or teacher aides, team planning is the norm. Team planning requires interdependent relationships among the staff. Interdependence enhances creativity and requires all staff members to work together to meet the developmental needs of children. Some programs try to include parents in curriculum planning, too.

Larger programs may have a curriculum coordinator, or an educational coordinator, who leads and supervises classroom planning. Regardless of how the curriculum and activities are selected, all selections require the program director's final approval. The following includes some of the most popular approaches to planning and teaching in early childhood classrooms.

Project Approach

In the **project approach** to teaching, care providers conduct projects that allow children to explore in developmentally appropriate ways. A project refers to children's in-depth investigation of a specific topic. The project topic is chosen both by children and care providers or teachers. Care providers make sure projects allow children to investigate topics of value that benefit them as people and learners. Effective topics stem from children's own interests and questions. The topic generates children's enthusiasm and curiosity. If a topic is particularly interesting, care providers will allow children to repeat activities, introducing new activities when the children are ready. See Fig. 24-7. Care providers and teachers should keep the following points in mind when using the project approach:

- **Grouping children.** Some projects involve all children; others may involve small groups. Project learning continues as long as children's interest is maintained and the care provider believes the learning is useful.

- **Project goals.** The main goal of the project is children learning to find answers to their own questions about a topic. Project topic investigations usually revolve around familiar objects, people, or events in children's daily lives. Once a topic is selected, care providers and children think of activities that will help them answer their questions. Care providers plan experiences that offer many different opportunities for hands-on learning. Some projects last a week, some a few months.

- **Use of resources.** In the project approach, children use a variety of resources to learn more about chosen topics. For instance, children learning about pets might look at books on the topic. Classmates' pets may visit the classroom with parents. Children would be encouraged to bring in resources that relate to the topic, such as photos of their own pets or supplies they use to groom pets. The care provider may invite a special visitor, such as a veterinarian, into the classroom to explain pet care.

- **Field trips.** Visits to field sites play an important role in project learning, too. Depending on children's interests, a project about pets might include a trip to a pet store, the animal humane society, or a pet breeder. Field site visits allow children to see how their topic, and the knowledge they learn about it, relates to the real world. In the project approach, trips usually occur early, so later activities can reflect learning that occurred on the field trip visit.

- **Gathering, organizing, and representing information.** During a project, children learn to gather, organize, and represent information in different ways. Explorations are integrated across curriculum areas as appropri-

FIG. 24-7. **The project approach involves in-depth investigation on a topic chosen by the class.** What role does the project approach play in the entire curriculum for early childhood programs?

ate. During a pet project, children use language skills to make a list of typical household pets. They use math skills to conduct a survey of pets owned by classmates. More math is used when they graph the survey results on a poster. In the art area, may draw pictures of pets or make clay sculptures. They may write stories about pets, put on a puppet show, or create a pretend pet shop for dramatic play. The field trips and other investigations allow children to add rich, realistic detail to all those play activities.

- **Assessing project learning.** To assess and record project learning, care providers frequently tape-record children's actual dialogue and photograph children during activities. This type of documentation allows children to refer back to experiences to help them gain greater understanding. Documentation also helps care providers keep parents informed about children's adventures and learning progress. It also helps teachers and care providers to note developmental delays in children.

Reggio Emilia Approach

A town in northern Italy, Reggio Emilia, has become internationally known for its unique approach to teaching young children. Its early childhood programs have been a strong inspiration for using the project approach around the world. The core features of the **Reggio Emilia Approach** include the following:

- Children are considered competent, capable, and motivated learners, full of potential.
- Collaborative learning is stressed. Children, care providers, parents, and community members explore and learn together. See Fig. 24-8.
- Physical environment is purposefully designed and organized. It is considered a very important influence on the learning process.
- Curriculum is project based, so children independently and cooperatively investigate topics.
- Children construct projects and represent learning in a variety of creative ways.

FIG. 24-8. **The environment is purposefully designed for collaborative learning in the Reggio Emilia Approach.** How can a purposefully designed environment influence the learning process?

Theme Approach

In some classrooms, curriculum activities are based on a theme approach. A **theme** is one central topic, or theme, selected by the care provider. The theme is not chosen based on children's interest. Care providers think of, plan, and conduct activities that relate to the theme for one or two weeks. The care provider gathers all the resources prior to conducting a theme activity.

There are many different types of themes for care providers or teachers to choose. However, themes are often used to teach specific concepts, such as colors, shapes, numbers, or letters. Themes are usually broad topics, rather than specific topics as used in the project approach. For instance, themes may cover all community helpers in general. In contrast, a project in the project approach would focus on a specific type of community helper, such as firefighters.

Care providers develop theme activities for each curriculum area. Field trips are usually the final step in the theme approach, rather than a beginning step, as in the project approach.

Implementing Curriculum

Regardless of the curriculum approach used, curriculum is implemented to encourage children's basic learning skills. All children need to gradually learn how to focus, pay attention, and concentrate. These skills help them learn to follow directions and cooperate. They need experiences in which they can learn to listen to others' ideas and clearly express their own ideas. Care providers foster listening skills by reading stories and introducing longer stories as children's attention spans grow. Learning how to work individually and in groups is also necessary. Practice in maintaining a positive learning attitude helps children persevere in the face of challenges.

Children need many different chances to show their understanding of concepts and topics. In early childhood, paper and pencil tests are not used to evaluate children's learning. Instead, learning is encouraged creatively through art construction, drawing, modeling with clay, block building, dictating stories, making books, and putting on plays and puppet shows. See Fig. 24-9.

Scheduling Curriculum Activities

As activities are planned, they are incorporated in the daily schedule. Chapter 9 discusses how schedules work. Regular routines—including arrival, meals, snacks, naps, toileting, and departure—form the core of the schedule. The remaining time is reserved for activities.

Timing affects when activities will be included in the schedule. Will there be enough time to accomplish what you want to do? What is the best time of day for the children to do this activity? Will the activity interfere with anything else going on in the center? Answering questions like these ahead of time will help the schedule flow more smoothly.

Developing Lesson Plans

It takes more than just an idea to make an activity happen in the classroom. Each activity must first be developed into a lesson plan. A **lesson plan** is a detailed, written explanation of an activity, including the purpose, any materials needed, the step-by-step method for carrying out the activity, and evaluation of the activity.

Lesson plans are an organization tool. They force you to think ahead about what you want to accomplish and why. They enable care providers and teachers to work through their ideas mentally and on paper before they conduct them. By doing so, they have a clear understanding of the purpose and objective behind each activity. Care providers and teachers apply major learning theories when planning developmentally appropriate learning experiences for children. Care providers can gather the right materials in the right quantity,

FIG. 24-9. A variety of activities encourage the development of creativity. How can working with modeling clay lead to creativity?

identify stimulating learning environments, and set up logical learning procedures with orderly steps. This helps implement developmentally appropriate lessons more clearly and calmly.

Many care providers and teachers use a preprinted form for preparing lesson plans. If you were making a lesson plan, you would fill out the form as shown in Fig. 24-10 on page 546. Although forms may vary, the basic information that you record on a lesson plan includes:

- **Age group.** Record the age or level of development of the children.

- **Activity title.** Give the lesson an appropriate title.

- **Objectives.** Briefly state the purpose of the lesson. List concepts and skills to be developed.

- **Materials required.** List all materials needed, including quantities.

- **Activity procedure.** Outline the steps for conducting the activity. Put them in order.

Lesson Plan

Sample Lesson Plan

Age Group: Four- and five-year-olds

Activity Title: Touch and Tell

Objectives:
- To develop the sense of touch, language and vocabulary skills.
- To become aware that objects vary in size, shape, and texture.

Materials Required
- Empty, clean, decorated coffee can.
- Large box filled with familiar toys, plastic fruit, blocks, etc., that will fit individually in the can.
- Blanket to cover box.
- Carpet squares.

Activity Procedure
1. Have children sit in a large circle on carpet squares.
2. **Introduction.** Ask the children to touch some items around them, such as their hair, clothing, or shoes. Then ask them to tell how these items feel.
3. Tell children they are going to learn how to gather information using just their sense of touch.
4. Place an object from the box in the coffee can. Use the blanket to keep all children from seeing the object.
5. Invite one child at a time to play the game as follows:
   - Have the child reach into the can and feel the object without looking.
   - Ask the child to describe what he or she is feeling without telling what it is.
   - The class then tries to guess what object is in the can.
6. Once the object is identified, repeat Steps 4 and 5 until all the children have had several turns.
7. **Closure.** Remind children that many objects around them are interesting to touch. Can they name any items that they especially like to touch? What objects are not safe to touch?

Evaluation
Six of the eight children were successful with this activity. Be sure to include a few less familiar objects to challenge the more developmentally advanced children. Begin activity with easier objects to identify. Allow 30 minutes the next time the activity is used.

FIG. 24-10. Preparing detailed lesson plans helps care providers have a clear understanding of the purpose and objective behind each activity. What may be the consequences of failing to plan adequately for children's learning experiences?

Try to be as thorough as possible in breaking down the sequence. Calculate and record the time needed to complete the activity. Well-planned activities begin with a short introduction that motivates children. You might use a question or show an object to create interest. The activity should be completed with something that brings it to closure. A question that generates thought or conclusions may be enough. A transition to the next activity on the schedule may also be included at the end.

- **Evaluation.** With your team members, briefly assess the effectiveness of the lesson. How many children were successful? How could the lesson be improved?

Teaching Styles

Lesson plans come to life in the hands of good care providers. A good lesson plan may not be effective when poorly presented. On the other hand, a skillful care provider might save a weak lesson plan. The manner used to teach a lesson or guide behavior is called teaching style.

Experienced, sensitive care providers and teachers are aware of their teaching styles. Those who are particularly skilled know how to adapt when necessary. They may have to change to meet children's needs or to handle an activity. With sharp observation skills, a versatile person does what is necessary when a situation demands it.

Just as personalities are different, teaching styles differ, too. Some care providers have theatrical energy, and others are calm and relaxed. Some are very precise about behavior; others are more informal. Some care providers prefer structure and orderly lessons; others are more spontaneous.

Integrating Style. When working with children, a care provider's teaching style becomes integrated with the activity. In fact, a care provider often plans the activity to fit with his or her teaching style. For example, after reading a story about a monkey, an outgoing care provider may join the children as they all walk around the room like monkeys. A quieter care provider might show pictures of different kinds of monkeys and lead a discussion or help the children write a group story about going to the zoo.

Beliefs of Care Providers. Beliefs also affect teaching style. What a care provider believes about children and how they learn impacts children's learning. Suppose care providers are working with two children who are shy and afraid of making mistakes. One care provider might believe that a gentle approach is the best way to gradually build their self-confidence. Another may believe the same children need to be drawn out by taking an outgoing approach, using humor. Carefully observing how the children react to a teaching style may give the best information regarding how these children will learn best.

Benefits of Different Styles. One teaching style is not necessarily better than another. Children can benefit from all types of styles. Some children may relate better to one style than another. A child who likes action, for example, might love to run around like a monkey but will become impatient with talk about the zoo. On the other hand, the need to sit still and practice listening as others talk about the zoo may help the energetic child learn self-control. When care providers with different styles interact with children throughout the day, children have chances to learn in different ways and adapt to varied situations. This also helps promote children's respect for diversity.

Encouraging Creativity

A care provider's style and behavior can either encourage or discourage children's creativity. Wise care providers respond to and interact with children, so that they learn creativity is valued. The following conditions encourage creativity:

- Freedom to explore materials without the risk of being judged or graded allows children to be more creative.
- Acceptance of creativity allows children to find new ways to play and interact.
- Variety in learning materials for independent use encourages children to be creative.
- Use of their own ideas, rather than copying those of a care provider, helps children develop resourcefulness.

- Time and support for problem solving helps children find new ways to accomplish their goals. They are more likely to be inventive and original if given time and support.

- Questions that cause children to think encourage creativity. For instance, the way in which a question is asked can either encourage or discourage creativity. **Open-ended questions** are those that require more than a yes or no answer. These questions often begin with *how, what, when, where,* and *why*. Open-ended questions encourage children to express feelings, explain ideas, and relate experiences. They stimulate both the creativity and the intellectual skills needed for language development. An example of a meaningful question might be, "What is happening in your drawing?" A question to encourage problem solving would be, "What's another way to stack the blocks so your building will not fall?" See Fig. 24-11.

Creativity Throughout the Curriculum.
Many people think creativity is only used in an art or music curriculum. However, children can apply creativity in all curriculum areas. It can be applied whether learning indoors or out. For example, sand play allows for creative sand sculptures as well as a variety of ways to apply science concepts. Children also can learn to creatively express themselves through storytelling,

FIG. 24-11. **Open-ended questions are an excellent way to get children to express their thoughts and feelings.** What questions might this teacher be asking this child?

puppetry, dramatic play, or writing. Dance and movement activities also allow plenty of room for creativity. Alert care providers never miss an opportunity to let children apply creative thinking during activities.

Section **24-2** Knowledge Check

1. What is a developmentally appropriate curriculum?
2. Name at least two approaches to curriculum development.
3. How does teaching style impact learning?

Mini-Lab

Interview an early childhood care provider who has used both the theme approach and the project approach to curriculum planning. What does the care provider see as the strengths and benefits of each approach? Report your findings to the class.

Section 24-3
Teaching Older Adults

OBJECTIVES

- Describe older adult learners.
- Identify learning styles of older adults.
- Determine ways to treat adult learners.

KEY TERMS

reinforcement
retention
transfer learning

People can learn and combine new information throughout life. However, the aging process affects the way older adults learn. Care providers must consider age-related changes when working with older adults.

Adults As Learners

Adult learners tend to be self-guided and wise, and they bring a wealth of information to the learning environment. Most adults are problem solvers and they seek solutions. Older adult learners want to learn information they can immediately use. They want information that helps them solve problems. Problem solving is one of the most beneficial educational activities for older adults.

Like children, older adults enjoy learning about topics of interest. Care providers should plan activities that reflect the interests of the older adults in their care. Activities also must represent the diversity of the participants. Considering cultural differences ensures that each person benefits from the activities.

Characteristics of Older Adult Learners

Older adults acquire knowledge differently than when they were young. Their knowledge, life experiences, and skills help them to use new information in making decisions. Older adults also have specific learning styles. Fig. 24-12 lists four learning styles that best represent the older adult learner. In addition to learning styles, older adults have certain characteristics.

- **Self-directed learning.** Due to their wealth of knowledge and life experiences, older adults seek active involvement in what they learn. Past education, work activities, and family provide the source for much of this knowledge. They need to connect new learning to this knowledge. During activities, care

FIG. 24-12.

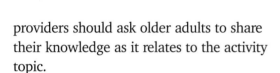

ADULT LEARNING STYLES

Learning Styles	Description
Environmental Learners	Environmental learners retain information best when they are in a place that is comfortable with appropriate lighting, seating, and room temperature.
Auditory Learners	Auditory learners learn new information best when it is spoken to them.
Visual Learners	Visual illustrations or demonstrations help these learners process information.
Kinesthetic Learners	Kinesthetic (kih-nuhs-THEH-tihk) learners learn best when they can touch and feel educational materials.

providers should ask older adults to share their knowledge as it relates to the activity topic.

- **Goal-oriented learning.** Older adults usually know what goals they want to attain when they enroll in a class or participate in an activity. They desire clearly defined goals and organization in program activities. This helps older adults achieve their activity goals. Care providers must be clear in showing how a program will meet older adults' goals. They also need to share the class objectives with the participants.

- **Applicable learning activities.** Older adults must know how learning new skills will apply to their home and work life. Before activities occur, care providers should describe the activity objectives. They should also give older adults activity choices as much as possible.

- **Practical learning activities.** Older adults want information and skills that are useful to them. They may not be interested in knowledge for its own sake. Care providers should explain how new information will be useful in the daily lives of older adults.

Because their cognitive ability may be slowing, older adults often need more time during activities. Many older adults also want detailed

information about a topic before making decisions. Care providers should tailor activities to the culture, age, and gender of older adults. Doing so ensures developmentally appropriate activities.

Care providers must also present information in a way that allows older adults to process it easily. Hands-on materials help older adults understand topics. Visuals, such as films, displays, and pictures, help some older adults see objects they might not see at home. These methods are effective because they appeal to different learning styles. Like many young learners, older adults often learn best when they can see and handle materials.

Motivation to Learn

Motivated learners typically achieve more than people who are not motivated. Older adults are motivated to learn when the topics relate to them. They also are motivated when they are allowed to help plan activities. When older adults help plan activities on relevant topics, they feel ownership of the activity. Some factors that motivate older adults include the following:

- **Social relationships.** Making new friends meets older adults' need for social interaction and friendship.

- **Authoritarian expectations.** Some older adults need to comply with instructions and fulfill another person's expectations.

- **Social welfare.** Some adults enjoy serving others and the community. Community work often motivates these learners.

- **Personal advancement.** Some older adults want to achieve higher status. These older adults like to perform well on a job, receive professional advancement, and stay informed about competitors.

- **Ability to change routines.** Some adults are motivated by a break in routines. Participating in a different activity relieves boredom and helps older adults feel motivated.

- **Cognitive interest.** Some older adults enjoy learning for the sake of learning. They seek knowledge because they like to learn.

Reinforcement of Learning

Reinforcement is a process used to strengthen and increase learning. It can be as simple as an encouraging word about a job well done. Or, reinforcement can occur using a different activity to reinforce a skill. Reinforcement ensures that older adults learn correct skills and behavior. For example, if an older adult were learning to use a computer, the care provider would provide varying experiences and numerous encouraging words to help an older adult learn this skill. Care providers should provide enough time for older adults to learn and practice new skills. An environment with limited distractions also helps older adults focus on specific activities. After the older adults have learned a skill, reinforcement helps them maintain it.

Retention of Learning

To benefit from the learning, **retention** of information—or the ability to remember information—is essential. Several conditions are necessary for older adults to retain learning. Older adults must:

ETHICS IN Action

Impact of Teaching Style. You have observed that a coworker almost always maintains a very structured environment that allows her complete control of the adult care facility where you are employed. She rarely involves participants in decision making or takes their learning styles into account. Although this style seems to suit her personality, you have observed signs of boredom and dissatisfaction among participants. *What would you do?*

- Believe the information is relevant.
- Believe the information is important.
- Believe the information is useful.

How much information older adults retain depends on how much they originally learned. If an older adult learns how to cook, and learns so very well, he or she will have an easier time retaining that learning. On the other hand, if an older adult did not learn to cook very well, he or she may not retain much information about cooking. To help older adults retain information, care providers should encourage them to practice skills. Training, practice, and support from family and care providers help older adults retain the information that they learn. See Fig. 24-13.

Transfer Learning

Transfer learning is the ability to use the information taught in an activity in a different setting. For example, older adults might learn to grow tomatoes in the activity center's garden.

Intergenerational Interactions

Elderhostel™ Intergenerational Programs

Elderhostel™ is an international travel organization for adults ages 55 and over. The organization offers older adults an opportunity to travel throughout North America and to faraway lands at reasonable rates. Elderhostel™ also hosts intergenerational programs for older-adult relatives and friends of young children. Programs, like those mentioned below, offer children and older adults a chance to learn together while sharing adventures.

- **Utah Dinosaur Triangle.** Visit the College of Eastern Utah Prehistoric Museum, Dinosaur National Monument, North American Museum of Ancient Life, and more as experts discuss the life, times, and characteristics of dinosaurs. As an added bonus, visitors will also river-raft through Split Mountain Gorge.

- **Hulbert Outdoor Center.** Enjoy the beauty of the Maine outdoors while camping and canoeing on the Rangeley Lakes. Participants will "rough it" as they sleep in tents, learn outdoor cooking tips, observe birds and wildlife, learn about astronomy, and more.

- **Denali National Park.** Children and older adults will be amazed by the beauty of the Alaskan wilderness. Daily tours allow visitors to see caribou, moose, bears, wolves, glacial rivers, wildflowers, and more.

- **An Interactive Rain Forest Adventure.** Visitors will travel mountain trails, jungle rivers, and cobblestone streets as they take in the beauty of Ecuador—from its snow-capped volcanoes to its lush Amazon Basin. Plus, they will visit with Native Americans whose heritage pre-dates Christopher Columbus.

- **Into Africa: An Eco-Safari.** On this trek through the wilderness of Zambia and Botswana, travelers will search for elephants, lions, zebras, giraffes, and more. They'll also visit the wetlands of Okavango Delta and Victoria Falls as they learn about the lives of ancient African tribes.

Follow-Up

Write a report on a place that you would like to visit. Include reasons why a trip to this place would be fun to experience with an older adult.

They show transfer learning when they later grow tomatoes at their own home or a relative's home.

Transfer learning is most likely to occur when older adults relate new ideas and information to their foundation of knowledge and experience. Care providers can help by explaining these similarities to older adults when the information is introduced.

Treatment of Older Adult Learners

Most older adults conribute a vast array of life experiences and knowledge to program activities. Through their contributions they earn the respect of others. Whenever possible, care providers should provide opportunities for older adults to share their viewpoints and knowledge. Together as equals, care providers and older adults can create enriching learning experiences.

FIG. 24-13. **Positive reinforcement increases learning and memory and promotes a healthy self-esteem in older adults.** *Investigate several memory-enhancing activities for older adults.*

Section **24-3** Knowledge Check

1. What are the four learning styles of adult learners?

2. What are the factors that motivate adults to learn?

3. How should older adults be treated in order for them to learn new information?

Mini-Lab

Assume that you are planning activities for an adult day center. Demonstrate how you would involve older adult participants in selecting the types of activities for a particular time period. Outline the steps you would take to get their involvement. Share your plan with the class.

Section **24-4**

Program Planning for Older Adults

- Identify the characteristics of developmentally appropriate programs for older adults.
- Identify various types of activities for older adults, including intergenerational activities.
- Determine the characteristics of effective program planning.
- Describe the use of facilitation with older adult learners.

KEY TERMS

**activity plan
facilitation**

Successful programs for older adults are planned and presented carefully. The programs are designed to meet the immediate needs of older adults. In successful programs, older adults help with planning and presenting the activities. It is important for care providers to know and use the principles of program planning for older adults.

Developmentally Appropriate Programs

Effective programs for older adults should be designed to improve their well-being. Developmentally appropriate programs:

- Increase self-esteem.
- Are useful to older adults.
- Reflect the insights, experience, and expertise of the older adults.
- Promote physical and mental health.
- Create opportunities for learning at every stage of development.
- Reduce stereotypes.
- Promote mutual respect for all ethnic groups.

Program Objectives

When planning activities, and during the activities, care providers should keep in mind the program's objectives and each individual's plan of care. When older adults are engaged in activities, care providers should observe and note any changes in the older adults or the environment. Care providers should respond to these changes to make sure learning continues. To be successful, care providers must be flexible and be willing to change an activity when it is not working. Offering a choice of activities during the activity time helps accommodate the interests and needs of the program participants. Many programs are not effective because they are inflexible and have too many detailed rules or a lack of varied activities.

Interaction Among Older Adults

Successful programs allow older adults to interact. Developing interaction among older adults takes time and sensitivity. Older adults may need to overcome their uncertainty about the program and their insecurity. To help develop interaction among older adults, arrange seating so that older adults can face each other to talk. Encourage older adults to help each other and ask them open-ended questions to generate conversation.

Appropriate Technology Use

Most older adults use technology in daily activities at home and in older adult care programs. Technology helps older adults have a productive lifestyle. The Internet helps older adults stay in touch with family members and friends. Older adults may also go online to shop for medical supplies, pay bills, or conduct banking activities. Some older adults also enjoy computer-based learning. This type of learning can help reduce social isolation. Technology can also be used in instruction. Television, computers, and other types of technology can motivate older adults and meet different learning styles and special needs. See Fig. 24-14.

Program Design

The program design depends on the information that older adults want to know and how they best learn. Programs can be presented in many places and in many ways to meet older adults' needs and learning styles.

Creating Activities

Involve older adults in creating the types of activities they need and want. They will more likely participate and assume responsibility for their learning when they have helped to create and select activities. Older adults understand their own needs and can create activities to fulfill them. They can also help care providers identify resources that are available for the activities.

Activity Plan. An **activity plan** provides an outline for the older adults and care providers to follow. It includes the objectives, the content, the teaching strategies, the outcome, and the evaluation methods. See Fig. 24-15.

Activities for Older Adults. Activities for older adults should be pleasurable and satisfying, so older adults will participate. Activities should also address cultural and personal interests and special needs of older adults. Older adults enjoy many different kinds of activities. Care providers should try to include as many diverse activities as possible, as long as the

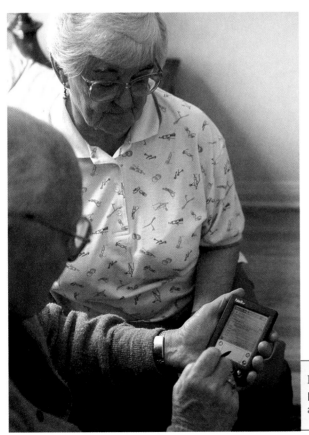

FIG. 24-14. **Technology can help older adults lead productive lives.** What are some ways that older adults might use technology?

FIG. 24-15. Activity plans help care providers effectively meet the needs of older adults. What are the consequences of having ineffective activity plans?

Activity Plan

Learning opportunities: Sessions will be held one day a week for four weeks.
Time: Each session will last 60 minutes (10:00 a.m.–11:00 a.m, November 1–30).
Resources: Computers and monitors, computer-based programs, food item labels, and medication labels.
Learners: English-speaking adults; 65–75 years of age; all have basic computer knowledge and skills.

Specific objectives:

- Read label on their medication bottle.
- Gain an understanding about how the medication works.
- Read labels on specific food items.
- Determine which foods to avoid when taking specific medications.

Planned learning experiences:

1. Participants will use computer-based programs to identify their medication.
2. Participants will use computer-based programs to identify food label content.
3. After becoming familiar with the content of the medication and food labels, participants will develop a plan that lists all food items to avoid when taking specific medications.
4. Participants will get printouts of the medication-food combination to track a daily plan.
5. As a follow-up activity, the group will view a videotape on combining food and medication.
6. A nutrition educator and pharmacist will answer questions.

Content outline: Develop a content outline for each of the sessions (introduction, activities, and summary).

activities meet the needs of older adults. Here are some possible types of activities:

- **Games, clubs, and cards.** Board games and special-interest clubs, such as chess and photography clubs, interest older adults. These activities stimulate cognitive skills and promote social interaction.

- **Art.** Activities—such as painting or sculpting—foster self-awareness, develop social skills, manage behavior, solve problems, reduce anxiety, and increase self-esteem.

- **Crafts.** Knitting, quilting, and woodworking create an appreciation for beauty and help older adults maintain small motor skills.

- **Music.** Singing, dancing, and playing instruments inspire older adults, help lighten their moods, and stimulate memory.

- **Gardening.** Planting, watering, and cutting plants and flowers builds motivation, stimulates cognitive thinking, helps manage stress, and creates a positive environment for older adults.

- **Fitness and exercise.** Head and body movements and relaxation techniques help older adults regain or maintain their strength and the use of their muscles and body parts.

- **Touring or traveling.** Travel and tour groups that involve cultural enrichment and historical events help motivate older adults and promote social interaction.

Intergenerational Activities. Intergenerational activities bring young people and older adults together. These activities promote learning and meet the needs of youth, older adults, and communities. Examples of intergenerational activities include:

FIG. 24-16. Outdoor activities, such as picnics, offer opportunities for interaction and enjoyment. What other outdoor activities might care providers plan for the old and young?

- **Intergenerational music.** All participants learn new songs together. A music activity can be a sing-a-long for young people and older adults.

- **Intergenerational art projects.** Examples of intergenerational art projects include creating collages or murals, painting, making videos, and taping songs. Participants may also create a dramatic performance to present at a community center.

- **Intergenerational language learning.** These activities allow older adults who speak a second language to teach young people their language.

- **Intergenerational community service projects.** These projects help older adults and young people appreciate and understand their community. Examples of community service projects include learning community history, participating in community clubs and events, or volunteering.

- **Intergenerational outdoor projects.** These projects include outdoor adventures, such as hiking and canoeing. See Fig. 24-16.

FIG. 24-17.

TEACHING STRATEGIES FOR OLDER ADULTS

- Care providers should use audiovisual materials, such as graphics, pictures, illustrations, and demonstrations.

- Care providers hold large- and small-group discussions. Invite guest speakers, such as a nutritionist or geriatric physical therapist.

- Care providers write activity plans for older adults to also use at home, encourage group activities, and instruct learners to take notes and explore objects.

- Care providers allow learning to take place in a nontraditional environment, such as learning at home over the Internet or independent study.

Roles of Program Planners

Program coordinators, the professionals who create programs for older adults, often include older adults in program planning. When beginning to plan, the coordinator first gathers together a group of older adults. This group represents the ages of all program participants. For example, if the program's participants are between ages 65 and 75, the program coordinator will include older adults between those ages for brainstorming activity ideas. The coordinator then guides the group in planning the activities. The coordinator must be able to:

- Identify activities they could do to improve the well-being of people in the group. For example, if the group decides they want fitness activities to help build strength, the coordinator would then plan activities accordingly.

- Identify resources needed to carry out the activity. For example, the center may need to purchase special small fitness balls to strengthen muscles.

- Establish priorities for activities.

- Identify what the older adults want to gain from completing this activity.

- Design an activity plan that provides good learning experiences and active involvement.

- Determine the program evaluation. For example, does the coordinator see improvement in the older adults' strength after six or more weeks?

- Share the plan with program sponsors or those who will provide funds. Positive activity results may lead to further program funding.

The Learning Environment

Care providers should design an informal environment that meets older adults' physical and psychological needs. For example, chairs should be arranged to encourage discussion. A learning environment should also:

- **Provide flexibility.** Care providers should allow for breaks from the traditional meeting routine. For example, care providers can arrange for a snack during a meeting to foster opportunities for interaction.

- **Use humor.** Humor helps older adult learners relax and build relationships. Care providers foster humor by laughing at themselves when they make a mistake. This also shows that making mistakes is a natural part of learning.

- **Provide for problem-solving support.** Older adults need support and resources to solve problems. One strategy care providers can use is to encourage older adults to work in groups.

Program Evaluation. After the activity is completed, take time to document what occurred. Reflect on the experience and write about the activity. Were the objectives met? Did the activity support the overall program goal? To extend the activity, care providers can encourage older adults to write a news release about the event for the local media.

Teaching Strategies

Teaching strategies should incorporate the learning styles of older adults. Older adults learn best by being involved. They bring knowledge and experience to the learning situation and also expect more from it. Sensitive care providers understand the learning styles of the older adults in their care, and should provide appropriate strategies that will be effective. Figure 24-17 shows the characteristics of teaching strategies.

Facilitation Styles

Facilitation helps bring about learning and makes new knowledge easier to learn. Facilitation differs from direct instruction, which tells

FIG. 24-18. **When care providers encourage participation among older adults, the older adults feel connected to the group.**

learners new knowledge as they listen. Facilitation allows learners to discover new knowledge through questioning, probing, and hands-on experiences. Care providers are not responsible for providing all the content to the learners. Instead, learners actively seek and share their knowledge. See Fig. 24-18.

Section 24-4 Knowledge Check

1. Name two qualities of developmentally appropriate programs for older adults.
2. Give three examples of activities for older adults.
3. How does facilitation differ from direct instruction?

Mini-Lab

Observe an activity at a local adult care center. Describe the activity. What teaching style does the care provider use? How does the care provider address the different learning styles of the older adults? Write a summary of your observations to share with the class.

Chapter 24 Review & Activities

Section Summaries

24-1 An early childhood curriculum provides a plan for educational experiences.

24-1 To plan appropriate activities, care providers must understand how children learn.

24-1 Play has a special role in children's learning. Play materials can be open-ended or close-ended.

24-1 Children have different learning styles.

24-2 Program goals determine curriculum objectives.

24-2 There are different approaches to early childhood curriculum planning.

24-2 For good organization, care providers use lesson plans.

24-2 Teaching styles affect how activities for children are handled.

24-2 Different care providers have different teaching styles.

24-3 Adult learners tend to be self-guided, wise, and bring a wealth of information to the learning environment.

24-3 As do children, older adults use hands-on materials to help them understand topics.

24-3 Older adults are motivated to learn by topics that are meaningful to them.

24-4 Older adults can play an active role in program planning and help create activities that are pleasurable, but meet the cultural and personal interests of all older adults.

24-4 The learning environment for older adults should be informal, yet meet their physical and psychological needs.

24-4 Facilitation helps older adult learners take responsibility for participating in learning.

Check Your Knowledge

1. Identify six principles that explain how children learn.
2. What is the difference between intelligence quotient and multiple intelligences?
3. Identify three qualities of a strong curriculum.
4. What is the role of play in children's learning?
5. Contrast the project and theme approaches to teaching.
6. List the components that should be included in a lesson plan for young children. What components should be included in activity plans for older adults?
7. What are open-ended and close-ended play materials? Give an example of each.
8. Contrast visual older adult learners with kinesthetic older adult learners.
9. List three teaching strategies that can be used with older adult learners.
10. How does facilitation differ from direct instruction?

Thinking Critically

1. Analyze methods care providers can use to assess developmental levels of children and adults during planned activities. Write a summary of your analysis.
2. Draw conclusions about how intergenerational activities can help prevent bias in a program.

Practical Applications

1. **Curriculum Projects for Children.** Describe five developmentally appropriate activities that might be used in a project approach curriculum and five themes that might be used in a theme approach curriculum for young children. Include in your description developmentally appropriate adaptations for children with special needs. Implement the activities, if possible.

2. **Activities for Older Adults.** Describe twenty activities that might be planned for older adults. Develop an activity plan for one of the activities. If possible, use the activity with a group of older adults.

3. **Researching Learning Styles.** Using the Internet and your library, research ways to assess learning styles. Select a questionnaire to use in determining the learning style of a young child or older adult. Use the questionnaire to assess the learning styles of several young children or older adults. Create a chart illustrating the results.

4. **Research Bilingual Communication.** Research methods for non-English-speaking parents to use when communicating with their children at home. Create a resource guide for parents, including your findings and any materials they can use, such as adult English classes, books, and tapes. Share your resource guide with a local child care center.

Building Your PORTFOLIO

Planning Activities

Program planning begins with a clear understanding of program goals, learning styles, grouping methods, and approaches to teaching or facilitating learning. Care providers also should consider resources and the activity budget.

Step 1: Assess your own teaching or facilitation style. How could you adjust your teaching style to meet the needs of young children or older adults whose style is different from your own? Write a report summarizing your ideas for your portfolio.

Step 2: Obtain a copy of the curriculum for a young children's program or program for older adults. Compare the program goals with the planned activities. Do you believe the program is developmentally appropriate? Why? Write an analysis of the strengths and weaknesses of the curriculum or program to include in your portfolio.

Step 3: Develop lesson plans in math, science, art, and music for young children or create activity plans in art, music, nutrition, and gardening for older adult learners. Consider the cultural backgrounds and special needs of the learners when planning. If possible, carry out the plans and evaluate the results. Include a copy of the plans in your portfolio.

Chapter 25
Language Arts & Social Skills

Section 25-1

Developing Language Skills

OBJECTIVES

- Explain how the early childhood environment can promote development of language skills.
- Plan a language arts learning center for preschoolers.
- Assess the suitability of specific books for children.
- Demonstrate the ability to read a story effectively to preschoolers.
- Explain how to prepare children for reading and writing.
- Plan and lead language arts activities.

KEY TERMS

language arts
bilingual children
emergent literacy
print-rich
   environment
whole language
auditory
   discrimination
finger plays
visual discrimination
invented spelling

From infancy, as children hear sounds and language on a daily basis, they gradually learn to understand language. During infancy, children understand much more language than they can speak. Their use of language increases during the toddler years. Preschoolers' vocabulary expands greatly. Interested adults who listen to children and respond with conversation encourage language development.

The Language Arts Curriculum

Children begin learning language at home as infants. They learn their native language, or the language spoken in the home. Care providers encourage this development by offering a language arts curriculum. **Language arts** include activities that teach children to listen, speak, read, and write. The goal is to help children learn to communicate well with others. Children need approximately two years of experience making the sounds of a language and listening to others make sounds before they can speak understandably. The ability to read and write language takes even longer. Time to master language is particularly important for **bilingual children**, who understand and speak two languages.

Encouraging Literacy

Literacy refers to the ability to use language through reading and writing. Children's literacy skills develop gradually over time. This is referred to as **emergent literacy**. "Readiness" is a key word when speaking about language and literacy development. Although some care providers take great pride when a child speaks, reads, or writes at an early age, rushing development is not the goal of a preschool program.

The care provider who creates interest in children instills confidence, and helps them develop coordination. Small motor skills build children's readiness to master language skills.

Effective early childhood classrooms are filled with language opportunities. Care providers model proper language usage throughout the day. Effective care providers encourage language use in all classroom activities. The following examples show how care providers can encourage language learning by:

- Using language during mealtimes to describe food, practice good manners, and talk with children about the day's activities.

- Involving children in a letter-writing activity to an ill classmate or writing a thank-you note to a guest speaker.

- Placing toy telephones in the dramatic play center to encourage conversation. See Fig. 25-1.

- Encouraging listening skills by telling stories and reading books aloud.

- Explaining procedures to children, such as how to tie shoes, clean the classroom, or wash after toileting.

- Observing and listening to children. Expand their language by asking questions while children work. For example, when working on tying shoes, ask, "What other kinds of shoes have you seen?" "Who wears them?" and "Why do they wear them?" This encourages children to use verbal skills and increases their vocabulary.

- Encouraging children to ask their own questions and talk about their own experiences and observations.

Early childhood care providers further encourage language skills by creating a **print-rich environment**. These settings use printed materials throughout the classroom in meaningful ways. For example, when playing restaurant, children use a telephone book to look up a telephone number to make reservations. Menus in the play restaurant help children understand why reading is helpful. Books placed in the dramatic play center allow children to read on the sofa as their parents do. The science center should be stocked with accessible nature books. Including reading and writing in meaningful classroom activities in this manner is practicing **whole language**.

FIG. 25-1. Encouraging conversation among children is one way to promote emergent literacy.
What activities encourage literacy?

Select Good Children's Literature

Not all children's books are of good quality. How can you tell whether a book is worthwhile for children? Look for these qualities:

- A simple, understandable plot.
- Characters that interest young children— such as children, families, and animals—or to whom they can easily relate.
- A focus on familiar topics that build on a child's firsthand knowledge of the world, such as home life.
- A theme that is appropriate for young children, such as friendship.
- Illustrations that clearly show the plot and characters' actions.
- No more than five sentences per page.
- Basic, but descriptive, vocabulary.
- Predictable phrases, repetition, and rhymes that encourage children to read along.
- Humor and suspense to maintain interest.
- Make-believe themes that do not frighten young children.
- Current, accurate information in nonfiction books.

- Characters of different cultural backgrounds.
- Respectful treatment of all people, regardless of gender, nationality, disability, religious beliefs, or age.

APPLY IT!

Begin keeping a card file on children's literature. Read at least 25 different children's books for infants, toddlers, preschoolers, and school-age children. Create an index card for each book. On each card write the book title, author's name, year published, a brief summary of the book content, and your comments on the visual appeal and plot for each book. Organize the cards alphabetically by age group and type of book.

The Language Arts Center

Although language skills can be practiced in all learning centers, the language arts learning center is specifically planned for this purpose. The center should be quiet and well lit. It includes a library corner, a storytelling area, and a writing area.

- **Library corner.** A library corner should be a quiet spot with few distractions. Rugs or carpeting, child-size rocking chairs, and stuffed animals all help make reading an enjoyable experience. Displaying book jackets on low bulletin boards and hanging mobiles helps build interest in reading. Books should also be prominently displayed. The focal point, of course, is a well-stocked bookshelf. A tape player with story recordings and books is also helpful, especially for children with visual impairments.

- **Storytelling area.** Here children should find items for acting out stories. These include puppets, a stage for puppet plays, and doll houses with dolls of different ethnic backgrounds and both genders. Pictures that stimulate ideas and a cassette recorder with blank tapes encourage children to invent stories and tell about personal experiences. See Fig. 25-2.

- **Writing area.** Preschoolers can practice their emerging writing skills at a writing area. Stimulate their interest in and appreciation for words with alphabet and number books, cookie sheets with magnetic letters, and writing toys, such as stencils for tracing letters. Provide children with child-size tables and chairs and plenty of writing tools and paper. Include envelopes and play stamps for letter writing. Computer programs with developmentally appropriate word games may also be provided.

FIG. 25-2. Encouraging children to act out stories helps them develop their language skills. What are three activities children could do in the language arts center to promote their language skills?

Language Arts Activities

Language arts activities offer children opportunities to use language in many different and engaging ways. These activities involve children in the basics of language, including listening, speaking, reading, or writing.

Reading to Children

Hearing good children's books read aloud motivates children to want to learn to read and eventually write. They like to look at books independently and practice early reading skills, such as turning pages and looking at books from front to back. Reading books to children helps them develop a love for language. Hearing stories is a special pleasure that captures children's imaginations and introduces them to a world of new knowledge.

Board books, those with sturdy cardboard pages, hold up best to wear and tear from toddlers. Preschoolers enjoy picture books. They have large, often full-page, illustrations. The pages may have no words or a few simple sentences. The plot of a good children's book is simple, so it can be told in pictures. The words and pictures are matched carefully. This shows children that words can create images to tell a story. Big books are oversized picture books, sometimes as large as 24 by 36 inches. This enlarged format enables groups of children to better see the pictures. See Fig. 25-3. When choosing books, be sure to think about the interests of each age level:

- **Infants and toddlers.** Infants and toddlers enjoy picture books with large illustrations and bright colors. Books for toddlers should emphasize words they already know. Toddlers enjoy stories about others their own age. Animal and vehicle books that emphasize sound words are other favorites. Rhythm, rhyme, and repetition make story time fun.

- **Preschoolers.** Preschoolers like books about familiar characters and experiences. Stories about other children, family, and community workers, such as police officers and doctors, appeal to them. They also enjoy make-believe and the world of talking animals. Preschoolers love books with funny situations, surprises, and exaggeration.

- **School-age children.** The reading tastes of school-age children vary according to their interests. Books and children's magazines about nature, science, and community life are popular. School-age children like fantasy and humor.

Reading Stories to Children. What do you like when you listen to a story? An expressive reader? Humorous characters? Gradual suspense? A surprise ending? Children like the same things. It takes practice to keep children's interest during book reading, but the effort is well worth it. Here are suggestions for success:

- Prepare by selecting an appropriate book and reading it aloud several times to yourself.

- As children seat themselves, do a simple hand game, chant, or sing songs until they settle down.

- Be certain that all children can see the book.

- Introduce the story with an interesting technique or prop to capture interest.

- Show children the jacket cover. Ask them if they can guess what the story will be about.

- Read the book title and the name of the author and illustrator before beginning to read.

- Hold it open beside you, facing the children as you read.

- Read with expression and enthusiasm. Use different voices for story characters.

- Whisper, talk louder, or include a child's name in the story to keep the entire group's attention.

- Occasionally move back and forth from the book to children to maintain eye contact.

FIG. 25-3. **Reading out loud to children helps them develop a love of language.** What types of books are appropriate for various ages of children?

Listening & Speaking Activities

Although some children are more talkative than others, all children need practice with talking and listening. Along with having books read to them daily, there are many other ways to promote children's listening and speaking skills. These activities help children learn to hear similarities and differences in sounds and words, a skill called **auditory discrimination**.

- **Sound-matching games.** These games require children to match sounds they hear. To make a sound game, provide pairs of plastic eggs (all one color) that contain identical materials. You might use rice, pebbles, and beans. When children shake the plastic eggs, they match the pairs by sound. You can also find ready-made sound-matching games. Toy catalogs sell games that have animal noises recorded on a tape. Children match an animal

Intergenerational Interactions

Succeeding at Storytelling

Children often enjoy being read to, but story time is even more interesting when an adult tells a story from memory. When telling stories, use the following tips:

- **Identify Your Audience.** You will likely tell your story differently to a group of older adults than to a group of small children. Use vocabulary, visual aids, and props that will be easily understood by your audience.

- **Use Props.** Puppets, pictures, hats, eyeglasses, noisemakers, and other items will help you tell your story. Make sure your props are close by before you begin.

- **Practice.** The only way to make sure your story will be heard and understood is to practice. Use a mirror to rehearse speech, facial expressions, actions, and timing.

- **Begin and End.** Before you start your story, use an introduction to give listeners a hint of what is to come. Then wrap up your story with an exciting ending.

- **Vary Your Voice.** Keep listeners interested by using different voices, especially as you change characters. Different voice tones, volumes, and speeds will help you point out character changes.

- **Stop the Clock.** Do not limit yourself to a set amount of storytelling time. You will not want to rush through your story, nor will you want to drag it out to fill time. Use pauses to collect your thoughts or build suspense.

- **Surprise the Audience.** If you are telling a story that may have been heard before, surprise your audience with a different high point or ending.

- **Listen.** Although you are the one telling the story, you will want to listen as well. Feedback can help you determine if your story is being told in a way that interests your audience.

Follow-Up

Prepare a story to share with a group of preschoolers or school-age children. Whether you make up your tale or talk about something that actually happened, start out by writing your story on paper. Then use the above tips to tell your story.

FIG. 25-4. Sound-matching games help children learn how to discriminate between sounds. How can this benefit children as they learn language?

picture with the sound the animal makes. Music activities are also great ways to encourage children to listen to sounds. See Fig. 25-4.

- **Finger plays, nursery rhymes, and songs.** The playful rhythms, patterns of repeating phrases, and rhyming of words make language fun. Children hear the parts of words (syllables) as they are stressed and stretched to the rhythm of the song or rhyme. **Finger plays** add a visual element to the words by accompanying a song with specific hand motions.

- **Sharing time.** Preschoolers love to talk about themselves—their pets, families, culture, and activities. By encouraging children to share information during group conversations, teachers promote self-confidence and self-esteem and communication skills. They also encourage children to take an interest in others. With open-ended questions, children give more complete answers.

- **Puppetry and dramatic play.** When groups of children play with puppets, they learn to listen and talk. Dramatic play themes that promote language skills include characters,

such as news reporters, weather and radio announcers, postal carriers, and restaurant servers. Try to choose plays and puppet shows from children's languages and cultures. Ask parents to participate, if possible.

- **Flannel board play.** Children and care providers tell stories when using flannel boards. These are large pieces of cardboard or wood covered with flannel or felt. They range in size from 12-inches square to those as large as a bulletin board. Small figures, such as people or animals, are cut from flannel or felt of different colors. These figures stay in position when placed against the flannel board, but can be easily repositioned. The storyteller moves the figures on the board as the story progresses.

Writing Activities

Preschoolers love to pretend to write. You may see them "write" a letter that contains zigzag markings that represent words. These early steps prepare children for real writing. They gradually learn to notice similarities and differences in shapes and alphabet letters. This is a necessary reading and writing skill called **visual discrimination**.

As children learn to write, they have to concentrate hard to control the writing tool. Writing requires strength in the thumb and fingers. It is not easy to control writing tools when these muscles are not fully developed. As small motor skills develop, the hand gains better control of a pencil. Playing with dough or clay and manipulative toys, such as connecting blocks, helps this skill develop. Using safety scissors, crayons, markers, and paintbrushes also prepares children to use writing tools.

Eye-hand coordination is another skill needed for writing. To form letters and words, children must make the hand and eye work together. Stringing beads and working puzzles develop this skill.

As with other developmental skills, not all children begin to write at the same time. When

FIG. 25-5. **Learning to write requires the coordination of many different skills.** How do small motor skills influence writing ability?

children are ready for writing, provide them with examples showing how to make printed letters. Several manuscript systems, or methods for printing letters and numbers, are used successfully with children. Find out which one is used in your program and follow it. Practice

your own printing skills to provide a good model. See Fig. 25-5.

Generally, the first word a child prints is his or her own name. Help children recognize their names by printing them on paintings, nametags, and cubbies. Provide children with properly printed copies of their names and encourage them to practice copying the letters. Children need patient support. Gather children's writing in a portfolio and show it to parents so they can see their children's literacy progress.

The need to communicate motivates children to learn to write. Young children can express ideas through writing by dictating their thoughts to a care provider, who writes their words on a poster board or a language chart. Children five years and older enjoy writing words themselves. They often begin by copying words others write for them.

The rules of spelling can be confusing and difficult for children to remember. Early writers often use **invented spelling**, spelling a word the way it sounds. Be patient with children's invented spelling. If you do not understand what a child writes, ask the child to read it to you. The more children write, the more they will want to learn to write accurately. When asked, help children with spelling and writing. You can reinforce writing efforts by asking children to share their writing during group times.

Section **25-1** Knowledge Check

1. What are the four areas of the language arts curriculum?
2. What is a print-rich environment?
3. What are characteristics of a children's picture book?

Mini-Lab

Select and read a good children's book to your class members. Then describe three suitable follow-up activities you could conduct with children after reading the book. Ask class members to identify strengths of your presentation and offer suggestions for improvement.

Section **25-2**
Developing Social Responsibility

OBJECTIVES

- Identify goals of a social studies curriculum.
- Describe areas of study in a social studies curriculum.
- Explain how preschoolers can learn about diversity, aging, and environmental issues.
- Identify methods of helping children become socially responsible citizens.
- Plan and lead social studies activities.

KEY TERMS

social studies
social responsibility

As a child care professional, you will influence how children think and behave. Research shows that attitudes form at an early age. During the preschool years children learn self-respect as well as appreciation for others. Through positive learning activities and social experiences, they develop attitudes of respect and acceptance that make life better for everyone.

The Social Studies Curriculum

Social studies is a curriculum area that teaches children about themselves, their families, communities, and the world. Through social studies, children discover that the world is a fascinating place. By learning how people live around the world, they realize there are many similarities and some differences. A social studies curriculum helps children develop skills for getting along peacefully with people from all backgrounds. The goals of a preschool social studies curriculum will help children to:

- Develop a positive attitude toward themselves and others.

- Understand their roles within the family unit.
- Recognize and appreciate how individuals and families are alike and different.
- Learn about their community.
- Explore how people in their community work and live.
- Acquire positive behaviors for living happily within the family, community, and society.
- See that people of all backgrounds bring special qualities and contributions to the world.
- Become aware of climates and environments on earth and how they affect lifestyle.
- Learn about the earth's resources and how to use and conserve them.

Social Studies Activities

Like all learning, social studies should start with what is most familiar to children. Thus, effective early childhood care providers begin their social studies curriculum with activities that help children learn about themselves.

Learning About Self

Children are very individualistic. Gradually they learn to act as members of families, neighborhoods, and communities. Understanding and liking oneself is the first step toward developing a well-rounded personality. It is also the first step to being able to function well in society. See Fig. 25-6.

People who have high self-esteem—people who accept and value their own traits and abilities—tend to participate more fully in life and

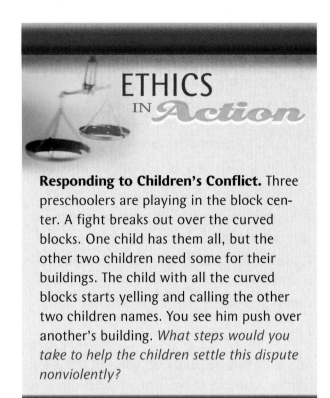

ETHICS IN Action

Responding to Children's Conflict. Three preschoolers are playing in the block center. A fight breaks out over the curved blocks. One child has them all, but the other two children need some for their buildings. The child with all the curved blocks starts yelling and calling the other two children names. You see him push over another's building. *What steps would you take to help the children settle this dispute nonviolently?*

get along better with others. Care providers help children become good community members by building their self-esteem. They do this by planning activities in which children can succeed. They acknowledge strengths and positive traits. They provide activities that explore children's likes, abilities, and interests.

Showing respect and appreciation for children's heritage helps develop self-pride. You can include items from different cultures in the classroom environment and curriculum. Respect for ethnic groups, for example, can be promoted with a collection of dolls that have different skin tones, features, and hair and eye colors. Dolls should have hairstyles and clothing that are typical of what people wear in everyday life, not costumes that are outdated or incorrect.

FIG. 25-6. Encouraging children to learn more about themselves is part of the social studies curriculum.

Learning About Families

After self, family is the next most familiar social concept to children. Through social studies activities, they can learn about different families. There are nuclear families with two parents and their child or children, extended families that may include grandparents, aunts, uncles, or cousins, blended families, and single-parent homes. Some children have siblings; others do not. Sharing experiences of family life with each other teaches children about the diversity of families.

Children can also learn that family types and roles vary among different cultures. Through pictures, stories, and guest speakers, they can see that family members have different jobs and expectations according to their culture and individual family beliefs.

Possibly the most important thing young children can learn about families is that strong families are the foundation of society. Family members take care of each other physically and emotionally. They guide children as they grow into happy, responsible adults.

FIG. 25-7. Teaching about community helpers gives children an opportunity to learn about the world immediately around them. What types of activities encourage children to learn about community helpers?

Learning About Community

Thinking abstractly is difficult for young children. For this reason, learning about people and places beyond their own family and home is more difficult. The progression from home to street to city to state to country is very hard for children to grasp.

Exploring community life with children should begin with their home and immediate neighborhood. Take walks around the neighborhood. Discuss what makes a neighborhood strong and why this is important.

Next, introduce children to neighborhoods beyond their own. As a class, ride the bus on community routes. Point out businesses where parents and neighbors work. Notice places of worship, libraries, museums, parks, the fire station, and schools. Visit such places on field trips to see what happens inside them. These activities gradually introduce children to the world and how it works.

Community Helpers. People whose job involves helping others within the community are called community helpers. Police officers, firefighters, doctors, nurses, and lifeguards are just a few examples. As part of the social studies curriculum, care providers plan experiences for children to investigate the jobs, duties, and skills of community helpers. They use a variety of activities, such as books, special visitors, field trips, puppets, and stories. See Fig. 25-7.

Community Diversity

Today's children live in a diverse world. They routinely see similarities and differences in people's music, dress, food, celebrations, art, and appearance. Creative teachers make learning about other people and their customs an exciting adventure. They encourage a positive attitude as they marvel at differences while celebrating a spirit of unity with all people.

As children learn about people in a diverse society, teach them how all people have the same basic needs and desires. Preschoolers are especially eager to learn about those similarities and differences. The following ideas will help you introduce children to a world of diversity.

- Read books that include children from a variety of cultures and races.

- Invite special visitors with different cultural backgrounds to visit the classroom. Ask them to talk about some of their customs.

- Serve ethnic or traditional foods regularly as part of meals, snacks, and cooking activities.

- Provide instruments from different cultures in the music center. Teach children simple cultural songs and dances.

Learning About Aging. Children also need to develop good attitudes toward aging. Misconceptions about aging occur when children have little opportunity to interact with older adults. Given information and closer contact, children learn to be comfortable with and sensitive to older adults. They discover that aging can mean wisdom, patience, and tenderness. Care providers can arrange visits to retirement homes and senior citizen centers. See Fig. 25-8.

Learning About the Environment

Children enjoy learning about the environment. Acquaint preschoolers with the characteristics of their local environment. Once children reach school age they can learn about distant climates, such as tropical rain forests.

Children like to investigate land characteristics, plants, and animals. Social studies concentrate on how these impact people's lives. To begin a study with children, take a walk around your facility. What kinds of trees, plants, and animals live there? Are there mountains or flatlands? What is the weather like? How do all these affect children's lives? For instance, can they go sledding in your climate? Do children need to carry umbrellas often? These questions help children analyze how location and climate affect how they live.

Conserving Resources. Young children can learn to respect and conserve community resources. Reduce, reuse, recycle—the three "Rs" of conservation—are appropriate concepts to explore. As a class, watch a garbage truck

FIG. 25-8. **Meeting regularly with older adults helps children learn to be comfortable with them.** What are the benefits of intergenerational activities for children and older adults?

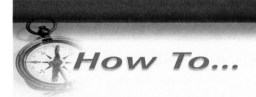

Reflect Diversity Throughout the Classroom

To become comfortable with diversity, children should see it reflected in many different ways in the classroom. From staff to materials, expose children to variety, so they can appreciate the richness of life. Following are ways to put this concept into practice:

- Provide opportunities for children to speak in the language of their choice.
- Employ both male and female care providers who are qualified.
- Include staff and volunteers of varying ages and different cultural backgrounds.
- Include dolls of diverse gender and ethnicity in the dress-up area.
- Give children ethnic costumes for playing dress-up.
- Provide instruments from different cultures to play during music time.
- Hang posters on walls that include children of varying abilities and backgrounds.

- Read children's books that include characters of varying abilities and backgrounds.
- Use recipes from different cultures for classroom cooking projects.
- In the dramatic play corner, include a variety of cooking utensils, such as a wok or tortilla press, for pretend cooking.
- Sing songs from different cultures.
- Play lullabies from different cultures during nap time.
- Make all classroom areas accessible to those with different abilities.
- Participate in continuing education about different cultures and languages, learn about cultural resources in the community, and help support parents' use of two languages in the home.

APPLY IT!

Create a lesson plan for an ethnically diverse social studies or language arts activity for preschoolers. If possible, conduct your activity with a group of preschool children. Evaluate the results of the activity.

---

making its rounds. Explain that garbage is buried in the earth. As children learn that trash does not just disappear, they will understand the purpose for practicing the three Rs. Here are other ways to teach respect for resources:

- Use both sides of paper for coloring activities.
- Conserve electricity by turning off classroom lights and computers when not in use.
- Reuse clean computer paper, egg cartons, and packing materials in art or math projects.
- Reuse clean paper or plastic bags.
- Create classroom recycling centers.

Encouraging Social Skills

When people make a positive contribution to the community and obey community laws, they practice **social responsibility**. To become productive members of society, children should learn from an early age to accept basic social skills and responsibilities. These range from respecting property to voting regularly in elections.

Through daily classroom routines, children learn attitudes and behaviors that prepare them to be responsible citizens. By following these practices, care providers show children that social responsibility is vital to a fair, orderly society:

- **Expect children to obey rules.** Include children in making classroom rules that protect individual safety as well as classroom property. Require children to put away toys once they are finished playing with them. Have them assist in cleaning up after activities.

- **Include children in classroom tasks.** Children develop pride when they participate in routine classroom chores. They can water plants, feed pets, and set tables for snack time. See Fig. 25-9.

- **Give children opportunities to make decisions.** Although many citizens don't realize it, their right to vote in a democracy is rare in today's world. Allowing children to vote on some classroom matters shows them that by expressing their preference, they can make a difference. Classroom voting opportunities may include choosing a class mascot, a favorite video, or a preferred snack.

- **Teach children to settle conflicts without violence.** Children can follow basic rules related to self-respect and respect for others. Insist that children settle problems with words, rather than by hitting. Never allow them to hurt another's feelings through teasing. When conflicts get out of hand, coach children through the steps of the problem-solving process. Help children develop positive social skills to use instead of aggression or violence. Such skills include expressing feelings; calmly discussing differing ideas; sharing, trading, or taking turns with toys; and compromising and negotiating. Remember to be a positive role model for children by always speaking in a courteous manner to the children and other adults.

FIG. 25-9. Successfully helping with classroom tasks gives a boost to children's self-esteem.

Section **25-2** Knowledge Check

1. What factors are important for preschoolers to learn about families?
2. What must children learn to become socially responsible?
3. What social skills help children to settle conflicts without violence?

Mini-Lab

Alone or with a partner, investigate various culturally diverse activities for teaching children about self and community. Plan an activity to use with preschoolers, including those with special needs. If possible, carry out the activity with a group of preschoolers and evaluate the results of your activity.

Section 25-3

Social Wellness for Older Adults

OBJECTIVES

- Define social well-being.
- Describe positive aging.
- Develop culturally diverse activities for older adults.
- Identify the care provider's role in assisting participants with social and language activities.

KEY TERMS

social well-being
positive aging
oral history

All people have some of the same social needs. We all desire to socialize with others, to build meaningful relationships, to be accepted as we are, and to receive respect from our friends and associates. Social wellness includes all these desires that are apart from physical wellness.

Social Well-Being

Taking care of the body by eating properly and getting regular exercise is a way to improve well-being. However, well-being goes beyond physical and mental health. Well-being also means making and sustaining friendships. Older adults value their social well-being. **Social well-being** means having meaningful relationships and maintaining a network of supportive friends. Older adults foster their own social well-being in various ways, and it is important for care providers to respect the choices of older adults.

Many older adults choose to reflect on their younger years. They eagerly share interesting stories about those wonderful days. Other older adults choose not to recall their pasts. They

maintain a positive social well-being simply by being satisfied with their lives. For example, some older adults receive contentment each day from participating in work and family and leisure activities. These activities are reassuring to older adults and help dispel their fears and prevent envy and anger. Figure 25-10 outlines qualities that can help you determine an older adult's social well-being and need of assistance.

Impact of Emotional Wellness

Emotions are a natural part of life and are a response to life events. There are many kinds of emotions, including happiness, sadness, or stress. Emotional wellness means being aware of and accepting your feelings. Achieving emotional wellness allows a person to experience

FIG. 25-10.

SOCIAL WELL-BEING CHECKLIST

Independent living	☑ Are older adults well-adjusted and able to help themselves? ☑ Do older adults lack resources that would help them be independent? Should they find a place to live where they can receive assistance?
Home assistance	☑ Do older adults need a support system to help them efficiently operate their homes? ☑ Do they have regular interaction with family and friends?
Safe/secure homes	☑ Are older adults' homes secure and do they have protection of family? ☑ Do older adults' homes lack proper security and protection of family?
Residential care	☑ Do older adults still operate satisfactorily in their homes? ☑ Do older adults need residential care to live properly?
Mental stability	☑ Do older adults have sound minds that help them to function properly? ☑ Are older adults forgetful and often confused?
Financial stability	☑ Do older adults have the ability to handle most financial situations? ☑ Do older adults lack the ability or the assistance to handle financial situations? ☑ Do older adults have support to help them cope with home conditions or financial problems?

life's ups and downs with enthusiasm and grace. It also allows people to maintain positive relationships with others when they experience difficult emotions. Learning to balance daily activities and having compassion toward others are ways to stay emotionally well. Dealing with issues of inner peace and developing a strong sense of personal ethics also help maintain emotional wellness.

The financial status of older adults can impact their emotional wellness. Some older adults have difficulty living on a fixed retirement income. Many older adults living on fixed incomes must buy expensive medication and pay medical and insurance bills along with buying food. Those who use credit cards to pay for necessities often find themselves further burdened. Then they owe for their purchases plus

credit card interest. The stress of debt can be overwhelming.

Care providers can help older adults by referring them to consumer financial counselors who will work with them to get them out of debt. Many of these consumer services are free of charge. The improvement of the financial state of older adults helps their emotional wellness.

The stress of everyday living can affect the health of older adults in negative ways, such as raising blood pressure. In order to help them learn to cope with problems of daily life, care providers can design activities that promote healthful lifestyles, such as fitness activities or nutrition classes. These activities help improve physical health and emotional wellness at the same time.

Positive Aging

Social well-being and emotional health are related to positive aging. **Positive aging** means having a positive attitude about life and having the ability to cope with change. It also means being responsible for one's own good health. Older adults who experience positive aging usually have a sense of humor and the ability to understand their needs and how to meet them. They usually think positively about life events, even when these events are sad. These older adults stay mentally and physically active and keep an optimistic attitude about the aging process. Care providers can encourage older adults to keep positive attitudes by suggesting that they spend time with friends and family, take walks, join a garden club project, engage in an enjoyable fitness activity, and eat healthful meals. Encourage them to plan ahead for the times when they may need more help and let them make their own life decisions. See Fig. 25-11.

FIG. 25-11. Having a positive outlook on life and accepting changes in life events lead to emotional health and positive aging. What can care providers do to encourage older adults to approach life changes in a positive manner?

Social & Language Arts Activities

People are social by nature. They interact in many ways, from playing games to sharing new skills. People thrive on meaningful social interactions with others. The same is true about older adults. Older adults should continue to interact daily with others to avoid disrupting their social network.

Social Skills Activities

Maintaining social skills is important for older adults. These skills help them interact with others in a variety of settings. As people age, there are many opportunities for continuous growth and development. Care providers can create and maintain a positive social environment for older adults by assisting them with social and leisure activities. These activities may include:

- Reading poetry or stories out loud. In an intergenerational setting, care providers can encourage older adults to read to young children.
- Playing games like "charades" offers many opportunities for participants to laugh and get to know each other.
- Playing a board game, such as chess, provides a relaxing activity for peer interaction.
- Taking day trips—such as tours, attending a play, or going out to lunch or to see a movie—with care providers serving as travel companions.

When planning and implementing social and leisure activities for older adults, care providers can assist them in identifying other areas of interest, such as community and political projects. As with all activities, care providers must evaluate the activities to be sure that the needs of all participants are met. The more knowledge the care providers have about the older adults they serve, the more effectively they can plan programs to meet their needs.

FIG. 25-12. **Oral history projects give older adults an opportunity to share the events of their lives.** How can oral history projects benefit children?

Oral History Projects

An **oral history** is information gathered from an older adult as the older adult speaks about past life events. This activity allows the older adult to be the center of attention and is a form of healing for him or her. Older adults often feel better about life as they recall and laugh at humorous events in the past. There are rewards for a young listener, too. Children learn about history and interesting social behaviors of the past. To gather information for an oral history project, the listener conducts an interview with the older adult and records the historical event. The *Intergenerational Interactions* feature in Chapter 16 offers more information on oral history projects. See Fig. 25-12.

Community Involvement

Many older adults improve their social well-being through community participation. This allows older adults to become more fully connected to the people in their communities. Care providers at senior centers can encourage older adults to serve their communities as volunteers for various projects that may include:

- Community festivals.
- Homeless shelters.
- Crisis nurseries.

Care providers can also assist older adults in organizing a community project of their own, such as sponsoring a fundraising event for an abuse shelter. Older adults might also volunteer as foster grandparents to local children. Some older adults might also enjoy helping their peers who have vision, hearing, or mobility disabilities. See Fig. 25-13.

Celebrating Diversity

Celebrating diversity is being able to accept differences among people, such as age, race, or religion. Care providers can help older adults accept and learn from each other by providing culturally diverse activities.

Cultural Food and Craft Activities. People from different cultures have different tastes in food and clothing. Encourage older adults to participate in cooking and sewing activities that allow them to learn about other cultures. For example, a group of older adults might enjoy making baklava or enchiladas. While they cook, they might share stories from their past, such as cooking with their parents or their children. These activities might also allow older adults to converse in their native language, which helps build their self-esteem. Some older adults might also enjoy sewing clothing or quilts. As they sew together, many share stories while they work or describe how cultural stories are sewn into the design of a quilt. In an intergenerational environment, young children can learn to cook and sew by observing or participating in activities with older adults. Experienced older adults might have a desire to teach a skill to a class of young children. Care providers must use their knowledge and skills to create an environment that is safe and beneficial for all.

Cultural Music Activities. Culture also can be shared through music. Encourage older adults to participate in sing-along sessions. First, choose music from various cultures. Make sure the music is appropriate and enjoyable for the older adults. Specify a day and select a leader for the sing-along. The leader can be an outgoing older adult or a member of the center's staff. Invite older adults to join the sing-along, even if they have disabilities. Incorporate hand motions, so older adults with hearing difficulties can follow along. Care providers can also arrange a big-band activity by inviting participants and community members to play instruments. Older adults can listen to music from other cultures, sing along with the band, and dance. Encourage requests so older adults can hear music they enjoyed when they were younger.

Cultural Movies, Plays, Tours, and Outings. Older adults often enjoy going to movies, plays, and tours of various communities that include varying cultural backgrounds. A care provider can encourage and make arrangements for older adults to go to movies, plays, and tours to explore various cultures. For example, care providers may schedule an art museum tour that is displaying Asian or Middle Eastern art. Older adults can discuss the various types of art

FIG. 25-13. When older adults get involved in community projects, they have an increased sense of worth.

and how they relate to their community. A care provider can gather information on other interesting and beneficial tours and outings. For example, some participants may welcome a fishing trip or a leisurely paddle-boat ride down a nearby river.

Section **25-3** Knowledge Check

1. Define social well-being.
2. Name four things older adults must do to maintain a positive outlook on aging.
3. Describe an activity that celebrates cultural diversity.

Mini-Lab

Assume that you are an activity coordinator for an adult day center that uses a social-medical model. Develop an intergenerational oral history project for older adults and high school students. Follow the steps in this chapter to guide your project. If possible, conduct your project at a local adult day center.

Section **25-4**

Education & Technology for Older Adults

OBJECTIVES	KEY TERMS
• Describe how technology impacts older adults. • Identify various types of assistive technology. • Describe ways to incorporate assistive technology into social and language activities. • Explain the care provider's role in helping older adults with assistive technology.	household automation assistive technology

Many people use technology every day. Technology is an important resource, particularly for older adults. Innovative technologies impact older adults by helping them maintain their independence.

Everyday Technology & Older Adults

Older adults are the fastest-growing group of technology users. Many older adults feel comfortable using technology because they used various types of technology in the workplace. Others learned about technology from their family members. The majority of older adults will continue to rely on technology to help them maintain their independence. For example, older adults might use the Internet to communicate with their families and friends to avoid long-distance phone bills. They might also use the Internet to pay bills, make banking transac-

tions, and purchase medications, groceries, or clothing. Using the Internet helps older adults who cannot travel conduct business on their own. Some of the everyday technologies older adults might use are listed in Fig. 25-14.

Household Automation. As adults grow older, household automation becomes more important. The technology that controls functions in a home is called **household automation**. Some household automation is fairly simple, such as a TV remote control. Others are more complicated, such as household automation systems. These technologies help older adults maintain their independence in their own homes, without diminishing their quality of life.

FIG. 25-14.

EVERYDAY TECHNOLOGIES

Technology Form	Available Options
Banking Tools	• **Telephone banking:** By using a touch-tone telephone or a voice-automated machine, older adults can conduct banking business over the telephone. • **Internet banking:** Special computer programs with which older adults can conduct banking business online from home, using the Internet. • **Automated teller machine (ATM):** These machines allow customers to withdraw or deposit money, 24 hours a day, without having to enter the bank.
Telephones	• **Touch-tone telephone:** A large-button variety helps people with limited vision or mobility problems use the telephone. • **Voice-activated, hands-free telephone:** A telephone that responds to a human voice for incoming calls that does not need to be picked up for use.
Household Technologies	• **Remote-control and sensor lighting:** As a person enters a room, special sensors trigger the lights to turn on. Older adults or those with impairments may also use a special remote-control device to turn on lights. • **Automated home security systems:** These systems automatically control home lighting and other household appliances. For example, these systems ensure that older adults can always enter a well-lit home or building. • **Video monitoring system:** This allows older adults to see who may be at their doors. It also allows care providers to monitor older adults from another room.

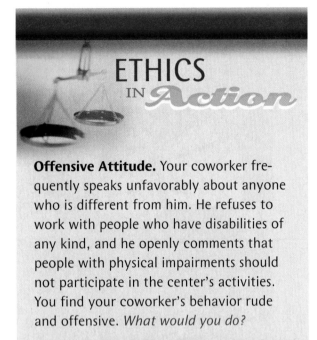

ETHICS IN *Action*

Offensive Attitude. Your coworker frequently speaks unfavorably about anyone who is different from him. He refuses to work with people who have disabilities of any kind, and he openly comments that people with physical impairments should not participate in the center's activities. You find your coworker's behavior rude and offensive. *What would you do?*

The Care Provider's Role. The growth of technology use means that care providers must also understand the different types of technology. As a care provider, at times you will need to explain different types of technology to older adults. Some older adults might feel anxious about using a device they have never seen or used. You will need to reassure them and instruct them in how to use it. You might also need to make technology suggestions to older adults who have trouble with certain tasks. For example, for older adults who

have arthritis in their hands, you might suggest a voice-activated, hands-free telephone to make it easier for them to use the telephone.

Assistive Technology

Remaining active is important to the health and well-being of older adults. Recreational and leisure activities help older adults feel happy and stay healthy. Some activities might seem impossible for older adults with disabilities. However, there is technology that helps ensure that everyone can participate in activities.

Equipment and services that allow older adults with limitations to continue to independently manage their lives is called **assistive technology**. For example, a wheelchair ramp is an assistive technology device—it helps older adults in wheelchairs go in and out of buildings. Some assistive technology devices are built into equipment. For example, automatic wheelchair sensors can be built into doors; they sense when wheelchairs approach and trigger the doors to open. Other assistive technology

FIG. 25-15. Assistive technologies make it easier for older adults to live independently.

FIG. 25-16.

LISTENING DEVICES

Device	Description
FM Systems	These special hearing aids are used in theaters, places of worship, museums, public meeting places, classrooms, and other large gathering areas. In an FM system, the microphone and transmitter are built into the room's sound system. The person with a hearing impairment is provided with an FM receiver, which connects to the hearing aid (or to a headset if the older adult does not wear a hearing aid).
Induction Loop Systems	These are most common in large group areas, but can also be purchased for individual use. An induction loop wire is installed (perhaps under a carpet) and connected to a microphone. When an individual system is used, a wire loop is laid on the floor. The person talking into the microphone creates a current in the wire, which makes an electromagnetic field in the room. The listener sets his or her hearing aid to pick up the electromagnetic signal.
Infrared Systems	These devices are often used with TV sets. They, like the FM system, are also used in large area settings, such as theaters. Sound is transmitted using infrared light waves. The TV is set at a volume comfortable for family members. The infrared system transmitter sends the TV signal to an older adult's receiver, and the older adult adjusts his or her own personal volume.

devices can be bought in local stores. One example of a separate device is a remote control. See Fig. 25-15. The following are just a few of the available assistive technology devices:

- **Specially designed furniture.** Some older adults might need chairs or beds that move so that they are easier to get into and out of. Special handrails mounted to walls also help older adults sit and stand. Adjustable height cabinets, which are lower than typical cabinets, allow older adults in wheelchairs to easily access cabinets and counters.

- **Van conversions and lifts.** Vans can be converted to include lifts for wheelchairs and modified driving controls. Ramps and wider doors permit older adults in wheelchairs to enter buildings and rooms.

- **Large-print assistive materials.** Books, clocks, and telephones with large print allow those with visual impairments to read on their own. Older adults with hearing impair-

ments might also benefit from closed captioning on television screens, which displays words as people speak them.

- **Wheelchair sensing systems.** These systems sense the approach of a wheelchair and activate lights and open doors.

- **Audio devices.** By elevating certain voice frequencies, these sound systems make it easier for older adults with hearing impairments to hear items, such as the telephone or television. For older adults with hearing impairments, flashing devices can be used in place of doorbells and telephones. Fig. 25-16 describes different types of listening devices.

- **Power doors.** Special sensors built into swing and slide doors allow people with limited mobility "hands-free" building access.

- **Full-spectrum lighting.** This type of lighting simulates the effects of natural sunlight. It is often used with people who experience

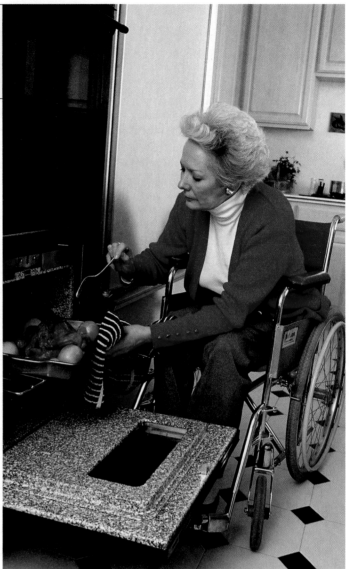

FIG. 25-17. Specially designed kitchens can help older adults do cooking tasks more easily. What other assistive technologies might be useful in the kitchen?

seasonal depression disorder due to lack of exposure to outdoor light. For people with limited vision, it provides a better light source.

- **Push-button water controls.** For people with limited strength and mobility, these controls are a beneficial resource. They allow older adults to control water flow and temperature.

- **Voice-activated computers.** By simply speaking to a computer, older adults have access to a variety of computer-related activities.

Assistive Technology & Activities

Older adults in day centers will use technology in different ways. Some will use it as part of an activity, such as using the computer to write letters. Others will use assistive technology devices to help them participate in typical recreational activities. Care providers should include technology as a part of other activities. Care providers should also observe participants and note any older adults who might need assistive technology devices. Offering a full range of activities that incorporates technology will help you address the needs of all older adults.

Assistive Technology for Cooking. Many older adults enjoy cooking, but might avoid it because they have difficulty performing cooking tasks. You can help them participate by providing specially designed utensils and cutting boards for older adults with limited hand

strength. Lowered cabinets allow those in wheelchairs to participate, and large-print calculators, timers, and cookbooks help older adults read and follow instructions. Flashing devices also work well as timers for older adults with hearing impairments. Encourage older adults with special needs to search the Internet for special recipes. See Fig. 25-17.

Assistive Technology for Reading. Many older adults enjoy reading, and some relish the chance to share books with others. You can help foster their reading hobby by providing large-print books, books on tape, and books on CDs. See Fig. 25-18. Most libraries provide these

FIG. 25-18. **For older adults with vision impairments, books on tapes or CDs provide an enjoyable alternative to reading.**

types of books, so older adults do not need to purchase them. Some older adults might enjoy researching their book topic or author on the Internet and then request the book through their local library. Older adults can get involved in online book clubs to discuss their favorite books. Some older adults who show interest in online book clubs might need assistance with using the Internet. Care providers should keep written instructions, in large print, next to each computer workstation. Let older adults know which staff members are available to answer their questions.

Assistive Technology for Community Activities. Many older adults enjoy being involved with their communities or participating in activities outside the center. You can assist older adults to participate in community activities by providing proper transportation, such as vans with lifts for older adults using mobility devices. If shopping, encourage older adults who have difficulty writing to use debit cards instead of checks. This way the older adult does not have to carry money for the purchase or take on a personal debt.

Section **25-4** Knowledge Check

1. List three examples of everyday technology.
2. What is assistive technology?
3. What are three types of listening devices?

Mini-Lab

Plan an appropriate physical activity, such as aerobics or dancing, for older adults with hearing impairments and for those in wheelchairs. Explain how to use assistive technology devices and other modifications to the activity so that the older adults with impairments can participate.

Chapter **25**
Review & Activities

Section Summaries

25-1 Language arts include: listening, speaking, reading, and writing.

25-1 Language should be emphasized throughout the daily schedule.

25-1 Children's literature encourages interest in reading.

25-1 Finger plays, rhymes, songs, dramatic play, and storytelling develop children's language skills.

25-2 Early childhood social studies focus on studying self, family, and community.

25-2 Learning about diverse ethnic groups and customs broadens children's worldview.

25-2 Field trips, special visitors, storybooks, music, and prop boxes are ways to help children learn about the community.

25-2 Children can help conserve resources by learning to reduce, reuse, and recycle.

25-3 Social well-being includes having meaningful relationships and friendships.

25-3 Positive aging means having a positive attitude about life and having the ability to cope with changes.

25-3 Care providers are responsible for encouraging older adults to participate in social activities and maintain friendships.

25-4 Older adults use various types of assistive technology to help them maintain their independence.

25-4 Care providers should try to integrate technology in activities and help provide assistive technology for older adults with special needs.

Check Your Knowledge

1. How do children acquire their native language?
2. What is the goal of a language arts curriculum?
3. What should be included in a language arts learning center?
4. What is included in a social studies curriculum? List three goals of a social studies curriculum for young children.
5. Why should the study of community begin with a child's own neighborhood?
6. Identify three ways of teaching children about different cultures and customs.
7. Why is social activity important for older adults?
8. Give three examples of activities that help older adults celebrate diversity.
9. What is community involvement and how does it help older adults?
10. What is assistive technology? Give four examples of assistive technologies for older adults.

Thinking Critically

1. Draw conclusions about how the social studies curriculum prepares young children to become socially responsible citizens.
2. Analyze why older adults often need support and encouragement to take advantage of new technologies.

Practical Applications

1. **Language Arts Center.** Plan a language arts center for preschoolers. Draw your plan to scale. Using equipment and supply catalogs, identify items you would include in a library corner, storytelling area, and writing area. Write a parent letter explaining the center. Provide language resources for parents who are not native English speakers.

2. **Rating Books.** Develop a rating scale for use in choosing books for young children. Use the rating scale to rate ten children's books. Include whether the book is also available in another language. Revise the rating scale based on your experience.

3. **Activity Centers.** Plan an activity center for older adults. Interview adult care providers and older adults to determine needs and interests. Draw your plan to scale. Using equipment and supply catalogs, identify items you would include in the center, such as puzzles, games, books, and audiotapes.

4. **Integrated Curriculum.** Plan language activities for children and older adults that integrate one or more of the following concepts: science, math, nutrition, safety, art, and diversity. Include the materials you would need to conduct the activity and provide adaptation devices for children and older adults with special needs.

Building Your PORTFOLIO

Promoting Communication & Social Interaction

Care providers help children develop language skills and prepare them for reading and writing. Adult care providers can help older adults learn about new technology and assist them in selecting and using technology to maintain their independence. Care providers play an important role in encouraging acceptance and diversity.

Step 1: Plan a curriculum to teach language arts or social studies to school-age or preschool children or a program to promote continuing education, use of technology, or social wellness for older adults. Present your curriculum or program to a child or adult care program director or to your teacher and ask for suggestions for improving it. Put your revised curriculum or program in your portfolio.

Step 2: Plan a language or social skills activity for preschoolers, school-age children, or older adults. Be sure to include materials and adaptations for those with special needs. If possible, carry out the activity with an appropriate group. Critique the results. Include a copy of the activity and your critique in your portfolio.

Step 3: Plan an activity for young children or older adults that encourages appreciation for differences. If possible, carry out the activity with an appropriate group. Critique the results. Include a copy of the activity and your critique in your portfolio.

Chapter *26*
Math & Science Explorations

Section 26-1
Math Skills for Children

Section 26-2
Science Skills for Children

Section 26-3
Nature & Gardening Activities

Section 26-4
Finances for Older Adults

Section 26-1

Math Skills for Children

OBJECTIVES

- Discuss how math skills are used in children's daily lives.
- Describe the goals of math curricula.
- Explain how math activities benefit children.
- Identify math materials for preschoolers.
- Plan math activities.

KEY TERMS

mathematical
    vocabulary
seriation
rote counting
rational counting
numerals

Math is used in everyone's daily life. As children become competent and comfortable with math, they will see how math is used in everyday life. For example, math is used in determining how much of the family budget can be spent on food. Career opportunities, from construction to computer programming, require good math skills. Effective care providers help children discover meaningful applications of math skills in daily life.

Math for Young Children

Helping children develop a positive attitude toward math as a helpful tool begins in preschool. Mathematics is the study of shapes and numbers and the use of numbers. Children experience math concepts daily without realizing it. For example, they may see many flowers in a field or discover that an object is heavier than it looks. All these general ideas become part of their **mathematical vocabulary**, or words that express numbers, quantities, shape, size, or volume. For example, children might say, "We make a sandwich with two slices of bread and one square slice of cheese." This

exposure to concepts of measurement and comparison is their first lesson in math. Children who frequently speak and hear these terms become fluent in math.

Math Curriculum Goals

True understanding of math occurs between ages five and seven. At this age children are in the middle to later part of Piaget's preoperational stage of intellectual development. The goal of a math curriculum for young children is to provide an environment that encourages the awareness and development of math skills. Math program objectives include:

- Identifying and classifying shapes.
- Understanding concepts of size and space.
- Sorting a variety of objects based on specific characteristics.
- Using math vocabulary that relates to numbers and establishes relationships between objects.
- Mastering one-to-one correspondence, which leads to counting.
- Organizing mathematical information and relating it in an understandable way.
- Establishing relationships between objects by comparing them.
- Using math concepts and applying them to everyday life.

Math Activities

As in other curriculum areas, hands-on experience with real objects is the best way to lead children to math mastery. When children group, sort, measure, weigh, and compare objects, they see how math skills apply to daily life. Children see math as a way of organizing and communicating information. See Fig. 26-1.

Care providers highlight math concepts in all classroom activities, regardless of the topic the children are investigating. For instance, children learning about supermarkets will learn about math. Children can visit a supermarket on a field trip. While there, they can learn about shapes, sizes, color, and quantity of foods. Back in the classroom, a care provider may help the children create a pretend supermarket in the dramatic play center. (See Chapter 27 for more information on dramatic play.) There they can play with cash registers and pretend money. They may weigh plastic vegetables on scales to determine weight and cost. Integrating math awareness and learning into all play activities helps children see why math skills are needed in real life. Care providers can also observe children as they play to determine each child's level of readiness for a new concept. They can also spot any learning problems children might have when they are involved in children's activities.

FIG. 26-1. **When math and science materials capture children's interest, they are more likely to work toward developing their math and science skills. What other materials could children use to practice their skills in measuring weight?**

Teachers and care providers use the following types of activities to encourage children to use math skills with confidence.

Recognizing Shapes. Children begin to notice different shapes as infants. By the preschool years, they are ready for activities that help build this skill. At snack time say, "Please put the round crackers on the square tray." Show children how different shapes can be put together—a triangular roof on a rectangular house with square windows. Encourage them to see relationships between shapes by giving them colorful paper shapes to use in creating their own designs and patterns. Shape-matching games also help children recognize shapes.

Sorting. Matching shapes is one way of sorting, or classifying, objects according to one or more characteristics. Children notice similarities and differences in objects, a valuable reasoning skill for both math and science. They can sort colors of clothes when "doing the laundry" during dramatic play. Have them sort tableware for meals. Give children small animals and have them create barnyards and zoos by including only those animals appropriate to each setting.

Seriation. Identifying size relationships between objects is called **seriation**. It is organizing objects according to increasing or decreasing size. While children look at a picture book about farming, the care provider might ask, "Which is taller—the farmer or the barn?" In the dramatic play center, the care provider could instruct, "Put the dishes away, with the smaller ones on top of the bigger ones." Anytime you can make a comparison, you can teach seriation. See Fig. 26-2.

Patterning. As children work with blocks, beads, or pegs of different shapes and colors, they begin to create predictable patterns. Children can continue patterns of repeated shapes or colors as they learn to observe, count, and sequence. For instance, stringed-bead necklaces can be made using a red, blue, red, blue pattern. Gradually, children will notice many other types of predictable patterns, such as designs in tiled floors or artistic paintings.

FIG. 26-2. Making comparisons about the size relationships of objects is seriation. What are some other ways that care providers can teach seriation?

Rote Counting. Many complex mental processes are used in learning to count. By age three, most children are capable of **rote counting**. That means they can memorize and recite numbers in order, but they have no real understanding of the quantity the numbers represent. Use activities to teach counting skills. Fill a basket with small items and tell each child to pick out a different amount. Make counting a physical activity by having children clap their hands, stomp their feet, or jump in place a certain number of times. Make a paper chain calendar, adding a link at the beginning of each day. Have the children count the number of links.

Independence Skills

Reinforcing Math Skills

Simple math concepts can be reinforced during snack time preparation or through cooking activities. Here are some ideas for turning food preparation into math activities.

1. Teach children about fractions when dividing foods into equal parts, such as fruits, sandwiches, pizza, or dough. Move the pieces around to show how fractions combine to make a whole, such as putting two of four pieces back together to make one-half.

2. The concepts of equal and unequal can be illustrated by cutting pieces of food into equal and unequal portions.

3. Teach children about sequence by asking them to recall what they did first, second, and third in a recipe.

4. Children can practice counting by counting out loud the number of times a food is stirred or by counting ingredients, such as raisins.

5. Have children identify the shapes of food, such as round, square, and triangle. Slices of cheese or bread work well for cutting into shapes. Older children may try more complex shapes, such as octagons.

6. Reinforce measurement by selecting recipes with ingredients children can measure. Show children how to use a ruler or measuring tape to measure a pan's size.

7. Teach children about addition and subtraction by putting food items together and taking items away.

8. The concept of time can be reinforced with recipes that require foods to sit, chill, or bake for a period of time.

Try It!

Design a food-preparation activity reinforcing math skills for a preschool age child. How many math concepts could be reinforced? Try the activity with one child or a group of children.

Rational Counting. To truly understand what numbers and their names represent, children must master **rational counting**, or learning to recognize the numerical symbols that represent quantities and place them in sequential order. Rational counting requires the understanding of one-to-one correspondence. Children learn to assign one number to each object counted. Care providers encourage this skill by counting objects with the child as each object is touched. You can count steps as the class goes up or down them. You can count graham crackers as the child places them on a tray at snack time. This is double reinforcement—the child realizes that the number of crackers corresponds to the number of students.

Recognizing Numerals. Once children understand rational counting, they can learn to recognize **numerals**, or written symbols that represent numbers. Care providers can help them make this association through simple activities. Mark bushel baskets with a numeral and have children place the corresponding number of apples in each one. Have children shape numerals from clay and then roll small bits of clay into the matching number of balls. Take photographs of the children in groups of different sizes. Provide them with numeral cards and have them pair the cards with the pictures showing the same number of children. When children build with blocks, talk about how many were used. See Fig. 26-3.

Ordering Numerals. As children advance intellectually, they combine their ability to count with their recognition of numerals. They order numerals, or place them in the correct sequence. Many activities help strengthen this skill. For instance, you could paint numerals on toy cars and have the children race the cars, finishing in numerical order. Children could place leis, each with a different number of flowers, around each other's necks in sequential order.

Making Charts and Graphs. Once children learn how to count correctly, they can gather information and organize it so it can be communicated. Charts and bar graphs allow children to relay mathematical information they gather. For instance, children can conduct a class survey of favorite pets. To do this, the care provider gives the children a sheet of paper with columns on it. At the top of each column is a photo or drawing of a typical childhood pet, such as dog, cat, and hamster. Children ask each classmate to pick his or her favorite pet. A tally mark is then made in the appropriate column. After responses are gathered, children count the tally marks in each column and write the total at the bottom. By comparing the column totals, children can announce which pet was picked as the class favorite. By ordering the column totals, they can also determine second-place and third-place favorites. Displaying this information on a poster board lets children refer back to results as they share their learning with parents.

FIG. 26-3. **Learning to recognize written numerals is a task common to the preschool years.** Investigate the use of "self-correcting" materials in helping children to recognize numerals.

Math Materials

Many materials are available for children to use to explore math concepts. The materials can be used in a variety of learning centers, from block play to art. See Fig. 26-4. The following are materials care providers should have on hand for children's creative use:

- One-inch square table blocks in many colors.
- Wood pattern chips and pegs and pegboards in many colors.
- Colored stringing beads of different shapes and inter-connecting plastic blocks or bricks.
- Nesting toys and measuring spoons and cups.
- Containers that hold from a half-pint to one gallon of liquid.
- Balance and weight scales.
- Height charts and tape measures and rulers.
- Counters—such as buttons, shells, or acorns—and counting table games.

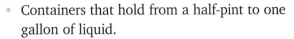

FIG. 26-4. Maintaining an interest-ing assortment of math materials encourages children to explore math concepts. What are the benefits of includ-ing culturally diverse math materials?

- Shape and number bingo, matching card games, and puzzles.
- Play cash register and play money.
- Clocks, kitchen timers, and plastic hour-glass timers.

Section 26-1 Knowledge Check

1. What is meant by the term mathematical vocabulary?
2. How can building with blocks help children develop math concepts?
3. Explain how children can use math skills in a dramatic play center.

Mini-Lab

Many toys and educational materials are designed to teach math principles to young children. Look through catalogs and sale flyers to find those that you believe would be effec-tive. Browse toy departments, too, for ideas. What math skills would the toys help develop? Could you adapt any of the toy ideas with homemade versions?

Section 26-2

Science Skills for Children

OBJECTIVES

- Explain how science activities benefit children.
- Describe the goals of a science curriculum.
- Plan a science learning center for preschoolers.
- Explain the care provider's role in making science interesting and enjoyable for children.
- Plan and lead science activities.

KEY TERMS

sensory table
light table
rebus recipe

Children learn to appreciate the wonders of the world at a young age. Young children have unending curiosity. They are full of questions and eager to explore. That curiosity naturally leads them to science.

Science for Young Children

Science is a process of collecting knowledge about the physical world and how the world works. Active discovery and investigation are the basics of science for children. Hands-on experiences let children witness and experiment with basic science concepts. Children enjoy messily exploring natural wonders, such as digging to find worms after a rain.

Topics for science are endless. They range from using magnets to caring for a classroom pet. Care providers need to guard against doing too much for children as they explore. However, showing children how to use some pieces of equipment and how to carefully treat animals and plants is necessary. Ethical treatment of all forms of life teaches compassion and respect.

Guiding Science Learning. Children discover science best when care providers set the stage for safe exploration. As children explore, care providers guide children's learning by asking questions to encourage observation, analysis, and problem solving. Care providers often ask open-ended questions to help focus children's thinking. Care providers might ask the following questions as children explore:

- How does it look?
- How does it feel?
- What is happening?
- Why do you think this is happening?

Care providers make the most of teachable moments to spark children's interest in science. If a butterfly is spotted on the play yard, an alert care provider gives children magnifying

FIG. 26-5. Outdoor science activities encourage curiosity and environmental awareness. What are some outdoor activities that encourage science skills?

glasses for closer observation. Children's books on butterflies will be displayed. Art materials will be provided so children can create butterfly drawings or paintings. Care providers might help children plant flowers that will feed the butterfly and provide shelter. Care providers know that children's active participation makes learning more meaningful. See Fig. 26-5.

Science Curriculum Goals

The science curriculum helps children satisfy their curiosity. Science encourages children to wonder and ask questions. It also helps children see that all things on the earth are interrelated. Weather and landscape affect how we live. The ways humans use land can impact other living things, such as plants and animals. There are also basic scientific laws that await children's discovery, such as the effect of temperature on objects, the effects of gravity, and how the sun and water help plants grow.

Regardless of the specific science topics children investigate, care providers pursue certain general science goals. Goals for a science curriculum include:

- Fostering children's appreciation of nature and themselves.
- Encouraging curiosity and providing chances to explore the world.
- Allowing children to investigate the world using their senses.
- Providing children with hands-on experiences that develop basic science concepts.
- Increasing children's ability to observe, describe, classify, see relationships, and solve problems.

Science Activities

Before you can develop science activities for children, you need to find ways to make the concepts simple and understandable. You want to spark interest, not overwhelm children with complicated, abstract lectures. A hands-on approach does this best. Relate science principles to everyday life. Some favorite science topics are the earth and its environments; properties of air, soil, and water; characteristics of foods and how they are cooked; and characteristics of plants, animals, and humans.

Care providers organize learning opportunities in response to children's questions or immediate experiences. For instance, if a child went fishing with her grandfather and wondered about the fish in the lake, a study of fish might begin. There are endless other topics that include trees, birds, insects, and seasons; animals, ocean, desert, or forest; colors and how they are made; rocks and minerals; how the body works; and types of transportation.

Young children can practice many skills through science activities. They like to collect, observe, and touch objects, plants, and animals. As they do, have them describe what their senses discover. Encourage them to question and think. Through exploration, they can compare and classify materials. They also note relationships, such as cause and effect. In addition, they notice similarities and differences in objects, plants, and animals. They use experimentation to test and retest scientific principles, such as what sinks and what floats.

Science activities need not be long-term projects. Some require little planning or preparation, yet they are rich with learning potential. Think of the science concepts you could explore through the following activities:

- Show children how to feel their pulse and heartbeat. Have them do this before and after a vigorous physical activity.

- Watch popcorn popping.

- Give children magnets of varied shapes, sizes, and strengths. Have them experiment with objects to find out what the magnets can and cannot pick up. See Fig. 26-6.

- Make a rainbow by spraying water from a garden hose in the sunshine.

- Place a bird feeder just outside the classroom window. Experiment to see what foods the birds prefer.

- Use objects to make shadows with a flashlight in a darkened room. Move them closer to and farther from the light. Hold the flashlight at different angles to the objects.

- Make static electricity. Rub an inflated balloon with a woolen cloth. Under some conditions—such as in dry weather—static electricity can also be produced by running a comb through your hair. Darken the room for the maximum effect.

Science Materials

Many classrooms for young children have a science learning center. The center includes at least one table and a set of chairs. Science collections, such as shells, fossils, or seeds, may be displayed on a low table or shelf. If live animals are included in the program, they may be housed in this learning center.

Because science activities sometimes require a group effort, provide enough materials for at least four children to use at the center at once. Providing more than one set of materials eliminates conflicts over the materials. It also encourages children to work together to develop their social skills. When looking for science materials, include items from nature, such as leaves and twigs, nuts and seeds, shells, fossils, rock and mineral kits, and ant farms. Aquariums, terrariums, kaleidoscopes, prisms, and color paddles also encourage science discovery.

Sometimes a **sensory table** is placed in the science learning center. This is a table with a box-like, hollow top that can hold water, sand, beans, or other substances for children to explore. The substance contained in the table can be changed periodically. Pitchers, funnels, rustproof spoons, shovels, pails, measuring cups, boats, and trucks are among the equipment children might use at the sensory table. See Fig. 26-7.

A **light table** may also be found in a science area. This is a low table with a plastic white

FIG. 26-6. Science activities do not have to take a lot of time. What can children learn from trying to pick up various objects with magnets?

FIG. 26-7. **Sensory materials lend themselves to dozens of different activities and sensory experiences.** What do children learn about the world from sensory experiences?

cover. Beneath the cover are low-wattage light bulbs. Children can place items, such as leaves or colored plastic connecting blocks, on the light table. When these items are lit up, they are very enticing to children. Veins on tree leaves can be traced or secondary colors made by laying two colored plastic shapes on top of each other. When creating a science area, be sure the space allows children to work and concentrate without distraction. For example, you might place the science area at the back of the room, away from the door and other learning centers. See Section 26-3 for outdoor opportunities for science instruction.

Cooking with Children

Though surprising to many, cooking is a science activity in itself. Recipe contents and the chemical processes that occur during cooking and baking reflect science. The equipment and tools used to cook with children are the results of scientific inventions.

Most children are familiar with at least some of the equipment and procedures used in cooking. They can carry out many tasks themselves. Cooking is a highly sensory experience, with many opportunities to observe, taste, smell, and handle ingredients and utensils. Children's interest and enjoyment peaks when the science project also produces a tasty snack.

Cooking activities lend themselves easily to topics that relate to vegetables, farming, or family traditions and home life. An activity for a unit on farm animals might include churning cream into butter. To learn about vegetables, children might visit an outdoor farmers' market to purchase some vegetables. Then they can use the vegetables and mix the dressing ingredients for a tossed vegetable salad. Cooking activities are also a perfect opportunity for parents to share their own expertise. Invite parents to join the class during cooking activities.

When cooking with children, print the recipe in large, bold letters on poster board. You may wish to make a **rebus recipe**, a recipe that illustrates ingredients and directions with picture symbols, to help the children follow the steps. See Fig. 26-8. For a successful cooking experience with young chefs, remember these guidelines:

- Look for simple recipes that illustrate the concept to be taught. For children whose native language is not English, try to find recipes in their native language and encourage them to speak their own language while working.

- Choose cooking activities that relate to other activities. For example, make carrot salad after reading *The Carrot Seed* during story time.

- Make cooking activities a cultural experience by preparing simple foods enjoyed in other parts of the world, such as baked plantain.

- Use foolproof recipes with children. Test them yourself before having children prepare them.

- Prepare foods over an easily cleaned surface, such as a tile floor.

- Limit group size to no more than six children and supervise them at all times.

peanut butter

grape jelly

butter knife

plate

1 tbsp. measuring spoon

whole wheat bread

1. Put 2 slices of whole wheat bread on the plate.

2. Spread 2 tablespoons of peanut butter on one slice of bread.

3. Spread 1 tablespoon of jelly on other slice of bread.

Put the slices of bread together.

4. Cut sandwich into quarters.

FIG. 26-8. Using rebus recipes allows children to follow the recipe ingredients and directions without being able to read.

• Avoid using kitchen appliances, if possible. Without them, there are more chances for hands-on learning and fewer safety hazards.

• Make sure everyone follows the rules of safety and sanitation described in Chapter 6. Wear aprons to keep clothing clean.

• Allow plenty of time. Hurrying can lead to carelessness and accidents. It can also hinder learning.

• Let each child participate in some way, adapting the activity or materials for children with special needs.

• Understand that the process of cooking is more important to learning than the finished product. Allow children to take their cooked treat home, if possible.

How To...

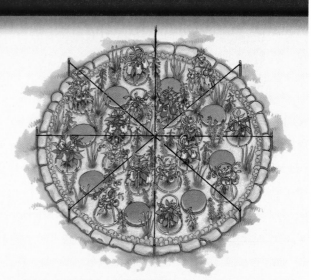

Make a Pizza Garden

Pizza gardens are shaped like a pizza and food items used by cooks when preparing pizzas are grown in them. Following are the steps to making your own edible pizza garden.

1. Select a sunny planting area.

2. Create a circular garden plot, measuring eight feet in diameter.

3. Remove grass and weeds from the plot.

4. Dig and loosen chunks of soil with a shovel to create fine dirt in which plant roots grow easily.

5. Add rich soil and compost to the garden plot during tilling. Vegetables do not grow well in soil that has too much sand or clay.

6. Use sticks and string to divide the circular garden into eight triangle pizza slices.

7. Plant seeds, bulbs, or small starter plants of pizza ingredients, such as tomatoes, red and green peppers, onions, basil, and oregano in each triangle.

8. Provide a climbing frame to support growth of the tomatoes and peppers.

9. Plant yellow marigolds or zinnias near the garden edges to represent pizza cheese.

10. Place stones around the plot to create a pizza crust. Place circular stepping stones throughout the pizza garden to represent pepperoni or sausage for meat lovers.

11. Weed and water as appropriate to your local growing climate.

12. Harvest the vegetables when they reach full ripeness and wash them thoroughly.

APPLY IT!

Use the produce to make a real pizza for a classroom snack. Include the children as much as possible in the process of planting, growing, harvesting, and cooking.

Section **26-2** Knowledge Check

1. What preschoolers' characteristic naturally leads them to science discovery?

2. What is a sensory table?

3. Why is cooking considered a science activity?

Mini-Lab

Draw your own design for a science learning center. Provide details that show the basic arrangement. List the equipment and materials you would include in the center. Identify the placement of equipment and materials on your drawing.

Section 26-3

Nature & Gardening Activities

- Explain how the natural world can be used for nature education.
- Discuss what can be learned from studying the natural world.
- Plan nature and gardening activities for young children.

KEY TERMS

nature education
field guide
birding

Learning about science and how the world works should not be confined just to the classroom. The outdoor environment and natural world offer many learning opportunities, too.

Exploring Natural Wonders

One of life's special pleasures is experiencing direct contact with nature. Daily experiences with natural elements are relaxing and rewarding for young and old alike. Studying nature helps people to be in tune with the life cycles of things on earth. Teaching about the environment and life on earth is called **nature education.**

There are many intergenerational programs in which older adults and young children can explore together the natural wonders of earth. For example, grandparents may take their grandchildren to an Elderhostel™ program. There they can build lasting memories through hands-on, nature activities. They might participate in activities that involve learning about the

forests and streams and develop skills in reading maps and compasses. These programs might also include hiking and building campfires.

Here are some ways to help children and older adults get the most out of nature education:

- **Savor the scents.** Smell flowers and blooming shrubs or trees. Notice smells after a rain or after grass is mowed.

- **Notice patterns and designs.** Patterns can be found in almost any natural object, such as ripples widening in puddles. Rainbows, tree leaves, bird feathers, seashells, or spider webs offer intriguing designs to admire. These patterns may inspire children's drawings, too.

- **Trace textures.** Gently touch nature items. Discuss textures, such as satiny tree buds,

FIG. 26-9. Gently touching items with texture in nature helps children develop discrimination skills. What are some other benefits of tracing textures?

mushy mud, and rough tree bark. Talk about how the breeze feels on the skin and hair. See Fig. 26-9.

- **Tune into sounds.** Sit quietly and listen to nature sounds, such as birds calling, wildlife rustling, and rain falling on a roof.

- **Observe the behavior of wildlife.** Observe a bird building a nest, caterpillars feeding, or a spider spinning a web. Find animal tracks. Notice what different animals eat and how they catch their food. How do they raise their young? Which animals have colors that blend with nature and help them hide? Notice basic characteristics of wildlife, such as body covering and number of legs.

- **Notice effects of climate and weather.** Observe sun and shadows and notice how wind affects pinwheels, wind chimes, banners, kites, and windsocks. Talk about the different types of clouds. Watch it rain and observe its effects. Enjoy snow activities, such as sledding or finding animals tracks in the snow.

- **Visit various nature areas.** Visit a lake or walk a woodland path. Parks and wildlife

preserves have many natural objects to investigate. Discover what creatures live in each habitat.

- **Examine various types of plant life.** Learn about seeds, stems, leaves, and roots. Find plants that grow in different types of soil, such as sandy, wet, clay, or dry soil.

- **Locate animal and insect homes.** Observe animals in their homes. What are the homes made of? How are they made?

Tools for Nature Exploration. Nature items can be explored safely, and in greater detail, when simple tools are provided. See Fig. 26-10. These tools may include:

- A magnifying glass to look closely at flowers, moss, or bird tracks.
- A pair of binoculars to see distant wildlife.
- Paper bags, grocery bags, or backpacks in which to collect nature items for art projects.
- Bug cages for looking at insects or worms.
- A tape recorder for recording nature sounds.
- Sketch pads and some colored pencils for drawing nature sights.
- Cameras or a camcorder to record nature experiences.
- **A field guide**—book for identifying natural items, such as flowers, insects, birds, or trees.
- A first aid kit for any nature field trip.

Health Precautions & Classroom Pets. Caution and good judgment are part of having animals in the classroom. The animals must be healthy. A veterinarian should certify that classroom pets are in good health. Be aware of any allergies to pets.

FIG. 26-10. Taking along tools for nature exploration helps children get the most benefit from their explorations.

Classroom Pets

Typical classroom pets include fish, rabbits, gerbils, hamsters, chameleons, and hermit crabs. Pets offer many lessons in science. They allow children to witness basic facts of the natural world up close. A pet's texture and color of body covering provide clues about the natural world. How an animal moves and eats is a great topic for investigation. How an animal communicates and plays is fun to observe as well.

Pets also respond to a human's social needs. Children and older adults practice compassion and responsibility as they care for pets during feeding or cleaning. People feel important and needed when they know a pet is depending on them. See Fig. 26-11.

When using pets with children and older adults, consider the following factors:

- The value of interaction between children, older adults, and pets. Do pets offer a source of comfort to children and older adults?

- The energy levels of older adults and children. Choosing a more mature pet may be better in many instances. For example, the high energy of a young puppy may overwhelm older adults and children. An older,

well-trained dog will likely be calmer around children and older adults.

- The limitations of people with disabilities, such as Parkinson's disease or mobility limitations. Will the pets interfere with mobility?

Some intergenerational programs use pets to stimulate learning in touring programs. For example, programs such as the OASIS Intergenerational Tutoring Program—based in St. Louis, MO—promotes literacy, builds children's self-esteem and positive attitudes toward learning, and strengthens reading skills. The program helps care providers develop units on pet care or pet health that can be taken into the classroom. Older adult mentors then use pets as a motivator for developing language or reading skills. OASIS has programs in many cities throughout the United States. Look for more information about OASIS on the Internet.

FIG. 26-11. Mature, well-trained pets are best to have around children and older adults. What are the benefits of using well-trained pets?

Bird Watching

Learning to identify birds is an enjoyable pastime for people of all ages. As well as being entertaining, bird watching refines skills in concentration, observation, and reasoning.

Birds can be found almost anywhere. To attract birds offer trees and shrubs, a birdbath, and a food source. Bird books and videos are good resources for learning about birds, too. Children and older adults can observe the following bird traits as they learn to identify birds: feather color, design, and shape; body size and shape; bill shape, size, and color; wing shape; eye color; flight pattern; bird songs and calls; nest site and materials; and foot details.

Gardening Adventures

Activities with plants and gardening are also great ways to connect people with the natural world. Gardening introduces children and older adults to the diversity of plants. Plant growth can be quick and dramatic. Eating plants grown in a garden makes learning rewarding.

Gardening also illustrates the life cycle, or the stages that living things go through during a lifetime. It shows what things are necessary for growth, including good soil, sun, and water. Children and older adults can also explore the different parts of plants, including seed, roots, stem, leaves, flower, and fruit.

Gardening shows how plants and insects depend on each other. Bees pollinate flowers as they feed. Caterpillars feed on plants before they turn into butterflies, which helps plant pollination. Birds eat flower seeds as well as carry them to new places. The flowers of plants attract insects, on which birds can feed. In those ways, gardening brings science concepts to life. See Fig. 26-12.

Gardening also provides good exercise, too. Muscle and motor control are put to use during raking, weeding, digging, hoeing soil, and planting, watering, and harvesting plants. Raised garden beds allow older adults and those in wheelchairs to participate in gardening, too.

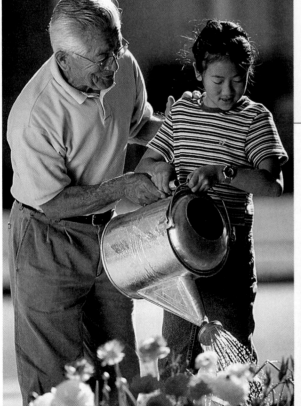

FIG. 26-12. Intergenerational gardening activities promote positive relationships between children and older adults. How can children and older adults help each other in gardening activities?

Intergenerational *Interactions*

Bird Watching

Perhaps the easiest way to see nature up close and at its finest is to watch birds. Bird watching, or **birding**, knows no boundaries. People of all ages, in all parts of the world, can appreciate birds. While people near the tropics and people near the Arctic circle will see vastly different types of birds, both groups can still enjoy the beauty and song of nature's feathered friends. The only equipment needed is a pair of binoculars. Bird watching:

- **Relaxes or Invigorates.** There are many levels of bird watching. As you observe birds in the wild, you can choose to do so from the comfort of your home. You can watch in your backyard from a lawn chair, or you can follow a nature trail in search of birds.

- **Joins Generations.** Like many activities, bird watching is a great intergenerational hobby. Whether watching birds at a backyard feeder or observing them on walks through a local park, people of all ages can enjoy identifying or simply watching birds.

- **Relieves Boredom.** For less-active older adults, time can pass very slowly. However, watching the graceful flight, song, and play of birds lessens boredom.

- **Soothes Emotions.** Watching the graceful flight or listening to the sweet song of a bird can help lower blood pressure, ease loneliness, and lessen symptoms of depression.

- **Increases Self-Worth.** Providing food and water for wild birds and caring for birds in aviaries give children and older adults a sense of independence and purpose.

Follow-Up

Take a walk around your school, home, or local park to observe birds in the wild. Identify and research the most interesting bird you see on your walk. Write a one-page report on the bird you identify. Explain how you might put this experience to practical use in creating a bird-watching activity for children and older adults.

For older adults, gardening is one of the low-intensity activities that can have some long-term health benefits, if done regularly. The activities associated with gardening help lower the risk of cardiovascular disease. Gardening and yard work are among the most popular moderate-intensity leisure activities. These activities also reduce the risk of falling and improve an older adult's ability to perform daily tasks.

Indoor Gardening

Activities with plants and gardening can take place indoors, too. Following are indoor gardening activities for children and older adults:

- **Growing houseplants.** Provide clay pots, soil, and seeds or nursery plants. Place near a good light source, such as a window. Children and older adults can water regularly and trim them when needed.

- **Experimenting with celery.** Place a stalk of celery in a jar of colored water. Children then can see how plants "drink."

- **Observing blooming buds.** Find a branch with buds on it that are about to bloom. Place the branch in a vase of water. Children and older adults can watch the buds blossom.

- **Growing green-haired funny faces.** Fill a coffee can with potting soil. Plant grass seed on top and keep it moist. Tape construction paper around the coffee can and draw a funny face on it. As grass grows, it becomes green hair!

- **Creating a mini-greenhouse.** Fill sections of an egg carton with soil. Plant marigold or alyssum seeds. Carefully wet soil using an eye dropper. Put the seeded carton into a plastic bag, seal it, and put in a sunny spot.

- **Making ivy sculptures.** Plant two small ivy plants in a large pot. Use a wire hanger to create a climber for the ivy. Hold the hanger upside down by the hook. Then bend into any shape, such as a circle, oval, or heart. Put the hook into the soil so that the hanger shape stands vertically. Gently train the vine to twine around the hanger as it grows.

- **Growing a pineapple.** Twist off the stem of a fresh pineapple. Remove the lower leaves to reveal two inches of stem. Put the stem in a glass and fill with water until the water reaches the bottom leaf. Maintain the water level until the glass is half-filled with strong roots. Once that happens, transplant to a pot of soil with good drainage.

- **Growing a sweet potato vine.** Poke four toothpicks around the middle of a fresh sweet potato. Letting the toothpicks rest on a clean jar of water, submerge half the potato. Observe as roots and a vine develop.

Section **26-3** Knowledge Check

1. What are tools for exploring nature?
2. What are ways to expose children and older adults to the natural world?
3. What safety precautions must be taken when using pets with children and older adults?

Mini-Lab

Explain how to modify an outdoor gardening activity for children or older adults with physical or visual impairments. List any special equipment the participants might need. Describe how you would meet the special needs of the children or older adults without being overprotective.

Section 26-4

Finances for Older Adults

Understanding finance is important when working with older adults. Many older adults have saved for their retirement; others have not. Older adults often depend on their families and care providers to help them make financial decisions so they will not be victims of financial abuse.

Finances & Older Adults

The financial status of older adults varies, depending on their work history and their financial stability. Factors that impact financial stability for older adults include:

- Have they worked and paid into a retirement plan?
- Have they worked long enough to receive Social Security income?
- Do they receive a spouse's Social Security income?
- Have they put money into a savings plan?

Older adults' financial status is based on their income, what they are paid, and their expenses, or what they owe. If they paid into a retirement plan when they worked, they will be eligible for retirement benefits. Retirement benefits are earnings that people receive after they retire. Social Security income is also one form of retirement plan that is run by the government. Most people pay Social Security taxes while they work. After they retire, they can receive Social Security income. To have enough money for retirement, many people also purchase stocks or bonds or put money into savings accounts while they work.

Financial Goals

Everyone who works or is retired generally has financial goals. By setting financial goals, people can be more financially secure. Planning for specific goals helps older adults plan their daily spending and live within their means. Care providers can invite guest speakers to come to the adult day care centers to conduct programs that will assist older adults in using their money wisely. A financial planner could point out better ways of paying bills. For example, it might be better for some older adults to use the automatic payment services to pay bills, such as monthly utility bills, rather than writing a check. When authorized by the older adult, money for certain bills can be automatically withdrawn from the individual's bank account each month. If for some reason, older adults are late paying a bill by check or cash, they will have to pay a late fee and may be charged interest on an outstanding balance.

Keeping Records

Managing finances requires consistent and accurate record keeping. Effective care providers help older adults organize and keep track of their financial records. They can help older adults by creating file folders that contain all the older adult's financial records. The goal is to help older adults to maintain their records independently. The filing system should be simple. Care providers might use color-coding to help older adults easily spot files. Try using expandable files for older adults who have trouble with small motor skills. See Fig. 26-13. Include the following in a financial records file:

- **Sources of regular income.** Include any pay stubs or statements that show money the older adult has received.
- **Social Security and Medicare information.** File any statements from the government related to financial and medical benefits the older adult has received.

FIG. 26-13. **Financial planners often help older adults evaluate and set financial goals. How might this benefit older adults on fixed incomes?**

- **Investment income.** If the older adult has investments, he or she will probably receive statements several times a year as well as important tax documents.
- **Insurance information.** It is important to keep copies of insurance policies in a fire safe. Also make sure the older adult has easy access to policy numbers.
- **Bank accounts.** File any bank statements or account information received from the bank.
- **Location of safe deposit boxes and contents.** Keep a separate list of valuables and documents stored in safe deposit boxes and names of the people authorized to access the box.
- **Copies of the most recent income tax returns.** File copies of state and federal income tax returns for three years.
- **Bills and liabilities.** Keep track of bills and liabilities (or debts) and how much is due on each. Place the bill statements in the appropriate file after each bill is paid.

- **Credit card numbers.** Make sure the older adult knows where his or her credit cards are located and keep the numbers in a separate place in case the credit cards are lost.
- **Location of personal items, such as jewelry and family heirlooms.** Make sure the older adult knows where his or her personal items are located. A family member might need to be told of the location if the older adult experiences memory problems.

Family Member Assistance

Many older adults feel more secure knowing that a trusted family member will make decisions for them and carry out their wishes if they are ever unable to do so. It is best for older adults to appoint a person to assist them and document it legally. Sensitive care providers are familiar with family members who assist older adults and understand the family's dynamics. Remember to respect the decisions that family members make for older adults. They are usually the ones that have to assist older adults with financial matters. Family members can be instrumental in helping them identify ways to

Financial Abuse. One of your colleagues is bragging to you that an older adult in his care has purchased sports equipment for him on several occasions. In addition, he has commented that he usually keeps the change when he makes small purchases for older adults as payment for doing their shopping. You know that your colleague is illegally taking advantage of the older adults in his care. *What would you do?*

keep up with their money. Care providers can assist family members by conducting workshops at the adult day care centers. They can also write articles in monthly newsletters that alert family members about programs and activities that can help them with money management.

Family members can assist older adults by paying close attention to their spending habits. With the older adult's help or permission, a trusted family member can review the older adult's checkbook and bank statements and canceled checks to help determine the need for additional help in managing money. When helping older adults with their finances, look for:

- Duplicate payments, such as payments for medical bills that have already been paid.
- Numerous payments to credit card companies, television shopping networks, sweepstakes or other contests. See Fig. 26-14.
- Unusually large donations to charitable or fraternal organizations.
- Failure to list or track deposits and income.
- Failure to record checks or track expenditures.
- Lost checkbooks or bank statements.
- Numerous transfers from savings to checking accounts.
- Consistent or unusual payments to a person unknown to you (a possible sign of financial exploitation).
- Past due notices or letters from creditors.

The review of this information may indicate that a daily money manager may be needed. A **daily money manager** is a person who offers financial services—such as establishing budgets, keeping track of financial records, and balancing checkbooks—for people who cannot manage their financial matters. Daily money managers charge a fee for their services.

If a family member care provider and the older adult decide that a daily money manager would be helpful, adult day care providers can set up interviews with several candidates. Get references from the daily money manager's

FIG. 26-14. **Care providers and family members can help older adults set up effective record-keeping systems for financial records. How can** older adults and their family members benefit from such an organized system?

clients and call to verify the references. Clients will gladly share how pleased or displeased they are. Also contact the local Better Business Bureau, Chamber of Commerce, local consumer protection agency, or area agency on aging for more information on daily money managers.

Banking

Many people have a lifelong business relationship with a bank or other financial institution, such as a savings and loan or a credit union. These institutions offer a variety of financial services that may include:

- Electronic direct deposit of income and other payment services.
- Checking and savings accounts and safety deposit boxes.
- Certificates of deposit and other investments.
- Mortgage and other loan services, or credit and debit card services.

Debit Cards

Many older adults have checking accounts and write checks. However, they sometimes fail to record them in the checkbook register. Some older adults have trouble writing checks because of physical limitations, such as arthritis. When older adults have trouble using checks, they may use a debit card. The debit card looks like a credit card and is used like one when making purchases. Care providers might have to work with an older adult to help him or her understand how to use a debit card.

Some older adults might not know the difference between a debit card and a credit card. Explain that a debit card takes money out of a bank account when the card is used. It works like cash or a check. A credit card charges the item, and the credit card company later sends a bill to the cardholder. Care providers might also need to help older adults remember their personal identification numbers for the debit cards.

Tell the older adults to keep the number written down in a safe place in case they forget it. See Fig. 26-15.

Older adults often become targets of financial abuse, such as commercial exploitation. **Commercial exploitation** can be defined as being overly influenced by commercial advertisements. Many older adults watch a lot of television and purchase unnecessary mail order items. Also, unethical people seek out older adults who are home during the day to telephone and coerce them to make purchases. Some people use other methods to get older adults to spend their money. Care providers can plan and implement programs to help older adults to be aware of schemes used to take advantage of them.

Older adults who are less able to handle their financial tasks often turn these tasks over to someone they trust, such as a durable power of atorney. A power of attorney document gives one or more people authority to make decisions on behalf of the older adults when they are not able. See Chapter 17 for more information.

FIG. 26-15. **Debit cards can be useful for older adults who have writing limitations due to arthritis and other conditions.** What precautions should older adults and their care providers take when using debit cards?

Section **26-4** Knowledge Check

1. What is Social Security?
2. How can a care provider assist older adults with their financial affairs?
3. What services are provided by daily money managers?

Mini-Lab

Outline the steps you would take to assist an older adult with his or her financial affairs. Include a timeline for paying bills and filing records.

Review & Activities

Section Summaries

26-1 Math activities should help children see how math is used in daily life.

26-1 Math concepts can be taught in daily routines.

26-1 Children learn math best through active participation with hands-on materials.

26-1 Math concepts should be included in other learning centers and curriculum topics.

26-2 A science curriculum encourages children to explore and analyze their world.

26-2 A science learning center consists of many different science materials.

26-2 Children learn science best through active participation.

26-2 Care providers should plan science activities in response to children's questions and immediate experiences.

26-2 Cooking activities allow children to explore and apply science concepts.

26-3 Animals and plants can teach children about biology and the life cycle.

26-3 Care providers should create environments that allow children and older adults to explore science concepts.

26-4 The financial status of older adults is influenced by their work history.

26-4 Relatives and friends sometimes must help older people manage their legal, medical, or financial affairs temporarily or even gradually assume these responsibilities.

26-4 A debit card looks like a credit card and works like cash or a personal check.

Check Your Knowledge

1. Name the goals of a math curriculum.
2. What are math skills children can develop?
3. List math materials children can use for play.
4. What are the goals of a science curriculum?
5. Explain how to implement science and math activities that also meet children's learning styles, home experiences, and cultural traditions.
6. What is the care provider's role in teaching science?
7. Identify two advantages of using pets to teach science concepts.
8. Explain how food-related activities can enhance participant development and social interactions.
9. List three ways a care provider can assist older adults with financial affairs.
10. When should family members consider using a daily money manager?

Thinking Critically

1. Draw conclusions about how the development of math and science skills in preschoolers contributes to future success in school.
2. Analyze why hands-on experiences are the best ways to teach young children basic math and science concepts.
3. What ethical issues might an adult care provider encounter in assisting older adults with their finances?

Practical Applications

1. **Math and Science Observation.** Observe a preschool teacher presenting a math or science concept to young children. Note the children's responses. Which responses indicated an understanding of the concept presented? Which responses indicated that the child has not yet grasped the concept? How does the teacher meet the different learning styles of the children?

2. **Transition Times.** Moving from active science and math activities to quiet times can be challenging. Determine five transition activities to use between an active activity and a quiet one. Describe the activities and how you would implement them successfully. Share your ideas with your classmates.

3. **Create a Directory.** Research local organizations that provide financial assistance to older adults, such as free tax planning or volunteer financial assistants. Create a directory of resources and share it with a local older adult day center.

Math & Science Experiences

Your future employer will look at how you effectively plan and carry out math and science activities for young children, or how well you can assist older adults with financial issues.

Step 1: Research typical goals for a math or science curriculum for young children or for a financial management program for older adults. Choose one goal and describe how you would develop it in a program for young children or older adults.

Step 2: Create three math or science activities for young children or three activities to assist older adults in managing their finances. Include information about how to provide learning experiences for those with special needs or second language learners. If possible, carry out one of these activities. Write a summary of the results.

Step 3: Write a personal philosophy statement regarding a care provider's role in stimulating young children's interest in math and science or a care provider's role in protecting older adults from financial abuse.

Step 4: Create a form for reporting to parents about their child's progress in math and science. Determine how often you will assess children and send the report home to parents.

Step 5: Include your work for Steps 1 through 4 in your portfolio.

Chapter 27
Movement & Drama Activities

Section 27-1

Motor Development & Fitness

OBJECTIVES

- Identify the benefits of movement for children.
- Plan and lead creative movement activities.
- Describe the physical skills development for older adults and determine the benefits.
- Determine the effects of motor development and fitness on activities of daily living.

KEY TERMS

creative movement
gait
locomotion
  compensation
joint mobilization

Physical fitness, body tone, and good coordination are important components throughout life. Developing and maintaining these attributes promote a healthy lifestyle and allow individuals to participate in activities of their choice.

Motor Development

Units 1 and 5 of this text discuss the physical development and motor abilities of children and older adults. Care providers plan and conduct activities that support participants' development and maintenance of physical skills.

Skill Development in Children

Developmental skills and abilities increase rapidly in healthy, growing children. Regardless of a child's level of development, the role of a care provider is to aid in the progression of those skills. Activities should be planned for areas of small and large motor coordination.

Over time, large and small motor development increases. Young children learn to coordinate their muscle movements and increase their motor skills. Through movement activities, children learn to make their bodies do what they want them to do. For example, first, children learn to purposefully touch an object, such as a ball. Next, they learn to pat the ball and then roll it. Within a couple of years, they begin tossing and throwing the ball. With experience, they ultimately learn to throw and catch with greater accuracy. See Fig. 27-1. Large motor activities, such as walking, must come before running and skipping. From a basic foundation, children can later learn to dance in different styles, such as tap, folk, or ballet. They can also participate in sports that are more physically demanding, such as tennis or gymnastics.

FIG. 27-1. **The way in which children learn to throw and catch a ball shows how they gain mastery over both small and large muscles.** What other activities show the progression of skills?

Exploring Creative Movement

Active participation is the key to children's mastery of motor skills. Care providers encourage participation by conducting creative movement activities. **Creative movement** is responding to music or a mental image through physical movement. A care provider may ask children to move across a room as if they were butterflies looking for flowers on which to feed. The children show their interpretation of this idea by how they move their bodies. With creative movement, children should be allowed to interpret the idea in any way they wish.

When conducting creative movement activities, use safe, large, open spaces with flat areas that offer safe footing. Keep children from window areas to avoid injuries. Care providers often supply materials and props for children to use when participating in movement activities. Sometimes a simple musical instrument is used, such as a drum. Whether using props or instruments, the goal is to help children become comfortable with their bodies and enjoy creative movement. The elements that make up creative movement are body awareness, force and time,

space, locomotion, weight, and moving in groups. Here are ideas to use with children:

Body Awareness. These activities familiarize children with the parts of their bodies and their range of movement.

- Play music with different tempos. Have children move parts of their bodies to the beat—first the head, then arms, legs, fingers, toes, and finally the entire body.

- Encourage expression and creativity in movement having children dance with props. Streamers, scarves, grass skirts, leis, boas, pom-poms, veils, and hats are a few examples.

- Have the children pretend to be sprouting seeds. Verbally guide them into pretending to be saplings and then mature trees. How would they move in a gentle breeze or a storm?

Force and Time. Force describes strength of movements. Time refers to how quickly or slowly children move.

- Have children respond to music with varying tempos, such as a wedding march, an Irish jig, or some popular music. Notice how their movements change.

- Adjust the volume of the music. How do children respond to louder music? To softer music?

Space. These activities encourage children to explore the use of physical space.

- In a large open area, play a steady drum beat. Encourage children to move to the beat—forward, backward, sideways, and in circles.
- Play circus music while children move through a safe obstacle course.

Locomotion. With locomotion, children experience different ways to move from place to place.

- Have children mimic animal movements. Ask them to gallop like ponies, slither like snakes, or crawl like turtles. Play appropriate music for each movement.

- Playing suitable music, have children mimic human movements. Can they march like a bandleader? Play a guitar or drums?

Weight. In these activities, children learn how weight affects body movements.

- Tell children to imagine they are carrying a heavy backpack. How would they walk going up a steep hill? Going down?
- Have children participate in a simple musical game, first holding streamers and later holding bottles or cartons filled with sand. Ask them to compare their movements in each case.

Moving in Groups. This requires personal coordination and coordinating movements with others.

- Playing music with a rapid tempo, have groups of children form themselves into a type of food, such as a bunch of bananas.
- Play musical follow the leader. Have children take turns setting a beat with a tambourine or drum. The leader also selects the movement the others make to the beat. See Fig. 27-2.

FIG. 27-2. Moving in groups and playing games, such as "Follow the Leader," help children learn to coordinate their body movements.

Physical Skills of Older Adults

Care providers must have some knowledge about the physical conditions and limitations of their older adult population. It is important to plan activities and programs that are designed to address the physical needs of these participants. Some older adults have minor physical problems, such as stiffness or aches. Others have more severe motor problems, such as impaired gait. **Gait** is the way a person walks. Gait disorders can cause pain in the knees, back, neck, or head. Older adults can experience changes in their gait. These changes may be caused by vision problems, lack of balance, or other medical factors. Physical movement, such as exercise, can improve the pain suffered by poor gait. Regular exercise has other benefits, such as reducing the number of accidents older adults suffer. Falls are particularly serious for older adults. Injuries from falling can reduce mobility and independence. These accidents may also create financial hardships for the individuals or their families due to additional hospitalization, medical, and physical therapy bills.

Gait and balance problems, visual impairments, and dizziness caused by medication can all lead to possible falls. Environmental hazards, such as slippery surfaces, uneven floors, poor lighting, loose rugs, unstable furniture, and objects on floors, can also cause accidents. To reduce the risk of falling, care providers can:

- **Maintain a regular exercise program.** Exercise improves strength, balance, and coordination.

- **Take steps to make living areas safe.** Remove tripping hazards. Install grab bars next to toilets. Also, install handrails on both sides of all stairways.

- **Promote wearing proper footwear.** Encourage older adults to wear shoes with wide heels and rubber soles to help prevent tripping and slipping. Wearing sturdy shoes may also help other older adults improve their balance.

FIG. 27-3. Shoes that are not slippery can help older adults avoid falls. What other compensations can help older adults with mobility?

- **Request a medication review.** Ask the doctor to review all of the older adult's medications to reduce side effects and interactions.

- **Schedule yearly vision exams.** Poor vision can increase the risk of falling. Care providers can encourage or schedule regular eye examinations.

Locomotion Compensation. It is important for older adults to be safe and to avoid accidents. The way people change their movements to be safe is called **locomotion compensation**. For example, some older adults might need a walking device, such as a cane or a walker. A physical therapist can help older adults select walking devices that best suit their individual needs. See Fig. 27-3.

Intergenerational Interactions

Parachute Play

Early childhood centers and elementary schools have used parachute play for years, but now older adults are getting involved. In fact, manufacturers even make smaller chutes for use with wheelchairs. Regardless of age or ability, parachute play is fun for all. It encourages teamwork, builds upper body strength, and boosts heart rates for better heart health in people of all ages. There are a variety of games that are sure to be fun. Spread the parachute out, surround it with people, and enjoy the activities.

- **Ball Roll.** Place a ball or two on top of the parachute. Chute holders can move the balls around by raising and lowering their arms. Try to get the balls to fall through the center hole.

- **Ocean.** Holders imagine the parachute is an ocean. A leader is chosen to give a weather report. Holders then move the chute to make waves that imitate the seas during that type of weather.

- **Musical Run or Walk.** While listening to music, parachute holders grasp the chute with one hand and walk in a circle. When the music stops, they switch directions.

- **Popcorn.** Place several beanbags on top of the parachute. Parachute holders should move the chute up and down so the beanbags bounce like popping corn.

- **The Wave.** Just as the fans do at sporting events, one by one have chute holders raise their hands. Raising their hands in a sequence creates a wave effect around the circle.

Follow-Up

Write a report on why you think parachute play would benefit children and older adults. In your report, include a list of additional games parachute holders could play.

FIG. 27-4. Stretching exercises help older adults maintain healthier joints and reduce pain and stiffness. What are the other benefits of stretching exercises?

Health care specialists recommend that older adults participate daily in physical activities. These activities can include walking, stretching, and muscle-challenging activities. Walking and other aerobic activities help strengthen the cardiovascular system. Stretching exercises are important for maintaining joint flexibility. See Fig. 27-4. **Joint mobilization** is defined as moving body joints evenly and consistently to avoid stiffness and pain. Muscle-challenging activities, such as weight lifting, can be instrumental in maintaining body strength and balance. Regular exercise helps older adults maintain their physical fitness. With reduced pain and stiffness, older adults may have more independence and a more fulfilling life.

Physical Activities for Older Adults

Older adults may vary in their range of abilities. Some can only move slowly or very little; others can move about quite freely and without pain. There are various types of physical activities that meet the individual needs of older adults. Some of the physical activities include:

Stretching. Stretching can help decrease aches and pains. Improvement in flexibility is often seen after only a few sessions. Other benefits of stretching include the limited injury risk and the ability to do the activity anywhere. Older adults can stretch in bed by pointing their toes, they can do gentle side bends while watching television, or stand on their toes while talking on the telephone.

Walking. Many older people can walk short distances for daily exercise. Walking stretches and strengthens muscles, works the joints, and improves cardiovascular health. If older adults can walk from room to room without stress, they have the basic skill needed for an exercise routine. Walking is also a way for them to socialize, such as with walking buddies.

Pool Exercise. Exercise done in the water can help older adults increase their strength, flexibility, and cardiovascular fitness. Older adults with health conditions, such as arthritis and osteoporosis, can often exercise in the water without additional pain. Almost everyone can participate because swimming ability is not needed for pool exercise. To make the exercise more pleasurable, provide music and allow older adults to bring tapes or CDs of their own to share.

Flexibility and Strength Training. There are many licensed programs that train older adults to increase flexibility and strength. Reaching, bending, and stretching are part of the program design. Recent studies show that older adults regain their strength, mobility, and overall general sense of wellness with any increase in physical exercise. Older adults may sit in chairs to exercise while a trained and certified instructor guides the class. Participants may use hand weights of varying weight, depending on the fitness level they need to achieve. These programs meet individual fitness levels, and each person can exercise at his or her own pace. Geriatricians, medical doctors, physical therapists, and other health care specialists review these programs for safety and appropriateness. Older adults should always consult their doctors before starting any new exercise program. See Fig. 27-5.

FIG. 27-5. Exercise that increases aerobic capacity and strengthens muscles benefits the health and independent functioning of older adults.

Section 27-1 Knowledge Check

1. What is creative movement?
2. What is a care provider's goal in encouraging children's physical development?
3. List three physical activities for older adults.

Mini-Lab

Using index cards, create a resource file of creative movement activities. First, think of images children or older adults can act out through creative movement. Include simple ideas, such as popcorn popping or tree limbs blowing in the wind. Then write down one idea per card. Maintain the activity resource file for use when you work with young children or older adults.

Section 27-2

Active Play & Recreation

Boundless energy and enthusiasm are hallmarks of childhood. Children are fueled by the excitement of discovering how fast they can run and how far they can jump. Older adults also enjoy fun, physical activities. Effective care providers plan and conduct appropriate and enjoyable physical activities for all generations.

OBJECTIVES

- Explain how active play benefits all areas of development.
- Plan active play learning centers (both indoor and outdoor) for pre-school children.
- List several ways of ensuring children's safety during active play.
- Identify some creative resources for active play.
- Plan and lead active play activities.

KEY TERMS

active play
maze
recreational therapy

Benefits of Active Play

Activities that engage children in fun physical participation are referred to as **active play**. Including active play in the daily curriculum promotes children's overall health and well-being. Active play helps children maintain energy and stamina needed for learning. Regular physical activity has long-lasting benefits. It helps develop the immune system so the body can fight off diseases. Physical activity strengthens the heart and lungs. It also helps control weight. Establishing good exercise habits during early childhood increases the chances that children will maintain a healthy lifestyle. Here are other ways active play promotes children's development:

- **Physical development.** Children's small and large muscles in the arms and legs become stronger during active play. They improve small and large motor coordination and perceptual motor skills.

- **Intellectual development.** Active play often means playing games that have rules. Remembering and following rules require thinking. Many games put language skills to use as children sing chants and talk to each other. Games that require strategy and purposeful action develop children's problem-solving and goal-setting skills.

- **Emotional development.** As children master physical skills, self-esteem and self-confidence grow. Active play offers them a constructive outlet for excess energy, which relieves stress.

FIG. 27-6. **Using outdoor play equipment allows children to test and strengthen their muscles.** What requirements does the Americans with Disabilities Act have for outdoor play yards?

Indoor Active Play. Some programs have a separate room for indoor active play, often large enough to allow for riding toys. This area may include small-scale climbers with mats placed underneath for safety in case of falls. Programs without separate indoor facilities depend on clever care providers who can conduct active play experiences in limited space. By moving classroom furniture to room edges, space can be made for active play. Using soft, flexible, active play props—such as sponge toys—prevents damage to classroom materials.

Guidelines for Safe Play

Chapter 12 discussed ways to design safe play environments for children. Those safety considerations are especially important for active play areas. Whether indoors or outdoors, children need plenty of open space to move freely with appropriate adult-to-child ratios. Play areas should also be free of items that could hurt children. Make daily checks for such dangers as broken glass, splintered climbing equipment, and tacks on the floor.

Care providers need to help children follow rules that help prevent accidents and injuries. State rules simply and clearly in positive terms. Focus on what children can do. Always keep a close eye on children during active play and remind them of rules when needed. Here are sample safety rules for active play equipment:

- **Climber rules.** Only one person may be on each part of the climber at a time. Play on the climber only when it is dry. Hold on with both hands when climbing.

- **Swing rules.** Only one person may use a swing at a time. Hold on with both hands

- **Social development.** When children play games, they learn to work well with others and to abide by the rules. By playing team games, children develop a sense of unity and belonging. They learn to cooperate with others to achieve common goals. Older children who play team sports learn positive character traits, such as fairness and teamwork.

Outdoor Active Play. As was discussed in Chapter 12, having separate, fenced play areas for infants and toddlers, preschoolers, and school-age children is best. Play yards should have plenty of climbing equipment scaled appropriately to children. Equipment and supplies should be versatile. Except for swings and slides, equipment should accommodate more than one child at a time. This gives more play opportunities for everyone. Teeter-totters, merry-go-rounds, swinging exercise rings, and high slides have been associated with many injuries to preschoolers. These and other similar items should not be included in the play yard. There should always be adequate staff to supervise outdoor play. See Fig. 27-6.

FIG. 27-7. **Teaching children to play safely on outdoor structures helps prevent accidents and injuries.** Give an example of three rules for using outdoor play equipment.

perceptual motor skills, and large motor skills. Scarves, streamers, and crepe paper strips encourage running and creative movement. Pinwheels and kites add variety to active play. Wheel toys—such as tricycles, scooters, and two-seater riding toys—build strong leg muscles. Games like hopscotch, rim ball (a basketball hoop placed low for preschoolers), and bowling with plastic balls and pins also help develop large motor and perceptual motor skills. Balance beams and hoops help develop balance and coordination.

while swinging. Sit in the middle of the swing with knees bent and feet down. Only an adult may push a child in a swing. Stop the swing before getting off. Stay away from the swing area when other children are swinging.

- **Slide rules.** Only one person may slide at a time. Hold onto the sides with both hands until ready to slide. Check that no one is at the bottom of the slide before going down. Slide in a sitting position with feet first. Move away from the bottom of the slide when you reach the ground. See Fig. 27-7.

Active Play Materials

The best active play materials are safe and encourage children to develop a whole range of physical skills. They should be fun to play with and allow children to experience success alone or while playing in a group.

Many toys and games meet these criteria. Rubber balls, beach balls, sponge balls, or beanbags all help refine eye-hand coordination,

Active Play Activities

Playing the same games repeatedly is not fun for children. They like new experiences. Start with simple activities and then gradually include more challenging ones as skills develop. Here are suggestions for active play activities:

Parachute Play. With parachute play, a group of children use a large circle of nylon fabric for active play. The parachute is between six and twelve feet in diameter. Some have handles. Parachute play is good for developing muscles in the arms and shoulders. See the feature on page 621 for more information on intergenerational parachute play. Parachute activities include:

- **Bounce the balls.** Have the children firmly grip the parachute edges and pull it tight. Toss sponge balls in the middle of the parachute. Have the children make the balls jump.
- **Catch.** With children holding the parachute on all sides, ask them to reach as high as possible toward the sky. Call out the name of a child, who runs under the parachute from

one side to the other. As the child crosses, the other children pull the parachute toward the ground, trying to catch the child under it. Repeat until all children have had a turn.

Beanbag Play. Beanbags are inexpensive play materials that can be used in many ways, indoors and out. Some simple games that use beanbags include:

- **Target toss.** Children toss beanbags into empty coffee cans, laundry baskets, plastic buckets, or plastic dishpans.

- **Moving target.** Using a sturdy rope, suspend a tire from a tree limb. Push the tire gently. Children try to toss the beanbag through the hole of the moving tire.

Balance Beam Play. A balance beam should be no higher than four inches off the ground. See Fig. 27-8.

- **Reverse walk.** Have children first walk forward, then backward, then sideways along the beam.

- **Two-level walk.** Have children walk with one foot on the beam and one foot on the ground.

Balloon Play. Balloons are another inexpensive choice for active play. They are best suited for indoor play. (Remember to blow up balloons yourself and throw away any broken pieces. Choking is always a possibility when playing with balloons.) Games using balloons include:

- **Balloon volleyball.** Stretch a string across the room. Divide children into two teams. Have them bat balloons to each other over the string.

- **Balloon table tennis.** Children can bat balloons to each other using nylon paddles. To make the paddle, bend a wire clothes hanger to form a circle. Straighten the hooked end to form a handle, taking care not to leave any sharp edges. Pull a nylon stocking tightly over the wire circle to create a paddle, allowing some of the stocking to come down onto

FIG. 27-8. Walking on the balance beam helps children develop balance and coordination. Balloon games are a good choice for developing perceptual motor skills. What other skills might a child gain from using the balance beam or playing balloon games?

the handle. With duct tape, attach the nylon to the handle and then wrap the handle completely with the tape.

Rope Play. Jumping rope is a longtime favorite activity, especially for school-age children. Ropes, however, also have other uses in active play. These include:

- **Long jump.** Lay two ropes parallel and close to each other. Allow children to jump over the ropes. Gradually make a larger space between the ropes. Challenge children to see how far they can jump.

- **Follow the wavy line.** Attach long pieces of rope together. Lay the rope throughout an area in a wavy design. Challenge children to follow the wave in different ways. Can they slither along the wave? Slide? Walk backwards?

Hoop Play. Large plastic hoops can be used as originally intended, which is to swivel the hips and abdomen to keep the hoop revolving around the waist. Also use hoops for:

- **Hoop hop.** Place six to ten hoops on the floor or playground. Children must hop from one hoop to the next. See Fig. 27-9.

- **Hoop walk.** Provide each child with a hoop. Call out directions for them to follow. For example, "Walk or skip around your hoop." "Hop on one foot in and out of your hoop."

Obstacle Courses and Mazes. During the following activities, children learn to problem solve and carefully control all body parts.

- **Obstacle course.** Arrange items so children can crawl under tables, creep through tunnels, step in and out of tires, and hop over teacher-built block walls.

- **Maze it.** Draw a large **maze**—a deliberately confusing series of pathways—on a concrete area, using chalk. Mark a beginning and an end to the maze. Children then walk, skip, and hop through the maze or, if there is enough space, drive through it on riding toys. For added fun, make the maze as challenging as space allows by including twists, turns, and dead ends.

Games. Games offer mental as well as physical exercise. These games are especially good for developing eye-hand coordination and perceptual motor skills:

- **Simon says.** Challenge children with directions that focus on parts of the body and positions. For example, "Put your hand beside your ear." "Put your elbow on your knee."

FIG. 27-9. Large plastic hoops can be used for any number of active play games. What motor skills will children develop by playing with hoops?

FIG. 27-10. Games, such as the "Mirror Game," help children develop perceptual motor skills. What activities might help children develop eye-hand coordination?

Active Water Play. Children enjoy water play during very warm weather. They can keep cool while having fun.

- **Water tag.** Provide plastic squirt and spray bottles, so children can spray each other.

- **Car wash.** Set up a car wash for riding toys by providing a hose, soap, sponges, and rags.

Active Snow Play. In cold climates, winter snow does not have to spell the end of outdoor active play. In fact, it can provide opportunities for new experiences. See Fig. 27-11. As with water play, make sure children are properly dressed.

- **Snow people and animals.** Children can express their creativity, learn about shape and size, practice memory skills, and strengthen muscles by building snow people and animals.

- **Treasure hunt.** Have children make tracks in newly fallen snow. Give them each a treasure to hide at the end of their tracks. Let children track down each other's treasures.

- **Mirror game.** Two children face each other. Choose one child as the leader, or the person who will move first. The other child tries to copy the exact movements of the leader. Have the children take turns being the leader. See Fig. 27-10.

- **Color touch.** Form groups of four to six children. Then direct children to touch someone wearing red. While still touching that person, they must touch someone wearing blue. Children may touch with hands, fingers, feet, knees, and head. Continue with as many colors and positions as possible.

- **Freeze tag or statue tag.** This is similar to regular tag, except that when touched by the person who is "it," children must freeze their body position (or turn into a statue). The game continues until all children are frozen, or until the care provider asks another child to be "it."

FIG. 27-11. Snow offers children many fun outdoor play experiences. What safety factors should care providers think about when children play in snow?

Active Play Safety. School-age children need active play opportunities that challenge their advanced physical development and skills. Children love group games and sports. However, some aggressive contact sports, such as rugby, boxing, and football, are not recommended for school-age children in a child care setting. These sports can cause serious injuries that interrupt normal bone and muscle development. Offer alternative activities, such as skating, T-ball or softball, soccer, volleyball, badminton, or basketball.

Activities for Older Adults

Regular recreational and fitness activities can provide important health benefits, even if people begin these activities later in life. Experts on aging agree that older adults need to be more physically active. To encourage this, care providers must consider age and skill level when planning activities. They should also consider the following:

- Changes in older adults that result in vision, hearing, balance, coordination, and muscle deficiencies.
- Chronic conditions and how they affect the ability of older adults to exercise safely.
- Psychological and emotional factors and how they can impact an older adult's ability to perform activities.
- Medical and physical restrictions, such as cardiovascular or mobility problems.

Activity Level. Care providers must determine the activity level when planning recreational and fitness activities. They need to know how much an older adult can endure when engaging in physical activities. Care providers should make certain that each older adult engages in activities at his or her own level. They should encourage older adults to stop exercising when they feel tired, short-winded, or are perspiring excessively. These factors may indicate a medical problem. A good knowledge of normal behavior, such as the breathing pattern of the older adults in your care, will be helpful during observation.

Recreational activities and fitness are important because they help older adults maintain good health while having fun. Many recreational activities can be integrated into a regular fitness plan. Older adults enjoy a variety of activities that may include fishing, camping, shuffleboard, yard darts, or table tennis along with walking, water aerobics, or dancing. When planning appropriate recreational and fitness activities for older adults, care providers should consider the following:

Fitness Programs for Older Adults. Family members must evaluate recreational and fitness programs carefully before enrolling older adult loved ones. Here are some warning signs about programs that may not be a good fit for older adults:

- Fitness programs that do not meet the individual needs of older adults.
- An environment that does not support or believe in older adult recreation.
- Inappropriate standard exercise classes that do not meet the needs of older adults.
- Programs that do not consider special needs of older adults with disabilities.

- **Length of activity.** Keep attention span in mind when designing activities. If an activity is enjoyable, older adults are more likely to continue participating.

- **Engagement in activity.** People engage in activities that they enjoy. Talk with older adults to find out the types of activities that appeal to them.

- **Benefits.** Older adults want to know that the activities are beneficial to them. Take the time to explain how the activity will help them and let participation be an option for them.

- **Modification of activities.** Recreational fitness activities should be inclusive, allowing people with special needs to participate. Make sure you have a way to modify the activity.

Recreational Therapy. Recreational therapy activities can help restore health and mobility. In **recreational therapy**, a therapist helps older adults with illnesses or disabilities maintain their physical, mental, and emotional health and well-being. The therapist uses many types of large and small motor activities. These activities might include sports, games, dance and movement, drama, and brief outdoor pleasure trips. For those older adults who experience depression, anxiety, stress, or limited mobility, recreational therapy can help restore motor functions and cognitive skills. Positive experiences in recreational therapy can lead to increased self-esteem, self-confidence, and independence. See Fig. 27-12.

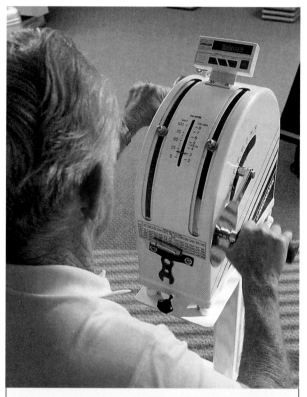

FIG. 27-12. **Physical fitness and recreational activities help older adults maintain health and wellness.**

General recreation and fitness activities that are usually performed for enjoyment should not be confused with recreational therapy. Professionals—such as physicians, occupational therapists, and psychologists—work closely with recreational therapists to meet the rehabilitation needs of older adults.

Section **27-2** Knowledge Check

1. What is active play?
2. How does active play promote children's development?
3. Give examples of recreational activities for older adults.

Mini-Lab

With a partner, list ten toys or games for active play that are popular with young children. (Look through store catalogs or newspaper advertisements for ideas.) Describe how—or whether—these items promote physical, intellectual, emotional, and social development.

Section 27-3

Self-Expression Through Drama

OBJECTIVES

- Explain how dramatic play encourages growth and how care providers encourage it.
- Plan a dramatic play learning center and dramatic play activities for preschoolers.
- Choose items for a prop box.
- Explain how to make and use puppets and how children benefit from play with puppets.
- Describe intergenerational dramatic storytelling and guidelines for its implementation.
- Identify creative self-expression activities for older adults.

KEY TERMS

dramatic play
spontaneous
   dramatic play
props
prop box

Children's ability to engage in make-believe is one of their most endearing qualities. This play does more than keep children pleasantly entertained. Through make-believe play, they learn to express their thoughts, ideas, and feelings. Those abilities will be used throughout life. This section will introduce you to ways to encourage dramatic play and ways that older adults can be involved in drama with children.

Types of Dramatic Play

When children create realistic or fantasy situations and act them out it is known as **dramatic play**. In dramatic play, children often imitate adults and act out situations they observe or imagine. They may even take on the role of inanimate objects or animals. Dramatic play allows children to safely explore what they are too young to experience in real life.

As part of dramatic play, children role play, or assume the identity of someone else. They "become" fascinating characters, such as parents, community helpers, and cartoon heroes. (Remember that to preschoolers, cartoon heroes can be as real as parents.) This most often occurs as **spontaneous dramatic play**, meaning that children engage in dramatic play without the suggestion or direction of adults.

Dramatic play can take place anywhere. Children may prepare and serve "dinner" in the housekeeping center or build a train and take a "vacation" in the block center. Sandboxes, water tables, and outside playgrounds are other common sites for dramatic play.

Benefits of Dramatic Play

Like real-life experiences, dramatic play helps children develop skills in all areas.

- **Physical.** When children button dress-up clothes, they develop small motor skills. Pretending to be jungle animals hunting food uses large muscles, too. See Fig. 27-13.

- **Intellectual.** Children use language skills to suggest and plan their dramatic play scenes. They develop problem-solving skills and imagination—especially symbolic thought—as they try to create plots. They use memory as they reenact events they witnessed or experienced.

- **Emotional.** During dramatic play, children can confront and try to understand their feelings and fears. Dramatic play allows children to try out different emotions, which is a good rehearsal for dealing with them later. They also learn about empathy for other people.

- **Social.** In dramatic play, children work together to create and carry out a story. They follow each other's lead as the play progresses, and sometimes compromise to work out small problems. They assume social and employment roles by pretending to be sister and brother or doctor and patient. They learn to appreciate the clothes and customs of other cultures.

Care Providers' Involvement

Because dramatic play involves plenty of action, care providers must allow ample time for it in the daily schedule. Children need at least a 45-minute block of time to decide on a theme and their roles, put on costumes, enact the scene, and then put away the equipment and materials.

Children like to have care providers join in their play; however, the care providers should follow the children's lead and resist taking over. Participation allows care providers to model appropriate play skills for children who have trouble cooperating with others. They can help children join dramatic play by suggesting roles they can play.

By observing dramatic play, care providers gain understanding of children's physical development, thinking abilities, and personal interests. Children reveal themselves through dramatic play. Care provider observations can be used for planning curriculum. Here are things care providers look for during dramatic play:

- Does the child participate regularly and easily in dramatic play? Are there recurrent themes?

- How does the child solve conflicts in dramatic play? Can the child be a leader and a follower? Does the child accept the ideas of others?

- Does the child use verbal and nonverbal communication skills effectively?

- What attitude does the child display? How does this compare with the child's usual attitude?

FIG. 27-13. **With dramatic play, children can practice dealing with emotions and developing their imaginations.** What other benefits can children gain from dramatic play?

- Do other children choose this child as a play-mate? Does the child play with peers or adults?
- How involved does the child become in the play's plot?
- Are there behaviors that cause concern for the child's physical or emotional well-being?

Dramatic Play Learning Center

Although drama happens everywhere, the dramatic play learning center is designed with specific furnishings. Dolls and stuffed animals quickly become characters in whatever drama is taking place. See Fig. 27-14.

What you see going on in this center one day may not be the same on another. Skilled care providers set the stage for play by creating different themes throughout the year. For example, the center could be equipped as a post office, campsite, florist shop, jewelry store, a home, or supermarket. By regularly rotating play themes, care providers encourage creativity.

FIG. 27-14. The dramatic play learning center should capture the imagination of children. As a care provider, what items would you include in the dramatic play learning center?

Dramatic Play Prop Boxes

Care providers create collections of **props**, or items that suggest themes for dramatic play. Children use props to add realism, detail, and interest to pretend play. For example, how might you emphasize that firefighters need oxygen to stay alive when working in smoke? One way is to provide face masks (from discarded scuba diving gear) and make-believe air tanks (oatmeal boxes covered with aluminum foil and strapped on with elastic). Children quickly see that these are important safety items for firefighters.

A **prop box** is a container for storing items used in a specific theme. Using prop boxes to follow up a story or help children explore a particular concept is a way to encourage dramatic play. After reading a book about astronauts, a care provider might put helmets (made from cardboard boxes) and other space-related items in a prop box. Using props, children develop a deeper understanding of the information in the story. See Fig. 27-15.

Care providers create community helper prop boxes so that children learn about jobs in society. These boxes might focus on helpers, such as medical professionals, police officers, judges, or veterinarians.

When creating prop boxes, make sure the contents are safe, clean, and durable. Items should be easy to use and familiar to the children. Choose real props, rather than toy ones. Secondhand stores and garage sales are possible sources for props. Put duplicate props in each box. This encourages cooperative play.

Puppetry. Preschool children love using puppets, with or without a puppet stage. They can use puppets to act out nursery rhymes and folktales. They also enjoy using puppets to act out the lyrics of songs during music time or in making conversation with another child. Playing with puppets develops skills such as:

- **Physical.** Children use both the large muscles in the arm and the small muscles in the fingers when playing with puppets. They also practice eye-hand coordination.

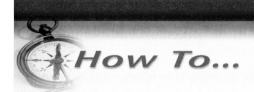

How To...

Make Homemade Puppets

Puppets come in all shapes and sizes. All should be well made and colorful, with no detachable or sharp parts that might cause choking or injury. Children like to make puppets themselves. Popular, easily made puppets include:

- **Stick Puppets.** Use a craft stick with a cutout character glued to the stick. Children can hold and move the stick to act out a story.

- **Sack Puppets.** A small, brown paper sack works well for this puppet. The flap is decorated with paper, fabric, ribbons, and other trims to make the character.

- **Glove Puppets.** Using a garden glove or child's knit glove, attach a face to each fingertip or make a face on the back of the hand while the fingers become the legs or hair.

- **Sock Puppets.** These are made with a sock and decorated with buttons, felt, yarn, moveable eyes, and other craft items. (Make sure children are old enough to use small objects without danger of choking.)

- **Hand Puppets.** Made from a simple pattern and fabric, these puppets can be sewn by hand or machine or glued with fabric glue. Attach a face directly to the puppet.

- **Finger Puppets.** Small pieces of felt or construction paper, folded to slip over a finger, are colored and decorated.

- **Puppet-in-a-Cup.** Stick puppets are used with a decorated paper cup. The sticks are pushed through the bottom of an inverted cup and moved up and down as needed during the story. The cup becomes the puppet stage.

APPLY IT!

Using a common children's story, create puppet characters using one or more of the methods described above.

- **Intellectual.** Puppets encourage children to listen, talk, and share. Children try to give their puppets personality, calling for imagination and creativity.

- **Emotional.** Children can express their feelings through puppets. Negative emotions, especially, are more easily shown through the safety and security of a puppet's character.

- **Social.** Puppets encourage cooperation and teamwork. The use of puppets may help shy children gain confidence in talking to others. Puppet play allows children to act out acceptable and unacceptable behavior.

FIG. 27-15. **With a sense of realism and some hands-on materials, children can create their own actions and words to tell a story.**

Intergenerational Dramatic Storytelling

Intergenerational dramatic storytelling is a way of sharing information in an imaginary form among people of different ages. Above all, dramatic storytelling is enjoyable.

Telling stories gives children and older adults a chance to creatively and dramatically express themselves by acting out specific roles. Dramatic storytelling is used to enhance self-worth, stimulate memory, and create peer support for older adults. To plan and implement intergenerational dramatic storytelling activities, use the following guidelines:

- Ask questions that are open-ended. See Fig. 27-16.

- Prepare children for story and drama interactions by asking them age-appropriate questions before they interact with older adults. Encourage the children to ask each other questions, too.

- Teach children how to ask questions of and listen respectfully to older adults.

- Ask the children to maintain eye contact with the older adults during the storytelling process.

Starting Stories. When grouping children and older adults for dramatic storytelling, care providers may need to ask questions to trigger the story content. Answering questions about who, what, where, when and why offers a foundation to forming stories. Here are some ways to get stories started:

- **Sharing favorite photographs.** Children and older adults can talk about their favorite pictures. They can tell stories about when a photograph was taken and the type of occasion at which it was taken.

- **Talking about families.** Have children and older adults talk about their families. How many brothers and sisters do they have? What are their favorite family activities?

- **Sharing favorite celebrations.** Ask children and older adults to talk about a favorite birthday or any other special day.

- **Talking about childhood experiences.** When older adults share their childhood experiences with young children, it offers common ground for storytelling and conversation.

FIG. 27-16. Using drama and storytelling is one way for older adults to connect with young children. How might care providers encourage children to participate in the dramas with older adults?

Intergenerational Drama & Play

Care providers can be helpful in involving children and older adults in drama and play activities. Both generations gain psychological and health benefits from these activities that promote relaxation and reduce stress. They also help maintain cognitive and physical skills. Care providers need to effectively plan and implement these activities to:

- Let imagination guide the activities. Using props in novel ways helps foster creativity.

- Encourage older adults to regain a playful childlike attitude as they become children's play partners.

- Choose games and toys that children and older adults will find fun, yet challenging.

- Promote props that are safe and suitable to the abilities of children and older adults.

- Let children show the older adults how to use props. Children delight in teaching what they know. See Fig. 27-17.

- Encourage children and older adults to just have fun.

- Encourage older adults to let children develop their own skills and solve their own problems. Taking charge and doing things for children can slow development and take the fun out of playing together.

Creative Expression for Older Adults

Older adults can benefit greatly by participating in creative expression activities that stimulate their cognitive and motor skills. Some creative activities include:

- **Charades.** The charades players must "act out" a phrase without speaking, while the other players of the team try to guess what the phrase is. This activity stimulates thinking skills.

- **Trivia games.** Questions on topics, such as early television, slang, and old product advertisements, serve to encourage reminiscing and promote entertaining discussion.

- **Personality game.** Identify famous individuals from the past. Players can act out a person's identity and others guess the name of the person. Each name or identity has two or three clues.

FIG. 27-17. **Older adults with a playful attitude can have fun learning new things from children.** What types of games and activities might children teach to older adults?

Section 27-3 Knowledge Check

1. Define dramatic play.
2. List three benefits of dramatic play.
3. Why is creative expression important for older adults? Give an example of creative expression.

Mini-Lab

Observe a variety of people on the job. List examples of simple, safe tools of the trade for each job you observe. Which tools could be used as props in a dramatic play center or dramatic storytelling? Prepare lists of the props that go with each of several careers.

Chapter **27**
Review & Activities

Section Summaries

27-1 Development and skills begin in childhood and progress gradually.

27-1 Creative movement encourages active participation.

27-2 Active play stimulates overall development and contributes to children's health and well-being.

27-2 Resources provided for active play should develop a wide range of physical skills.

27-2 Children who learn to appreciate physical activity at an early age are more likely to carry that interest into adulthood.

27-3 Dramatic play helps children experience and practice different roles.

27-3 Dramatic play learning centers and prop boxes use themes to stimulate pretend play.

27-3 Puppet play can contribute to all areas of development.

27-3 Children and older adults benefit from intergenerational dramatic storytelling.

27-3 Creative activities for older adults stimulate cognitive and motor skills.

Check Your Knowledge

1. What are the elements of creative movement?
2. Name one way active play benefits each area of development: physical, intellectual, emotional, and social.
3. What types of equipment should not be provided in an outdoor play area?
4. Identify guidelines for a safe active play area.
5. Explain how dramatic play can contribute to growth in any three areas of development.
6. Contrast dramatic play and spontaneous dramatic play.
7. List five things a teacher might look for when observing children in dramatic play.
8. What are the benefits of using puppets with children?
9. How can care providers help initiate dramatic storytelling?
10. What are three suggestions for implementing intergenerational drama and play activities?

Thinking Critically

1. Contrast ways physical skills develop through movement activities for children and older adults. How are they similar and different?
2. Why is safety an important concern when planning movement activities for young children or older adults?

Practical Applications

1. **Movement Activity.** Analyze a movement activity for young children or older adults. What skills does the activity develop?

2. **News Article.** Read an article describing safety issues related to children's play areas or older adults' living areas. Write a summary of the key points in the article.

3. **Observation.** Observe an early childhood teacher guiding a dramatic play activity. Write a summary of your observations. How did the teacher introduce the activity? What props were provided? How did the children respond? To what extent was the teacher involved? How successful was the activity?

4. **Investigating Storytelling.** Investigate the history behind effective storytelling. Why is dramatic storytelling important? Share your findings with the class.

Building Your PORTFOLIO

Movement & Drama for Young & Old

Understanding the benefits of movement and drama activities for young children and older adults will enhance your skills as a caregiver.

Step 1: Select a movement activity for young children or older adults. With the program director's approval, use the activity with an appropriate group of young children or older adults. Write a description of the activity and the results to include in your portfolio.

Step 2: Develop a safety checklist for use in inspecting children's play areas or one for inspecting older adults' living areas for hazards that might cause falls. Use the checklist to inspect an appropriate area. Revise the checklist, if needed. In your portfolio, include a copy of the checklist and a summary of your findings after using it.

Step 3: Select a theme appropriate for a dramatic play learning center for young children. Collect the props needed for the center. Place the items collected in a dramatic play learning center. Observe a group of young children as they play in the center. Write a report summarizing your observations. Include a description of the dramatic play learning center you created and your observation report in your portfolio.

Section 28-1

Developing Artistic Expression

OBJECTIVES

- List the goals of an art curriculum.
- Describe the stages of children's artistic development.
- Plan an art learning center for preschoolers.
- Explain appropriate methods for guiding children's art experiences.
- Plan and lead art activities for children.

KEY TERMS

proportion
process versus
   product
three-dimensional
collage

Art is the use of skills and imagination to produce something that expresses thoughts, ideas, or emotions. Art provides children with many opportunities for growth in all developmental areas. This chapter will explain how care providers help that growth occur.

Art Curriculum Goals

At first glance, a toddler's scribbles and a preschooler's drawings seem unimportant. With a closer look, you will notice that much learning is taking place during art. Well-planned art activities develop:

- **Physical skills.** Children practice eye-hand coordination and small motor skills through coloring, cutting, and pasting.
- **Language skills.** As children participate in art and explain their ideas to others, they build their vocabulary skills. Children also learn to observe and listen to others' ideas.
- **Thinking skills.** Creating art requires children to make decisions about their projects. They use creativity, imagination, and thinking skills as they work with art materials.

- **Emotional skills.** Increased self-esteem and confidence result when children succeed at creating their own projects.
- **Social skills.** Art activities often are cooperative efforts. Children work together and see how each child's contribution adds to the final product. This builds respect for others' ideas.
- **Appreciation of diversity.** Cultural art activities allow children to discover the use of art in cultural traditions and events. These activities explore art techniques and help children value the creativity of all people. See Fig. 28-1.
- **Basic concepts.** Art experiences give children a hands-on method of learning about color, shape, size, and other basic concepts. Skills from many curriculum areas are used in art. For example, mixing paint for different colors is science in action.

FIG. 28-1. Multicultural art activities help give children an appreciation for art around the world. Investigate some ways in which art techniques and styles are used in other cultures.

Stages of Children's Art

Children go through predictable stages in learning to create art. Remember that children go through these stages at individual rates and ages. Physical maturation and how often art activities occur impact how children work through the stages. See Fig. 28-2.

Scribble and Mark-Making (Ages One to Three). Children gain control of shoulder muscles before the wrist and finger muscles. Therefore, early drawings tend to sprawl in wide loops over a piece of paper. During this stage, children first use many different types of scribbles. They progress from scribbling to patterns, such as zigzags or spirals.

Symbolic and Design (Ages Three to Five). At this stage, there is very deliberate placement of lines and geometric shapes. Children frequently repeat shapes. At this stage, specific marks begin to represent real objects to children. However, the object may not be recogniz-

able to others. One shape may represent many things. For instance, a circle might represent a whole body before children learn how to draw body parts.

Representational (Ages Four to Seven). Drawings and symbols are more accurate and recognizable to others at this stage. Children give greater attention to detail. For instance, eyelashes and earrings may begin to appear on drawings of people.

Realistic (Ages Five to Ten). Children make increasingly complex designs. They are concerned about making people and objects look real. Children's drawings reflect features of people and differences in gender and skin tone. They also more accurately use perspective and **proportion**, or the size relationship of the parts.

The Art Center

A well-stocked art learning center is important. This invites children to select art activities on their own according to their interests and abilities. Provide many different materials, occasionally substituting new ones. Store materials on shelves with labels.

The best location for the center is in an uncarpeted area. Having a sink nearby is very helpful for cleanup. Shelves, tables and chairs, easels, and drying racks should be easy to clean. Refer to Chapters 12 and 13 for more information. See Fig. 28-3.

Remember to be cautious with art materials since some are hazardous. Substances, such as spray paints and liquid dyes, can trigger allergic reactions or asthma attacks. Make sure art supplies, especially safety scissors, are in good repair. Supervise activities continuously when using objects small enough to put in the nose, ears, or mouth. Other safety tips include:

- Buy premixed clays that are talc-free.

- Buy water-based, nontoxic glues, pastes, markers, and paints.

FIG. 28-2. Children go through predictable stages as they develop their art skills. What are the differences between the art of a three-year-old and the art of a five-year-old?

- Do not let children use paints or markers on their skin. Wash promptly after activities.

- Make sure the art center has good ventilation. Use a fan to circulate air, if needed.

- Use a vacuum or a wet mop to clean up dusty debris. Sweeping stirs up dust.

FIG. 28-3. A safe, well-equipped art center allows children to creatively explore art. What are some important safety tips for the art center?

Guiding Art Experiences

Children enjoy working on their own in the art center. They also enjoy art activities that are care provider led. Use the following principles:

Value the Process. Children learn through the process of creating art. In fact, what they learn is more important than the art product they create. This teaching principle is referred to as **process versus product**. When the emphasis is on the process, art experiences are less apt to aim for a specific result—allowing children to make decisions about their projects.

Encourage Creativity. Activities that require children to assemble products that look exactly like the care provider's leave no room for creativity. Open-ended art activities encourage creativity and imagination.

Respond Sensitively. When children proudly show you pictures or paintings, it is tempting to ask, "What is it?" This question can disappoint children who think, "Can't you tell?" An encouraging response is, "You've been working hard. Please tell me about your picture." This recognizes children's efforts and encourages language, confidence, and self-esteem.

Accept and Appreciate Children's Art. It is important to view art with an eye of objectivity. During childhood, it is inappropriate to grade children's art or to label it as bad. These practices lower self-esteem and can stifle interest and creativity.

Respect Children's Art. As children learn to draw, their pictures are not usually accurate. With years of experience, accuracy improves. In the meantime, care providers should not redraw, or complete children's creations. Working on projects for children only sends the message that they cannot do it right. Self-esteem suffers in these instances. Help children take pride in their accomplishments.

Display Children's Art. Displaying children's art increases their self-esteem. When displaying art, write the artist's name in an upper corner, using capital and small letters. Whenever possible, hang the art at children's eye level. Rotate items often to show appreciation for every child's effort. Return art to the artists to display at home. See Fig. 28-4.

FIG. 28-4. **Creatively displaying children's art at eye level gives a boost to children's self-esteem. Providing children with large sheets of plain paper allows them to draw and color their own creations.** Why is this developmentally appropriate?

How To...

Plan Art for School-Age Children

School-age children enjoy more challenging art activities. They are ready to use smaller brushes, ⅛- to ¼-inch wide, for easel painting. They can use clay or dough to make more intricate projects, such as necklaces or flower vases. Weaving, sewing, woodworking, and assembling model kits are all creative crafts school-age children enjoy. They maintain interest and are developmentally appropriate. They might try these projects:

- **Mobiles.** These are a collection of items or pictures suspended on wire by string. Once all items are attached to the mobiles, they are hung from the ceiling. Children might make mobiles of paper songbirds to hang in the science center.

- **Origami (OR-uh-GAH-mee).** A Japanese art form in which squares of tissue paper are folded into representational forms, such as birds, is called origami.

- **Dioramas (DY-uh-RA-muhs).** These are three-dimensional pictures made with small, cutout designs. Making a large, detailed diorama can be a group effort.

APPLY IT!

Plan an art project for school-age children. Choose one or more of the projects above and gather the needed materials. Work with a group of school-age children to complete the project. Write an evaluation of this experience.

Art Activities

Many art activities can be available daily for children to use in the art center. Drawing and easel painting materials, for example, may always be available. Provide other materials, such as sponge painting tools, occasionally. Some activities require more supervision than others which impacts how and when they occur. Try the following art activities.

Drawing & Coloring

Provide paper of different sizes, shapes, and colors on which children can draw and color. Supply plenty of crayons, chalk, colored pencils, and markers, including duplicates of each color.

Avoid using coloring books with children. Experts believe that overexposure to coloring books can limit creativity.

Children practice decision making as they plan how to use the space on the paper. They also become more aware of specific object characteristics, such as flower petals.

Art Safety. Even young toddlers can participate in art. They enjoy finger painting. Because they still like to put things in their mouths, use homemade, edible finger paint. Try instant pudding (mixed with water) and partially set flavored gelatin. The same mixtures can be thinned to use as easel paint.

Painting

With limited vocabularies, children may be able to "speak" or express emotion through their artwork. Through painting, they learn to blend primary colors into secondary colors. The art center should include:

- **Paint.** Water-based tempera paint is inexpensive, washable, and nontoxic. It comes in ready-to-use and powdered forms. To help prevent spills, pour only small amounts of the paint into individual containers. For younger children, offer only two colors at a time. Be sure to label and store paint in sealed containers out of children's reach.

- **Easels.** These slanted boards hold paper for painting at children's height. Use easels that allow two to four children to paint at once.

- **Paper.** Newsprint, the paper used for newspapers, is good for easel painting. For variety, use old sheets of wallpaper or poster board.

- **Painting tools.** For easel painting, use long-handled brushes ½- to 1-inch wide. Younger children may need wider brushes. Place one brush in each paint container and remind children to put each brush back in its own container. Experiment with using other items as painting tools, such as feathers and cotton swabs. After painting, have children help wash the painting tools. See Fig. 28-5.

- **Cover-Ups.** Plastic aprons and old shirts can be used to keep children's clothes clean during painting.

- **Drying area.** Do not leave paintings on an easel to dry. Instead, use a drying rack, clothesline, or a spare table on which to dry paintings.

Finger Painting

The sensory experience of finger painting can be very soothing to children. At first, some children may be hesitant to try finger painting. Encourage them to watch others or to begin by painting with just one finger.

Finger-paint paper is slick and glossy. You can buy ready-to-use finger paint or make your own from recipes in art resource books. Create finger-paint substitutes by adding food coloring to cold cream, hand lotion, shaving cream, or mild liquid soap.

FIG. 28-5. Provide enough nontoxic painting materials to allow children to be creative without conflicts.

Modeling & Shaping

Playing with dough or clay is relaxing. Using dough or clay, children can create objects that are **three-dimensional**, having height, width, and depth. Doughs, which are softer and easier to handle than clays, can be made from flour or cornstarch, salt, and water. See Fig. 28-6.

As they mold and shape the dough or clay, children practice small motor skills and eye-hand coordination. Include many objects and utensils for cutting and shaping the dough.

Cutting & Tearing

Cutting activities develop small motor skills and eye-hand coordination. Toddlers can develop these skills by simply tearing pieces of paper. For cutting activities, provide safety scissors for children. Right- and left-handed scissors should be available. Magazines and flower catalogs are colorful favorites to cut and tear.

Pasting, Gluing & Attaching

Children like to attach objects to each other. They may use glue, tape, staples, paper clips, string, or hook-and-loop tape to attach objects to paper. Supervise these activities carefully.

Children can practice cutting, pasting, and making decisions by creating a collage. A **collage** (kuh-LAHZH) is a picture or design made

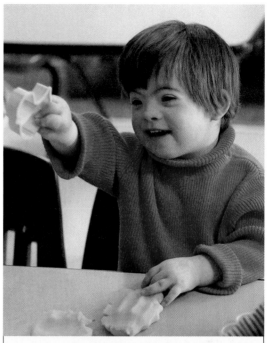

FIG. 28-6. **Homemade doughs are soft and easy for children to manipulate.** Investigate various types of clays and doughs to use in the early childhood classroom.

by gluing or pasting many different materials to a backing. Many materials work well in collages, such as pictures, paper, fabric scraps, colorful string, or different types of seeds. Varying the sizes, shapes, colors, and textures of materials enchances this sensory experience. Label and store items for collages in separate containers in the art center for easy access.

Section **28-1**   Knowledge Check

1. What is art for young children?
2. What safety considerations should care providers be aware of when planning art activities?
3. How can toddlers participate in art experiences?

Mini-Lab

Demonstrate how to make homemade dough. Compare the cost of making it to that of purchased modeling compound.

Section 28-2

Developing Musical Expression

OBJECTIVES

- Identify the benefits of music to children.
- Plan a music learning center for preschoolers.
- Explain the care provider's role in music.
- Describe how basic skills and concepts are reinforced through music activities.
- Plan and lead music activities.

KEY TERMS

lyrics
tempo
pitch
melody
rhythm instruments
call-and-response
  songs

Music can be a source of pleasure for everyone, not just the musically talented. Those who acquire an appreciation of music from an early age enjoy it throughout life. As adults they may create music, dance to it, or simply listen to it. Music, in all its forms, adds quality to life.

Music Curriculum Goals

Musical enjoyment and expression begin early. Infants eagerly respond to music during basic routines. Care providers can sing to infants as they rock them to sleep.

As children grow in early childhood, their musical interest expands further. They learn to produce and order sounds and tones with their voices and musical instruments. During music activities, they learn to recognize and enjoy all kinds of music styles and compositions. They also learn to recognize a variety of musical instruments and the sounds they make. Music activities benefit development in many areas.

Physical Development. As children move rhythmically to music, they develop their large muscles and refine their motor coordination skills. Hopping, wiggling, swaying, bouncing, or twirling to music are acceptable ways to release energy. To play basic instruments, such as drums or tambourines, children use small motor skills and eye-hand coordination.

Intellectual Development. Language skills develop as children sing. Memory develops as they learn **lyrics**—words to songs—and follow directions to musical games. Vocabularies grow and concepts become clearer as children sing songs about shape, color, and size. Listening skills develop, too. Children have to listen carefully to the sounds, words, and music before they can respond appropriately. Attention span lengthens and concentration improves. In addition, children learn about music itself. They

FIG. 28-7. **Working with different musical tempos can encourage thinking skills.** In what other ways can music help promote intellectual skills in children?

identify **tempo**, the speed at which a song is sung, as well as beat, the recurring pulse that gives a song rhythm. To sing tunefully, children must be able to recognize **pitch**, the highness or lowness of musical sounds, and to listen for **melody**, the tune of a song. Putting all of these together to make music causes children to use reasoning skills. As musical skills improve so do thinking skills. See Fig. 28-7.

Emotional Development. Through music, children express and cope with their emotions. Music can calm frustration and provide an outlet for anger. Children gain self-confidence with success in musical activities. Sharing songs from family backgrounds affirms cultural heritage.

Social Development. During music activities, children learn to obey rules and share materials. Playing instruments in harmony requires cooperation and taking turns. Group singing promotes feelings of togetherness that help friendships develop. Folk songs from all cultures pass on important social values, such as friendliness, cooperation, honesty, and caring for family.

The Music Center

A music center is a classroom area set aside just for music experiences. It should be available to children during choice time. There they can explore the sounds that instruments make and listen to recorded music. In addition, care providers conduct small-group activities in the music center and use materials from the center for large-group activities.

Recordings and a machine on which to play them are basic to the music center. A well-stocked center has recordings, ranging from relaxing melodies to fast-paced music for active play. Suitable music should be available for group singing, musical games, dancing, and other movement activities. Be sure to include folk music of many cultures.

Children understand beat and tempo before they master following a melody or singing on pitch. Therefore, the music center should have child-size versions of **rhythm instruments**, musical instruments that allow children to experiment with making their own rhythms. Maracas and drums are two simple rhythm instruments that children can master. See Fig. 28-8.

Most programs also have musical instruments for care providers to use as they lead activities. These might include a piano or guitar.

FIG. 28-8. **Rhythm instruments are part of every culture.** What are three different lessons you could teach using authentic cultural instruments?

Guiding Music Experiences

Children enjoy singing and playing simple instruments, as well as moving and dancing to music. They find it especially enjoyable when their care providers play along.

Many care providers are not musically inclined. This does not have to limit their students' musical experiences. Most songs can be sung without instrumental accompaniment. Children's records are also helpful to care providers who do not play an instrument.

When guiding music experiences, be sure to follow many of the same principles for guiding art. Consider the children's process of making music more important than their final performance. Encourage children to explore and experiment.

As children participate, care providers encourage creativity and reinforce independence as they allow children to express themselves uniquely. Sensitive care providers refrain from passing judgment. They avoid pressuring children to perform alone in front of others.

Some children take longer than others to feel at ease in group music activities. Asking parents what music the children listen to at home and then using that music in activities is helpful. Planning individual and small-group activities also helps children feel more at ease. Some children feel more secure and confident when they have an instrument to play; they focus on the instrument instead of themselves.

Music Activities

Singing is not the only way for children to enjoy music. Music can also be related to other curriculum areas. For instance, prop boxes for dramatic play can have a musical theme, such as a ballet dancer or orchestra conductor. Field trips—such as visits to a high school band rehearsal, radio station, or dance studio—allow children to see community music in action. Care providers may invite special visitors to the classroom, such as a piano tuner. They may also have musicians perform for children. Other music experiences include:

- **Exploring familiar sounds.** Before learning specifics about music, children need to learn about sounds in general. Then children can enjoy creating new sounds through music. See Fig. 28-9.

- **Going on listening walks.** What nature sounds can children identify? Are there birds, frogs, or crickets? What city sounds do they hear? How does a train's whistle differ from a truck's horn? Listen for quiet sounds, harsh sounds, pretty sounds, and scary sounds. Can children guess how these sounds are made?

- **Exploring sounds in daily life.** Clock buzzers wake them up or alarms warn of fire and storms. What other sounds can children remember hearing?

- **Exploring the sounds of the human body.** Children should experiment making sounds with their own bodies. They can slap, clap, snap, hum, or stamp to a tune.

Boosting **Brain Power**

Music Builds Math Skills. **If provided with a solid foundation of music experiences in early childhood, school-age children are ready for formal instruction. This is typically provided through schools or private teachers. Brain research has shown that children who begin to play a musical instrument by age 10, especially the piano or violin, also develop better math skills. School performance will be supported if school-age children are allowed to practice their musical instrument at the child care center after school.**

FIG. 28-9. **Leading children in singing activities helps children learn how sounds are made and how to match pitch.** What are some other benefits of singing?

- **Identifying the uses of music.** Music is used on car radios, in places of worship, in elevators, in baby nurseries, on television programs, and in movies. Can children guess why music is used in these ways?

- **Singing with children.** The human voice is the finest musical instrument of all. Young children love to sing and make up their own songs. They sing as they bathe, dress, eat, and play. The ability to sing in tune develops slowly. Children have limited singing range that gradually expands as they grow older. They learn to sing by imitating others.

- **Singing in groups.** When choosing songs for group singing, consider developmental level and interests. Select a simple melody within voice range. Make sure songs have an identifiable beat or rhythm. Children enjoy songs that have an interesting story to tell. Look for songs with verses that repeat and have understandable vocabulary. **Call-and-response songs**, in which an adult sings questions and children sing back the answers, are popular. Children also enjoy using hand or body motions with songs.

- **Moving to music.** Action songs, those for which children act out the motions in the lyrics, require children to use their minds and their bodies. In the song "Grey Squirrel," for example, children sing about a squirrel collecting acorns for the winter. The song lyrics give children cues on how to imitate the squirrel's actions. Pairing music with action helps increase attention span and helps children learn more quickly. Musical games also promote active involvement. Such songs as

"London Bridge" and "Hokey Pokey" allow children to explore body movements. Use short games with very simple rules. Small groups are easier to manage and motivate than larger ones.

Playing Instruments. Children love to play simple rhythm instruments, such as triangles and wood blocks. These materials may be purchased or can be made inexpensively. See Fig. 28-10. Many multicultural rhythm instruments are available. They can be exciting additions to music centers. Introduce instruments a few at a time. Demonstrate how to use each instrument appropriately so it does not break. Show children where and how to store instruments. Set basic rules for playing with instruments to avoid misuse. See Fig. 28-11. Here are some ways to include musical instruments:

- Use instruments in a marching parade.

- Give children instruments to use as sound effects during stories. Before the story begins, identify when each child should play an instrument. Give cues as needed.

- Behind a screen, play an instrument familiar to the children. Have them guess what it is.

- Play a tune on an instrument. Have the children guess the song.

FIG. 28-10.

RECYCLED RHYTHM: HOMEMADE RHYTHM INSTRUMENTS

Instrument	Materials	Procedure
Shakers and Rattles	Plastic eggs, salt and pepper shakers, or 35 mm film canisters; buttons, raw rice, or dried beans.	Fill containers with varying amounts of buttons, rice, or beans; secure lids or seams with tape.
Sandpaper Blocks	Two wooden blocks, about 3 by 5 by 2 inches; two 3- by 5-inch rectangles of coarse sandpaper.	Glue sandpaper onto blocks; replace sandpaper as needed.
Drum	Cylinder-shaped snack container, oatmeal canister, or coffee can with snug-fitting plastic lid; strip of nylon or other sturdy fabric.	Attach fabric strip to can; sling over shoulder to carry drum on opposite hip and play it with both hands.
Tambourine	Embroidery hoop, paper plate, or aluminum pie tin; small bells; string or pipe cleaners.	Attach bells to hoop, plate, or pie tin with string or pipe cleaners.
Cymbals	Two aluminum pie tins; two empty thread spools.	Glue spools to center of insides of pie tins; use spools as handles.

ETHICS IN Action

Including Everyone's Music. Imagine that music from your culture was never recognized or sung on the radio. How would you feel? Would you feel ignored? Would you come to believe your cultural music wasn't as good as others? Now imagine you are an early childhood care provider with Latino or Asian children in your early childhood class. *How might such children feel if their cultural music was not reflected in your classroom? What steps could you take to make sure their culture was included in classroom music activities?*

• Create a pattern of beats with a drum. Have the children repeat your pattern, using their own instruments. Vary the beat to add challenge. Let children take turns playing patterns for others to follow.

• Experiment with tempo and volume by asking children to follow your lead. Can they play loud, soft, slow, and fast?

• Ask one child to hide in the room and play an instrument quietly. Have the other children find their playmate by following the sound.

FIG. 28-11. **Teaching children appropriate use of instruments helps ensure that instruments are not misused.** Why should children be exposed to a variety of musical instruments?

Music Throughout the Day. Care providers find ways to incorporate music into classroom routines. Greeting and farewell activities are good times to include music. Songs may be used as a calming transition from outside play. At nap time, children are eased into sleep with lullabies and other soft music. Appreciation for music of all kinds grows when teachers include many types of music. Playing light classical music during nap time can help children appreciate its soothing qualities. Listening to calypso music during lunch encourages children to associate it with friendship and informality.

Section **28-2**   Knowledge Check

1. When does musical enjoyment and expression begin?
2. What should be included in a music center?
3. List the guidelines for teaching songs to children.

Mini-Lab

Work in groups to make rhythm instruments. Find and perform a song using these instruments.

Section **28-3**

Art for Older Adults

Art can play an important role in helping people age with dignity. Creativity and expression through art helps to maintain health and well-being throughout all stages of life. Art is a creative medium that can encourage cognitive stimulation and active engagement in life for older adults. This section describes some ways older adults can participate in art activities to help them maintain their quality of life.

Art for Older Adults

As a branch of learning, art requires the conscious use of skill and imagination to create objects of beauty for people to purely enjoy. As people age, art appreciation and participating in art activities may become more important. It can bring communities together and provide older adults with a positive and healthy feeling about the aging process. Older adults who are involved in art activities often experience a sense of freedom and independence. Care providers can collaborate with art museums and other community art groups to plan art programs. Some activities include acrylic painting, watercolor painting, pottery, and other art forms.

The Older Americans Act recognizes and supports art therapy. **Art therapy** is a human service profession that uses art media and the creative art process as helpful tools in treating people who experience developmental, medical, social, or psychological concerns. **Art therapists** are professionals trained in the field of art therapy at the master's degree level following the requirements established by the American Art Therapy Association. They often work as part of a team of professionals including physicians, psychologists, social workers, or teachers.

Art Therapy & Aging

Art therapy produces successful results with people of all ages. As older adults participate in art therapy, the creative art process helps them express their thoughts and emotions in a non-verbal way. For those who experience low self-esteem and lack of control over their lives, art therapy can help restore mental health and enhance self-esteem. It can also give older adults a sense of accomplishment and may increase independence. See Fig. 28-12.

The goal of art therapy is to help older adults increase communication with others and increase feelings of self-confidence. As confidence builds, many older adults are better able to responsibly carry out activities of daily living. Since the needs of participants vary, art therapy activities are geared toward those needs. Some benefits of art therapy include:

- A change in how much control older adults feel they have over their lives. Art therapy helps them to feel more in control and better able to make decisions.

- A change in identity from aging adult to creative artist that includes using skills in problem solving and imagination.

- Increased socialization and communication.

- Improved small motor functions and eye-hand coordination.

- An emotional outlet, providing an acceptable alternative for unacceptable behavior.

The role of art therapists is to establish a safe environment for older adults to be creative. They help older adults appreciate their work. Older adults come to understand that there is not a right or a wrong way to do art and that experimenting is good. Art therapists encourage independence by noting and reinforcing older adults' creative choices.

Health Benefits of Art

Various forms of art are used in health care. Participating in different types of art programs can be soothing to the body, mind, and soul. For example, painting can be relaxing to the mind. Simple hand weaving can help older adults with stiff finger joints increase dexterity, while giving them a sense of accomplishment with their finished work. Most older adults can benefit from art in some way. See Fig. 28-13.

FIG. 28-12. **Art therapy gives older adults a creative outlet and a way to express themselves visually.** How does art therapy benefit the self-esteem of older adults?

Art Activities for Older Adults

Older adults have more leisure time and want to feel needed. Many older adults enjoy volunteering in local community organizations, such as child care centers and public libraries, because they enjoy working and feeling needed.

Reading and art activities, such as those in summer library programs and community centers, work well. These organizations often design intergenerational art activities. Successful programs include older adults in planning the art-related activities. Some art activities that older adults enjoy include:

- Making dough beads to paint and string.

- Painting ceramics. Some may also build and paint clay pots.

- Making jewelry that may include working with metals and other materials to create earrings, bracelets, and other jewelry.

FIG. 28-13.

ART BENEFITS FOR OLDER ADULTS

Benefits of Art Activities	Involvement of Older Adults
Helps to understand and define aging.	Uses a method to explore a "conversation" about what it means to grow old through writing, holding forums, painting pictures, acting in the theater, and dancing.
Offers opportunities for self-expression during loss.	It fills the space of voids and uncertainty. Many older adults face frequent loss in their lives—jobs, health, spouses, friends, leadership positions, or income.
Provides ample opportunities for lifelong learning and service to others.	Older adults have increased leisure time with their unprecedented longer lives. Volunteerism enriches the quality of life for older adults.
Offers contributions and resources to people.	Older adults are creators, mentors, teachers, tutors, and advisors, sharing the wisdom that they have gained through a lifetime of experience. As role models, they show people how to age creatively by sharing their unique perspectives on life and teach others what it is like to grow old.

Adapted from the National Endowment for the Arts, *The Arts and Older Americans—Arts Participation: The Greying of America.*

- Creating shadow boxes that include collections of family materials or other meaningful memorabilia.
- Making sewing cards from collections of old greeting cards. The cards can be sewn together to create table runners or placemats.
- Puppet making for grandchildren and other young children.
- Making gift baskets lined with colorful fabrics and stuffed with special treats, such as cookies and candies.
- Creating a nuts-and-bolts collage.
- Making dollhouse furniture.
- Creating homemade jigsaw puzzles.
- Making bird houses out of old dollhouses.

Intergenerational Art Activities

Intergenerational art programs are important to connecting generations and cultures. By building relationships through the creative arts, children and older adults can celebrate culture and build community. These shared experiences give them chances to practice teamwork and new skills and gain respect for one another.

Care providers can plan intergenerational art activities that will be enjoyable for children and older adults. Adult mentors can guide young people in art activities. Care providers can identify older adults who are retired artists and have them teach art classes. These individuals can coach both children and other older adults in carrying out art projects.

Creating an Intergenerational Art Program. Intergenerational art programs can be very successful when all people involved help plan, create, and manage the activities. Members of the planning team include administrators, care providers, artists, older adults and their families, and parents of young children. Each team member takes responsibility for a different job. Some members might conduct fundraising activities. Others might recruit artists from the community to teach classes. Another team member might create the schedule and send out information flyers that advertise the program. See Fig. 28-14.

Age-Awareness Training. Age-awareness training for children, older adults, and professional volunteer artists is also essential. Age-awareness training helps undo misunderstandings and stereotypes many people hold about older adults. For example, some people think that all older adults are senile or a burden on society. Age-awareness training positively influences the way people interact with older adults, eliminating poor relationships.

FIG. 28-14. **Working together on visual arts is just one way children and older adults can celebrate diversity and help rebuild communities. What are some other benefits of intergenerational arts programs?**

Section **28-3** Knowledge Check

1. What is art therapy?
2. List three art activities for older adults.
3. Who is involved in planning an art program?

Mini-Lab

Create three appropriate art activities for an intergenerational art program. List needed materials for the activities and who will lead the activities—an older adult, a guest artist, or a care provider. Conduct your activity at a local care center, if possible.

Section **28-4**

Music for Older Adults

Whether through listening or performing, music provides a creative outlet for many people. It also can help people feel better physically and emotionally.

Music for Older Adults

Music that is purely for social and personal enjoyment is called **recreational music**. It offers sensory stimulation and social experiences. During planned music activities, older adults might sing, dance, and reminisce about their favorite music from years passed. In planning activities, care providers should work closely with older adults and their families to offer meaningful music activities.

Music Therapy & Aging

In contrast to recreational music, **music therapy** uses music to help meet the physical, psychological, cognitive, and social functioning of older adults. For example, music therapy may be used with older adults who struggle with physical disabilities, dementia, depression, severe pain, high blood pressure, or social isolation. The goal of music therapy is to use musical experiences to create positive changes in human behavior. Music therapy is nonthreatening and can be used successfully with people in all stages of development.

Certified music therapists plan music therapy activities for individuals or groups of people. They assess the needs of older adults, design music sessions according to those needs, and participate in the activities. Music therapy in group sessions provides older adults with social interaction. These activities may include:

- Listening to music and discussing feelings and memories brought about by the music.
- Writing songs to encourage emotional expression.
- Performing instrumental and vocal music.

FIG. 28-15. **Music therapists help encourage emotional well-being in older adults.** What are some other benefits of music therapy?

Participating in music activities increases older adults' self-esteem and positive thinking. Like art, music helps older adults maintain their quality of life. See Fig. 28-15.

The Benefits of Music

Most people enjoy music, and it has many benefits. Care providers who plan and conduct age-appropriate and culturally sensitive music activities do much for the self-esteem and attitudes of older adults. See Fig. 28-16. Here are some additional benefits of music activities:

- Better quality of life.
- Increased independence.
- Reduced depression and stress.
- Cognitive and sensory stimulation.
- Increased physical exercise.
- Opportunities to share musical interests with younger generations.
- Relaxation.
- Increased social interaction.
- Opportunity to explore personal feelings.
- Improved attitude.
- Increased problem-solving skills.

Intergenerational Music Activities

Music is often the most effective bridge between generations. Even older adults with limited memory respond to the music that was popular when they were younger.

A person who is a trained musician or someone with an interest in music can conduct music activities. A person that provides music activities does not need to be formally trained in

FIG. 28-16. **Along with providing relaxation for older adults, music can be used to provide sensory stimulation.** How can music be used to strengthen non-music skills?

Intergenerational *Interactions*

Intergenerational Music

Music stirs emotions and memories among people of all ages. That's one reason intergenerational music programs are so successful. Programs can be as simple as mingling preschoolers with older adults to sing holiday carols at an assisted living facility, or as complex as the following orchestras.

- **New Jersey Intergenerational Orchestra (NJIO).** Since 1993, NJIO has been joining generations around music. Currently, 140 members, ranging in age from 4 to 88, are placed within three divisions according to experience. The Nouveau Group is open to people just learning an instrument. Those with some training make up the Full Orchestra, and the Chamber Group includes musicians with advanced skills. NJIO has performed at many famous places, including Lincoln Center, the steps of the United States Capitol, the Sam Rayburn Building, and more.

- **Encore Community Music Association (ECMA).** This nonprofit organization brings people ages 8 to 70 together in an effort to create beautiful music and lasting experiences. ECMA, which performs a variety of music from classical to pop, currently includes a string orchestra, symphonic band, and symphony orchestra.

- **Lawrence Philharmonic.** Created in 1994, the Lawrence Philharmonic is supported by the Lawrence Public Schools in New York.

The group includes musicians ranging in age from 13 to 80, and plays a variety of music, from classical to contemporary. The Lawrence Philharmonic strives to build relationships among musicians of all ages.

- **Ridgewood Symphony Orchestra (RSO).** RSO is an intergenerational orchestra that welcomes talented musicians ranging from high school students to older adults. The group allows students to learn from more experienced musicians while preparing for ongoing education and/or careers in music. Over the last several years, RSO has proudly awarded thousands of dollars in scholarship money to its high school members in northern New Jersey.

Follow-Up

Write a report on how your community could benefit from an intergenerational music program.

music. Care providers can lead songs and conduct music games without knowing how to sing or play an instrument. Some intergenerational music activities that older adults enjoy include:

- **Sing-alongs.** Instead of performing for older adults, teach young people old songs they can sing with older adults. Ask young people to share their favorite songs, too. Older adults enjoy hearing what young people enjoy, including rock-and-roll and rap music. Be sure to consider the age and cultural background of the participants. Try to include songs from the past or from different cultures.

- **Musical events.** Children and older adults could attend an opera or symphony performance at a local theater. Outdoor concerts are also enjoyable.

- **Playing instruments.** Many older adults and children know how to play instruments, and they enjoy teaching their skills to others. Provide instruments for participants to use. If possible, recruit musicians to teach music classes to adults and children.

- **Musical studio.** Care providers can encourage music activities by designing a musical studio. A musical studio is usually placed in an open area that is used for music, dance, and drama activities. A musical studio allows older adults and children to come together

FIG. 28-17. Dancing to a variety of musical forms helps children and older adults appreciate diversity. How might a child dance with an older adult in a wheelchair?

to engage in creative expression of ideas, thoughts, and feelings related to music. Stock the musical studio with a stereo, musical recordings, and instruments.

- **Dancing to music.** Older adults may teach young children dance steps to music from their "era." Dancing is not only a fun music activity, but it is also a good form of exercise for young and old alike. See Fig. 28-17.

Section *28-4* Knowledge Check

1. What is music therapy?
2. List three benefits of music activities.
3. List five music activities.

Mini-Lab

Assume that you are the director of an intergenerational day center. Design an intergenerational musical studio. Include in your description the size of the studio, the materials used, and the types of activities offered. Be sure to include any modifications for older adults and children with special needs.

Chapter **28**
Review & Activities

Section Summaries

28-1 Through art, children learn to express feelings and ideas, practice skills, develop self-esteem, and develop creativity.

28-1 Art activities should be appropriate to children's age and level of development.

28-1 Artistic ability develops in stages.

28-1 Stock the art center with a variety of art materials that give children choices.

28-1 Common art activities include coloring, painting, finger painting, modeling with dough or clay, cutting, pasting, and making collages.

28-2 Music activities benefit children's overall development.

28-2 Music activities include listening to sounds, singing, playing musical instruments, and moving to music.

28-2 Children can make music and also learn to move creatively to it.

28-3 Art therapy uses art to help people understand themselves, while making positive changes in their behavior.

28-3 The goal of art therapy is to help people feel good about themselves, help them communicate with others, and help them take charge of their lives responsibly.

28-3 Intergenerational art activities allow young and old to participate together in art activities.

28-4 Music has many benefits, including lowered blood pressure, increased self-esteem, and reduced anxiety and depression.

28-4 Music therapy addresses the physical, psychological, cognitive, and social functioning of older adults.

Check Your Knowledge

1. List four goals of the art curriculum.
2. Identify and describe the three stages of artistic development. Include the general age range for each stage.
3. Describe an art learning center.
4. Give three safety suggestions for preschool art activities.
5. How does music benefit children?
6. Suggest two strategies for involving hesitant children in music activities.
7. List the benefits of art therapy.
8. What are the physical benefits of art activities?
9. What is a major benefit of intergenerational art programs?
10. Give four examples of art activities for older adults.

Chapter **28** Review & Activities

Thinking Critically

1. How might a child's or an older adult's development be affected if art or music were not included in center activities?
2. What effect could a care provider's negative comments regarding a child's artwork have on the child?
3. Draw conclusions about why you think art and music are therapeutic for older adults.

Practical Applications

1. **Analyzing Artwork.** Collect artwork from children of different ages. Analyze the artwork to determine each child's stage of artistic development. Compare your analyses with those of classmates. Do you agree on the stage of artistic development represented by each piece of artwork?

2. **Multicultural Music.** Survey participants at a local child development center or adult day center to find the names of popular songs from other cultures. Research the songs to find the lyrics. Ask a parent or older adult to translate the songs into English. Compile your song lyrics and make them available to care providers during music activities.

3. **Activity Guidelines.** Observe a care provider conducting an intergenerational art or music activity. Based on your observations, create a list of guidelines for leading an intergenerational art or music activity.

4. **Planning Activities.** Using print or Internet resources, plan and implement music activities with children and older adults. Evaluate the success of your experience.

Building Your PORTFOLIO

Art & Music Activities

Planning and leading art and music activities are among the most rewarding responsibilities of child and adult care providers. Both children and older adults enjoy these activities. Use your understanding of human development and your creativity in these areas to enhance your skills as a care provider.

Step 1: Plan and carry out an art activity with a group of young children, a group of older adults, or an intergenerational group. In your portfolio, include your activity plan and a summary of the results, along with changes you would make if you did the activity again.

Step 2: Plan and carry out a music activity with a group of young children, a group of older adults, or an intergenerational group. In your portfolio, include your activity plan and a summary of the results, along with changes you would make if you did the activity again.

Step 3: Using supply catalogs, select items to include in a music or art center for young children or older adults. Set a realistic budget for the center and then select items that fit the budget. (A program director can help you establish a realistic budget.) Design an appealing music or art center. Include your plan for the music or art center in your portfolio.

Glossary

A

accessible—Easily used by those with disabilities. (22-2)

accommodation—Children change their thinking about concepts to make better sense of information. (19-1)

accommodations—Classroom changes made to more fully meet the special needs of some children. (22-1)

accreditation criteria—A list of desirable features related to a high-quality early childhood program. (12-1; 14-1)

action plan—A plan that provides written feedback, summary of personal comments, and documents solutions. (11-3)

active listening—Paying attention to and interacting with the speaker. (4-1)

active play—Fun physical activities in which children participate. (27-2)

activity plan—A plan for care providers and older adults that includes objectives, content, teaching strategies, outcomes, and evaluation methods. (24-4)

adult protective service agencies—Agencies that receive and investigate reports on suspected abuse and neglect of adults. (8-2)

advanced directive—A document that states how an individual wants his or her medical decisions handled if he or she becomes unable to make those decisions. (17-2)

advisory board—A group of people that give directors recommendations on decisions to be made. (14-2)

advocacy—The process of pleading a cause to influence change for the best interest of others. (5-3)

advocates—People who inform legislators (or policymakers) of their clients' needs. (5-3)

agitated—The feeling of being uptight, disturbed, or nervous. (7-2)

amino acids—The building blocks of protein. (10-1)

anecdotal record—A written description that focuses on a specific incident. (7-1)

anemia—A condition in which there are not enough red blood cells in the body to carry the appropriate amount of oxygen. (10-2)

antioxidants—Substances that inhibit oxidation. (10-2)

anxiety—Extreme or unrealistic worry about something for a prolonged time. (23-2)

aphasia—A language impairment the affects a child's (or adult's) use of speech and understanding of language. (22-1)

art therapist—A professional trained in the field of art therapy at the master's degree level. (28-3)

art therapy—A profession that uses art media and the creative art process to treat people who experience developmental, psychological, medical, or social concerns. (28-3)

assessment—A tool that measures a person's ability to function and helps to identify needed help and services. (23-2)

assimilation—Children take in new information and try to make it fit with what they already know and understand. (19-1)

assistive technology—Equipment and services that allow older adults with limitations to independently manage their lives. (25-4)

at-risk—Environments that interfere with proper development and well-being of children. (1-2)

attachment behavior—A sign of bonding, or a strong preference for one person. (18-1)

attention deficit hyperactivity disorder—A disorder of the central nervous system that is caused by lack of certain brain chemicals. Characteristics include being aggressive, impulsive, or having difficulty paying attention. (22-1)

auditory discrimination—Hearing similarities and differences in sounds and words. (25-1)

au pair—A person coming from another country to live with a family and take care of the children. (14-1)

autism—A brain disorder that impacts normal development, communication, and social interaction. (22-1)

automated external defibrillation (AED)—An electrical shock that reestablishes normal heart rhythm. (6-3)

autonomy—A sense of independence. (19-1)

B

baby boomers—People born between 1946 and 1964 following World War II. (2-1)

bilingual—Able to speak more than one language. (20-1)

biohazardous—Potentially hazardous materials when in contact with bodily fluids. (6-1)

birding—Bird watching. (26-3)

Bloom's taxonomy—A system of ranking educational objectives from very basic thinking skills to very complex. (24-2)

board (board of directors)—A group designated to make decisions about a program or company. Board members are not employees. (14-2)

body language—A form of nonverbal communication that does not use words but communicates through what a person sees when he speaks or listens to you. (4-1)

burnout—Physical or mental exhaustion due to long periods of stress and frustration. (3-2)

C

caesarean birth—Birth by surgical delivery. (1-2)

call-and-response songs—Songs in which an adult sings questions and children sing back the answers. (28-2)

cardiopulmonary resuscitation—A life-saving technique used when the heartbeat has stopped. (6-2)

care provider report form—A form used to organize and record the routine care provided to children. (18-2)

centration—Children's ability to focus on one characteristic at a time. (20-1)

checklist—Specific information that can be checked off indicating completion. (7-1)

child abuse—An intentional injury afflicted on a child. (8-1)

Child Development Associate (CDA)—A nationally recognized credential program for early childhood professionals. (3-1)

child neglect—The failure to provide a child with basic life necessities, including food, clothing, shelter, and medical care. (8-1)

chronic—Conditions that have no cure. (23-1)

close-ended materials—Items used in primarily one way with an expected result. (24-1)

cognitive—Intellectual development. (1-1)

cognitive ability—Thinking that includes memory, learning, reasoning, and problem solving. (23-2)

collage—A picture made by gluing many different pieces of materials to a backing. (28-1)

collective bargaining—The process of workers and employees agreeing to working conditions, contracts, and other job benefits. (4-3)

commercial exploitation—Overly influenced by commercial advertisements. (26-4)

communication barriers—Obstacles that prevent people from sending or receiving information. (5-1)

community service directory—A reference guide for making referrals or obtaining information related to programs. (17-1)

compassion—The ability to respond sensitively to others' feelings and experiences. (11-1)

compensatory time—Extra pay or time off for hourly employees who work overtime. (4-3)

complete protein—Protein that contains all essential amino acids. (10-1)

con artists— People who are able to manipulate situations and other people to benefit themselves. (8-2)

concrete operations—Piaget's developmental stage during which children ages seven to 11 learn to think logically. (21-1)

conferences—Large gatherings at which members of a specific profession exchange information, attend workshops, or network within their field. (5-2)

confidentiality—The practice that the privacy of others must always be maintained. (5-2)

conflict-management plan—A plan that involves the use of problem solving to identify needs and goals. (11-3)

congregate meals—A nutritionally based program allowing people to eat together in a central place. (10-2)

consequences—Events that occur as a result of choices—good or bad, positive or negative. (11-2)

conservation—Understanding that an object's physical weight and properties remain the same even when its appearance changes. (20-1)

constituents—The residents of electoral districts. (5-3)

consumable supplies—Items that are used up. (13-2)

consumer-directed care—Care in which older adults have an opportunity to make choices based on their likes and dislikes. (23-2)

continuing education—Updating career knowledge and acquiring of new job skills. (5-2)

continuity theory—Holds that older adults continue to build on their lifetime of likes, dislikes, experiences, and preferences. (23-2)

cool down moment—A short period of time in which the child must sit apart from the other children and/or activities. (11-2)

cooperative learning—A child's ability to investigate a specific topic of interest with other children. (20-2)

cooperative play—Children playing together and agreeing on play activities and themes. (20-1)

creative movement—Responding to music or a mental image with physical motion. (27-1)

crisis nursery—A 24-hour service for parents who feel at risk to abuse their child. (8-1)

cross-training—Training about the needs and development of children and older adults. (16-2)

curriculum—Experiences and activities that support and guide children's learning. (24-2)

D

daily care plan—A written description of the person and his or her daily needs. (17-3)

daily money manager—A person who offers financial services for people who cannot manage their financial matters. (26-4)

deficiency—A lack (in this case, in one or more nutrients which can cause additional medical issues). (10-1)

dehydrated—Abnormal loss of water or fluids. (12-2)

depression—Feelings of sadness, hopelessness, helplessness, and worthlessness over a period of time. (23-2)

depth perception—The ability to judge distance and see objects in perspective. (21-1)

developmentally appropriate—Fitting the age of a child or person. (13-1)

developmentally appropriate curriculum—Activities geared to the specific abilities and levels of development in a group of children. (24-2)

discretionary income—The money left after paying for basic needs. (2-2)

discrimination—Unfair treatment based on age, gender, race, ethnicity, religion, physical appearance, disability, or other factors. (4-3)

disparities—Inconsistencies (in this case, related to health care). (6-2)

diversity—The qualities that people have that make them different from one another. (21-1)

documenting—Providing a written record of activities or information (in this case, related to child abuse or neglect). (8-1)

dramatic play—Realistic or fantasy situations that children act out. (27-3)

durable power of attorney—A document giving one or more persons authority to handle financial matters and decisions if a dependent person becomes unable to do so. (17-2)

dyscalcula—A math-skills disorder in which children may be unable to count objects or recognize basic shapes. (22-1)

dyslexia—A reading disorder in which a child (or adult) may have trouble recognizing alphabet letters or difficulty reading. (22-1)

E

early intervention programs—Programs for special needs children under age three that are usually sponsored by public schools. (22-2)

egocentric—Children's way of thinking about the world only from their own point of view. (18-1; 21-1)

elder—One of the oldest persons in a family who is respected for his or her wisdom. (2-1)

elder abuse—Any act that harms the health of an older adult. (8-2)

Elderly Nutrition Program (ENP)—Workers help older adults improve their diets and lifestyle choices, along with daily physical exercise. (10-2)

emergent literacy—Literacy skills that develop over time. (25-1)

empathy—Putting yourself in another's place and attempting to understand his or her feelings. (4-3; 11-1)

engagement—The extent to which an older person is involved and active with others and with activities in the environment. (23-2)

entrepreneur—A person who owns and operates a business. (3-1)

ethics—Internal guidelines for distinguishing right from wrong. (4-3)

eye-hand coordination—The ability to move the hands and fingers precisely in relation to what is seen. (18-1)

F

facilitate—To help or bring about learning without controlling it. (24-1)

facilitation—An indirect form of instruction that allows learners to discover new knowledge through questioning and hands-on experience. (24-4)

fall zones—Zones designated to keep children from walking into unsafe areas, or safety factors that will eliminate injuries. (12-2)

family care management—The process through which family members and service providers work together to manage the care of a dependent family member. (17-3)

family care manager—A person who best understands the wants and needs of the dependent family member and speaks on his or her behalf. (2-2; 17-3)

fee-agreement contracts—Written agreements related to child care facilities and what they provide and cost. (17-2)

fiber—A plant material that doesn't break down when the body digests food. (10-1)

field guide—A book for identifying natural items, such as flowers, insects, trees, and birds. (26-3)

fight talk—A defensive way of talking. (11-3)

financial abuse—Taking unfair advantage of someone in regard to money or possessions. (8-2)

financial management—Managing income and expenses in a working program. (14-2)

finger plays—Hand motions added to songs. (25-1)

flexibility—The ability to adapt willingly to changing circumstances. (4-1)

Food Guide Pyramid—A guide to daily food choices based on the recommendations of nutrition experts. (10-1)

foodservice sanitation certificate—A state document indicating that proper foodservice practices are being followed. (6-3)

formal support—Paying care providers to care for and support older adults. (23-2)

for-profit—Programs that are designed to bring in more income than they cost. (14-1)

fraud—Intentional misrepresentation for financial gain. (8-2)

frequency count—A record of how many times a particular behavior or situation occurs during a specific period of time. (7-1)

frostbite—The freezing of body tissue, usually in feet, hands, face, and ears. (6-1)

functional ability—The ability of older adults to take care of themselves and manage their environments. (23-1)

functional furniture—Furniture that is practical, durable, and easy to care for. (12-1)

functionally dependent—Relying on others for help with basic activities. (23-1)

G

geriatrician—Provides care specifically for older adults. (6-2)

geriatrics—A field of medicine that focuses on preventing or managing common diseases for older adults. (2-1; 15-1)

gerontology—The study of the aging process. (2-1; 15-1)

governing board—Has the ability to tell directors what actions to take; serves as the decision-making power. (14-2)

grief—Extreme sadness related to a loss. (23-2)

growth plateau—Slow and steady growth for younger school-age children. (21-1)

H

health department inspector—A person who evaluates the health practices of a program. This will include food service areas. (10-1)

heat exhaustion—Caused by the loss of fluid and salt through profuse sweating; can result in dizziness and fatigue. (6-1)

Heimlich maneuver—A technique for dislodging an object or food from the throat. (6-3)

heredity—Qualities and traits passed from parents to children through their genes at conception. (1-1)

hormones—Chemical substances carried in the blood that impact growth and development. (21-1)

hospice—A facility or program with staff members who are trained to provide a caring environment that meets the needs of the terminally ill. (2-2)

household automation—Technology that controls functions in a home. (25-4)

hypothermia—Body temperature reaching dangerously low numbers. (6-1)

I

I-messages—Spoken words that do not attack the character of the person they are directed to—instead, the behavior is addressed. (11-2)

immunizations—Vaccines that protect people from certain diseases. (6-1)

inclusion—A federal law that states children with disabilities must be educated whenever possible with children who are not disabled. (22-2)

incomplete protein—Protein that doesn't contain all of the essential amino acids. (10-1)

Individualized Education Plan (IEP)—A written document that outlines how to encourage the development of a child with special needs. (22-2)

Individualized Family Service Plan (IFSP)—A plan that sets goals to meet the overall special needs of a child, including assessment, goals for development, and ways to promote family support and involvement. (22-2)

industry—The desire to perform skills, succeed at tasks, and make social contributions. (21-1)

inferiority—A feeling of not having met expected standards. (21-1)

informal support—Nonpaid care that includes helping provide for social and emotional needs, as well as assisting with ADLs and IADLs. (23-2)

instrumental activities of daily living (IADL)—Includes six home management activities relating to activities of daily living. (9-2)

intergenerational coordinator—A trained staff person who plans and implements activities for children and older adults collectively. (16-2)

intergenerational programs—Those programs that involve two or more generations, such as older adults and children. (3-2)

intergenerational support—Help given to older adults by those from another generation, including family members. (23-2)

integrated services—Programs that care for both young children and older adults. (16-1)

intelligence quotient—The ratio between mental age and chronological age. (24-1)

interpersonal relationships—Relationships that are positive, caring, and respectful. (17-3)

intervention services—Specialized help and resources for children and their parents. (1-2)

invented spelling—Spelling a word the way it sounds. (25-1)

inventory—A detailed record of the quantity of supplies on hand. (13-2)

inventory record—A list of equipment and materials on hand. (14-2)

isolation room—A room set apart for sick children. (12-1)

J

job description—A written list of duties and responsibilities for each employee. (14-2)

joint mobilization—Moving body joints evenly and consistently to avoid stiffness and pain. (27-1)

K

keywords—Significant words that make it easier for employers to search the Internet for relevant information. (4-2)

L

labor union—An organization of workers in a similar field. (4-3)

lap pool—A pool designed for people to swim in small areas. (13-2)

latchkey children—Children who stay home alone before or after school. (21-2)

learned helplessness—Loss of ability to do things for oneself because someone else takes over. (23-1)

learning centers—Clearly defined spaces for specific types of learning or play. (12-1)

learning disability—A disorder that affects the way the brain processes information. (22-1)

learning specialists—Professionals trained to identify learning disorders and help children overcome them. (22-1)

lesson plan—A detailed, written explanation of an activity, including the purpose, materials needed, step-by-step instructions, and evaluation. (24-2)

license exempt—Not required to have a license to operate a program. (14-1)

light table—A low, lighted table with a white plastic top on which children can put objects for close inspection. (26-2)

literacy—The ability to read and write language. (20-2)

living will—A will that allows a person to make the decision to initiate or remain on life support or not to initiate or maintain life support before that decision has to be made. (17-2)

locomotion compensation—The way people change their movements to be safe. (27-1)

longevity—The length of an extended life span. (2-1)

lyrics—Words to songs. (28-2)

M

mandated—Required by law, such as to report suspected abuse or neglect cases. (3-1)

manipulatives—Toys or materials that children can operate and change with their hands. (24-1)

material safety data sheets (MSDS)—Records that OSHA requires employers to keep identifying hazardous chemicals and their components. (15-1)

mathematical vocabulary—Words that express numbers, quantities, shape, size, or volume. (26-1)

maze—A deliberately confusing series of pathways. (27-2)

Meals on Wheels—A national program supplying meals to elderly or infirm people. (10-2)

Medicaid—A health insurance program for low-income people established as part of the Social Security Act. (3-2)

Medicare—A health insurance program for older adults established as part of the Social Security Act. (3-2)

melody—The tune of a song. (28-2)

minimum wage—The lowest hourly amount a worker can earn. (4-3)

multidisciplinary—A combination of two or more fields of study. (3-2)

multiple intelligences—Gardner's belief that people vary in terms of type of intelligence and learning strengths just as they differ in learning styles. (24-1)

multipurpose senior center—A community-based facility for older adults, offering a variety of programs and usually sponsored by the city and county. (15-1)

music therapy—Using music to help meet the physical, psychological, cognitive, and social functioning of older adults and others. (28-4)

N

native language—The language spoken in a person's home. (20-1)

naturalistic observation—A record of natural behaviors as they occur (in this case, with children). (7-1)

nature education—Teachings about the environment and life on earth. (26-3)

negativism—A toddler's behavior of refusing to do what is asked or doing just the opposite. (19-2)

networking—Making use of all your personal and professional contacts to further your career goals. (4-2)

neurons—Nerve cells in the brain. (1-1)

nonprofit—No stockholders who receive money from the program's income. (14-1)

nontoxic—Not poisonous. (12-2; 13-1)

numerals—Written symbols that represent numbers. (26-1)

nutrients—Substances in food that the body uses to function, grow, repair tissue, and produce energy. (10-1)

nutrition—The process through which the body uses the nutrients in food. (10-1)

O

objective observations—Recorded facts without personal opinion or bias. (7-1)

objective reporting—Reporting that doesn't include any personal judgments. (7-2)

objectives—Learning outcomes for children to achieve or experience through participation in a specific curriculum activity. (24-2)

object permanence—Understanding that an object continues to exist even when out of sight. (18-1)

on demand—Conduct routines (in this case) according to each child's individual needs. (18-2)

one-to-one correspondence—Counting one number for each object counted. (20-1; 26-1)

open door policy—Any parent or legal guardian (or approved family members) can observe the child at any time. (17-1)

open-ended materials—Items that can be used in a variety of ways, with no single correct outcome. (24-1)

open-ended questions—Questions that require more that a yes or no answer and often begin with *how, what, when, where,* and *why.*

oral history—Information gathered from older adults about past events. (25-3)

organizational chart—A document letting staff know to whom they report. (14-2)

osteoporosis—A disease in which the bones become brittle and weak. (10-2)

P

parallel play—Children playing near each other, but not with each other. (19-1)

parent report form—A document parents complete that details an infant's activities and behavior before arrival at the center. (18-2)

participant observer—Someone who interacts with children while observing them. (7-1)

partnership—A bringing together of separate parts (in this case, the bringing together of separate programs for joint activities). (16-1)

pathogens—Disease-causing organisms. (6-1)

pediatrician—A physician who provides care specifically for children. (6-2)

perceptual motor skills—Skills that require the coordination of vision, intellect, and movement. (18-1)

perishable—Foods that will become spoiled if not refrigerated or frozen. (10-1)

pitch—The highness or lowness of musical sounds. (28-2)

polypharmacy—Problems that can occur when more medications are taken than needed. (6-2)

positive aging—Having a positive attitude about life and the ability to cope with change. (25-3)

positive reinforcement—A consequence that rewards a particular behavior and encourages its repetition. (11-2)

prenatal—Before birth. (1-2)

preoperational period—Piaget's second period of children's intellectual development. (19-1)

primary care provider—A care provider assigned to a child with special needs who makes sure the child participates in all routines and activities in a meaningful way. (22-2)

print-rich environment—Using printed materials throughout the classroom in meaningful ways. (25-1)

prioritize—Putting tasks in order of importance. (4-1)

proactive—Having the know-how to solve problems. (16-2)

probation—A period of time in which an employer observes the employee's work and behavior in order to assess whether the employee is right for the job. (4-3)

process versus product—What children learn is more important than the product they create. (28-1)

productive language—The ability to use words to express oneself. (19-2)

professional ethics—The standards of right and wrong that apply to your professional behavior. (5-2)

program goals—Basic skills, concepts, and attitudes to develop and encourage in children. (14-1)

program governance—The director and board make decisions about policies and procedures. (14-2)

program's philosophy—General beliefs, concepts, and attitudes about learning (in this case, programs for children). (14-1)

program sponsors—Specific groups or individuals that fund or manage a program. (14-1)

project approach—A method of teaching that allows children to explore projects in developmentally appropriate ways. (24-2)

prop box—A container for storing items (props) used for specific dramatic-play themes. (27-3)

proportion—The relationship of the parts. (28-1)

props—Collections of items that suggest themes for dramatic play, such as face masks for firefighters. (27-3)

puberty—The transition stage when children undergo a series of physical changes and begin to look like adult men and women. (21-1)

public relations—Positive communication with the general public regarding your program or company. (5-1; 14-2)

Q

quackery—Misrepresenting, being dishonest, or trying to fool someone into believing something else (in this case, about medical claims). (8-2)

R

radial pulse—A pulse rate taken at the wrist. (7-2)

rating scale—A recorded verbal or numerical evaluation by an observer. (7-1)

rational counting—Recognizing numerical symbols and placing them in sequential order with the understanding that the last number counted in a group represents the entire number of objects in the group. (20-1; 26-1)

rebus recipe—A recipe that shows ingredients and directions with picture symbols. (26-2)

receptive language—The ability to understand spoken words. (19-2)

recreational music—Music purely for social and personal enjoyment. (28-4)

recreational programs—Activity programs (often hobby-related), usually city-funded, for persons of similar ages. (15-1)

recreational therapy—Activities that help restore health and mobility. (27-2)

redirection—The steering or redirecting (in this case, the steering of disruptive behavior to more acceptable behavior). (11-2)

reference checks—Checking the applicant's character and abilities with former employers. (14-2)

referral(s)—Sending parents who need assistance to another support service, such as a local family-centered agency or parenting Web site. (1-2; 17-1) A job lead from others. (4-2)

reflexes—Instinctive, involuntary reactions to a stimulus, such as a noise or touch. (18-1)

Reggio Emilia Approach—A unique approach to using the project approach that originated in Reggio Emilia, Italy. (24-2)

registration—Recording of pertinent information instead of a formal program license. (14-1)

reinforcement—A process used to strengthen and increase learning. (24-3)

resilience—Coping with and bouncing back from situations (in this case, recovering from the hardships of neglect and abuse). (8-1)

respite care—Temporary relief care for family members taking care of a sick relative. (15-2)

résumé—A summary of your career objectives, work experience, job qualifications, education, and training. (4-2)

retention—The ability to remember information. (24-3)

rhythm instruments—Musical instruments with which children experiment to make their own rhythms. (28-2)

risk-management plan—Written emergency procedures. (6-1)

rote counting—Memorizing and reciting numbers in order. (20-1; 26-1)

routine—A regular, expected procedure that is followed to accomplish a goal. Can be daily, weekly, or monthly. (9-1; 9-2)

S

schedule—A plan for how time will be used. (9-1; 9-2)

screenings—Examinations given to a group of children to look for one specific health problem. (6-1)

search talk—Trying to find the right word(s) in a conversation. (11-3)

self-directed—Learn and are motivated in an independent fashion. (9-1)

self-discipline—The ability to guide your own behavior. (11-2)

self-help skills—Skills that allow children to help take care of their personal needs. (19-1)

self-perception—How people picture themselves. (2-2)

sensorimotor—A period of time when children explore through their senses of sight, touch, taste, hearing, or smell. (1-1; 18-1)

sensory—Experiences that involve the senses. (1-1; 12-1)

sensory table—A table with a boxlike, hollow top that can hold water, sand, beans, or other substances for children to explore. (26-2)

separation anxiety—A child's fear of separation from familiar people. (19-2)

seriation—The ability to organize objects according to increasing or decreasing size. (20-1; 26-1)

service learning—Community service that becomes part of your schoolwork. (4-2)

sexual harassment—An act of discrimination; any unwelcome verbal or physical behavior of a sexual nature. (4-3)

shareholders—People who have funds invested in a program, center, or company. (15-2)

small talk—Light, casual conversation. (11-3)

social competence—A person's ability to get along with others in an acceptable and appropriate way. (11-1)

social responsibility—Making a positive contribution to a community and obeying community laws. (25-2)

social studies—A curriculum area that teaches about self, families, communities, and the world. (25-2)

social well-being—Having meaningful relationships and maintaining a network of supportive friends. (25-3)

sociocultural theory—Children learn their culture's beliefs, customs, and skills through social interactions with skilled peers and adults. (20-1)

sociology—The study of society, its institutions, and social relationships. (2-1)

solitary play—Children play alone rather than with other children. (19-1)

special activities—Program activities for school-age children, such as gymnastics, swimming lessons, or organized sports. (21-2)

special needs—Circumstances that cause physical, cognitive, and behavioral development to vary significantly from the norm. (22-1)

spite talk—A resentful and disrespectful way to talk to another person. (11-3)

spontaneous dramatic play—Dramatic play in which children engage without direction from adults. (27-3)

staff turnover—The rate at which employees leave their jobs, creating the need for hiring new employees. (18-2)

stranger anxiety—An infant's fear of unfamiliar people. (18-1)

subjective description—An observation based on personal judgments. (7-1)

subjective reporting—A recorded observation based on personal ideas, thoughts, feelings, and attitudes. (7-1)

support groups—Meetings to discuss common concerns and needs. (17-1)

support services—Programs that provide interaction between two or more groups for a specific cause. (16-1)

symbolic thinking—Children's more advanced thought process characterized by increased attention span and memory. (19-1)

synapses—Electrical connections between neurons in the brain. (1-1)

T

teachable moments—Unplanned opportunities for learning. (24-1)

temperament—A typical way children respond to people, situations, and their environment. (1-1; 18-1)

temper tantrum—An episode in which a child shows anger or frustration in an aggressive or destructive way. (19-2)

tempo—The rhythm and speed at which a song is sung. (28-2)

theme—One central topic around which activities are selected. (24-2)

therapeutic—Assist with healing. (12-2)

three dimensional—Shapes and objects that have height, width, and depth. (28-1)

toxins—Harmful substances that can cause disease or illness. (6-3)

trade publications—Magazines and newsletters written for people in an industry by organizations that support the industry. (4-2)

traffic pattern—The pattern of the room and the direction the children (people) take to get from one area to another. (12-1)

transfer learning—The ability to use the information taught in an activity in a different setting. (24-3)

transition—A short activity to guide children from one activity (routine) to another. (9-1)

transition techniques—The specific activities or techniques used in transition. (9-1)

trend—The overall direction in which a society moves within a given time frame. (3-1)

V

visual discrimination—The ability to notice similarities and differences in shapes and alphabet letters and other objects. (25-1)

vocalizations—Sounds made by infants that imitate adult language. (18-1)

vulnerable—Open to acts of unkindness or mistreatment. (8-2)

W

whole language—A practice of using reading and writing in meaningful classroom activities. (25-1)

workers' compensation—Employers' provision for injured employees to cover their medical expenses and lost wages if they cannot work. (4-3)

Index

D

S

Credits

Ralf-Finn Hestoft, 30
Michael Keller, 111
Alyx Kellington, 87
Kathleen Kliskey-Geraghty, 395
Kent Knudson, 225 b
Ed Lallo, 416
Chris Lowe, 447
Jim McGuire, 80
Sally Moskol, 62, 295
Larry Mulvehill, 43
Omni Photo Communications, Inc., 53 t, 266
Frank Pedrick, 631
David Porter, 251
Lindy Powers, 623
Frank Primelife, 60 b
RO-MA Stock, 85
Chuck St. John, 444
Nancy Sheehan, 34, 646
Frank Siteman, 102, 146 l, 303 l
Inga Spence, 402, 418
SW Productions, 61
Table Mesa Prod., 388, 400
Shmuel Thaler, 633
Aneal Vohra, 88, 562, 588
Zephyr Picture, 89, 100
Zeth Visual Media-Germany, 28 r
International Stock, Dick Dickinson, 622
Steve Karp, 258 r
Kompan, Inc., 315 l, 316
Robert F. Kusel, 217, 503
Laerdal Medical Corporation, 186 b, 372
Landscape Structures, Inc., 315 r
Ken Lax, 454
LifeScan, Inc., 209
Masterfile, 458, 472, 512
Rommel, 163
Kevin May, 11, 35 r, 36 l, 57 r, 63 t, 64, 69, 82, 86, 90, 98, 104, 107 b, 112, 116 t, 124, 130, 136, 138, 156, 162, 165, 171, 178 b, 181 lr, 184, 190, 196, 210, 218, 236 tl, 237, 240 t, 243 b, 245, 250, 253, 255, 257 t, 259, 263, 265, 296, 305 l, 305 r, 309, 311, 318 r, 321, 326 lr, 329, 330 r, 334, 335, 343 t, 344, 347 tb, 351 tr, 356, 358 bt, 359, 360, 369, 378, 394, 405, 407, 412, 414, 424 tbr, 433, 435, 437,

440, 442, 455, 456, 461, 469, 490, 515 bt, 534, 536, 537, 539, 544, 545, 565, 566, 569, 574, 576, 587, 593, 596 r, 599, 605 t, 606 r, 619, 620, 621, 626, 627 rl, 628, 629 t, 643 b, 644 r, 647, 651, 659 t
Michael Marsland/Yale University, Office of Public Affairs, 54 l
Ted Mishima, 31
Nasco, 10, 596 l, 649 b
PhotoDisc, 146 r, 127, 143, 477 t, 479, 485, 558
S. Wanke/PhotoLink, 572
Keith Brofsky, 522
PhotoEdit
Bill Aron, 406 t, 477 m
Davis Barber, 186 t
Robert Brenner, 216
Peter Byron, 404
Myrleen Ferguson Cate, 6, 149, 159, 188, 484 l, 604
Kathy Ferguson-Johnson, 262
Cindy Charles, 345
CLEO PHOTOGRAPHY, 396 t, 481
Paul Conklin, 308, 340, 362, 504, 556 t, 568
Gary Conner, 110
Mary Kate Denny, 101 t, 343 b, 462, 487
Laura Dwight, 303 r, 592
Tony Freeman, 164, 273, 478, 640, 662
Jose Galvez, 9, 510
Spencer Grant, 183, 409, 636, 655
Jeff Greenberg, 192 t
Richard Hutchings, 482 r, 642
Bonnie Kamin, 330 l, 590, 614
Dennis MacDonald, 272
Felicia Martinez, 242, 324
Stephen McBrady, 567
Michael Newman, 151, 166, 167, 200, 219, 240 b, 376, 383, 390, 391, 392 t, 399, 406 b, 453, 543, 625
A. Ramey, 230, 246, 525
Elena Rooraid, 353
Robin Sachs, 581
James Shaffer, 507
Rhoda Sidney, 580
Frank Siteman, 6, 227, 292
Barbara Stitzer, 629 b
Susan Van Etten, 361, 379

Merritt Vincent, 5, 154, 209 t
Dana White, 107 t, 160
David Young-Wolff, 10, 11, 135, 153, 161, 192 b, 203 t, 226, 285, 289, 313, 336, 430, 463, 471, 497, 500, 538, 555, 559, 595, 598, 606 l, 635, 645
Psychology Archives-The University of Akron, 33 l
Scholastic, 33 r
SkillsUSA-VICA, 106
Barb Spink, 56, 115, 161, 195, 197, 198, 199, 203, 204, 205, 342, 352, 370, 380, 521, 546, 556 b
Stock Food/Snowflake Studios, Inc., 261 b
Stockbyte, 207, 297
SuperStock, 40, 319 r
Jim Arbogast, 36 b
The National Center on Elder Abuse, supported in part, by grant No. 90-AP-2144, from the Administration on Aging, Dept. of Health and Human Services, 221 b
USDA, 252
Welch Allyn, Inc., 165, 206
Dana White, 172, 235, 258 l, 269, 278, 283 r, 351 tl, 426 b, 451 t, 499, 541, 649 t
Williams Sound Corp., 132

Special thanks to the following individuals, schools, businesses and organzations for their assistance with photographs in this book: Karen Rose and Lori Covey, Senior World; Susie Champion, PALS Praise & Leadership Schools; Elaine Lundberg, Bright Horizons—Little Friends Learning Center; Mo Miller, Heartland Community College—Child Development Lab and Learning Center; Susie Doubet, Lakeview YWCA Child Care Center Peoria Public Library Bookmobile; Peoria Police Department; Annette Scherer, Rural Peoria County Council on Aging; Kathy Chapman, Methodist Medical Center; Barb Yoder, Noah's Ark Children's Center; Maple Lawn Homes.